BRITISH GOVERNMENT
AND THE CONSTITUTION

LAW IN CONTEXT

Editors: Robert Stevens (Haverford College, Pennsylvania),
William Twining (University College, London) and
Christopher McCrudden (Lincoln College, Oxford)

ALREADY PUBLISHED

Accidents, Compensation and the Law (Third Edition), P. S. Atiyah
Company Law and Capitalism (Second Edition), Tom Hadden
Karl Llewellyn and the Realist Movement (reissue), William Twining
Cases and Materials on the English Legal System (Fourth Edition), Michael Zander
Computers and the Law, Colin Tapper
Tribunals and Government, J. A. Farmer
Government and Law (Second Edition), T. C. Hartley and J. A. G. Griffith
Land, Law and Planning, Patrick McAuslan
Landlord and Tenant (Second Edition), Martin Partington
How to do Things with Rules (Second Edition), William Twining and David Miers
Evidence, Proof and Probability (Second Edition), Richard Eggleston
Family Law and Social Policy (Second Edition), John Eekelaar
Consumers and the Law (Second Edition), Ross Cranston
Law and Politics, Robert Stevens
Obscenity, Geoffrey Robertson
Labour Law (Second Edition), Paul Davies and Mark Freedland
Charities, Trusts and Social Welfare, Michael Chesterman
The Law-Making Process (Second Edition), Michael Zander
An Introduction to Law (Second Edition), Phil Harris
Sentencing and Penal Policy, Andrew Ashworth
Law and Administration, Carol Harlow and Richard Rawlings
Legal Foundations of the Welfare State, Ross Cranston

KD
3989
.T87
1985

British Government and the Constitution
Text, Cases and Materials

COLIN TURPIN

Fellow of Clare College, Cambridge
University Lecturer in Law

WEIDENFELD AND NICOLSON
London

369723

Tennessee Tech. Library
Cookeville. Tenn.

To Monique

© 1985 Colin Turpin

All rights reserved. No part of this publication may
be reproduced, stored in a retrieval system, or
transmitted, in any form or by any means,
electronic, mechanical, photocopying, recording or
otherwise, without the prior permission of the
copyright owner.

George Weidenfeld and Nicolson Ltd
91 Clapham High Street, London SW4 7TA

British Library Cataloguing in Publication Data

Turpin, Colin C.
  British government and the constitution: text,
  cases and materials. – (law in context)
  1 Great Britain – Constitutional law
  I. Title   II. Series
  344.102′2   KD3989

ISBN 0–297–78651–2 cased
ISBN 0–297–78652–0 paperback

Photoset by Deltatype, Ellesmere Port
Printed in Great Britain by Butler & Tanner Ltd
Frome and London

'Government without a Constitution is power without a right.'

Thomas Paine, *Rights of Man*

CONTENTS

Preface

This book is concerned with the organization, powers and responsibility of government in the British constitution. It has been written from a lawyer's perspective, modified by an awareness that the British constitution is not the sole handiwork of lawyers. Judges and other practitioners of the discipline of law have made a notable contribution to it, but so have politicians, polemicists, noble lords, rebels in and out of Parliament, party members and the legions of special interests. Yet lawyers sometimes pretend that the constitution is theirs, teaching and writing about it in precarious isolation.

I have written this book in the conviction that the law student obtains an incomplete and fragmentary view of the constitution unless he is encouraged to travel beyond the boundaries of the law's domain. He has much to learn from writers and practitioners in politics, government and public administration, just as students of these subjects can enrich their studies by learning something of the values, constraints and possibilities of the law. If asked a question, say, about the power of Parliament, the lawyer and the political scientist will give very different answers. But they are describing the same institution, and for a full understanding of its place in the constitution each of them needs to take account of the other's viewpoint, and may have to modify his own.

I have set out in this book to present essential features of British government and the constitution in a way that offers a wider range of view to students of law and I hope also to students of politics and government. The materials in the book are taken not only from law reports, statutes and legal works but from a variety of official publications and from the writings of political scientists, parliamentarians and other commentators on the constitution and the practice of government. I have tried in this way to show the variegated texture of a constitution which consists not only of rules – legal, quasi-legal and customary or conventional – but of values, habits of mind and shared understandings: a constitution continually re-shaped in the daily practice of politics and administration as well as by the deliberate law-making of legislators and judges.

The student of the British constitution soon finds that there are present in it two opposite principles: a principle of change and a principle of continuity. The former principle was expressed by a member of Parliament who once remarked that 'we make up our constitution as we go along'. The constitution appears to be composed of impermanent laws and a constantly changing practice – a fluid mass of formal instruments, unwritten rules, customs and procedures – something always in movement and about to become something else. The other principle emphasizes certain continuing themes, traditions and values in the constitution: these include parliamentary sovereignty, the rule of law, responsible government, free elections, the legitimacy of opposition. In this study of the constitution I have tried to give due weight to both principles. Perennial themes such as parliamentary sovereignty and the rule of law are considered in their modern setting, together with recent trends in constitutional scholarship and questions raised by the practice of twentieth-century government.

In formal terms the British system of government is a constitutional monarchy. British governments are not confined by a written constitution but exercise their powers within a framework of constitutional theory, law, conventions and political understandings. The elements of this brief description are developed in Part I of this book, which also considers the case for a new constitutional settlement.

British government is carried on in a unitary state which, by its accession to the European Communities, has become subject to a European legal order which has modified in some respects the terms of our domestic constitutional arrangements. Part II is concerned with the organization of British government, the territorial and supra-national contexts of its operations, and the powers available to it for carrying out its tasks.

A fundamental value claimed for our constitutional system is that it provides for responsible government. By this is meant that government is both 'responsive' and 'accountable' to the people and to Parliament. Part III is concerned with the forms and techniques for assuring the responsibility of government in Britain.

I have not attempted to provide a comprehensive account of the British system of government – or the book would have been two or three times as long – and some topics are treated in greater depth than others, according to my judgement of their interest and importance, or of how fully they are covered in other books. For a detailed exposition of the legal rules, reference should be made to one or other of the standard textbooks on constitutional and administrative law. My aim has been to provide information, points of view and discussion on issues of lasting importance or which have acquired a new significance in our own time.

I have quoted from or cited a large number of books, articles and other sources, and I hope that these will provide a helpful indication of further reading for the student who wishes to make a fuller study of particular topics.

Acknowledgements

I wish to thank a number of people for their help and encouragement. I have dedicated this book to my wife, Monique, in gratitude for her unfailing support and for her help with typing and other technical aspects of the book. My colleagues Professor Bob Hepple and Professor Paul O'Higgins have helped me in numberless ways over the years and I owe much to their scholarship and their friendship. Again, while I have not consulted him in writing this book, I should like to acknowledge a like debt of long standing to Professor Lord Wedderburn of Charlton.

I am grateful to the Fellows of Clare College who have provided a collective, friendly stimulus, and who relieved me of collegiate duties to enable me to write this book. Mrs Elizabeth Freeman, in particular, willingly undertook an additional burden of teaching and direction of studies in my absence.

I am indebted to the academic editors of this series, Professor Robert Stevens, Professor William Twining and Mr Christopher McCrudden, for their most helpful comments and advice. Weidenfeld and Nicolson Ltd have shown much patience and consideration, and I am particularly grateful to Mr Benjamin Buchan for his efficiency in piloting the book on its way to publication.

I wish also to thank the staff of the Cambridge University Library – in particular those working in the Official Publications Room and in the Squire Law Library – for their helpfulness in responding to my numerous inquiries.

The author and publishers would like to thank the following for permission to reproduce copyright material:

H. J. Abraham (Oxford University Press, N.Y., *Freedom and the Court*); S. H. Beer (Faber and Faber, *Modern British Politics*); A. W. Benn (*Political Quarterly*, 'Democracy in the Age of Science'); K. Berrill (University of London, *Strength at the Centre – The Case for a Prime Minister's Department*: Stamp Memorial Lecture 1980); A. H. Birch (George Allen & Unwin, *Representative and Responsible Government*); Lord Blake (The British Academy and Oxford University Press, *The Office of Prime Minister*: available only from The British Academy); V. Bogdanor (Cambridge University Press, *The People and the Party System* and *Multi-Party Politics and the Constitution*; Oxford University Press, *Devolution*); R. L. Borthwick and the Study of Parliament Group (Fontana, 'The Floor of the House' in *The Commons Today*); Lord Boston of Faversham and C. Campbell (Maurice Temple Smith, 'Arguments Against a Bill of Rights' in *Do We Need a Bill of Rights?*); A. W. Bradley (British Broadcasting Corporation/The Listener, 'The

Tameside Affair'); R. Brazier (Stevens & Sons, 'The Constitution in the New Politics');
I. Burton and G. Drewry (Macmillan Press, *Legislation and Public Policy*); D. Butler
(Collins, *Governing Without a Majority*); D. Butler and Gareth Evans (Heinemann
Educational Australia, *Labor and the Constitution 1972–1975*); R. Butt (Constable, *The
Power of Parliament*); Butterworth & Co. (extracts from the All England Law Reports);
J. Callaghan (Personal Minute to Ministers); Lord Carrington (Letter to the Prime
Minister); J. A. Chandler (Butterworth Scientific Ltd, 'The Plurality Vote: A
Reappraisal'); M. Charlot (*Political Quarterly*, 'A Changing Britain? A View from
France'); D. N. Chester and the Study of Parliament Group (Fontana, 'Questions in
the House' in *The Commons Today*); D. N. Chester and F. M. G. Willson (George Allen &
Unwin, *The Organization of British Central Government 1914–1964*); Commission and Court
of Justice of the European Communities (extracts from European Court Reports,
Treaty of Rome and official publications); Controller of Her Majesty's Stationery
Office (Hansard, Parliamentary papers and government publications); B. Crick
(Weidenfeld and Nicolson, *The Reform of Parliament*); R. H. S. Crossman (Hamish
Hamilton and Jonathan Cape, *The Diaries of a Cabinet Minister*; Mrs Anne Crossman,
Inside View); K. C. Davis (Louisiana State University Press, *Discretionary Justice*); S. R.
Davis (University of California, *The Federal Principle*); A. V. Dicey (Macmillan Press,
The Law of the Constitution); G. Drewry (Butterworths, 'Passing the Buck'); P. Dunleavy
and R. A. W. Rhodes (Macmillan Press, 'Beyond Whitehall' in *Developments in British
Politics*); S. E. Finer (Anthony Wigram, *Adversary Politics and Electoral Reform*; Royal
Institute of Public Administration, 'The Individual Responsibility of Ministers'); I.
Gilmour (Hutchinson, *The Body Politic*); Lord Gordon Walker (Jonathan Cape, *The
Cabinet*); W. Green & Son Ltd (extracts from *Scots Law Times*); J. A. G. Griffith (*Modern
Law Review*, 'The Place of Parliament in the Legislative Process'); J. A. G. Griffith and
the Study of Parliament Group (Fontana, 'Standing Committees in the House of
Commons' in *The Commons Today*); Lord Hailsham of St Marylebone (British
Broadcasting Corporation, *Elective Dictatorship*: Richard Dimbleby Lecture; *The Times*,
'The Case for a New, Written Constitution'); A. H. Hanson and M. J. Walles (Fontana
Paperbacks, *Governing Britain*); M. L. Harrison (*New Society*, 'The Coming Welfare
Corporatism'); H. L. A. Hart (Oxford University Press, *The Concept of Law*); O. Hood-
Phillips (*The Times*, Letter to the Editor); C. Howard, C. A. Saunders and Gareth
Evans (Heinemann Educational Australia, *Labor and the Constitution 1972–1975*); The
Incorporated Council of Law Reporting for England and Wales (extracts from the Law
Reports); International Commission of Jurists (*The Rule of Law in a Free Society*); I.
Jennings (Cambridge University Press, *Cabinet Government*); N. Johnson (Pergamon
Press, *In Search of the Constitution*); G. W. Jones ('Development of the Cabinet' in *The
Modernization of British Government*, by permission of Pitman Publishing Ltd, London); J.
Barry Jones and R. A. Wilford (University of Wales Press, 'Implications: Two Salient
Issues' in *The Welsh Veto*); JUSTICE (*Freedom of Information*; 'Statement on the War
Damage Bill'); Juta & Co. Ltd (extracts from the South African Law Reports); M. J.
Keating and A. F. Midwinter (Mainstream Publishing, *The Government of Scotland*); P.
Kellner and Lord Crowther-Hunt (Macdonald Futura Publishers, *The Civil Servants*); J.
Kerr (Letter and Statement of 11 November 1975); Anthony Lewis (*Sunday Times*, 'The
Crossman Diaries and the Legal Lessons of the Pentagon Papers'); Liberal/SDP
Alliance (Report on Electoral Reform); J. F. Lively (Basil Blackwell, *Democracy*); J. R.
Lucas (*The Times*, 'Commonsense before the Law'); J. P. Mackintosh (Stevens & Sons,
The British Cabinet; Hutchinson, *The Government and Politics of Britain*); C. B. Macpherson

(Oxford University Press, *The Life and Times of Liberal Democracy*); G. Marshall and G. C. Moodie (Hutchinson, *Some Problems of the Constitution*); D. R. Miers and A. C. Page (Sweet and Maxwell, *Legislation*); R. Miliband (Oxford University Press, *Capitalist Democracy in Britain*; Weidenfeld and Nicolson, *The State in Capitalist Society*); G. C. Moodie (Thomas Y. Crowell, *The Government of Great Britain*); P. Norton (Martin Robertson, *The Commons in Perspective*; Oxford University Press, 'The House of Commons and the Constitution: The Challenges of the 1970s'); P. Paterson (Macgibbon & Kee, *The Selectorate*); G. R. Peele (Macmillan Press, 'Government at the Centre' in *Developments in British Politics*); L. W. Pye (Princeton University Press, *Political Culture and Political Development*); Lord Rawlinson of Ewell (Commonwealth Parliamentary Association, 'Dissolution in the United Kingdom'); R. Rose (Faber and Faber, *Politics in England*; Macmillan Press, *The Problem of Party Government* and *Studies in British Politics*); G. Sawer (Pitman Publishing, *Modern Federalism*); Lord Scarman (Stevens & Sons, *English Law – The New Dimension*); Scottish Council of Law Reporting (extracts from Session Cases); C. Seymour-Ure (Royal Institute of Public Administration, 'British "War Cabinets" in Limited Wars'); B. Smith and Basil Blackwell (Martin Robertson, *Policy-Making in British Government*); Times Newspapers Limited (extracts from Leading Article, articles by Lord Hailsham, J. R. Lucas and A. Lewis, and the Times Law Reports); H. W. R. Wade (Cambridge University Press, 'The Basis of Legal Sovereignty'; Stevens & Sons, *Constitutional Fundamentals*; Memorandum to the Foreign Affairs Committee); Lord Wade (Austicks Publications, *Behind the Speaker's Chair*; Bill of Rights Bill); S. A. Walkland (George Allen & Unwin, *The Legislative Process in Great Britain*); P. Wallington and J. McBride (The Cobden Trust, *Civil Liberties and a Bill of Rights*); D. Wass (Routledge & Kegan Paul, *Government and the Governed*); K. C. Wheare (Oxford University Press, *Modern Constitutions*); Lord Wilson of Rievaulx (Weidenfeld and Nicolson, *The Governance of Britain*; Minute on Cabinet Committee Procedure); M. Zander (Barry Rose, *A Bill of Rights?*)

The author and publishers are also grateful to the following:

Mr S. Alderson, for an extract from *Yea or Nay? Referenda in the United Kingdom*: originally published by Cassell and Co. Ltd, reprinted by permission of Macmillan Publishing Company. Copyright © Stanley Alderson 1975.

Canada Law Book Inc., 240 Edward Street, Aurora, Ontario, L4G 3S9, Canada, publishers of the Dominion Law Reports, for extracts from *Reference re Amendment of the Constitution of Canada*.

The Hansard Society for Parliamentary Government, for an extract from *Paying for Politics*: the Report of the Commission upon the Financing of Political Parties. (While the Council of the Hansard Society congratulates Edmund Dell and his colleagues on the excellence of their work, it neither accepts nor rejects the findings of the Commission it has sponsored.) The Hansard Society is also thanked for permission to quote from the Report of the Hansard Society on Electoral Reform. (Since the Society exists simply to promote research and discussion, it does not either accept or reject the findings of the Commission which it has sponsored but merely commends the work to the public as a worthwhile contribution to the subject.)

The Princeton University Press, for an extract from Lucian W. Pye and Sidney Verba (eds.), *Political Culture and Political Development*, Copyright © 1965 by Princeton University Press.

Cases

Page numbers in **bold** type indicate extracts.

Statutes

Abbreviations

The standard abbreviations are used for law reports.

PART I

The British Constitution

I

The constitutional order

What do we mean when we speak of the British constitution? The fact that we do not have a written constitution – a formal document setting out the main rules which govern the political system – adds something to the difficulty of describing our constitution. Even if a country has a written constitution the inquirer will soon discover that not all the arrangements for its government are to be found in the formal document (or documents, for there may be more than one): much of the constitution will have to be looked for elsewhere. (The formal constitution may even be misleading, for we are warned by a Frenchman, Léon Duguit, that 'the facts are stronger than constitutions', and by an American, Roscoe Pound, that the 'law in books' is not necessarily the same as the 'law in action'.) But at all events a written constitution is a place where a start can be made. Lacking this, how do we set about describing the British constitution?

We might begin in a specific way by taking note of particular rules and practices observed in the working of the political system – for example, the rule that a Parliament can continue for no more than five years before dissolution (Parliament Act 1911, section 7), or the practice by which the Prime Minister answers Questions in the House of Commons for 15 minutes every Tuesday and Thursday. Rules and practices like these, relating to the government of the country, are of great number and variety: if it were possible to make a complete statement of them, that could no doubt be presented as a formal description of the British constitution. (It would include much that elsewhere would be put into a written constitution and much more that would be left out.) We should then have the material for a definition of the British constitution, which might run something like this:

a body of rules, conventions and practices which describe, regulate or qualify the organization and operation of government in the United Kingdom.

But such a definition, even if formally adequate, would fail to reveal some important dimensions of the constitution.

Shifting our point of view slightly, we might think next of the institutions and offices which constitute the machinery of British government. An institutional description of the constitution would include Parliament, the Cabinet and the courts, the Queen and her ministers, and such offices as those of the Parliamentary Commissioner for Administration (Ombudsman), the Comptroller and Auditor General, and the Director of Public Prosecutions. Of course these institutions and offices are themselves to be explained by reference to rules and practices which constitute them or define their powers and activity. But we do not think of them simply as bundles of rules but as having their own reality – often loaded with history and tradition – in the living constitution.

Reflecting further on the constitution, there would come to mind certain ideas, doctrines or organizing principles which have influenced or inspired the rules and practices of the constitution, or which express essential features of our institutions of government or of relations between them. There can be no true understanding of the British constitution without an appreciation of the role within it of such principles as those of democracy, parliamentary sovereignty, the separation of powers, ministerial responsibility and the rule of law.

We have now assembled the different elements of which the constitutional order seems to be composed. In the rest of this chapter we shall look more closely at the rules and practices, the institutions, and the informing ideas or principles of the British constitution, in an attempt to deepen our understanding of its nature.

1 Constitutional rules

Until now I have spoken rather loosely of 'rules and practices' of the constitution, and we need to be more definite. The *legal* rules that make up part of the constitution are either statutory rules or rules of common law. Many of the more important practices of the constitution also have the character of rules and, like legal rules, are the source of obligations and entitlements. These non-legal rules are called conventions. (The nature of conventions and their relation to law is one of the fundamental problems of the constitution, and will be more fully explored in the next chapter.)

As already indicated, the attempt might be made to enumerate all the rules relating to the system of government in a comprehensive statement of the contents of the British constitution (even though it would not remain up to date for long). The problem that would arise in doing this would be one of deciding whether rules were sufficiently connected with government to count as part of the constitution. Should the statement include the rules and practice relating to the control of immigration, or the organization of the armed forces, or the administration of social security? This sort of question would have to be answered rather arbitrarily, for there are no natural boundaries of the system of government or of the constitution. No comprehensive list or statement of the kind under consideration has been attempted, but a list presented in 1973 by Albert P. Blaustein and Gisbert H. Flanz (eds.) in *Constitutions of the Countries of the World*, of the constitutional *statutes* of the United Kingdom, named over 300 statutes, from Magna Carta 1215 to the European Communities Act 1972, including the Riot Act 1715, the Metropolitan Police Act 1839, the Parliament Acts 1911 and 1949, the Government of Ireland Act 1920, the National Service Act 1948, the Television Act 1964, the Race Relations Acts 1965 and 1968, and the Courts Act 1971.

A comprehensive list of constitutional rules would not tell us what is distinctive in the British constitution or what is of especial value. For the constitution is not mere machinery for the exercise of public power, but establishes an order by which public power is itself to be constrained. Some constitutional rules express social or political values that we think it important to preserve, or help to maintain a balance between different institutions of government or an accommodation of different interests or groups, or safeguard minorities or protect individual rights. These rules, we may say, have 'something fundamental' about them, and are distinguishable from much that is specific, temporary, simply convenient or merely mechanical in the constitution.

This distinction is of immense importance but is also very problematic. There is often disagreement about what is vital in the constitution and what is inessential. It is easy to fall into a very conservative way of regarding the constitution and to categorize what is old and traditional in our rules and practices as necessarily to be cherished and preserved, although no longer conformable to a changed society, a transformed public consciousness and new conceptions of justice and morality. There is a contrary tendency to view the whole constitution in an instrumental way, holding all its rules to be equally malleable or dispensable in the interest of immediate political ends or administrative convenience.

The present time is one in which the constitution shows signs of stress, perhaps because it has not adapted itself to the political realities of the post-industrial, multi-racial, multi-party, relatively non-deferential and egalitarian (if still unequal) society of the late twentieth century. Samuel Beer observes, for example, that 'the new stress on participant attitudes and behavior collides with values anciently embedded in the political system' (*Britain Against Itself*, 1982, p. 112). Constitutional rules which were formerly supported by a consensus or at least a general acquiescence have come under severe scrutiny and criticism in recent years – the electoral system, for example, and the rules for maintaining governmental secrecy. Reform is often inhibited by lack of agreement on alternative arrangements, combined with official inertia or preference for the *status quo*. Nevertheless ours is a time in which constitutional changes are on the agenda – or even are apt to take place without deliberation or public debate. It is important therefore that we should be searching for agreement on what is fundamental in the constitution and should be defended.

Earlier in this century an American constitutional lawyer remarked that a 'fundamental constitution' means a set of rules that are not subject to the will of the sovereign authority in the state, and he added that such rules 'have existed and must exist in any state worthy of the term "constitutional" ' (C. H. McIlwain, *Constitutionalism and the Changing World*, 1939, p. 279). This might seem to exclude the United Kingdom, with its sovereign Parliament, but McIlwain denied that this country failed the test of constitutionalism. In England, he said, 'there are many fundamental rights of the subject that parliament in modern times has never dreamt of infringing and could only infringe at the cost of revolution' – therefore 'no formal written constitution has ever been needed' (pp. 279–80). The possibility of revolution to which McIlwain refers, as our only sanction of constitutionalism, assumes a strong popular consensus supporting a set of rules thereby made fundamental. This sustaining public sentiment is nowadays often explained as a body of shared beliefs, values and expectations said to constitute the *political culture* of a society.

> Lucian W. Pye in L. W. Pye and Sidney Verba (eds.), *Political Culture and Political Development* (1965), pp. 7–8

The concept of political culture . . . suggests that the traditions of a society, the spirit of its public institutions, the passions and the collective reasoning of its citizenry, and the style and operating codes of its leaders are not just random products of historical experience but fit together as a part of a meaningful whole and constitute an intelligible web of relations. For the individual the political culture provides controlling guidelines for effective political behavior, and for the collectivity it gives a systematic structure of values and rational considerations which ensures coherence in the performance of institutions and organizations. . . .

[P]olitical culture is a recent term which seeks to make more explicit and systematic much of the understanding associated with such long-standing concepts as political ideology, national ethos and spirit, national political psychology, and the fundamental values of a people. Political culture, by embracing the political orientations of both leaders and citizens, is more inclusive than such terms as political style or operational code which focus on elite behavior. On the other hand, the term is more explicitly political and hence more restrictive than such concepts as public opinion and national character.

Not all the political attitudes and sentiments of a people are necessarily relevant in defining their political culture, for many are too ephemeral and lightly held to affect fundamental development. . . .

Samuel Beer (*Modern British Politics*, 3rd edn 1982, p. 390) observes that

a peaceful and orderly political process does require as an essential condition the presence of substantial consensus on values and beliefs in the political culture.

Public sentiment and convictions, or the political culture, support values and principles embodied in the constitution, rather than the precise technical forms these may take as rules. A rule may be said to have a fundamental character even though it is too technical to have entered the public consciousness, if it is a key element in a structure of rules which does reflect a common political understanding or consensus. Fundamental rules may have to be adjusted or modernized from time to time, so as to express in a more rational way the lasting values or principles which are grounded in the political culture.

The view that there are fundamental rules in our constitution, deriving that status directly or indirectly from a shared public consciousness, has to contend with what seems a self-evident fact, that the political culture is not constant or in all respects uniform. It certainly changes over time and it seems to include variations of attitude which amount to separate and differing sub-cultures in the community. Rules may reflect only the culture of an élite rather than of the community as a whole. We may find, in the words of R. M. Unger (*Law in Modern Society*, 1977, p. 173), that

What seems at first glance the outcome of a long tradition of agreement turns out, on closer inspection, to represent the beliefs and interests of the dominant groups who shaped the tradition.

These possibilities should put us on our guard; at the least they exacerbate the problem of identifying what is really fundamental.

But if McIlwain is right, to reject the notion of fundamental rules would be to abandon the idea of constitutionalism, which is the antithesis of arbitrary power. The idea is worth holding on to, as part of the effort to keep government to certain limits and standards. And if the link between fundamental rules and public consensus should be obliterated, it would be hard to find any other basis for such rules in our unwritten and informal constitution. Even going over to a written constitution with express guarantees might not, by itself, be enough: could there be fundamental rules in a society in which agreement on the essentials of political life had broken down? All this emphasizes the need to strive for the continuance of the widest possible consensus in the operation of the principal rules of our constitution and in the making of major changes.

If there are fundamental rules, we are entitled to expect that Parliament, the government and the courts will treat them with particular respect and will not abolish, subvert or disregard them – at least until it has been demonstrated that the rule no longer helps to support those 'essential' parts of the constitution that are rooted in the convictions of society.

Unfortunately this expectation is sometimes disappointed. Here is an example of what seems to have been an unjustified subversion of a fundamental rule – although happily it was only a temporary aberration, and after a time the rule was restored.

The writ of habeas corpus, for securing a judicial inquiry into the legality of a person's detention, has its origin in early common law and a series of Habeas

Corpus Acts. Section 3 of the Act of 1816 provides that when a writ of habeas corpus has been issued, and the custodian of the person detained has made his return to the writ, showing cause for the detention, the court may 'examine into the truth of the facts set forth in such return'. The efficacy of the writ of habeas corpus will often depend in practice on the onus of proof, and the courts established the rule (surely implicit in section 3 of the Habeas Corpus Act 1816) that the custodian must prove, to the satisfaction of the court, the circumstances alleged to justify the detention. This rule, in assuring effective protection of the right of the individual to personal freedom, certainly has the appearance of 'something fundamental': it is not confined to habeas corpus proceedings and was expressed as follows by Lord Atkin in *Eshugbayi Eleko* v. *Government of Nigeria* [1931] AC 662, 670: 'In accordance with British jurisprudence no member of the executive can interfere with the liberty or property of a British subject except on the condition that he can support the legality of his action before a court of justice.' However in a number of cases arising under the Immigration Act 1971 the courts reversed the rule as to onus of proof in habeas corpus proceedings, holding that the onus was on the applicant to establish that his detention was unlawful. It was further held that this onus could only be discharged by showing that the immigration authority – immigration officer or Secretary of State – had *no reasonable grounds* for reaching the conclusions on which the detention was based. (See in particular *R.* v. *Secretary of State for the Home Department, ex p. Choudhary* [1978] 1 WLR 1177; *R.* v. *Secretary of State for the Home Department, ex p. Zamir* [1980] AC 930.) The effect of these rulings upon the administration of immigration law was, as Templeman LJ observed in *R.* v. *Secretary of State for the Home Department, ex p. Akhtar* [1981] QB 46, 52, to deny 'the effective recourse of an individual to the courts which administer justice in this country'. Would it be an exaggeration to describe this development, by which the courts overturned the rule of the Habeas Corpus Act and robbed the individual of an effective remedy for unlawful detention, as unconstitutional? Fortunately in *R.* v. *Secretary of State for the Home Department, ex p. Khawaja* [1984] AC 74, the House of Lords restored the true principle, holding that the burden of proof rested on the custodian, and that the issue was not whether he had reasonable grounds for his decision but whether the detention was lawful. (See further Newdick, 'Immigrants and the Decline of Habeas Corpus' [1982] PL 89.)

To whom are we to look for the defence of what is fundamental in the constitution – for the preservation of 'constitutionalism'?

In the first place, the courts have undoubtedly an important role to play although, as we have seen, they have themselves a power to reinterpret or displace constitutional rules which calls for vigilance: *quis custodiet ipsos custodes*? We rely upon the courts to maintain fundamental legal rules against the exuberance or malpractice of administrators and others who exercise public power, but their role as constitutional guardians is subject to certain limits.

They are restricted, as regards legislation, by the doctrine of parliamentary sovereignty; and they work within a tradition (itself resting on a fundamental idea of the constitution) of judicial restraint, for they are unelected, unaccountable, and not qualified to resolve issues of political judgement and policy. In recent years the courts have, however, found a new boldness in developing the principles of judicial review, and one constitutional lawyer declares that they have brought about a 'renaissance of administrative law' in asserting their power to control public authorities. (H. W. R. Wade, *Constitutional Fundamentals*, 1980, ch. 5.) The balance between a proper judicial restraint and a legitimate judicial activism remains a critical feature of the constitution. (See further p. 41 *et seq.* below.)

Secondly, we depend on the political actors themselves to observe the 'rules of the game': ministers, civil servants and parliamentarians operate in a framework of generally well-understood procedures which are designed to make the governmental machine work, not merely efficiently but with respect for fundamentals. A leading parliamentarian showed an awareness of this in remarking, 'We have no constitution in this country: we have only procedure – hence its importance' (Mr St John-Stevas, HC Deb. vol. 991, col. 721, 30 October 1980). Procedures cannot, it is true, necessarily be relied on in a time of crisis. Admitting this, J. W. Gough nevertheless asked whether, in 'a time of crisis or of embittered emotions', we should be 'any safer with laws, even with fundamental laws and a written constitution' (*Fundamental Law in English Constitutional History*, 1955, p. 212). The observance of procedures is checked in certain respects by parliamentary select committees – such as the Public Accounts Committee and the Joint Committee on Statutory Instruments (see chapter 7 below) – and by the Comptroller and Auditor General and the Parliamentary Commissioner for Administration.

Thirdly, and in the last resort, we depend on the force of public opinion, pronounced in the general verdicts of elections and expressed in more specific ways through the media, political parties, and private interest groups and organizations of many kinds. A valuable role is performed by those organizations, like the National Council for Civil Liberties, that exist for the purpose of defending individual rights. Officially constituted bodies may also play a part in advancing the cause of civil and political rights: in Northern Ireland the Standing Advisory Commission on Human Rights, established under section 20 of the Northern Ireland Constitution Act 1973, seeks through advice and pressure to encourage respect for human rights in the laws and administration of the province.

In considering the nature of constitutional rules I have suggested that some of them may be characterized as 'fundamental'. A sceptic might comment as follows. The rules of the constitution are the result of the interplay of social and political forces and represent unstable compromises – or, some would say, the prescriptions of a state élite. What is fundamental is at best a matter of subjective judgement, or may simply reflect a dominant ideology. In any event the nineteenth-century French writer de Tocqueville spoke the truth when he said (*Democracy in America*, Fontana edn 1968, vol. 1, p. 122):

In England Parliament has the right to modify the Constitution. In England, therefore, the Constitution can change constantly, or rather it does not exist at all.

Are these comments well-founded?

2 Institutions

Definitions of the constitution often make use of the concept of the state and its organs. For example, Hood Phillips and Jackson, in *Constitutional and Administrative Law* (6th edn 1978, p. 5), define a constitution as

the system of laws, customs and conventions which define the composition and powers of organs of the state, and regulate the relations of the various state organs to one another and to the private citizen.

Regarded from the perspective of international law the United Kingdom is undoubtedly a state, but our own constitutional system has been constructed largely without the use of the concept of the state. With us there is no legal entity called 'the state' in which powers are vested or to which allegiance or other duties are owed. In this respect we are a 'stateless society', unlike 'societies which have a historical and intellectual tradition of the state as an institution that embodies the "public power" ' (Kenneth H. F. Dyson, *The State Tradition in Western Europe*, 1980, p. 19, n. 2). The non-admission of the idea of the state helps to explain the tardy and partial development, in Britain, of the distinction between public and private law. As Dyson remarks (op. cit., p. 117), there was 'no conception of the state to which principles and rules could be attributed', and the ordinary private law occupied much of the field in which relations between public officers and private citizens were conducted. For issues savouring more of policy than of property, the courts were inclined to resign to Parliament the function of controlling governmental action. (See further J. D. B. Mitchell, 'The Causes and Effects of the Absence of a System of Public Law in the United Kingdom' [1965] *PL* 95; Carol Harlow, ' "Public" and "Private" Law: Definition without Distinction' (1980) 43 *MLR* 241.)

The written constitutions of many countries adopt the idea of the state as expressing the whole political organization of the people. We find, for instance, the following provisions in the Constitution of Ireland of 1937.

The Constitution of Ireland

Article 4. The name of the State is *Éire*, or, in the English language, *Ireland*.
Article 5. Ireland is a sovereign, independent, democratic state.
Article 6. (1) All powers of government, legislative, executive and judicial, derive, under God, from the people, whose right it is to designate the rulers of the State. . . .

(2) These powers of government are exercisable only by or on the authority of the organs of State established by this Constitution.

Article 9. . . . (2) Fidelity to the nation and loyalty to the State are fundamental political duties of all citizens.

A number of the fundamental rights defined by the Irish Constitution are expressed in terms of guarantees or obligations assumed by the state. For instance, the state 'guarantees liberty for the exercise' *inter alia* of 'The right of the citizens to express freely their convictions and opinions' (art. 40(6)(1)).

The idea of the state has not been entirely absent from English political thought, and lawyers are familiar with such expressions as 'offences against the state', 'act of state', and the 'interests of the state'. There is, however, no single legal definition of the state for all purposes. In *D.* v. *National Society for the Prevention of Cruelty to Children* [1978] AC 171, it was argued that the NSPCC, a voluntary body incorporated by royal charter and authorized by statute to bring care proceedings for the protection of children, was not part of 'the state' and accordingly could not rely on 'public interest immunity' as justifying it in refusing to disclose the identity of its informants. Lord Simon of Glaisdale disposed of this argument in the following words (pp. 235–6):

'[T]he state' cannot on any sensible political theory be restricted to the Crown and the departments of central government (which are, indeed, part of the Crown in constitutional law). The state is the whole organisation of the body politic for supreme civil rule and government – the whole political organisation which is the basis of civil government. As such it certainly extends to local – and, as I think, also statutory – bodies in so far as they are exercising autonomous rule.

The phrase 'the interests of the state' occurs in the Official Secrets Act 1911, and was considered in the following case.

Chandler v. Director of Public Prosecutions [1964] AC 763 (HL)

The appellants had attempted to enter and immobilize an airfield, which was a 'prohibited place' within the Official Secrets Act 1911, as a demonstration of opposition to nuclear weapons. They were charged with conspiracy to commit a breach of section 1 of the Act, which makes it an offence *inter alia* to enter any prohibited place 'for any purpose prejudicial to the safety or interests of the State'.

It was argued for the appellants that what they had intended to do was not *in fact* prejudicial to the safety or interests of the state, and further that it was their *purpose* to benefit and not to harm the state. Counsel argued also that the word 'State' in the Act meant the inhabitants of the country and not the organs of government.

LORD REID: . . . Next comes the question of what is meant by the safety or interests of the State. 'State' is not an easy word. It does not mean the Government or the Executive. 'L'Etat c'est moi' was a shrewd remark, but can hardly have been intended as a definition even in the France of the time. And I do not think that it means, as counsel argued, the individuals who inhabit these islands. The statute cannot be referring to the interests of all those individuals because they may differ and the interests of the majority are not necessarily the same as the interests of the State. Again we have seen only too clearly in some other countries what can happen if you personify and almost deify the State. Perhaps the country or the realm are as good synonyms as one can find and I would be prepared to accept the organised community as coming as near to a definition as one can get. . . .

Lord Hodson also took the state to mean 'the organised community' (p. 801).

LORD DEVLIN: . . . What is meant by 'the State'? Is it the same thing as what I have just called 'the country'? Mr Foster, for the appellants, submits that it means the inhabitants of a particular geographical area. I doubt if it ever has as wide a meaning as that. I agree that in an appropriate context the safety and interests of the State might mean simply the public or national safety and interests. But the more precise use of the word 'State', the use to be expected in a legal context, and the one which I am quite satisfied . . . was intended in this statute, is to denote the organs of government of a national community. In the United Kingdom, in relation at any rate to the armed forces and to the defence of the realm, that organ is the Crown. . . .

In the view of all their Lordships, the interests of the state were identical with those of the Crown or at all events were determined by the Crown – i.e., by the government of the day. Lord Pearce, for example, said (p. 813):

In such a context the interests of the State must in my judgment mean the interests of the State according to the policies laid down for it by its recognised organs of government and authority. . . .

Consequently it could not be argued that the military dispositions decided upon by the *government* were not in the interests of the *state*.

The arguments for the appellants having failed in this and other respects, their convictions were confirmed. (See further Donald Thompson [1963] *PL* 201.)

The speeches in this case reflect the relative unfamiliarity to English lawyers of the concept of the state. Lord Reid appears to have had it in mind that the state is an entity to which attributes of sovereignty or absolutism may easily be applied. On the other hand the French jurist Léon Duguit has stripped the state of the borrowed purple of its sovereignty, insisting that it is only an organ of society set up to perform services. (See *Law in the Modern State*, tr. F. & H. Laski, 1921, pp. 29–31.)

If the interests of the state and of the government are in law to be considered the same, the possibility remains that those interests may differ from what is in the real interest of the community as a whole. This was perceived by Lord Radcliffe when he said, in *Glasgow Corporation* v. *Central Land Board* 1956 SC (HL) 1, 18–19, that 'The interests of government . . . do not exhaust the public interest.'

Legal argument about the nature of the state and its relation to the government is directed to limited and practical purposes, and may cause us to lose sight of wider political realities. These receive their due in the following passage.

Ralph Miliband, *The State in Capitalist Society* (1969), pp. 49–54

There is one preliminary problem about the state which is very seldom considered, yet which requires attention if the discussion of its nature and role is to be properly focused. This is the fact that 'the state' is not a thing, that it does not, as such, exist. What 'the state' stands for is a number of particular institutions which, together, constitute its reality, and which interact as parts of what may be called the state system.

The point is by no means academic. For the treatment of one part of the state – usually the government – as the state itself introduces a major element of confusion in the discussion of the nature and incidence of state *power*; and that confusion can have large political consequences. Thus, if it is believed that the government is in fact the state, it may also be believed that the assumption of governmental power is equivalent to the acquisition of state power. Such a belief, resting as it does on vast assumptions about the nature of state power, is fraught with great risks and disappointments. To understand the nature of state power, it is necessary first of all to distinguish, and then to relate, the various elements which make up the state system.

It is not very surprising that government and state should often appear as synonymous for it is the government which speaks on the state's behalf. It was the state to which Weber was referring when he said, in a famous phrase, that, in order to be, it must 'successfully claim the monopoly of the legitimate use of physical force within a given territory'. But 'the state' cannot claim anything: only the government of the day, or its duly empowered agents, can. Men, it is often said, give their allegiance not to the government of the day but to the state. But the state, from this point of view, is a nebulous entity; and while men may choose to give their allegiance to it, it is to the government that they are required to give their obedience. A defiance of its orders is a defiance of the state, in whose name the government alone may speak and for whose actions it must assume ultimate responsibility.

This, however, does not mean that the government is necessarily strong, either in relation to other elements of the state system or to forces outside it. On the contrary, it may be very weak, and provide a mere façade for one or other of these other elements and forces. In other words, the fact that the government does speak in the name of the state and is formally *invested* with state power, does not mean that it effectively *controls* that power. How far governments do control it is one of the major questions to be determined.

A second element of the state system which requires investigation is the administrative one, which now extends far beyond the traditional bureaucracy of the state, and which encompasses a large variety of bodies, often related to particular ministerial departments, or enjoying a greater or lesser degree of autonomy – public corporations, central banks, regulatory commissions, etc. – and concerned with the management of the economic, social, cultural and other activities in which the state is now directly or indirectly involved. The extraordinary growth of this administrative and bureaucratic element in all societies, including advanced capitalist ones, is of course one of the most obvious features of contemporary life; and the relation of its leading members to the government and to society is also crucial to the determination of the role of the state.

Formally, officialdom is at the service of the political executive, its obedient instrument, the tool of its will. In actual fact it is nothing of the kind. Everywhere and inevitably the administrative process is also part of the political process; administration is always political as well as executive, at least at the levels where policy-making is relevant, that is to say in the upper layers of administrative life. . . . Officials and administrators cannot divest themselves of all ideological clothing in the advice which they tender to their political masters, or in the independent decisions which they are in a position to take. The power which top civil servants and other state administrators possess no doubt varies from country to country, from department to department, and from individual to individual. But nowhere do these men *not* contribute directly and appreciably to the exercise of state power. . . .

Some of these considerations apply to all other elements of the state system. They apply for instance to a third such element, namely the military, to which may, for present purposes, be added the para-military, security and police forces of the state, and which together form that branch of it mainly concerned with the 'management of violence'.

In most capitalist countries, this coercive apparatus constitutes a vast, sprawling and resourceful establishment, whose professional leaders are men of high status and great influence, inside the state system and in society. Nowhere has the inflation of the military establishment been more marked since the second world war than in the United States, a country which had previously been highly civilian-orientated. And much the same kind of inflation has also occurred in the forces of 'internal security', not only in the United States; it is probably the case that never before in any capitalist country, save in Fascist Italy and Nazi Germany, has such a large proportion of people been employed on police and repressive duties of one kind or another.

Whatever may be the case in practice, the formal constitutional position of the administrative and coercive elements is to serve the state by serving the government of the day. In contrast, it is not at all the formal constitutional duty of judges, at least in Western-type political systems, to serve the purposes of their governments. They are constitutionally independent of the political executive and protected from it by security of tenure and other guarantees. Indeed, the concept of judicial independence is deemed to entail not merely the freedom of judges from responsibility to the political executive, but their active duty to protect the citizen *against* the political executive or its agents, and to act, in the state's encounter with members of society, as the defenders of the latter's rights and liberties. . . . But in any case, the judiciary is an integral part of the state system, which affects, often profoundly, the exercise of state power.

So too, to a greater or lesser degree, does a fifth element of the state system, namely the various units of sub-central government. In one of its aspects, sub-central government constitutes an extension of central government and administration, the latter's antennae or tentacles. In some political systems it has indeed practically no other function. In the countries of advanced capitalism, on the other hand, sub-central government is rather more than an administrative device. In addition to being agents of the state these units of government have also traditionally performed another function. They have not only been the channels of communication and administration from the centre to the periphery, but also the voice of the periphery, or of particular interests at the periphery; they have been a means of overcoming local particularities, but also platforms for their expression, instruments of central control and obstacles to it. For all the centralisation of power, which is a major feature of government in these countries, sub-central organs of government, notably in federal systems such as that of the United States, have remained power structures in their own right, and therefore able to affect very markedly the lives of the populations they have governed.

Much the same point may be made about the representative assemblies of advanced capitalism. Now more than ever their life revolves around the government; and even where, as in the United States, they are formally independent organs of constitutional and political power, their relationship with the political executive cannot be a purely critical or obstructive one. That relationship is one of conflict *and* cooperation.

Nor is this a matter of division between a pro-government side and an anti-government one. *Both* sides reflect this duality. For opposition parties cannot be wholly uncooperative. Merely by taking part in the work of the legislature, they help the government's business. . . .

As for government parties, they are seldom if ever single-minded in their support of the political executive and altogether subservient to it. They include people who, by virtue of their position and influence must be persuaded, cajoled, threatened or bought off.

It is in the constitutionally-sanctioned performance of this cooperative and critical function that legislative assemblies have a share in the exercise of state power. That share is rather less extensive and exalted than is often claimed for these bodies. But . . . it is not, even in an epoch of executive dominance, an unimportant one.

These are the institutions – the government, the administration, the military and the police, the judicial branch, sub-central government and parliamentary assemblies – which make up 'the state', and whose interrelationship shapes the form of the state system. It is these institutions in which 'state power' lies, and it is through them that this power is wielded in its different manifestations by the people who occupy the leading positions in each of these institutions – presidents, prime ministers and their ministerial colleagues; high civil servants and other state administrators; top military men; judges of the higher courts; some at least of the leading members of parliamentary assemblies, though these are often the same men as the senior members of the political executive; and, a long way behind, particularly in unitary states, the political and administrative leaders of sub-central units of the state. These are the people who constitute what may be described as the state elite.

The political scientist, aware of the ramifications of state power, may recognize as parts of the 'state system' institutions which the constitutional lawyer may regard as being outside his province. For here, too, the problem arises of drawing the boundaries of the constitution. Are political parties, for example, to be excluded as private law associations with no legally defined role in the political system? Yet our form of representative government is essentially one of *party* government. Parties dominate elections, the work of Parliament, the formation of governments: could any realistic description of the constitution fail to take account of them? Again, does the pale of the constitution include the public corporations and other quasi-autonomous public bodies that are linked with government and perform a variety of executive and advisory functions? The National Economic Development Council, for example, with its tripartite representation of government, employers and unions, has at certain times had a significant role in industrial policy-making. (Others of this numerous class of 'fringe' bodies which have public functions and stand in a close relation with government are the Bank of England, the Health and Safety Commission and the Export Guarantees Advisory Council. See further pp. 153–6 below.) Perhaps no one today would agree with Gladstone's dictum that the public schools were part of the constitution, despite the numerical preponderance of their products in Mrs Thatcher's Cabinet.

The structure of our major institutions is not fixed, and alterations are made to them from time to time. When these seem to affect fundamentals, prudence and respect for constitutionalism may argue a need to proceed on the basis of consensus.

When a Labour Government proposed in 1967 to reform the composition and powers of the House of Lords, it announced (in the Queen's speech) that it was 'prepared to enter into consultations appropriate to a constitutional change of such importance' (HC Deb. vol. 753, col. 7, 31 October 1967). Representatives of the official Opposition and of the Liberal Party joined with members of the Government in an inter-party conference which reached agreement on a scheme of reform. Although the inter-party discussions were broken off after the House of Lords had voted in June 1968 to reject the Southern Rhodesia (United Nations Sanctions) Order, the Government's Parliament (No. 2) Bill was based substantially on the agreed scheme. In the result, however, cross-party opposition to the bill in the House of Commons forced the Government to abandon it: there was insufficient support in the House for what would have been a radical alteration of the composition and powers of the second chamber.

The House of Lords as at present constituted would seem to be an irrational element in the constitution of twentieth-century Britain. The frequent emergence of proposals for its reform – and lately for its abolition – in the major political parties would suggest that, at least in its present form, it is not firmly supported by the political culture. Some believe that the existence of a second chamber in some form is an essential constitutional safeguard; others that if the House of Commons were reformed the need for a second chamber would disappear. The Labour Party favours abolition of the House of Lords. Would such action by a Labour Government be justified if the proposal had been included in its election manifesto? Should the issue be submitted to a referendum? (On the question whether Parliament can *lawfully* abolish the House of Lords see Peter Mirfield (1979) 95 *LQR* 36 and George Winterton, id., 386.)

The particular form that institutions may take is often less important than a principle embodied in them. 'What has to be ensured', says J. D. B. Mitchell ((1955) 67 *Juridical Review* 1 at 9), 'is that in changing constitutional forms the effective operation of old principles is preserved . . . .' For instance, the system of superior courts has often been modified: considerations of efficiency may require the amalgamation or replacement of courts or changes in their organization and procedures. But we should think that severe damage had been done to constitutionalism if there were to be any infringement of the principle of the independence of the judiciary, which rests on a foundation of legal rules (e.g. the rule of the Act of Settlement of 1701, now found in section 12(1) of the Supreme Court of Judicature (Consolidation) Act 1925, that a judge holds office during good behaviour, being removable from office on an address from both Houses of Parliament), conventions (e.g. the convention obliging judges to be politically neutral) and the law and custom of Parliament (e.g. the *sub judice* rule, prohibiting parliamentary consideration of matters before the courts). (On the independence of the judiciary see further Hartley and Griffith, *Government and Law*, p. 179 *et seq.*)

In the study of the constitution we are concerned not only with the structure of institutions but with the relations between them. It is in these relations – between the Crown (or ministers) and Parliament, ministers and the civil service, Parliament and political parties, the Lords and the Commons, the courts and the executive, and so on – that we may look for the effective distribution of power in the constitutional system. But relations of power are not something constant, and in the shifting ground of the relations between institutions there is a continuous interplay of ideas of separation and coordination, effectiveness and control, authority and accountability. We find, too, within the institutions themselves a dispersion of power and conflicts of interest or ideology – as in Parliament, between government and opposition, between ministers or opposition leaders and backbenchers, and between party factions. We need to be alert to the tensions and complexities – the organic life – within the solid-seeming forms of institutions like the Cabinet, Parliament and the courts.

3 The idea of the constitution

'Successful constitutions and institutions', says Ian Gilmour (*Inside Right: A Study of Conservatism*, 1978, p. 70), 'are not mere pieces of machinery. If they work, it is because of the ideas and beliefs of those who try to work them.' In Britain, he adds, the 'idea of the constitution' is more important than the constitution itself.

The British constitution, having evolved over centuries, does not embody any single constitutional theory. It is the product of a long period of kingly rule, parliamentary struggle, revolution, many concessions and compromises, a slow growth of custom, the making and breaking and alteration of many laws. Although we lack a general theory of the constitution, there has come down to us the idea of constitutionalism – of a *constitutional order* which acknowledges the power of government while placing conditions and limits upon its exercise. The British version of constitutionalism has been shaped by a number of leading ideas or principles: some of these have crystallized as rules or doctrines of the constitution; others have influenced constitutional thought or have gained currency as explanations or justifications of particular features of the constitution. In this section we shall consider some of these commanding ideas or doctrines and their place in the modern constitution.

(a) Democracy and the constitution

Since the achievement of universal suffrage with the enactment of the Representation of the People Acts 1918 and 1928 it can be claimed that the British constitution has embodied the principle of democracy.

There had been advocates of the principle much earlier, but democracy was 'still a pejorative term on both sides of the House in 1831–2' (D. G. Wright, *Democracy and Reform 1815–1885*, 1970, p. 38) and the idea of government by the whole people, as it would be understood today, was not accepted by political leaders at any time in the nineteenth century. Even after the Third Reform Act of 1884 only about 60 per cent of the adult male population, or about 28 per cent of the total adult population, had the vote. The Representation of the People Act 1918 introduced universal adult male suffrage (on condition of six months' residence in a constituency) and gave the right to vote to women aged over 30. The Act of 1928 lowered the voting age for women to 21, which was the same as for men, and the principle of 'one man or woman, one vote' was finally achieved when the Representation of the People Act 1948 abolished the business and university franchises which had qualified certain persons to cast more than one vote.

The First Reform Act of 1832 began a process by which the claims of democracy were progressively accommodated with the existing institutions of government. There was no sudden triumph of democracy such as might have been accompanied by new political institutions and a new foundation for the constitution upon the principle of rule by the people. But at all events in the present century the idea of democracy has taken root in the British political culture and is embraced, in one or other form, by all political parties of any significance.

Samuel Beer, *Modern British Politics* (3rd edn 1982), pp. 69–71

We expect a political party to take a distinctive approach to public policy. It is likely also to have its own view of how political power should be organized and exerted. In this century, the Labour Party introduced the question of Socialism into British politics. It has also been the principal means by which a new theory of representation has been propagated. It introduced into the political culture of Britain not only a new concept of public policy – Socialism – but also a new view of political organization which we may designate as 'Socialist Democracy'. This includes a distinctive view of party, interest groups, and indeed of the British constitution and the meaning of democracy.

But in Britain the old – and not least, the very old – often blends with the new. The

Toryism of the Conservative Party is a case in point. This pre-capitalist, pre-individualist, pre-liberal creed ought surely to have died out in the nineteenth century. Yet not only has it survived into the era of the Welfare State and the Managed Economy, it can also claim credit for having helped create them. British Tories are in some degree Collectivists, not only in certain aims of policy, but also in certain methods of political action. In both respects, they often have more in common with Socialists than with their contemporaries in the Liberal Party. Old traditions of strong government, paternalism, and the organic society have made easier the massive reassertion of state power that has taken place in recent decades, often under Conservative auspices. Old ideals of authority have been adapted to the conditions of mass suffrage in a theory of representation which we may call 'Tory Democracy'.

Socialist Democracy and Tory Democracy have a great deal in common. Both of course accept the basic legal structures of modern British government – universal suffrage, periodic elections, freedoms of speech and press, an elected legislature, a career civil service. Both accept the basic conventions of Cabinet Government, although there are aspects of these conventions that are interpreted differently. But what is most interesting is the extent to which they agree on how political power is to be organized within this legal and constitutional framework. This agreement sets both Tory and Socialist Democracy apart from nineteenth-century political individualism and constitutes a common theory of politics in the Collectivist era. This theory is not confined to the closets of political philosophers, but pervades the political culture of twentieth-century Britain and functions powerfully as an operative ideal in daily political life.

The major theme of this Collectivist theory of representation is party government; its minor theme, functional representation. In this Collectivist guise, democratic thought legitimizes a far greater role for group and party than did Liberal and Radical thought. To put the matter negatively: both Tory and Socialist Democracy reject parliamentarism. Both reject the notion that Members of Parliament should freely follow their own judgment when deciding how to vote and that the House of Commons is, or should be, in Bagehot's phrase, in 'a state of perpetual choice'. On the contrary, both demand that the MP should be not a 'representative' but a 'delegate' (although, to be sure, a party delegate, not a local delegate), and that the Government's majority should stand stoutly with it, as should the Opposition's minority. Both accept the great organized producer groups of a modern industrial society and attribute to them an important role in government and administration. Both, in short, depart in major respects from the political individualism of the nineteenth century.

But the political culture of a country is rarely monolithic. In modern Britain Liberal and Radical currents of opinion still run strongly. Even more important, however, is the dialectic between Tory and Socialist Democracy within the consensus of Collectivist politics. Conflict exists between Tory and Socialist views over the function of party and the meaning of democracy – and it is tempting to call this conflict fundamental.

Democracy as established in the United Kingdom is a form of that 'liberal democracy' which is associated with the countries of Western Europe and the United States. With us it occurs as a system of representative and responsible government in which voters elect the members of a representative institution, the House of Commons, and the government is accountable to the House and ultimately to the electorate.

Jack Lively, *Democracy* (1975), pp. 43–4

What then are the conditions necessary for the existence of responsible government? What is needed to ensure that some popular control can be exerted over political leadership, some governmental accountability can be enforced? Two main conditions can be suggested, that governments should be removable by electoral decisions and that some alternative can be substituted by electoral decision. The alternative, it should be stressed, must be more than an alternative governing group. It must comprehend alternatives in policy, since it is only if an electoral decision can alter the actions of government that popular control can be said to be established. The power of replacing Tweedledum by Tweedledee (the 'Ins' by the 'Outs', as Bentham had it) would be an insufficient basis for such control. To borrow the economic analogy, competition is meaningless, or at any rate cannot create consumer sovereignty, unless there is some product differentiation.

In detail there might be a great deal of discussion about the institutional arrangements necessary to responsible government, but in general some are obvious. There must be free elections, in which neither the incumbent government nor any other group can determine the electoral result by means other than indications of how they will act if returned to power. Fraud, intimidation and bribery are thus incompatible with responsible government . . . . Another part of the institutional frame necessary to responsible government is freedom of association. Unless groups wishing to compete for leadership have the freedom to organize and formulate alternative programmes, the presentation of alternatives would be impossible. Lastly, freedom of speech is necessary since silent alternatives can never be effective alternatives. In considering such arrangements, we cannot stick at simple legal considerations; we must move from questions of 'freedom from' to questions of 'ability to'. The absence of any legal bar to association will not, for example, create the ability to associate if there are heavy costs involved which only some groups can bear. Nor will the legal guarantee of freedom of speech be of much use if access to the mass media is severely restricted.

This could be summed up by saying that responsible government depends largely upon the existence of, and free competition between, political parties.

The degree of influence or control over government which is exercisable by the electorate depends upon a variety of factors, among them the electoral system adopted, party organization, and the particular concept of representation ('delegation' or 'authorization') which the constitution embodies. These are matters to which we shall return in chapter 8.

The kind of liberal democracy that is reflected in our present constitutional arrangements is neither flawless nor immutable. Should we not consider the claims of other models of democracy?

C. B. Macpherson, *The Life and Times of Liberal Democracy* (1977), pp. 6–8

Would it not be simpler to set up a single model of present liberal democracy, by listing the observable characteristics of the practice and theory common to those twentieth-century states which everyone would agree to call liberal democracies, that is, the systems in operation in most of the English-speaking world and most of Western Europe? Such a model could easily be set up. The main stipulations are fairly obvious. Governments and legislatures are chosen directly or indirectly by periodic elections with universal equal franchise, the voters' choice being normally a choice between political parties. There is a sufficient degree of civil liberties (freedom of speech, publication, and association, and freedom from arbitrary arrest and imprisonment) to make the right to choose effective. There is formal equality before the law. There is some protection for minorities. And there is general acceptance of a principle of maximum individual freedom consistent with equal freedom for others.

. . . It is all too easy, in using a single model, to block off future paths; all too easy to fall into thinking that liberal democracy, now that we have attained it, by whatever stages, is fixed in its present mould. Indeed, the use of a single contemporary model almost commits one to this position. For a single model of current liberal democracy, if it is to be realistic as an explanatory model, must stipulate certain present mechanisms, such as the competitive party system and wholly indirect (i.e. representative) government. But to do this is to foreclose options that may be made possible by changed social and economic relations. There may be strong differences of opinion about whether some conceivable future forms of democracy can properly be called *liberal* democracy, but this is something that needs to be argued, not put out of court by definition. One of the things that needs to be considered is whether liberal democracy in a large nation-state is capable of moving to a mixture of indirect and direct democracy: that is, is capable of moving in the direction of a fuller participation, which may require mechanisms other than the standard party system.

The democratic ideal is imperfectly realized in existing political institutions: the processes of government are remote from the mass of the people, who participate only indirectly and to a limited extent in political decision-making. Macpherson indicates that the theory of representative democracy may be opposed by one of *participatory* democracy which would accord a more active political role to the people. Is participatory democracy reconcilable with a system of party government? Could new institutional arrangements be devised which would provide for greater participation by the people in the political system? (See Carole Pateman, *Participation and Democratic Theory*, 1970.)

The idea of democracy stands so high on the western scale of values that our satisfaction in having achieved a democratic constitution may have a tendency to inhibit deeper inquiry. C. B. Macpherson reminds us in *The Real World of Democracy* (1972), p. 4, that a liberal democracy like any other organization of government is a system of power – a system 'by which power is exerted by the state over individuals and groups within it', and further that

a democratic government, like any other, exists to uphold and enforce a certain kind of society, a certain set of relations between individuals, a certain set of rights and claims that people have on each other both directly, and indirectly through their rights to property. These relations themselves are relations of power – they give different people, in different capacities, power over others.

This suggests that for a proper evaluation of our kind of democratic system we must ask some searching questions about it. Does it protect individual rights and ensure social justice? Do people rule, or does the system foster the emergence of remote and uncontrollable centres of power, dominated by élites? Does government act, without bias, for the general good, or does it chiefly serve the interests of the economically powerful?

(b) **Parliamentary sovereignty**

For Dicey, whose magisterial *Law of the Constitution* was first published in 1885, it was 'the very keystone of the law of the constitution' that Parliament is the sovereign or supreme legislative authority in the state.

Dicey, *The Law of the Constitution*, pp. 39–40

The principle of Parliamentary sovereignty means neither more nor less than this, namely, that Parliament . . . . has, under the English constitution, the right to make or unmake any law whatever; and, further, that no person or body is recognised by the law of England as having a right to override or set aside the legislation of Parliament.

The legislative supremacy of Parliament was assured by the Glorious Revolution of 1688, which established the primacy of statute over prerogative. Academic lawyers, drawing on works on political science, embraced it as orthodox doctrine, and the courts have propounded it as law. It is at once historical reality, theory of the constitution, and a fundamental principle of the common law. In accordance with this principle the courts hold that statutes enacted by Parliament must be enforced, and must be given priority over rules of common law, international law binding upon the United Kingdom, the enactments of subordinate legislative authorities, and earlier enactments of Parliament itself.

Cheney v. *Conn* [1968] 1 All ER 779 (Ungoed-Thomas J)

A taxpayer appealed against an assessment to income tax made under the Finance Act 1964. One of the grounds of the appeal was that, since the money would be used in part for the construction of nuclear weapons, and since (it was argued) such use was contrary to international law, the illegal purpose to which the statute was being applied invalidated the assessment. This argument failed; in dealing with it Ungoed-Thomas J said:

What the statute itself enacts cannot be unlawful, because what the statute says and provides is itself the law, and the highest form of law that is known to this country. It is the law which prevails over every other form of law, and it is not for the court to say that a parliamentary enactment, the highest law in this country, is illegal.

See also *Mortensen* v. *Peters* (1906) 14 SLT 227; *R.* v. *Secretary of State for the Home*

Department, ex p. Thakrar [1974] QB 684. In *Salomon* v. *Commissioners of Customs and Excise* [1967] 2 QB 116, 143, Diplock LJ observed that 'the sovereign power of the Queen in Parliament extends to breaking treaties'. On the other hand a court will as far as possible *interpret* a statute as being in conformity with international law and treaty obligations: *Salomon's* case, above, at p. 143.

Principles of common law, however fundamental, are not proof against statute. For example, until 1962 every British subject had the right at common law to enter and live in the United Kingdom, but this right was taken away by the Commonwealth Immigrants Acts 1962 and 1968 and the Immigration Act 1971. (See, too, *R.* v. *Jordan* [1967] Crim. LR 483, and pp. 92–3 below.)

The legal sovereignty of Parliament, from time to time positively asserted by the courts, is also sustained in a negative way by a consistent judicial disclaimer of any power of interference with Acts of Partament. In *Ex p. Canon Selwyn* (1872) 36 JP 54 a question was raised as to the validity of the Irish Church Act 1869. Cockburn CJ said:

[T]here is no judicial body in the country by which the validity of an act of parliament could be questioned. An act of the legislature is superior in authority to any court of law.

More recently Sir Robert Megarry VC said in *Manuel* v. *Attorney-General* [1983] Ch. 77, 86:

I am bound to say that from first to last I have heard nothing in this case to make me doubt the simple rule that the duty of the court is to obey and apply every Act of Parliament, and that the court cannot hold any such Act to be ultra vires. Of course there may be questions about what the Act means, and of course there is power to hold statutory instruments and other subordinate legislation ultra vires. But once an instrument is recognised as being an Act of Parliament, no English court can refuse to obey it or question its validity.

The qualification that the instrument before the court must be recognized as being an Act of Parliament was insisted upon long ago in *The Prince's Case* (1606) 8 Co. Rep. 1a, where it was said that if an Act of Parliament, although entered on the Parliament Roll,

be penned, that the King, with the assent of the Lords, or with the assent of the Commons, it is no Act of Parliament, for three ought to assent to it, *scil.* the King, the Lords, and the Commons or otherwise, it is not an Act of Parliament.

In *Bowles* v. *Bank of England* [1913] 1 Ch. 57, Parker J held that a resolution of the House of Commons was not enough to empower the Crown to levy income tax: only an Act of Parliament could authorize taxation.

But if an Act is expressed to have been enacted by Queen, Lords and Commons, the courts will not inquire whether it was properly passed, or represents the will of Parliament. This was affirmed in a famous dictum of Lord Campbell in *Edinburgh and Dalkeith Railway Co.* v. *Wauchope* (1842) 8 Cl. & Fin. 710. In this case it had been argued in the court below that a private Act of

Parliament was inoperative because notice to those affected by it had not been given as required by parliamentary standing orders. (Private Acts commonly affect private rights and are subject to a special parliamentary procedure.) Although this argument was abandoned in the House of Lords, Lord Campbell expressed a clear view on the point:

[A]ll that a Court of Justice can do is to look to the Parliamentary roll: if from that it should appear that a bill has passed both Houses and received the Royal Assent, no Court of Justice can inquire into the mode in which it was introduced into Parliament, nor into what was done previous to its introduction, or what passed in Parliament during its progress in its various stages through both Houses.

Some years later in *Lee* v. *Bude and Torrington Junction Rly Co.* (1871) LR 6 CP 576 there was again a challenge to the validity of a private Act, this time on the ground that the promoters of the Act had fraudulently misled Parliament as to the facts and the promoters' true purposes. In rejecting this argument, Willes J said:

Are we to act as regents over what is done by parliament with the consent of the Queen, lords, and commons? I deny that any such authority exists. If an Act of Parliament has been obtained improperly, it is for the legislature to correct it by repealing it: but, so long as it exists as law, the Courts are bound to obey it. The proceedings here are judicial, not autocratic, which they would be if we could make laws instead of administering them.

Despite these authorities the question of the validity of a private Act was once more to be argued in the courts.

British Railways Board v. *Pickin* [1974] AC 765 (HL)

In Acts of Parliament by which the old railway companies acquired land for laying railway lines it was provided that, if the lines should be discontinued, the land taken was to revert to the adjoining landowners. In 1968 the British Railways Board promoted a private bill which would extinguish the rights of reverter; it was passed as the British Railways Act 1968. The plaintiff (respondent in the House of Lords), who had acquired land adjoining a railway line that had been discontinued, brought an action in which he claimed that the relevant provision (section 18) of the Act of 1968 was invalid and ineffective to deprive him of his rights in the track. The Act, he maintained, had been improperly got through Parliament as an unopposed private bill, in that notice had not been given to affected landowners as required by standing orders, and Parliament had been misled by false statements in the preamble to the bill that notices and plans of the land had been published.

On the application of the Railways Board these contentions were ordered to be struck out of the pleadings as an abuse of the process of the court, but they were restored by the Court of Appeal as raising a triable issue. The Board's appeal against this decision was allowed by a unanimous House of Lords.

LORD REID: . . . The idea that a court is entitled to disregard a provision in an Act of Parliament on any ground must seem strange and startling to anyone with any knowledge of the history and law of our constitution, but a detailed argument has been submitted to your Lordships and I must deal with it.

I must make it plain that there has been no attempt to question the general supremacy of Parliament. In earlier times many learned lawyers seem to have believed that an Act of Parliament could be disregarded in so far as it was contrary to the law of God or the law of nature or natural justice, but since the supremacy of Parliament was finally demonstrated by the Revolution of 1688 any such idea has become obsolete.

The respondent's contention is that there is a difference between a public and a private Act. There are of course great differences between the methods and procedures followed in dealing with public and private Bills, and there may be some differences in the methods of construing their provisions. But the respondent argues for a much more fundamental difference. There is little in modern authority that he can rely on. The mainstay of his argument is a decision of this House, *Mackenzie* v. *Stewart* in 1754.

The Court of Appeal had been persuaded that in *Mackenzie* v. *Stewart* the House of Lords had refused to give effect to a private Act obtained by fraud. Lord Reid re-examined this old and ill-reported case, and concluded that it had been decided by putting a particular construction upon the Act in question, and not by holding it invalid. Lord Reid continued:

The function of the court is to construe and apply the enactments of Parliament. The court has no concern with the manner in which Parliament or its officers carrying out its Standing Orders perform these functions. Any attempt to prove that they were misled by fraud or otherwise would necessarily involve an inquiry into the manner in which they had performed their functions in dealing with the Bill which became the British Railways Act 1968. . . .

For a century or more both Parliament and the courts have been careful not to act so as to cause conflict between them. Any such investigations as the respondent seeks could easily lead to such a conflict, and I would only support it if compelled to do so by clear authority. But it appears to me that the whole trend of authority for over a century is clearly against permitting any such investigation.

The respondent is entitled to argue that section 18 should be construed in a way favourable to him and for that reason I have refrained from pronouncing on that matter. But he is not entitled to go behind the Act to show that section 18 should not be enforced. Nor is he entitled to examine proceedings in Parliament in order to show that the appellants by fraudulently misleading Parliament caused him loss. I am therefore clearly of opinion that this appeal should be allowed. . . .

Their Lordships gave express approval to the observations of Lord Campbell in *Wauchope's* case and Willes J in *Lee's* case quoted above. Lord Simon of Glaisdale relied in particular upon the privilege of Parliament declared in Article 9 of the Bill of Rights 1689 as disallowing any investigation of parliamentary proceedings. (See p. 62 below.) He also drew attention to a practical consideration:

[I]f there is evidence that Parliament may have been misled into an enactment, Parliament might well – indeed, would be likely to – wish to conduct its own inquiry. It would be unthinkable that two inquiries – one parliamentary and the other forensic – should proceed concurrently, conceivably arriving at different conclusions; and a parliamentary examination of parliamentary procedures and of the actions and understandings of officers of Parliament would seem to be clearly more satisfactory than one conducted in a court of law – quite apart from considerations of Parliamentary privilege.

Lord Morris was mindful of Parliament's original character as the supreme judicial body:

It would be impracticable and undesirable for the High Court of Justice to embark upon an inquiry concerning the effect or the effectiveness of the internal procedures in the High Court of Parliament or an inquiry whether in any particular case those procedures were effectively followed.

(See further Wallington (1974) 37 *MLR* 686.)

The principle of the 'sovereignty' or legislative supremacy of Parliament does not imply any statement about the location of *political* authority in the modern constitution. Dicey was himself careful to distinguish the 'legal conception' of sovereignty, which 'means simply the power of law-making unrestricted by any legal limit', from political sovereignty, which he saw as residing in the electorate (*Law of the Constitution*, pp. 72–6). As to this, the editor of Dicey (E. C. S. Wade) commented (op. cit., p. cxciv):

The power of the electorate is qualified by the recognition of the increased power of the Cabinet, which is able to utilise the power entrusted to it by the electorate to change the law at its will. But every Government is disposed to keep its ear to the ground to detect electoral rumblings. In other words, there is a change of emphasis. It is the Cabinet system which is fundamental to parliamentary government. That system depends for its efficiency as an instrument of government upon being able to use the legal supremacy of Parliament (or rather of the Commons) to serve its ends; it is saved from being an autocratic instrument by the knowledge that at intervals the electorate may alter the composition of the Commons and so place the supremacy of Parliament in other hands.

Wade added a warning:

Indeed the legal instrument of parliamentary supremacy stands in some risk of actually facilitating the creation of an extreme form of government at the present time, since any change, however fundamental, can be accomplished in law by an ordinary enactment of Parliament.

Notwithstanding the absolute terms in which parliamentary sovereignty is usually expressed, it is argued that there are certain legal limitations of Parliament's legislative competence which qualify that sovereignty. Arguments of this kind are based on the terms of England's union with Scotland in 1707 and on the accession of the United Kingdom to the European Communities in 1972, and will be considered in chapters 4 and 5. For the present we shall consider limitations of a different sort, which it is said that the sovereign Parliament can impose upon itself.

Transfers of sovereignty

First, it is argued (with equivocal support from Dicey, op. cit., p. 69 note) that Parliament can surrender its sovereign authority over particular territory to some other body of persons. The Statute of Westminster 1931 may be thought to have accomplished this. The Statute removed limitations upon the competence of Dominion parliaments and reinforced this conferment of legislative power with a provision, in section 4, intended to give a legal underpinning to the convention (itself reaffirmed in the preamble to the Statute) that the United Kingdom Parliament should not legislate for a Dominion without its consent. Section 4 provides:

No Act of Parliament of the United Kingdom passed after the commencement of this Act shall extend, or be deemed to extend, to a Dominion as part of the law of that Dominion unless it is expressly declared in that Act that that Dominion has requested, and consented to, the enactment thereof.

In more recent times Acts have been passed to transfer sovereign authority to former colonies and dependencies which have gained independence. In most of these independence Acts the renunciation of legislative competence is not qualified by a 'request and consent' provision like that in section 4 of the Statute of Westminster. For example the Zimbabwe Act 1979, section 1(2), provides:

On and after Independence Day Her Majesty's Government in the United Kingdom shall have no responsibility for the government of Zimbabwe; and no Act of the Parliament of the United Kingdom passed on or after that day shall extend, or be deemed to extend, to Zimbabwe as part of its law.

The majority opinion has held that the transfers of sovereignty effected by the Statute of Westminster and the independence Acts are in strict law only conditional, in that Parliament can at any time repeal or disregard these enactments and resume its entire legislative authority over the countries concerned. This was the view expressed in an obiter dictum of Lord Sankey, with reference to the application of section 4 of the Statute of Westminster to the Dominion of Canada, in *British Coal Corporation* v. *The King* [1935] AC 500, 520:

It is doubtless true that the power of the Imperial Parliament to pass on its own initiative any legislation that it thought fit extending to Canada remains in theory unimpaired: indeed, the Imperial Parliament could, as a matter of abstract law, repeal or disregard s.4 of the Statute.

But he went on to say:

But that is theory and has no relation to realities.

The position taken by Lord Sankey as a matter of 'abstract law' was countered by the assertion of a South African Judge (Stratford ACJ in *Ndlwana* v. *Hofmeyr*, 1937 AD 229, 237) that 'Freedom once conferred cannot be revoked.' This was echoed by Lord Denning in *Blackburn* v. *Attorney-General* [1971] 1 WLR 1037, 1040:

We have all been brought up to believe that, in legal theory, one Parliament cannot bind another and that no Act is irreversible. But legal theory does not always march alongside political reality. Take the Statute of Westminster 1931, which takes away the power of Parliament to legislate for the Dominions. Can any one imagine that Parliament could or would reverse that Statute? Take the Acts which have granted independence to the Dominions and territories overseas. Can anyone imagine that Parliament could or would reverse those laws and take away their independence? Most clearly not. Freedom once given cannot be taken away. Legal theory must give way to practical politics.

These constitutional issues arose in the following case.

> *Manuel* v. *Attorney-General* [1983] Ch. 77, 95 (Sir Robert Megarry
> v–c and the Court of Appeal)

The Canada Act 1982, making provision for a new constitution of Canada, had been passed by the United Kingdom Parliament on a request submitted by the Senate and the House of Commons of Canada with the agreement of nine of the ten provincial Governments. The plaintiffs were Canadian Indian Chiefs whose complaint was that the new constitution took away the special protection which had been accorded to the rights of the Indian peoples of Canada under the prior constitutional arrangements. They sought a number of declarations claiming that (1) the United Kingdom Parliament had no power to amend the constitution of Canada so as to prejudice the Indian nations of Canada without their consent; (2) the Canada Act 1982 was ultra vires and void. The defendant, the Attorney-General, moved that the statement of claim be struck out as disclosing no reasonable cause of action.

SIR ROBERT MEGARRY V–C: . . . On the face of it, a contention that an Act of Parliament is ultra vires is bold in the extreme. It is contrary to one of the fundamentals of the British Constitution. . . . As was said by Lord Morris of Borth-y-Gest [in *British Railways Board* v. *Pickin*, above] it is not for the courts to proceed 'as though the Act or some part of it had never been passed'; there may be argument on the interpretation of the Act, but 'there must be none as to whether it should be on the Statute Book at all'. . . .

Mr Macdonald [counsel for the Manuel plaintiffs] was, of course, concerned to restrict the ambit of the decision in *Pickin* v. *British Railways Board*. He accepted that it was a binding decision for domestic legislation, but he said that it did not apply in relation to the Statute of Westminster 1931 or to the other countries of the Commonwealth. . . . [This point] is founded upon the theory that Parliament may surrender its sovereign power over some territory or area of land to another person or body. . . . After such a surrender, any legislation which Parliament purports to enact for that territory is not merely ineffective there, but is totally void, in this country as elsewhere, since Parliament has surrendered the power to legislate; and the English courts have jurisdiction to declare such legislation ultra vires and void.

Before I discuss this proposition, and its application to Canada, I should mention one curious result of this theory which emerged only at a late stage. In response to a question, Mr Macdonald accepted that as the theory applied only to territories over which Parliament had surrendered its sovereignty, it did not affect territories over which Parliament had never exercised sovereignty. Thus if one adapts an example given by Jennings [*The Law and the Constitution*, 5 edn 1959] at pp. 170, 171, an English statute making it an offence to smoke in the streets of Paris or Vienna would be valid, though enforceable only against those who come within the jurisdiction, whereas an English statute making it an offence to smoke in the streets of Bombay or Sydney would be ultra vires and void, and an English court could make a declaration to this effect. At this stage I need say no more than that I find such a distinction surprising.

The plaintiffs had argued that the Statute of Westminster had transferred sovereignty to Canada, subject to section 7 of the Statute by which the United Kingdom Parliament retained power to enact amendments to the Canadian Constitution (contained in the British North America Acts). This power could be exercised (in what was argued to be the true meaning of section 4) only on condition that the actual request and consent of the Dominion had been forthcoming, and such consent must be expressed by all the provincial legislatures and by the Indian nations of Canada as well as by the federal Parliament. No such general consent of the Dominion had been given, and without it the United Kingdom Parliament could not legislate for Canada on any subject.

SIR ROBERT MEGARRY V–C: . . . In the present case I have before me a copy of the Canada Act 1982 purporting to be published by Her Majesty's Stationery Office. After reciting the request and consent of Canada and the submission of an address to Her Majesty by the Senate and House of Commons of Canada, there are the words of enactment:

> 'Be it therefore enacted by the Queen's Most Excellent Majesty, by and with the advice and consent of the Lords Spiritual and Temporal, and Commons, in this present Parliament assembled, and by the authority of the same, as follows: . . . .'

There has been no suggestion that the copy before me is not a true copy of the Act itself, or that it was not passed by the House of Commons and the House of Lords, or did not receive the Royal Assent . . . . The Canada Act 1982 is an Act of Parliament, and sitting as a judge in an English court I owe full and dutiful obedience to that Act.

I do not think that, as a matter of law, it makes any difference if the Act in question purports to apply outside the United Kingdom. I speak not merely of statutes such as the Continental Shelf Act 1964 but also of statutes purporting to apply to other countries. If that other country is a colony, the English courts will apply the Act even if the colony is in a state of revolt against the Crown and direct enforcement of the decision may be impossible: see *Madzimbamuto* v. *Lardner-Burke* [1969] 1 AC 645 . . . . Similarly if the other country is a foreign state which has never been British, I do not think that any English court would or could declare the Act ultra vires and void. No doubt the Act would normally be ignored by the foreign state and would not be enforced by it, but that would not invalidate the Act in this country. Those who infringed it could not claim that it was void if proceedings within the jurisdiction were taken against them. Legal validity is one thing, enforceability is another. Thus a marriage in Nevada may constitute statutory bigamy punishable in England (*Trial of Earl Russell* [1901] AC 446), just as acts in Germany may be punishable here as statutory treason: *Joyce* v. *Director of Public Prosecutions* [1946] AC 347. Parliament in fact legislates only for British subjects in this way; but if it also legislated for others, I do not see how the English courts could hold the statute void, however impossible it was to enforce it, and no matter how strong the diplomatic protests.

I do not think that countries which were once colonies but have since been granted independence are in any different position. Plainly once statute has granted independence to a country, the repeal of the statute will not make the country dependent once more; what is done is done, and is not undone by revoking the authority to do it . . . . But if Parliament then passes an Act applying to such a country, I cannot see why that Act should not be in the same position as an Act applying to what has always been a foreign country, namely, an Act which the English courts will recognise and apply but one which the other country will in all probability ignore.

Sir Robert Megarry accordingly held that the plaintiffs' statement of claim disclosed no reasonable cause of action. He concluded with the following observation:

Perhaps I may add this. I have grave doubts about the theory of the transfer of sovereignty as affecting the competence of Parliament. In my view, it is a fundamental of the English constitution that Parliament is supreme. As a matter of law the courts of England recognise Parliament as being omnipotent in all save the power to destroy its own omnipotence. Under the authority of Parliament the courts of a territory may be released from their legal duty to obey Parliament, but that does not trench on the acceptance by the English courts of all that Parliament does. Nor must validity in law be confused with practical enforceability.

The plaintiffs appealed. The Court of Appeal was content to assume in favour of the plaintiffs (while expressly refraining from deciding) the correctness of the proposition 'that Parliament can effectively tie the hands of its successors, if it passes a statute which provides that any future legislation on a specified subject shall be enacted only with certain specified consents'. But was this what Parliament had done in enacting section 4 of the Statute of Westminster? The judgment of the court (delivered by Slade LJ) proceeded on the basis that precise compliance with section 4 was necessary if the Canada Act 1982 was to be valid and effective. (This involved a further assumption in favour of the plaintiffs, that section 4 was not made inapplicable to the Canada Act 1982 by section 7(1) of the Statute of Westminster, which provided that 'Nothing in this Act shall be deemed to apply to the repeal, amendment or alteration of the British North America Acts . . . .')

SLADE LJ: . . . What then are the conditions which section 4 imposes? It is significant that, while the Preamble to the Statute of 1931 recites that 'it is in accord with the established constitutional position that no law hereafter made by the Parliament of the United Kingdom shall extend to any of the said Dominions as part of the law of that Dominion otherwise than at the request and with the consent of that Dominion . . . .'

Section 4 itself does *not* provide that no Act of the United Kingdom Parliament shall extend to a Dominion as part of the law of that Dominion unless the Dominion has *in fact* requested and consented to the enactment thereof. The condition that must be satisfied is a quite different one, namely, that it must be 'expressly declared in that Act that that Dominion has requested, and consented to, the enactment thereof'. Though Mr Macdonald [counsel for the plaintiffs] submitted that section 4 requires not only a declaration but a true declaration of a real request and consent, we are unable to read the section in that way. There is no ambiguity in the relevant words and the court would not in our opinion be justified in supplying additional words by a process of implication; it must construe and apply the words as they stand . . . . If an Act of Parliament contains an express declaration in the precise form required by section 4, such declaration is in our opinion conclusive so far as section 4 is concerned.

There was, we think, nothing unreasonable or illogical in this simple approach to the matter on the part of the legislature, in reserving to itself the sole function of deciding whether the requisite request and consent have been made and given. The present case itself provides a good illustration of the practical consequences that would have ensued, if section 4 had made an actual request and consent on the part of a Dominion a condition precedent to the validity of the relevant legislation, in such manner that the courts or anyone else would have had to look behind the relevant declaration in order to ascertain whether a statute of the United Kingdom Parliament, expressed to extend to that Dominion, was valid. There is obviously room for argument as to the identity of the representatives of the Dominion of Canada appropriate to express the relevant request and consent. Mr Macdonald, while firm in his submission that all legislatures of the Provinces of Canada had to join the Federal Parliament in expressing them, seemed less firm in his submission that all the Indian Nations had likewise to join. This is a point which might well involve difficult questions of Canadian constitutional law. Moreover, if all the Indian Nations did have to join, further questions might arise as to the manner in which the consents of these numerous persons and bodies had to be expressed and as to whether all of them had in fact been given. As we read the wording of section 4, it was designed to obviate the need for any further inquiries of this nature, once a statute, containing the requisite declaration, had been duly enacted by the United Kingdom Parliament. Parliament, having satisfied itself as to the request and consent, would make the declaration and that would be that.

Mr Macdonald submitted in the alternative that, even if section 4 on its proper construction does not itself bear the construction which he attributed to it, nevertheless, in view of the convention referred to in the third paragraph of the preamble, the actual request and consent of the Dominion is necessary before a law made by the United Kingdom Parliament can extend to that Dominion as part of its law. Whether or not an argument on these lines might find favour in the courts of a Dominion, it is in our opinion quite unsustainable in the courts of this country. The sole condition precedent which has to be satisfied if a law made by the United Kingdom Parliament is to extend to a Dominion as part of its law is to be found stated in the body of the Statute of 1931 itself (section 4). This court would run counter to all principles of statutory interpretation if it were to purport to vary or supplement the terms of this stated condition precedent by reference to some supposed convention, which, though referred to in the preamble, is not incorporated in the body of the Statute.

In the present instance, therefore, the only remaining question is whether it is arguable that the condition precedent specified in section 4 of the Statute of 1931 has not been complied with in relation to the Canada Act 1982. Is it arguable that it has not been 'expressly declared in that Act that that Dominion has requested, and consented to, the enactment thereof'? In our judgment this proposition is not arguable, inasmuch as the preamble to the Canada Act 1982 begins with the words 'Whereas Canada has requested and consented to the enactment of an Act of the Parliament of the United Kingdom to give effect to the provisions hereinafter set forth . . . .'

. . . [W]e conclude that, if and so far as the conditions of section 4 of the Statute of 1931 had to be complied with in relation to the Canada Act 1982, they were duly complied with by the declaration contained in the preamble to that Act . . . .

The attack on the validity of the Act therefore failed. By construing section 4 of the Statute of Westminster as requiring no more than a declaration in an Act that the Dominion had requested and consented to it, the Court of Appeal avoided having to decide the constitutional issues, whether Parliament can give up its sovereignty over a particular territory, and whether it can make the consent of some other body necessary for the validity of its Acts.

What answers to these questions are suggested by the judgment of Sir Robert Megarry (p. 28 above)?

See further the note on *Manuel* by Brigid Hadfield [1983] *PL* 351, and Marshall, *Constitutional Conventions*, ch. XII.

Continuing sovereignty and the 'new view'

Let us now put on one side the unlikely prospect of legislation by the United Kingdom Parliament purporting to alter the law of a state such as Zimbabwe (or Canada, since the Canada Act 1982) to which it has ostensibly made an unqualified transfer of legislative sovereignty.

The wider question remains, which has important practical implications, whether Parliament can bind itself (including succeeding Parliaments). The sovereignty of the United Kingdom Parliament is generally held to be of that transcendent kind that cannot be limited even by Parliament itself:

Godden v. *Hales* (1686) 11 St. Tr. 1165 (KB)

HERBERT CJ: . . . [I]f an act of parliament had a clause in it that it should never be repealed, yet without question, the same power that made it, may repeal it.

Professor H. L. A. Hart holds that the rule of parliamentary sovereignty is part of what he calls the 'rule of recognition' of our legal system. This is the fundamental or ultimate rule of the system which states the criteria for identifying valid rules of law: unlike all the other rules the rule of recognition is binding simply because it is accepted by the community, in particular by its judges and officials. Courts in the United Kingdom act upon a rule of recognition which includes the proposition that Parliament cannot bind itself.

H. L. A. Hart, *The Concept of Law* (1961), pp. 145–6

Under the influence of the Austinian doctrine that law is essentially the product of a legally untrammelled will, older constitutional theorists wrote as if it was a logical necessity that there should be a legislature which was sovereign, in the sense that it is free, at every moment of its existence as a continuing body, not only from legal limitations imposed *ab extra*, but also from its own prior legislation. That Parliament is sovereign in this sense may now be regarded as established, and the principle that no earlier Parliament can preclude its 'successors' from repealing its legislation constitutes part of the ultimate rule of recognition used by the courts in identifying valid rules of law. It is, however, important to see that no necessity of logic, still less of nature, dictates that there should be such a Parliament; it is only one arrangement among others, equally conceivable, which has come to be accepted with us as the criterion of legal validity. Among these others is another principle which might equally well, perhaps better, deserve the name of 'sovereignty'. This is the principle that Parliament should *not* be incapable of limiting irrevocably the legislative competence of its successors but, on the contrary, should have this wider self-limiting power. Parliament would then at least once in its history be capable of exercising an even larger sphere of legislative competence than the accepted established doctrine allows to it. The requirement that at every moment of its existence Parliament should be free from legal limitations including even those imposed by itself is, after all, only one interpretation of the ambiguous idea of legal omnipotence. It in effect makes a choice between a *continuing* omnipotence in all matters not affecting the legislative competence of successive parliaments, and an unrestricted *self-embracing* omnipotence the exercise of which can only be enjoyed once. These two conceptions of omnipotence have their parallel in two conceptions of an omnipotent God: on the one hand, a God who at every moment of His existence enjoys the same powers and so is incapable of cutting down those powers, and, on the other, a God whose powers include the power to destroy for the future his omnipotence. Which form of omnipotence – continuing or self-embracing – our Parliament enjoys is an empirical question concerning the form of rule which is accepted as the ultimate criterion in identifying the law. Though it is a question about a rule lying at the base of a legal system, it is still a question of fact to which at any given moment of time, on some points at least, there may be a quite determinate answer. Thus it is clear that the presently accepted rule is one of continuing sovereignty, so that Parliament cannot protect its statutes from repeal.

The rule of recognition, which affirms the sovereignty of Parliament, may change over time; political developments may eventually cause the courts to give obedience to a modified or new rule of recognition. But while it stands it has, as Hart says, a 'unique authoritative status'. The rule of parliamentary sovereignty is not alterable even by Parliament itself.

H. W. R. Wade, 'The Basis of Legal Sovereignty' [1955] *CLJ*
172, at 187–9

But to deny that Parliament can alter this particular rule [that the courts will enforce statutes] is not so daring as it may seem at first sight; for the sacrosanctity of the rule is an inexorable corollary of Parliament's continuing sovereignty. If the one proposition is asserted, the other must be conceded. Nevertheless some further justification is called for, since there must be something peculiar about a rule of common law which can stand against a statute.

The peculiarity lies in this, that the rule enjoining judicial obedience to statutes is one of the fundamental rules upon which the legal system depends. That there are such rules, and that they are in a very special class, is explained with great clarity by Salmond:

> 'All rules of law have historical sources. As a matter of fact and history they have their origin somewhere, though we may not know what it is. But not all of them have legal sources. Were this so, it would be necessary for the law to proceed *ad infinitum* in tracing the descent of its principles. It is requisite that the law should postulate one or more first causes, whose operation is ultimate and whose authority is un-derived. . . . The rule that a man may not ride a bicycle on the footpath may have its source in the by-laws of a municipal council; the rule that these by-laws have the force of law has its source in an Act of Parliament. But whence comes the rule that Acts of Parliament have the force of law? This is legally ultimate; its source is historical only, not legal. . . . It is the law because it is the law, and for no other reason that it is possible for the law itself to take notice of. *No statute can confer this power upon Parliament, for this would be to assume and act on the very power that is to be conferred.*'

Once this truth is grasped, the dilemma is solved. For if no statute can establish the rule that the courts obey Acts of Parliament, similarly no statute can alter or abolish that rule. The rule is above and beyond the reach of statute, as Salmond so well explains, because it is itself the source of the authority of statute. This puts it into a class by itself among rules of common law, and the apparent paradox that it is unalterable by Parliament turns out to be a truism. The rule of judicial obedience is in one sense a rule of common law, but in another sense – which applies to no other rule of common law – it is the ultimate *political* fact upon which the whole system of legislation hangs. Legislation owes its authority to the rule: the rule does not owe its authority to legislation. To say that Parliament can change the rule, merely because it can change any other rule, is to put the cart before the horse.

For the relationship between the courts of law and Parliament is first and foremost a political reality. Historical illustrations of this are plentiful. When Charles I was executed in 1649 the courts continued to enforce the Acts of the Long Parliament, the Rump, Barebones' Parliament, and the other Commonwealth legislatures. For a revolution took place, and the courts (without any authority from the *previous* sovereign legislature) spontaneously transferred their allegiance from the King in Parliament to the kingless Parliaments. In other words, the courts altered their definition of 'an Act of Parliament' and recognised that the seat of sovereignty had shifted. This was a political fact from which legal consequences flowed. But in 1660 there was a counter-revolution: Charles II was restored, and it was suddenly discovered that all Acts passed by the Commonwealth Parliaments were void for want of the royal assent. The courts, again without any prior authority, shifted their allegiance back to the King in Parliament, and all the Commonwealth legislation was expunged from the statute book. The 'glorious revolution' of 1688 was, in its legal aspect if in no other, much like the revolution of 1649, for the courts, recognising political realities but without any *legal* justification, transferred their obedience from James II to William and Mary. Had the

Jacobite rebellions of 1715 and 1745 succeeded, the courts might once again have held all intervening legislation – including the Bill of Rights and Act of Settlement – void for lack of the assent of the proper monarch. The fact that William and Mary's Parliament had passed Acts confirming their title to the Crown and its own legislative authority would obviously not have availed in the least.

What Salmond calls the 'ultimate legal principle' is therefore a rule which is unique in being unchangeable by Parliament – it is changed by revolution, not by legislation; it lies in the keeping of the courts, and no Act of Parliament can take it from them. This is only another way of saying that it is always for the courts, in the last resort, to say what is a valid Act of Parliament; and that the decision of this question is not determined by any rule of law which can be laid down or altered by any authority outside the courts. It is simply a political fact.

It is argued by some constitutional theorists (whose argument derives a gratuitous advantage from being sometimes described as the 'new view' of parliamentary sovereignty) that the orthodox doctrine of sovereignty does not prevent Parliament from binding itself as to the 'manner and form' (as opposed to the content) of future legislation. (See, e.g., R. F. V. Heuston, *Essays in Constitutional Law*, 2nd edn 1964, ch. 1.) According to this view, Parliament could effectively provide that an Act might be repealed or amended only by a specified majority in both Houses, or only with the approval of the electorate in a referendum, or only by the use of a specified verbal formula in the amending Act. We saw an example of the last sort in section 4 of the Statute of Westminster 1931 as that section was interpreted by the Court of Appeal in *Manuel* v. *Attorney-General* (requiring only a declaration of request and consent in an Act extending to a Dominion) but the court did not decide what would have been the effect of an Act not including the required verbal formula. The 'new view' that such self-imposed procedural limitations would be binding on Parliament relies mainly on Commonwealth cases, of which the following is an example.

Harris v. *Minister of the Interior*, 1952 (2) SA 428
(Appellate Division of the Supreme Court
of South Africa)

The South Africa Act 1909, an Act of the United Kingdom Parliament, joined together four colonies as the Union of South Africa, and created the Parliament of the Union. This was initially a non-sovereign legislature which by reason of the Colonial Laws Validity Act 1865 had no general power to legislate inconsistently with United Kingdom statutes extending to South Africa. But section 152 of the South Africa Act empowered the Union Parliament to 'repeal or alter any of the provisions of this Act'.

Those who framed the South Africa Act were concerned to protect and entrench existing voting rights, in particular the rights of the 'Cape Coloured' voters of the former Cape Colony. Accordingly section 35(1) of the Act provided that no Act of the Union Parliament should disqualify any person in the Cape Province as a voter by reason of his race or colour, unless the bill be passed by both Houses of Parliament sitting together, and at the third reading be agreed to by not less than two-thirds of the total number of members of both Houses.

Section 35 was itself entrenched in a proviso to section 152, by which any repeal or alteration of section 35, or indeed of section 152, could be effected only by the same method of a bill passed by a two-thirds majority at a joint sitting of both Houses.

In 1948 a National Government came into power and initiated an intensified policy of white supremacy under the name of *apartheid*. By that date South Africa had, as a result of constitutional convention and the Statute of Westminster 1931, shed its colonial status and was acknowledged to be an independent and sovereign state within the Commonwealth. In 1951 the Union Parliament passed by a simple majority, the two Houses sitting separately, a Separate Representation of Voters Act (Act 46 of 1951) which deprived Cape Coloured voters of their existing voting rights, by providing for their registration on a separate voters' roll. Some of the disqualified voters brought proceedings to challenge the validity of the Act.

The argument of counsel for the Government was that the Union Parliament, having acquired full legislative sovereignty as a result of the Statute of Westminster, was free to disregard the limitations contained in sections 35 and 152 of the South Africa Act 1909.

A unanimous Appellate Division held that the Separate Representation of Voters Act was null and void:

CENTLIVRES CJ: . . . It is common cause that Act 46 of 1951 was passed by the House of Assembly and the Senate sitting separately and assented to by the Governor-General and that it was not passed in conformity with the provisions of sec.35(1) and sec.152 of the South Africa Act. . . .

If Act 46 of 1951 had been passed before the Statute of Westminster, it is clear . . . that that Act would not have been a valid Act, as it was not passed in accordance with the procedure prescribed by secs 35(1) and 152. . . .

The effect of sub-sec.(1) of sec.2 [of the Statute of Westminster] is that the Colonial Laws Validity Act no longer applies to any law made . . . by the Union Parliament. Consequently the Union Parliament can now make a law repugnant to a British Act of Parliament in so far as that Act extends to the Union. . . . [I]t is clear that when [the Statute of Westminster] refers to a law made by a Dominion, such law means in relation to South Africa a law made by the Union Parliament functioning either bicamerally or unicamerally in accordance with the requirements of the South Africa Act.

[The judge referred to the argument of counsel for the Government that the effect of the Statute of Westminster was that the Union was a sovereign state and that all fetters binding the Union Parliament had fallen away, and continued:]

A State can be unquestionably sovereign although it has no legislature which is completely sovereign. As Bryce points out in his *Studies in History and Jurisprudence* legal sovereignty may be divided between two authorities. In the case of the Union, legal sovereignty is or may be divided between Parliament as ordinarily constituted and Parliament as constituted under . . . the proviso to sec.152. Such a division of legislative powers is no derogation from the sovereignty of the Union and the mere fact that that division was enacted in a British Statute (viz., the South Africa Act) which is still in force in the Union cannot affect the question in issue.

. . . The South Africa Act, the terms and conditions of which were, as its preamble shows, agreed to by the respective Parliaments of the four original Colonies, created the Parliament of the Union. It is that Act and not the Statute of Westminster which prescribes the manner in which the constituent elements of Parliament must function for the purpose of passing legislation. While the Statute of Westminster confers further powers on the Parliament of the Union, it in no way prescribes how that Parliament must function in exercising those powers.

. . . [T]he Statute of Westminster has left the entrenched clauses of the South Africa Act intact, and, that being so, it follows that . . . courts of law have the power to declare Act 46 of 1951 invalid on the ground that it was not passed in conformity with the provisions of secs 35 and 152 of the South Africa Act. . . . To hold otherwise would mean that Courts of law would be powerless to protect the rights of individuals which were specially protected in the constitution of this country. . . .

(The judicial vindication in this great case of the rule of law and the rights of individuals was countered by further measures taken by the National Government which succeeded eventually in removing the Cape Coloured voters from the common roll. The whole course of the constitutional battle is considered by Geoffrey Marshall, *Parliamentary Sovereignty and the Commonwealth* (1957), ch. 11.)

The *Harris* case established the principle that a Parliament may be sovereign and yet be subject to requirements of manner and form for the legally effective expression of its will. But this does not justify us in concluding that the United Kingdom Parliament can impose legally binding requirements of manner and form upon itself. The Union Parliament owed its existence to the South Africa Act, which therefore had a special status as the constituent instrument of that Parliament. Only when functioning in accordance with the procedural requirements of the constituent Act could it be said that the Union Parliament functioned at all. Other Commonwealth cases that are invoked in support of the 'new view' of parliamentary sovereignty, such as *Attorney-General for New South Wales* v. *Trethowan* [1932] AC 526 and *Bribery Commissioner* v. *Ranasinghe* [1965] AC 172, also depend upon the special authority of the instrument containing the limiting provisions. In the constitution of the United Kingdom, on the other hand, as the Privy Council observed in *Ranasinghe*'s case, 'there is no governing instrument which prescribes the law-making powers and the forms which are essential to those powers'.

As regards requirements of manner and form imposed by the United Kingdom Parliament upon itself, the following case gives no encouragement to exponents of the 'new view'.

Ellen Street Estates Ltd v. *Minister of Health* [1934] 1 KB 590 (CA)

The Acquisition of Land (Assessment of Compensation) Act 1919 laid down the principles on which compensation was to be assessed for the compulsory acquisition of land for public purposes. Section 7(1) said that the provisions of any Act authorizing compulsory acquisition 'shall . . . have effect subject to this Act, and so far as inconsistent with this Act those provisions shall cease to have or shall not have effect'. On one view section 7(1) is correctly construed as applying only to past enactments, but it was argued in this case that it applied also to later Acts and that, as a consequence, inconsistent provisions in the Housing Act 1925 were of no effect. It was held by the Court of Appeal that even if section 7(1) of the Act of 1919 was intended to apply to later Acts, it could not control future Parliaments, and the provisions of the Housing Act 1925 therefore overrode those of the Act of 1919.

SCRUTTON LJ: . . . Such a contention involves this proposition, that no subsequent Parliament by enacting a provision inconsistent with the Act of 1919 can give any effect to the words it uses. . . . That is absolutely contrary to the constitutional position that Parliament can alter an Act previously passed, and it can do so by repealing in terms the previous Act . . . and it can do it also in another way – namely, by enacting a provision which is clearly inconsistent with the previous Act.

MAUGHAM LJ: . . . The Legislature cannot, according to our constitution, bind itself as to the form of subsequent legislation, and it is impossible for Parliament to enact that in a subsequent statute dealing with the same subject-matter there can be no implied repeal. If in a subsequent Act Parliament chooses to make it plain that the earlier statute is being to some extent repealed, effect must be given to that intention just because it is the will of the legislature.

The same conclusion on this point had been reached earlier by the Divisional Court in *Vauxhall Estates Ltd* v. *Liverpool Corporation* [1932] 1 KB 733. But these cases are not necessarily conclusive of the matter. T.R.S. Allan, 'Parliamentary Sovereignty: Lord Denning's Dexterous Revolution' (1983) 3 *Oxford J. Legal Stud.* 22, argues that the 'fundamental' rule about parliamentary sovereignty is in fact indeterminate: it does not specify whether sovereignty is 'continuing' or 'self-embracing'. It is therefore for the judges to decide on the effectiveness of any self-imposed limitation of manner and form as and when the question arises, and they may respond to a 'readiness of the political climate for change' in upholding such a limitation. See further on the entrenchment of fundamental rights, pp. 99–104 below, and on sovereignty and the European Community, pp. 275–84 below.

The rule of parliamentary sovereignty is the keystone of the constitution. It provides a party elected into office by the people with the legal capacity to put its policies into effect, and in this respect serves the claims of democracy. Governments have been able to call on the sovereign power of Parliament in attacking the great issues of poverty and inequality and in establishing a welfare state. But is a legally unlimited power something alien to the idea of constitutionalism, creating a constant danger of arbitrary rule? It is 'Parliament's sovereign power', says Lord Scarman, 'more often than not exercised at the will of an executive sustained by an impregnable majority, that has brought about the modern imbalance in the legal system' (*English Law – The New Dimension*, 1974, p.74).

(c) **The separation of powers**

A doctrine of the separation of powers was formulated by English writers and controversialists of the seventeenth century who argued for the separation of the legislative and executive (then including judicial) functions of government, seeing in this a means to restrain the abuse of governmental power. The theory of the separation of powers was further developed by John Locke in his *Second Treatise of Civil Government* (1690) and more systematically in France by Montesquieu in *The Spirit of Law* (1748). Montesquieu, in the context of his description of an idealized English constitution, distinguished the legislative, executive and judicial functions of government, which he maintained should be exercised by different persons, and insisted on the independence of the judiciary. (Montesquieu also held that the judiciary should not be identified with any one estate or class of persons in the state.) 'All would be lost', he wrote (*The Spirit of Laws*, Book xi, ch. 6), 'if the same man or the same ruling body, whether of nobles or of the people, were to exercise these three powers, that of law-making, that of executing the public resolutions, and that of judging crimes and civil causes.' He held also that the legislature and the executive should have powers to enable each to check or limit the other.

Montesquieu's work ensured the lasting influence of the theory of the separation of powers. In England, however, this theory was opposed in the eighteenth century by the doctrine of the mixed or balanced constitution, in which monarchical, aristocratic and democratic elements were joined and held in equilibrium. Despite Blackstone's acceptance of a modified theory of the separation of powers (in his *Commentaries on the Laws of England*, 1765) this theory was not to prevail as an explanation of English constitutional arrangements; nor did it provide a focus for constitutional reform. It was in America that the theory was to be accepted by political leaders and makers of constitutions, and the federal constitution adopted in 1789 was based on a conception of the separation of powers qualified by a machinery of checks and balances.

The system of parliamentary government that evolved in the United Kingdom in the nineteenth century under the impetus of the Reform Act of 1832 was evidently not based on the separation of powers, and the modern constitution is even less conformable to that theory, for nowadays 'rules are made by civil servants and by judges as well as by legislatures; rules are applied by the courts as well as by "the executive"; and judgements are made by civil servants and ministers as well as by judges' (M. J. C. Vile, *Constitutionalism and the Separation of Powers*, 1967, p. 317). On the other hand the Donoughmore Committee, in inquiring into delegated legislation and administrative adjudication, did not consider that the idea of the separation of powers was wholly without relevance to the British constitution.

Report of the Committee on Ministers' Powers
(Donoughmore Committee),
Cmd 4060/1932, pp. 4–5

In the British Constitution there is no such thing as the absolute separation of legislative, executive, and judicial powers; in practice it is inevitable that they should overlap. In such constitutions as those of France and the United States of America, attempts to keep them rigidly apart have been made, but have proved unsuccessful. The distinction is none the less real, and for our purposes important. One of the main problems of a modern democratic state is how to preserve the distinction, whilst avoiding too rigid an insistence on it, in the wide borderland where it is convenient to entrust minor legislative and judicial functions to executive authorities.

It is customary to-day for parliament to delegate minor legislative powers to subordinate authorities and bodies. Ministers of the Crown are the chief repositories of such powers; but they are conferred also, in differing degrees, upon Local Authorities, statutory corporations and companies, Universities, and representative bodies of solicitors, doctors and other professions. Some people hold the view that this practice of delegating legislative powers is unwise, and might be dispensed with altogether. A similar view is held with regard to the delegation to Ministers by statutory authority of judicial and quasi-judicial functions. It has even been suggested that the practice of passing such legislation is wholly bad, and should be forthwith abandoned. We do not think that this is the considered view of most of those who have investigated the problem, but many of them would like the practice curtailed as much as possible. It may be convenient if on the threshold of our report we state our general conclusion on the whole matter. We do not agree with those critics who think that the practice is wholly bad. We see in it definite advantages, provided that the statutory powers are exercised and the statutory functions performed in the right way. But risks of abuse are incidental to it, and we believe that safeguards are required, if the country is to continue to enjoy the advantages of the practice without suffering from its inherent dangers.

The Donoughmore Committee was appointed in a political atmosphere which was generally hostile to the delegation by Parliament of legislative and judicial functions to ministers and other public authorities. It had been asserted that the practice of delegation, in its denial of the separation of powers, presented a threat to parliamentary sovereignty and the rule of law. The Committee, however, declined to give its imprimatur to a strict separation of powers, seeing the doctrine as no more than a 'rule of political wisdom' which 'must give way where sound reasons of public policy so require' (p. 95). Moreover it rejected the view that the delegation of law-making and judicial powers had led to a 'new despotism' of officials.

The doctrine of the separation of powers cannot explain the complex and overlapping processes of law-making, administration and adjudication in contemporary Britain. But the idea contained in the doctrine is not spent, and still today, as Vile (op. cit. p. 10) aptly says,

We are not prepared to accept that government can become, on the grounds of 'efficiency', or for any other reason, a single undifferentiated monolithic structure, nor can we assume that government can be allowed to become simply an accidental agglomeration of purely pragmatic relationships.

And he goes on to say (p. 15): 'The diffusion of authority among different centres of decision-making is the antithesis of totalitarianism or absolutism.' Values which were once associated with a doctrine of the formal separation of legislative, executive and judicial powers may now be represented by the pluralist arrangements of the modern state, in which the powerful departments of central government operate in a world of countervailing powers exercised by Parliament, courts, political parties, local government and the empire of pressure groups.

The courts in the constitution

In particular, the idea of a separation of powers still has value in explaining and justifying the role and authority of the courts in the constitution. There are issues that are most appropriately resolved by a process of adjudication, in which decisions are reached after hearing argument and by reference to legal rules and principles. Certain of these issues are best adjudicated by courts which are independent of the executive. In deciding whether a particular matter is suitable for judical determination, account must be taken of the nature of the process of adjudication and of the limits of the expertise and resources available to the courts. Some questions are 'non-justiciable' because they cannot be satisfactorily decided by the process of legal argument and rule-application, or because they raise wide issues of policy or the public interest of which it is impossible for the courts to inform themselves adequately within the limits of existing judicial procedures. These questions should be referred to other agencies which are better equipped to decide them. (See Harlow and Rawlings, *Law and Administration*, ch. 3.)

The courts will themselves decline to undertake inquiries into matters which they identify as non-justiciable: for example, one of the grounds of decision in *Chandler* v. *Director of Public Prosecutions* [1964] AC 763 (p. 11 above) was that the question whether it was in the interests of the state for the armed forces to be provided with nuclear weapons was a political question which was not appropriate for judicial determination.

We can discern the idea of the separation of powers in the constitutional role of the courts in reviewing the exercise of power by public authorities, at the instance of individuals whose interests are affected: here the separation of powers supports the 'rule of law' (pp. 46–58 below) for, as R. M. Unger says (*Law in Modern Society*, 1977, p. 177):

For the administrator to act within the boundaries set by the laws, there must be some other person with final authority to determine what the laws mean, and to do so by a method different from the administrative one. This official is the judge.

By the constitutional power of judicial review, which is only considered to be excluded by the most explicit language in an Act of Parliament, the courts will intervene if a public authority acts unlawfully or abuses its power. The essence of judicial review, as Lord Devlin has said, 'is that all power, however plenary in form, is given for a purpose and that, if it is exercised for any other purpose, it is abused' (*The Times*, 27 October 1976). The principle of judicial review was explained as follows by Kerr LJ in *R. v. London Transport Executive, ex p. Greater London Council* [1983] QB 484, 490:

Authorities invested with discretionary powers by an Act of Parliament can only exercise such powers within the limits of the particular statute. So long as they do not transgress their statutory powers, their decisions are entirely a matter for them . . . subject, however, to one important proviso. This is . . . that they must not exercise their powers arbitrarily or so unreasonably that the exercise of the discretion is clearly unjustifiable. . . .

If an authority misdirects itself in law, or acts arbitrarily on the basis of considerations which lie outside its statutory powers, or so unreasonably that its decisions cannot be justified by any objective standard of reasonableness, then it is the duty and function of the courts to pronounce that such decisions are invalid when these are challenged by anyone aggrieved by them and who has the necessary locus standi to do so.

Applying these principles the courts can exercise a far-reaching control. Most powers of the administration are statutory and the courts, in interpreting the statute and ascertaining its objects and policy, can mark out the limits of the power. The courts have, indeed, shown themselves willing to make a bold use of the principles of judicial review, and it is right that they should check any abuse of power by public authorities: this is essential for the maintenance of the rule of law. But the separation of powers also requires an observance of judicial restraint, for otherwise the courts might themselves be guilty of a usurpation of power. This danger was adverted to by Lord Brightman in *Chief Constable of the North Wales Police v. Evans* [1982] 3 All ER 141 at 154, and Lord Hailsham warned in the same case (p. 143) that the function of the courts in exercising judicial review 'is to see that lawful authority is not abused by unfair treatment and not to attempt itself the task entrusted to that authority by the law'. It follows that the courts do not interfere with the merits of decisions reached by the executive as a matter of policy: this is where the boundary runs between the courts and the executive.

The separation of powers also defines the role of the courts in relation to Parliament, as was emphasized in *Duport Steels Ltd v. Sirs* (below). In this case the House of Lords reversed the decision of the Court of Appeal in which a restrictive interpretation had been placed on section 13(1) of the Trade Union and Labour Relations Act 1974 (as amended in 1976), which conferred immunity from liability in tort for an act done by a person 'in contemplation or furtherance of a trade dispute'.

Duport Steels Ltd v. *Sirs* [1980] 1 WLR 142 (HL)

LORD DIPLOCK: . . . My Lords, at a time when more and more cases involve the application of legislation which gives effect to policies that are the subject of bitter public and parliamentary controversy, it cannot be too strongly emphasised that the British constitution, though largely unwritten, is firmly based upon the separation of powers; Parliament makes the laws, the judiciary interpret them. When Parliament legislates to remedy what the majority of its members at the time perceive to be a defect or a lacuna in the existing law (whether it be the written law enacted by existing statutes or the unwritten common law as it has been expounded by the judges in decided cases), the role of the judiciary is confined to ascertaining from the words that Parliament has approved as expressing its intention what that intention was, and to giving effect to it. Where the meaning of the statutory words is plain and unambiguous it is not for the judges to invent fancied ambiguities as an excuse for failing to give effect to its plain meaning because they themselves consider that the consequences of doing so would be inexpedient, or even unjust or immoral. In controversial matters such as are involved in industrial relations there is room for differences of opinion as to what is expedient, what is just and what is morally justifiable. Under our constitution it is Parliament's opinion on these matters that is paramount.

A statute passed to remedy what is perceived by Parliament to be a defect in the existing law may in actual operation turn out to have injurious consequences that Parliament did not anticipate at the time the statute was passed; if it had, it would have made some provision in the Act in order to prevent them. It is at least possible that Parliament when the Acts of 1974 and 1976 were passed did not anticipate that so widespread and crippling use as has in fact occurred would be made of sympathetic withdrawals of labour and of secondary blacking and picketing in support of sectional interests able to exercise 'industrial muscle'. But if this be the case it is for Parliament, not for the judiciary, to decide whether any changes should be made to the law as stated in the Acts, and, if so, what are the precise limits that ought to be imposed upon the immunity from liability for torts committed in the course of taking industrial action. These are matters on which there is a wide legislative choice the exercise of which is likely to be influenced by the political complexion of the government and the state of public opinion at the time amending legislation is under consideration.

It endangers continued public confidence in the political impartiality of the judiciary, which is essential to the continuance of the rule of law, if judges, under the guise of interpretation, provide their own preferred amendments to statutes which experience of their operation has shown to have had consequences that members of the court before whom the matter comes consider to be injurious to the public interest. The frequency with which controversial legislation is amended by Parliament itself (as witness the Act of 1974 which was amended in 1975 as well as in 1976) indicates that legislation, after it has come into operation, may fail to have the beneficial effects which Parliament expected or may produce injurious results that Parliament did not anticipate. But, except by private or hybrid Bills, Parliament does not legislate for individual cases. Public Acts of Parliament are general in their application; they govern all cases falling within categories of which the definitions are to be found in the wording of the statute. So in relation to section 13 (1) of the Acts of 1974 and 1976, for a judge (who is always dealing with an individual case) to pose himself the question: 'Can Parliament really have intended that the acts that were done in this particular case should have the benefit of the immunity?' is to risk straying beyond his constitutional role as interpreter of the enacted law and assuming a power to decide at his own discretion whether or not to apply the general law to a particular case. The legitimate questions for a judge in his role as interpreter of the enacted law are: 'How has Parliament, by the words that it has used in the statute to express its intentions, defined the category of acts that are entitled to the immunity? Do the acts done in this particular case fall within that description?' . . . .

LORD SCARMAN: . . . My basic criticism of all three judgments in the Court of Appeal is that in their desire to do justice the court failed to do justice according to law. When one is considering law in the hands of the judges, law means the body of rules and guidelines within which society requires its judges to administer justice. Legal systems differ in the width of the discretionary power granted to judges: but in developed societies limits are invariably set, beyond which the judges may not go. Justice in such societies is not left to the unguided, even if experienced, sage sitting under the spreading oak tree.

In our society the judges have in some aspects of their work a discretionary power to do justice so wide that they may be regarded as law-makers. The common law and equity, both of them in essence systems of private law, are fields where, subject to the increasing intrusion of statute law, society has been content to allow the judges to formulate and develop the law. The judges, even in this, their very own field of creative endeavour, have accepted, in the interests of certainty, the self-denying ordinance of 'stare decisis', the doctrine of binding precedent: and no doubt this judicially imposed limitation on judicial law-making has helped to maintain confidence in the certainty and evenhandedness of the law.

But in the field of statute law the judge must be obedient to the will of Parliament as expressed in its enactments. In this field Parliament makes, and un-makes, the law: the judge's duty is to interpret and to apply the law, not to change it to meet the judge's idea of what justice requires. Interpretation does, of course, imply in the interpreter a power of choice where differing constructions are possible. But our law requires the judge to choose the construction which in his judgment best meets the legislative purpose of the enactment. If the result be unjust but inevitable, the judge may say so and invite Parliament to reconsider its provision. But he must not deny the statute. Unpalatable statute law may not be disregarded or rejected, merely because it is unpalatable. Only if a just result can be achieved without violating the legislative purpose of the statute may the judge select the construction which best suits his idea of what justice requires. Further, in our system the rule 'stare decisis' applies as firmly to statute law as it does to the formulation of common law and equitable principles. And the keystone of 'stare decisis' is loyalty throughout the system to the decisions of the Court of Appeal and this House . . . .

Within these limits, which cannot be said in a free society possessing elective legislative institutions to be narrow or constrained, judges, as the remarkable judicial career of Lord Denning himself shows, have a genuine creative role. Great judges are in their different ways judicial activists. But the constitution's separation of powers, or more accurately functions, must be observed if judicial independence is not to be put at risk. For, if people and Parliament come to think that the judicial power is to be confined by nothing other than the judge's sense of what is right (or, as Selden put it, by the length of the Chancellor's foot), confidence in the judicial system will be replaced by fear of it becoming uncertain and arbitrary in its application. Society will then be ready for Parliament to cut the power of the judges. Their power to do justice will become more restricted by law than it need be, or is today . . . .

J. R. Lucas commented on this case (*The Times*, 17 September 1980):

> Lord Diplock is right in thinking that judges should not put themselves above Parliament, and that when Parliament has spoken, even if wrongly, its word should none the less stand.
>
> But although Parliament speaks often, it does not always speak clearly, nor is it quick to clear up ambiguity or remedy injustices. Legislation which is badly drafted and inadequately scrutinized is often difficult to interpret and often leads to unintended injustices.
>
> 'The words that Parliament has approved as expressing its intention' often fail to express its real intention, because Parliament has not had time to consider what the words might be construed as meaning or what their effect might be in particular cases. In a golden age, when Parliament enacted few laws, carefully vetting every clause of every bill, and could quickly put right any unintended injustice arising from some previous enactment, Lord Diplock's separation of powers was feasible. But now it is not. Parliament's approval is a general, not a detailed one.
>
> Between the publication of a bill and its application in individual cases, there is relatively little time in Parliament and relatively much in the courts for considerations of expediency, justice and morality to be adduced. Therefore, if we want our laws to be expedient, just and moral – which they need to be if they are to be respected and obeyed – we should do well to allow judges to be guided by those considerations. But, of course, in being guided by these considerations, they are not to be guided by them alone.
>
> The judges should not take it on themselves to decide the law independently of Parliament, but only to interpret Parliament's enactments as sensibly as they can. It is not the judge's task to say what Parliament should have enacted, but only to say, given that Parliament has enacted a general law, what its decision would have been in an individual case if it had been apprised of all the particular circumstances of the case.

(See also Hood Phillips (1977) 93 *LQR* 11.)

It is nowadays generally recognized that judges make law, and that the development of the common law is part of the constitutional role of the courts. As Lord Wilberforce said in *British Railways Board* v. *Herrington* [1972] AC 877, 921, 'the common law is a developing entity as the judges develop it, and so long as we follow the well tried method of moving forward in accordance with principle as fresh facts emerge and changes in society occur, we are surely doing what Parliament intends we should do'. This dictum indicates that there are limits beyond which the courts should not go in creating new rules. Lord Reid, too, sounded a note of caution in *Pettitt* v. *Pettitt* [1970] AC 777, 794–5:

> Whatever views may have prevailed in the last century, I think that it is now widely recognised that it is proper for the courts in appropriate cases to develop or adapt existing rules of the common law to meet new conditions. I say in appropriate cases because I think we ought to recognise a difference between cases where we are dealing with 'lawyer's law' and cases where we are dealing with matters which directly affect the lives and interests of large sections of the community and which raise issues which are the subject of public controversy and on which laymen are as well able to decide as are lawyers. On such matters it is not for the courts to proceed on their view of public

policy for that would be to encroach on the province of Parliament.

(See also *Morgans* v. *Launchbury* [1973] AC 127.) In a recent case the House of Lords declined to introduce a new rule which Parliament appeared to have decided, as a matter of policy, not to introduce by legislation, saying that to do so could be seen as 'an unjustifiable usurpation by your Lordships' House of the functions which belong properly to Parliament': *President of India* v. *La Pintada Cia Navegacion SA* [1984] 2 All ER 773, 789 (*per* Lord Brandon). While judges frequently advert in such terms as these to a separation of powers between Parliament and the courts, the boundary cannot be precisely drawn. Opinions differ as to the proper scope of judicial law-making, and judges themselves act on differing conceptions of their role. (Compare the views of Lords Bridge and Scarman with that of Lord Edmund-Davies in *McLoughlin* v. *O'Brian* [1983] 1 AC 410 as to consideration by the courts of matters of policy.) Judicial restraint in this matter is supported by an argument from democracy, that the courts should not assume power to make law on questions which ought properly to be settled by the elected legislature. On this ground there was widespread criticism of the case of *Shaw* v. *Director of Public Prosecutions* [1962] AC 220, in which the House of Lords made a ruling which amounted to the creation of a wide new criminal offence of 'conspiracy to corrupt public morals'.

It is a corollary of the separation of powers that the authority conferred on judges to decide disputes and develop legal principles is given on the condition that they will not be influenced by considerations of political (or party) policy. Sir John Donaldson MR affirmed this principle in *British Airways Board* v. *Laker Airways Ltd* [1984] QB 142, 193, in saying:

It is a matter of considerable constitutional importance that the courts should be wholly independent of the executive, and they are. Thus, whilst the judges, as private citizens, will be aware of the 'policy' of the government of the day, in the sense of its political purpose, aspirations and programme, these are not matters which are in any way relevant to the courts' decisions and are wholly ignored.

But can we be sure that this condition is always observed if judges, by virtue of their background, training and associations, are generally deeply conservative and have attitudes which may lead them to look with favour upon property owners, employers and the established social order? (See J. A. G. Griffith, *The Politics of the Judiciary*, 1977, and compare Ronald Dworkin, 'Political Judges and the Rule of Law' (1978) 64 *Proceedings of the British Academy* 259.)

See further Colin Munro, 'The Separation of Powers: Not Such a Myth' [1981] *PL* 19.

(d)　**The rule of law**

The idea of the rule or supremacy of law is rooted in the history of European constitutionalism, although with us it was first given a clear definition in

Dicey's *Law of the Constitution* in 1885. Edward McWhinney rightly sees the English version of the concept as a 'historically received notion' and says that it is, in essence, 'a distillation of English common law legal history from the great constitutional battles of the seventeenth century onwards' (*Constitution-making: Principles, Process, Practice*, 1981, p. 10). (See further Jaffe and Henderson, '*Judicial Review and the Rule of Law: Historical Origins*' (1956) 72 *LQR* 345.)

The ideal of the rule of law has been formulated in many ways, both broad and narrow, and there is much disagreement as to the values or principles that it embraces. The argument has often focused on Dicey's classic exposition of the rule of law, and in particular on the first two meanings he gives to this expression.

Dicey, *The Law of the Constitution*, pp. 202–3

[The rule of law] means, in the first place, the absolute supremacy or predominance of regular law as opposed to the influence of arbitrary power, and excludes the existence of arbitrariness, of prerogative, or even of wide discretionary authority on the part of the government. Englishmen are ruled by the law, and by the law alone; a man may with us be punished for a breach of law, but he can be punished for nothing else.

It means, again, equality before the law, or the equal subjection of all classes to the ordinary law of the land administered by the ordinary law courts; the 'rule of law' in this sense excludes the idea of any exemption of officials or others from the duty of obedience to the law which governs other citizens or from the jurisdiction of the ordinary tribunals . . . .

Government under law

The minimal, and surely uncontroversial, element in these propositions is that the government is subject to the law and may exercise its power only in accordance with law. A government that claimed to be above the law and to be subject to no legal restraint in issuing commands to give effect to its view of the public (or its own) interest, would undoubtedly be a government that did not acknowledge the rule of law. In England it was established long ago in the following case that the use of public power must be justified by law and not by the claims of state necessity.

Entick v. *Carrington* (1765) 19 St. Tr. 1030
(Court of Common Pleas)

The King's messengers, armed with a warrant of the Secretary of State to arrest the plaintiff, John Entick, alleged to be the author of seditious writings, and to seize his books and papers, broke and entered his house and took away his papers. Entick sued the officers for trespass to his house and goods, and the defendants sought to justify the legality of the warrant. Unable to find specific authority in law, they argued that such warrants had been issued frequently in the past and executed without challenge, and that the power of seizure was essential to government.

LORD CAMDEN CJ: . . . This power, so claimed by the secretary of state, is not supported by one single citation from any law book extant . . . .

If it is law, it will be found in our books. If it is not to be found there, it is not law.

. . . By the laws of England, every invasion of private property, be it ever so minute, is a trespass. No man can set his foot upon my ground without my licence, but he is liable to an action, though the damage be nothing . . . . If he admits the fact, he is bound to shew by way of justification, that some positive law has empowered or excused him. The justification is submitted to the judges, who are to look into the books; and [see] if such a justification can be maintained by the text of the statute law, or by the principles of common law. If no such excuse can be found or produced, the silence of the books is an authority against the defendant, and the plaintiff must have judgment. . . .

I come now to the practice since the Revolution, which has been strongly urged, with this emphatical addition, that an usage tolerated from the era of liberty, and continued downwards to this time through the best ages of the constitution, must necessarily have a legal commencement. . . .

With respect to the practice itself, if it goes no higher, every lawyer will tell you, it is much too modern to be evidence of the common law. . . .

This is the first instance I have met with, where the ancient immemorable law of the land, in a public matter, was attempted to be proved by the practice of a private office.

The names and rights of public magistrates, their power and forms of proceeding as they are settled by law, have been long since written, and are to be found in books and records. . . . [W]hoever conceived a notion, that any part of the public law could be buried in the obscure practice of a particular person?

To search, seize, and carry away all the papers of the subject upon the first warrant: that such a right should have existed from the time whereof the memory of man runneth not to the contrary, and never yet have found a place in any book of law; is incredible. . . .

But still it is insisted, that there has been a general submission, and no action brought to try the right.

I answer, there has been a submission of guilt and poverty to power and the terror of punishment. But it would be strange doctrine to assert that all the people of this land are bound to acknowledge that to be universal law, which a few criminal booksellers have been afraid to dispute. . . .

It is then said, that it is necessary for the ends of government to lodge such a power with a state officer; and that it is better to prevent the publication before than to punish the offender afterwards. . . . [W]ith respect to the argument of state necessity, or a distinction that has been aimed at between state offences and others, the common law does not understand that kind of reasoning, nor do our books take notice of any such distinctions. . . .

It was held that the warrant was illegal and void, and the plaintiff was awarded damages.

The principle affirmed in this great case, that a public officer must show express legal authority for any interference with the person or property of the citizen, is still the law. But nowadays there are many statutes which authorize such interferences and some do so in very general terms. One statute of this sort, the Taxes Management Act 1970, was said by Lord Scarman in *R.* v. *Inland Revenue Commissioners, ex p. Rossminster Ltd* [1980] AC 952, 1022, to make 'a breath-taking inroad upon the individual's right of privacy and right of property'. The Act authorizes officers of the Board of Inland Revenue, acting under a search warrant, to enter premises by day or night, if necessary by force, and seize 'any thing whatsoever' reasonably believed to be evidence of any offence 'involving any form of fraud' in connection with tax. The search warrant is issued by a judge who must be satisfied that there is reasonable ground for suspecting that an offence of fraud in relation to tax has been committed. The warrant in the *Rossminster* case simply followed the wording of the statute without specifying what particular offence was suspected, and the Court of Appeal ([1980] AC 967) held the warrant invalid for this reason. Lord Denning cited *Entick* v. *Carrington* among other cases and said (p. 974):

When the officers of the Inland Revenue come armed with a warrant to search a man's home or his office, it seems to me that he is entitled to say: 'Of what offence do you suspect me? You are claiming to enter my house and to seize my papers.' And when they look at the papers and seize them, he should be able to say: 'Why are you seizing these papers? Of what offence do you suspect me? What have these to do with your case?' Unless he knows the particular offence charged, he cannot take steps to secure himself or his property. So it seems to me, as a matter of construction of the statute and therefore of the warrant – in pursuance of our traditional role to protect the liberty of the individual – it is our duty to say that the warrant must particularise the specific offence which is charged as being fraud on the revenue.

The House of Lords, however, reversed the Court of Appeal's ruling and held that there was nothing in the statute to require the particular offence to be stated in the warrant. Since the provisions of the statute had been complied with, there was no violation of the principle of *Entick* v. *Carrington*.

The requirement of the rule of law that express legal authority must be shown for interferences with individual rights was doubtless formally satisfied in this case. But is it diluted in substance, when the legal power is conferred in very wide terms which do not have to be particularized before the power is used against an individual?

The rule of law was vindicated in the following case.

Commissioners of Customs and Excise v. *Cure & Deeley Ltd* [1962]
1 QB 340 (Sachs J)

The Finance (No. 2) Act 1940 introduced and regulated purchase tax. Section 33(1) provided:

The commissioners may make regulations providing for any matter for which provision appears to them to be necessary for the purpose of giving effect to the provisions of this Part of this Act and of enabling them to discharge their functions thereunder. . . .

The commissioners made the Purchase Tax Regulations 1945. Regulation 12 was as follows:

If any person fails to furnish a return as required by these Regulations or furnishes an incomplete return the commissioners may, without prejudice to any penalties which may be incurred by such person, determine the amount of tax appearing to them to be due from such person, and demand payment thereof, which amount shall be deemed to be the proper tax due from such person and shall be paid within seven days of such demand unless within that time it is shown to the satisfaction of the commissioners that some other amount is the proper tax due. . . .

The defendants having submitted incomplete returns, the commissioners made a determination under Regulation 12 of the amount of tax appearing to them to be due, and sent a demand for payment of that sum. The defendants contended, *inter alia*, that the commissioners had no authority under the statute to make Regulation 12.

SACHS J: . . . Regulation 12 . . . has the following effects as regards determinations made under it when once an inaccuracy appears in a return. On the matters thus determined it excludes the subject from access to the courts; it substitutes for the liability imposed by the charging section and schedules to pay the appropriate tax in law due a liability to pay whatever the commissioners believe to be the appropriate tax; it enables the commissioners to take into account evidence obtained under conditions of secrecy upon the footing that it is not to be disclosed to the subject; it enables the commissioners so to announce their determination as not to reveal what they considered to be wrong in the return; it enables them to withhold from the taxpayer information even as to what are the goods or transactions upon which the tax is determined to be due. The regulation upon the face of it is one that can hardly even faintly be argued to provide for the appearance of justice being done: and it is capable of producing results adversely different, so far as the subject is concerned, from those which would result from a judicial determination of the tax payable.

. . . I reject the view that the words 'appear to them to be necessary' when used in a statute conferring powers on a competent authority, necessarily make that authority the sole judge of what are its powers as well as the sole judge of the way in which it can exercise such powers as it may have. It is axiomatic that, to follow the words used by Lord Radcliffe [in *Attorney-General for Canada* v. *Hallet & Carey Ltd* [1952] AC 427, 449], 'the paramount rule remains that every statute is to be expounded according to its manifest or expressed intention'. . . .

To my mind a court is bound before reaching a decision on the question whether a regulation is intra vires to examine the nature, objects, and scheme of the piece of legislation as a whole, and in the light of that examination to consider exactly what is the area over which powers are given by the section under which the competent authority is purporting to act. . . . [T]he court has to interpret the words 'for the purpose of giving effect to the provisions of this Part of the Act and of enabling them to discharge their functions thereunder' to see what is the area over which the power of the commissioners to make regulations extends. . . .

On the above footing it is, to my mind, clear that regulation 12 is ultra vires on at any rate three grounds, which, to my mind, are distinct in law though they overlap in so far as they may be different ways of expressing the result of certain facts. First, it is no part of the functions assigned to the commissioners to take upon themselves the powers of a High Court judge and decide issues of fact and law as between the Crown and the subject. Secondly, it renders the subject liable to pay such tax as the commissioners believe to be due, whereas the charging sections impose a liability to pay such tax as in law is due. Thirdly, it is capable of excluding the subject from access to the courts and of defeating pending proceedings. . . .

In the result this attempt to substitute in one segment of the taxpayer's affairs the rule of tax collectors for the rule of law fails. . . .

Although in cases like this the courts have refused to countenance action against the citizen that was not justified by law, a contrary tendency in our legal system allows certain kinds of interference with private interests to be committed by public authority without express legal justification. This is because there are in our constitution relatively few legally constituted civil rights: the 'rights' of the citizen are often no more than the residue of liberty which is beyond the limits of lawfully exercised public power. If the citizen's interest is not supported by a legally acknowledged right, a public authority may be able to act to the detriment of that interest without having to show specific legal authority for its action.

Malone v. *Metropolitan Police Commissioner* [1979] Ch. 344
(Sir Robert Megarry v–c)

The plaintiff had been charged with handling stolen property; in the course of the trial, counsel for the Crown admitted that the plaintiff's telephone line had been 'tapped' in order to hear and record his conversations, for the purpose of criminal investigation. The tapping had been done on the authority of a warrant issued by the Home Secretary in accordance with usual practice.

The plaintiff brought proceedings against the Metropolitan Police Commissioner for declarations that the tapping was unlawful, *inter alia* on the ground that it was authorized neither by statute nor by common law.

SIR ROBERT MEGARRY v–c: . . . England, it may be said, is not a country where everything is forbidden except what is expressly permitted: it is a country where everything is permitted except what is expressly forbidden.

. . . If the tapping of telephones by the Post Office at the request of the police can be carried out without any breach of the law, it does not require any statutory or common law power to justify it: it can lawfully be done simply because there is nothing to make it unlawful. The question, of course, is whether tapping can be carried out without infringing the law.

. . . [T]here is admittedly no statute which in terms authorises the tapping of telephones, with or without a warrant. Nevertheless, any conclusion that the tapping of telephones is therefore illegal would plainly be superficial in the extreme. The reason why a search of premises which is not authorised by law is illegal is that it involves the tort of trespass to those premises: and any trespass, whether to land or goods or the person, that is made without legal authority is prima facie illegal. Telephone tapping by the Post Office, on the other hand, involves no act of trespass. The subscriber speaks into his telephone, and the process of tapping appears to be carried out by Post Office officials making recordings, with Post Office apparatus on Post Office premises, of the electrical impulses on Post Office wires provided by Post Office electricity. There is no question of there being any trespass on the plaintiff's premises for the purpose of attaching anything either to the premises themselves or to anything on them: all that is done is done within the Post Office's own domain. As Lord Camden CJ said in *Entick* v. *Carrington*, 'the eye cannot by the laws of England be guilty of a trespass'; and, I would add, nor can the ear. . . .

Sir Robert Megarry was also of the opinion that where tapping was carried out under warrant its lawfulness had been recognized by the Post Office Act 1969. Arguments for the plaintiff based upon alleged infringements of rights of privacy and confidentiality and breaches of the European Convention on Human Rights were also unsuccessful.

Mr Malone subsequently complained to the European Commission of Human Rights that the tapping of his telephone, considered in the context of United Kingdom law and practice, had violated the European Convention on Human Rights. The case was referred by the Commission to the European Court of Human Rights, which ruled that there had been a violation of Article 8 of the Convention (right to respect for private life and correspondence). Since the law of England failed to provide a clear delimitation of the power of interception, 'the minimum degree of legal protection to which citizens are entitled under the rule of law in a democratic society is lacking' (*Malone Case*, ECHR 1984, Series A, No. 82.) Following this ruling the Government brought forward legislation to provide a 'comprehensive framework' for the interception of communications (Interception of Communications Act 1985).

According to the principle affirmed by Sir Robert Megarry in the *Malone* case, the act of a public authority will be upheld if it was 'in accordance with law' in the sense that it did not infringe any law. In this respect the administration is treated like a private individual, who is free to do whatever the law does not prohibit. The individual, for instance, is free to choose with whom he will make contracts: so is the government, which places many thousands of contracts worth many millions of pounds every year. From 1975 to 1978 the Government, in pursuance of a counter-inflation policy, maintained a blacklist of firms that had agreed to wage settlements in excess of non-statutory government guidelines, and withheld government contracts from the offending firms. Blacklisted firms were unable to challenge the Government's action in the courts, for their legal rights had not been infringed: there is no right to the award of a government contract. (See further pp. 341–2 below.) Is it not, however, a dubious constitutional principle that places government, with the great resources at its command and its responsibility for the public interest, on the same footing as a private individual? (See further George Winterton, 'The Prerogative in Novel Situations' (1983) 99 *LQR* 407.)

In the limited sense that governmental action must not contravene the law, the rule of law is a part of the law of England. This is not to say that breaches of the principle do not occur; a notorious instance was the officially authorized but unlawful physical ill-treatment applied to detainees in Northern Ireland in 1971. (See the Compton Report, Cmnd 4823/1971; Brownlie (1972) 35 *MLR* 501; *Ireland* v. *United Kingdom*, ECHR 1978, Series A, No. 25.) Nor is it unknown for the police to exceed or abuse their powers in dealing with suspected offenders or people taking part in political demonstrations or industrial action. (See, e.g., the *Report of the Inquiry into the Death of Maxwell Confait*, HC 90 of 1977–8; Editorial, 'Right of Protest and Police Power' (1978) 128 *NLJ* 941.) The rule of law is undermined if the government itself connives at breaches of the law. In 1965 the Wilson Government decided to apply oil sanctions against the illegal regime in Southern Rhodesia (now Zimbabwe) and Orders in Council were made to implement the policy. It was subsequently established that the embargo was circumvented by multi-national oil companies under both Labour and Tory administrations until 1978. (See the *Report on the Supply of Petroleum and Petroleum Products to Rhodesia*, HMSO 1978.) What was not determined was whether or to what extent senior officials and ministers connived at and concealed illegal conduct, as they were alleged to have done. In circumstances like these there can be no assurance, without an independent and searching investigation of the events and the government's role in them, that the rule of law has been observed. Although the House of Commons resolved on 1 February 1979 that a commission of inquiry into the operation of oil sanctions should be set up, this was not done.

The rule of law: a wider conception

The rule of law in its minimal sense of government according to law is a relatively unexacting principle, for it is satisfied by any state that has taken the trouble to invest its officers with legal authority to do what is required of them. The rule of law in this limited sense is not inconsistent with despotic government, if the despot is scrupulous about using the forms of law. But the rule of law is generally considered to include other elements, of which some, at least, are present (if not fully elaborated) in Dicey's formulation (p. 47 above).

In its wider sense the rule of law demands that laws should be general, prospective, open, clear and stable. (See especially Joseph Raz, 'The Rule of Law and its Virtue' (1977) 93 *LQR* 195, who sees these and other principles of the rule of law as resting on the 'basic idea that the law should be capable of providing effective guidance' and on respect for the dignity and autonomy of the individual.) While each of these elements of the rule of law expresses a valuable constitutional principle, we must keep in mind that the rule of law is not something absolute and has at times to be balanced against other values of a legal system.

The *generality* of a legal order would distinguish it from a regime in which specific commands were issued without regard to reasoned principle – or in which, in the words of Lon Fuller, governmental power expressed itself in 'unpredictable and patternless interventions in human affairs' (*The Morality of Law*, 2nd edn 1969, pp. 157–8). It is impossible to conceive of a legal *system* of which this was the characteristic feature, but a government might show a tendency to act in this way in particular branches of administration.

The law should be *prospective*, and should not, as Willes J observed in *Phillips* v. *Eyre* (1870) LR 6 QB 1, 23, 'change the character of past transactions carried on upon the faith of the then existing law'. In *Lauri* v. *Renad* [1892] 3 Ch. 402, 421, Lindley LJ held it to be a 'fundamental rule of English law that no statute shall be construed so as to have a retrospective operation unless its language is such as plainly to require such a construction. . . .' Retrospective *penal* legislation is open to particular objection, and is contrary to Article 7 of the European Convention on Human Rights: see *Waddington* v. *Miah* [1974] 1 WLR 683. But retrospective legislation is sometimes justified, as Willes J conceded in *Phillips* v. *Eyre* (above), to avoid 'practical public inconvenience and wrong'. (See further Ian S. Dickinson, 'Retrospective Legislation and the British Constitution' (1974) *Scots Law Times* 25.)

Laws should be *open*, that is to say, made known by sufficient publication. Legislation in the United Kingdom generally satisfies this requirement, but many rules and guidelines adopted by the administration in its dealings with the citizen are not published. (See p. 328 below.)

If laws are to be an effective and reliable guide to conduct it is evident that they should be *clear*: Fuller (op. cit., p. 63) holds this to be 'one of the most essential ingredients of legality'. Our laws do not always achieve this: see p. 303 below.

Laws should be *stable* because frequent changes in them make it difficult to know the law or to plan for the future. (See Raz, op. cit., p. 199.)

Discretion and the rule of law

I have said that the principles included in the rule of law are not absolute: this becomes apparent when we consider the subject of discretion. If the decisions of public authorities are to be taken in accordance with known and clear general rules, that might seem to exclude decision-making by the exercise of discretion. Dicey was of this mind in saying (p. 47 above) that the rule of law excluded 'wide discretionary authority on the part of the government'. Since Dicey's time we have come to a fuller recognition of the necessity and value of discretionary power in many branches of public administration, in order that changing circumstances as well as the needs of justice in individual cases can properly inform the making of decisions.

Kenneth Culp Davis, *Discretionary Justice* (1971), pp. 17, 42

Rules without discretion cannot fully take into account the need for tailoring results to unique facts and circumstances of particular cases. The justification for discretion is often the need for individualized justice. This is so in the judicial process as well as in the administrative process.

Every governmental and legal system in world history has involved both rules and discretion. No government has ever been a government of laws and not of men in the sense of eliminating all discretionary power. Every government has always been *a government of laws and of men.* . . .

Elimination of all discretionary power is both impossible and undesirable. The sensible goal is development of a proper balance between rule and discretion. Some circumstances call for rules, some for discretion, some for mixtures of one proportion, and some for mixtures of another proportion. . . . [T]he special need is to eliminate *unnecessary* discretionary power, and to discover more successful ways to confine, to structure, and to check necessary discretionary power.

(See further Titmuss, 'Welfare "Rights", Law and Discretion' (1971) 42 *Political Quarterly* 113, and Harlow and Rawlings, *Law and Administration*, pp. 130–35.)

We may see it as a function of the rule of law today to identify the branches of government in which discretionary power is a proper technique of administration, to ensure that civil liberties are not at the mercy of uncontrolled discretion, and generally to prevent discretionary power from degenerating into arbitrariness by insisting upon effective limits, standards and controls.

Courts and the rule of law

The rule of law is most seriously threatened when government itself exceeds or abuses the powers which it has under the law, and a state can only claim to uphold the rule of law if it provides effective means for the prevention and redress of illegal action by the administration. A further requirement of the rule of law is therefore that there should be courts or other agencies which will supervise public authorities and check their breaches of the law, and these agencies must themselves act independently, with respect for the law and not in deference to the government. (See pp. 41–2 above.) Dicey maintained in his *Law of the Constitution* that officials must be subject to the ordinary law administered by the ordinary tribunals (p. 47 above), but he later modified his insistence that a separate system of administrative law and administrative courts, such as exists in France, is inimical to the rule of law. The system was not then well understood in England; it is now recognized as being entirely compatible with justice and the rule of law.

It is not demanded by the rule of law that the administration should necessarily be liable in the courts on the same principles and to the same extent as private individuals: the public interest may justify special immunities and particular rules of procedure in proceedings against public authorities. But it is an evident requirement of the rule of law that the government should comply with judgments of the courts given against it. In particular it would not be consistent with the rule of law for a government to resort to retrospective legislation in order to nullify those judgments which it preferred not to obey. The issue arises in an acute form if the court's decision appears to go beyond the previous general understanding of the law, for in this aspect of the rule of law we meet again the idea of the separation of powers, by which courts and government should each respect the proper domain of the other.

In *Burmah Oil Co. Ltd* v. *Lord Advocate* [1965] AC 75 the Burmah Oil Company claimed compensation for the wartime destruction of its installations in Burmah, which had been ordered by the British military authorities to prevent their falling into the hands of advancing Japanese forces. The destruction had been a lawful exercise of the war prerogative of the Crown, but the House of Lords held that its exercise in these circumstances imported an obligation to pay compensation. In a dissenting speech Lord Radcliffe observed that in no previous case had a court of law awarded compensation for a taking or destruction of property under the prerogative, and that there was no clear body of legal opinion which would justify the declaration, for the first time, of a legal right to compensation.

The company's victory in this case opened up a possible governmental liability (to other claimants also) in a considerable amount, greatly exceeding the sum it had made available for a partial compensation of war losses, out of which many claims had already been settled. The Government then, arguing that it was necessary to maintain the integrity of its scheme of compensation, brought about the enactment of the War Damage Act 1965, which provided:

1. (1) No person shall be entitled at common law to receive from the Crown compensation in respect of damage to, or destruction of, property caused (whether before or after the passing of this Act, within or outside the United Kingdom) by acts lawfully done by, or on the authority of, the Crown during, or in contemplation of the outbreak of, a war in which the Sovereign was, or is, engaged.

    (2) Where any proceedings to recover at common law compensation in respect of such damage or destruction have been instituted before the passing of this Act, the court shall, on the application of any party, forthwith set aside or dismiss the proceedings, subject only to the determination of any question arising as to costs or expenses.

After the introduction of the bill which became the War Damage Act, JUSTICE (the British Section of the International Commission of Jurists) published the following statement:

At a recent meeting of the Executive Committee of JUSTICE the members present, who included lawyers who are members of all the main political parties, considered the War Damage Bill in the context of the principles of the Rule of Law which JUSTICE is pledged to uphold.

It was the unanimous view of the meeting that the passage of this Bill into law would constitute a serious infringement of the Rule of Law by which is understood the supremacy of the Courts. The refusal to meet a legitimate claim for compensation affirmed by the highest Court in the land, namely the House of Lords, is in the view of JUSTICE an action inconsistent with the Rule of Law and a dangerous precedent for the future. It is entirely wrong that when a litigant has won his case, legislation should be produced revising decisions retrospectively so that the successful plaintiff is deprived of his victory.

The fact that a threat of legislative action was made during an early stage of the proceedings, and long after the right of legal action had arisen, so far from justifying the enactment of this Bill, makes it clear, in the opinion of JUSTICE, that both Conservative and Labour Governments have failed to recognise the over-riding need to respect the decisions of the judiciary.

But the issues raised by the *Burmah Oil* case and the Government's response to it are perhaps more complex than this statement would suggest. (See further Harlow and Rawlings, *Law and Administration*, pp. 377–82.)

The rule of law as we have so far considered it is neutral as regards the content or quality of legal rules. It is also neutral with respect to the distribution of power in society and may even help to sustain a legal order founded on inequality and vested interests. (Cf. E. P. Thompson, *Whigs and Hunters*, 1975, pp. 258–69.) R. M. Unger (*Law in Modern Society*, 1977) observes that the rule of law has failed to solve the problem of power: it is, he says (p. 239),

the liberal state's most emphatic response to the problems of power and freedom. But ... whatever its efficacy in preventing immediate government oppression of the individual, the strategy of legalism fails to deal with these issues in the basic relationships of work and everyday life.

(See also pp. 179–81.)

In recent times the rule of law has been invoked in defence of private interests against the actions of 'interventionist' government directed to social reform and public welfare. W. Friedmann (*The State and the Rule of Law in a Mixed Economy*, 1971, p. 95) has replied:

The proposition that the rule of law in modern democracy is incompatible with any kind of economic planning by the state or ... that the planned state 'commands people which road to take', whereas the rule of law only provides 'signposts', [F. A. von Hayek, *The Road to Serfdom*, 1944, p. 54] is of course incompatible with the reality of any contemporary democracy. It would be a useless exercise for us to attempt to define the rule of law in a way that bears no relation to the minimum functions of social welfare, urban planning, regulatory controls, entrepreneurship and other essential functions of the state in a mixed economy.

The achievement of great social ends, such as the removal of economic, racial and sexual injustice, and the provision of welfare services, are impossible without state activity and the assumption of the necessary powers. We can demand of a constitution that it should assist, not frustrate, the attainment of these ends, while also providing against arbitrariness and the abuse of power.

There are some who argue for an enlarged conception of the rule of law which would include an ideal of justice or the recognition of moral and political rights. The International Commission of Jurists has led the way in urging that the rule of law should move beyond an exclusive insistence on requirements of legality and procedural fairness, and should incorporate fundamental rights and standards of social and economic justice. The Congress of the International Commission of Jurists held in Delhi in 1959 declared:

that the Rule of Law is a dynamic concept for the expansion and fulfilment of which jurists are primarily responsible and which should be employed not only to safeguard and advance the civil and political rights of the individual in a free society, but also to establish social, economic, educational and cultural conditions under which his legitimate aspirations and dignity may be realized.

The impulse to redefinitions of this kind comes from an awareness that a neutral conception of the rule of law seems to distance lawyers and the ideals of law from the most compelling issues of our time – of poverty, social deprivation and the denial of political rights and elementary justice by authoritarian governments. The lawyers at Delhi were conscious that law is, too often, mainly of service to limited and powerful interests in unequal societies.

Others still insist on a stricter definition of the rule of law, saying with Raz (op. cit., pp. 195–6): 'If the rule of law is the rule of the good law then to explain its nature is to propound a complete social philosophy. But if so the term lacks any useful function. We have no need to be converted to the rule of law just in order to discover that to believe in it is to believe that good should triumph.'

Can the wider objectives declared in Delhi be accommodated within a workable concept of the rule of law? (See generally T. R. S. Allan, 'Legislative Supremacy and the Rule of Law' [1985] *CLJ* 111.)

(e) **Ministerial responsibility**

At the end of the nineteenth century the legal and political responsibility of ministers was, as M. J. C. Vile says (*Constitutionalism and the Separation of Powers*, 1967, p. 231), 'the crux of the English system of government'. The legal responsibility of ministers to the courts was complemented by their political responsibility to Parliament. Ministerial responsibility in the political sense was the result of the development of conventions by which the Sovereign had become bound to act on the advice of ministers, and ministers had become answerable to Parliament for the advice given. The principle of ministerial responsibility, as an element in the theory of the British constitution, was inferred from the reality of constitutional practice. 'The accountability of ministers to Parliament, and through Parliament to the nation, is the theoretical basis of our modern English Constitution': so wrote Sidney Low in 1904 (*The Governance of England*, p. 133).

According to this theory the power of government was 'placed under the check of a strict responsibility and control' (Earl Grey, *Parliamentary Government*, new edn 1864, p. 5). But it was only for a few decades in the middle of the nineteenth century, when a Parliament not yet infiltrated by disciplined parties showed its ability to bring down governments, that so strong a statement of the theory might have been justified by the facts. Since then the government has established an ascendancy over Parliament, and the traditional parliamentary techniques of control and accountability, focused on ministers, have proved inadequate for checking the use of power in the corridors of the departmental bureaucracies and in the outworks of Government occupied by quasi-autonomous organizations.

This modern development has led some to dismiss the theory of ministerial responsibility as mere fiction: it is now 'little more than a formal principle used by ministers to deter parliamentary interference in their affairs' says Vile (op. cit., p. 341). But no other theory of government has taken its place; it still explains much of what happens in government and Parliament, and it is through the mechanisms of ministerial responsibility that Parliament persists in its effort to 'watch and control' the government. The extent to which it is able to do so in practice is considered in chapter 7.

The theory of ministerial responsibility has in one respect had a baleful effect upon the control of public power. The courts have in a number of cases been influenced, in declining to question the exercise of powers by ministers, by the principle that ministers are answerable to Parliament for the use of their powers. In the words of J. D. B. Mitchell: 'The respect for, and belief in, the efficacy of parliamentary controls moved courts to assume an attitude of restraint in the exercise of their admitted powers of control, which otherwise they might not have assumed' ([1965] *PL* 95 at 100). For example, in *Liversidge* v. *Anderson* [1942] AC 206 the House of Lords interpreted a wartime regulation which authorized the Home Secretary to order the detention of any person whom he had 'reasonable cause to believe' to be of hostile origin or associations as giving the minister a subjective discretion which could not be controlled by the courts. In justification of this ruling their Lordships observed that the Home Secretary was answerable to Parliament for his decisions. (The ruling in *Liversidge* v. *Anderson* has since been repudiated by the House of Lords in *R.* v. *Inland Revenue Commissioners, ex p. Rossminster Ltd* [1980] AC 952.) More recently in *R.* v. *Secretary of State for Home Affairs, ex p. Hosenball* [1977] 1 WLR 766 the Court of Appeal declined to review the Home Secretary's decision to deport a journalist in the interest of national security: 'He is answerable to Parliament as to the way in which he did it and not to the courts here' (*per* Lord Denning MR at p. 783). A different view of ministerial responsibility was taken by the High Court of Australia in *Re Toohey, ex p. Northern Land Council* (1981) 38 ALR 439, in asserting its jurisdiction to control the exercise of power by the Crown. Gibbs CJ said (p. 457) that 'under modern conditions of responsible government, Parliament could not always be relied on to check excesses of power by the Crown or its Ministers', and Mason J said (p. 481) that 'the doctrine of ministerial responsibility is not in itself an adequate safeguard for the citizen whose rights are affected'.

2

Law, convention and liberty

In chapter 1 we saw that for a true view of the constitution we must take account of its rules, its institutions, and the 'idea' or theory of the constitution, consisting of a set of leading principles.

In this chapter we shall give further attention to the rules, which are the building blocks of the constitution. Some of these are legal rules, making up the 'law of the constitution'; others are rules of practice, or constitutional conventions. We shall look for distinctive features of constitutional laws and conventions and consider the relationship between these two kinds of rules.

It will appear that our constitution is highly flexible and that even fundamental rules are liable to change or abolition. This has led to concern that civil rights and liberties are imperfectly protected in the United Kingdom, and we shall consider arguments for a new constitutional settlement which would give stability to the constitution and a guarantee of individual rights.

1 The law of the constitution

Dicey (*Law of the Constitution*, p. 203) held it to be one aspect of the rule of law in England that

the principles of private law have with us been by the action of the courts and Parliament so extended as to determine the position of the Crown and of its servants; thus the constitution is the result of the ordinary law of the land.

Dicey's statement needs qualification. It fails to take account of the 'law and custom of Parliament', which has developed separately from the 'ordinary' law. But the statement is more seriously misleading in that a large part of modern constitutional law consists of enactments conferring powers on public authorities, principles developed by the courts in interpreting those enactments, and remedies of exclusive application to public bodies: a corpus of public law, in short, which cannot be explained as a mere extension of private law rules to the administration. The scope of public law in the United Kingdom and the boundary between it and private law are still being worked out by the courts. (See, e.g., *O'Reilly* v. *Mackman* [1983] 2 AC 237, *Davy* v.

Spelthorne BC [1984] AC 262, *Wandsworth LBC* v. *Winder* [1984] All ER 976, and Carol Harlow, ' "Public" and "Private" Law: Definition without Distinction' (1980) 43 *MLR* 241.)

It remains true that the legal rules of the constitution have, in general, evolved by the same processes, and from the same sources, as the law governing the relations between private persons. We find constitutional rules mingled with the rest of the law, in statutes and subordinate legislation, in the common law and decisions of judges.

(a) **Statutes**

Although our constitution is described as 'unwritten', a considerable part of it consists of Acts of Parliament which regulate the system of government or the exercise of public power. These include statutes which have established fundamental features of the constitution, as by defining the terms of the Union between England, Scotland and Northern Ireland (Acts of Union with Scotland 1707 and with Ireland 1800) or fixing the duration of Parliaments (Septennial Act 1715, amended by the Parliament Act 1911). Among 'constitutional' statutes we may also number those directed against public disorder (Public Order Acts 1936 and 1963), remedying maladministration in government (Parliamentary Commissioner Act 1967), providing for civil proceedings by and against the Crown (Crown Proceedings Act 1947), and regulating the franchise and the conduct of elections (Representation of the People Act 1983). There are others far too numerous to mention.

Among these statutes are certain great constitutional Acts which were enacted in confirmation of the results of political upheaval or revolution, or as emphatic statements of what were conceived as fundamental rights or privileges. The antiquity of these Acts, or the great historical events with which they are associated, or the lasting worth of the principles contained in them – or a combination of these features – have invested them with a kind of sanctity (in the minds of lawyers and to some extent in public sentiment) which is not unlike that elsewhere attaching to written constitutions. They include Magna Carta 1215, the Habeas Corpus Act 1679, the Bill of Rights 1689, the Act of Settlement 1701, the Act of Union with Scotland 1707, and the Statute of Westminster 1931.

The following extracts are taken from the Bill of Rights 1689:

[The] Lords Spirituall and Temporall and Commons pursuant to their respective Letters and Elections being now assembled in a full and free Representative of this Nation. . . . Doe in the first place (as their Auncestors in like Case have usually done) for the Vindicating and Asserting their auntient Rights and Liberties, Declare

That the pretended Power of Suspending of Laws or the Execution of Laws by Regall Authority without Consent of Parlyament is illegall.

That the pretended Power of Dispensing with Laws or the Execution of Laws by Regall Authoritie as it hath beene assumed and exercised of late is illegall.

. . . That levying Money for or to the Use of the Crowne by pretence of Prerogative without Grant of Parlyament . . . is Illegall.

. . . That the raising or keeping a standing Army within the Kingdome in time of Peace unlesse it be with Consent of Parlyament is against Law.

That the Subjects which are Protestants may have Arms for their Defence suitable to their Conditions and as allowed by Law.

That Election of Members of Parlyament ought to be free.

That the Freedome of Speech and Debates or Proceedings in Parlyament ought not to be impeached or questioned in any Court or Place out of Parlyament.

That excessive Baile ought not to be required nor excessive Fines imposed nor cruell and unusuall Punishments inflicted.

. . . And that for Redresse of all Grievances and for the amending strengthening and preserveing of the Lawes Parlyaments ought to be held frequently.

The provisions of the Bill of Rights are not inviolate, and some have been altered by subsequent legislation; for example, it hardly needs saying that Protestant subjects no longer enjoy a special privilege in the keeping of arms. Some other provisions have lost their importance. There remains however a core of provisions which the courts will still uphold against the Crown or government (but not against Parliament).

Attorney-General v. *Wilts United Dairies Ltd* (1921) 37 TLR 884 (CA)

It was the statutory duty of the Food Controller to regulate the supply and consumption of food, and he had power under the Defence of the Realm Acts and Regulations to make orders for this purpose. He made orders which fixed maximum prices for milk and provided for the licensing of wholesale dealers. The maximum price fixed for the more productive counties of Cornwall, Devon, Dorset and Somerset was 2d a gallon less than for other areas, but dealers who took milk from these counties for sale elsewhere were required to pay 2d a gallon to the Food Controller. Licences were granted to the defendants to purchase milk in the four counties on the express condition that they should pay the 2d a gallon, but they afterwards refused to pay, and proceedings were brought to recover the amount claimed to be due.

The Court of Appeal held that the statutory provisions relied upon by the Food Controller did not give him power to levy a financial charge, and accordingly that the imposition of the charge was illegal.

SCRUTTON LJ: . . . [T]he Bill of Rights . . . forbids 'levying money for the use of the Crown without grant of Parliament', and the requirement of this twopence appears to me clearly to come within these words. It is true that the fear in 1689 was that the King by his prerogative would claim money; but excessive claims by the Executive Government without grant of Parliament are, at the present time, quite as dangerous, and require as careful consideration and restriction from the Courts of Justice. . . .

The judgment of the Court of Appeal was affirmed by the House of Lords: (1922) 38 TLR 781. (See also *Congreve* v. *Home Office* [1976] QB 629.)

In *Williams* v. *Home Office (No.2)* [1981] 1 All ER 1211 it was argued that the plaintiff's detention in a special control unit, while serving a sentence in Wakefield Prison, violated the prohibition in the Bill of Rights of the infliction of cruel and unusual punishments. Since the regime in the control unit was authorized only by delegated legislation (the prison rules) and not by the Prison Act 1952, it would be illegal if contrary to the Bill of Rights. It was held, however, on the evidence, that the regime in the control unit was neither cruel nor unusual and therefore that there had been no breach of the Bill of Rights.

In *R.* v. *Secretary of State for the Home Department, ex p. Phansopkar* [1976] QB 606, the Court of Appeal held that a person seeking a certificate of entitlement to enter the United Kingdom as a patrial (one having the 'right of abode' under provisions of the Immigration Act 1971 then in force) had the right to prompt and fair consideration of her application for the certificate, and could not be required first to return to her country of origin, there to suffer the same delays as affected those requiring leave to enter the United Kingdom. The court cited Magna Carta: 'To none will we sell: to no one will we delay or deny right or justice.'

Despite the special deference with which the Bill of Rights, Magna Carta and other great constitutional statutes are cited by the courts, none of them is immune from repeal by Parliament, and many of their provisions have in fact been so repealed. In this respect their legal status is no greater than that of the Bees Act 1980. (But see pp. 5–7 above and cf. Philip Allott, 'The Courts and Parliament: Who Whom?' [1979] *CLJ* 79.)

Chester v. *Bateson* [1920] 1 KB 829 (DC)

A wartime regulation made under statutory authority provided that no person should bring proceedings for the ejectment of a tenant of any dwelling-house situated in certain areas of armament manufacture without the consent of the Minister of Munitions. In proceedings brought by a landlord, without the consent of the Minister, for the ejectment of a tenant, the validity of the regulation was challenged.

DARLING J: . . . [Counsel for the landlord] has contended that this regulation violates Magna Carta, where the King declares: 'To no one will we sell, to no one will we refuse or delay right or justice.' I could not hold the regulation to be bad on that ground, were there sufficient authority given by a statute of the realm to those by whom the regulation was made. Magna Carta has not remained untouched; and, like every other law of England, it is not condemned to that immunity from development or improvement which was attributed to the laws of the Medes and Persians. . . .

Nevertheless the regulation was held invalid since the 'grave . . . invasion of the rights of all subjects' which it effected had not been expressly authorized by the empowering Act of Parliament.

The fact that constitutional statutes are made and repealed by the ordinary parliamentary process attracted the following comment by a French observer.

Monica Charlot, 'A Changing Britain? A View from France'
(1981) 52 *Political Quarterly* 450, 451–2

Once under challenge, an unwritten constitution weathers the day as best it can. Little is needed for it to change course, for there are no qualified majorities, no complex procedures or statutory delays. There was, for instance, nothing to prevent the Labour Party from introducing a referendum Bill [on EEC membership, in 1975] as any other Bill, and getting it passed since they commanded a parliamentary majority. Thus it is that with little real debate and no constitutional need to clarify things, important changes can be made. The very concept of sovereignty, for instance, has been modified by British entry into the EEC, and the notion of the unitary state was challenged by projects aiming at altering the relationship of the various parts of the kingdom – the devolution bills had they been accepted by the public would have changed the very essence of the British political system. And yet there was no constitutional debate on the subject, no presentation of the problem to English voters who were not asked to express any opinion on the weakening of the constitutional unity of Britain. Supreme judges of the 'constitutionality' of laws – as the French *Conseil Constitutionnel* – may be derided because they do on occasion seem to lack the courage of their convictions, but their very existence means the government must pause while constitutional lawyers argue the matter – not only in the Conseil but in the press and on radio and television. Constitutional issues interest the French because they are taught to appreciate their importance.

For ordinary public bills (other than Appropriation Bills, the annual Finance Bill and some others) the committee stage in the House of Commons, when their clauses are discussed in detail, is normally taken 'upstairs' in a standing committee, rather than in committee of the whole House. The Select Committee on Procedure recommended in 1945 (First Report, HC 9–1 of 1945–6, para. 6) that the committee stage of bills of 'first-class constitutional importance' should be taken on the floor of the House so that every member should have the opportunity of discussing their detailed provisions. This principle was approved by the House of Commons (HC Deb. vol. 415, col. 2402, 15 November 1945) and has since been followed, though there is sometimes disagreement as to whether a bill is 'constitutional' or of the first class of importance. (Cf. the controversy as to the 'constitutional' character of the British Nationality Bill 1980: HC Deb. vol. 995, cols. 649 *et seq.*, 4 December 1980; vol. 996, col. 1138, 12 January 1981.)

From time to time the deliberate attempt has been made to invest an Act of Parliament with a special 'constitutional' character. Betty Kemp, writing of the seventeenth and eighteenth centuries, says (*London Review of Books*, 22 December 1983, p. 13):

The distinction between constitutional and ordinary Acts of Parliament was made by legislators as well as by dissentients from parliamentary sovereignty. Some Acts of Parliament were tacitly designated 'constitutional' or 'fundamental' by the insertion of the words 'for ever'. The Bill of Rights, the Act of Settlement and the Acts of Union with Scotland and Ireland had these words, and the Triennial and Septennial Acts used a phrase with the same meaning. Of course the words 'for ever' in an Act of Parliament are, and were, no legal obstacle to its repeal by any future Parliament: they were, however, a moral obstacle. But what is important is that the words express a feeling of need for a way of distinguishing between constitutional, or fundamental, and ordinary acts of parliament.

(On the Acts of Union with Scotland and Ireland see pp. 176, 190 below. Compare too the Northern Ireland Constitution Act 1973, s.1, and the European Communities Act 1972, pp. 271, 272 *et seq*, below.)

The authority of statute is supreme, but statutes are interpreted by judges with the aid of principles which the courts have themselves evolved. In particular, statutes that allocate powers to public authorities often do so in terms which may be understood in a wide or narrow sense, so that it is left to judges, in interpreting the Act, to settle the precise limits of the power conferred. The decisions of judges can therefore be crucial in fixing the range of freedom of action of public bodies – for example, the freedom of local authorities to develop and apply policies for the government of their areas, as in *Bromley London Borough Council* v. *Greater London Council* [1983] 1 AC 768, in which the House of Lords interpreted and applied the Transport (London) Act 1969 in such a way that the GLC's 'Fares Fair' policy of transport subsidy was overthrown as ultra vires and illegal. (See p. 234 below.) In other cases the judicial interpretation of Acts of Parliament has marked out the powers of ministers in relation to local authorities, as in *Secretary of State for Education and Science* v. *Tameside Metropolitan Borough Council* [1977] AC 1014 (p. 211 below).

(b) Subordinate legislation

With the exception of prerogative Orders in Council (p. 315 below), subordinate legislation is made under the authority of Acts of Parliament. Normally such delegated legislation is concerned with matters of detail, but it is sometimes of wider significance, and some Orders in Council and regulations made by ministers have a place among the sources of constitutional law. Subordinate legislation of this kind may, for example, reallocate functions of central government or regulate the exercise of powers by local or other public authorities.

The Secretary of State for the Environment Order 1970, SI 1970
No. 1681

2(1) The Ministry of Housing and Local Government, the Ministry of Public Building and Works and the Ministry of Transport are hereby dissolved, and all functions of the Minister of Housing and Local Government, of the Minister of Public Building and Works or of the Minister of Transport (including functions belonging to any of them jointly) are hereby transferred to the Secretary of State or, in the case of functions described in Schedule 1 to this Order, to the Secretary of State for the Environment.

This Order in Council, made under the Ministers of the Crown (Transfer of

Functions) Act 1946 (see now the Ministers of the Crown Act 1975), dissolved three government departments and vested some of their functions in the Secretary of State for the Environment and the remainder in 'the Secretary of State'. By the Interpretation Act 1978, s.5 and Sched.1, 'Secretary of State' means 'one of Her Majesty's Principal Secretaries of State'. Powers and functions entrusted to 'the Secretary of State' can accordingly be exercised by *any* of the Principal Secretaries of State, of whom there are at present 13. In practice the functions of the dissolved departments were assumed by the Secretary of State for the Environment. There is now again a separate Department of Transport with its own Minister. (Secretary of State for Transport Order 1976, SI 1976 No. 1775.)

(c) **Common law**

A substantial part of the law of the constitution is common law. It is in the common law that we find a number of important powers of government (notably the prerogative powers, of which most are at the disposal of ministers of the Crown) and also certain principles by which the exercise of public powers is qualified. Some of these latter are considered to have a 'fundamental' character. We may take as an example the 'great web of natural justice' (*R. v. Police Complaints Board, ex p. Madden* [1983] 1 WLR 447, 470) which covers a wide range of judicial and administrative decision-making and requires the deciding authority to act without bias (*nemo judex in causa sua*), to allow those affected by the decision to be heard (*audi alteram partem*), and to reach its conclusion honestly and fairly. The obligation to give a hearing was declared long ago in the case of *Dr Bentley* (1723) 1 Stra. 557, who had been deprived of his degrees by the University of Cambridge without notice. Fortescue J said in this case (at p. 567):

[T]he objection for want of notice can never be got over. The laws of God and man both give the party an opportunity to make his defence, if he has any. I remember to have heard it observed by a very learned man upon such an occasion, that even God himself did not pass sentence upon Adam, before he was called upon to make his defence. Adam (says God) where art thou? Hast thou not eaten of the tree, whereof I commanded thee that thou shouldst not eat? And the same question was put to Eve also.

The growth in modern times of governmental powers affecting the individual has extended the reach of natural justice, and the courts continually work out its content and application in a great variety of circumstances. Lord Morris of Borth-y-Gest said in *Wiseman* v. *Borneman* [1971] AC 297, 309:

Natural justice, it has been said, is only 'fair play in action'. Nor do we wait for directions from Parliament. The common law has abundant riches: there may we find what Byles J called 'the justice of the common law' (*Cooper* v. *Wandsworth Board of Works* (1863) 14 CBNS 180, 194).

Lord Reid said in the same case (p. 308) that where a procedure for decision-making was laid down by statute, the courts might supplement it with further safeguards if that was necessary to ensure the observance of natural justice, provided that 'to require additional steps would not frustrate the apparent purpose of the legislation'.

Again, it is to the common law made by the judges – case law – that we must look for the rules relating to *locus standi* ('standing'), or the right to apply to the courts for the review of actions of public authorities. As Lord Diplock said in *Inland Revenue Commissioners* v. *National Federation of Self-Employed and Small Businesses Ltd* [1982] AC 617, 639,

The rules as to 'standing' for the purpose of applying for prerogative orders, like most of English public law, are not to be found in any statute. They were made by judges, by judges they can be changed; and so they have been over the years to meet the need to preserve the integrity of the rule of law. . . .

The common law is (subject to Parliament) under the control of the judges, who may by their decisions modify and reinterpret constitutional powers and relationships, and redefine the rights of citizens. In the following case the court extended a common law principle and added to the government's armoury for the protection of Cabinet secrecy.

Attorney-General v. *Jonathan Cape Ltd* [1976] QB 752
(Lord Widgery CJ)

Richard Crossman, a Minister in the 1964–70 Labour Government, kept a diary of Cabinet proceedings which he meant to publish in full, with the object of challenging the traditional secrecy of British government and giving a detailed public account of the working of the Cabinet. Crossman died before the diaries could be published, but after his death *The Sunday Times* began to publish extracts from them, and Crossman's literary executors proposed to publish the diaries in full as a book. In accordance with the usual practice as to ministerial memoirs, *The Sunday Times* and the executors first submitted the diaries to the Secretary to the Cabinet for his comments. Ordinarily if the Cabinet Secretary required the deletion of particular items which he thought infringed the confidentiality of Cabinet proceedings, or would be damaging to national security, the publishers would comply. In this instance, however, *The Sunday Times*, faithful to Crossman's intentions, began to publish the extracts although the Cabinet Secretary had refused to give them clearance.

The Attorney-General brought proceedings for injunctions to prevent the further publication of the diaries. In no previous case had an injunction been granted or sought in similar circumstances, but the Attorney-General argued that the courts had power to protect the confidentiality of Cabinet proceedings in the public interest. Counsel for the defendants contended, on the other hand, that if publication of Cabinet proceedings was contrary to the public interest, that was a matter to be remedied by legislation.

LORD WIDGERY CJ: . . . It has always been assumed by lawyers and, I suspect, by politicians, and the Civil Service, that Cabinet proceedings and Cabinet papers are secret, and cannot be publicly disclosed until they have passed into history. It is quite clear that no court will compel the production of Cabinet papers in the course of discovery in an action, and the Attorney-General contends that not only will the court refuse to compel the production of such matters, but it will go further and positively forbid the disclosure of such papers and proceedings if publication will be contrary to the public interest.

The basis of this contention is the confidential character of these papers and proceedings, derived from the convention of joint Cabinet responsibility whereby any policy decision reached by the Cabinet has to be supported thereafter by all members of the Cabinet whether they approve of it or not, unless they feel compelled to resign. It is contended that Cabinet decisions and papers are confidential for a period to the extent at least that they must not be referred to outside the Cabinet in such a way as to disclose the attitude of individual Ministers in the argument which preceded the decision. Thus, there may be no objection to a Minister disclosing (or leaking, as it was called) the fact that a Cabinet meeting has taken place, or, indeed, the decision taken, so long as the individual views of Ministers are not identified.

There is no doubt that Mr Crossman's manuscripts contain frequent references to individual opinions of Cabinet Ministers, and this is not surprising because it was his avowed object to obtain a relaxation of the convention regarding memoirs of ex-Ministers. . . . There have, as far as I know, been no previous attempts in any court to define the extent to which Cabinet proceedings should be treated as secret or confidential, and it is not surprising that different views on this subject are contained in the evidence before me. The Attorney-General does not attempt a final definition but his contention is that such proceedings are confidential and their publication is capable of control by the courts at least as far as they include (a) disclosure of Cabinet documents or proceedings in such a way as to reveal the individual views or attitudes of Ministers; (b) disclosure of confidential advice from civil servants, whether contained in Cabinet papers or not; (c) disclosure of confidential discussions affecting the appointment or transfer of such senior civil servants.

The Attorney-General contends that all Cabinet papers and discussions are prima facie confidential, and that the court should restrain any disclosure thereof if the public interest in concealment outweighs the public interest in a right to free publication. . . .

I do not understand . . . the Attorney-General to be contending, that it is only necessary for him to evoke the public interest to obtain an order of the court. On the contrary, it must be for the court in every case to be satisfied that the public interest is involved, and that, after balancing all the factors which tell for or against publication, to decide whether suppression is necessary.

The defendants' main contention is that whatever the limits of the convention of joint Cabinet responsibility may be, there is no obligation enforceable at law to prevent the publication of Cabinet papers and proceedings, except in extreme cases where national security is involved. In other words, the defendants submit that the confidential character of Cabinet papers and discussions is . . . founded in conscience only. Accordingly, the defendants contend that publication of these Diaries is not capable of control by any order of this court.

If the Attorney-General were restricted in his argument to the general proposition that Cabinet papers and discussion are all under the seal of secrecy at all times, he would be in difficulty. It is true that he has called evidence from eminent former holders of office to the effect that the public interest requires a continuing secrecy, and he cites a powerful passage from the late Viscount Hailsham to this effect. . . .

The defendants, however, in the present action, have also called distinguished former Cabinet Ministers who do not support this view of Lord Hailsham, and it seems to me that the degree of protection afforded to Cabinet papers and discussion cannot be determined by a single rule of thumb. Some secrets require a high standard of protection for a short time. Others require protection until a new political generation has taken over. In the present action against the literary executors, the Attorney-General asks for a perpetual injunction to restrain further publication of the Diaries in whole or in part. I am far from convinced that he has made out a case that the public interest requires such a Draconian remedy when due regard is had to other public interests, such as the freedom of speech. . . .

I have already indicated some of the difficulties which faced the Attorney-General when he relied simply on the public interest as a ground for his actions. That such ground is enough in extreme cases is shown by the universal agreement that publication affecting national security can be restrained in this way. It may be that in the short run (for example, over a period of weeks or months) the public interest is equally compelling to maintain joint Cabinet responsibility and the protection of advice given by civil servants, but I would not accept without close investigation that such matters must, as a matter of course, retain protection after a period of years.

However, the Attorney-General has a powerful reinforcement for his argument in the developing equitable doctrine that a man shall not profit from the wrongful publication of information received by him in confidence. This doctrine, said to have its origin in *Prince Albert* v. *Strange* (1849) 1 H & T1, has been frequently recognised as a ground for restraining the unfair use of commercial secrets transmitted in confidence. . . . It is not until the decision in *Duchess of Argyll* v. *Duke of Argyll* [1967] Ch. 302, that the same principle was applied to domestic secrets such as those passing between husband and wife during the marriage. It was there held by Ungoed-Thomas J, that the plaintiff wife could obtain an order to restrain the defendant husband from communicating such secrets, and the principle is well expressed in the headnote in these terms, at p. 304:

> 'A contract or obligation of confidence need not be expressed but could be implied, and a breach of contract or trust or faith could arise independently of any right of property or contract . . . and that the court, in the exercise of its equitable jurisdiction, would restrain a breach of confidence independently of any right at law.'

This extension of the doctrine of confidence beyond commercial secrets has never been directly challenged, and was noted without criticism by Lord Denning MR in *Fraser* v. *Evans* [1969] 1 QB 349, 361. I am sure that I ought to regard myself, sitting here, as bound by the decision of Ungoed-Thomas J.

Even so, these defendants argue that an extension of the principle of the *Argyll* case to the present dispute involves another large and unjustified leap forward, because in the present case the Attorney-General is seeking to apply the principle to public secrets made confidential in the interests of good government. I cannot see why the courts should be powerless to restrain the publication of public secrets, while enjoying the *Argyll* powers in regard to domestic secrets. Indeed, as already pointed out, the court must have power to deal with publication which threatens national security, and the difference between such a case and the present case is one of degree rather than kind. I conclude, therefore, that when a Cabinet Minister receives information in confidence the improper publication of such information can be restrained by the court, and his obligation is not merely to observe a gentleman's agreement to refrain from publication. . . . I find overwhelming evidence that the doctrine of joint responsibility is generally understood and practised and equally strong evidence that it is on occasion ignored. The general effect of the evidence is that the doctrine is an established feature of the English form of government, and it follows that some matters leading up to a Cabinet decision may be regarded as confidential. Furthermore, I am persuaded that the nature of the confidence is that spoken for by the Attorney-General, namely, that since the confidence is imposed to enable the efficient conduct of the Queen's business, the confidence is owed to the Queen and cannot be released by the members of Cabinet themselves. I have been told that a resigning Minister who wishes to make a personal statement in the House, and to disclose matters which are confidential under the doctrine obtains the consent of the Queen for this purpose. Such consent is obtained through the Prime Minister. I have not been told what happened when the Cabinet disclosed divided opinions during the European Economic Community referendum. But even if there was here a breach of confidence (which I doubt) this is no ground for denying the existence of the general rule. I cannot accept the suggestion that a Minister owes no duty of confidence in respect of his own views expressed in Cabinet. It would only need one or two Ministers to describe their own views to enable experienced observers to identify the views of the others. . . .

The Cabinet is at the very centre of national affairs, and must be in possession at all times of information which is secret or confidential. Secrets relating to national security may require to be preserved indefinitely. Secrets relating to new taxation proposals may be of the highest importance until Budget day, but public knowledge thereafter. To leak a Cabinet decision a day or so before it is officially announced is an accepted exercise in public relations, but to identify the Ministers who voted one way or another is objectionable because it undermines the doctrine of joint responsibility.

It is evident that there cannot be a single rule governing the publication of such a variety of matters. In these actions we are concerned with the publication of diaries at a time when 11 years have expired since the first recorded events. The Attorney-General must show (a) that such publication would be a breach of confidence; (b) that the public interest requires that the publication be restrained, and (c) that there are no other facets of the public interest contradictory of and more compelling than that relied upon. Moreover, the court, when asked to restrain such a publication, must closely examine the extent to which relief is necessary to ensure that restrictions are not imposed beyond the strict requirement of public need.

Applying those principles to the present case, what do we find? In my judgment, the Attorney-General has made out his claim that the expression of individual opinions by Cabinet Ministers in the course of Cabinet discussion are matters of confidence, the publication of which can be restrained by the court when this is clearly necessary in the public interest.

The maintenance of the doctrine of joint responsibility within the Cabinet is in the public interest, and the application of that doctrine might be prejudiced by premature disclosure of the views of individual Ministers.

There must, however, be a limit in time after which the confidential character of the information, and the duty of the court to restrain publication, will lapse. Since the conclusion of the hearing in this case I have had the opportunity to read the whole of volume one of the Diaries, and my considered view is that I cannot believe that the publication at this interval of anything in volume one would inhibit free discussion in the Cabinet of today, even though the individuals involved are the same, and the national problems have a distressing similarity with those of a decade ago. It is unnecessary to elaborate the evils which might flow if at the close of a Cabinet meeting a Minister proceeded to give the press an analysis of the voting, but we are dealing in this case with a disclosure of information nearly 10 years later.

It may, of course, be intensely difficult in a particular case, to say at what point the material loses its confidential character, on the ground that publication will no longer undermine the doctrine of joint Cabinet responsibility. It is this difficulty which prompts some to argue that Cabinet discussions should retain their confidential character for a longer and arbitrary period such as 30 years, or even for all time, but this seems to me to be excessively restrictive. The court should intervene only in the clearest of cases where the continuing confidentiality of the material can be demonstrated. In less clear cases – and this, in my view, is certainly one – reliance must be placed on the good sense and good taste of the Minister or ex-Minister concerned.

In the present case there is nothing in Mr Crossman's work to suggest that he did not support the doctrine of joint Cabinet responsibility. The question for the court is whether it is shown that publication now might damage the doctrine notwithstanding that much of the action is up to 10 years old and three general elections have been held meanwhile. So far as the Attorney-General relies in his argument on the disclosure of individual ministerial opinions, he has not satisfied me that publication would in any way inhibit free and open discussion in Cabinet hereafter.

It remains to deal with the Attorney-General's two further arguments, namely, (a) that the Diaries disclose advice given by senior civil servants who cannot be expected to advise frankly if their advice is not treated as confidential; (b) the Diaries disclose observations made by Ministers on the capacity of individual senior civil servants and their suitability for specific appointments. I can see no grounds in law which entitle the court to restrain publication of these matters. A Minister is, no doubt, responsible for his department and accountable for its errors even though the individual fault is to be found in his subordinates. In these circumstances, to disclose the fault of the subordinate may amount to cowardice or bad taste, but I can find no ground for saying that either the Crown or the individual civil servant has an enforceable right to have the advice which he gives treated as confidential for all time.

For these reasons I do not think that the court should interfere with the publication of volume one of the Diaries, and I propose, therefore, to refuse the injunction sought but to grant liberty to apply in regard to material other than volume one if it is alleged that different considerations may there have to be applied.
Injunction refused.

The report of the case concludes with an afterword by the Chief Justice:

Lord Widgery CJ said that the statement in his judgment that the courts would not restrict publication of confidential communications between civil servants and Ministers was restricted to the present proceedings and did not amount to a general ruling that the courts had no power to do so in any circumstances.

The Attorney-General may be said to have been victorious in this case in gaining judicial acceptance of the *principle* that a legal obligation of confidentiality attaches to Cabinet proceedings, even though the court decided that the Crossman diaries no longer, after the lapse of ten years, retained their confidential character, and so fell outside the protection of the law. The court fashioned from the 'developing equitable doctrine' of confidentiality, which had in previous cases found its application in commercial and domestic relations, a new rule for maintaining the secrecy of Cabinet proceedings.

In the course of the trial an American lawyer commented as follows:

Anthony Lewis, *The Sunday Times*, 3 August 1975

One of the main differences between the political systems of our two countries, we are always told, is the much more active role of American judges; they feel free, as expounders of a written Constitution, to change the law and to decide social and political questions that would never be deemed appropriate for judicial decision in Britain. Felix Frankfurter, an American Supreme Court justice who deplored his countrymen's habit of looking to the courts for salvation, often pointed to Britain as the happy example of a society that left political issues to a democratic political institution, Parliament.

We have been taught also that the British system relies less than the American on legal restraints, and more on the invisible restraints of honour and custom and responsibility. . . .

Yet in the Crossman Diaries case the Attorney-General asked the court to make new law in a highly political area, that of State secrecy. (Political, that is, not in the partisan sense but in the sense of affecting the nature of the governmental system.) And the result sought in the suit would be to subject to law, and to Civil Service views, a personal discretion and responsibility long exercised by Ministers.

The new common law rule established in *Attorney-General* v. *Jonathan Cape Ltd* was not considered by the Government to give sufficient protection to the confidentiality of government business. More stringent rules of non-disclosure, recommended by a Committee of Privy Counsellors (the Radcliffe Committee, Cmnd 6386/1976), were adopted by the Government in 1976 as rules of practice to which ministers would be required to agree. These rules do not supplant the common law but impose obligations, of a non-legal kind, which are more precise and of wider scope than the legal obligations of confidentiality established in the Crossman Diaries case.

Judges have not hesitated to extend legal principles in matters which they see as touching the safety of the state, public order, or the moral welfare of society. In *R.* v. *Chief Constable of Devon and Cornwall, ex p. Central Electricity Generating Board* [1982] QB 458, a case concerning protestors who were passively obstructing exploratory work for a nuclear power station, Lord Denning took the meaning of 'breach of the peace' (allowing intervention by the police) beyond previous case law in saying (at p. 471):

I think that the conduct of these people, their criminal obstruction, is itself a breach of the peace. There is a breach of the peace whenever a person who is lawfully carrying out his work is unlawfully and physically prevented by another from doing it. He is entitled by law peacefully to go on with his work on his lawful occasions. If anyone unlawfully and physically obstructs the worker – by lying down or chaining himself to a rig or the like – he is guilty of a breach of the peace.

(See, too, *Shaw* v. *Director of Public Prosecutions* [1962] AC 220 and in particular the remarks of Viscount Simonds at pp. 267–8.)

Statutes are interpreted by the courts against a background of common law principles, and some of these are regarded as having so fundamental a character that only very clear statutory language is accepted by the courts as effective to displace them.

Pyx Granite Co. Ltd v. *Ministry of Housing and Local Government*
[1960] AC 260 (HL)

By statute a person wishing to develop his land had normally to obtain the permission of the local planning authority or of the Minister. The Act also provided that the Minister's decision on the question whether permission was needed in a particular case should be final. The appellant company had applied for planning permission, and the Minister, having ruled that permission was required, refused permission for part of the land and granted it for another part only upon conditions. The company brought proceedings in which it claimed that the proposed developments did not require planning permission and that as a consequence the Minister's decisions were invalid. It was argued against the company that the courts had no jurisdiction to entertain the action because the Act had provided the only procedure for having the question of the need for permission determined.

VISCOUNT SIMONDS: . . . The question is whether the statutory remedy is the only remedy and the right of the subject to have recourse to the courts of law is excluded. . . . It is a principle not by any means to be whittled down that the subject's recourse to Her Majesty's courts for the determination of his rights is not to be excluded except by clear words. That is, as McNair J called it in *Francis* v. *Yiewsley and West Drayton Urban District Council*, a 'fundamental rule' from which I would not for my part sanction any departure. . . . There is nothing in the Act to suggest that, while a new remedy, perhaps cheap and expeditious, is given, the old and, as we like to call it, the inalienable remedy of Her Majesty's subjects to seek redress in her courts is taken away. . . .

Their Lordships held that the jurisdiction of the courts was not excluded, and that the company did not require planning permission for the proposed development.

Compare *Chester* v. *Bateson* [1920] 1 KB 829, p. 63 above, and see *Raymond* v. *Honey* [1983] 1 AC 1 at 12–13, 14–15.

Common law principles, however fundamental they may seem, have always to yield to unequivocal statutory provision, and besides it may be clear that a statute is intended to implement a policy which runs counter to older ideas enshrined in common law. An example is the opposition between private

rights of property, traditionally defended by the common law, and modern
public welfare legislation. (See, e.g., *Belfast Corporation* v. *OD Cars Ltd* [1960]
AC 490, 523–4, *per* Lord Radcliffe.)

2 Conventions

It is a rule of law that the Queen may give or refuse assent to a bill passed by
both Houses of Parliament; it is a constitutional convention that she should
always (or in all but very exceptional circumstances: see de Smith, *Constitutional and Administrative Law*, 4th edn 1981, p. 128) give her assent. It is the law that
a writ for a parliamentary by-election must be issued by the Clerk of the Crown
when he has received a warrant from the Speaker of the House of Commons
(Representation of the People Act 1983, Sched. 1, paras. 1, 3); it is a
convention that when a vacancy occurs in the House the Chief Whip of the
party to which the former member belonged shall, within three months, move
that the Speaker should issue his warrant for a writ (see (1974) 42 *The Table*
143–4; HC Deb. vol. 41, cols. 164–8, 19 April 1983). Convention prescribes
that there should be a prime minister who is a member of the House of
Commons; the law directs that he or she should receive a salary (Ministerial
and other Salaries Act 1975).

Dicey formulated the distinction between the law of the constitution and
constitutional conventions as follows.

Dicey, *The Law of the Constitution*, pp. 23–4

[T]he rules which make up constitutional law, as the term is used in England, include
two sets of principles or maxims of a totally distinct character.

The one set of rules are in the strictest sense 'laws', since they are rules which
(whether written or unwritten, whether enacted by statute or derived from the mass of
custom, tradition, or judge-made maxims known as the common law) are enforced by
the courts; these rules constitute 'constitutional law' in the proper sense of that term,
and may for the sake of distinction be called collectively 'the law of the constitution'.

The other set of rules consist of conventions, understandings, habits, or practices
which, though they may regulate the conduct of the several members of the sovereign
power, of the Ministry, or of other officials, are not in reality laws at all since they are
not enforced by the courts. This portion of constitutional law may, for the sake of
distinction, be termed the 'conventions of the constitution', or constitutional morality.

To put the same thing in a somewhat different shape, 'constitutional law', as the
expression is used in England, both by the public and by authoritative writers, consists
of two elements. The one element, here called the 'law of the constitution', is a body of
undoubted law; the other element, here called the 'conventions of the constitution',
consists of maxims or practices which, though they regulate the ordinary conduct of the
Crown, of Ministers, and of other persons under the constitution, are not in strictness
laws at all.

The distinction made by Dicey in this passage has been rejected by some who have denied that there is any difference in principle between laws and conventions. Sir Ivor Jennings, in particular, argued that enforceability by the courts was not a valid basis for a distinction between laws and conventions and that both rested essentially on the acquiescence of those to whom they applied (*The Law and the Constitution*, 5th edn 1959, pp. 103–36). But Dicey's analysis can be defended, for it can be shown that laws are given effect or 'enforced' by courts or tribunals in a sense which cannot be applied to the treatment of conventions by these bodies. Moreover law is not usually defined in terms that can include conventions, and those who are involved in or observe the political process are aware of a difference between laws and conventions and are rarely uncertain as to the category to which a particular rule belongs. A civil servant who, without authority, sends a confidential departmental minute to a newspaper is in no doubt that he is breaking the law (Official Secrets Act 1911, s.2(1)); a Cabinet Secretary knows that it is convention and not law that prevents him from disclosing to a new administration the papers of the previous government of a different party (see p. 89 below). See further Colin Munro, 'Laws and Conventions Distinguished' (1975) 91 *LQR* 218.

Madzimbamuto v. *Lardner-Burke* [1969] 1 AC 645 (PC)

After the unlawful declaration of independence by the Government of the Crown colony of Southern Rhodesia in 1965, the United Kingdom Parliament passed the Southern Rhodesia Act 1965 to deal with the circumstances arising from this unconstitutional action. In the *Madzimbamuto* case the question arose whether Parliament could properly legislate for Southern Rhodesia, the colony having already progressed, before the declaration of independence, to a substantial degree of self-government. The United Kingdom Government had indeed formally acknowledged in 1961 that

it has become an established convention for Parliament at Westminster not to legislate for Southern Rhodesia on matters within the competence of the Legislative Assembly of Southern Rhodesia except with the agreement of the Southern Rhodesia Government.

Lord Reid (delivering the majority judgment) referred to the convention set out in the United Kingdom Government's statement of 1961, and continued:

That was a very important convention but it had no legal effect in limiting the legal power of parliament.

It is often said that it would be unconstitutional for the United Kingdom Parliament to do certain things, meaning that the moral, political and other reasons against doing them are so strong that most people would regard it as highly improper if Parliament did these things. But that does not mean that it is beyond the power of Parliament to do such things. If Parliament chose to do any of them the courts could not hold the Act of Parliament invalid. It may be that it would have been thought, before 1965, that it would be unconstitutional to disregard this convention. But it may also be that the unilateral Declaration of Independence released the United Kingdom from any obligation to observe the convention. Their Lordships in declaring the law are not concerned with these matters. They are only concerned with the legal powers of Parliament. . . .

Although conventions are not *enforced* by courts, the existence of a convention may form part of the reasoning that leads a judge to his decision. For example in *Attorney-General* v. *Jonathan Cape Ltd* (above) the court held that an injunction can in a proper case be granted to protect the confidentiality of Cabinet proceedings, on the ground that confidentiality is necessary for the maintenance of the convention of joint (or collective) Cabinet responsibility, a convention which the court considered to be in the public interest. Here the court's evaluation of the convention of collective ministerial responsibility as an essential feature of our governmental system was a crucial element in its argument and conclusions.

See also the *Reference re Amendment of the Constitution of Canada* case, below.

How do conventions arise?

Conventions, as Geoffrey Marshall says, 'are unlike legal rules because they are not the product of a legislative or of a judicial process' (*Constitutional Conventions*, p. 216). Many conventions are the result of a gradual hardening of usage over a period of years or generations. This is true of the cardinal convention of our constitutional monarchy, that the Queen must act upon the advice of her ministers. Queen Victoria might not have assented to this obligation (see G. H. L. Le May, *The Victorian Constitution*, 1979, p. 74), but in 1910 the Prime Minister reminded King George v of what had become an incontrovertible convention. The King had proposed to meet the leader of the Unionist Opposition in the House of Lords, Lord Lansdowne, to discover his views on the progress of the Liberal Government's Parliament Bill, in the light of the Liberal victory in the general election of December 1910.

Mr Asquith's Minute to King George v, December 1910

The part to be played by the Crown, in such a situation as now exists, has happily been settled by the accumulated traditions and the unbroken practice of more than 70 years. It is to act upon the advice of the Ministers who for the time being possess the confidence of the House of Commons, whether that advice does or does not conform to the private and personal judgment of the Sovereign. Ministers will always pay the utmost deference, and give the most serious consideration, to any criticism or objection that the Monarch may offer to their policy; but the ultimate decision rests with them; for they, and not the Crown, are responsible to Parliament. It is only by a scrupulous adherence to this well-established Constitutional doctrine that the Crown can be kept out of the arena of party politics.

It follows that it is not the function of a Constitutional Sovereign to act as arbiter or mediator between rival parties and policies; still less to take advice from the leaders on both sides, with the view to forming a conclusion of his own. George III in the early years of his reign tried to rule after this fashion, with the worst results, and with the accession of Mr Pitt to power he practically abandoned the attempt. The growth and development of our representative system, and the clear establishment at the core and centre of our Constitution of the doctrine of Ministerial responsibility, have since placed the position of the Sovereign beyond the region of doubt or controversy. . . .

(The Prime Minister withdrew his objection to the interview with Lord Lansdowne upon the King's assurance that his purpose was to obtain information and not advice.)

It may be difficult to say with certainty that a usage or practice has come to be acknowledged as a binding convention. We can often only infer that those affected by a supposed convention consider themselves bound by it from the consistency of their behaviour over a period: the shorter the period, the more doubtful the inference. Between 1964 and 1983 no new hereditary peerages were created, and it seemed that a new convention in this sense was on the way to becoming established. But in 1983 hereditary peerages were again conferred, on the recommendation of the Prime Minister (Mrs Thatcher), and it was not objected that there had been a breach of convention. Conventions are always emerging, crystallizing and dissolving, and it is sometimes questionable whether a convention has been broken or has simply changed.

Conventions may also arise from an agreement by the interested parties to conduct their mutual relations in a particular way. Conventions affecting the status and relations of member countries of the Commonwealth have been agreed upon from time to time at Commonwealth (formerly Imperial) conferences: for example, statements of fundamental constitutional usages of the Commonwealth were agreed at the Imperial Conference of 1930 and were afterwards recorded in the preamble to the Statute of Westminster 1931. (See p. 79 below.) Again, the convention that a Chief Whip should normally move for the issue of a by-election writ within three months of a vacancy occurring (p. 74 above) resulted from agreement in an all-party Speaker's Conference (Cmnd 5500/1973, para. 1(a)).

Is agreement really an independent source of convention? Eric Colvin, 'Constitutional Jurisprudence in the Supreme Court of Canada' (1982) 4 *Supreme Court Law Review* 3 at 15, says: 'Unless such an agreement reflects past practice it is perhaps best regarded as an anticipatory convention, since the claim that the rule exists will be unsustainable in the event that subsequent practice departs from it.'

The sources of convention, as Colin Munro remarks (op. cit., pp. 232-3), are 'open-ended and diverse'. In the following case a new principle of administrative conduct was accepted by the Government as a result of parliamentary and public pressure.

The 'Crichel Down principle'

In 1953 there occurred the notorious incident of Crichel Down. Some land in Devon had been compulsorily acquired from its owners by the Air Ministry in 1937 for use as a bombing range. After the war the land was no longer needed for this purpose, and eventually it was transferred to the Commissioners for Crown Lands, who let it to a tenant of their choice. Attempts by one of the former owners to buy back his land were rebuffed, and assurances given to neighbouring landowners that they would be given an opportunity of tendering for tenancies of the land were not honoured. After vigorous public criticism there was an official inquiry which revealed that civil servants had acted in a high-handed and deceitful manner. The result of these events was the resignation of the responsible Minister, Sir Thomas Dugdale. (The bearing of this case on the convention of individual ministerial responsibility is considered in chapter 7.) In the course of his resignation speech in the House of Commons, Sir Thomas Dugdale announced a new procedure for dealing with land that had been compulsorily acquired. If the land was no longer wanted by the acquiring department, or immediately by any other department which could have purchased the land under compulsory powers, it would normally be offered to the former owner, or a successor who could establish his claim, at the current market price. (HC Deb. vol. 530, cols. 1190–92, 20 July 1954.)

This new administrative practice, based upon the results of an independent inquiry and announced as a corrective of actions which had caused widespread public concern, was approved by a majority vote in the House of Commons after the subsequent debate. Successive administrations accepted the correctness of the 'Crichel Down principle' after that time, and the terms of its application were laid down in a Treasury circular.

(For controversial applications of the Crichel Down principle see *The Times*, 6 June 1980, and *Fourth Report of the Parliamentary Commissioner*, HC 322 of 1980–81.)

It hardly needs saying that conventions (like laws) are not always obeyed, and that those who obey them may do so for a variety of reasons, whether from sense of obligation or respect for tradition, from habit, expediency or administrative necessity. But when political practices are observed with a sufficient degree of regularity there will arise an expectation that they will continue to be observed – and often also a general conviction that they *ought* to be observed. Such conviction is most likely to be present if the practice can be seen to contribute to the rational functioning of the political system. As long as practices are supported by a general, tacit agreement (among participants and commentators) that they ought to continue, we can speak of them as conventional rules. When the agreement is only partial, the existence of the convention is doubtful.

In a case decided in 1982 the Supreme Court of Canada assumed jurisdiction to decide on the existence and content of a convention. Its ruling on the disputed convention was a landmark in a controversy which raised important issues about the nature of constitutional conventions. The issues arose from a proposal to 'patriate' the Canadian constitution, which rested upon a United Kingdom statute, by bringing it wholly under the control of

Canadian institutions.

Patriation of the Canadian Constitution 1980–82

The basic constitutional structure of Canada was established by the British North America Act 1867, an Act of the United Kingdom Parliament which incorporated the terms upon which the Canadian Provinces were united in the Federation of Canada. Any necessary amending legislation was to be enacted by the United Kingdom Parliament.

Although Canada was a fully independent state at least after the Statute of Westminster 1931, the Canadian Parliament remained incompetent to amend the British North America Acts. There was in 1931 no agreement in Canada as to the terms on which the power of constitutional amendment might be transferred to Canadian institutions, and the Statute of Westminster left this power with the United Kingdom Parliament. While section 2 of the Statute allowed full efficacy in general to the legislation of the Canadian Parliament (and the parliaments of the other independent Dominions), section 7(1) provided:

Nothing in this Act shall be deemed to apply to the repeal, amendment or alteration of the British North America Acts, 1867 to 1930. . . .

And section 7(3) provided:

The powers conferred by this Act upon the Parliament of Canada or upon the legislatures of the Provinces shall be restricted to the enactment of laws in relation to matters within the competence of the Parliament of Canada or of any of the legislatures of the Provinces respectively.

The British North America (No. 2) Act 1949, which transferred a power of constitutional amendment to the Parliament of Canada, excepted amendments affecting the distribution of powers between the provincial and Federal Governments.

Even before 1931 a convention had become established which governed legislation by the United Kingdom Parliament for the self-governing Dominions. This convention was formally reaffirmed in the preamble to the Statute of Westminster in the following words:

It is in accord with the established constitutional position that no law hereafter made by the Parliament of the United Kingdom shall extend to any of the said Dominions as part of the law of that Dominion otherwise than at the request and with the consent of that Dominion.

(A *legal* reinforcement of this convention was provided by section 4 of the Statute, considered above: pp. 27–32.)

On a number of occasions, both before and after 1931, the British North America Act 1867 was amended by the United Kingdom Parliament, in each case upon the request of the Canadian Parliament. When the requested legislation would directly affect federal-provincial relations, the request was made and acted upon only after the Federal Government had obtained the agreement of the governments of the affected provinces.

In 1980 the Canadian Government decided that the time had come to 'patriate' the Canadian constitution, i.e., to terminate the power of the United Kingdom Parliament to legislate for Canada and provide for all future constitutional amendments to be effected in Canada in accordance with a prescribed procedure. It was proposed at the same time to incorporate in the patriated constitution a Charter of Rights and Freedoms which would prevail over inconsistent federal or provincial laws.

Only the United Kingdom Parliament could pass the necessary legislation to bring about the desired patriation of the constitution. The legislation would clearly affect the distribution of powers in the Canadian Federation, and the Federal Government tried to obtain the agreement of the Provincial Governments to the proposal. However only two Provinces (Ontario and New Brunswick) agreed, while the remaining eight Provinces were opposed to patriation on the Federal Government's terms. Neverthless the Federal Government decided to proceed on the basis of this limited agreement. A proposed resolution was submitted to the Canadian Parliament in the form of an address to the Queen, requesting her to cause a bill to be introduced in the United Kingdom Parliament which would incorporate a Constitution Act for Canada, including a Charter of Rights and Freedoms and a procedure for constitutional amendment in Canada.

In response to these developments the Foreign Affairs Committee of the British House of Commons undertook an inquiry into the role of the United Kingdom Parliament in the expected event that a request for patriation should be supported only by the Federal Government and Parliament and two Provincial Governments. Would the United Kingdom Parliament be bound to accede to such a request? The answer would depend on the applicable conventions rather than on law.

The following Memorandum was submitted to the Foreign Affairs Committee.

First Report from the Foreign Affairs Committee (Kershaw Report),
vol. II, HC 42–II of 1980–81: Memorandum by
Professor H. W. R. Wade (p. 102)

1. The Government of Canada claims that the United Kingdom Parliament is obliged to enact, without questions asked, any amendment of the British North America Acts which is submitted by the Government of Canada and backed by the usual resolutions of the two Houses of Parliament in Ottawa, even though the amendment affects the rights of the Provinces.

2. The Government of the UK may be tempted to accept this claim since it would enable the Parliament of the UK to play a purely formal and automatic part and to avoid embroiling itself in a Canadian constitutional controversy which ought to be

decided in Canada alone and in which no one in the UK wishes to intervene.

3. Are the Government and Parliament of the UK entitled to take this line of least resistance? The answer depends upon constitutional convention rather than upon law. In law there is no doubt that the Canadian courts recognise that in matters affecting the Provinces the British North America Acts can be amended only by the UK Parliament in accordance with the Statute of Westminster 1931, section 7. They may be expected to recognise also (a) that no law sets any limit upon this amending power of the UK Parliament; and (b) that no law sets any limit upon the freedom of the Canadian Government to submit amendments affecting the constitutional powers and position of the Provinces – though if they should decide otherwise this will be an internal Canadian matter. The important question for the UK Government and Parliament is whether it is required by constitutional convention that any amendment legislation should be enacted without question at Westminster, even though it affects and is opposed by some or all of the Provinces.

4. In British constitutional theory and practice there is a clear-cut distinction between law and convention. Law derives from common law and statute and is enforceable by the courts. Convention derives from constitutional principle and practice and is not enforceable by courts. Law remains in force until changed by statute. Convention may change with changing times. Law, at least if statutory, is ascertainable in precise form. Convention is often imprecise and may be nowhere formulated in categorical terms.

5. The correct attitude for the UK Government and Parliament to adopt must be found by looking at (a) constitutional principle and (b) past practice.

A. CONSTITUTIONAL PRINCIPLE

6. The essential elements of a federal constitution are that powers are divided between the central and provincial governments and that neither has legal power to encroach upon the domain of the other, except through the proper process of constitutional amendment. The system of local government in the UK, for example, contains no element of federalism because the powers of local authorities are wholly at the mercy of Parliament. The same would have been true of the proposed devolution of powers to Scotland and Wales.

7. If it were correct that the UK Parliament is obliged to enact any amendment of the British North America Acts proposed by the Canadian Government, this would obviously contradict the federal principle. It would then lie wholly within the power of the Canadian Government, *de facto*, to obtain amendments derogating from the powers of the Provinces and against the will of the Provinces. The Canadian constitution would cease to be federal in the true sense, since the Provinces would be at the mercy of the central government. By agreeing to act merely as an automaton at the direction of the Canadian Government, the UK Parliament would be subverting the whole foundation of the Constitution of Canada. It would put into the hands of the Canadian government powers which are not possessed by the central government of the United States, Australia, India and other federal countries, and which cannot be possessed by the central government without destroying the federal basis of the constitution. It would be idle then to say that the UK was refraining from taking sides in a Canadian controversy. In fact the UK would be taking sides with the Canadian government in undermining the constitutional rights and powers of the Provinces, contrary to the whole system of the British North America Acts and the fundamentals of Canadian

constitutional law. . . .

9. Section 7 of the Statute of Westminster 1931 was inserted at the instance of the Provinces expressly for the purpose of preserving the federal principle. Had that not been done, the Canadian Parliament would have obtained full legal power to amend the British North America Acts under section 2. Full powers of enacting and amending legislation were conferred upon the Federal Government by section 2 and upon the Provincial Governments by section 7(2), but with the restriction set out in section 7(3) so as to prevent either from encroaching upon the other's sphere of independence.

10. The provisions of the Statute of Westminster make it quite clear that it cannot have been supposed in 1931 that convention required the UK Parliament to enact without question any British North America Bill put forward by the Canadian Government and Parliament. If there had been any such convention, section 7 would have been useless to the Provinces, and the security which it was intended to give them would have been nugatory, since the Canadian Government could at any time have called upon the UK Parliament to enact an amendment taking away constitutional powers of the Provinces. It is inconceivable that the Provinces would have been satisfied with this situation. Yet they were satisfied with section 7, thus clearly disproving the existence of any convention of the kind now claimed. They must have felt fully assured that they enjoyed not only strictly legal but also genuinely constitutional protection for their rights.

11. Constitutional principle, therefore, is entirely opposed to any alleged convention that the UK Parliament is obliged to enact amendments of the Constitution of Canada which reduce the rights of the Provinces without the consent of the Provinces concerned and without inquiring whether that consent has been given.

B. PAST PRACTICE

12. It would be unprofitable to itemise all the amendments of the British North America Acts effected by the UK Parliament since 1867. The majority of them had no effect on the legislative powers of the Provinces and the fact that provincial consent was not obtained is immaterial.

13. The only amendments affecting the legislative powers of the Provinces were those of 1940, 1951, 1960 and 1964. In each one of these cases all the Provinces were consulted and their agreement was obtained. The amendment of 1940 was delayed for some years until the agreement of Quebec could be obtained. By accepting this delay of the amendment (which gave the Canadian Parliament power to legislate for unemployment insurance) the Canadian Government (in the words of the federal Prime Minister)–

'avoided the raising of a very critical constitutional question, namely, whether or not in the amending of the British North America Act it is absolutely necessary to secure the consent of all the Provinces, or whether the consent of a certain number of Provinces would of itself be sufficient.' (Canadian Commons Debates, 1940 (25 June), pp. 1117–18.)

It is clear from this remark that the Canadian Government accepted that in the case of such amendments convention made it 'absolutely necessary' that the consent of at least some Provinces was obtained. In principle it would seem right that the consent of all Provinces suffering any diminution of their legislative powers should be obtained, and this is corroborated by the fact that unanimous consent was obtained for the amendments of 1951, 1960 and 1964.

14. In addition, there is the very significant case of non-amendment represented by the Statute of Westminster 1931. This would have gravely affected Provincial legislative independence, as already pointed out, had not section 7 been inserted at the instance of the Provinces. In this case not only the Canadian Government but also the UK Government and Parliament felt bound to take account of the Provinces' objections.

15. It hardly seems necessary to argue that convention requires the prior agreement of Provinces whose powers will be affected by the amendment, since the Canadian Government expressly admitted as much in the White Paper of 1965 entitled 'The Amendment of the Constitution of Canada'. It said:

> '*The fourth general principle* is that the Canadian Parliament will not request an amendment directly affecting federal-provincial relationships without prior consultation and agreement with the provinces. This principle did not emerge as early as others but since 1907, and particularly since 1930, has gained increasing recognition and acceptance. The nature and the degree of provincial participation in the amending process, however, have not lent themselves to easy definition.'

This statement, it is important to observe, was agreed by all the Provinces before the White Paper was published. . . . It therefore represents a 'convention' in the literal sense, being an agreed statement of the federal-provincial relationship. It is thus as authoritative a source of constitutional convention as can be imagined.

16. It is therefore acknowledged by all concerned that as the conventions of the Canadian constitution have developed they have hardened in favour of the protection of the rights of the Provinces. The Statute of Westminster evidently represents the watershed. That was the outstandingly important occasion when the Provinces made good their claim for protection of their rights, and it is not surprising that thereafter the convention requiring Provincial consent became clearer and more positive.

17. The 'fourth general principle' quoted above is framed in terms of convention binding the Canadian Parliament rather than the UK Parliament. But it by no means follows that it will not concern the UK Parliament. The whole object of section 7 of the Statute of Westminster was to make the UK Parliament the guardian of the rights of the Provinces and as already shown, constitutional principles make it essential that the UK Parliament should not act as a mere automaton at the Canadian Government's instance. It is inexorably necessary, therefore, that the UK Parliament should be assured that the Canadian conventions for the protection of the Provinces have been duly observed. If the UK Parliament failed to satisfy itself of this, it would be acting as an automaton and failing in its function of constitutional guardian. Where the requested amendment will affect the Provinces, therefore, the UK Parliament must make sure that the Provinces concerned have consented. As the precedents since 1930 make clear, the consent of the Provinces to amendments affecting them has in fact always been sought and obtained by the Canadian Government, so that the UK Parliament has not had to make any inquiry. But it would be entirely wrong to conclude from that that the UK Parliament will never look behind the Canadian Government's request. That will be true only where it is clear that the requisite Provincial consent has already been obtained. If the Canadian Government has failed to observe the conventions established in Canada, the UK Parliament will not be bound by the supposed convention that it should ask no questions.

18. Conventions are the rules of the game of politics, and it may be necessary to

correct one infringement by another. If for example a British government were to refuse to resign after being defeated on a motion of no confidence, the Queen would be justified in dismissing the ministers against their will. The fact that the UK Parliament does not in practice look behind amendments requested by Canada is entirely dependent upon those requests being in conformity with Canadian conventions. If those conventions are infringed, the duty of the UK Parliament is to take corrective action. . . .

20. The inescapable conclusion is that section 7 of the Statute of Westminster 1931 has left the UK Parliament with not only legal but also political responsibility for upholding the federal constitution of Canada and acting as guardian of the rights of the Provinces. Anachronistic and unwelcome as this responsibility may be, it was deliberately preserved in 1931 and nothing has since happened to alter it. The UK Parliament therefore has the duty, when requested to amend the British North America Acts, to ask itself two questions: first, does the amendment adversely affect Provincial legislative powers; and secondly, if so, have the Provinces affected signified their consent?

In its report to the House of Commons, the Foreign Affairs Committee concluded that the United Kingdom Parliament was not bound by law or convention to act automatically upon a request from the Canadian parliament for the repatriation of the Canadian constitution. The Committee advised that it was 'in accord with the established constitutional position for the UK Government and Parliament to take account of the federal character of Canada's constitutional system, when considering how to respond' to such a request (para. 14.4). On the other hand the Committee was not persuaded that the United Kingdom Parliament could properly act upon a request for patriation only if it was supported by *all* the Provinces. In the Committee's view the request must have a sufficient degree of provincial support for Parliament to be satisifed that it represented 'the wishes of the Canadian people as a federally structured community' (para. 114). The committee proposed a criterion for determining whether the required degree of support existed (para. 114).

Meanwhile some of the dissenting Provinces had instituted proceedings in the Canadian courts to obtain a ruling on the constitutionality of the action being taken by the Federal Government to secure patriation. Appeals from the rulings of three provincial Courts of Appeal were heard by the Supreme Court of Canada, which gave its judgment before the resolution of the Canadian Parliament had been submitted to the Queen.

Reference re Amendment of the Constitution of Canada (1982) 125 DLR
(3d) 1 (Supreme Court of Canada)

The Supreme Court decided by a majority of seven to two that there was no *legal* impediment to the submission by the Canadian Parliament, without the agreement of the Provinces, of a request for the constitutional amendments necessary to effect patriation, and no legal restraint upon the power of the

United Kingdom Parliament to act on such a request. But the court had also been asked to decide the following question:

Is it a constitutional convention that the House of Commons and Senate of Canada will not request Her Majesty the Queen to lay before the Parliament of the United Kingdom of Great Britain and Northern Ireland a measure to amend the Constitution of Canada affecting federal-provincial relationships or the powers, rights or privileges granted or secured by the Constitution of Canada to the provinces, their legislatures or governments without first obtaining the agreement of the provinces?

The Supreme Court decided by a majority of six to three that this question should be answered in the affirmative, and further that 'at least a substantial measure of provincial consent' was required for compliance with the convention. Since the necessary measure of provincial agreement was wanting it would be 'unconstitutional in the conventional sense' for the proposed request for constitutional amendment to be submitted to the Queen. Passages quoted below are from the majority opinion of Martland, Ritchie, Dickson, Beetz, Chouinard and Lamer JJ.

In giving general consideration to the nature of conventions the court said:

The conventional rules of the Constitution present one striking peculiarity. In contradistinction to the laws of the Constitution, they are not enforced by the Courts. One reason for this situation is that, unlike common law rules, conventions are not judge-made rules. They are not based on judicial precedents but on precedents established by the institutions of government themselves. Nor are they in the nature of statutory commands which it is the function and duty of the Courts to obey and enforce. Furthermore, to enforce them would mean to administer some formal sanction when they are breached. But the legal system from which they are distinct does not contemplate formal sanctions for their breach.

Perhaps the main reason why conventional rules cannot be enforced by the Courts is that they are generally in conflict with the legal rules which they postulate and the Courts are bound to enforce the legal rules. The conflict is not of a type which would entail the commission of any illegality. It results from the fact that legal rules create wide powers, discretions and rights which conventions prescribe should be exercised only in a certain limited manner, if at all.

The following example was given to illustrate this point:

As a matter of law, the Queen, or the Governor General or the Lieutenant-Governor could refuse assent to every bill passed by both Houses of Parliament or by a Legislative Assembly [of a Province] as the case may be. But by convention they cannot of their own motion refuse to assent to any such bill on any ground, for instance because they disapprove of the policy of the bill. We have here a conflict between a legal rule which creates a complete discretion and a conventional rule which completely neutralizes it. But conventions, like laws, are sometimes violated. And if this particular convention were violated and assent were improperly withheld, the courts would be bound to enforce the law, not the convention. They would refuse to recognize the validity of a vetoed bill.

It had been argued that a question about the existence of a convention was a political one and did not raise a justiciable issue appropriate for a court to decide. This argument was dismissed on the ground, *inter alia*, that the statutes empowering the Provincial Governments to put questions for resolution by the Courts did so in terms wide enough to entitle them to obtain an answer to a question of this kind. Although the question was 'not confined to an issue of pure legality', it had to do with 'a fundamental issue of constitutionality and legitimacy'. The court had not been asked to enforce a convention but rather 'to recognize it if it exists'. This the courts in England and the Commonwealth had done many times:

In so recognizing conventional rules, the Courts have described them, sometimes commented upon them and given them such precision as is derived from the written form of a judgment. They did not shrink from doing so on account of the political aspects of conventions, nor because of their supposed vagueness, uncertainty or flexibility.

In our view, we should not, in a constitutional reference, decline to accomplish a type of exercise that Courts have been doing of their own motion for years.

Did the convention exist? In addressing this question the court adopted Sir Ivor Jennings's view of the requirements for establishing a convention, stated as follows in *The Law and the Constitution* (5th edn 1959, p. 136):

We have to ask ourselves three questions: first, what are the precedents; secondly, did the actors in the precedents believe that they were bound by a rule; and thirdly, is there a reason for the rule? A single precedent with a good reason may be enough to establish the rule. A whole string of precedents without such a reason will be of no avail, unless it is perfectly certain that the persons concerned regarded them[selves] as bound by it.

(Not everyone agrees that there is a requirement of a 'good reason' for a convention. See Brazier and Robilliard [1982] *PL* 28, and cf. Marshall, *Constitutional Conventions*, pp. 10–12.)

The court proceeded to examine in turn the precedents, the beliefs of the 'actors' or participants in government, and the reason for the alleged rule.

The court found five precedents where constitutional amendments had changed provincial legislative powers and so had directly affected federal-provincial relationships:

Every one of these five amendments was agreed upon by each Province whose legislative authority was affected.

In negative terms, no amendment changing provincial legislative powers has been made since Confederation when agreement of a Province whose legislative powers would have been changed was withheld. . . .

The accumulation of these precedents, positive and negative, concurrent and without exception, does not of itself suffice in establishing the existence of the convention; but it unmistakedly points in its direction. Indeed, if the precedents stood alone, it might be argued that unanimity is required.

Turning to the question whether the convention had been acknowledged by the 'actors in the precedents', the court cited the official statement of Federal

Government policy, endorsed by all the Provinces and published in the White Paper of 1965. (This statement, affirming the general principle of prior consultation and agreement with the Provinces on amendments affecting federal-provincial relationships, is quoted in Professor Wade's Memorandum, above, para. 15.) Government ministers, the court found, had expressed themselves in similar terms on a number of occasions, and successive discussions between the Federal and Provincial Governments on the subject of constitutional amendment had proceeded on the assumption that a substantial degree of provincial consent was required. It was clear to the court that not all the actors concerned had accepted a principle of *unanimous* provincial consent. The court concluded as follows:

It would not be appropriate for the Court to devise in the abstract a specific formula which would indicate in positive terms what measure of provincial agreement is required for the convention to be complied with. Conventions by their nature develop in the political field and it will be for the political actors, not this Court, to determine the degree of provincial consent required.

It is sufficient for the Court to decide that at least a substantial measure of provincial consent is required and to decide further whether the situation before the Court meets with this requirement. The situation is one where Ontario and New Brunswick agree with the proposed amendments whereas the eight other Provinces oppose it. By no conceivable standard could this situation be thought to pass muster. It clearly does not disclose a sufficient measure of provincial agreement. Nothing more should be said about this.

Finally the court considered the reason for the rule, finding this in the federal principle embodied in the constitution of Canada as a federal union. The court cited Lord Watson's observations on the British North America Act in *Liquidators of Maritime Bank* v. *Receiver-General of New Brunswick* [1892] AC 437, 441–2:

The object of the Act was neither to weld the provinces into one, nor to subordinate provincial governments to a central authority, but to create a federal government in which they should all be represented, entrusted with the exclusive administration of affairs in which they had a common interest, each province retaining its independence and autonomy.

This federal principle, said the court,

cannot be reconciled with a state of affairs where the modification of provincial legislative powers could be obtained by the unilateral action of the federal authorities. . . . The purpose of [the] conventional rule is to protect the federal character of the Canadian Constitution and prevent the anomaly that the House of Commons and Senate could obtain by simple resolutions what they could not validly accomplish by statute.

In the result the conclusion of the Supreme Court was that while the law did not require provincial consent to the proposed resolution of the federal Houses of Parliament, the evolution of convention had made a substantial measure of provincial consent constitutionally necessary. Convention had become settled in this sense without affecting the legal position for, as the court held, it is impossible for a convention to crystallize into law.

(On this case see further Marshall, op. cit., ch. xi; Eric Colvin (1982) 4 *Supreme Court Law Review* 3; and Richard S. Kay, id., 23.)

The court's judgment did not indicate what would be a 'substantial measure of provincial consent', but its decision that the support of only two Provinces did not meet this condition caused the Federal Government to seek wider agreement on a revised set of proposals for patriation. In the result nine Provinces (all except Quebec) agreed to support the revised scheme. In pursuance of this agreement an Address to the Queen was approved by both Houses of the Canadian Parliament in December 1981, requesting the passage of legislation which would enact a new Constitution for Canada, incorporating a charter of rights, and transfer the power of constitutional amendment to Canadian institutions. The Canada Bill 1982, of which the long title was 'A Bill to give effect to a request by the Senate and House of Commons of Canada', was accordingly laid before the United Kingdom Parliament. The Lord Privy Seal, Mr Humphrey Atkins, moved the second reading of the bill in the House of Commons.

House of Commons, 17 February 1982 (HC Deb. vol. 18, cols. 295, 297)

MR ATKINS: It is, of course, a matter for regret that the present proposals do not have the unanimous support of the Canadian provinces. But . . . the Supreme Court of Canada considered that the consent of all the provinces was not required, either by law or by constitutional convention, to the making of a request to us. No one would deny that nine out of 10 provinces constitutes the substantial measure of provincial consent to which the Supreme Court referred.

After referring to the preamble to the Statute of Westminster 1931 (see p. 79 above), Mr Atkins continued:

It would, of course, be inconsistent with this 'request and consent' convention for Parliament to make amendments which have not been requested and consented to by Canada in the first place. . . . In the light of this, I have to state the clear view of the Government that any amendment to the Canada Bill which may be put forward should not be passed by the House.

The Canada Bill was duly passed by both Houses without amendment.

Richard S. Kay (op. cit., p. 33) remarks that the Canadian Supreme Court's part in the process which resulted in agreement between the Federal Government and nine of the ten Provincial governments was crucial, and that perhaps it was only the court's intervention that could have broken the political logjam. He adds: 'But the Court intervened as another political actor, not as a court of law.' Do you agree?

We owe mainly to Dicey the identification of the conventional part of the constitution (see p. 74 above). But Dicey was of the opinion that the lawyer has no direct concern with conventions, which 'vary from generation to generation, almost from year to year'. Yet some conventions are firmly based on generally accepted constitutional principles or values and may be very long lasting, while some constitutional laws have been short-lived. In any event if we were to limit our attention to legal rules we should get a very incomplete and misleading picture of the system of government, for the legal structure of the constitution is everywhere penetrated, transformed and given efficacy by conventions.

The 'major purpose of the domestic conventions', says Marshall (op. cit., p. 18), 'is to give effect to the principles of governmental accountability that constitute the structure of responsible government'. The relations between the Crown and Parliament are fundamental to this structure, and are mainly regulated by convention. For example, while the Triennial Act 1694 requires only that 'a Parliament shall be holden once in the three years at the least', by convention Parliament is summoned to meet every year. (This convention is fortified by the need to obtain the consent of Parliament to annual Acts providing for the raising of revenue and the expenditure of public money.) Governmental accountability depends on the conventions of ministerial responsibility to Parliament (pp. 58–9 above and chapter 7 below) and a host of ancillary conventions which help to safeguard the rights of opposition parties, parliamentary select committees and individual members of Parliament. The rules of parliamentary procedure are supplemented by conventions which exist, in the words of Erskine May, 'for the purpose of securing fair play between the majority and the minority, and due consideration of the rights of individual Members': these conventions are enforced 'by the public opinion of the House' (*The Law, Privileges, Proceedings and Usage of Parliament*, 20th edn 1983, p. 208). (We shall meet with some of these conventions in chapter 7.)

Other conventions serve a variety of purposes connected with many different aspects of government. A recently developed conventional rule governs access by ministers to the papers of a previous administration of a different political party. The terms of the convention are set out in a note of guidance to officials, which declares it to be

an established rule that after a General Election a new Administration does not have access to the papers of a previous Administration of a different political complexion. This rule applies especially to Cabinet papers.

In general, documents are withheld from the new administration if they reveal the personal views of the previous ministers on matters of policy or administration, or advice submitted to them on matters which they had under consideration. (For further details see HC Deb. vol. 977, cols. *305–7*w, 24 January 1980.)

What is the constitutional utility of this convention? (See further Lord Hunt

[1982] *PL* 514.)

Conventions are not usually precisely formulated and there is often uncertainty about their scope. This imprecision may give rise to constitutional controversies but also allows for a congruous development of the constitution in response to experience and the pressure of events. It would doubtless be possible to give a more exact definition to most conventions by enacting them as rules of law. In modern constitutions constructed on the Westminster model we often find familiar conventions expressed with more precision as rules of the written constitution. For example, the United Kingdom convention of an annual meeting of Parliament appears in the Constitution of Zimbabwe in the following terms:

Zimbabwe Constitution Order 1979, SI 1979 No. 1600

62(2). There shall be a session of Parliament beginning in every calendar year so that a period of more than one hundred and eighty days shall not intervene between the last sitting of either House in any one session and the first sitting of Parliament in the next session.

If the United Kingdom were to adopt a written constitution it would have to be decided which conventions should be incorporated in the constitution, and whether they should be made justiciable by the courts. In this regard Professor Hood Phillips asks (*Reform of the Constitution*, 1970, p. 147):

Are some of the conventions sufficiently definite to be capable of formulation in a statute? Are there some conventions that it would be undesirable to crystallise in statutory form? Are the Courts a suitable forum for adjudicating upon the proper observance of conventions?

(See further Geoffrey Marshall and Graeme C. Moodie, *Some Problems of the Constitution*, 5th edn 1971, pp. 34–6.)

3 The constitution and liberty

(a) A flexible constitution

In constitutional theory the British constitution is of the kind described as 'flexible', which is to say that the law of the constitution can be altered by the ordinary processes of amendment of the law. The conventional part of the constitution can change without formal process of any kind. This flexibility may seem to allow of an easy and prompt adaptation of constitutional forms and practices to new ideas and needs and the changing conditions of society. This does not always happen, perhaps because powerful groups in society have an interest in the maintenance of the *status quo*.

K. C. Wheare, *Modern Constitutions* (2nd edn 1966), p. 17

The fact is that the ease or the frequency with which a Constitution is amended depends not only on the legal provisions which prescribe the method of change but also on the predominant political and social groups in the community and the extent to which they are satisfied with or acquiesce in the organization and distribution of political power which the Constitution prescribes. If the Constitution suits them, they will not alter it much, even if the alteration requires no more than an ordinary act of parliament. Against their opposition, too, attempts at amendment by dissatisfied minorities cannot hope to succeed. If, on the other hand, enough of them wish to see the Constitution altered, it will be done, even if the process involves the surmounting of special legal obstacles.

In recent times the flexibility of our constitution has been more often perceived as a danger than as a virtue. It is pointed out that those parts of the constitution which are meant to ensure that the government is responsible to Parliament and to the electorate, that government will be conducted in accordance with law, and that the interests of individuals and minorities will be protected, are no more immune from alteration, erosion or abolition than any other part. It is questioned whether we can still safely rely on the cultural props of the constitution.

Nevil Johnson, *In Search of the Constitution* (1977), pp. 32–4

[The British Constitution] appears to eschew rules and principles as far as possible, proclaiming instead that the rights and procedures which it claims to protect have their security and continuance in particular political habits and understandings, and only there. Unfortunately, whilst the Constitution may have rested safely on such a basis in the past, and more particularly in the last century when such theory of it as we still have was elaborated, there can be no guarantee that it will always be so. Nor do we need to look far for reasons to account for the uncertainty and dangers which stem from a total reliance on convention and habit. The distribution of power in a society is never static: it can change in ways which strain and dissolve the conventions; the role of government has vastly increased, bringing dangers for the protection of individual rights undreamt of half a century ago; political values and attitudes change, weakening particular conventions and blurring such understanding as may have been present of the purpose of earlier constitutional understandings. But most serious of all, the uncritical acceptance of flexibility and adaptation as the supreme values of the Constitution expresses an unhistorical view of the conditions in which such values come to play a major part in the definition of that very Constitution.

I have referred to an unhistorical view of the role of convention and habit. This merits a little more explanation. The contemporary account of the Constitution of this country still owes nearly everything in it to the writers of the last century, and notably to A. V. Dicey. For it was he who gave such a large place to convention and attempted to explain how it operated as an indispensable complement to constitutional law proper. But the crucial point is that the power of Victorian constitutional convention was incomparably greater than that of any contemporary convention of the same kind. In saying this I am to some extent doing no more than pointing out how much more seriously our forefathers were committed to the firm observance of a range of moral and political conventions far wider than would be conceivable today. In contrast it is a hallmark of our age that virtually every aspect of social life is caught up in a process of change, is open to challenge, and has lost the kind of predictability which it once had. But for the builders of the Victorian theory of the Constitution there was no need to question the reliance on convention or to believe that they were not building on solid ground. The large place then given to convention was precisely the result of a belief that it was founded on habits and traditions expressive of the genius of the people which, like the rock of ages, would endure. (It is immensely important to remember how keen a sense of the force of opinion in society was expressed by Dicey, the constitutionalist.)

When we begin to think about the character and role of convention in our present political life we can see that this confidence was misplaced and over-optimistic. There is no longer that degree of commitment to particular procedures, that respect for traditional values and habits, nor that breadth of agreement about how political authority should be exercised and for what purposes, which would justify the belief that convention alone is a sheet-anchor on which we can rely for the protection of civil rights or for the survival of a particular form of government. Flexible and adaptable the Constitution remains, but these are qualities which can be used for different purposes, and increasingly it becomes clear that they serve chiefly to justify the relentless extension of public power and the erosion of such notions as may survive of the limits within which it may properly be exercised. Thus what was a valuable element in the British constitutional tradition, a sign of political wisdom, has been perverted: it has begun to absorb all else and to obscure the very sense of a constitution.

What we all tend to forget nowadays is that most elementary truth about a constitution, that is to say that it is a means of establishing limits, constraints or boundaries for the exercise of power both by office-holders and by one citizen against another. A constitution is a kind of corset for us all: if it is not that, then it is nothing, it is degraded to pure formalism. This was still understood in the late nineteenth century and on into our own. But now that sense of what it means to conduct political life within the framework of a constitutional order has passed away. We no longer seem to appreciate that having a constitution entails setting limits to the exercise of powers. The very categories of constitutional reasoning have atrophied.

(b) Rights and liberties

Since nothing in the British constitution is guaranteed against alteration, the rights that the individual has against the state are in no way entrenched (except to the extent that the United Kingdom is bound by international conventions to respect certain human rights). In any event, as we have already seen (p. 51 above), the 'rights of Englishmen' usually turn out to be a merely residual liberty to act within the limits of what the law does not prohibit. Even liberty in its primary sense of freedom from physical restraint has this residual character: the writ of habeas corpus, for securing the subject against unlawful detention, is unavailing if the detainor can justify the detention in terms of, for example, the Immigration Act 1971, Sched. 2, para. 16, the Mental Health Act 1983, ss.2, 3 or 4, or the Prevention of Terrorism (Temporary Provisions) Act 1984, s.12.

The qualified and precarious nature of our rights becomes apparent if we consider the 'right' of persons to take part in a public meeting or procession. Lord Scarman, in his *Report on the Red Lion Square Disorders of 15 June 1974* (Cmnd 5919/1975), numbered amongst our 'fundamental human rights' the rights of 'peaceful assembly and public protest' (p. 1). But when a meeting or procession is held, for greatest effect, on a public highway, the limits of lawful conduct by those attending are narrow and uncertain. Lord Scarman said that here too the right to demonstrate 'of course exists, subject only to limits required by the need for good order and the passage of traffic' (p. 38). But the restrictions are far-reaching. Those attending a stationary meeting on the highway will very likely be guilty of the offence of wilful obstruction of the highway, contrary to the Highways Act 1980, s.137, and may also be guilty of public nuisance. (See the restrictive judgment of Forbes J in *Hubbard* v. *Pitt* [1976] QB 142.) Lord Scarman, indeed, said also in the Report cited above that 'it is open to question whether a public meeting held on a highway could ever be lawful' (pp. 34–5). Those who take part in a procession on the highway may be guilty of the offences already mentioned if the procession is 'unreasonable in extent'. (Cf. *R.* v. *Clark (No. 2)* [1964] 2 QB 315.) Demonstrators on the streets, even if acting peacefully, may in certain ill-defined circumstances be guilty of obstructing police officers in the execution of their duty (contrary to the Police Act 1964, s.51(3)) if they do not disperse when directed to do so. (See *Duncan* v. *Jones* [1936] 1 KB 218; *Piddington* v. *Bates* [1961] 1 WLR 162.)

On the other hand in the Court of Appeal in *Hubbard* v. *Pitt* (above) Lord Denning, in a dissenting judgment, vindicated the right to demonstrate. The defendants in this case had picketed the premises of a firm of estate agents in protest against the firm's alleged anti-social practices directed against tenants in the area. The firm having sued for an injunction and damages for the tort of nuisance, the majority of the Court of Appeal held in interlocutory proceedings that there was a serious issue of private nuisance to be tried, and upheld an interim injunction granted (on different grounds) by the court below. Lord Denning, who would have discharged the injunction, said (p. 178):

Here we have to consider the right to demonstrate and the right to protest on matters of public concern. These are rights which it is in the public interest that individuals should possess; and, indeed, that they should exercise without impediment so long as no wrongful act is done. It is often the only means by which grievances can be brought to the knowledge of those in authority – at any rate with such impact as to gain a remedy. Our history is full of warnings against suppression of these rights. Most notable was the demonstration at St Peter's Fields, Manchester, in 1819 in support of universal suffrage. The magistrates sought to stop it. At least 12 were killed and hundreds injured. Afterwards the Court of Common Council of London affirmed 'the undoubted right of Englishmen to assemble together for the purpose of deliberating upon public grievances'. Such is the right of assembly. So also is the right to meet together, to go in procession, to demonstrate and to protest on matters of public concern. As long as all is done peaceably and in good order, without threats or incitement to violence or obstruction to traffic, it is not prohibited. . . .

It was time, Lord Denning went on to say, for the courts to recognize the right to demonstrate and to protest. (See Wallington [1976] *CLJ* 82 for comment on this case.)

Lord Denning has also declared that the common law recognizes freedom of association and the right to join a union of one's choice: *Cheall* v. *Association of Professional, Executive, Clerical and Computer Staff* [1983] QB 126, 136. In *Home Office* v. *Harman* [1983] 1 AC 280, 311, Lords Scarman and Simon, dissenting, said that freedom of communication was a basic right at common law. But the affirmation of fundamental rights in such terms as these is unusual in the English courts, which generally prefer to develop specific remedies without committing themselves to declarations of broad principle. The courts do indeed apply certain presumptions in favour of fundamental rights when interpreting statutes, and in this way may be able to protect personal liberty, private property, access to the courts, etc. (See p. 73 above, and *R.* v. *Bhagwan* [1972] AC 60: right of British subject to enter UK; *Central Control Board* v. *Cannon Brewery Co* [1919] AC 744, 752: rights to property.) But they have lacked the authority and perhaps the vision to go beyond this. Nor can it be denied that judicial decisions have sometimes drastically narrowed rather than broadened the rights of individuals against the state. (See, e.g., *Duncan* v. *Jones* [1936] 1 KB 218: free speech and police powers; *Liversidge* v. *Anderson* [1942] AC 206 (p. 59 above): personal freedom and executive discretion; *Azam* v. *Secretary of State for the Home Department* [1974] AC 18: right of residence in UK; *Home Office* v. *Harman* (above): freedom of communication and contempt of court; *R.* v. *Secretary of State for Home Affairs, ex p. Hosenball* [1977] 1 WLR 766: natural justice and national security; cf. *Council of Civil Service Unions* v. *Minister for the Civil Service* [1984] 3 All ER 935 (p. 159 below).

(c) A new constitutional settlement?

Royal Commission on the Constitution, vol. II, Memorandum of Dissent, Cmnd 5460–1/1973, paras. 5, 8

In investigating whether our institutions of government today match the needs and aspirations of the people of the United Kingdom, it is natural to start by considering the vast expansion in the functions and responsibilities of government which has taken place particularly since the end of the nineteenth century. In the reign of Queen Victoria, the tasks of government were for the most part relatively simple; they were mainly passive and regulatory. Since then its traditional regulatory functions have multiplied in size and greatly broadened. . . . This enlargement of the role of government and the increased complexities of the problems it is called on to handle have not been matched by any correspondingly large changes in our main institutions of government. This is not to say that there have been no changes in the role and working of Parliament and the Cabinet, in the administration of justice, or in the responsibilities and organisation of local government. Nor is it to say that no new institutions have been developed to meet new needs. But at best the changes have been piecemeal improvisations following no coherent pattern or plan; at worst they have often been self-contradictory and self-defeating.

There are those who argue for a written constitution for the United Kingdom which would bring order to what is seen as a 'constitutional wasteland', set limits to the sovereignty of Parliament, and incorporate a new 'bill of rights', with specific guarantees of individual liberties.

The written constitutions of other countries have often been established in the aftermath of great events: a successful revolution, a union of states, the achievement of independence. No such political convulsion has occurred in the United Kingdom in modern times, which might have induced us to make a new constitutional beginning. But this country has a considerable vicarious experience of written constitutions through having provided them for others. Constitutions conferred upon countries that have achieved independence from British rule have incorporated definitions and guarantees of fundamental rights. (A recent example is the Declaration of Rights contained in the Constitution of Zimbabwe: see the Zimbabwe Constitution Order, SI 1979 No. 1600.)

The arguments for a written constitution and for a bill of rights are really separate; it would be quite possible to have one of them without the other. If, however, it were proposed to fortify or 'entrench' a bill of rights by protecting it from repeal or amendment by the ordinary legislative process, there would have to be a change in the present structure of constitutional powers and relationships, and this might be effected as part of a general reorganization of the system of government in a written constitution – the 'new constitutional settlement' that some have called for.

> Sir Leslie Scarman, *English Law – The New Dimension* (1974),
> pp. 74–5

The common law system is part of our constitution: a new settlement is needed, which will retain its strengths, while eradicating its features of weakness and obsolescence. In times past the strength of the common law was its universality together with its origin in a customary law which owed nothing to the legislative activity of Parliament; indeed, it preceded it. This strength, when ranged alongside the power of Parliament, gave it victory over the King in the seventeenth century and led to the constitutional settlement of 1688–1689. But the true victor in that settlement was Parliament, whose sovereignty then began. Today, however, it is Parliament's sovereign power, more often than not exercised at the will of an executive sustained by an impregnable majority, that has brought about the modern imbalance in the legal system. The common law is no longer the strong, independent ally, but the servant of Parliament. This, perhaps, did not matter quite so much so long as the constitution of Parliament itself contained effective restraints upon the will of a bare majority in one House. The

Parliament Act 1911 [which made it possible for a public bill to be passed without the consent of the House of Lords] was, no doubt, a valuable democratic reform: but it did remove from our constitution an important check on legislative power and introduce an imbalance at its very centre – an imbalance which, if no redressing factor be found or devised, could well prove to be the precursor of further freedoms from restraint to be enjoyed by a bare majority in the Commons. I suggest that the less internal control Parliament is prepared to accept the greater the need for a constitutional settlement protecting entrenched provisions in the field of fundamental human rights, and the universality of the rule of law.

Lord Hailsham, *Elective Dictatorship* (1976), pp. 12–14

The advocates of a Bill of Rights are for limiting the powers [of Parliament]. They argue, correctly, that every other civilised nation has imposed some limits upon its legislature, and has laws which make changes in the Constitution either difficult or impossible. In such cases the judges, or some special constitutional Court, can strike down legislation which exceeds the bounds. But how can these limitations be made effective? Under our present arrangements, Parliament could always take away what it has given, by amending or repealing the Bill. To this the advocates of the Bill always reply that Governments would be restrained by public opinion from doing that sort of thing. I am afraid that I regard that view as extremely naïve. I fully accept that a Bill of Rights might, in some cases, prevent interference with individual rights by some oversight in an ill-drafted Act of Parliament. But I do not accept that a party government of either colour would hesitate for a moment, with its main programme bills, to insert when it wished to do so, the necessary exempting words: 'Notwithstanding anything in the Bill of Rights or any other rule of law or statute to the contrary'. . . . Surely if it is to be worth the paper it is written on, a Bill of Rights must be part of a written constitution in which the powers of the legislature are limited and subject to review by the courts. Otherwise it will prove to be a pure exercise in public relations.

Even if I were wrong about this I would be bound to point out that a Bill of Rights could only solve a relatively small part of the problem. Infringement of individual rights is an important weakness of our elective dictatorship, but it is not the most important nor is it the one which occurs most frequently. Should we not be more concerned with its remoteness, its over-centralisation, its capacity for giving control to relatively small minorities, and its dependence upon the enthusiasm of political caucuses and other outside bodies and pressure groups whose zeal, ideological bigotry and desire for irreversible change all too often outrun their discretion? If, as I think, the powers of Parliament need restricting at all, the restrictions should not be limited to the protection of individual rights. . . .

I have . . . reached the conclusion that our constitution is wearing out. Its central defects are gradually coming to outweigh its merits, and its central defects consist in the absolute powers we confer on our sovereign body, and the concentration of those powers in an executive government formed out of one party which may not fairly represent the popular will. . . .

I envisage nothing less than a written constitution for the United Kingdom, and by that I mean one which limits the powers of Parliament and provides a means of enforcing these limitations either by political or legal means.

Many remain unconvinced of the need either for a written constitution or for a new bill of rights. We do well to recall the words of K. C. Wheare (p. 91 above) that if enough of the predominant groups in the community wish to see a written constitution altered, 'it will be done, even if the process involves the surmounting of special legal obstacles'. A written constitution is no guarantee of stability in the state or, ultimately, of the rights which the constitution may enshrine. Doubtless it can provide a limited safeguard; it may focus opposition to tyranny and put difficulties and delay in the way of attempts to deprive individuals or minorities of their rights. On the other hand a written constitution, in setting limits to governmental power, can be a means to the obstruction of necessary reform; retrogressive forces in a society may wear the colours of its written constitution, and march to the trumpet-sound of its bill of rights. In the United States, rights guaranteed by the Constitution were at one time used by Supreme Court justices, imbued with ideas of *laissez-faire* capitalism, as weapons against progressive social welfare legislation. (See, e.g., *Lochner* v. *New York*, 198 US 45 (1905), in which the Supreme Court held that a statute limiting employment in bakeries to 60 hours a week and ten hours a day was invalid as an arbitrary interference with the freedom to contract guaranteed by the Fourteenth Amendment to the Constitution.)

Henry J. Abraham, *Freedom and the Court* (4th edn 1982), p.8

The chief concern of this long era [1888–1930] was to guard the sanctity of property. Socio-economic experimentation by the legislatures, such as minimum-wage, maximum-hour, and child-labor regulations, was regarded with almost unshakable disapproval by a solid majority of the Court. Again and again the justices struck down, as unconstitutional violations of *substantive* due process of law, legislation that large majorities on both the national and state levels deemed wise and necessary. Their grounds were that, because of the *substance* of the legislation involved, such statutory experimentations deprived 'persons' (i.e., property owners, chiefly businessmen) of their liberty and property without due process of law.

Again, the New Deal programme, undertaken by President Roosevelt to counter the results of economic depression, was substantially nullified by Supreme Court decisions in the years 1934 to 1936. On the other hand, advocates of a British bill of rights to be defended by the judiciary take encouragement from the more recent history of the United States Supreme Court. After 1937 the court turned away from attempts to control the social and economic policies of elected legislatures. Since then, and especially under the 'Warren Court' presided over by Chief Justice Earl Warren from 1953 to 1969, the Supreme Court has defended and extended individual rights and protected the interests of minorities.

In its active phases the Supreme Court has been the source of far-reaching judicial legislation, whether of a conservative or a liberal tendency, and has had a substantial influence on social and political affairs in the United States.

This is the kind of role that may be assumed by a court which has power to interpret a written constitution and vindicate fundamental rights.

In Britain the arguments of recent years about the constitutional protection of fundamental rights have revealed that opposing political views may be reflected in different conceptions of a bill of rights. There are those who see it as providing ammunition against legislation associated with the aims of one or other political party. (See, e.g., Viscount Lambton's remarks in support of his proposed bill 'to preserve the rights of the individual': HC Deb. vol. 782, cols. 474–5, 23 April 1969.) But a bill of rights, if it is to be successful, must rest on a broad consensus that certain rights transcend political differences and are to be defended against governments of every colour. The quest for a 'neutral' but effective bill of rights leads many to favour the incorporation into English law of the provisions of the European Convention for the Protection of Human Rights and Fundamental Freedoms. A Bill of Rights Bill introduced in the House of Lords by Lord Wade in 1976 adopted the provisions of the Convention.

A
BILL
Intituled
An Act to declare the inalienable rights and liberties of the subject.
BE IT ENACTED by the Queen's most Excellent Majesty, by and with the advice and consent of the Lords Spiritual and Temporal, and Commons, in this present Parliament assembled, and by the authority of the same, as follows:-
1. The Convention for the Protection of Human Rights and Fundamental Freedoms signed by Governments being Members of the Council of Europe at Rome on 4th November 1950, together with the five Protocols* thereto, shall without any reservation immediately upon the passing of this Act have the force of law, and shall be enforceable by action in the Courts of the United Kingdom. For the purposes of this Act the texts of the said Convention and Protocols shall be those set out in Schedules 1 to 6 hereto.
2. In case of conflict between any enactment prior to the passing of this Act and the provisions of the said Convention and Protocols, the said Convention and Protocols shall prevail.
3. In case of conflict between any enactment subsequent to the passing of this Act and the provisions of the said Convention and Protocols, the said Convention and Protocols shall prevail unless subsequent enactment shall explicitly state otherwise.
4. (1) This Act may be cited as the Bill of Rights Act 1976.
　(2) This Act extends to Northern Ireland.

Lord Wade's bill lapsed, was re-introduced, with modifications, in 1979 and 1980, but on each occasion was lost in the House of Commons after passing through all stages in the House of Lords.

---

*The Fourth Protocol to the Convention (liberty of movement etc.) has not been ratified by the United Kingdom. Neither has the Sixth Protocol (abolition of the death penalty) or the Seventh Protocol (rights of aliens to procedural guarantees in the event of expulsion, etc).

Entrenchment

Many proponents of a bill of rights argue that it would be necessary to entrench it against abrogation or amendment by the ordinary parliamentary process.

Sir Leslie Scarman, *English Law – The New Dimension* (1974), p. 15

When times are normal and fear is not stalking the land, English law sturdily protects the freedom of the individual and respects human personality. But when times are abnormally alive with fear and prejudice, the common law is at a disadvantage: it cannot resist the will, however frightened and prejudiced it may be, of Parliament. . . . It is the helplessness of the law in face of the legislative sovereignty of Parliament which makes it difficult for the legal system to accommodate the concept of fundamental and inviolable human rights. Means therefore have to be found whereby (1) there is incorporated into English law a declaration of such rights, (2) these rights are protected against all encroachment, including the power of the state, even when that power is exerted by a representative legislative institution such as Parliament.

Entrenchment of a bill of rights would bring about a transfer of power to judges, who would be called upon to interpret the guaranteed rights and uphold them even against Acts of Parliament. The Liberal Party, in giving support to an entrenched bill of rights in its memorandum to the House of Lords Select Committee on a Bill of Rights (HL 276 of 1976–7), said:

We concede that this would increase the power of the judiciary but prefer it to the present position of rule of an unrepresentative Parliament by the executive.

But judges would certainly seem to be unrepresentative: they are drawn from a narrow and relatively privileged segment of society and, even though they make strenuous efforts to be impartial, may be thought to reflect the values of a conservative Establishment. These considerations make it questionable whether the judges should be given a new constitutional role in which they would be called on – much more than at present – to resolve conflicts of public, private and group interests in intensely political contexts.

Perhaps this objection could be met by the creation of a new constitutional court, separate from the ordinary courts and with a different procedure of appointment. Edward McWhinney (*Constitution-making: Principles, Process, Practice*, 1981, p. 127) argues the need 'for broadening the recruitment of . . . constitutional judges, by opening up the processes of appointment to public scrutiny and by involving the legislatures as much as possible in the election or, at the very least, the confirmation of judicial candidates'. (See also Wallington and McBride, op. cit. below, pp. 104–5.) The creation of a specialized court could also help to overcome more speedily the relative lack of experience of English judges in the techniques of constitutional interpretation.

It is argued against proposals for an entrenched bill of rights that the entrenched provisions might become inapposite to the conditions of future times.

Peter Wallington and Jeremy McBride, Civil Liberties and a Bill of Rights (1976), p. 84

Entrenching a Bill of Rights assumes that the perspective of the present gives a unique insight into humanity and the needs of individuals in organised society. But manifestly we do not have such insight; needs will change, as societies will change in ways we may not have foreseen. To fetter future generations may be to frustrate their attempts to improve the human condition; if the political system has not the capacity to meet the demands for change, it may be the political system itself which will crack. That is a legacy which it would be a disservice to bequeath.

Might a bill of rights be an effective safeguard even though its provisions could be repealed or amended by the ordinary legislative process? It might be given a lesser degree of entrenchment, by which the courts would be empowered to strike down an Act that conflicted with the protected rights *unless* the Act included an express statement that it was to take effect notwithstanding the provisions of the bill of rights. This would preserve the ultimate power of Parliament to pass whatever legislation was considered necessary in the public interest, but the bill of rights would have a special status and would be protected from accidental, covert or unconsidered alteration. Various formulae for achieving this partial entrenchment have been suggested. One can be seen in clause 3 of Lord Wade's 1976 bill (above); this was altered in his 1979 bill, in a more scrupulous deference to parliamentary sovereignty, to read as follows:

In any case of conflict between any enactment subsequent to the passing of this Act and the provisions of the said Convention and Protocols, such enactment passed after the passing of this Act shall be deemed to be subject to the provisions of the said Convention and Protocols and shall be so construed unless such subsequent enactment provides otherwise or does not admit of any construction compatible with the provisions of this Act.

Compare the more radical formula included in the draft bill of rights proposed by Wallington and McBride (op. cit., App. 1):

9(1) Any Act passed after this Act shall be so construed and applied as not to abrogate, abridge or infringe, or to require, authorise or permit any abrogation, abridgement or infringement of, any of the rights or freedoms mentioned in the Bill of Rights; and any such Act shall be so construed and applied as not to repeal or amend, or permit the repeal or amendment of, any provision of this Act. . . .

(2) Insofar as any Act passed after this Act, or any part of such an Act, is incapable of such construction or application as may be required by subsection (1), it shall not have effect.

(3) Subsections (1) and (2) shall not apply to any Act or part of an Act as to which it is expressly declared in an Act of Parliament that it shall have effect notwithstand-

ing this Act.

Cf. the sceptical view of partial entrenchment expressed by Lord Hailsham, p. 96 above.

Professor Zander sums up the case for a (partially entrenched) bill of rights as follows:

> Michael Zander, *A Bill of Rights?* (2nd edn 1979), pp. 87–8

In my own view a Bill of Rights is desirable not because human rights are grossly abused in Britain, nor to provide against the danger of future tyranny. The former is untrue; the latter unlikely. The case for a Bill of Rights rests rather on the belief that it would make a distinct and valuable contribution to the *better* protection of human rights. Certainly it would not solve all problems. The extent of the contribution it could make must, in the end, depend on how it is regarded and interpreted by the judges. It would give them greater scope than exists in the ordinary common law and statute law. It would require of them a broader, more wide-ranging approach than has been customary. There would be more argument on matters of importance in courts of law. Some of the courts' decisions would not merely be controversial but would be unacceptable to the prevailing orthodoxy whether of the Left or of the Right. But ultimate authority would remain where it belongs in a democracy, in the legislature. I am not unaware of the problems of entrusting major issues to the English judges. I feel nevertheless that on balance, this is an experiment that should be tried.

Others, like Lord Boston of Faversham, remain unconvinced.

> Lord Boston of Faversham, 'Arguments Against a Bill of Rights', in Colin Campbell (ed.), *Do We Need a Bill of Rights?* (1980), pp. 24–5, 29.

One of the most fundamental objections to incorporation of the [European Convention on Human Rights] is that it would . . . graft onto the existing law, an Act of Parliament which would be in a form totally at variance with any existing legislation and in a way which would be incompatible with such legislation. It has long been accepted under our constitution that Parliament legislates in a specific form, and that the role of the courts is to *interpret* that legislation. If we took the course proposed by those who wish to incorporate the Convention, we would be opening up a wide variety of legislative policies in a very general way and handing them over to the judiciary for detailed *development* (not just interpretation) on such subjects as, say, race relations, freedom of speech, freedom of the Press, privacy, education, and forms of punishment. Yet those are matters which, under our constitution, have been the province of the legislature. . . .

I share the view of those who say that under a Bill of Rights it would not be the case that the role of the courts would remain similar to the role they have always had at common law. For at common law the development of legal principles has been a slow process – evolving from case to case. Under a Bill of Rights incorporating the European Convention, however, the courts would start off with a set of broad principles and would then have a free hand to decide how to apply those principles to the individual cases that came before them. . . .

Another matter of great concern is the *uncertainty* in the law which those of us who are against a Bill of Rights foresee arising. . . . I am sure we would all agree that, so far as possible, the law should be clear and certain. . . . But if the European Convention which is couched in broad terms proclaiming wide generalisations open to a variety of interpretations were made part of our domestic law, it would introduce a vast area of uncertainty into our law. It would become much more difficult for individual people as well as companies and other bodies to get confident advice about their rights and obligations, their powers and their liabilities.

Is entrenchment possible?

Entrenchment might be considered for an Act incorporating a bill of rights or for a new written constitution in its entirety, so that none of its provisions would be alterable except by some special process. This might be a specified parliamentary majority (e.g. a two-thirds majority in each House), but a requirement of approval by the people in a referendum has also been suggested. Alternatively a partial entrenchment might be preferred, requiring only the use of a prescribed formula in the amending Act. Either form of entrenchment would somehow have to overcome the obstacle of parliamentary sovereignty.

It is generally held, as we have seen (pp. 37–8 above), that an Act of Parliament cannot effectively prescribe that its provisions may not be altered except by express words or the use of some specified formula. This principle may seem to rule out schemes of partial entrenchment, but it is possible that the courts would take a different view of an entrenching provision of this kind in a Bill of Rights Act, which was clearly intended to provide an effective machinery for the protection of fundamental rights. After the enactment (on the basis of a broad political consensus, let us suppose) of such an Act, the judges might come to accept that an amending Act which did not use the prescribed form was not an authentic expression of parliamentary intent. (Cf. T. R. S. Allan, (1983) 3 *Oxford J. Legal Stud.* 22 at 30–33.)

On the other hand the full entrenchment of a bill of rights or of other constitutional provisions – as by a requirement of specified majorities in Parliament – encounters head-on the issues of parliamentary sovereignty and whether the ultimate 'rule of recognition' of the English legal system assumes the continuing sovereignty of Parliament *as ordinarily constituted*. (See pp. 32–8 above.) But it is for the courts to identify and delimit the rule of recognition, and it might be possible to persuade them that a change had occurred in the foundations of the legal system. Perhaps this could be done by contriving a 'legal revolution' or break in legal continuity, as a result of which a new constitutional order would be established, incorporating limitations upon the power of Parliament.

Lord Hailsham, 'The Case for a New, Written Constitution',
The Times, 20 May 1975

If Parliament can ... grant a new constitution there is no reason why a successor Parliament should not withdraw it, modify it, or proceed to legislate in terms inconsistent with it. Countries with 'written' constitutions with entrenched provisions have secured them by means of some discontinuity with the past, either by successful revolution, as with the United States, or the successive French Republics; or, as in the case of India, Canada, Australia, New Zealand and all subsequent enfranchised ex-colonies, by a grant by the colonial power, followed by the colonial power divesting itself of sovereignty and leaving the new nation to govern itself as a separate entity recognized in international law.

The problem is whether, if it should be found otherwise desirable, it would be possible to create such a discontinuity artificially so that Parliament could divest itself of its absolute sovereignty without leaving it open to a subsequent Parliament to recall it.

Professor O. Hood Phillips, QC, letter to the editor, *The Times*,
2 June 1975

... There is a logical and legal objection to 'self-limitation' which suggests that a legislature cannot bind itself unless it is empowered to do so by some 'higher law', that is, some prior law not laid down by itself.

In order that a new written constitution should be wholly or partly entrenched, it seems that we must have a new legislature which would owe its existence to a constitution not enacted by itself, from which it would derive both its powers and its limitations, including restrictions on amendment. Our existing Parliament would have to extinguish itself, having made provision for the drawing up of a new constitution, probably transferring its powers to a Constituent Assembly (not identical with the present Parliament because its Second Chamber is unreformed). The statute setting up the Constituent Assembly, as well as the new constitution itself, would require existing and future judges to take an oath of loyalty to the new constitution. The ultimate court of appeal in constitutional cases might be a body like the Judicial Committee of the Privy Council.

Professor Wade argues that there is an easier way out: entrenchment requires only that there should be a 'change in the breasts of the judges'.

H. W. R. Wade, *Constitutional Fundamentals* (1980), pp. 37–9

All that need be done in order to entrench any sort of fundamental law is to secure its recognition in the judicial oath of office. The only trouble at present is that the existing form of oath gives no assurance of obedience to statutes binding later Parliaments. But there is every assurance that if the judges undertake upon their oath to act in some particular way they will do so. If we should wish to adopt a new form of constitution, therefore, all that need be done is to put the judges under oath to enforce it. An Act of Parliament could be passed to discharge them from their former oaths, if that were thought necessary, and to require them to be resworn in the new terms. All the familiar problems of sovereignty then disappear: a fresh start has been made; the doctrine that no Parliament can bind its successors becomes ancient history; and the new fundamental law is secured by a judiciary sworn to uphold it. . . .

This is, as it appears to me, the one and only way in which we can take command of our constitution without having to wait for some sort of political revolution, which is most unlikely to arrive just when we want it, and without having to contrive some artificial legal discontinuity. . . . [M]erely by a change in the judicial oath a new judicial attitude can be created, and that is all that is needed. Fundamentally the question simply is, what will the judges recognise as a valid Act of Parliament? If they solemnly undertake to recognise a new grundnorm and to refuse validity to Acts of Parliament which conflict with a Bill of Rights or other entrenched clauses, that is the best possible assurance that the entrenchment will work. Always in the end we come back to the ultimate legal reality: an Act of Parliament is valid only if the judges say it is, and only they can say what the rules for its validity are.

Can we by this simple device 'take command of our constitution'? Or might the Act requiring the new oath 'itself be amended or repealed, expressly or impliedly'? (Winterton (1981) 97 *LQR* 265, 271.)

PART II
The Government in context

In this part of the book we shall consider the structure and powers of British government in the territorial context of the United Kingdom and the legal framework established by the European Community.

British government is founded on a principle of constitutional monarchy, and the institution of the Crown is still at the centre of our governmental arrangements. In chapter 3 we shall first consider the meaning and role of the Crown in the modern constitution and then give attention to the elements of 'government under the Crown' – that is to say, the central government of the United Kingdom.

In chapter 4 we shall adopt the territorial standpoint, to survey the arrangements for the government of the four countries of the United Kingdom and also the organization of local government.

Chapter 5 widens our perspective to encompass the new legal order of the European Community and its impact on government and law in the United Kingdom.

In chapter 6 we consider the tasks of modern government and the range of powers which are available for carrying them out – as well as certain restraints and limits upon the exercise of these powers.

3
The Crown and the government

1   The Crown

We have already seen (p. 10 above) that constitutional thought and doctrine
in the United Kingdom have largely dispensed with the concept of the state.
Instead of the state we have the Crown, which serves as a central, organizing
principle of government. The Crown is associated with the idea of executive
authority rather than with that of the common interest: the major public
powers are vested in the Crown, or in ministers who are servants of the Crown.

    The Crown is characterized in law as a corporation, though of what kind
there is some doubt.

> *Town Investments Ltd* v. *Department of the Environment* [1978] AC
> 359 (HL)

A Minister of the Crown had acquired a leasehold interest in certain premises
for use by civil servants as government offices. The House of Lords held that it
was the Crown, not the Minister, that became the tenant of the premises, and
further that the Crown was in occupation for the purposes of a business carried
on by it. The premises were therefore occupied under a 'business tenancy' and
were subject to a rent freeze imposed on such tenancies by statutory
instrument.

LORD DIPLOCK: . . . [I]t is not private law but public law that governs the relationships
between Her Majesty acting in her political capacity, the government departments
among which the work of Her Majesty's government is distributed, the ministers of the
Crown in charge of the various departments and civil servants of all grades who are
employed in those departments. These relationships have in the course of centuries
been transformed with the continuous evolution of the constitution of this country from
that of personal rule by a feudal landowning monarch to the constitutional monarchy of
today; but the vocabulary used by lawyers in the field of public law has not kept pace
with this evolution and remains more apt to the constitutional realities of the Tudor or
even the Norman monarchy than to the constitutional realities of the 20th century. To

use as a metaphor the symbol of royalty, 'the Crown', was no doubt a convenient way of denoting and distinguishing the monarch when doing acts of government in his political capacity from the monarch when doing private acts in his personal capacity, at a period when legislative and executive powers were exercised by him in accordance with his own will. But to continue nowadays to speak of 'the Crown' as doing legislative or executive acts of government, which, in reality as distinct from legal fiction, are decided on and done by human beings other than the Queen herself, involves risk of confusion. We very sensibly speak today of legislation being made by Act of Parliament – though the preamble to every statute still maintains the fiction that the maker was Her Majesty and that the participation of the members of the two Houses of Parliament had been restricted to advice and acquiescence. Where, as in the instant case, we are concerned with the legal nature of the exercise of executive powers of government, I believe that some of the more Athanasian-like features of the debate in your Lordships' House could have been eliminated if instead of speaking of 'the Crown' we were to speak of 'the government' – a term appropriate to embrace both collectively and individually all of the ministers of the Crown and parliamentary secretaries under whose direction the administrative work of government is carried on by the civil servants employed in the various government departments. It is through them that the executive powers of Her Majesty's government in the United Kingdom are exercised, sometimes in the more important administrative matters in Her Majesty's name, but most often under their own official designation. Executive acts of government that are done by any of them are acts done by 'the Crown' in the fictional sense in which that expression is now used in English public law.

The executive acts of government with which the instant case is concerned are the acceptance of grants from lessors who are private subjects of the Queen of leasehold interests in premises for use as government offices and the occupation of the premises by civil servants employed in the work of various government departments. The leases were executed under his official designation by the minister of the Crown in charge of the government department to which, for administrative and accounting purposes, there is entrusted the responsibility for acquiring and managing accommodation for civil servants employed in other government departments as well as that of which the minister himself is the official head. In my opinion, the tenant was the government acting through its appropriate member or, expressed in the term of art in public law, the tenant was the Crown. . . .

Later in his speech Lord Diplock (with whose speech Lord Edmund-Davies expressed his agreement) characterized the Crown as a 'corporation sole'. Lord Simon of Glaisdale took a different view on this point:

LORD SIMON OF GLAISDALE: . . . [Y]our Lordships are concerned with symbolic language which cannot be understood without regard to constitutional history. The crown as an object is a piece of jewelled headgear under guard at the Tower of London. But it symbolises the powers of government which were formerly wielded by the wearer of the crown; so that by the 13th century crimes were committed not only against the king's peace but also against 'his crown and dignity'. . . . The term 'the Crown' is therefore used in constitutional law to denote the collection of such of those powers as remain extant (the royal prerogative), together with such other powers as have been expressly conferred by statute on 'the Crown'.

So too 'The Queen' indicates the person who by right of succession is entitled to wear the crown. But 'Her Majesty' is evidently a symbolic phrase, betokening the power, the 'mana', which is embodied in the person entitled to wear the crown – as 'His Holiness', 'His Beatitude' or 'Mr Justice' are descriptive of the power believed to inspire and characterise the person so entitled. 'Her Majesty' in constitutional legal usage thus generally personifies the powers of 'the Crown' – powers the nucleus of which legally and historically are those of The Queen, but which by constitutional convention (i.e. in political reality) are exercised in the name of The Queen by those who are nominally and legally her servants or agents.

. . . '[T]he Crown' and 'Her Majesty' are terms of art in constitutional law. They correspond, though not exactly, with terms of political science like 'the Executive' or 'the Administration' or 'the Government', barely known to the law, which has retained the historical terminology.

. . . [T]he legal concept which seems to me to fit best the contemporary situation is to consider the Crown as a corporation aggregate headed by the Queen. The departments of state including the ministers at their head (whether or not either the department or the minister has been incorporated) are then themselves members of the corporation aggregate of the Crown. But on this approach two riders must be added. First, the legal concept still does not correspond to the political reality. The legal substratum is overlaid by constitutional convention. The Queen does not now command those legally her servants who are heads or subordinate members or subject to the control of the departments of state. On the contrary she acts on the formally tendered collective advice of those ministers who constitute the Cabinet. Secondly, when the Queen is referred to by the symbolic title of 'Her Majesty', it is the whole corporation aggregate, the Crown, which is generally indicated. . . .

The Minister of Works and the Secretary of State for the Environment are aspects or members of the Crown, incorporated and charged for administrative convenience with holding and administering property required by other Crown servants, who are also aspects or members of the Crown. A demise to the Minister of Works or to the Secretary of State for the Environment for and on behalf of Her Majesty is a demise to the Crown. Therefore the Crown was the tenant in the case of each of the premises with which your Lordships are concerned, and the Crown as tenant occupied them. . . .

Professor H. W. R. Wade sounds a cautionary note as to the reasoning adopted in the *Town Investments* case: 'the case did not concern statutory powers and it should presumably not be taken to alter the rule that powers conferred upon ministers belong to them personally and not to the Crown' (*Administrative Law*, 5th edn 1982, p. 50, n. 2). When statutory powers are vested in specified ministers (or 'the Secretary of State': see p. 66 above) they are themselves legally answerable for any excess or improper exercise of such powers and cannot shelter behind immunities of the Crown.

Whether the Crown is a corporation aggregate or a corporation sole remains unresolved, and is perhaps not of importance. (See further Geoffrey Marshall, *Constitutional Theory*, 1971, pp. 18–19.)

Notwithstanding its continuing formal centrality, the constitutional concept of the Crown has suffered a substantial decay. The original or inherent powers of the Crown embraced in the royal prerogative, although still significant, have been greatly reduced in extent by the operation of statute.

Powers are nowadays normally vested in individual ministers rather than in the Crown, and the legal characterization of ministers as Crown servants is something markedly fictional, as appears from the speeches in the *Town Investments* case. From the viewpoint of political science, if not of law, the concept of the Crown distorts reality in representing the different elements of the executive as a unified whole, concealing their inter-relationships – for example, the conflicts and accommodations that take place between the prime minister and other ministers, the Treasury and the spending departments, ministers and civil servants, departments and their quasi-autonomous 'fringe' bodies, irregular or special advisers and established civil servants, and so on. As Rodney Barker observes (in R. L. Borthwick and J. E. Spence (eds.), *British Politics in Perspective* 1984, p. 5):

Constitutional theory is concerned to determine coherent principles, and as such the notion of the crown has a limited use since it cannot be employed over a wide range of constitutional behaviour without losing precisely that coherence, and referring to powers which are separate, conflicting or independent of one another.

In law, however, the Crown is (within the United Kingdom) one and indivisible. All ministers are in law 'servants of the Crown' (or of the Queen); civil servants work under the direction of ministers but are themselves also servants of the Crown, not of the departmental minister. (See *Bainbridge* v. *Postmaster-General* [1906] 1 KB 178.) In *Robertson* v. *Minister of Pensions* [1949] 1 KB 227 the appellant was assured by an official of the War Office that a disability from which he suffered had been accepted as attributable to military service, so entitling him to certain disablement benefits. Later the Minister of Pensions decided that the appellant's disability was not attributable to war service. The court (Denning J) held that the assurance given by the War Office was legally binding, and since the War Office was the agent of the Crown, it was binding on the Crown, and therefore bound the Minister of Pensions, who was also only a servant or agent of the Crown.

In the larger realm of the Commonwealth, however, the Crown is divisible, and the Queen's government is a separate legal entity in each of the territories: see *R.* v. *Secretary of State for Foreign and Commonwealth Affairs, ex p. Indian Association of Alberta* [1982] QB 892.

2 Privileges of the Crown

In a vivid aphorism, Walter Bagehot remarked of the England of Queen Victoria that 'A Republic has insinuated itself beneath the folds of a Monarchy' (*The English Constitution*, Fontana edn 1963, p. 94). Modern governments, having assumed the attributes of the Crown, are invested with most of those common law powers, privileges and immunities that formerly constituted the 'royal' prerogative, but of which relatively few are now exercised or enjoyed by the Queen in her own person. Some of these are necessary governmental powers which, if they did not belong to the government as part of the prerogative, would have to be provided by statute. (The prerogative powers of government are further considered in chapter 6.) The prerogative also includes, however, certain privileges and immunities which, as the legacy of a former royal pre-eminence, may lack justification in a modern democratic state.

It is a principle generally considered to derive from the prerogative that the Crown is not bound by a statute unless it is shown to be the clear intention of the statute that its provisions should bind the Crown. In effect the principle functions as a rule of construction or a presumption (one that is rebuttable) that the Crown is not bound. It is preserved by section 40(2)(*f*) of the Crown Proceedings Act 1947, which provides that nothing in the Act shall 'affect any rules of evidence or any presumption relating to the extent to which the Crown is bound by any Act of Parliament'.

Madras Electric Supply Corporation Ltd v. *Boarland* [1955]
AC 667 (PC)

In this case the liability of the appellant company to income tax was in issue, the company having transferred its business to the Crown in the course of the year of assessment. It was not disputed that the Crown itself was immune from the taxing provisions of the relevant statute, but some of their Lordships found it necessary, in dealing with the contentions of the parties, to consider the basis of the Crown's immunity.

LORD MACDERMOTT: . . . Whatever ideas may once have prevailed on the subject, it is, in my opinion, today impossible to uphold the view that the Crown can find in the prerogative an immunity from tax if the statute in question, according to its true construction, includes the Crown amongst those made liable to the tax it imposes. The appropriate rule, as I understand it, is that in an Act of Parliament general words shall not bind the Crown to its prejudice unless by express provision or necessary implication. . . .

LORD REID: . . . I do not think that it has ever been suggested, at least since 1688, that, if an Act in its terms and on its true construction applies to the Crown, its operation can be prevented by the royal prerogative. It is true that there does not appear to be in the authorities any statement which precisely negatives this argument, but that is not surprising. As the point has never been raised it has not been necessary to formulate the answer to it.

Chitty states the rule as follows: 'But Acts of Parliament which would divest or abridge the King of his prerogatives, his interests or his remedies, in the slightest degree, do not in general extend to, or bind the King, unless there be express words to that effect.' (*Prerogatives of the Crown*, [1820] p. 383.) I draw attention to the words 'extend to, or bind the King'. It is not a matter of the King preventing the operation of an Act which extends to the Crown, but of the scope of provisions which prejudice the Crown being so limited that they never extend to the Crown. . . .

The following observations of Lord Keith have a somewhat old-fashioned ring and appear to invest the prerogative with a higher status than is nowadays accorded to it.

LORD KEITH OF AVONHOLM: . . . The contention for the company seems indistinguishable from the proposition that it is a principle of statutory construction that words used do not include the Crown, or Crown property, unless the contrary is expressed, or clearly implied. But, if so, no question of the prerogative arises. The matter is just a rule of statutory construction that calls for no invocation of the prerogative. If so, all the previous decisions are unexplained in their reference to and reliance on the prerogative. The true explanation, easily understandable on historical and legal grounds, is that words in a statute capable of applying to the Crown may be overridden by the exercise of the prerogative. That is necessarily involved in the oft-repeated phrase that the King is not bound by a statute unless by express words or by clear implication. If the statute does not apply to him there can be no question of his being bound by it. It is only because it can apply to him that appeal to the prerogative is necessary. The conception of the prerogative, in my view, is of something that stands outside the statute, on which the Crown can rely, to control the operation of the statute so far as it prejudices the Crown. . . .

Since the decision of the Privy Council in *Province of Bombay* v. *Municipal Corporation of the City of Bombay* (below), a remarkably stringent test has been applied in deciding whether a statute is effective to bind the Crown. Instead of taking a broad view of what the policy and objects of the statute require, the courts apply the rule that the Crown is bound only if it is made subject to the Act by express words or *necessary implication*. The requirement of necessary implication is strictly interpreted.

Province of Bombay v. *Municipal Corporation of the City of Bombay*
[1947] AC 58 (PC)

The City of Bombay Municipal Act 1888 gave power to the Bombay Municipality to carry water-mains 'into, through or under any land whatsoever within the city'. The municipality wished to lay a water-main in certain Crown land within the city, but its right to do so was contested by the Crown. The High Court of Bombay was satisfied that the Act could not operate with reasonable efficiency unless it applied to Crown land, and accordingly held that it must be taken to bind the Crown by necessary implication. This decision was reversed by the Privy Council. The judgment of the Board was delivered by Lord du Parcq.

LORD DU PARCQ: . . . The maxim of the law in early times was that no statute bound the Crown unless the Crown was expressly named therein, 'Roy n'est lie par ascun statute si il ne soit expressement nosme'. But the rule so laid down is subject to at least one exception. The Crown may be bound, as has often been said, 'by necessary implication'. If, that is to say, it is manifest from the very terms of the statute, that it was the intention of the legislature that the Crown should be bound, then the result is the same as if the Crown had been expressly named. It must then be inferred that the

Crown, by assenting to the law, agreed to be bound by its provisions. . . . [T]heir Lordships are of opinion that to interpret the principle in the sense put on it by the High Court would be to whittle it down, and they cannot find any authority which gives support to such an interpretation.

It was contended on behalf of the [municipality] that whenever a statute is enacted 'for the public good' the Crown, though not expressly named, must be held to be bound by its provisions and that, as the Act in question was manifestly intended to secure the public welfare, it must bind the Crown. . . . The proposition which the [municipality] thus sought to maintain is supported by early authority . . . but in their Lordships' opinion it cannot now be regarded as sound except in a strictly limited sense. Every statute must be supposed to be 'for the public good', at least in intention, and even when, as in the present case, it is apparent that one object of the legislature is to promote the welfare and convenience of a large body of the King's subjects by giving extensive powers to a local authority, it cannot be said, consistently with the decided cases, that the Crown is necessarily bound by the enactment. . . . Their Lordships prefer to say that the apparent purpose of the statute is one element, and may be an important element, to be considered when an intention to bind the Crown is alleged. If it can be affirmed that, at the time when the statute was passed and received the royal sanction, it was apparent from its terms that its beneficent purpose must be wholly frustrated unless the Crown were bound, then it may be inferred that the Crown has agreed to be bound. Their Lordships will add that when the court is asked to draw this inference, it must always be remembered that, if it be the intention of the legislature that the Crown shall be bound, nothing is easier than to say so in plain words.

The Crown's (qualified) immunity from statute may enable Crown bodies to escape the operation of social welfare and other legislation enacted in the public interest. Indeed some statutes make express provision for the Crown's immunity; for example, section 13 of the Rent Act 1977 provides that tenants of the Crown shall not qualify for the protection of the Act. (However, the Housing Act 1980, s.73(1), brings tenancies of land managed by the Crown Estate Commissioners under the protection of the Rent Act.) Again, planning permission is not required for the development of Crown land – see the Town and Country Planning Act 1971, s.266 – although a non-statutory, administrative procedure provides equivalent safeguards (see Department of the Environment Circular 7/77). Exemptions of the Crown are also to be found in the Fire Precautions Act 1971, s.40, and the Control of Pollution Act 1974, s.105(3).

Even when an Act is expressed to be binding on the Crown, the exemption may be retained in respect of some of its provisions. Part I of the Health and Safety at Work etc. Act 1974 which deals with the health, safety and welfare of employees and the protection of public health and safety, is declared to be binding on the Crown, but with important exceptions relating to enforcement procedures (section 48).

Report of the Health and Safety Commission, 1977–78, paras.
81–2, 85

Crown bodies have the same obligations under the HSW Act as other employers but, unlike other employers, they can neither be issued with statutory improvement or prohibition notices, nor be prosecuted. . . .

The Chairman of the Commission has frequently drawn attention to our view that it is not right that Crown employers should be in a privileged position. From evidence given to us by the [Health and Safety] Executive we have concluded that the attitude of Crown employers to health and safety is in general no better and no worse than other employers and the same provisions relating to enforcement seem to be necessary if the legislation is to be effective in Crown establishments. In particular the arguments used to justify the introduction of improvement and prohibition notices are just as telling in the case of Crown employers as elsewhere.

. . . [W]e have decided on the introduction of a non-statutory procedure of issuing special Crown improvement and prohibition notices in situations where, but for Crown immunity, statutory notices would have been issued. . . . Failure to comply will lead to approaches by the Executive to higher authorities in the Crown body concerned.

The Health and Safety Commission reported in 1980 that the non-statutory notices issued to Crown employers generally gained the desired result (Report for 1979–80, p. 18).

Can you suggest a more satisfactory rule for the operation of statute with respect to the Crown?

While the Crown is in principle not *bound* by statute, it is generally held that it is entitled at common law to take the *benefit* of a statute although not named in it. Section 31(1) of the Crown Proceedings Act 1947 provides:

This Act shall not prejudice the right of the Crown to take advantage of the provisions of an Act of Parliament although not named therein; and it is hereby declared that in any civil proceedings against the Crown the provisions of any Act of Parliament which could, if the proceedings were between subjects, be relied upon by the defendant as a defence to the proceedings, whether in whole or in part, or otherwise, may, subject to any express provision to the contrary, be so relied upon by the Crown.

(See further Hartley and Griffith, *Government and Law*, pp. 316–19.)

The Crown has in the past benefited from a far-reaching privilege relating to the production of evidence in court, to which the name 'Crown privilege' was aptly applied. This doctrine, rooted in the royal prerogative, enabled a minister of the Crown to disallow the production of any document in a court of law by invoking the public interest. Crown privilege has in recent years been judicially reinterpreted as a rule of 'public interest immunity' which gives a qualified protection to documents bearing on the interests of the state: the courts have assumed the power to review and, in an appropriate case, to set aside the objection of the executive to disclosure. It is still rare, however, for a court to override a minister's contention that the production of a document would be harmful to the public interest. (See further Hartley and Griffith, op. cit., pp. 320–25; *Burmah Oil Co. Ltd* v. *Bank of England* [1980] AC 1090; *Air Canada* v. *Secretary of State for Trade* [1983] 2 AC 394.)

The Crown still enjoys certain privileges and immunities in legal proceedings to which it is a party – for example, the remedies of injunction and specific performance are not available against the Crown: Crown Proceedings Act 1947, s.21. A declaration, which can be granted against the Crown, is usually as effective a remedy as an injunction, but where interim relief is needed against the Crown no substitute for an injunction is available: it follows that 'there is a lacuna in [the] court's power to control exercises of executive discretion' (*per* Mann J in *R. v. Secretary of State for the Home Department, ex p. Kirkwood* [1984] 2 All ER 390, 394).

3 Personal powers of the Sovereign

We have already seen that most of the surviving powers, privileges and immunities which were once aspects of the *royal* prerogative have been appropriated by the government. Even when it is the Queen who acts, she is normally obliged by convention to do so in accordance with the advice of her ministers. There remain, however, a few prerogative powers which may still be exercised by the Queen at her own discretion in exceptional circumstances.

(a) Appointment of prime minister

The Queen appoints the prime minister, but her choice is governed by the convention, grounded in political necessity, that she must appoint the man or woman who can form a government which will have the confidence of the House of Commons. Normally this convention clearly indicates the party leader who, having majority support in the House, has an indisputable claim to be appointed as prime minister.

Formerly if a prime minister died or personally resigned (his colleagues remaining in office) the Sovereign might have had to use his own judgement in making an appointment, but now the main parties all have procedures for electing a successor in such an event. When Mr Harold Wilson announced his resignation as Prime Minister in March 1976 he did so in terms that it would take effect when the Parliamentary Labour Party had elected a new leader. Mr Callaghan having been elected, Mr Wilson formally tendered his resignation to the Queen and informed her of the result of the election, probably adding his opinion that Mr Callaghan was assured of majority support in Parliament. (See Harold Wilson, *The Governance of Britain*, 1976, pp. 21–2.) There was no room for the exercise of discretion by the Sovereign.

In the event of a sudden death or resignation of the prime minister the governing party would doubtless expedite its election procedures. If there were still to be substantial delay before a successor could be chosen, the Cabinet could be expected to bring forward a minister who would assume temporary leadership of the government, the Sovereign being invited to confirm his authority to act.

If in a general election the main opposition party wins an overall majority of seats, the government will resign and the Sovereign will call on the leader of the Opposition to form a new government. But if no party gains an overall majority it may not be immediately clear whether the existing prime minister, or the leader of the Opposition (or some other party leader), will have sufficient support in the House of Commons to govern effectively. This indeed was the position after the general election of February 1974.

Rodney Brazier, 'The Constitution in the New Politics' [1978]
PL 117, 117–20

What may be said with confidence about the February 1974 General Election is that the Conservative Government lost it. Its 323 seats out of 630 at the dissolution were reduced to 296 out of the newly-enlarged House of 635, and the Ulster Unionists no longer took the Conservative whip. Labour gained the largest number of seats, 301, but no overall majority. Such a result had not occurred since 1929. What, if anything, is constitutionally prescribed in such an event?

It was expected on the Friday after polling that Mr Heath would resign: after all, Labour had a clear majority of five seats over the Conservatives. And the Labour Shadow Cabinet had issued a statement announcing that the Labour Party was prepared to form a minority government, without coalition or inter-party pacts. But Mr Heath saw the Queen merely to inform her of the political situation, and then tried to form a coalition with the 14 Liberal M Ps, or, failing that, at least to reach agreement on a parliamentary and administrative programme. The negotiations failed, and on Monday, March 4, 1974, Mr Heath resigned and Mr Wilson kissed hands on appointment as Prime Minister.

Those who must work the constitution at the centre must decide what a Prime Minister should do if he loses a General Election in circumstances in which no opposition party has captured a majority of Commons seats. A Parliament so composed is very unusual in modern times, for every General Election since 1931 had produced a majority government. The precedents are unhelpful. In the December 1923 Election Baldwin's majority was destroyed, the Conservatives holding 258 seats but Labour achieving 191 and the combined Liberals 159 – Labour thus becoming the second largest parliamentary party for the first time in its history. The new Parliament did not assemble until January 1924. Baldwin reluctantly accepted George v's advice not to resign in the interim but to meet the new House of Commons, where he was duly beaten on an amendment to the address in reply to the King's Speech. MacDonald then became Prime Minister on Baldwin's resignation, to hold office at Liberal sufferance. After the 1929 General Election Labour formed the largest grouping in the House (with 288 seats) followed by the Conservatives (260), the Liberals holding only 59 seats but again having the balance of power. This time Baldwin resigned forthwith, to allow MacDonald to form his second minority Government. It is of no help to recall that ever since that resignation a Prime Minister who has lost his majority in the House at the polls has, with the exception of Mr Heath, resigned immediately, because in every case with that exception there has been a Leader of the Opposition with a parliamentary majority waiting in the wings. And as in 1923–24 and in 1929 the sitting Prime Minister made no attempt to construct a workable Commons majority, these precedents are of even less use in considering the constitutionality of Mr Heath's delayed resignation or that of any future Prime Minister who might be placed in his predicament. If it is accepted that many constitutional conventions mean what the current set of politicians say they mean, then with both Mr Heath and Mr Wilson being of the view that it was right for the former to try to form a fresh government from the new House [see Harold Wilson, *The Governance of Britain*, 1976, pp. 25–6], we are propelled to the view that if a House of Commons is elected in which no single party has an overall majority it falls first to the Prime Minister to see if he can construct an administration enjoying the confidence of that House, and that if he cannot do so within a reasonable time, he should offer to resign. . . . [I]t seems that the Queen acted in a wholly appropriate manner after the February Election. Given a Labour minority government in waiting, it was surely correct for her to stay out of the political arena and to allow the parties to resolve the difficulties of the electorate's making. Had she on the day after polling insisted on Mr Heath's immediate resignation, when a Conservative-Liberal coalition was on the cards, then that would have been an entirely unjustifiable use of the prerogative which would have caused the Queen to become, in Asquith's phrase, 'the football of contending factions'.

'Hung' Parliaments, with no party enjoying an overall majority, will doubtless recur in Britain, and may do so with frequency if a system of proportional representation should be introduced at some future time. A general election might produce a result allowing of either a minority government or one formed from any of various combinations of parties under one or other of a number of party leaders. In these circumstances the existing conventions and precedents might fail to give an unequivocal indication of the way in which the prerogative should be exercised.

David Butler, *Governing Without a Majority* (1983), pp. 92–4

Let us consider one particularly difficult scenario – an outcome, after a Conservative government had appealed to the country, such as this:

Conservative	230
Labour	270
Alliance	120
Other	20

The Alliance indicate that they would work under a Conservative government but not under its current Leader. The Labour party makes plain (as it did in 1974) that it is ready to form a minority government but not to make deals with any other party. The Conservative Prime Minister goes to the Palace and, before resigning, indicates that the Conservative Deputy Leader should be asked to form a government, assured of Alliance support. Should the Queen accept this advice or should she send for the Leader of the largest party, Labour? It is a no-win situation. Whichever course was followed would be regarded as violently objectionable by a large section of the political community. Here two widely accepted principles are irreconcilable:

1. If a party is defeated in an election, the sovereign sends for the Leader of the Opposition in the previous parliament, especially if it is now the largest party.
2. The sovereign sends for the leader most likely to command a majority in the House of Commons.

There are many people, from all points in the political spectrum, who would argue that the Queen should certainly send for the Labour Leader, ask him to form a government and, if he is defeated at the first vote, grant a request for a dissolution. She would be following precedent and she would be referring the decision to the voters. But she would also, at a time when Parliament offered a viable government, be giving to Labour the chance of choosing a polling day and going to the country with all the prestige of a government in office. There is, moreover, a paradox. If the Conservative Leader (by private agreement with the Alliance) stayed in office until Parliament met and confirmed a coalition government in power, then there could be no objection in the event of a Prime Minister resigning if a successor was found from within the ranks of the coalition. Once a government is established, there is no reason for the sovereign to send for the Leader of the Opposition, even if it is the largest party in the House, should the Prime Minister resign or die in office.

But, in the event of the Prime Minister resigning immediately, the snag about the alternative course is that the coalition might not stick together. How far could the Queen accept the assurance that there was a working majority? In 1926 Lord Byng [the Governor-General of Canada] was told by Mr Meighen that he could command a majority in the Canadian House of Commons. Events proved that he did not – to the humiliation of Lord Byng and his office.

If multi-party politics should become normal in Britain, the conventions of a two-party system would be of limited use in guiding the Sovereign's choice of a prime minister. Doubtless the question would generally be resolved by the process of bargaining between political parties, whose agreement on a leader would simply be ratified by the Sovereign. But agreement might not always be reached, and it could then fall to the Sovereign to exercise a personal judgement in choosing between party leaders who each claimed substantial support in the House.

The appointment of a prime minister, in circumstances in which the choice was not plainly dictated by convention, would be likely to have major political repercussions. Vernon Bogdanor (*Multi-party Politics and the Constitution*, 1983, p. 137) observes that

the duty of safeguarding the Constitution belongs less to the Sovereign than to the politicians. It lies with them to develop conventions and understandings which can preserve the values of constitutional monarchy in a multi-party system, and ensure that the monarchy is not unwittingly brought into the arena of party politics.

But while the choice of a prime minister may still call for the exercise of political judgement, is the decision best left with the Queen and her personal advisers, or should it be given instead to the Speaker of the House of Commons, or a panel of eminent citizens, or a ballot of MPs?

See further Bogdanor, op. cit., ch. 6; Rodney Brazier, 'Choosing a Prime Minister' [1982] *PL* 395; and Michael Steed, 'The Formation of Governments in the United Kingdom' (1983) 54 *Political Quarterly* 54.

(b) Dismissal of ministers

The Queen has a prerogative power to dismiss 'her' ministers, singly or collectively, but the power is overlaid by convention.

In practice the fate of individual ministers is in the hands of the prime minister. Although constrained by political factors he has by convention the power to require the resignation of any minister. (In the last resort he could advise the Queen to exercise her power of dismissal.)

In *Adegbenro* v. *Akintola* [1963] AC 614, the Privy Council had to decide a question about the power vested by the Constitution of Western Nigeria in the Governor of the Region to dismiss the regional Premier if he had lost the confidence of the elected House. Arguments addressed to the court had sought to draw analogies from the Queen's prerogative of dismissal in the United Kingdom. Lord Radcliffe said (p. 631):

British constitutional history does not offer any but a general negative guide as to the circumstances in which a Sovereign can dismiss a Prime Minister. Since the principles which are accepted today began to take shape with the passing of the Reform Bill of 1832 no British Sovereign has in fact dismissed or removed a Prime Minister, even allowing for the ambiguous exchanges which took place between William IV and Lord Melbourne in 1834. Discussion of constitutional doctrine bearing upon a Prime Minister's loss of support in the House of Commons concentrates therefore upon a Prime Minister's duty to ask for liberty to resign or for a dissolution, rather than upon the Sovereign's right of removal, an exercise of which is not treated as being within the scope of practical politics.

Having regard to the facts that a government holds office by virtue of the support of a democratically elected House of Commons, and that no prime minister has been dismissed by the Sovereign since 1783 (or perhaps 1834, when the circumstances of Melbourne's departure were equivocal), it must now be unconstitutional for the Sovereign to dismiss the prime minister and his colleagues in all but the most exceptional circumstances. The power is said to survive for use if a government should act to destroy the democratic or parliamentary bases of the constitution. But unless the Sovereign's judgement of the necessity to dismiss her ministers on these grounds should be generally supported by public opinion, the monarchy itself would be placed in jeopardy.

What consequences might follow if a government, defeated on a vote of confidence in the House of Commons, refused to resign or request a dissolution of Parliament? Would this be an occasion for the exercise of the prerogative of dismissal? Cf. Marshall, *Constitutional Conventions*, p. 27.

When in 1975 the Governor-General of Australia, Sir John Kerr, acting in the name of the Queen but on his own initiative, dismissed the Prime Minister of Australia, Mr Whitlam, and all the ministers of the Labour Government with the object of resolving a political and constitutional impasse, his action provoked much controversy and reactions of an intense and bitter kind. The crisis had resulted from the refusal of the Upper House of the Australian Parliament, where the Opposition had a majority, to pass Appropriation Bills providing necessary supply (authorization of expenditure) for the Government. This unprecedented action of the Senate was designed to bring down the Government, which attempted to extricate itself from a critical situation by devising unorthodox expedients for raising money. In this crisis the Governor-General acted by dismissing Mr Whitlam and his Government and appointing as Prime Minister the Leader of the Opposition, Mr Fraser, who had first assured the Governor-General that the Appropriation Bills would be passed and that he would as Prime Minister advise a dissolution of both Houses of Parliament in order that the deadlock might be resolved by the verdict of the people. The subsequent election was convincingly won by the opposition Liberal and Country Parties, and a coalition government was formed under Mr Fraser.

> Letter and statement by the Governor-General of Australia,
> Sir John Kerr, 11 November 1975

Dear Mr Whitlam,

In accordance with section 64 of the Constitution I hereby determine your appointment as my Chief Adviser and Head of the Government. It follows that I also hereby determine the appointments of all the Ministers in your Government.

You have previously told me that you would never resign or advise an election of the House of Representatives or a double dissolution and that the only way in which such an election could be obtained would be by my dismissal of you and your ministerial colleagues. As it appeared likely that you would today persist in this attitude I decided that, if you did, I would determine your commission and state my reasons for doing so. You have persisted in your attitude and I have accordingly acted as indicated. I attach a statement of my reasons which I intend to publish immediately.

It is with a great deal of regret that I have taken this step both in respect of yourself and your colleagues.

I propose to send for the Leader of the Opposition and to commission him to form a new caretaker government until an election can be held.

> Yours sincerely,
> (signed) JOHN R. KERR

STATEMENT BY THE GOVERNOR-GENERAL

I have given careful consideration to the constitutional crisis and have made some decisions which I wish to explain.

Summary

It has been necessary for me to find a democratic and constitutional solution to the current crisis which will permit the people of Australia to decide as soon as possible what should be the outcome of the deadlock which developed over supply between the two Houses of Parliament and between the Government and Opposition parties. The only solution consistent with the Constitution and with my oath of office and my responsibilities, authority and duty as Governor-General is to terminate the commission as Prime Minister of Mr Whitlam and to arrange for a caretaker government able to secure supply and willing to let the issue go to the people.

I shall summarise the elements of the problem and the reasons for my decision which places the matter before the people of Australia for prompt determination.

Because of the federal nature of our Constitution and because of its provisions the Senate undoubtedly has constitutional power to refuse or defer supply to the Government. Because of the principles of responsible government a Prime Minister who cannot obtain supply, including money for carrying on the ordinary services of government, must either advise a general election or resign. If he refuses to do this I have the authority and indeed the duty under the Constitution to withdraw his commission as Prime Minister. The position in Australia is quite different from the position in the United Kingdom. Here the confidence of both Houses on supply is necessary to ensure its provision. In the United Kingdom the confidence of the House of Commons alone is necessary. But both here and in the United Kingdom the duty of the Prime Minister is the same in a most important respect – if he cannot get supply he must resign or advise an election.

If a Prime Minister refuses to resign or to advise an election, and this is the case with Mr Whitlam, my constitutional authority and duty require me to do what I have now done – to withdraw his commission – and to invite the Leader of the Opposition to form a caretaker government – that is one that makes no appointments or dismissals and initiates no policies until a general election is held. It is most desirable that he should guarantee supply. Mr Fraser will be asked to give the necessary undertakings and advise whether he is prepared to recommend a double dissolution. He will also be asked to guarantee supply.

The decisions I have made were made after I was satisfied that Mr Whitlam could not obtain supply. No other decision open to me would enable the Australian people to decide for themselves what should be done.

Once I had made up my mind, for my own part, what I must do if Mr Whitlam persisted in his stated intentions I consulted the Chief Justice of Australia, Sir Garfield Barwick. I have his permission to say that I consulted him in this way.

The result is that there will be an early general election for both Houses and the people can do what, in a democracy such as ours, is their responsibility and duty and theirs alone. It is for the people now to decide the issue which the two leaders have failed to settle.

(See Sir John Kerr, *Matters for Judgment*, 1978, pp. 361–4, for a Detailed Statement of Decisions.)

Colin Howard and Cheryl Saunders in Gareth Evans (ed.),
Labor and the Constitution 1972–1975 (1977), p. 280

The deadlock which occurred between the two Houses of Parliament in 1975 was the result of a political struggle between the headstrong leaders of two political parties. Its genesis and character was such that it should have been solved by political means. It follows that intervention by the Governor-General inevitably would be construed as political intervention. On 11 November, there were some signs that a political solution was, if not imminent, at least approaching. It seems likely that the ultimate solution would have been a negotiated surrender of the Opposition parties and the passage of the Appropriation Bills through the Senate. This analysis derives from the mounting body of public opinion at the time that it was for the politicians to resolve a deadlock which they themselves had deliberately created; from the responsiveness of politicians to adverse public opinion; and from the fact known to one of the authors, and doubtless to many others, that the ranks of the Opposition in the Senate were not as united as they appeared. Viewed purely as a political struggle, it strains credulity that the resolve of the Opposition would have proved greater than that of the Government in these circumstances.

Preference for a political and parliamentary solution rather than vice-regal intervention depends on the degree of faith placed in the processes of parliamentary democracy. In 1975 a great deal of faith was required. Funds for the maintenance of the ordinary services of government were becoming depleted rapidly. It was said that unless Parliament was dissolved on 11 November, an election could not be held in time to solve the deadlock before the money ran out. Nevertheless it was apparent to cool heads that the tightening time pressure was virtually dictating a political compromise. The knowledge that November 11 was the last day for solution by election inevitably increased the likelihood on and from 12 November that the solution would be otherwise, which meant the passage of supply by the Senate. It is impossible to credit that both leaders would have maintained their stand to the point where there was a total breakdown in civil order, still less that party discipline could have been maintained to that point.

> David Butler, Introduction to Gareth Evans (ed.), *Labor and the Constitution 1972–1975* (1977), pp. xvii–xviii

[I]t is possible to make a case for [Sir John Kerr's] action on November 11, to argue that, with the situation that had then been reached, the course he followed was the only one which could guarantee that the Australian government would not default on its financial obligations. . . . By putting Mr Fraser in office, Sir John secured the immediate passage of the blocked Supply legislation; without that, there could be no certainty that there would have been any legal way of meeting public service salaries and other Federal liabilities after early December. Moreover, by the form in which he provided for the election, he ensured that the verdict on the political deadlock would be put immediately in the hands of the electorate and that, if they opted for Mr Whitlam, Labor could get through its programme, even without a Senate majority. As it turned out, Labor was defeated. But that does not necessarily mean that a conscientious Governor-General should have acted differently.

See further Sir John Kerr, *Matters for Judgment* (1978), especially chs. 16–22.

(c) **Dissolution of Parliament**

The exercise of the prerogative of dissolution depends in ordinary circumstances on the judgement of the prime minister.

> Lord Blake, *The Office of Prime Minister* (1975), pp. 58–60

Until the First World War no one doubted that the decision to advise the Crown to dissolve Parliament was a collective decision of the Cabinet, or at any rate of those members of it who sit in the House of Commons. (When Disraeli took the opinion of his Cabinet in 1880 on the question of dissolution, only the Commoners gave voice, but whether this was a normal practice I do not know. In any case it was a Cabinet decision.) For reasons which are not wholly clear the practice since 1918 has been for the decision to rest with the Prime Minister alone, taking such advice (or none) as he sees fit. The Cabinet was not consulted over the timing of the Coupon Election [in 1918] nor, as far as is publicly known, has it been consulted since.

. . . [I]t seems clear that the responsibility now lies with the Prime Minister alone. No doubt the point is usually academic. No Prime Minister would take such a decision without informally consulting his principal colleagues and getting their support.

It seems that the appropriation by the prime minister of the power to request a dissolution came about, in the early years of the century, through a misunderstanding of the precedents: see Lord Blake, op. cit., p. 59 and Marshall, *Constitutional Conventions*, pp. 48–51. Marshall argues that the justification for the present practice is weak. In any event it is normal, as Lord Blake notes, for the prime minister to consult the Cabinet or senior colleagues before asking for a dissolution.

May the Queen in any circumstances refuse a dissolution requested by the prime minister? The question was canvassed after the general election of February 1974, when Labour took office with five more seats in the House of Commons than the Conservatives but no overall majority. The new Government faced the threat of immediate defeat in the House in a division on the Address in reply to the Queen's Speech, which would have obliged the Prime Minister either to resign, with his Government, or seek a dissolution of Parliament. The Prime Minister, Mr Wilson, publicly declared his intention to request a dissolution in such an event. As it happened the expected challenge to the Government did not materialize and the Queen was not asked to dissolve Parliament until some months later. It has, however, been asserted that if a dissolution had been requested in March 1974 or shortly thereafter, the Queen would have been justified in refusing.

Sir Peter Rawlinson, 'Dissolution in the United Kingdom'
(1977) 58 *The Parliamentarian* 1, 2

When Mr (Sir) Harold Wilson in March 1974 formed a minority government in succession to Mr Edward Heath, following the failure of the latter to find allies from the minor parties, the Crown could have rejected advice (if proffered, which it was not) to dissolve the Parliament elected in February 1974 within days or weeks of the succession of Mr Heath by Mr Wilson. For it was the duty of the new minority Wilson Administration to face Parliament and to discover whether the new Administration was viable. There was always the possibility of another attempt at coalition between the Conservatives and Liberals and other parties as an alternative to the Wilson Government. As Lord Balfour has said. . . . 'No constitution can stand a diet of dissolutions', and advice to dissolve very shortly after March 1974, when Supply was being effected and major Bills presented by the new Wilson Government were being accepted by the House of Commons, could and should have been rejected by the Sovereign certainly until at least six months of minority government had been experienced. Advice to dissolve prior to a period of trial would have been advice wrongly proffered and, therefore, wrong to have been accepted. The Sovereign on her personal responsibility could have taken into account the time since the previous election and the incidence that government was not being impossibly thwarted.

On the other hand the Queen's personal advisers are doubtless fully aware of the necessity to shield the monarchy from the winds of political controversy, which would certainly have been unleashed if the Queen had refused a dissolution in these circumstances. Contemporary reports suggest – though the matter cannot be stated with certainty – that soundings at the Palace on behalf of the Conservative Party revealed that there would be no question of refusal if the Prime Minister were to request a dissolution. (See *The Times*, 6 May 1974, p. 14; David Watt, (1974) 45 *Political Quarterly* 346 at 349.) Refusal would have been followed by Mr Wilson's resignation. The obvious person to succeed him, Mr Heath, had already failed to gain Liberal support for a Government headed by himself.

Governors-General have refused prime ministerial requests for dissolutions in the present century, but there has been no refusal by the Sovereign in the United Kingdom since the Reform Act of 1832.

> Geoffrey Marshall and Graeme C. Moodie, *Some Problems of the Constitution* (5th edn 1971), pp. 40–41

The Governor-General of Canada in 1926 and the Governor-General of South Africa in 1939, wielding the powers of the Crown, refused a dissolution to the then Prime Minister. In each case, therefore, he had no option but to resign. In each case an alternative Government was available – the Canadian one lasting only a few days before being forced itself to request a dissolution (which was granted), and the South African one maintaining a majority until after the war had been won. In each case, too, the Governor-General became the target of criticism coming mainly from supporters of the government which had, in effect, been dismissed. Even were it universally agreed that the Governors-General had acted constitutionally, which it is not, one could not safely conclude that the same judgment would apply to similar action by a Monarch in the United Kingdom (or elsewhere). It is not certain, for one thing, that precisely the same rules must always apply in the United Kingdom as in the other Commonwealth countries whose constitutions derive from it. More important, it is not certain that the same rules apply to a Governor-General as to the Sovereign in person. Admittedly the powers of a Governor-General are officially the same as those of the Monarch in the United Kingdom but, in the absence of any clear formulation of the latter, it is not easy precisely to enumerate those powers. It cannot be disputed that in 1926 and 1939 the Governors-General exercised powers which had once belonged to the Monarch. Furthermore, had these actions been taken by the Monarch personally, and been accepted as constitutional at the time, it could not be disputed that they were instances of powers properly belonging to Governors-General. That is to say that what the Queen may do, her representatives may do also, in the absence of any legal provision to the contrary. But it does not necessarily follow that what is done by them may constitutionally be done by the Queen. The essential point to remember is that a Governor-General is, nowadays, appointed for a limited term on the advice of the Commonwealth government concerned, and thereafter acts on the advice of Commonwealth Ministers, and not on the advice or instruction either of Ministers or of the Monarch in the United Kingdom. It follows that his involvement in controversy concerns himself alone, and not necessarily the place of the Crown. The temporary and appointive nature of his office, moreover, means that the real or apparent partisanship of any one incumbent need imperil nothing more than his own tenure. Neither of these statements can safely be made about the Monarch personally. It must be concluded, therefore, that these precedents provide no clearer guidance than do the opinions of constitutional authorities.

According to some constitutional authorities, the Sovereign might properly refuse a dissolution if it were clearly contrary to the public interest for a general election to be held in the circumstances prevailing at the time, on condition that an alternative government could be formed that would be able to carry on with a working majority in the House. Others would say that assessment of the national interest is rather a matter for the prime minister, constrained by the counsels or warnings of his colleagues, and accountable to the electorate. Marshall and Moodie (op. cit., p. 43) come to the following conclusion:

In present times the Monarch is expected to refrain from political intervention to an extent unknown a century and more ago. What was accepted as legitimate political influence then is not so accepted now when a greater emphasis is placed on such conceptions as 'the sovereignty of the people'. Whether in fact people would vote for or against a government which was believed to possess royal support, it is now generally felt to be undesirable that this be an issue at all. Governments and parties should be supported or opposed on their merits and their record, and not on their acceptability to the Monarch. Only if a dissolution is felt to be the decision of the Prime Minister, not of the Monarch, can an election be freed from the essentially irrelevant question of royal preferences. And only thus may the Monarch satisfy the constitutional requirement that she be, in fact and appearance, politically impartial.

There is, however, a need for a safeguard against abuse of the conventional rules by a prime minister devoted more to retaining office than to the public interest. Marshall (*Constitutional Conventions*, p. 42) refers to 'the possibility in an era of multi-party governmental groupings that requests for dissolution might be disputed or resisted within the governmental party or that the coalition leader might be held to be requesting dissolution to preserve his own position or for narrow party political reasons'. At present the safeguard depends on the political judgement of the Sovereign, and again the question arises whether it is best left there, or whether a new mechanism should be devised to take the place of the prerogative. (See p. 118 above and Vernon Bogdanor, *Multi-party Politics and the Constitution*, 1983, pp. 159–63; Marshall, op. cit., pp. 35–44.)

On the prerogative powers to give or refuse assent to bills and to create peers, see Marshall, op. cit., pp. 21–5.

4 The central government

(a) Ministers of the Crown

In the theory of the constitution, holders of ministerial office in the government are servants of the Crown. Ministers are chosen by the prime minister and are then appointed by the Queen. As they hold office 'at the pleasure of the Crown' they can be lawfully dismissed by the Queen, but in this she must act in accordance with convention. (See above.)

Town Investments Ltd v. *Department of the Environment* [1978] AC
359 (HL)

LORD SIMON OF GLAISDALE: . . . Once central government was firmly established in England, power – what in modern political science would be known as executive, judicial and legislative power – was concentrated in the King. No line was drawn at first between the private and the public business of the King. But, as the latter grew, administrative convenience called for some devolution. Offices were hived off from the King's household. There was the Chancery presided over by the Chancellor. Then there was the Privy Seal office under a Keeper of the Privy Seal, and the Exchequer with a Treasurer and a Chancellor of its own. And so on. All these officials holding offices of ancient origin had their action 'confined within rigid limits, expressed by the commissions by which they were appointed and the procedure which their acts must follow'. The motive force behind their departments

> 'was the King's command. They all existed to give effect to his will. The officials who presided over them were appointed and dismissible by him. Each was charged with the fulfilment of the royal pleasure within his own appropriate sphere.'

However, for centuries thereafter the King's secretary remained within the royal household. Unlike the officials holding offices of ancient origin, the King's secretary was therefore 'free to enter every new branch of royal administration as it developed'. So it was that with the increase in the powers of the Crown in the 16th century the Secretary rose to the first rank among the King's servants. But under the Restoration the Secretaries (for their office was now duplicated) too became heads of departments of state, charged like the holders of the ancient offices with executing the royal will. (For the foregoing historical development, see D. L. Keir, *The Constitutional History of Modern Britain 1485–1937* . . ., whence also came the quotations.)

With the development of modern government fresh departments were formed to be headed by ministers or by Secretaries of State. Just as all were originally appointed to carry out departmentally the royal will, so today all ministers are appointed to exercise the powers of the Crown, together with such other powers as have been statutorily conferred upon them directly.

In theory there is still only one office of Secretary of State, but several may be invested with the title and powers of the office. At present there are 13 Secretaries of State, each heading a government department and with a seat in the Cabinet. Some ministers have traditional titles reflecting their historical functions as servants of the Crown: they include the Lord Chancellor, the Chancellor of the Exchequer, the Lord Privy Seal, the Lord President of the Council and the Chancellor of the Duchy of Lancaster. The last three are not departmental ministers (excepting the Lord President's responsibility for the small Privy Council Office) and may be given whatever non-departmental responsibilities the prime minister thinks appropriate. For example, the Chancellor of the Duchy of Lancaster in the Heath Government (1970–74) had responsibility for the conduct of negotiations for British entry into the European Communities. The Lord Privy Seal answered for the Foreign Office in the House of Commons from 1979 to 1982 when the Foreign Secretary was a member of the Upper House. The present Lord Privy Seal acts as leader of the House of Commons.

The Attorney-General and the Solicitor-General, as law officers of the Crown for England and Wales, and the Lord Advocate and Solicitor-General for Scotland with similar functions in respect of Scotland, are (non-Cabinet) ministers who act as the government's chief legal advisers and have important responsibilities in relation to the law and its enforcement. The Attorney-General has certain discretionary powers to authorize, institute or stop criminal proceedings. (See S. A. de Smith, *Constitutional and Administrative Law*, 4th edn 1981, p. 380.) While he may properly consult his colleagues before taking action of these kinds in cases raising political issues, he is required by convention to exercise an independent judgement uninfluenced by considerations of party advantage. In September 1984 allegations were made that the prosecution of a civil servant, Mr Ponting, under section 2 of the Official Secrets Act 1911 had been undertaken on the insistence of the Secretary of State for Defence, supported by the Prime Minister. Mrs Thatcher denied the allegation in a letter to Dr David Owen, saying that the decision to prosecute had been taken by the law officers without consulting any of their ministerial colleagues, and adding:

. . . you must know that the Attorney-General acts in a totally independent and non-political capacity in making decisions on prosecutions. It would be improper for me or my colleagues to interfere in any way with his discretion in the exercise of that function and I confirm that we did not do so in Mr Ponting's case. [*The Times*, 17 September 1984.]

(See further on this question John Ll. J. Edwards, *The Attorney General, Politics and the Public Interest*, 1984, chs. 11 and 12.)

Should the office of Attorney-General be separated from the political arena, as an independent office outside government? How might such an independent officer be held accountable for his actions? (Cf. Edwards, op. cit., pp. 62–7.)

Next in rank below full or senior ministers (most of whom head departments and sit in the Cabinet) are ministers of state, who are attached to departments headed by Cabinet ministers. Some ministers of state are appointed to take charge (under the departmental minister) of a particular section of a department and are designated accordingly – e.g. the Ministers for Local Government and for Housing and Construction in the Department of the Environment. Others have tasks allotted to them by the departmental minister at his discretion. Departments also include junior ministers known as Parliamentary Secretaries (or Parliamentary Under-Secretaries of State if the senior minister is a Secretary of State). In the Department of the Environment after the June 1983 election there were, besides the Secretary of State, two Ministers of State (one of them a peer) and three Parliamentary Under-Secretaries of State. Statutory powers are not conferred on ministers of state or junior ministers, who act as delegates of the Secretary of State or other departmental minister in whom powers are legally vested and who remains responsible to Parliament for their exercise. Ministers may be assisted, in their parliamentary and political work, by Parliamentary Private Secretaries, who are unpaid and do not themselves rank as ministers.

Government Whips have posts with titles which do not indicate their functions of backbench liaison and party discipline: the Chief Whip has the title of Parliamentary Secretary to the Treasury and his deputy that of Treasurer of Her Majesty's Household.

By statute there can be no more than 95 holders of ministerial office in the House of Commons at any time: House of Commons Disqualification Act 1975, s.2(1). (See also the Ministerial and Other Salaries Act 1975, Sched. 1.) In 1979 the number of MPs involved in government (including Whips and Parliamentary Private Secretaries) was 114 (David Butler and Ann Sloman, *British Political Facts 1900–1979*, 5th edn 1980, p. 78) and nowadays the number is unlikely to fall very much below this. The principle of collective responsibility (pp. 146–52 below) generally assures the Cabinet of the support at least of this substantial body of parliamentarians for its policies and bills.

Since the financial responsibilities of Parliament are exercised by the House of Commons alone, the Chancellor of the Exchequer and other senior Treasury ministers (the Chief Secretary and the Financial Secretary to the Treasury) are invariably members of the Lower House. The two leading parties differ in their readiness to entrust major departmental responsibilities to peers. In the 1964–70 and 1974–9 Labour Governments the only departmental heads who were peers were the Lord Chancellor and (briefly in 1965–6) the Colonial Secretary. A peer, Lord Carrington, held successively the portfolios of Defence, Energy, and Foreign and Commonwealth Affairs in the 1970–74 and 1979–83 Conservative administrations.

Ministers of the Crown generally have a quite short tenure of office. In the period from the formation of the first government after the First World War to the end of 1971, the average length of tenure for the holders of seven leading ministerial portfolios ranged from 22.6 months (Defence) to 36.7 months (Agriculture). The average tenure of office in the seven ministries taken together was 27.5 months. (Valentine Herman in V. Herman and J. E. Alt,

Cabinet Studies: A Reader, 1975, p. 55.) In the 1964–70 Labour Government there was an especially rapid turnover of ministerial office, the median tenure of Cabinet ministers being 19 months. (Bruce Headey, *British Cabinet Ministers: The Roles of Politicians in Executive Office*, 1974, pp. 95–6.) Donald Shell records that of 85 ministers appointed to departmental posts in 1979, 60 had been moved at least once by 1983: (1983) 36 *Parliamentary Affairs* 154. (See further the articles by R. K. Alderman and J. A. Cross in (1979) 9 *British Journal of Political Science* 41 and (1981) 29 *Political Studies* 425.) Few ministers bring to their departments an appropriate specialized knowledge, and few remain long enough to acquire it.

Collective ministerial responsibility for the whole of government policy entitles each Cabinet minister to claim a share in general policy-making, including policies on important issues emerging from other departments. But ministers immersed in the 'urgent minutiae' of departmental life (Barbara Castle, *The Castle Diaries, 1974–76*, 1980, p. 523) seldom have time to inform themselves adequately about extra-departmental matters. When these arise in Cabinet or Cabinet committee the departmental minister may simply remain passive, or else take a position urged on him previously by ministerial colleagues, or follow a brief prepared by his own civil servants. Some ministers are more assertive and try to take a full part in government policy-making. Whether they are able to do so will depend upon their standing with their colleagues and the prime minister, their membership of the inner Cabinet, if there is one, and of relevant Cabinet committees, and their ability to limit their involvement in departmental administration, as by delegating responsibility to subordinate ministers. (The help given to ministers by political advisers is also important in this connection: see pp. 163–5 below.)

A former minister, Mr Edmund Dell, has argued (in *Policy and Practice: the Experience of Government*, RIPA 1980, ch. 2) that British government should be built on 'the rock of individual ministerial responsibility' and that there should be a move away from the collective decision-making in Cabinet and Cabinet committees which 'confers upon every Minister an equal right to be awkward, even ignorantly awkward' in the business of his colleagues. In government on the collective principle, says Dell, '[c]lear decision-making is compromised and real responsibility is confused'. The solution, in his view, is that there should be stronger central (prime ministerial) control in matters of general policy combined with clearer ministerial authority in departmental matters. (Keep Dell's arguments in mind as you read the remaining sections of this chapter.)

(b) The Cabinet

The prime minister decides on the membership of the Cabinet, but the heads of the dozen or so principal departments are nowadays always given places. In this century the size of the Cabinet has varied between 16 and 24 members. At the end of 1984 Mrs Thatcher's Cabinet had 22 members (including four peers) as follows:

> Prime Minister, First Lord of the Treasury and Minister for the Civil Service
> Lord President of the Council and Leader of the House of Lords
> Lord Chancellor
> Secretary of State for Foreign and Commonwealth Affairs
> Home Secretary
> Chancellor of the Exchequer
> Secretary of State for Education and Science
> Secretary of State for Energy
> Secretary of State for Defence
> Secretary of State for Scotland
> Secretary of State for Wales
> Secretary of State for the Environment
> Lord Privy Seal and Leader of the House of Commons
> Secretary of State for Social Services
> Secretary of State for Trade and Industry
> Secretary of State for Employment
> Minister of Agriculture, Fisheries and Food
> Chief Secretary to the Treasury
> Secretary of State for Transport
> Secretary of State for Northern Ireland
> Chancellor of the Duchy of Lancaster and Minister for the Arts
> Minister without Portfolio

All members of the Cabinet have an equal voice, but it is not usual for a vote to be taken. The prime minister sums up at the end of a discussion and declares what he or she takes to be the Cabinet view.

Patrick Gordon Walker, *The Cabinet* (rev. edn 1972), p. 15

A secret of the smooth adaptability of the British Constitution is that the Cabinet, which is central to the political life of the nation, is unknown to the law and thus extra-constitutional. Many constitutional changes and amendments that in other countries might have to be formally made are in Britain brought about by developments in the form and functions of the Cabinet. All that is necessary is that these developments should be accepted and carried on by successive Governments: often they may scarcely be noticed as constitutional innovations and may not be recognized and analysed until after they have passed into normal practice.

The modern Cabinet is the result of the slow growth of constitutional convention and has received only incidental recognition from the law (e.g. in the Ministerial and Other Salaries Act 1975, Sched. 1). It is not, however, correctly described as 'extra-constitutional' simply because it belongs to the conventional part of the constitution rather than to the part governed by law. The fact that firm rules about its composition, functions and procedure are lacking does mean, as Gordon Walker indicates, that changes in its role and *modus operandi* may occur without formality or publicity.

Richard Rose, *Politics in England* (3rd edn 1980), p. 65

Notwithstanding its formal importance, meetings of the Cabinet normally ratify rather than make decisions. One reason for this is the pressure of time. The Cabinet usually meets only one morning a week, and its agenda is extremely crowded with routine business. A second reason is bureaucratic: the great majority of matters going up to Cabinet have normally been discussed in great detail beforehand in Whitehall committees. Any major measure is likely to be considered first by senior civil servants from the departments affected by it. Civil servants are meant to confine their discussions and recommendations to technical matters, so that ministers can concentrate upon controversial political acts. The distinction is easier to state than to apply. Ministers meet in Cabinet committees to review the preliminary reports of civil servants, and to dispute and resolve outstanding political issues. On crisis issues of the economy and foreign affairs, committees may be constituted informally, meeting late at night at 10 Downing Street, with the Prime Minister conferring with chosen advisers from within and outside the Cabinet.

Ministers prefer to resolve their differences by bargaining in committee or by informal negotiations in order to present Cabinet an agreed recommendation difficult to challenge. In Cabinet, a minister finds it difficult to upset a recommendation agreed by informed and affected colleagues. A minister is more likely to let settlements hammered out in committee go through without great debate, in anticipation of having decisions affecting his department similarly endorsed another time.

Douglas Wass, *Government and the Governed* (1984), pp. 10–12, 24–6

[O]verriding almost all the individual responsibilities of ministers and departments runs the doctrine of the collective responsibility of the Cabinet. The Cabinet, some would say in formal terms, though I would say in real terms as well, is the ultimate embodiment of the executive government in this country. A minister may have statutory responsibilities peculiar to himself, but if the exercise of those responsibilities affects his colleagues, if, for example, he exposes the whole government to criticism and attack, or if he imposes costs on his fellow ministers, he must expect to submit his decision to collective endorsement.

The way issues are presented to Cabinet, indeed, the way issues are settled between departments, is crucially affected not only by these conventions, but also by the organisation of government. An issue which is brought to Cabinet for approval or resolution is always presented by the minister whose business it is. If it impinges other than tangentially on another minister he too may make a presentation to Cabinet, supporting or opposing the case of the minister who is principally concerned. But the essence of any collective Cabinet discussion is that it takes place on the basis of statements by interested parties, and they can always be relied on to do their best by argument and presentation to secure approval for what they want to do. Where the proposals are contested by a colleague whose departmental interests are adversely affected, the discussion assumes an adversarial character and the Cabinet acts in what amounts to a judicial role. But where as so often happens, there is no adversary, the Cabinet simply hears the case which the minister concerned presents, and this case is inevitably put in terms which suit the minister himself.

Now it may be that in ideal circumstances the minister will present the issue with the same objectivity that his own officials have employed in presenting it to him. The Cabinet will then, as a minimum, have the same information as the minister, and its decision can be presumed to be an efficient one. But if for any reason the minister does not present all the relevant information to his colleagues, how then can the Cabinet be said to be taking an efficient decision?

In no area of policy-making does this problem arise more acutely than in the management of the economy and, in particular, the Budget. The minister who brings these issues to Cabinet is of course the Chancellor of the Exchequer. No other minister has at his command the back-up of analytical support that the Chancellor receives from his Treasury and Revenue Department officials and from the Bank of England. How can his colleagues be assured that they are getting the whole story and not just the one which the Chancellor wishes them to hear? They have no independent staff. They have indeed no direct access to the official advice which the Treasury provides. Yet they are obliged to come to a view on the basis of what one of their colleagues, a committed party, is telling them. And they will be expected to defend that view in public as though it had been reached on the basis of full information.

. . . The machinery which exists within departments to give ministers a perspective of all their activities, a set of suggested objectives and a ranking of priorities, is missing in the collective forum of the Cabinet. Ministers in Cabinet rarely look at the totality of their responsibilities, at the balance of policy, at the progress of the government towards its objectives as a whole. Apart from its ritual weekly review of foreign affairs and parliamentary business, Cabinet's staple diet consists of a selection of individually important one-off cases or of issues on which the ministers departmentally concerned are unable to agree. . . .

The characteristics I have described carry with them two main consequences. The first consequence is that the general thrust of the government's policies is seldom if ever reviewed and assessed by Cabinet; strategic changes of course in response to substantial shifts in circumstances are not subjected to collective consideration; and the ordering of priorities is discussed in only the most general terms. I am not saying that these matters are never reviewed by governments: I can recall several important policy changes in the field of economic management which governments have made as the result of a deliberate reassessment. But they were not usually Cabinet reviews; and none of them was the result of a systematic study. The second consequence is that Cabinet does not have adequate safeguards against a strong departmental minister. An issue which comes to Cabinet is presented by the minister whose interests and reputation are involved, and he is bound to be partisan. No mechanism exists to enable the Cabinet to challenge his view unless the interests of another minister are involved, and even then the challenge itself may be partisan. Cabinet can too easily be railroaded.

For Bagehot, writing in 1867, the Cabinet was a body chosen 'to rule the nation' and was 'the most powerful body in the State' (*The English Constitution*,

Fontana edn 1963, pp. 67, 68). Since then power has drained away from the Cabinet – to the great departments of state, the prime minister, Cabinet committees, coteries of senior ministers, and even to organizations and groups outside government.

John P. Mackintosh, *The British Cabinet* (3rd edn 1977),
pp. 629–30

[T]he Cabinet is the place where certain categories of decisions are taken, disagreements ironed out and compromises registered but the principal policies of a government may not be and often are not originated in Cabinet. The key decisions of Mr Macmillan's Government to seek a summit meeting with Russia, America and France, to try to enter the Common Market and to go for industrial expansion, though shared with certain key ministers, were in a real sense his own. Similarly the central policies of Mr Wilson's first three years, again to mediate on Vietnam, to retain a presence East of Suez, to enter Europe and to defend the existing parity of the pound, though concerted with Mr Brown or Mr Callaghan, were his policies rather than those of the whole Cabinet. When a member of the Cabinet who wished to devalue the pound both after Labour took office and in July 1966, was later asked if a change of economic strategy was ever discussed in the Cabinet, he said 'No. And in any case I am keeping my head below the parapet.' This was one of the policies that was above or beyond the Cabinet and when it was adopted in November 1967, the decision was taken by Mr Wilson and Mr Callaghan and reported to the Cabinet.

In the 1945–51 Attlee Government the decision to develop a British atomic bomb was made by the Prime Minister and an inner group of leading ministers, Mr Attlee taking the view that 'the fewer people who were aware of what was happening, the better' (John P. Mackintosh, op. cit, p. 502). Similarly, in the 1974–9 Labour Government the critical decisions on development of the improved Polaris missile (Chevaline) and on support for a NATO programme of new theatre nuclear weapons in Europe, were taken not by the Cabinet but by small groups of ministers. In 1984 a controversial decision by the Government to ban trade union membership at the Government Communications Headquarters at Cheltenham was reported to have been taken by a group of ministers without discussion in the Cabinet. (See, e.g., *The Times* 7 February 1984.)

Richard Crossman expressed the view in 1963 that the Cabinet was becoming one of the 'dignified' (rather than 'efficient') elements of the constitution (Introduction to Bagehot, op. cit., p. 54); he repeated this view in his *Diaries of a Cabinet Minister* (3 vols. 1975–7), but his account of the actual working of the Cabinet gives a more equivocal impression of Cabinet power. Cabinet may have declined, but is not yet moribund. It is still possible to take a sanguine view of Cabinet government, as the following passage shows.

G. W. Jones, 'Development of the Cabinet', in William
Thornhill (ed.), *The Modernization of British Government*
(1975), pp. 31–32

The Cabinet has been belittled over the last 15 years by some commentators who
have relegated it from the 'efficient' to the 'dignified' part of the British Constitution.
They have discarded 'Cabinet Government', along with 'Parliamentary Government',
as apt descriptions of the nature of British central government in favour of 'Party
Government', 'Administrative Government', 'Prime Ministerial Government' or more
subtly 'Government by Prime Minister in Cabinet'. Even some who sensibly avoid
such titles and depict decision-making at the top as complex tend to denigrate the
Cabinet and allege that it has become so fragmented or diluted as now to be barely an
institution. It has disintegrated, they claim, into a number of other gatherings that take
the important decisions: inner cabinets, partial cabinets, Cabinet committees,
ministerial meetings and sessions between the Prime Minister and his ministers. For
this committee system the Cabinet is a kind of holding company: its meetings keep its
members informed of major policy developments, settle inter-departmental conflicts
and test opinion on large policy-issues, but rarely is it an effective decision-making
body. The Cabinet simply ratifies.

Assessing the validity of these assertions, while Cabinet records are closed to public
view under the 30-year rule, is a hazardous venture. Reliance must be placed on partial
accounts in biographies and memoirs of participants, on gossip purveyed by
journalists, and on scattered nuggets unearthed by academics. What emerges is that
the Cabinet is alive and doing well. Of course, many decisions are not taken by the
Cabinet, even decisions which have great consequences for millions of people, cost
millions of pounds and alter the development of the country, especially in the long-
term. But for the most politically important issues the Cabinet is the effective decision-
making body. These issues may not be the most 'objectively' or 'intrinsically'
important, particularly in terms of their long-run implications, but they are the most
contentious at the time. The Cabinet is no university seminar: it is a meeting where
divisive matters are settled. It has neither the time nor the inclination to discuss topics
on which its members are agreed or about which there is unlikely to be controversy in
the near future. The Cabinet meets to resolve conflicts between its members, and this
very purpose makes it a place of genuine collective decision-making.

The importance of the Cabinet is not diminished because much preliminary work is
carried out before it meets; in fact, its role is strengthened. Beforehand, non-
controversial points can be cleared away, so that the Cabinet can concentrate on the
undetermined items. Indeed, what has enabled the Cabinet to survive . . . as the central
decision-making institution, while government business has increased in amount and
complexity, is the elaborate network of arrangements through which government
business is transacted before the meetings of the Cabinet.

The Cabinet remains the prize of the political battle. Politics in Britain involves the
struggle between parties to win a majority at an election so as to be able to form a
Cabinet, and once formed it is the central driving force in government, arbitrating as
the final tribunal of policy and issuing authoritative directions, like the medieval
monarchs whose governmental powers it has inherited. The Cabinet is now the
political Crown of Britain, its supreme 'directive'. It responds to the political and
administrative pressures that demand governmental decisions. Since the demands are

mutually exclusive, contradictory, and seek more than resources allow, the Cabinet faces a gigantic task of satisfying, of reconciling, of persuading and of managing the conflicting forces. It can approve, reject or alter any proposal put to it; schemes carefully worked-out on prior occasions can be jettisoned.

Inner Cabinets

It is often said – by former Cabinet ministers among others – that the Cabinet is not an effective body for discussing matters of broad political principle or for working out general government policies. With the object of achieving a stronger strategic control prime ministers have from time to time formed groups or committees of leading ministers to formulate major policies and decide issues of great importance. Confirmation by the full Cabinet of decisions so taken by the inner group may be sought after the event but often in such a way as to leave little scope for reconsideration.

John P. Mackintosh, *The Government and Politics of Britain* (5th edn 1982), p. 68

Most Premiers have prior discussions with senior ministers and this has led to talk of 'inner Cabinets' or 'partial Cabinets'. Only Mr Wilson formally announced his arrangements at this level when he set up a 'Parliamentary Committee' in April 1968 to act as a steering committee on acute political issues which he replaced in April 1969 with a slightly smaller inner Cabinet with the same functions. But it appears that despite these bodies, Mr Wilson's conduct altered very little, most of his preliminary discussions being with the relevant ministers or with members of his own staff, though in 1969 he did dismiss Mr Callaghan from the Parliamentary Committee (leaving him in his office and in the Cabinet) for opposing a Cabinet decision on the National Executive of the party. In practice, no Prime Minister likes to go into the Cabinet without some idea of how his senior colleagues will react and he will usually consult some more than others. If this becomes frequent and convenient, talk of an inner Cabinet will arise.

In 1970 Mr Wilson denied the existence of an inner Cabinet, declaring that nothing of the kind was known to the constitution. (HC Deb. vol. 801, col. 198, 5 May 1970.)

An inner or partial Cabinet may be set up in response to a crisis. Small 'War Cabinets' controlled operations in the Suez War of 1956 and the Falklands War of 1982. The 'Egypt committee' set up in 1956 had a fluctuating membership and, as Seymour-Ure remarks (op. cit. below, p. 192), it is difficult to be certain how far the committee itself took decisions and how far discretion was exercised 'by the Prime Minister with a few colleagues *ad hoc*'. The full Cabinet ratified the most critical decisions, and took the final decision to launch the invasion. The War Cabinet which assumed the direction of the Falklands War was technically a sub-committee of the Cabinet's Defence Committee, but reported directly to the Cabinet. It consisted of the Prime

Minister, the Home Secretary, the Foreign Secretary, the Secretary of State for Defence, and the Paymaster General (who was the chairman of the Conservative Party). Major War Cabinet decisions were approved by the full Cabinet. Professor Seymour-Ure concludes an analysis of these War Cabinets and of the role of the Defence Committee in the Korean War as follows ('British "War Cabinets" in Limited Wars: Korea, Suez and the Falklands' (1984) 62 *Pub. Adm.* 181 at 199):

Luck and extemporization are intrinsic to crisis management. *Ad hoc* committees with flexible membership and terms of reference are probably a natural response . . . . For the political control of limited wars in a Cabinet system, however, War Cabinets, natural or not, do seem an uncomfortable arrangement. On one side, the War Cabinet has specialist support, day-to-day involvement and increasing experience. On the other side stands Parliament, a body, on the basis of Suez and the Falklands, liable to outbreaks of group hysteria – the very last assembly to determine war policy. In the middle sits the full Cabinet, flanked by a powerful executive committee too close to the war and an excited assembly too far away and too conscious of its electorate. In principle, the full Cabinet is the one group which in such queasy times can link the 'specialists' running the war to the 'politicians' in Parliament. Yet in practice, is it ever so weak as now? Where it should provide balance, perspective and steadiness, it seems to blink and nod. Like Parliament, it has a veto. But the dynamics of circumstance tend to preclude its use.

(c) **Cabinet committees**

Much of the work on government policy is done not in Cabinet but in committees of the Cabinet. Such committees have existed since the early nineteenth-century, but a fully organized committee system only became established as a normal part of Cabinet government after the Second World War. Standing committees of the Cabinet deal with matters of continuing governmental concern such as foreign affairs, economic policy, and the European Communities, and a new administration may retain much of the previous government's standing committee structure. *Ad hoc* committees are appointed to deal with specific and immediate issues of policy, or with current legislation, and are wound up when the work entrusted to them has been completed. At any time there may be between 15 and 25 standing committees and as many or more *ad hoc* committees (the latter customarily designated by the labels GEN or MISC), but the number is variable, and the present Government has fewer Cabinet committees than is usual.

Patrick Gordon Walker, *The Cabinet* (rev. edn 1972), p. 51

The Prime Minister sets up and disbands committees, appoints the chairmen and members and sets the terms of reference. Normally, besides the Ministers departmentally concerned, some other Ministers are put on committees to ensure that policies are broadly considered. Ministers can be represented by their junior Ministers. Often a non-departmental Minister is in the Chair: indeed a Cabinet today needs some such Ministers for this purpose – probably about four.

Considerable arguments and even dispute can arise over these matters. A Minister may consider that his prestige or his departmental interests are involved: where various departments have overlapping interests there may be competition for the chairmanship of a key committee. When a Cabinet Committee on Prices and Incomes was set up in 1967, Mr Roy Jenkins, Chancellor of the Exchequer, and Mrs Barbara Castle, the Minister in charge of administering the policy, both claimed the chairmanship. The Chancellor was given the chair by the Prime Minister.

Occasionally 'mixed' *ad hoc* committees are set up which include civil servants as well as ministers.

Cabinet committees consider some matters with a view to making a recommendation to the full Cabinet, but many questions are decided by the committees themselves. Every Cabinet committee, said Richard Crossman, 'is a microcosm of the Cabinet' (*Inside View*, 1972, p. 56); decisions of the committees have the same authority as those of the Cabinet itself.

> Minute on Cabinet Committee Procedure from Mr Harold Wilson to Ministers, 1970 (quoted by Richard Crossman, *The Diaries of a Cabinet Minister*, vol. 3 (1977), p. 861)

[I]t is clearly understood that Cabinet Committees operate by a devolution of authority from the Cabinet itself, and their procedure therefore follows the Cabinet's own procedure, particularly in the sense that it is the chairman's responsibility at the end of a discussion to specify clearly the decision which has been reached, and that he does so, not by counting heads, but by establishing the general consensus of view around the table. Nothing in these arrangements derogates or should be allowed to derogate from the right of any Minister to dissent from the final decision of a Committee, or to reserve his position to say that he wishes to appeal to the Cabinet. This is the basic right of all Ministers, and it must be maintained. Nevertheless like all rights it can be abused, and the abuse will weaken both the right itself and the whole system, which exists to preserve it. If the Cabinet system is to function effectively, appeals to Cabinet must clearly be infrequent. Chairmen of Committees must clearly be free to exercise their discretion in deciding whether to advise me to allow them. It goes without saying that they must not be made lightly, still less for reasons of mere obstructiveness, and if they are made they must carry with them the full authority of the Minister concerned, and must be supported by very compelling arguments. It is for these reasons that I decided some time ago that I would not entertain appeals to the Cabinet except after consultation with the chairman of the Committee concerned.

An arrangement of this sort made by one prime minister may be changed by his successor and it is rarely possible to be certain of the details of current practice concerning the Cabinet and its committees.

The system of Cabinet committees is not a publicly acknowledged part of the constitution. Governments normally do not announce the establishment or admit the existence of Cabinet committees and refuse to publish details of their responsibilities or membership.

Personal Minute from the Prime Minister, Mr James
Callaghan, to Ministers in Charge of Departments,
February 1978

Consistently with the practice of all former Prime Ministers I have always refused to
publish details of Cabinet Committees or to answer Questions in the House about
them. . . . There is, however, now some evidence that Select Committees would like to
interest themselves in the Committee system and may be seeking to erode the present
convention. I have therefore been considering the case for taking the initiative and
disclosing details of the Committee structure.

I accept that the present convention has certain disadvantages for us. In particular
non-disclosure makes it difficult to answer charges that the Government's policies are
not properly co-ordinated. For example the Select Committee on Overseas Development has recommended the establishment of a Cabinet Committee to co-ordinate
political, trade and aid policies towards the developing world largely because the
Ministry for Overseas Development were not able to disclose that such a committee
(RD) already exists. It is also arguable that non-disclosure is inconsistent with a policy
of greater openness. In any case some parts of the Committee structure are quite widely
known outside Government: in these cases what is at issue therefore is a refusal to admit
publicly what a lot of people know about privately.

It is important therefore to understand the reasons for the current practice of non-
disclosure. They are as follows: the Cabinet Committee system grew up as the load on
the Cabinet itself became too great. It allows matters of lesser importance to be decided
without troubling the whole Cabinet: and major issues to be clarified in order to save
the time of the Cabinet. The method adopted by Ministers for discussing policy
questions is however essentially a domestic matter: and a decision by a Cabinet
Committee, unless referred to the Cabinet, engages the collective responsibility of all
Ministers and has exactly the same authority as a decision by the Cabinet itself.
Disclosure that a particular Committee had dealt with a matter might lead to argument
about the status of the decision or demands that it should be endorsed by the whole
Cabinet. Furthermore publishing details of the Committees would be both misleading
and counter-productive. The existence of some could not be disclosed on security
grounds: others are set up to do a particular job and are then wound up. The absence of
a Committee on a particular subject (e.g. agriculture or poverty) does not mean that
the Government do not attach importance to it: and the fact that a particular Minister
is not on a committee does not mean that he does not attend when his interests are
affected. Publication would almost inevitably lead to pressures for both more and
larger Committees, and for disclosures of information about their activities.

I do not believe that we could in any event disclose the existence of the GEN [ad hoc]
groups. This is partly because of their ephemeral nature and partly because disclosure
would often reveal either that very sensitive subjects were under consideration or that
we had something in train about which we were not ready to make an announcement.
Disclosure of the main standing Committees would thus give a partial picture only.
Moreover having gone as far as this I do not believe that it would be possible for me to
hold the line and refuse to answer any further questions about the composition and
activities of the Committees. At the minimum we would be under pressure to reveal the
names of the Chairmen. This would make it harder for me to make changes: and it
would have implications for the responsibilities of Departmental Ministers since Select

Committees would try to summon the Chairmen of Cabinet Committees to give evidence in addition to the responsible Minister. I should also be under continuing pressure to say that a committee was considering a particular subject (and often it would be a GEN group): and there would be questions about when Committees were meeting, the work they were doing, whether particular Ministers are on them, the details of under-pinning Official Committees, etc.

I have therefore decided that we should not change our stance on this matter. The present convention is long established and provides a basis on which we can stand. Any departure from it would be more likely to whet appetites than to satisfy them. I ask my colleagues therefore to rest on the position that the way in which we co-ordinate our decisions is a matter internal to Government and not to answer questions about the Cabinet Committee system.

Mr Callaghan's successor, Mrs Thatcher, modified the practice by disclosing the existence (but not the membership or terms of reference) of four standing committees of the Cabinet: a defence and overseas policy committee, an economic strategy committee (both under the chairmanship of the Prime Minister), a home and social affairs committee (with the Home Secretary as chairman) and a legislation committee (with the Lord Chancellor as chairman). (See HC Deb. vol. 967, col. *179*w, 24 May 1979, and for some later changes: HC Deb. vol. 45, cols. 7–8w, 4 July 1983.)

Is it right to say that the arrangements for discussion of policy questions in government are 'essentially a domestic matter'? Would greater openness about the structure of Cabinet committees really be damaging to the process of decision-making in government?

(d) **The prime minister**

The office of prime minister is the creation of convention, and the role and powers of the prime minister still depend mainly on convention and political circumstances. It is now a firm convention that the prime minister should be a member of the House of Commons. The last peer to hold the office was Lord Salisbury (from 1895 to 1902); the Earl of Home disclaimed his peerage and sought election to the House of Commons when he became Prime Minister in 1963.

Since the person appointed by the Queen as prime minister will, as we have seen, normally be the leader of one or other of the political parties, eligibility for the office of prime minister is in practice determined by the election procedures of the parties. Indeed the Labour Party in 1957 formally adopted the principle that a Labour prime minister must have been elected as leader of the party. Before the June 1983 election the Liberal and Social Democratic parties jointly nominated a Prime Minister-designate (Mr Roy Jenkins) in case the Alliance should have the strongest claim to provide the prime minister.

The prime minister customarily holds the titular position of First Lord of the Treasury, and since 1968 has held the office of Minister for the Civil Service, with another minister exercising day-to-day responsibility. Exceptionally the prime minister takes control of a major department, as when Mr Harold Wilson assumed responsibility for the Department of Economic Affairs from 1967 to 1968 (assisted by a Secretary of State). In any event the prime minister has a general authority to intervene in any sphere of government and often takes a leading role in foreign relations, dealing directly with other heads of government.

John Mackintosh wrote in 1962 that the description of British government simply as 'Cabinet government' had become misleading, for 'the country is governed by the Prime Minister' (*The British Cabinet*, 1st edn 1962, p. 451; see also the 3rd edn, 1977, ch. 20). R. H. S. Crossman agreed with, and developed, this thesis.

Richard Crossman, *Inside View* (1972), pp. 62–7

I now turn to the role of Prime Minister and will try to explain why I think that Cabinet government has been developing into Prime Ministerial government. Here is my list of the relevant powers the Prime Minister wields.

(1) First of all, remember that each Minister fighting in the Cabinet for his Department can be sacked by the Prime Minister any day.... [E]ven though he is balancing forces in the Cabinet rather than ordering them, he has, in my view, tremendous power – something which any Cabinet Minister is aware of every day of his life. I am aware I am there at the Prime Minister's discretion. The Prime Minister can withdraw that discretion on any day he likes without stating a reason. And there's nothing much I can do about it – except succeed, and so build up my own strength.

(2) The second of the powers of the Prime Minister is that he decides the agenda of the Cabinet. Say that I think something is terribly important: I must get it through and I've had a row in the Cabinet committee. I register my dissent and ask for it to go to Cabinet. Somehow it does not occur on the agenda week after week. I fume – but the Prime Minister has the last word. The agenda is fixed in Number 10; and the two men who fix the agenda – the Prime Minister and the Secretary to the Cabinet – decide what issues shall be fought out, what shall not.

(3) Thirdly, the Prime Minister decides the organization of the Cabinet committees. What committees exist, how they are manned – above all, who are the chairmen – all this is entirely a matter for the Prime Minister.... [T]here are many ... issues, awkward issues where it is up to the Prime Minister to decide what kind of Cabinet committee the issue is put to. Shall it contain ten departmental Ministers; shall it be limited to Junior Ministers; or shall it be only three Senior Ministers? He's absolutely free to adjudicate to which members of the Cabinet or of the Government the issue shall be put in committee. He can in fact virtually decide whether the proposition is buried without ever coming to Cabinet, or whether it comes with certain amendments, or whether it is given top priority and pushed through intact.

Of course, all this has a tremendous effect on the doctrine of collective responsibility. This is a doctrine which many people ... regard as the distinguishing characteristic of British Cabinet government, but I am not so sure they all understand how it works today. In Bagehot's time collective responsibility used to mean that every member of the Cabinet had the right to take part in the Cabinet discussion; but after the discussion was over, he was bound by the decision which had been reached. That was the original notion; that's what you find in Bagehot.

Collective responsibility now means something totally different. It means that everybody who is in the Government must accept and publicly support every Cabinet decision, even if he was not present at the discussion or, frequently, was completely unaware the decision had been taken. As we have seen, collective decision-taking is now fragmented, and many major decisions may be taken by two, three, four or five Ministers. But the moment they have been taken, *and minuted*, they have the force of a decision taken by the whole Cabinet, and are binding on a hundred-odd members of the Government.

This is an interesting transformation of the old notion of collective responsibility, and it enormously increases Prime Ministerial power. There is all the difference in the world between a Prime Minister who had to carry twenty colleagues with him when anything of importance was being decided, and a new-style Prime Minister who has appointed some eighty members of his Government, each with a specific job to do, each permitted to hear only after the event nine-tenths of the decisions for which he shares collective responsibility. It is by this transformation that Cabinet government, in my view, has been evolved into what I call Prime Ministerial government.

(4) But that does not conclude the powers of the Prime Minister. . . . [H]e has almost a monopoly of patronage. He personally controls the Honours List. He has an unchallenged free hand in selecting new members of the House of Lords. This latter gives him a useful device for retiring ageing or incompetent Ministers without disgrace – purging his Government by promotion into the Upper Chamber. . . .

As for other appointments, paid and unpaid, there are many, many thousands which departmental Ministers make. All the important ones have to be approved, however, by Number 10 Downing Street. . . .

(5) Even more important than the control of patronage is the control of the Civil Service which a Prime Minister has exercised . . . since the period of Lloyd George. During World War 1, and up until 1919, the heads of the various Departments in Whitehall were mostly selected from inside the Department; and it was the Minister who made the decision . . . Lloyd George . . . sent out a minute which said that in future all heads of Departments would be appointed by the Permanent Secretary of the Treasury, in consultation with the Prime Minister. [Crossman goes on to describe the appointments system as it was in 1972. Today appointments to the two highest grades in the departments are made by the Prime Minister with the advice of a Senior Appointments Selection Committee, a group of Permanent Secretaries chaired by the Head of the Home Civil Service. The present Prime Minister, Mrs Thatcher, is reported to have played a more active role than her predecessors in the selection process.]

(6) His final power is his personal control of Government publicity. . . . [T]he media of mass publicity tend to personalize politics; and as our politics centre on Number 10, and as much of the political news is announced from Number 10, you can see how natural it is for the press to be fed with the Prime Minister's interpretation of Government policy, and to present him as the champion and spokesman of the whole Cabinet in the battle against the Shadow enemy on the other side.

Now I have listed his powers, do you see what I meant by Prime Ministerial government? It does not mean that he is a dictator; it does not mean he can tell his Ministers what to do in their Departments. But it does mean that in the battle of

Whitehall this man in the centre, this chairman, this man without a Department, without apparent power, can exert, when he is successful, a dominating personal control.

(See also Crossman's Introduction to Walter Bagehot, *The English Constitution*, Fontana edn 1963. The thesis of prime ministerial government recurs, but is also significantly qualified, in Crossman's *The Diaries of a Cabinet Minister*, 3 vols. 1975–7.)

Another former Cabinet minister, Mr Tony Benn, has emphasized the 'immense concentration of power in the hands of the prime minister', and the need to bring it under greater democratic control (*Arguments for Democracy*, 1981, ch. 2). Other writers have taken a more sceptical or qualified view of prime ministerial power. Graeme Moodie (*The Government of Great Britain*, 3rd edn 1971, pp. 99–100) points out that 'no powers are legally vested in the prime minister as such, but only in individual ministers or in the crown', and continues:

It is as chief adviser to the crown that the prime minister exercises governing power. With this may be contrasted the position of the American president with whom the prime minister is more and more frequently compared, but in whom alone, by the letter of the Constitution, is vested responsibility for the executive power of the federal government. To a greater extent than a president, therefore, the prime minister is constitutionally constrained to work with and through others. These others must, in virtue of this fact alone, place some limit on the prime minister's power, and thus share the burden of responsibility – a fact that may assist him in carrying the load of office as much as it may frustrate his personal wishes.

Moodie observes that even a 'strong' Prime Minister like Harold Wilson had to yield to opposition in the Cabinet as well as from Labour MPs and trade union leaders to his proposed reform of trade union law in 1969.

A. H. Hanson and Malcolm Walles, *Governing Britain* (4th edn 1984), pp. 134–5

It would, naturally, be too simplistic if, in our discussion of where power lies, we ignored the multiple sources of policy initiative that exist. Declared party policy, civil service recommendations, administrative necessities, the personal policies of Departmental Ministers, group representations, the pressure of events, all contribute to the composite that is a party's programme. The Prime Minister will make his own contribution – a contribution which may be especially valuable in the light of his special position – but he is not often in a position to *impose* his will. For example, when Harold Macmillan decided to promote British entry into the Common Market he could not force the policy upon the Cabinet. It took several months of persuasion before the climate of opinion was such that attempts to implement the policy could be made. . . .

The Prime Minister's most significant task does still remain one of persuasion and negotiation. He is undoubtedly the most important member of the Cabinet, and this increases the persuasiveness of his arguments, but this is some way from a totally 'Prime Ministerial system' that would have him the sole fount of policy and the master of his colleagues. He is Prime Minister because his fellow party members are prepared to accept him as such. He remains in office for just so long as that acceptance continues. What he makes of the power of the office is dependent upon many factors – such variables as his own ability and personality; the ability and status of the principal members of the Cabinet; the existence or not of an obvious and acceptable alternative leader; the state of the nation; the ends he is seeking to promote. What is certain is that, unless certain Cabinet members are prepared to abdicate, in the sense that they are ready to accept without question his policies and his leads, the Prime Minister is very much a member of a team and must act accordingly.

> Gillian Peele, 'Government at the Centre', in Henry Drucker *et al*. (eds.), *Developments in British Politics* (1983), pp. 101–2

Thatcher's premiership [from 1979–83] appears to divide into two parts. The first part, which lasted from May 1979 until the reshuffle of September 1981, saw Thatcher as an assertive premier but one whose cabinet was in many ways not her own. She had felt the need in forming her government to bring in men such as Peter Walker, a close associate of Edward Heath's, had tried to balance the cabinet between 'wets' and 'dries' and had few really close supporters among the most senior figures in the cabinet. Thus, although prime minister, she often seemed to be in a minority position within her own cabinet. . . . [T]his early period was one in which cabinet disagreements both occurred regularly and were reported regularly.

From the autumn reshuffle of 1981 onwards, however, she appeared much more in control. The removal of Lord Soames, Sir Ian Gilmour and Norman St John Stevas and the promotion of Lady Young made the cabinet more reflective of her views; and the Falklands campaign enabled her to rebuild her national popularity (which had slumped) and to acquire a massive dominance over the cabinet. . . .

Such . . . features of Thatcher's style of cabinet government as can be discerned from the evidence point to an emphasis on efficiency rather than prolonged debate. She seems to favour a more streamlined cabinet committee structure than her predecessors and is unsympathetic to extensive debate in full cabinet.

How would the position and authority of the prime minister be likely to be affected if coalition government should become usual in Britain?

(On the question of prime ministerial power see further A. H. Brown, 'Prime Ministerial Power' [1968] *PL* 28, 96; Patrick Weller, 'The Vulnerability of Prime Ministers: A Comparative Perspective' (1983) 36 *Parliamentary Affairs* 96; Robert Blake, *The Office of Prime Minister* (1975); and a good summing-up by James Barber in R. L. Borthwick and J. E. Spence (eds.), *British Politics in Perspective* (1984).)

A Prime Minister's Department?

Cabinet government assumes a collective leadership of ministers, even if one of their number is *primus inter pares*. This indeed is the basis of the 'collective responsibility' of ministers to Parliament. Some maintain that the collective leadership of Cabinet government, in accommodating the views of different ministers through bargain and compromise, cramps decision-making and results in makeshift policies. (See p. 129 above.) These argue for *strengthened* power at the centre, with more resources of information, policy analysis and advice being made available to the prime minister to assist him or her in developing the general strategy of the government. Some take this further in arguing for the establishment of a Prime Minister's Department.

> Sir Kenneth Berrill, *Strength at the Centre – The Case for a Prime*
> *Minister's Department* (Stamp Memorial Lecture, 1980), pp. 4–7

The power of a Prime Minister to intervene in any field at any time is clear enough (and prime ministerial intervention is a significant force indeed). The more interesting question is why they should feel the need to do so? There are a number of reasons and taken together they seem to me both to explain the increase in the role of the head of government in most industrial democracies and to suggest that this increase will continue inexorably.

The first and perhaps the most powerful reason for prime ministerial intervention can be expressed in the form 'The Centre is the guardian of the strategy and the Prime Minister is the mainstay of the Centre'. In opposition shadow cabinets can spend a considerable amount of time working out their strategy for putting the country to rights when they get back to power. Each member of the shadow cabinet has a department he is shadowing but since he is not actually in charge its problems do not pre-occupy his mind. Inevitably things are different when the shadow cabinet becomes the real cabinet and each member moves into his department, for the basis of the departmental system is that each 'fights its own corner'. . . . Their job is to fight for their own programmes, their own public expenditure, their own share of the legislative timetable. Inevitably they come to see the world and any proposed action in terms of the possible effect on their particular interests and objectives. . . .

But the sum of spending departments' interests can be a long way from adding up to a coherent strategy and no one is more aware of this than a Prime Minister. A Prime Minister knows only too well that the Government will be judged at the next election more on its overall performance than on its success or failure in particular departmental areas. . . . Hence the importance of sufficient 'strength at the centre' to hold the balance in any decision between the requirements of the strategy and the crosspulls of the interests of the different spending departments. . . .

The second reason for widespread prime ministerial concern and involvement is less basic but is a powerful influence nonetheless. It is the tendency of the media and the public to hold the Government responsible for virtually any problem that arises in both the public and the private sectors and to identify the Government's reaction to the problem with the persona of the Prime Minister. Internationally as well as domestically governments are expected to have a view, a policy, a programme of action for virtually everything. . . .

This wide public expectation of the role of government is allied to the increased personalisation of government. . . . [A]t bottom the media and the public think and talk of Mrs Thatcher's government or Mr Callaghan's. They lay the ultimate responsibility for virtually every act or omission by the Government at the door of the Prime Minister who must expect to be attacked on any of them and be ready to answer in any interview and at Question Time in Parliament. Small wonder then that a Prime Minister should feel the need to try to keep an eye on everything and be tempted into fire-fighting intervention on issues which look like causing political difficulties.

The first two reasons for very wide prime ministerial involvement are then (1) the need for the centre to keep the balance on every decision between departmental objectives and strategic objectives and (2) the need to be ready to answer to the media and Parliament for virtually every government action. The third reason, and in recent years it has become one of ever increasing weight, is the growth in personal contact between heads of government, to such an extent that we expect to read daily in our newspapers of personal visits by one head of government to another.

These contacts take place at formal 'summits' in a variety of different fora (EEC, Commonwealth, major OECD countries, etc.); by bilateral visits, and through unpublicised messages and telephone conversations. . . . A head of government cannot always have the relevant cabinet minister by his side nor leave it to him to do all the talking. The head of government must know the facts and have views on the objectives, the strategy and the tactics across a very wide range of issues in their international context. The importance of this preparation and briefing hardly needs stressing for if heads of government come to an understanding, even an informal one, that is bound to have a major influence on policy.

No matter what his priorities, in today's world it is just not open to a head of government to devote himself very largely to his country's domestic problems. In a country like Britain the Prime Minister is involved every week and sometimes every day in international visits and contacts, and the frequency seems continually to rise. This international involvement provides the third powerful force which is moulding the role of head of government towards a wider and more interventionist role.

The prime minister has a private office which provides administrative services, advice and information, and maintains the lines of communication to the departments. Its resources are not comparable with those of a government department. In addition a small Policy Unit at 10 Downing Street employs specialists from outside the Civil Service to advise the prime minister from a standpoint of political sympathy with the government. The Cabinet Office works for the prime minister and for the Cabinet as a whole. Sir Kenneth Berrill questions whether this support system has developed adequately 'in parallel with the degree and width of prime ministerial involvement', and finds that other countries with prime ministerial systems (such as Australia) have substantially larger supporting staffs for the premier. He concludes as follows (pp. 13–15):

In today's world the support system for the head of government is a subject of increasing importance. Our competitors have, by and large, faced this issue and come to some structured solutions which have put rather more resources into the area than we have been prepared to do. We have preferred to keep a very small staff at No. 10 and rely on incremental changes in the Cabinet Office and on the flexibility of those who work there.

If there were to be a more public discussion my own argument would not be for massive change. Britain is a prime ministerial democracy, not a presidential form of government. . . . The prime ministerial load is already too heavy to take on yet more detailed responsibilities. What in my view is at issue is whether a Prime Minister should have a support system with time to work on problems in some depth across the width of government activities. . . .

An across the board support system for a Prime Minister of adequate depth seems a simple enough issue and one where the expense involved is tiny in relation to the issues involved. A simple question but it raises many issues. Would these extra staff just be added to the Cabinet Office secretariat and work both for the Prime Minister and cabinet or would they work for the Prime Minister alone? would they all be drawn from the public service or from outside? would they be political or non-political appointments? etc.

. . . Of one thing I am sure: we *do* need strength at the centre if as a nation we are to find a way out of our troubles. The role of a Prime Minister at the centre has increased, is still increasing and will not be diminished. We will be foolish if we do not face up to that fact and structure our arrangements adequately.

Sir Douglas Wass, a former Joint Head of the Home Civil Service, is not persuaded that a Prime Minister's Department is desirable. In his opinion the fact that it is the Cabinet, and not the prime minister alone, that has the power to take major policy decisions 'has provided us with a valuable constitutional check', and he believes that it would be inconsistent with the principle of collective responsibility and a significant step towards a 'presidential' form of government for the prime minister to be given 'the responsibility and the means to co-ordinate policy, to order priorities and to challenge in detail the proposals of individual departments' (*Government and the Governed*, 1984, pp. 32–4). (Compare the views of Edmund Dell, p. 129 above, and see further Patrick Weller, 'Do Prime Ministers' Departments Really Create Problems?' (1983) 61 *Pub. Adm.* 59, and the Rejoinder by G. W. Jones, id. p. 79.)

(e) Ministerial solidarity

The convention of collective ministerial responsibility obliges ministers to support and defend the policies and decisions of the government to which they belong. The classic or strict version of this principle requires a minister to resign from office if he feels bound to express public dissent from government policies.

The principle of collective solidarity began as a political expedient for opposing the authority of the King and managing Parliament; it was fortified by the development of party cohesion in the nineteenth century. Lord Salisbury gave his emphatic endorsement to the principle in 1878.

House of Lords, 8 April 1878 (Parl. Deb. 3rd series, vol. 239, cols. 833–4)

LORD SALISBURY: Now, my Lords, am I not defending a great Constitutional principle, when I say that, for all that passes in a Cabinet, each Member of it who does not resign is absolutely and irretrievably responsible, and that he has no right afterwards to say that he agreed in one case to a compromise, while in another he was persuaded by one of his Colleagues. Consider the inconvenience which will arise if such a great Constitutional law is not respected. . . . It is, I maintain, only on the principle that absolute responsibility is undertaken by every Member of a Cabinet who, after a decision is arrived at, remains a Member of it, that the joint responsibility of Ministers to Parliament can be upheld, and one of the most essential conditions of Parliamentary responsibility established.

The principle is in the interest of the government, which is able to present a united front against the Opposition. In this respect it seems to be essentially a feature of the party political system, and we find that a similar convention is observed by the Opposition, whose frontbench spokesmen are expected to uphold Opposition party policies. But it can also be claimed that the convention has a wider 'constitutional' function, in that it makes for coherent and accountable government and the loyalty of ministers to policies which have been approved by the electorate.

But the convention of collective responsibility exacts its price. By stifling open dissent it contributes to secrecy in government: questions of public importance which may be strongly contested between ministers are not aired in a way that enables public opinion to be expressed before decisions are reached – the argument goes on behind the screen of collective responsibility. Also, since the convention extends to all ministers (not only those in the Cabinet) and even, if perhaps in a weaker form, to Parliamentary Private Secretaries to ministers, over 100 MPs on the government side are required to give unqualified support to government policies, as a condition of retaining their positions. In this way the convention helps to strengthen the government's control over Parliament.

In practice, however, prime ministers often find it impolitic to insist on a strict observance of the obligations of ministerial solidarity. Indeed, on a few occasions the convention has been formally suspended, with a publicly announced 'agreement to differ' on some issue of importance. A famous instance of this occurred in 1932. The National Government, constituted the year before under Ramsay MacDonald to deal with a financial crisis, proposed to introduce tariffs; four Cabinet Ministers, convinced free-traders, were unable to agree. In the emergency it was considered important to keep the Government together, so a compromise was reached by which the dissenting Ministers were allowed to speak and vote against tariffs, while remaining in the government. This arrangement has been regarded with disfavour by most writers on the constitution. Jennings described it as 'an attempt to break down the party system and to substitute government by individuals for government by political principles' (*Cabinet Government*, 3rd edn 1959, p. 281). In 1975 there was again an agreement to differ on the issue of United Kingdom membership of the European Communities. The Labour Government had decided to submit the question of continued membership (on the terms renegotiated by the Government) to a referendum and to recommend the electorate to vote for remaining in the Community. Seven Cabinet Ministers who dissented from the Government's recommendation were allowed to oppose it in the referendum campaign.

House of Commons, 23 January 1975 (HC Deb. vol. 884, col. 1746)

The Prime Minister (MR HAROLD WILSON): . . . When the outcome of renegotiation is known, the government will decide upon their own recommendation to the country, whether for continued membership of the Community on the basis of the renegotiated terms, or for withdrawal, and will announce their decision to the House in due course. . . .

The circumstances of this referendum are unique, and the issue to be decided is one on which strong views have long been held which cross party lines. The Cabinet has, therefore, decided that, if when the time comes there are members of the government, including members of the Cabinet, who do not feel able to accept and support the Government's recommendation, whatever it may be, they will, once the recommendation has been announced, be free to support and speak in favour of a different conclusion in the referendum campaign.

House of Commons, 7 April 1975 (HC Deb. vol. 889, col. 351w)

THE PRIME MINISTER: In accordance with my statement in the House on 23rd January last, those Ministers who do not agree with the Government's recommendation in favour of continued membership of the Euopean Community are, in the unique circumstances of the referendum, now free to advocate a different view during the referendum campaign in the country.

This freedom does not extend to parliamentary proceedings and official business. Government business in Parliament will continue to be handled by all Ministers in accordance with Government policy. Ministers responsible for European aspects of Government business who themselves differ from the Government's recommendation on membership of the European Community will state the Government's position and will not be drawn into making points against the Government recommendation. Wherever necessary Questions will be transferred to other Ministers. At meetings of the Council of Ministers of the European Community and at other Community meetings, the United Kingdom position in all fields will continue to reflect Government policy.

I have asked all Ministers to make their contributions to the public campaign in terms of issues, to avoid personalising or trivialising the argument, and not to allow themselves to appear in direct confrontation, on the same platform or programme, with another Minister who takes a different view on the Government recommendation.

This arrangement helped to keep the Government together. Was it also in the public interest?

In 1977 collective responsibility was again suspended, to allow dissenting ministers to vote against the principle of the European Assembly Elections Bill – which provided, in accordance with government policy, for direct elections to the European Parliament – at its second reading. Questioned in the House of Commons about collective responsibility the Prime Minister (Mr Callaghan) replied (HC Deb. vol. 933, col. 552, 16 June 1977):

I certainly think that the doctrine should apply, except in cases where I announce that it does not.

This was brusquely said, and has been cited as a cynical disregard of constitutional proprieties. But we must ask with Marshall (*Constitutional Conventions*, p. 8) whether it does 'represent a breach of any constitutional duty to the House of Commons if freedom to speak or vote against cabinet policy [is] willingly conceded by the Cabinet to individual Cabinet Ministers?'

Formal suspensions of the convention have been rare and controversial; a more commonplace and frequent mitigation of collective responsibility is provided by the 'unattributable ministerial leak'.

Patrick Gordon Walker, *The Cabinet* (rev. edn 1972), pp. 33–4, 35, 38–9

The unattributable leak involves the disclosure of . . . matters that are secret only because of the doctrine of collective responsibility – such as the subject of Cabinet discussion, Cabinet decisions, views assigned to different Ministers and the like. The leak gives information known only to members of the Cabinet; being unattributable, it does not breach the doctrine that Ministers do not attack one another in public.

An element of concealment was inherent in the very concept of collective responsibility. The doctrine that the Cabinet must appear to be united presupposed Cabinet divisions that had not been reconciled. Ministers must in the nature of things have differences but they must outwardly appear to have none. Collective responsibility must therefore to some extent be a mask worn by the Cabinet.

The self-same conditions of mass democracy that gave rise to collective responsibility produced the unattributable leak. The maintenance of secrecy imposed by the doctrine became intolerable. This for two main reasons.

First, Ministers were political creatures living in a political world. As party leaders they accepted the need for the doctrine of collective responsibility: but as political creatures they felt it sometimes necessary to let their political views be unofficially known.

Secondly, the Press began to try and tear away the mask from the face of the Cabinet: their readers became increasingly interested in being informed about 'secrets' that were felt to be of a political and not a security nature. . . . From [the 1880s] the unattributable leak became a feature of the Cabinet system. The main motives for leaks by Ministers became the desire to inform – or to mislead – their followers in the Parliamentary party about the stand they had taken in the Cabinet on a particular issue; or the attempt to mobilize party or public opinion behind a view that was being argued in Cabinet. . . .

Thus the doctrine of collective responsibility and the unattributable leak grew up side by side as an inevitable feature of the Cabinet in a mass two-party system. In every Cabinet the leak will be deplored and condemned; but it is paradoxically necessary to the preservation of the doctrine of collective responsibility. It is the mechanism by which the doctrine of collective responsibility is reconciled with political reality. The unattributable leak is itself a recognition and acceptance of the doctrine that members of a Cabinet do not disagree in public.

Leaking is practised by prime ministers as well as by other members of the Cabinet. If a necessary palliative of collective responsibility, it is no substitute for open government: leaked information is often unreliable and at its worst the practice is a technique for misleading the public. (See Michael Cockerell, Peter Hennessy and David Walker, *Sources Close to the Prime Minister*, 1984, ch. 7.)

It happens from time to time that a minister flouts convention by disagreeing in public with government policy. This may result in his dismissal. When a junior naval minister made a speech in 1981 criticizing the Government's proposed reduction of the surface fleet he was promptly dismissed by Mrs Thatcher, who said, 'Ministers should fight departmental battles within the Department and not outside' (HC Deb. vol. 5, col. 151, 19 May 1981). But sometimes the breach results in nothing more than a prime ministerial rebuke or is simply overlooked. In 1974 after a Minister of State had publicly criticized a government decision to complete the delivery of warships to a tyrannical regime in Chile, the Prime Minister (Mr Harold Wilson) was asked in the House of Commons to say what his policy was with regard to collective responsibility. He replied (HC Deb. vol. 873, col. 1103, 14 May 1974):

All members of the Government share a collective responsibility for the policies of Her Majesty's Government. I have recently reminded my right hon. and hon. Friends in the administration that, where any conflict of loyalties arises, the principle of the collective responsibility of the Government is absolute and overriding in all circumstances.

Dissenting ministers sometimes choose to resign in emphatic repudiation of government policy, and in these instances we seem to see the convention of collective responsibility dramatically confirmed. But resignations (like dismissals) by no means automatically follow breaches of ministerial solidarity and are largely a matter of political calculation; in this respect it appears that we are dealing with an 'optional convention' (P. J. Madgwick in V. Herman and J. E. Alt (eds.), *Cabinet Studies: A Reader*, 1975, p. 98).

The relaxation of the convention in recent times has alarmed some observers.

'The Principle that Counts', leading article, *The Times*, 1 May 1976

... A number of Labour Ministers over the years have experienced a conflicting tug of loyalties between the party on the one hand and the government on the other. They may be elected to office within the party as well as appointed to office within the government. It is therefore often argued that in such cases they have a double obligation, to those who have elected them to party office as well as to the government in which they serve, and that when they speak in the National Executive Committee [of the Labour Party] they cannot do so only as Ministers. On top of that, there is the knowledge that many Ministers down the years have made an open secret of their disagreements with colleagues – not only when they have been licensed to do so at such a special time as a referendum – and that the case for taking a personal stand is all the greater at a time of national doubt and confusion.

There is a seductive logic in these arguments. But the principle of collective responsibility matters if anything even more at such a time. It is the government collectively who are responsible to Parliament and the nation. If Ministers are not prepared to stand up for the unpopular as well as any popular decisions then the exercise of government becomes more haphazard and uncoordinated than it need be. It is one of the weaknesses of the British system that the policies of one department all too often fail to support the policies of another, that these bureaucratic boundaries are allowed to be an impediment to the public good. That evil, great enough as it is, would be even worse if Ministers had no obligation to take responsibility for anything that happened beyond their own departmental walls. At a time when the old loyalties of British politics are dissolving it becomes all the more essential to hold fast to certain principles of good government.

Professor Nevil Johnson discerns a 'retreat into constitutional anarchy' if collective responsibility can at any time be waived by the prime minister, and expresses the sombre belief that 'our constitution has atrophied to a point at which it expresses only one principle, namely that any rule or convention thought to be part of it may be suspended or evaded if the government of the day believes that this is required for the sake of holding together the party in power' (letter to *The Times*, 22 June 1977). But an inflexible insistence on ministerial solidarity is not manifestly for the public good, and its relaxation might contribute to more open and honest government and better informed public debate. Political controversy often takes place *within* rather than *between* the political parties – especially when there is a consensus on particular policies between the party leaderships – and collective responsibility may confine or even effectively suppress this necessary conflict.

Anthony Wedgwood Benn, 'Democracy in the Age of Science'
(1979) 50 *Political Quarterly* 7, 18–19

... [T]he constitutional convention of collective Cabinet responsibility which is thought to be central to the working of the British Constitution has considerable implications for secrecy of government. Under this doctrine the myth of Cabinet unity on all matters discussed is fostered. Cabinets are, of course, rarely united in their views. Indeed, were it so there would be no Cabinet discussion at all. . . .

Common sense and ordinary personal loyalty must require defeated minorities to accept the majority decision and to explain and defend it. But there is no reason whatsoever why this necessary and sensible principle should be extended to the necessarily false pretence that no alternative policies were considered, no real debate took place, and that everyone present was convinced of the merits of the majority view –

as distinct from accepting that it was the majority view and that as such it should be supported. The narrow interpretation of collective Cabinet responsibility denies citizens essential knowledge of the processes by which their government reaches its decisions.

Ian Gilmour, *The Body Politic* (2nd edn 1971), pp. 13–15

Conflict within a government department is shielded from the public and parliament by the dogma of [individual] ministerial responsibility. Similarly, conflict within the Cabinet is hidden by the doctrine of Cabinet responsibility. Conflict between departments at a lower level is concealed because of the belief that there is only one government and it must not disagree with itself in public.

. . . [T]here is too much agreement and compromise in British government. The absence of conflict causes weakness. The essence of the British political system is that it is more important to travel peacefully than to arrive. . . .

More public conflict in the governmental system would not in the long run produce more social conflict. There is a clear distinction between the two things. It is the job of politicians to reconcile conflicts and to diminish social dissension. . . . But it is not the job of politicians to abolish or conceal all public conflict in the governmental system. More governmental conflict would produce more public awareness and a more active consensus, not the consensus of stagnation.

(f) **Government departments**

D. N. Chester and F. M. G. Willson, *The Organization of British Central Government 1914–1964* (2nd edn 1968), pp. 16–17, 391, 399

The Ministers are assisted by departments. A departmental Minister is responsible for one or more departments: thus . . . the Chancellor of the Exchequer is responsible for several departments in addition to the Treasury. A department may have one of a variety of titles. If it is a large department established during the last half century it is quite likely to have the formal name 'Ministry', and the bigger departments are sometimes referred to collectively as 'Ministries'. There is no important constitutional distinction between the term 'Ministry' and the term 'Department'.

. . . [D]espite the existence of a number of marginal cases, it is possible without too much equivocation to draw a line round about thirty major departments, together with some forty or fifty minor departments, and refer to them collectively as the central administration. . . . [T]he work of Ministers and the major departments has always been the core of British central government. The work of the various departments differs very much and their autonomy is real and important. But . . . [t]hey share a number of common features of organization, they are nearly all staffed by the members of a unified Civil Service (who may pass from one department to another in the course of their careers), and they are bound by the collective responsibility of Ministers to co-ordinate their work so as to ensure that policies do not conflict. . . .

A variety of factors influences the upper and lower limits to the number of departmental Ministers at any one time. In British experience the most powerful pressure forcing an increase in the number has been the relentless growth in the functions and responsibilities of the central government, which in turn has resulted in some ministries becoming too large for their Ministers to control effectively. . . . [T]he distribution of functions between different Ministers must as far as possible be such as to make it clear who is responsible for any major issue of governmental policy. Any distribution which blurred the responsibility for any important field of government policy over two or three Ministers would be most unlikely to work satisfactorily as regards Parliament and the public and even as regards the working of the Cabinet system as a whole.

A feature of the 1960s and early 1970s was the bringing together of a number of related governmental functions in new departments, some of them of considerable size and popularly described as 'giant' departments. A reconstituted Ministry of Defence absorbed the Admiralty, the War Office and the Air Ministry in 1964, and in 1968 two new departments were created by merging the Foreign Office with the Commonwealth Office and the Ministry of Health with the Ministry of Social Security. The Department of the Environment, set up in 1970, took over the functions of three former Ministries – Housing and Local Government, Public Building and Works, and Transport. (But Transport has since been reconstituted as a separate department: see p. 66 above.) Another 'giant' established in the same year, the Department of Trade and Industry, was short-lived, its functions devolving for a time upon the three Departments of Energy, Industry and Trade. But Trade and Industry were re-united in 1983. At present the departments which account for the bulk of government expenditure and civil service manpower are the Departments of Health and Social Security, Employment, Trade and Industry, and Environment, the Ministry of Defence, and the Boards of Inland Revenue and Customs and Excise.

The departmental system is a flexible one and alterations are frequently made in the structure and responsibilities of departments. But repeated changes are costly and disruptive of the work of administration. The present Prime Minister has extinguished three departments – the Ministry of Overseas Development, the Department of Prices and Consumer Protection, and the Civil Service Department – besides merging Trade and Industry. Christopher Pollitt points out that of 28 new departments created between 1960 and 1979, 13 had died by 1981 ((1982) 60 *Pub. Adm.* 73). There are altogether about 70 departments, great and small. For each of them some or other senior minister has ultimate responsibility.

(g) Non-departmental public bodies

On the fringes of central government there is a large constellation of commissions, boards, committees and other bodies which are involved in manifold ways in the process of government. *Advisory* committees are set up to provide specialized advice and to enlist the cooperation of outside interest groups in government policy-making. Our present concern is rather with *executive* bodies which perform various administrative or regulatory functions on behalf of government. These are sometimes termed 'fringe bodies', and the acronym QUANGO (quasi-autonomous non-governmental organization) has been coined for them, but they are in fact closely linked with central government and their functions are of a governmental nature. (We are not concerned in this section with the bodies managing nationalized industries.) Although publicly funded, fringe bodies generally enjoy a high degree of autonomy, but 'departmental forces of varying power operate upon them' (Gordon Bowen, *Survey of Fringe Bodies*, 1978, p. 7). Some have been set up by statute, others under the prerogative or by administrative acts of ministers. The following are a few of the better-known ones:

> Advisory, Conciliation and Arbitration Service
> Arts Council of Great Britain
> Civil Aviation Authority
> Commission for Racial Equality
> Council on Tribunals
> Criminal Injuries Compensation Board
> Equal Opportunities Commission
> Gaming Board for Great Britain
> Health and Safety Commission
> Manpower Services Commission
> Medical Research Council
> National Economic Development Council
> Police Complaints Authority

These and many other bodies have been set up to harness expertise only available outside the civil service or to carry out functions which it is thought should be removed from political influences or be free from the constraints of civil service organization.

Gordon Bowen, *Survey of Fringe Bodies* (1978), pp. 33–4

There is no single criterion which would serve as an unambiguous indicator of a fringe body. Nor is there any accepted concise definition. It therefore seems only practicable to proceed by setting out a group of characteristic features of fringe bodies. Although few of them will display all of these characteristics, many fringe bodies will possess a number of them and can thereby be recognised as belonging to the category of governmental instruments to which the term 'fringe bodies' is applied. The main characteristics are:

a. A fringe body derives from a ministerial decision to establish a special institution to perform a particular defined function on behalf of the Government, or a decision to take over or adapt an existing institution for that purpose.

b. A fringe body is responsible to a Minister for carrying out the designated function. It is free to do this in its own way within the limits set by its terms of reference and by the resources conditionally allocated to it. A Minister is generally answerable to

Parliament for terms of reference of a fringe body and any statement of its functions as well as for the financial provision made for Exchequer funds for its work. He is not however answerable for particular acts of a fringe body nor does he normally concern himself with its day-to-day operations.

c. A fringe body's existence is characteristically sanctioned by an Act of Parliament or an Order under an Act. There is however a range of constitutional instruments by which a fringe body can be established. Some fringe bodies are registered under the Companies Act as companies limited by guarantee to establish their corporate status; some are registered as Charities.

d. Fringe bodies are not normally Crown bodies nor do they act on behalf of the Crown; there are however some important exceptions to this statement. [E.g., the Manpower Services Commission.]

e. A fringe body is normally financed by a grant-in-aid or by a statutory levy and not off the face of a departmental Vote but there are some so financed. Fringe bodies may draw funds through more than one channel and Non-Exchequer funds may be a significant part of their income.

f. The Chairman and Members of the board or council of a fringe body are appointed by a Minister (in a dozen instances by the Prime Minister) and they can presumably be dismissed by him. . . .

g. The Board of a fringe body recruits and employs its own staff who are not civil servants; there are some exceptional instances of fringe bodies whose staff are civil servants. . . .

h. The accounts of most fringe bodies are audited commercially and are then submitted to the Minister. . . . The annual accounts are normally laid before Parliament by the sponsoring Minister.

j. Most fringe bodies are required to produce an Annual Report which the responsible Minister lays before Parliament.

Fringe bodies have not developed in a coherent fashion and there is an evident lack of consistency in their legal status, organization, funding and degree of autonomy.

Over 20,000 members of non-departmental public bodies are appointed by ministers, assisted by a Public Appointments Unit in the civil service which maintains a list of 'the Great and the Good' considered suitable for appointment. This places a considerable number of posts, many of them carrying salaries or other emoluments, in the gift of ministers. (See Anne Davies, 'Patronage and Quasi-Government: Some Proposals for Reform', in Anthony Barker (ed.), *Quangos in Britain*, 1982, p. 167.)

An official survey in 1980 discovered 489 'executive' and 1561 'advisory' non-departmental bodies (*Report on Non-Departmental Public Bodies*, Cmnd 7797). The Thatcher Government had by then begun a critical scrutiny of the work of these bodies and since 1979 a number have been abolished as 'non-essential' and others reduced in size and scope. But a considerable number of fringe bodies have survived this culling and new ones continue to be created. No government can do without the expert services that can be secured by this means, and the desirability of keeping some executive functions separate from government departments is generally admitted.

Control and accountability

The independence which is believed necessary to the proper functioning of non-departmental bodies gives rise to problems of control and accountability. Organizations to which governmental functions and public money are entrusted cannot be left to operate as uncontrolled seigniories. Powers of intervention – e.g. to give binding directions or to call for information – are generally reserved to the minister, who also has the ultimate power of dismissal (or non-renewal of appointments). Ministers are accountable to Parliament for the exercise of these powers, but beyond this are not answerable for the day-to-day activities of fringe bodies.

The annual reports of many of the fringe bodies are laid before Parliament. The select committees of the House of Commons which monitor the work of the principal government departments are empowered to examine the 'associated public bodies' of these departments, but the resources of the committees do not allow of a regular and systematic scrutiny of all of them. A few fringe bodies are within the jurisdiction of the Parliamentary Commissioner for Administration – e.g., the Advisory, Conciliation and Arbitration Service and the Manpower Services Commission – but the great majority are not.

The National Audit Act 1983 now empowers the Comptroller and Auditor General to carry out 'value for money' audits of many of the fringe bodies, and to report the results to the House of Commons. (See sections 6, 7 and 9 of the Act.)

A degree of control is also exercised by the courts. Bodies created by statute are held by the courts to the limits of their statutory powers under the doctrine of ultra vires: a case of this kind was *Anisminic Ltd* v. *Foreign Compensation Commission* [1969] 2 AC 147, in which the House of Lords struck down a decision of the Commission as having been made outside its jurisdiction. A public body is also open to legal challenge on the ground that it misapplied the rules (even if non-statutory) under which it operates (*R.* v. *Criminal Injuries Compensation Board, ex p. Schofield* [1971] 1 WLR 926), or that it failed to act fairly in deciding a question affecting the rights or interests of an individual (cf. *R.* v. *Gaming Board, ex p. Benaim and Khaida* [1970] 2 QB 417).

An Australian Royal Commission on Government Administration has warned (Parliamentary Paper No. 185/1976, para. 4.4.26) that, taken to extremes, the creation of non-departmental bodies

could represent a substantial modification of the constitutional system through the addition of what would amount to a fourth branch of government, separate from the executive branch and largely exempt from the operation of the constitutional conventions which harness the executive to the legislature.

On fringe bodies see further P. P. Craig, *Administrative Law* (1983), pp. 107–26.

(h) **The Civil Service**

Civil servants are servants of the Crown employed in a civil capacity in government departments. There is no all-purpose legal definition of a civil servant, but a definition adopted by the Fulton Committee in 1968 (Cmnd 3638, App. A) declares that civil servants are

servants of the Crown, other than holders of political or judicial offices, who are employed in a civil capacity and whose remuneration is paid wholly and directly out of monies voted by Parliament.

Besides judges and ministers of the Crown this definition excludes members of the armed forces, the police, local government employees, and the employees of nationalized industries and the National Health Service. The total number of civil servants on 1 January 1984 was 632,591, of whom 123,724 were industrial and 508,867 non-industrial employees (*Civil service statistics*, 1984).

Many Acts of Parliament affect the rights, duties and liabilities of civil servants (e.g. the Official Secrets Acts 1911–39 and the Superannuation Act 1972), but their conditions of service are regulated mainly by Orders in Council made under the royal prerogative and by regulations and instructions issued by the Minister for the Civil Service and the Treasury under the authority of the Civil Service Order in Council 1982. The rules are collected in the Civil Service Pay and Conditions of Service Code (formerly Estacode). The code is supplemented by regulations made by individual departments for their staff.

At common law, civil servants hold office at the pleasure of the Crown and can be dismissed at any time. (See *Dunn* v. *The Queen* [1896] 1 QB 116; *Hales* v. *The King* (1918) 34 TLR 589; *Denning* v. *Secretary of State for India* (1920) 37 TLR 138.) This rule has in the past sometimes been explained as resting upon an implied term in the contract of employment, but is better regarded as a rule of constitutional law established by the courts on the basis of public policy (and attributed by the majority of their Lordships in *Council of Civil Service Unions* v. *Minister for the Civil Service* (below) to the prerogative). But public policy changes over time, and the modern view of the nature of public employment is expressed in legislation which extends to civil servants, with some exceptions, the protection against unfair dismissal enjoyed by other employees. (See the Employment Protection (Consolidation) Act 1978, Part v and s.138.) In practice civil servants enjoy a high degree of security in their employment, although dismissals for inefficiency, disciplinary offences and redundancy do occur. Civil servants benefit from the provisions of the Equal Pay Act 1970 and the Sex Discrimination Act 1975; and the provisions of the Race Relations Act 1976 relating to discrimination against employees apply to employment under the Crown. (Equal Pay Act 1970, s.1(8); Sex Discrimination Act 1975, s.85; Race Relations Act 1976, ss.4(2), 75.)

It has been a matter of controversy whether the relationship between a civil servant and the Crown is contractual, the denial of a contract seeming to justify both the Crown's power of dismissal and the view, upheld in some cases, that a civil servant cannot sue for his pay. One such case was *Mulvenna* v. *The Admiralty* 1926 SC 842 in which Lord Blackburn, while not eschewing the language of contract, declared (at pp. 859–60):

[T]he rule based upon public policy which has been enforced against military servants of the Crown, and which prevents such servants suing the Crown for their pay on the assumption that their only claim is on the bounty of the Crown and not for a contractual debt, must equally apply to every public servant. . . . It also follows that this qualification must be read, as an implied condition, into every contract between the Crown and a public servant, with the effect that, in terms of their contract, they have no right to their remuneration which can be enforced in a civil court of justice, and that their only remedy under their contract lies 'in an appeal of an official or political kind'.

Lord Blackburn's reasoning was followed by Pilcher J in *Lucas* v. *Lucas* [1943] P 68 (criticized by Logan (1945) 61 *LQR* 240), but in *Kodeeswaran* v. *Attorney-General of Ceylon* [1970] AC 1111 Lord Diplock, in delivering the judgment of the Privy Council, quoted Lord Blackburn's statement and continued:

The only cases cited in support of this proposition were the well-known cases which establish that the Crown has power to determine the employment of a public servant at will. He treated as an ineluctable consequence of this, too plain to call for further explanation, that a civil servant had no claim in law to arrears of salary accrued due before his dismissal.

In their Lordships' view this is a non sequitur. A right to terminate a contract of service at will coupled with a right to enter into a fresh contract of service may in effect enable the Crown to change the terms of employment in futuro if the true inference to be drawn from the communication of the intended change to the servant and his continuing to serve thereafter is that his existing contract has been terminated by the Crown and a fresh contract entered into on the revised terms. But this cannot affect any right to salary already earned under the terms of his existing contract before its termination.

In the opinion of their Lordships, Lord Blackburn's reasoning in *Mulvenna*'s case . . . is defective and his conclusion is contrary to authority and is wrong.

The courts habitually use the terminology of contract with reference to employment in the civil service (see, e.g., *Waite* v. *Government Communications Headquarters* [1983] 2 AC 714), but in *Council of Civil Service Unions* v. *Minister for the Civil Service* [1984] 3 All ER 935 it was common ground in the proceedings before the House of Lords that there was no contractual relationship between the Crown and civil servants employed at the Government Communications Headquarters (GCHQ). Perhaps the relationship is to be characterized as *sui generis*, with some contractual features including the right of a civil servant to sue for arrears of pay.

In 1983 the Prime Minister (as Minister for the Civil Service) issued an instruction which had the effect of revising the conditions of service of civil servants employed at GCHQ, a military and signals intelligence centre, so as to exclude the right of trade union membership. Contrary to the regular practice, this action was taken without prior consultation with trade unions representing staff at GCHQ. In *Council of Civil Service Unions* v. *Minister for the Civil Service* (above) it was argued, *inter alia*, that the prerogative power to vary the terms and conditions of employment of civil servants was subject to review by the courts, and further that the staff at GCHQ had a legitimate expectation, which the courts should protect, that the Minister would not vary such terms and conditions without first consulting the staff or their trade union representatives. These contentions were accepted in principle by the House of Lords, although the Minister's action was upheld as lawful in this instance because it had been taken on the ground of national security. (See further p. 344 below.)

Personnel matters in the civil service are excluded from the jurisdiction of the Parliamentary Commissioner for Administration to investigate complaints of maladministration against government departments: Parliamentary Commissioner Act 1967, Sched. 3, para. 10. The Commissioner has had to reject a substantial number of complaints as falling within this excluded area, and in 1978 he observed that it was 'an area of administrative action giving rise to much discontent' (Memorandum to the Select Committee on the Parliamentary Commissioner: Fourth Report, HC 615 of 1977–8, p. 150). Both the Select Committee on the Parliamentary Commissioner and the Commissioner himself have repeatedly urged that civil service personnel matters should, within certain limits, be brought within the Commissioner's jurisdiction.

Civil service power and impartiality

By convention the British civil service is non-political and is expected to give loyal service to governments of every political complexion. A new government, while it may introduce a small number of political advisers of Cabinet ministers into the departments, keeps in office the senior civil service personnel who have advised its predecessors. In each department the Permanent Secretary as its official head, having ensured the removal of files and documents of the previous minister from the sight of his successor – what Richard Crossman called 'the purging of the files' (*Inside View* (1972), pp. 12–13: see further p. 89 above) – assumes the role of impartial adviser to the new political head of the department. Recruitment of civil servants has long been insulated from political influence by entrusting responsibility for appointments to an independent Civil Service Commission. By the House of Commons Disqualification Act 1975, s. 1(1)(*b*), civil servants are ineligible for membership of the House of Commons, and under rules first laid down in 1953 (Cmd 8783) they are subject to restrictions on participation in political activities. In 1978 the Armitage Committee recommended relaxations of the rules so as to allow a wider freedom to take part in political activity (Cmnd

7057). The Government accepted the recommendations in principle and revised rules were introduced in 1984. The rules divide civil servants into three groups: the politically free (mainly industrial civil servants); a politically restricted group of civil servants (of the grade of Principal and above) who are debarred from national political activity but may be given permission to take part in local politics; and an intermediate group, comprising all other staff, who may, with permission, take part in national or local politics.

It does not sufficiently explain the role of civil servants to say that they advise ministers on policy and execute ministers' decisions. In the modern government department very many decisions are necessarily taken by civil servants themselves without reference to ministers, and these decisions will often involve an element of policy-making. Moreover the senior civil servants who advise ministers can draw on an accumulated departmental experience and specialized study in pressing for acceptance of the 'departmental view'.

Peter Kellner and Lord Crowther-Hunt, The Civil Servants
(1980), pp. 172, 187, 203–4

The policy work of 2,000 Assistant Secretaries and above are channelled through to 100 ministers. It is inevitable that even hard-working ministers can only see a small fraction of the policy work that is done for them. Information, analysis, and policy options must be carefully selected in order to provide ministers with manageable briefs on which to pass judgment. That process of selection is done – and self-evidently must be done – by civil servants. At the same time the *method* of selection and presentation can make a decisive difference to the view any minister then takes. The control over this process gives senior civil servants considerable power. The issue is not whether this power exists, but how it is wielded – and by whom. A diligent Deputy Secretary working to an enthusiastic minister can open up the choices available on any given subject; a less flexible Deputy Secretary working to a more idle minister is likely to limit the choices *and to receive the gratitude of the minister for having done so.*

The authors consider the formation of a 'departmental view' on matters of policy:

The concept of the departmental view is difficult to define, or to reconcile with any conventional constitutional theory. Broadly it consists of the ideas and assumptions that, independently of which party is in office, flow from the knowledge and experience that are generated by civil servants working together. However much civil servants as individuals move around, they add their increment of information to the pool of knowledge about motorway building, or kidney machines, or food subsidies. Such knowledge does not exist in a moral or political vacuum: and so, by an often complex chemistry, a department's knowledge translates into a departmental view. Some of the greatest conflicts between ministers and their Permanent Secretaries occur when the minister's intentions conflict with the departmental view. . . .

Civil service power is a principal theme of the study by these authors:

But what if power does not reside exclusively in the hands of the directly elected representatives of the people? What if non-elected civil servants can, and often do, thwart or modify the will of ministers and Parliament by devising and operating policies of their own? How can that be squared with parliamentary democracy and ministerial responsibility? Yet perhaps today there has to be at least some bureaucratic power. The solution of (and, indeed, the understanding of) the complex economic, social and technological problems of our day, not only needs an expertise which politicians do not usually possess, but also requires a much longer period of gestation and continuous application than the frequent changes of ministers and governments make possible. So, perhaps, it is inevitable that civil servants should have much more power and influence than our traditional democratic theory would allow.

Much of the groundwork in developing new policies is done in departmental and inter-departmental committees of officials, which Richard Crossman said were 'the key to the control by the Civil Service over the politicians' (*The Diaries of a Cabinet Minister*, vol. 1, 1975, p. 616). Of particular importance are the official committees which shadow the Cabinet committees of ministers and do the preparatory work for them, often recommending conclusions which they wish to see adopted. Ministers may find it difficult to reject a proposal coordinated by officials and based on detailed prior study. There is also a weekly meeting of Permanent Secretaries of the departments which is a kind of shadow to the Cabinet itself.

Questions of civil service power and impartiality were raised in the following report of a House of Commons select committee.

Eleventh Report from the Expenditure Committee, 'The Civil Service',
vol. 1, HC 535–1 of 1976–7

137. All civil servants naturally say that they exist solely to serve the Government and that they take their policy instructions automatically from Ministers. . . . However, many who have been, or who are, Ministers believe that Ministers do not always get the service which it is claimed that they get. They say that they find on their coming into office that some Departments have firmly held policy views and that it is very difficult to change these views. When they are changed, the Department will often try and reinstate its own policies through the passage of time and the erosion of Ministers' political will. Many Departments are large and it is not difficult to push forward policies without a Minister's knowledge, particularly if there is any lack of clarity in defining demarcation lines between different Ministers' responsibilities, as has been known to happen.

138. Further it is often said to be extremely difficult to launch a new policy initiative which is not to the liking of a Department. Delay and obstruction are said to be among the tactics used, together with briefing Ministers in other Departments to oppose the initiative in Cabinet or Cabinet Committee. The workload on Ministers is immense and procrastination or repetition of the difficulties of a policy would be tactics that Ministers would find difficulty in overcoming.

139. In considering these allegations it is necessary to make two points which to some extent would justify these practices to the extent that they may exist. First, the workload of most Departments is so great that all decisions cannot be taken by

Ministers. It is natural in these circumstances that Ministers would want to delegate some matters for decision to the civil service. We merely observe that any such delegation should be decided by Ministers, not by civil servants, and the succeeding incumbents in the relevant ministerial offices should be informed of it.

140. Secondly, the civil service has a duty to preserve the overall consistency of Government policy when a Minister embarks on a course conflicting with that of a Minister in another Department. It may be right for the one Minister to be frustrated, and the other (or the Prime Minister) alerted, until such time as the two have met and argued the matter out to a decision, either in or out of Cabinet. In addition, when a Permanent Secretary considers that his Minister is acting improperly he has a right to appeal to the Prime Minister and should do so.

141. Beyond these instances, however, there seems to us to be no justification for any of the practices mentioned in paragraphs 137 and 138. It is often argued that the civil service is entitled to prevent what is called 'the worst excesses of left or right' in the interests of stable Government policy. This point of view used to be argued, particularly in relation to the French civil service, but also in relation to Britain in the years following the last war. It is still thought by some to be a justification for the civil service resisting measures which Ministers might wish to take, which in the opinion of the civil service are 'going too far'. In the opinion of Your Committee the duties of the civil service should be limited to pointing out the possible consequences, including the political consequences, of any policy but should not include opposing or delaying the policy. If the policy indeed turns out to be unwise or destabilising, the political party in office pays the price. They carry the responsibility, they should have the power to implement their policies.

142. The danger with the argument of preventing 'the worst excesses' is that it becomes open to civil servants to decide what are and what are not 'worst excesses'. If they assume the right to do that, then the step to assuming views on all party matters is but a small one. . . .

Former ministers have differed in their view of the commitment of departments to their 'own' policies and in their estimation of the power of civil servants to deflect ministerial policies into more congenial channels. A former Head of the Civil Service, Lord Armstrong, has said (*The Times*, 15 November 1976, p. 6):

Obviously I had a great deal of influence. The biggest and most pervasive influence is in setting the framework within which the questions of policy are raised. We, while I was in the Treasury, had a framework of the economy basically neo-Keynesian. We set the questions which we asked ministers to decide arising out of that framework and it would have been enormously difficult for any minister to change the framework, so to that extent we had great power. . . .

But since then the framework of economic policy has indeed been changed.

Should civil servants give total and unqualified loyalty to the government, or do they have, in any circumstances, an overriding responsibility to Parliament and the public? What should be their duty if they become aware that ministers are concealing politically embarrassing facts from the public, or are misleading Parliament and the public with false information? At present civil servants are strictly constrained by section 2 of the Official Secrets Act 1911 and, although the section acknowledges that a civil servant may have a *duty in the interest of the state* to disclose officially secret information, this exemption was narrowly construed by McCowan J in *R.* v. *Ponting* [1985] Crim. LR 318 in holding 'duty' to refer to *official* duty, and in identifying the 'interest of the state' with the policies of the government in power.

It can be fairly claimed that British governments have been able to rely upon the *political neutrality* of the civil service. Government policies have not, perhaps, hitherto imposed undue strains upon that neutrality.

> Ralph Miliband, *Capitalist Democracy in Britain* (1982), p. 102

The fact that senior civil servants hold conventional views, which are part of the predominant 'common sense' of people in power, helps them to bring to their work the 'non-partisan' attitude which is thought appropriate to it. This in effect means two things. One of them is that, so far as they are concerned, it matters very little if at all that a particular policy is labelled Conservative or Labour, provided it is squarely within the framework of accepted ideas. Secondly, it means that the approved professional attitude is one of relative detachment towards any policy within that framework. Samuel Brittan wrote in 1971 [*Steering the Economy*, p. 44] of the 'air of civilized scepticism' which was to be found in many parts of Whitehall; and he went on to say that 'it is still regarded as inappropriate to show excessive enthusiasm for a new idea; and the words "There is nothing new under the sun" seem to be written on the wall in invisible ink. . . .' British official scepticism is more often directed towards new reforming ideas than towards accepted beliefs and is not necessarily a prelude to anything at all.' This seems right; and the scepticism towards new ideas of which Brittan speaks can of course quite easily turn into strong opposition. Scepticism of this sort is a version of conservatism and of the defence of the status quo: such defence not only admits of cautious and moderate reform, but often requires it.

Miliband concludes that 'there is at the heart of British government a very powerful braking mechanism against radical change' (p. 108).

(i) **Special advisers**

In recent years ministers have looked outside the departments for more committed advice from persons sympathetic to their policies. With prime ministerial approval they have appointed temporary advisers to provide them with political advice or the benefit of specialized skills (e.g. in economics).

> Statement by the Prime Minister, Mr Harold Wilson, to the Commonwealth Heads of Government Conference, May 1975 (Appendix to Harold Wilson, *The Governance of Britain*, 1976)

The general doctrine is of course that Ministers take political decisions and civil servants carry them out. Why then do we want political advisers? What can they do that Ministers cannot?

There are two reasons which have caused us to experiment in this way.

The first is the pressure of work on Ministers. In less hectic days Ministers were their own political advisers. To a large extent this is still true. A politician with decades of experience and accountable to his electors can only survive if he can scent the changes of mood in the country and in his Party. But the burdens of modern government as developed in our country, the immense volume of papers, the exhausting succession of departmental committees, of Party gatherings and meetings with outside interests make it almost impossible for him to carry out his departmental and political responsibilities and at the same time sustain a detailed analysis of all the various political nuances of policy. If he can keep on top of his own department's work he is doing very well, but he finds it increasingly difficult to play a constructive part in the collective business of the Government as a whole.

The second is the nature of our Civil Service. The British Civil Service takes a pride in its political impartiality. As a result – unlike for example the United States – political change does not mean drastic changes in the Civil Service. This gives our system a degree of continuity and stability which is often admired. The ability of senior civil servants to change and often reverse policies is achieved both by a genuine wish to serve the Government of the day to the best of their ability and also by a certain amount of contingency planning in a pre-electoral period based on a careful on-going study of the proposals of potential Governments.

This system has not been without its critics however. There are those who say that the social and educational background of senior Civil Servants remains too narrow and that the 'Whitehall mandarin', coming as he does from such a background and guaranteed stability and continuity in his office, can become isolated from changes of mood and structure in our society. . . .

Accordingly when we came into office in March 1974 I authorised the appointment by Cabinet Ministers of Political Advisers. This is not of course a wholly new concept – previous administrations had brought in advisers from outside, normally chosen from political sympathisers – and even now we have only 30 such advisers spread around 15 departments. The increase is however of considerable significance and Political Advisers now play a definite role in our affairs.

Since a Political Adviser is the personal appointment of his Minister his specific role within any particular department will vary to some degree or another. His role will also depend on his particular background and experience. . . .

Political and other 'special' advisers were intended to counter the conventional wisdom of the departments, follow up the implementation of ministerial decisions, and maintain direct links with the party and with outside interest groups. Ministers in the present Conservative Government have continued the practice of appointing special advisers, although in smaller numbers. The experiment has so far been on too modest a scale to have brought about a fundamental change in the process of policy-making. The view is gaining ground that if ministers are to take effective command of departmental policy they must have the political support of a strong executive team of outsiders brought into the department to advise on policy and supervise its execution. This is what is proposed by a former adviser to the Prime Minister, Sir John Hoskyns, who writes ((1983) 36 *Parliamentary Affairs* 137 at 146):

[W]e need to replace a large number of senior civil servants with politically appointed officials on contracts. . . . They might number between ten and twenty per department. Some of them would fill senior positions in the department. Others might work as policy advisers to the Cabinet minister concerned. There is no reason why, in some cases, the Permanent Secretary should not be an outsider, with a career official as Second Permanent Secretary responsible for the day-to-day running of the department.

What objections might there be to this proposal?

4

The structure
of the United Kingdom

1 The United Kingdom as a unitary state

The United Kingdom has a *unitary* constitution, like those of France, Italy, Sweden and New Zealand, and unlike the *federal* constitutions of West Germany ('The Federal Republic of Germany'), the United States, Australia, Canada and Nigeria.

K. C. Wheare, *Modern Constitutions* (2nd edn 1966), p. 19

In a federal Constitution the powers of government are divided between a government for the whole country and governments for parts of the country in such a way that each government is legally independent within its own sphere. The government for the whole country has its own area of powers and it exercises them without any control from the governments of the constituent parts of the country, and these latter in their turn exercise their powers without being controlled by the central government. In particular the legislature of the whole country has limited powers, and the legislatures of the states or provinces have limited powers. Neither is subordinate to the other; both are co-ordinate. In a unitary Constitution, on the other hand, the legislature of the whole country is the supreme law-making body in the country. It may permit other legislatures to exist and to exercise their powers, but it has the right, in law, to overrule them; they are subordinate to it.

From this it appears that the essential features of a federal constitution are that the central and regional governments have limited powers and that, within those limits, each government is independent of the other.

Other definitions of federalism have been proposed. Preston King, *Federalism and Federation* (1982), pp. 140–41, sees the distinguishing feature of a federation as the entrenched role of the regional units in national decision-making:

a federation may conveniently be defined as a constitutional system which instances a division between central and regional governments and where special or entrenched representation is accorded to the regions in the decision-making procedures of the central government.

Sawer identifies the 'basic federal principles' as follows:

Geoffrey Sawer, *Modern Federalism* (new edn 1976), p. 1

(1) A country which, taken as a whole, is a nation state, an independent unit from the point of view of international relations and law, is provided with a set of institutions required for the work of government, having authority over the whole of that country. (We shall call this set of institutions the CENTRE.)

(2) This country is also divided into a number of geographical areas, each of which is also equipped with a set of institutions required for the work of government in that area. (We shall call each such set of institutions a REGION.)

(3) The power to govern is distributed between the centre and the regions in such a way that each set of governmental institutions has a direct impact on the individual citizens and other legal persons within its area of competence.

(4) The distribution of competence between centre and regions is effected by a constitution (usually written) having a fair degree of rigidity, so that its basic terms are 'entrenched' – that is, cannot be amended at the sole discretion of the centre or of any region or combination of regions. This implies the inability of a region to secede, unless the terms of the constitution specifically authorise such a step.

(5) The constitution provides rules to determine any conflict of authority between centre and regions, where but for the conflict the activity in question would have been within the competence of each of the conflicting authorities. Theoretically the rule could favour either regions or centre, and could vary with the subject of power; in all known cases the general rule is that the centre law prevails.

(6) The distribution of competence between centre and regions is interpreted and policed by a judicial authority which can make authoritative determinations as to the validity of governmental acts (including legislation) where these are alleged to be beyond the competence of the centre or a region, or where the conflict rules referred to under (5) have to be applied.

This is not to say that all systems commonly regarded as federal will necessarily possess all these features, and there are considerable variations in the ways in which they are worked out in different federal constitutions.

The regions in a federation will often have been independent countries which agreed to join together in a federal union; but an existing unitary state may transform itself into a federation by redistributing sovereign powers between central and regional governments. However created, a federal system seems to embody a *contractual* idea in that the central and the regional governments each hold their powers upon a condition of respect for the independence of the other. The terms of the 'contract' under which power is distributed are expressed in a written constitution, and are unalterable by either the central or the regional legislatures acting unilaterally. To that extent the constitution is supreme.

The formal analysis of federal and unitary constitutions assumes a regularity which is not always to be found in the shifting and diverse patterns of modern governmental systems. Wheare observed that a federal constitution might include elements that diverged from the federal principle as formally defined; indeed if it had 'considerable unitary modifications' it would be better classified as 'quasi-federal'. (K. C. Wheare, *Federal Government*, 4th edn 1963, p. 19.) Moreover when we consider the actual practice of governments it appears that a country 'may have a federal constitution, but in practice it may work that constitution in such a way that its government is not federal', or again that 'a country with a non-federal constitution may work it in such a way that it provides an example of federal government' (op. cit., p. 20).

History and our own time show us such a variety of systems for the distribution of power between central and regional governments, and so many exceptions, qualifications, understandings and compromises in the working of constitutions, that there is often disagreement about whether a system of government is federal or unitary. The Constitution of the United States is generally regarded as the paradigm of federal constitutions, yet even there the limits on the powers of the federal and state governments are blurred by innumerable arrangements for shared or cooperative governmental activity, and the central government, with its vast financial resources, has gained an ascendancy that transcends its formal powers. A centralizing tendency is, indeed, a general feature of modern federal systems, and in all of them the formal location of power is less important than the actual network of central-regional governmental relations. This means that the classification of a governmental system as federal or unitary (if we can agree upon it) does not tell us much about how the system actually works. Equally it is open to doubt whether either a federal or a unitary system, in the abstract, has the advantage in assuring good, efficient or strong government. S. Rufus Davis disposes in the following passage of judgements like that of Dicey, who concluded (in *The Law of the Constitution*, pp. 171–2) that 'federal government means weak government' and that a federation 'will always be at a disadvantage in a contest with unitarian states of equal resources'.

S. Rufus Davis, *The Federal Principle* (1978), pp. 211–12

The truth of the matter is – and experience has been the teacher – that some 'federal' systems fail, some do not; some are able to resist aggression, some are not; some inhibit economic growth, some do not; some frustrate *some* kinds of economic planning, some frustrate *other* kinds; some develop a great diversity of public services, some do not; some promote a great measure of civil liberty, some do not; some are highly adaptive, some are not; some are highly efficient in servicing the needs of a modern state, some are not; some gratify values that others do not. Indeed, over a long or short span of time, some are always something (socially, economically, politically, administratively, constitutionally) which other federal systems are not. But whatever their condition at any one time (e.g., adaptive/maladaptive, conservative/progressive, efficient/ inefficient, etc.), it is rarely clear that it *is* so because of their federalness, or the particular character of their federal institutions, or the special way they practise federalism, or in spite of their federalness. And further: when at some moment federal systems resemble or differ from each other in some respect or other (e.g., efficiency or inefficiency in the delivery of public services, tepidity or zealotry in the pursuit of civil liberties), the reasons, though sometimes traceable to similarities or differences in their constitutional structure, flow more often than not from the things they share in common as societies or the things that distinguish them as societies.

In a word, we are dealing with things that are only partly the same. And if there is . . . a common 'logic' running through all federal systems, it lacks the force to transcend their different political cultures and impose a common political direction. This is the massive fact we have come to learn. To expect to give a common explanation for, say, the failure of the Weimar Federal Republic and the Central African Federation in any other than trivial generalizations, or to expect that political performance will necessarily differ because states are federal or unitary, is to exaggerate the limited potentialities of contemporary federal theory and mistake the limited value of the distinction between federal and unitary systems.

This agnosticism is not shared by everyone. Sawer (op. cit., p. 125) remarks that

by contrast with wholly centralised systems a federal one will tend to place checks on speedy and resolute action by either regions or centre, to discourage rapid social change, and to leave to Court action the resolution of policy disputes which elsewhere are settled by political action.

Sawer sees federalism as a 'prudential' system best suited to the more stable or conservative societies.

The United Kingdom, at all events, is clearly recognizable as a unitary state, even if we can discern in the practical arrangements for its government some elements of a 'federal principle'. There are at present no separate governments established for England, Scotland, Wales or Northern Ireland. A Government and Parliament of Northern Ireland were constituted by the Government of Ireland Act 1920, but these institutions were subordinate to the Parliament of the United Kingdom, as was expressly declared by section 75 of the Act:

Notwithstanding the establishment of the Parliament of . . . Northern Ireland . . . or anything contained in this Act, the supreme authority of the Parliament of the United Kingdom shall remain unaffected and undiminished over all persons, matters, and things in [Northern] Ireland and every part thereof.

(Was there any constitutional necessity for this express reservation of the authority of the United Kingdom Parliament?) In practice the United Kingdom Parliament refrained from exercising its power to legislate on matters 'transferred' to the Parliament of Northern Ireland, and it may therefore be correct to describe the *system of government* in Northern Ireland – at all events until the period of crisis which began in 1968 – as 'quasi-federal'. (See Vernon Bogdanor, *Devolution*, 1979, pp. 50–51.) The overriding sovereignty of the Parliament at Westminster was, however, demonstrated when the government of Northern Ireland was suspended and its Parliament prorogued by the Northern Ireland (Temporary Provisions) Act 1972. (See further p. 194 below.)

Institutions of *local* government in the United Kingdom owe their existence and powers to Parliament and can at any time be reorganized, abridged in their powers, or extinguished by Parliament.

There has never been serious official consideration of a re-structuring of the United Kingdom on a federal plan. The Kilbrandon Commission, in a rather sketchy survey of federalism (Cmnd 5460/1973, paras. 501–23), concluded that 'in the modern world federal countries are hampered by an inflexible system of government', and rejected federalism as inappropriate for the United Kingdom.

Report of the Royal Commission on the Constitution, vol. 1, Cmnd
5460/1973

Acceptability of federalism

527. We have noted that a federal system of government would require a written constitution, a special procedure for changing it and a constitutional court to interpret it. None of these features has been present in our constitutional arrangements before, and we doubt very much whether they would now find general acceptance.

528. Although there are many Acts of Parliament dealing with constitutional matters, there is no separate body of entrenched law which enshrines the basic rules of our system of government. Parliament is sovereign and can make or alter any law by a simple majority. Its Acts are interpreted by the courts, but this is done strictly by reference to the words of the statute itself, not in the light of any general constitutional principles or supposed limitations on the powers of Parliament. Ultimately Parliament cannot be overruled by the courts. If it does not like the interpretation put on the law by the courts, it can change the law.

529. In a federal system, however, there is more than one legislature and the powers of each are strictly defined. There may be provision for federal law to override provincial law where the two conflict, but this rule is designed for those fields in which the federal and provincial governments have joint responsibility. It cannot be used by the federal government to encroach upon legislative territory specifically assigned under the constitution to the provinces. Disputes about governmental powers which cannot otherwise be resolved go to a constitutional court. The effect is therefore to place elected bodies in a position subordinate to the judiciary. Inevitably there are some constitutional questions which have to be decided more as a matter of individual judgement than in accordance with the rules laid down in the constitution. . . . The work of the judges therefore tends to become political, and their known political views are taken into account when they are appointed. This situation, probably unavoidable in a federal system, is foreign to our own tradition of unitary government based upon the complete sovereignty of Parliament and upon the complete dissociation of the judiciary from matters of political policy.

530. Although there are circumstances in which the benefits to be derived from federalism may outweigh those of any practicable alternative, in our view such circumstances do not exist in the United Kingdom. We believe that to most people a federal system would appear strange and artificial. It would not provide continuity with the past or sufficient flexibility for the future, and it is unlikely that it would be generally acceptable.

The dominant position of England

531. As far as we are aware no advocate of federalism in the United Kingdom has succeeded in producing a federal scheme satisfactorily tailored to fit the circumstances of England. A federation consisting of four units – England, Scotland, Wales and Northern Ireland – would be so unbalanced as to be unworkable. It would be dominated by the overwhelming political importance and wealth of England. The English Parliament would rival the United Kingdom federal Parliament; and in the federal Parliament itself the representation of England could hardly be scaled down in such a way as to enable it to be out-voted by Scotland, Wales and Northern Ireland, together representing less than one-fifth of the population. A United Kingdom federation of the four countries, with a federal Parliament and provincial Parliaments in the four national capitals, is therefore not a realistic proposition.

532. The imbalance would be corrected if England were to be divided into a number of units, each having the status of a federal province. It is clear, however, that this artificial division into provinces with independent sovereign powers would be unacceptable to the people of England. Advocates of federalism have attempted to get round the difficulty by an arrangement in which the regions of England would not have the full status of federal provinces; they would have elected assemblies with fewer powers than the legislatures of Scotland, Wales and Northern Ireland, and a separate body would be established to deal with all-England affairs. But no matter how this body were to be constituted and its powers shared with the regional assemblies, the fact would remain that England by its weight of numbers and wealth would continue to dominate the federation.

533. Proposals designed to accommodate federalism by splitting England up into several provinces tend to overlook one further point, which is that the province which included south-east England might well itself dominate the federation. Out of a United Kingdom population of 55 million, over 17 million live in this region, and since it includes London, the headquarters of both government and business, its general influence on the economic life of the country as a whole is proportionately even greater.

534. For these reasons, stated here only in brief terms, we have concluded that there is no satisfactory way of fitting England into a fully federal system.

The consequences for political and economic unity

535. We have said that we regard as essential the maintenance of political and economic unity. Federalism would tend to undermine that unity and make the objectives of the United Kingdom more difficult to attain. There is a possibility that provinces with sovereign powers would not always be very ready to co-operate with each other and with the central government in the wider interest. . . . They might be tempted to withhold co-operation in order to assert their sovereignty, and to use their sovereign powers in provincial matters as a bargaining counter to gain advantages in federal matters. In our view there is a real danger that provincial sovereignty would lead to intergovernmental rivalry and contention to an extent that would be damaging to the interests of the United Kingdom. In the international field, and particularly in European Community matters, it would add to the difficulties of the United Kingdom Government's negotiating position.

536. A federal system would be less suitable than a unitary system for meeting the economic needs of the United Kingdom, which has a more open economy than most federal countries and is more dependent on overseas trade. Its governments also tend to

pursue more radical objectives: a highly developed regional policy is one example. For these reasons it has a greater need for instruments of central economic management. In a federal system the base of taxation and expenditure available to the United Kingdom Government for economic adjustments would be substantially reduced. A large part of taxation and public expenditure would be under the sovereign control of provincial governments primarily concerned with pursuing their own policies in provincial matters; their independent decisions about provincial taxation and expenditure would be geared to that end. The circumstances of most federal countries are such that this obstacle to economic management can be successfully overcome. For United Kingdom governments concerned with performing the economic role which has come to be expected of them the difficulties would be a good deal greater. . . .

(See also *Devolution: the English Dimension*, HMSO 1976, para. 17.)

The political impetus for the introduction of a federal system of government does not at present exist in the United Kingdom, although federalism does have its protagonists. (See, e.g., Jenny Chapman *et al.*, *Scottish Self-Government*, 1976; Bernard Burrows and Geoffrey Denton, *Devolution or Federalism?* 1980.) It would very likely prove a more expensive system, with its separate layers of government, than the present one, and there would be high costs in money and effort in introducing the new system and 'running it in', with no certainty that better government would result. Are there nevertheless compelling arguments for reconstituting the United Kingdom on a federal basis? Would federalism give fuller expression than any other system, within a still undivided United Kingdom, to the national and cultural identities of the Scots and Welsh?

2 The countries of the United Kingdom

The United Kingdom is a multi-national state in which the inhabitants of Scotland, Wales and Northern Ireland identify themselves not only (if at all) as 'British' but most often primarily as Scots, Welsh, Ulstermen, or Irish. (See Richard Rose (ed.), *Studies in British Politics*, 3rd edn 1976, p. 127, Table 5.) In law there is, however, a single British citizenship for all those sufficiently connected by birth or descent with the United Kingdom (British Nationality Act 1981).

> Richard Rose, 'The United Kingdom as a Multi-National
> State', in Richard Rose (ed.), *Studies in British Politics*
> (3rd edn 1976), pp. 115–16

Legally, there is no such thing as an English regime. In international law as in the title of the Queen, the regime is the United Kingdom of Great Britain and Northern Ireland, a composite of jurisdictions joined in one state. The prolonged and continuing refusal of some Irish people to give allegiance to this regime has meant that at no time has it been fully legitimate everywhere in the realm. Scotland and Wales have not shown the same measure of political disaffection and violence, but the resurgence of distinctive parties such as the Scottish Nationalists and Plaid Cymru in the 1960s is a reminder that generalisations about political allegiance in the United Kingdom cannot automatically be extended beyond England's boundaries.

Unfortunately, many who write about British politics confuse England, the largest part, with the whole of the United Kingdom, or ignore any possibility of differences within it. For instance, Bagehot's study of *The English Constitution*, published in 1867, gives no hint of the constitutional problems that followed the Fenian Rising in Ireland in the same year. Latter-day writers have also ignored differences between English and United Kingdom politics. L. S. Amery, an active politician during the Irish troubles, gave careful attention in his *Thoughts on the Constitution* (1953), to the integration of colonies into the British Empire and Commonwealth, but none to the problems of the integration and disintegration of parts of the United Kingdom.

The structure of the United Kingdom as we now know it dates from 1922, when southern Ireland withdrew from the Union as the Irish Free State.

Legislation of the United Kingdom Parliament can and usually does extend to all parts of the Kingdom, but some public Acts apply only to Scotland, Wales or Northern Ireland (rarely only to England). Scotland has its own legal system, and the former Parliament of Northern Ireland (1921–72) enacted many laws for the province which are still in force. There is freedom of movement throughout the United Kingdom for those settled there, but this is qualified by the Prevention of Terrorism (Temporary Provisions) Act 1984, by which a person may in certain circumstances be excluded either from Great Britain or from Northern Ireland.

(a) **England**

England is the largest of the four countries of the United Kingdom, and its population of 46,362,836 (1981 census) is over 80 per cent of the total United Kingdom population of 55,773,499. While there are no significant nationalist or separatist political movements in England, there are cultural differences associated with particular regions, and differences both cultural and linguistic among the immigrant populations of English cities.

England has 523 of the 650 seats in the House of Commons, and is under-represented in comparison with the rest of the United Kingdom: if average constituency electorates were equal throughout the United Kingdom, England would have 541 seats.

In the central government of the United Kingdom there is no separate department for England like the 'territorial' departments for Scotland, Wales and Northern Ireland, but some departments – Agriculture and Fisheries, Education and Science, the Environment – are predominantly concerned with the affairs of England because equivalent functions in the other countries of the United Kingdom are mainly discharged by the territorial departments. (See Richard Rose, *The United Kingdom as an Intellectual Puzzle*, 1977, pp. 3–4.)

With the First World War there began a process of 'deconcentration' of administrative functions to outstations of Whitehall departments in regions of

England (and in Scotland and Wales). (This is not the same thing as a 'decentralization' of powers to autonomous bodies outside central government.) Regional offices carry out departmental policies, in some cases through a network of local offices, in administering social services, agricultural grants, aid to industry, road construction and maintenance, export services, and so on. There are also regional organizations of the National Health Service (regional hospital boards), of nationalized industries such as gas and electricity, and for water resources (regional water authorities).

There is no single organizational map of English regions, for different departments and public authorities have adopted regional areas and boundaries suitable for their particular services, with little attempt to achieve a uniform system. The Treasury had some success in 1946 in getting departments with regional offices to conform to the same nine Standard Regions of England, but variations in regional boundaries soon reappeared.

The authors of the minority report of the Royal Commission on the Constitution asked themselves whether it was necessary to retain the regional tier of government.

> *Royal Commission on the Constitution*, vol. II, *Memorandum of Dissent*
> *by Lord Crowther-Hunt and Professor A. T. Peacock*, Cmnd
> 5460–I/1973

193. Clearly, there are only three ways of getting rid of this level of government. One is for the different units of local government to take over the functions now being performed at this intermediate level. Another is for the functions to be reabsorbed by the central government departments in Whitehall. Thirdly, we might consider that many of the intermediate level functions are unnecessary anyway and could be abolished. Though a very detailed examination might well identify some functions which fall into this last category, there can be little doubt that the vast number of decisions which are now made in the outposts of central government and in the 'regional' organisations of the *ad hoc* authorities [e.g. regional water authorities] have got to be made somewhere or other in our governmental machine. So only the first two alternatives – or a combination of them – offer a possible solution.

194. As far as the first alternative is concerned, it is difficult to see how the . . . local authorities could efficiently absorb more than a mere handful of the functions now concentrated at this intermediate level.

195. Virtually none of the functions performed in England by the regional outposts of central government could be handed over to individual local authorities in a way which would make it possible for the departments concerned to abolish their regional organisations. This is because for the most part the *raison d'être* of government departments carrying out these functions and making this large number of decisions at this intermediate level is the need to comprehend a wider area of the country than is covered by one individual local authority. . . .

197. Just as the great bulk of the intermediate level functions of the outposts of central government and of the *ad hoc* authorities cannot be absorbed by local government, so it would make no sense for them to be reabsorbed by the central

government departments in Whitehall. The purpose of developing departmental regional structures has been to lighten the load on Whitehall and to try to ensure that decisions are taken by those with a more intimate knowledge of the day-to-day problems involved; similar purposes are behind the development of regional *ad hoc* executive bodies. Clearly it would be wrong to reverse these trends and concentrate government authority in all these matters back in Whitehall.

198. So, in the end we need to recognise that we have this very substantial intermediate tier of government and decision-making for one very important reason. It is quite simply that there are a large number of important problems and functions which cannot be satisfactorily handled except by bodies operating at this level. So the question we have to face is not whether we need an intermediate level, but what is the best way of running the one we have. . . .

Two comments may be made about the system of regional deconcentration in England.

(1) The diversity of boundaries is an obstacle to regional planning (supposing the government to be in favour of planning) and the coordination of departmental policies in the regions.

(2) Ministerial responsibility for the actions of civil servants, something tenuous at best (see chapter 7 below), has least reality where the activities of regional offices are concerned, remote as these are from ministerial supervision.

A House of Commons Standing Committee on Regional Affairs was set up in 1975 to consider matters relating to the regions of England. The Committee consists of all members representing English constituencies (together with not more than five other members). It debates matters referred to it on the motion of a minister: objection by any 20 members defeats the motion. The Committee is essentially a forum for debate and reports to the House only that it 'has considered' the matter referred to it: a vote carried against a motion to this effect has no practical consequences. The *raison d'être* of the Committee is to provide more time for debates on regional questions than is available on the floor of the House; some members have regretted the loss of publicity attending debates in the chamber, and have doubted the usefulness of the Committee's proceedings. But the Committee does provide additional opportunities for publicity to be given to regional problems, and for the interests of regions to be pressed upon ministers.

(b) Scotland

Scotland covers about a third of the area of the United Kingdom and has a population (1981 census) of 5,130,735 or about 9 per cent of the total United Kingdom population.

Scotland and England, under the same Crown from 1603 but with separate institutions of government, were joined in the United Kingdom of Great Britain in 1707 by the Treaty and Acts of Union. Articles of Union, agreed in 1706 by Commissioners acting on behalf of the Parliament of each country, were adopted by the Acts of Union passed by the Scottish and English Parliaments in 1707. In terms of these instruments the two Parliaments were superseded by a Parliament of Great Britain – 'a new Parliament for a new State' (Scottish Law Commission, Memorandum No. 32, 1975, p. 16). This was to be a unitary, not a federal state; as K. C. Wheare observes (*Federal Government*, 4th edn 1963, p. 43), there was no model of federal government in existence which might have been urged against the unitary scheme then proposed and adopted. Scottish arguments for retention of the Scottish Parliament did not prevail.

In entering the Union the Scots were concerned to ensure, as far as they could, that certain of their cherished rights and institutions should not be at risk from a Parliament in which English members would be in a majority. The Union legislation accordingly declared, as a 'fundamental and essential condition' of the union, that the Presbyterian religion and Church of Scotland should 'remain and continue unalterable' in Scotland, and affirmed that the Scottish superior courts (Court of Session and Court of Justiciary) should remain 'in all time coming', with their authority and privileges. While the Parliament of Great Britain was authorized to alter the laws of Scotland, it was stipulated that no alteration should be made in private law 'except for evident utility of the subjects within Scotland'. From a modern point of view the Acts of Union are defective in that they include no safeguards against violation of their 'fundamental' provisions, nor any special machinery for amending these as changed conditions might require. At least one of the fundamental provisions, obliging professors of Scottish universities to make a formal submission to Presbyterianism, was repealed by the Universities (Scotland) Acts 1853 and 1932; the issue was not a contentious one and the Scots may be said to have acquiesced in the repeal.

It would seem to follow from the doctrine of parliamentary sovereignty that an Act of Parliament is valid even if it violates fundamental provisions of the Union legislation. Against this it is argued that the Acts of Union are constituent Acts which, in creating the Parliament of the United Kingdom, imposed limitations upon its powers which remain effective. English constitutional lawyers have not in general accepted this argument. It has been heard in the Scottish courts where it has neither prevailed nor been summarily dismissed.

MacCormick v. *Lord Advocate* 1953 SC 396 (Court of Session, Inner House)

The chairman and secretary of the Scottish Covenant Association petitioned the Court of Session for a declaration that a proclamation describing the Queen as 'Elizabeth the Second of the United Kingdom of Great Britain' was illegal. They argued that the adoption of the numeral 'II', since it implied that Elizabeth I had been Queen of Great Britain, was contrary to Article I of the

Treaty and Acts of Union which brought about the union of the two Kingdoms in 1707. For the Crown the Lord Advocate denied that the proclamation conflicted with Article 1, and maintained further that the use of the numeral 'II' was authorized by the Royal Titles Act 1953. The petitioners contended that the Act could not validly permit the violation of a fundamental provision of the Treaty.

The Lord Ordinary (Lord Guthrie) dismissed the petition on the grounds (1) that the Royal Titles Act had authorized the adoption of the numeral, and an Act of Parliament could not be challenged as being in breach of the Treaty or on any other ground; (2) that in any event the Treaty did not expressly or impliedly prohibit the use of the numeral; and (3) that the petitioners had no sufficient interest to bring the proceedings.

The petitioners' appeal to the First Division of the Inner House was dismissed, the court agreeing with Lord Guthrie that there was nothing in Article 1 of the Treaty against the use of the numeral, and that the petitioners had no title to sue. The court was of the opinion that the Royal Titles Act had no relevance in the case: it was enacted only after the proclamation of the Queen as Elizabeth II, and was not concerned in any way with the numeral adopted. The Lord President nevertheless expressed his opinion on the questions of the validity of an Act of Parliament that conflicted with the Treaty, and the jurisdiction of the courts if such an issue were to arise.

LORD PRESIDENT COOPER: ... The principle of the unlimited sovereignty of Parliament is a distinctively English principle which has no counterpart in Scottish constitutional law. It derives its origin from Coke and Blackstone, and was widely popularised during the nineteenth century by Bagehot and Dicey, the latter having stated the doctrine in its classic form in his *Law of the Constitution*. Considering that the Union legislation extinguished the Parliaments of Scotland and England and replaced them by a new Parliament, I have difficulty in seeing why it should have been supposed that the new Parliament of Great Britain must inherit all the peculiar characteristics of the English Parliament but none of the Scottish Parliament, as if all that happened in 1707 was that Scottish representatives were admitted to the Parliament of England. That is not what was done. Further, the Treaty and the associated legislation, by which the Parliament of Great Britain was brought into being as the successor of the separate Parliaments of Scotland and England, contain some clauses which expressly reserve to the Parliament of Great Britain powers of subsequent modification, and other clauses which either contain no such power or emphatically exclude subsequent alteration by declarations that the provision shall be fundamental and unalterable in all time coming, or declarations of a like effect. I have never been able to understand how it is possible to reconcile with elementary canons of construction the adoption by the English constitutional theorists of the same attitude to these markedly different types of provisions.

The Lord Advocate conceded this point by admitting that the Parliament of Great Britain 'could not' repeal or alter such 'fundamental and essential' conditions. He was doubtless influenced in making this concession by the modified views expressed by Dicey in his later work entitled *Thoughts on the Scottish Union*, from which I take this passage (pp. 252–253):- 'The statesmen of 1707, though giving full sovereign power to the Parliament of Great Britain, clearly believed in the possibility of creating an absolute sovereign legislature which should yet be bound by unalterable laws.' After instancing the provisions as to Presbyterian Church government in Scotland with their emphatic prohibition against alteration, the author proceeds:- 'It represents the conviction of the Parliament which passed the Act of Union that the Act for the security of the Church of Scotland ought to be morally or constitutionally unchangeable, even by the British Parliament. . . . A sovereign Parliament, in short, though it cannot be logically bound to abstain from changing any given law, may, by the fact that an Act when it was passed had been declared to be unchangeable, receive a warning that it cannot be changed without grave danger to the Constitution of the country.' I have not found in the Union legislation any provision that the Parliament of Great Britain should be 'absolutely sovereign' in the sense that that Parliament should be free to alter the Treaty at will. However that may be, these passages provide a necessary corrective to the extreme formulations adopted by the Lord Ordinary, and not now supported. In the latest editions of the *Law of the Constitution* the editor uneasily describes Dicey's theories as 'purely lawyer's conceptions', and demonstrates how deeply later events, such as the Statute of Westminster, have encroached upon the earlier dogmas. As is well known, the conflict between academic logic and political reality has been emphasised by the recent South African decision as to the effect of the Statute of Westminster – *Harris* v. *Minister of Interior*. [See p. 35 above.]

But the petitioners have still a grave difficulty to overcome on this branch of their argument. Accepting it that there are provisions in the Treaty of Union and associated legislation which are 'fundamental law,' and assuming for the moment that something is alleged to have been done – it matters not whether with legislative authority or not – in breach of that fundamental law, the question remains whether such a question is determinable as a justiciable issue in the Courts of either Scotland or England, in the same fashion as an issue of constitutional *vires* would be cognisable by the Supreme Courts of the United States, or of South Africa or Australia. I reserve my opinion with regard to the provisions relating expressly to this Court and to the laws 'which concern private right' which are administered here. This is not such a question, but a matter of 'public right' (articles 18 and 19). To put the matter in another way, it is of little avail to ask whether the Parliament of Great Britain 'can' do this thing or that, without going on to inquire who can stop them if they do. Any person 'can' repudiate his solemn engagement but he cannot normally do so with impunity. Only two answers have been suggested to this corollary to the main question. The first is the exceedingly cynical answer implied by Dicey (*Law of the Constitution*, 9th edn, p. 82) in the statement that 'it would be rash of the Imperial Parliament to abolish the Scotch law courts, and assimilate the law of Scotland to that of England. But no one can feel sure at what point Scottish resistance to such a change would become serious.' The other answer was that nowadays there may be room for the invocation of an 'advisory opinion' from the International Court of Justice. On these matters I express no view. This at least is plain, that there is neither precedent nor authority of any kind for the view that the domestic Courts of either Scotland or England have jurisdiction to determine whether a governmental act of the type here in controversy is or is not conform to the provisions of a Treaty, least of all when that Treaty is one under which both Scotland and England ceased to be independent states and merged their identity in an incorporating union. From the standpoint both of constitutional law and of international law the position appears to me to be unique, and I am constrained to hold that the action as laid is incompetent in respect that it has not been shown that the Court of Session has authority to entertain the issue sought to be raised. . . .

[Lord Carmont expressed agreement with the views of the Lord President, and Lord Russell in a concurring judgment was in general agreement with those views.]

It would not appear that any procedure exists for obtaining an advisory opinion from the International Court of Justice on an issue of the sort that arose in this case. (See further Neil MacCormick, 'Does the United Kingdom have a Constitution? Reflections on *MacCormick* v. *Lord Advocate*' (1978) 29 *NILQ 1.*)

Gibson v. *Lord Advocate* 1975 SLT 134 (Court of Session, Outer House)

Section 2(1) of the European Communities Act 1972 provides that regulations of the European Communities are to have the effect of law in the United Kingdom. Article 2 of Regulation 2141/70 made by the Council of the European Communities required member states to allow equal access to fishing grounds in their maritime waters for all fishing vessels of other member states.

The pursuer (plaintiff) in this case was the skipper and part-owner of an inshore fishing vessel with which he fished waters off the west coast of Scotland. He sued the Lord Advocate, as representing the Crown, for a declarator (declaration) that section 2(1) of the European Communities Act, in purporting to give legal effect to Article 2 of the EEC Regulation, was contrary to Article XVIII of the Act of Union 1707 and was null and of no effect.

Article XVIII enacted:

That the laws concerning regulation of trade customs and such excises to which Scotland is by virtue of this treaty to be liable be the same in Scotland from and after the union as in England and that all other laws in use within the Kingdom of Scotland do after the union and notwithstanding thereof remain in the same force as before . . . but alterable by the Parliament of Great Britain with this difference betwixt the laws concerning publick right policy and civil government and those which concern private right that *the laws which concern publick right policy and civil government may be made the same throughout the whole United Kingdom but that no alteration be made in laws which concern private right except for evident utility of the subjects within Scotland* [italics added].

The pursuer maintained that before 1707 Scottish subjects had exclusive fishing rights in Scottish waters, and that the laws which assured those rights were laws concerning private right within the meaning of Article XVIII: the alteration of the fishing rights by the EEC Regulation (in making them non-exclusive) was not for the evident utility of Scottish subjects, and therefore section 2(1) of the European Communities Act, so far as it gave effect to Article 2 of the Regulation, was null and void.

LORD KEITH: . . . The defender pleads that the court has no jurisdiction to entertain the action, that the pursuer has no title to sue, that the action is incompetent on a number of grounds, and he has a general plea to the relevancy of the pursuer's averments.

. . . [S]enior counsel for the defender placed the matter of relevancy in the forefront of his argument. I propose to consider first his contention that the law which the pursuer claims to have been altered by s.2(1) of the 1972 Act is a law concerned with public right, not with private right. The right of the public to white fishing in the sea around Scotland goes back to time immemorial, and it was affirmed by an Act of Queen Anne, the statute of 1705, c.2. This was entitled an 'Act for advancing and establishing the fishing trade in and about this Kingdom', and by it Her Majesty, with advice and consent of the estates of Parliament, 'authorises and impowers all her good subjects of this Kingdom to take, buy and cure herring and white fish in all and sundry seas, channels, bays, firths, lochs, rivers, etc. of this Her Majesty's ancient Kingdom'. There is no suggestion that any foreigners were authorised and empowered to take herring and white fish in the seas etc. in question, so it may be taken that the right affirmed by the statute extended only to the subjects in Scotland. The juridical position is stated as follows in Rankine on *Landownership*, 4th edition [1909], p. 251: – 'The narrow seas, and a strip formed by an imaginary line drawn three miles out to sea from low-water mark along the general line of the coast, disregarding gulfs and minor inlets, are regarded as belonging to the sovereign, as custodian of, or trustee for, the public rights of navigation and the national rights of fishing.' The extent of territorial waters, however, depends upon what is recognised by foreign states as being within the territorial sovereignty of the Crown, and is therefore in substance a matter of international law. Originally the extent was such as was capable of being commanded by cannon shot from the shore, which came to be crystallised at three nautical miles. But the extent is capable of being and has been altered following conventions with foreign states. At present British fishery limits stand at twelve nautical miles, by virtue of the Fishery Limits Act 1964, this distance of twelve nautical miles being divided into 'the exclusive fishery limits', which extend up to six nautical miles, and the remainder, which is described in the Act as 'the outer belt'.

The exclusion of foreigners from fishing in territorial waters depends upon the exercise of sovereign power, and is capable of being achieved only by the use of fishery protection vessels to arrest foreign ships illegally fishing and the prosecution of offenders in the criminal courts of the land. Provision for these matters has been made in a series of Sea Fisheries Acts of which the earliest still in force, at least in part, is that of 1868.

The dichotomy between public right and private right, which appears in article XVIII of the Act of Union is one familiar to Scottish institutional writers. In Stair's *Institutions*, I.i.23, it is stated 'Rights, in respect of the matter, are divided into public and private rights. Public rights are those which concern the state of the commonwealth. Private rights are the rights of persons, and particular incorporations.' Erskine's *Institute*, I.i.29, states: 'Positive law may be divided into public and private. The public law is that which hath more immediately in view the public weal, and the preservation and good order of society; as laws concerning the constitution of the state, the administration of the government, the police of the country, public revenues, trade and manufactures, the punishment of crimes etc. Private law is that which is chiefly intended for ascertaining the civil rights of individuals.' In my opinion, that branch of law which is concerned with the control of fishing in territorial waters round the coasts of Scotland is a branch of public law. These waters are regarded as belonging to the sovereign as custodier or trustee for public, not private, rights of navigation and fishing. Sea fishing is a trade, which contributes to the public good, and laws relating to trade are specifically mentioned by Erskine as falling within the field of public law. Article xviii of the Act of Union specifically provided that the laws concerning regulation of trade were to be made the same throughout Great Britain. That was one of the principal objects of the Union. Further, the exclusion of foreign vessels from fishing in territorial waters was and is capable of being achieved only by the exercise of sovereign power, by the employment of fishery protection officers, and the prosecution of offenders in the criminal courts of the Crown. Erskine allocates to the domain of public law police matters and the prosecution of crime, and this is plainly right. There is the further consideration that mutual recognition of the extent of territorial waters and such rights of fishing, if any, as subjects of foreign states are to be accorded within them are matters of foreign policy and diplomacy, as well as international law, as evidenced by the negotiation over many years of the Conventions referred to in various Sea Fisheries Acts. No private individual possesses any right enabling him personally to prevent a foreign vessel from fishing in territorial waters. For these reasons I am of opinion that the law which the pursuer founds upon as the basis of his case is a law concerned with public right, within the meaning of article xviii of the Act of Union. Carried to its logical conclusion, the pursuer's case must necessarily involve that inhabitants of England should never have been allowed to fish in Scottish waters. This was, however, a right specifically conferred upon them by the Act 29 Geo. 2, c.23, entitled 'an Act of encouraging the fisheries in that part of Great Britain called Scotland'. This Act is, in my opinion, evidence that the matter of sea fishing was at the time regarded as falling within the domain of public law.

It was also argued for the defender that s.2(1) of the 1972 Act does not, on a proper construction, have the effect of making article 2 of the EEC Regulations part of the domestic law of Scotland. Article 189 of the Treaty of Rome, which I have already quoted, provides that a regulation made by the Commission and Council 'shall be binding in its entirety and directly applicable in all member states'. Section 2(1) of the 1972 Act apparently seeks to give effect to this provision, and I have no doubt that it has the effect of causing to be binding on individual subjects in Scotland such EEC regulations as are capable of being so binding. Some EEC regulations, however, do not purport to impose any obligation upon individual citizens, and I regard the particular regulation now under consideration as falling into this category. That regulation, in my view, operates in the field of public law. The obligations which it imposes are imposed upon the member states, not upon any individuals. Each member state is in substance required to operate its system of fishery control and its code of criminal law in such a way as to avoid discrimination against the fishing vessels of other member states. I am accordingly of opinion that s.2(1) of the 1972 Act and article 2 of the EEC Regulations do not effect any alterations in the private laws of Scotland.

Lord Keith also accepted an argument for the defender that access by fishing vessels of other Community states to Scottish waters was in any event authorized by an Order made under the Fishery Limits Act 1964, so that a declarator in the terms sought by the pursuer, relating only to section 2(1) of the European Communities Act 1972 and EEC Regulation 2141/70, would have no practical effect. He continued:

For these reasons I am of opinion that the pursuer's case is irrelevant and should be dismissed.

In addition to the argument on relevancy there were addressed to me interesting arguments upon the question of jurisidiction and the competency of the action. These arguments raised constitutional issues of great potential importance, in particular whether the Court of Session has power to declare an Act of the United Kingdom Parliament to be void, whether an alleged discrepancy between an Act of that Parliament and the Treaty or Act of Union is a justiciable issue in this court, and whether, with particular reference to article XVIII of the Act of Union, this court has power to decide whether an alteration of private law bearing to be effected by an Act of the United Kingdom Parliament is 'for the evident utility' of the subjects in Scotland. Having regard to my decision on relevancy, these are not live issues in the present case. The position was similar in *MacCormick* v. *Lord Advocate* [above], a case concerned with the validity of the proclamation as Queen of Her present Majesty under a title which incorporated the numeral 'second'. The First Division held that no question properly arose concerning the validity of the Royal Titles Act 1953, but delivered certain obiter dicta upon the constitutional position as regards the Treaty and Act of Union. . . . Like Lord President Cooper, I prefer to reserve my opinion on what the question would be if the United Kingdom Parliament passed an Act purporting to abolish the Court of Session or the Church of Scotland or to substitute English law for the whole body of Scots private law. I am, however, of opinion that the question whether a particular Act of the United Kingdom Parliament altering a particular aspect of Scots private law is or is not 'for the evident utility' of the subjects within Scotland is not a justiciable issue in this court. The making of decisions upon what must essentially be a political matter is no part of the function of the court, and it is highly undesirable that it should be. The function of the court is to adjudicate upon the particular rights and obligations of individual persons, natural or corporate, in relation to other persons or, in certain instances, to the state. A general inquiry into the utility of certain legislative measures as regards the population generally is quite outside its competence. . . .

Lord Keith dealt finally with the question of the pursuer's title to sue and said that, had the court been competent to review the utility, from the point of view of the people of Scotland generally, of an alteration in the law brought about by a particular Act of Parliament, he could see no reason why such review 'should not be instituted at the instance of any person who has an interest to invoke the powers of the court'.

The action was accordingly dismissed. (See comment by J. M. Thomson (1976) 92 *LQR* 36.)

These two cases contain interesting dicta but give no definite ruling on the question whether Parliament's powers are limited by the Treaty and Acts of Union. It is evident however that any challenge to an Act on this ground encounters two preliminary obstacles: the need for the plaintiff to have a sufficient interest, giving standing to sue (one of the reasons for the failure of the action in *MacCormick*'s case); and the necessity of persuading a court to assume jurisdiction to decide the question – the prospects of any such attempt are doubtful. Even if a court agreed to entertain the matter, it *might* decide that the new Parliament created in 1707 succeeded to the sovereignty of its English predecessor and was unlimited in *law* by the terms of the Treaty of Union; or alternatively that any initial limitations upon the power of the United Kingdom Parliament have been overcome by the full maturing of the doctrine of parliamentary sovereignty since 1707.

It is nevertheless the fact that the essential conditions of the Treaty of Union have in substance been respected. Scottish lawyers, politicians and others still hold them to be significant (but the Scottish National Party, with 11.8 per cent of the Scottish vote in the 1983 general election, rejects the British political system). Custom, Scottish national sentiment, and political calculation are factors which qualify the exercise of Parliament's powers with regard to the Treaty of Union.

The government of Scotland

After the Union of 1707 the Scottish administration was absorbed into an administration of Great Britain centred in London. The Lord Advocate, besides being a Law Officer of the Crown, kept some responsibilities for Scottish administration, and public boards with governmental functions were established in Scotland in the nineteenth century. But these arrangements did not satisfy the Scots and in 1885 a Secretary of Scotland was appointed as ministerial head of a Scottish Office in Whitehall. The Scottish Secretaryship was replaced in 1926 by the more senior office of Secretary of State, and in 1939 the Scottish Office was moved to Edinburgh.

The Secretary of State for Scotland always has a seat in the Cabinet – necessary if he is to be able to press the case for Scotland on equal terms. At present his ministerial team includes a Minister of State and three Parliamentary Under-Secretaries of State. His responsibilities cover a wide range of Scottish affairs, corresponding to functions which are spread over several Whitehall departments. The Scottish Office is a 'federal' organization comprising five departments:

> Department of Agriculture and Fisheries for Scotland
> Scottish Development Department (housing, local government, town and country planning, etc.)
> Scottish Economic Planning Department (economic development, assistance to industry, new towns, etc.)
> Scottish Education Department (schools and colleges, arts, social services, etc.)
> Scottish Home and Health Department (National Health Service, police, prisons, criminal justice, etc.)

The authors of the following passage consider 'the extent to which the Scottish Office "makes" its own policy or simply "administers" policy made elsewhere'.

Michael Keating and Arthur Midwinter, *The Government of Scotland* (1983), pp. 19–23

The process for handling major policy initiatives is fairly standard. Proposals are formulated in the department which is to take the 'lead', with, normally, a considerable amount of outside consultation. Often, it is outside interest groups who have raised the issue in the first place and where the issue has been raised is the first factor determining which department is to take the lead. At a very early stage, other departments are sounded out through the civil service grapevine and the Treasury is consulted on any financial implications. Policy clearance will then be sought from the appropriate Cabinet committee, where bargaining and negotiation are likely. To clarify this, let us divide policy proposals into three types: Scottish Office proposals for Scotland alone; proposals from 'UK departments' for England and Wales; and proposals for the whole of the UK (or Britain), in which the initiative and lead will almost invariably be taken by a UK department. A purely Scottish or purely English proposal may be passed on the nod, with provision made only for the copying of the relevant papers to the other territorial departments. Alternatively, major objections, amounting to a veto, may be made and the initiating department forced to withdraw the proposal. More likely, the proposal will be the subject of negotiation and emerge from the committee in a modified form. If the proposal requires legislation, then this, too, will have to be approved by the committee, which will continue to monitor the passage of the bill and approve any amendments to it. So policy is agreed interdepartmentally and can be presented as the policy of the Government, no matter which department takes the lead. On the other hand, the amount of bargaining and the influence which departments can bring to bear will vary greatly. We can see the Scottish Office role in the policy process in terms of a spectrum ranging from, at one extreme, almost complete autonomy in policy making to, at the other extreme, complete dependence, following, more or less exactly, the line laid down by a UK lead department. Where an issue involves more than one department, the process by which that policy is forged depends on a complex interplay of forces, the principal ones of which we will now examine.

The first of these is the *statutory responsibilities* of the departments concerned. Where the Scottish Office has administrative responsibility for a function, it will have staff working on policy development and automatic membership of the appropriate interdepartmental committee. Its civil servants will be part of the grapevine. The degree of administrative responsibility for a function can vary greatly. In the case of education, it is almost total, allowing considerable autonomy. In the case of energy, the Scottish Office has responsibility only for electricity. However, this still gives it membership of committees on energy policy and allows the Secretary of State to maintain a small group of civil servants working on energy policy generally. While this group is too small to formulate much in the way of policy initiatives, it does enable the Scottish Office to keep abreast of policy development in the Department of Energy and to provide a Scottish input where appropriate. Similarly, the Secretary of State's rather ill-defined but official role as an economic and industrial minister and his limited range of economic responsibilities give him an entree into the industrial and economic policy network. A great deal of Scottish activity here is reactive, trying to modify proposals coming from a UK lead department, but, as far as possible, Scottish ministers and officials do try to contribute to the making of overall UK policy rather than just harping on the 'Scottish angle'. In this way they are able to maximise their impact.

The extent of *cross-border spillover* effects is, of course, of great importance in determining the degree of autonomy allowed to the Scottish Office. Where a matter has few repercussions for England, UK departments are often content to let the Scots go ahead on their own. Where Scottish actions would affect England or vice versa, on the other hand, there may be a need for a unified policy. Professional education provides two contrasting examples. Because the Scottish primary/secondary school system and its teaching profession are largely self-contained, teacher-training and teacher supply can be handled independently in Scotland. In social work, however, there is a UK-wide job market, so that qualifications and supply have to be co-ordinated closely. . . .

In many areas, UK departments are prepared to recognise the existence of a separate *Scottish tradition* providing for autonomy. Where such a tradition exists, with separate legislation and administrative structures, then it may be difficult in any case, to obtain uniformity of policy. On the other hand, this autonomy only exists within the constraints which we are examining.

The *public expenditure* implications of a policy proposal will largely determine the role of the Treasury. In the past, expenditure considerations were a major constraint on the autonomy of the Scottish Office, as . . . any policy change involving expenditure required the approval of the Treasury, which was also involved in monitoring expenditure. Now most Scottish Office expenditure is expressed as a block allocation within which the Secretary of State has scope for virement [transfers of funds between programmes]. The Treasury has, consequently, retreated to a concern mainly with the Office's overall cash limits. However, the Scottish Office block allocation is built up functionally and based on the budgets of the corresponding UK departments. So the total of Scottish expenditure can only be influenced by the Secretary of State by his supporting UK functional ministers in their battles for more resources. . . .

The need or otherwise for *legislation* will also affect the Scottish Office's freedom of manoeuvre. If the Office requires legislation for its own policy proposals, this will need the approval of the Cabinet, which rarely allows more than one major Scottish bill per parliamentary session. UK departments will also have to consider whether a change in Scottish law will affect them. Where a UK department proposes legislation, the Scottish Office will consider whether it wishes Scotland to be included or excluded and, if the former, will usually try to secure a separate Scottish bill which, as well as producing clearer law for Scotland, will give it greater control over the legislative process.

Party policy and the *political salience* of an issue are important factors. Though there are some variations in party policy on either side of the border, the basic ideological thrust is the same and, on partisan matters, there is a tendency to uniformity, even where Scottish ministers might try to resist it. So the last Labour Government's legislation on private beds in National Health Service hospitals, on which the lead was taken by [the Department of Health and Social Security], was applied to Scotland despite the objections of Scottish ministers, who believed that the conditions in Scotland were quite different and that the problem was being dealt with satisfactorily by other means. Generally, both civil servants and ministers try to minimise policy divergence on either side of the border to prevent the spectacle of a government apparently believing in two different policies for the same issue. . . .

Where *finance* or *charges* for public services are involved, there are usually political objections to variations so that these tend to be uniform.

Where policy is, formally, made separately in Scotland and England, it may nevertheless develop on the same lines because of common *professional views* and fashions. Thus, developments in health care or the social services will be transmitted through UK-wide professional networks and suggested at the same time to both Scottish and English departments.

Leadership and the balance of influence are also affected by the *relative importance* of the issue for Scotland and England and the relative size of the corresponding sections of the Scottish and English departments. On most matters it is the UK or 'English' department which is the larger and more senior but, occasionally, Scotland is of equal weight, for example in fisheries, where it accounts for over half the UK industry, and in some aspects of agriculture. Here joint policy making is the rule, with the Scottish Office having equal weight and sometimes taking the lead. . . .

The policy process is, finally, influenced by *personal and political factors* which can vary from time to time. Ministers can smooth their way by personal friendships and log-rolling and an energetic and determined minister will be able to achieve more than one who sees his role in terms of keeping the department ticking over or following leads given elsewhere. The status of the Scottish Office depends, too, on the political rank of the Secretary of State and on the perceived importance of Scotland to the Government. In recent years, Labour governments have been much more dependent on their Scottish seats than have Conservative ones and this, combined with the threat to those seats from the SNP, gave Secretaries of State in the late 1960s and late 1970s added political weight. . . .

The chief law officer for Scotland is the Lord Advocate, who advises the government on matters of Scots law and heads the Crown Office in Edinburgh, which is responsible for criminal prosecutions. His department in London does the work of drafting Scottish legislation.

Since 1975 it has been the practice to appoint a Scottish MP to the office of Minister of State in the Department of Energy.

Scottish Ministers are responsible to a United Kingdom Parliament in which there are 72 members representing Scottish constituencies in a House of Commons of 650 members. The Labour Party has won a majority of Scottish seats in every general election since 1959, with the result that Conservative Ministers in the Scottish Office have ruled a 'Labour' Scotland in 1959–64, 1970–74 and since 1979. In 1983 the Conservative Party won only 28.4 per cent of the Scottish vote.

Scotland is over-represented in the House of Commons for, if average constituency electorates were the same in all four countries of the United Kingdom, Scotland would have not 72 but 60 seats. (A minimum of 71 seats for Scotland is prescribed by the House of Commons (Redistribution of Seats) Act 1949, Sched. 2.)

Scottish affairs in the House of Commons

Special arrangements exist for the conduct of Scottish business in the House. A Scottish Grand Committee consisting of all 72 Scottish MPs debates Scottish 'matters and estimates' on up to 12 days in each session. In addition bills certified by the Speaker as relating exclusively to Scotland are usually referred, on the motion of a minister, to the Grand Committee for a 'second reading' debate, when the bill is considered in principle. (Objection by ten members prevents the reference of a bill to the Grand Committee.) After debate the Committee reports to the House that it has considered the bill, and there is normally no debate on the floor of the House before the bill's formal second reading. (There can be a further reference of the bill to the Grand Committee for its report stage, but this does not happen in practice.) The Grand Committee, which holds some of its sittings in Edinburgh, is like a sub-parliament for Scotland within the House of Commons, but one that is essentially a forum for debate, without independent powers.

The detailed examination of Scottish bills at their committee stage, after second reading, is undertaken by one of the two Scottish standing committees. These committees are made up of Scottish MPs but in such a way as to reflect the party balance in the House.

As a fairly typical example of the passage of Scottish legislation we may take the Housing (Financial Provisions) (Scotland) Bill which was introduced by the Secretary of State for Scotland and had its first (formal) reading in the House of Commons on 17 November 1977. The bill introduced a new system of housing support grants for local authorities in Scotland and made provision for repair grants for old houses. It was certified by the Speaker as relating exclusively to Scotland, and on the motion of the Minister – no members objecting – it was referred to the Scottish Grand Committee.

The bill, which had broad cross-party support, was considered for one day in the Grand Committee. (At one point proceedings had to be suspended because attendance had fallen below the quorum of 17.) A member on the Government side severely criticized the bill for not giving a fair deal to tenants. At the end of the debate it was agreed after a division (24 to two) to report to the House 'that the Committee have considered the Housing (Financial Provisions) (Scotland) Bill in relation to the principle of the Bill'.

The next day in the House the Minister moved that the bill 'be committed to a Scottish Standing Committee', and this having been agreed to, the bill was deemed under standing orders to have been read a second time. (Any six members could have given notice of an amendment, and so secured a second reading debate on the floor of the House.)

The standing committee, which consisted of 16 Scottish MPs, spent five days on the clause-by-clause discussion of the bill, which was piloted through the Committee by a Parliamentary Under-Secretary of State for Scotland. Several amendments were made to the bill on the proposal of the Minister or with his agreement; one was carried against the Government.

The bill was then 'reported to the House as amended'; in the report stage debate in the House only Scottish MPs spoke. The Government took the opportunity of removing the amendment carried against it in committee. The bill was given its third reading, without a division, on the same day, and was sent to the House of Lords. It continued its relatively uneventful passage (returning to the Commons for consideration of some Lords' amendments, which were agreed) and received the royal assent on 25 May 1978. In the whole course of the proceedings on the bill only Scottish members took part.

Besides the arrangements for general debate and the consideration of Scottish bills, there is machinery for the critical scrutiny of the Scottish Office, with its wide-ranging powers and general responsibility for the social and economic welfare of Scotland. A Select Committee on Scottish Affairs set up in 1969 was not a success and expired after the 1971–2 session of Parliament. When a new system of select committees for the scrutiny of government departments was established in 1979 (see chapter 7 below), a Committee on Scottish Affairs was set up to examine the 'expenditure, administration and policy' of the Scottish Office and its associated public bodies (e.g., the Highlands and Islands Development Board and the Scottish Development Agency). It inquires into aspects of Scottish administration (such as youth unemployment and training, and rural road passenger transport) and its aim has been 'to select matters of current concern in Scotland on which we could hope to influence decisions through the publication of a report or influence discussion through the publication of evidence' (First Report from the Liaison Committee, *The Select Committee System*, HC 92 of 1982–3, p. 109).

The system that has been described provides much work for Scottish MPs and involves them closely and constantly in Scottish business at Westminster. This business is, however, firmly set in a United Kingdom context where collective ministerial responsibility and centralized policy-making are the rule.

(c) **Wales**

Wales is about one-twelfth the size of the United Kingdom and has a population (1981 census) of 2,791,851 or about 5 per cent of the total United Kingdom population. Wales came under the rule of the English Crown in the thirteenth century. There was no treaty of union, then or later, between the two countries, and the Act of Union of 1536 was a unilateral Act of the English Parliament, extending the English administrative system to Wales and providing for Welsh representation in Parliament.

In the early years of the twentieth century a number of departments with Welsh responsibilities were created (e.g. the Welsh Board of Health and the Welsh Department of the Board of Education) and from 1951 a senior departmental minister (at first the Home Secretary) was given a general responsibility for Wales with the title of Minister for Welsh Affairs. A Secretaryship of State for Wales was created by the Wilson Government in 1964, and since then there has been a Secretary of State for Wales with a seat in the Cabinet. At present there are also a Minister of State and a Parliamentary Under-Secretary of State in the Welsh Office, which has its headquarters in

Cardiff.

The responsibilities of the Secretary of State for Wales have been substantially increased since 1964 and now include economic and industrial development, agriculture, water resources, town and country planning, local government, roads, housing, health and social services, and education (except universities). These functions are not quite so wide-ranging as those of Scotland's Minister, for, as we have seen, the Scottish Office has a longer history of 'separateness' and administers Scotland's own judicial and legal systems.

The Secretary of State and the Welsh Office have probably been of benefit to Wales in bringing Welsh interests into account when government policies are being formulated. Moreover a Welsh Office in Cardiff is more accessible to Welsh pressure groups and local authorities than a distant and preoccupied Whitehall. But a note of scepticism is sounded in the following passage.

Vernon Bogdanor, *Devolution* (1979), pp. 138–9

[I]t would be wrong to believe that current governmental arrangements in Wales offer a satisfactory solution to the problem of adjusting national policies to Welsh needs. For the conventions of British government are bound to limit the autonomy of the Secretary of State, even if to a lesser extent than was the case with the Welsh departments of UK ministries. The Welsh Secretary is bound by the policies of his party even if these do not coincide with the desires of the majority of Welsh voters, a situation particularly likely to arise when the Conservatives are in government; and the traditions of the civil service remain hostile to excessive experimentation in one part of the country, lest it create an undesirable precedent for other areas.

Moreover, the Welsh Secretary is unlikely to be a powerful figure in Cabinet. The post is not one that is likely to be offered to a politician of the front rank, and promotion to one of the leading offices of state is unlikely to result from competence in the office. Indeed, the Welsh Secretary, now that this office is a separate one, is far junior in Cabinet rank to his predecessors, the Home Secretary and the Minister for Housing and Local Government, when they exercised responsibility for Wales. . . .

The convention of Cabinet secrecy makes it difficult for voters in Wales to attribute clear responsibility for policy decisions affecting Wales. The Secretary of State may often have to defend policies with which he disagrees, and he will be unable to parade his triumphs except surreptitiously. He is also in a peculiarly anomalous position, in that he is popularly regarded as the 'Minister for Wales' even though he is statutorily responsible for only a limited range of government policy in Wales. Where he fails to prevent pit or rail closures he may be blamed by Welsh public opinion, even though these matters do not fall within his statutory competence.

Wales is guaranteed a minimum of 35 seats in the House of Commons (by the House of Commons (Redistribution of Seats) Act 1949, Sched. 2) and has at present 38. Like Scotland, Wales is over-represented in the House on the basis of the size of its electorate, which would strictly entitle it to no more than 33 seats. From 1880 to 1910 Wales was a Liberal stronghold; the Labour Party has won a majority of Welsh seats in every election since 1935.

A Welsh Grand Committee of the House of Commons was first set up in 1960 to debate Welsh affairs and review the administration of Wales; it now consists of all MPs for Wales and up to five other members. The Grand Committee considers bills and other matters relating exclusively to Wales that are referred to it on the motion of a minister. (Objection by 20 MPs keeps a bill on the floor of the House.) The Committee reports to the House that it has considered any 'matter' referred to it, and recommends that any bill considered by it should, or should not, be given a second reading. Legislation relating exclusively to Wales is rare: some examples are the Welsh Courts Act 1942, the Welsh Language Act 1967, and the Welsh Development Agency Act 1975.

There are no Welsh standing committees, like those for Scotland, established to examine Welsh bills, but an ordinary standing committee appointed for any such bill must include all Welsh MPs (SO 65).

A Select Committee on Welsh Affairs was created in 1979 'to examine the expenditure, administration and policy of the Welsh Office and associated public bodies' (e.g. the Welsh Water Authority). The Committee sometimes meets in Wales and has taken evidence in Welsh. It has inquired into such matters as employment opportunities in Wales, broadcasting in the Welsh language, and the impact of the European Community on Wales. Its scrutiny of the Welsh Office provides a safeguard against the emergence of an 'unaccountable' bureaucracy in Wales.

(d) Northern Ireland

Northern Ireland, a land of 5,000 square miles, has a population (1981 census) of 1,488,077 or less than 3 per cent of the total United Kingdom population. Catholics compose between 31 and 42 per cent of the population of the six counties. (The figure is very uncertain: see *The Times*, 29 August 1983, p. 1.)

Ruled by the English Crown since the twelfth century, all Ireland was united with Great Britain by Acts of Union of the British and Irish Parliaments in 1800. (The Act of the Irish Parliament was passed in unedifying circumstances but was doubtless formally valid.) The Acts of Union ended the life of the Irish Parliament and transferred its authority to a Parliament of the United Kingdom, which was to include Irish members. The two countries were to be united into one Kingdom 'for ever after'; and the union of the Churches of England and Ireland was declared to be established for ever as 'an essential and fundamental part' of the Union.

As with the earlier Acts of Union between England and Scotland (see above), it can be argued that the Acts of Union of 1800 were constituent Acts of a new (United Kingdom) Parliament which set legal limits to the powers of that Parliament. But in this instance the argument has not fared well. The Irish Church Act 1869 disestablished the Church of Ireland, dissolving its union with the Church of England, notwithstanding the explicit provision of the Acts of Union. A challenge to the validity of the Act (although not expressly for its non-conformity with the Acts of Union) was unsuccessful: *ex p. Canon Selwyn* (1872) 36 JP 54. The Acts of Union were abrogated in a fundamental respect in 1921–2 when the Irish Free State was separated from the United Kingdom as a free dominion within the Commonwealth. (See the Irish Free State (Agreement) Act 1922, the Irish Free State Constitution Act 1922 and the Irish Free State (Consequential Provisions) Act 1922.) It became a republic with the name Eire in 1937 and withdrew from the Commonwealth in 1949.

The six counties of the north-east remained within the United Kingdom with their own Parliament and Government in Belfast established by the Government of Ireland Act 1920. The Ireland Act 1949 included, in statutory form, a political assurance to the Unionist (mainly Protestant) community of Northern Ireland which was reaffirmed in the following terms in section 1 of the Northern Ireland Constitution Act 1973:

It is hereby declared that Northern Ireland remains part of Her Majesty's dominions and of the United Kingdom, and it is hereby affirmed that in no event will Northern Ireland or any part of it cease to be part of Her Majesty's dominions and of the United Kingdom without the consent of the majority of the people of Northern Ireland voting in a poll held for the purposes of this section. . . .

Has this statutory declaration any effect in law? See Brigid Hadfield [1983] *PL* 351. The *Report of the New Ireland Forum* (Dublin, 1984, para. 5.1(4)) says of the guarantee in section 1 that it 'has in its practical application had the effect of inhibiting the dialogue necessary for political progress. It has had the additional effect of removing the incentive which would otherwise exist on all sides to seek a political solution' to the problem of Northern Ireland.

Devolved government

The constitution of Northern Ireland established by the Government of Ireland Act 1920 endured until 1972. The Act provided for a system of 'devolved government', with a bicameral Parliament and an Executive headed (from 1922) by a Governor of Northern Ireland as representative of the Crown. Section 1 of the Act read as follows:

(1) On and after the appointed day there shall be established . . . for Northern Ireland a Parliament to be called the Parliament of Northern Ireland consisting of His Majesty, the Senate of Northern Ireland, and the House of Commons of Northern Ireland.

(2) For the purposes of this Act, Northern Ireland shall consist of the parliamentary counties of Antrim, Armagh, Down, Fermanagh, Londonderry and Tyrone, and the parliamentary boroughs of Belfast and Londonderry. . . .

Elections to the House of Commons were by proportional representation until

1929, and from then by the plurality ('first past the post') system used in United Kingdom parliamentary elections. The United Kingdom Parliament retained its entire sovereignty in matters affecting Northern Ireland, but there was an extensive transfer of legislative power to the Parliament at Belfast, the Act specifying the subjects to be *reserved* to Westminster rather than those to be *transferred*. The convention was soon established that the United Kingdom Parliament should not legislate for Northern Ireland in the 'transferred' area unless requested to do so by the Northern Ireland Government. Representation of Northern Ireland in the United Kingdom Parliament continued, but with a reduced number of seats (13 until 1948, thereafter 12).

Report of the Royal Commission on the Constitution (Kilbrandon Report), vol. 1, Cmnd 5460/1973

170.   . . . The world in which the home rule ideas were to operate was very different from the one in which they were conceived. The [Government of Ireland Act 1920] was passed at a time when it was still possible to believe that, following the end of the First World War, both legislatures and governments would be able to limit their activities to those of the Edwardian era, the subject matter being neatly divided into the great 'imperial' issues on the one hand and purely domestic matters, which could safely be left to a regional legislature, on the other. The Act was designed in this way, the 'imperial' matters being reserved to Westminster and a contribution levied to pay for them, while nearly all other matters were transferred to the Northern Ireland Parliament, which was to have complete legal freedom to make of them what it wished and the independent finance needed to underpin that freedom. But almost before the Act had come fully into force this dream had collapsed and the mounting crisis of unemployment, in Northern Ireland as elsewhere, forced the state into activities which had hardly been known before the war, and started the long escalation of expenditure which has continued to the present.

171.   This collapse of the financial arrangements laid down in the 1920 Act, and its wider consequences for the working of the home rule provisions, owed nothing to the peculiarities of the Northern Ireland situation, except to the extent that the province is a part of the United Kingdom, but by no means the only part, which is unable to pay for its own domestic services out of the proceeds of taxes collected there. Measures began to be devised soon after 1920 to provide additional revenue for Northern Ireland . . . . An important consequence of the way arrangements developed was a reduction in Northern Ireland's freedom to pursue independent policies on transferred matters, since financial adjustment was inevitably accompanied by a degree of United Kingdom Treasury control which was certainly not contemplated when the Act was passed. The free exercise of legislative powers was inhibited also by popular pressures for the adoption of standards in the public services no lower than those obtaining in other parts of the United Kingdom.

172.   . . . [T]he constitution was placed under additional stresses stemming from the division of the population into two sharply distinct communities, a majority, predominantly Protestant and in favour of the maintenance of the union with Great Britain, and a minority, predominantly Roman Catholic and opposed to the union. For the whole period of the existence of the Northern Ireland Parliament, politics in the

province were dominated by this single issue. Parliamentary elections were concerned almost exclusively with it, and only those political parties whose positions in relation to it were clearly defined were able to attract substantial support. . . .

1251. . . . [T]he Act applied to Northern Ireland the system of Parliamentary democracy in use at Westminster, which depends for its smooth working on an alternation between Government and Opposition. The rule that the 'winner takes all' – that the Government is formed exclusively from the party that has a majority, be it large or small, in the legislature, and that the Opposition is totally excluded – is far easier to accept when electoral victory passes from party to party. Balance and equity are achieved by alternation. But in Northern Ireland the winner was always the Unionist Party. There was nothing contrived or improper about this; whatever may have been true, from time to time and from place to place, about local government elections, there is no room for doubt that at every general election for the Northern Ireland House of Commons a clear majority of the electors deliberately intended the Unionist Party to form the government. The permanent majority was a permanent and cohesive majority in the electorate. But such a result, so often repeated, and apparently so likely to continue, inevitably produced great dissatisfaction in the minority and raised the question of the suitability of that particular form of government in the special circumstances of Northern Ireland.

Despite these flaws the Kilbrandon Commission was in agreement with other commentators who have judged the devolved or 'home rule' government of Northern Ireland to have been broadly successful in providing laws and administration suitable to the particular needs of the province. It had been an instrument of progress at all events 'in the large areas of government which were unaffected, or at least were not dominated, by the community problem' (para. 1264). But a different aspect of the period of home rule is emphasized in the 1984 *Report of the New Ireland Forum* (composed of representatives of democratic nationalist parties of North and South). The identity of the nationalist community in the North, it said (para. 3. 9), had been effectively disregarded:

The symbols and procedures of the institutions to which nationalists are required to give allegiance have been a constant reminder of the denial of their identity. . . . [T]hey have had virtually no involvement in decision-making at the political level. For over 50 years they lived under a system of exclusively unionist power and privilege and suffered systematic discrimination. They were deprived of the means of social and economic development, experienced high levels of emigration and have always been subject to high rates of unemployment.

For the whole period 1921–72 the Unionist Party had an absolute majority in the Northern Ireland House of Commons. (No such long-lasting single-party hegemony has been known at Westminster since the Reform Act of 1832.) The dominance of the Unionist Party extended to local government, where Unionist majorities were sometimes assured by gerrymandering and the manipulation of housing allocations. Inflexible single-party rule contributed to the resentments of a disadvantaged Catholic community in the poorest part of the United Kingdom, and these resentments were at last to explode in the disorders of 1968 and the following years.

There was a series of constitutional reforms in Northern Ireland between 1968 and 1972. Electoral law was reformed and local government reorganized. A Northern Ireland Parliamentary Commissioner for Administration and a Commissioner for Complaints were appointed to investigate complaints of maladministration by public authorities. A Community Relations Commission was set up to promote action to improve community relations, and a Housing Executive took over responsibility for public housing in the province. Despite these reforms, the nationalist community was 'still discriminated against in social, economic, cultural and political terms' (*Report of the New Ireland Forum*, para.3.17) and the province experienced continuing violence and disorder, the despatch of troops, and the introduction of internment. The deepening crisis elicited increasing involvement by the United Kingdom Government in the affairs of Northern Ireland, and finally in March 1972 direct rule from Whitehall was imposed on the province. By the Northern Ireland (Temporary Provisions) Act 1972 the Parliament of Northern Ireland was prorogued, and provision was made for legislation by Order in Council on the subjects within its competence. The powers of the Northern Ireland Government were transferred to a Secretary of State for Northern Ireland.

Direct rule

The first period of direct rule ran from 1972 to 1974. A considerable amount of time was given at Westminster to legislation for Northern Ireland (Acts and Orders in Council). A Northern Ireland (Border Poll) Act 1972 provided for a referendum in the province on the question whether Northern Ireland should remain part of the United Kingdom or be joined with the Republic of Ireland. In the 'border poll' of March 1973, only 58.7 per cent of the electorate cast their votes (nationalist political leaders had urged their supporters not to vote): 591,820 voted to remain part of the United Kingdom, 6,463 to join with the Republic of Ireland.

A new system of devolution, based on the principle of power-sharing between the two communities, was instituted by the Northern Ireland Constitution Act 1973 and the Northern Ireland Assembly Act 1973. There were to be an Assembly, with legislative powers, elected by proportional representation, and an Executive constituted from parties representative of both communities. The Assembly was duly elected and an Executive, composed of members of the Official Unionist Party, the Social Democratic and Labour Party (SDLP), and the Alliance Party, took office. The Executive entered into discussions with the Government of the Irish Republic on the formation of a Council of Ireland which would be an instrument for cooperation between the province and the Republic.

This first attempt to achieve an inter-communal constitutional settlement in Northern Ireland collapsed when a general strike of loyalist workers organized by the Ulster Workers' Council brought down the Executive in May 1974, after only five months. The Assembly was dissolved and direct rule from Whitehall was resumed under arrangements made by the Northern Ireland Act 1974. Direct rule was to be for an 'interim period' of one year; it has been extended annually by orders made under the Act, in the conviction that a return to single-party government in Northern Ireland would offer no prospect of a solution to the problems of the province.

A renewed attempt to induce agreement between Northern Ireland political parties was made in 1975, when a Constitutional Convention was elected (in terms of the Northern Ireland Act 1974) to devise a scheme of devolved government which would have broad support in the two communities. But the Convention was dissolved after failing to agree on fundamentals, the loyalist members having insisted on majority rule in any new Executive.

In 1982 a further attempt was made to fill the political vacuum resulting from the resumption of direct rule. The new scheme was announced in a White Paper (*Northern Ireland: A Framework for Devolution*, Cmnd 8541/1982) and implemented by the Northern Ireland Act 1982.

The Act made arrangements for a reconstituted Northern Ireland Assembly, to be elected by proportional representation, which would, from the first, debate the affairs of the province, establish committees to scrutinize the work of the Northern Ireland departments, and report on matters (including proposed Orders in Council) referred to it by the Secretary of State. In the longer term the Assembly could claim the devolution to itself, and to a sufficiently widely based Executive, of those matters previously designated by the Northern Ireland Constitution Act 1973 as 'transferred matters' and considered appropriate for devolution. These do not include 'excepted' matters (such as the armed forces, international relations and immigration, elections and the franchise) which are to remain the responsibility of United Kingdom departments, and 'reserved' matters (such as law and order) which are also to remain with Whitehall departments but may be transferred once a durable and stable system of government has been established in Northern Ireland. It is provided that a devolution of legislative and executive powers in the 'transferred' category may be effected either *en bloc* or partially – the functions of some Northern Ireland departments being devolved while others remain subject to direct rule. A transfer of powers can take place only if a draft Order in Council is laid by the Secretary of State before Parliament and is approved by it. 'The crucial requirement', the Government has said, 'is that the Assembly's proposals should be likely to command widespread acceptance throughout the community: in forming a judgment on this the Government would only consider a proposal to command sufficiently widespread acceptance if it appeared to be acceptable to both sides of the community' (*Northern Ireland: A Framework for Devolution*, Cmnd 8541/1982, para. 42). (See the Northern Ireland Act 1982, s.1.)

The first elections to the new Northern Ireland Assembly were held in

October 1982, an absolute majority of seats being won by the Unionist parties. The two nationalist parties (the SDLP and Sinn Fein) declined to take their seats. The Assembly has begun its 'scrutinizing, deliberative and consultative' functions, but no powers have yet been devolved to it.

Direct rule continues while results are awaited from the scheme of 'rolling devolution'. The government of Northern Ireland is the responsibility of a Secretary of State assisted by two ministers of state and two Parliamentary Under-Secretaries of State. Policy on law and order, constitutional development, etc., is directed by the Northern Ireland Office in Whitehall; departments in Belfast (staffed by the Northern Ireland Civil Service, which is a distinct service under the Crown) administer agriculture, economic development, education, the environment, and health and social services.

Acts of Parliament may be enacted for or extended to Northern Ireland, but the Northern Ireland Act 1974 confers power to legislate specifically for Northern Ireland by Order in Council, subject to affirmative resolutions of both Houses of Parliament, and this is the method usually adopted. Orders in Council do not receive the same full parliamentary consideration as bills and they cannot be amended.

The representation of Northern Ireland in the United Kingdom Parliament was increased by the House of Commons (Redistribution of Seats) Act 1979, which provided (section 1) that the number of constituencies for Northern Ireland should be 17 (unless the Boundary Commission for Northern Ireland should find it necessary to vary this number to 16 or 18 for the time being). There are at present 17 Northern Ireland seats in the House of Commons. The Northern Ireland Committee, a standing committee of the House, debates Northern Ireland affairs referred to it; the departmental select committees which review the work of United Kingdom Government departments can inquire into matters within their ambit which are the responsibility of the Secretary of State for Northern Ireland.

'There are at present', says the *Report of the New Ireland Forum* (para. 2.4), 'no political institutions to which a majority of people of the nationalist and unionist traditions can give their common allegiance or even acquiesce in'. The Forum sees the solution in terms of a united Ireland: 'The immense challenge facing political leaders in Britain and Ireland is . . . to create the conditions for a new Ireland and a new society acceptable to all its people.'

3 Devolution

The arrangements for the government of Scotland and Wales through the 'territorial' ministers and departments for those countries, together with 'regional' deconcentration to Scottish and Welsh outstations of other government departments, are sometimes described as a system of 'administrative devolution'. This system preserves in full the sovereignty of the United

Kingdom Parliament and the principle of collective decision-making by a Cabinet responsible to Parliament for the government of the United Kingdom as a whole.

A more thoroughgoing scheme of devolution, although still falling short of the fragmentation of sovereignty associated with federalism, was drawn up under the 1974–9 Labour Government, but failed to be put into effect. The devolution experiment is interesting because it illuminated the existing constitutional structure, highlighting its distinctive features and its strengths and weaknesses. Although the scheme has been abandoned, we cannot be sure that political events in the future will not cause it, or elements of it, to be revived.

Radical constitutional change is perhaps more often the result of political disaffection or pressures than of a cool appraisal of constitutional weaknesses and the need for reform. So it was with the devolution venture.

An upsurge of Scottish nationalism in the 1960s was heralded by a sharp rise in the vote for the Scottish National Party (SNP) at a by-election in West Lothian in 1962. There were notable increases in the SNP vote in the 1964 and 1966 general elections, followed by a striking by-election victory for the SNP at Hamilton in 1967, in what had been a safe Labour seat, and substantial SNP gains in the municipal elections of the following year.

The Labour Government, conscious of the importance of Scottish and Welsh votes for its survival, received another shock when Plaid Cymru took Carmarthen from Labour in a by-election in 1966 and came close to winning the safe Labour seat of Rhondda West in 1967.

Both the Government and the Conservative Opposition responded to the nationalist threat. In 1968 the Leader of the Opposition, Mr Heath, called for a Scottish Assembly and set up a constitutional committee under Sir Alec Douglas-Home to examine the question. This committee reported in 1970, recommending an elected Scottish Convention which would have advisory and scrutinizing functions and would take the initial stages of Scottish bills, returning them to the Commons for third reading. Meanwhile, in 1969, the Wilson Government had announced the appointment of a Royal Commission on the Constitution chaired by Lord Crowther (and after his death in 1972 by Lord Kilbrandon):

To examine the present functions of the central legislature and government in relation to the several countries, nations and regions of the United Kingdom;

to consider, having regard to developments in local government organisation and in the administrative and other relationships between the various parts of the United Kingdom, and to the interests of the prosperity and good government of Our people under the Crown, whether any changes are desirable in those functions or otherwise in present constitutional and economic relationships;

to consider, also, whether any changes are desirable in the constitutional and economic relationships between the United Kingdom and the Channel Islands and the Isle of Man.

The 1970 general election seemed to show that the nationalist challenge was fading: the SNP won only one seat, and Plaid Cymru none. The H‹ ath Government which came to power in 1970 took no action on the Douglas-Home recommendations, waiting instead for the report of the Royal Commission. This, the Kilbrandon Report, was published in 1973 (Cmnd 5460 and 5460–1).

How was the Royal Commission to interpret its terms of reference? These could be taken as authorizing a very wide-ranging inquiry into the constitution, opening to question everything except the continuance of a government of 'Our people under the Crown'. The Commissioners found the mere identification of their task 'a major preoccupation'; the majority took the view that a wide review of the whole constitution 'was not intended, and would not be practicable', and saw it as their main concern to investigate the case for 'devolution' of governmental functions to new institutions in the countries and regions of the United Kingdom (Report, paras. 12–19).

The Kilbrandon Report adopted a broad meaning of the term 'devolution', so as to include both the 'deconcentration' of functions within the governmental hierarchy, which it termed 'administrative devolution', and the more advanced devolution which involves a *transfer* of central government powers to regional bodies, although 'without the relinquishment of sovereignty'. Devolution of the more advanced kind might extend to the transfer of powers to determine policies and enact legislation to put them into effect – *legislative devolution*; alternatively major policies and primary legislation might be kept at the centre, while powers of subordinate policy-making and administration were transferred to the regions – *executive devolution*. The question was whether the case had been made out for going beyond the existing system of administrative devolution in favour of either legislative or executive devolution to any of the countries or regions of the United Kingdom.

All the Commissioners were persuaded that central government had become overloaded and remote, and that there had been a weakening of public confidence in the democratic process. As a remedy for these infirmities of the body politic, 12 Commissioners – all but one – prescribed the introduction of schemes of legislative or executive devolution, but there was disagreement about the application of the schemes. Eight Commissioners proposed a scheme of legislative devolution for Scotland, six wished to see it extended to Wales, two favoured executive devolution for Scotland, Wales and eight English regions, three wanted an elected assembly for Wales with advisory functions only, nine recommended non-elected regional advisory councils for England. In a Memorandum of Dissent two Commissioners proposed a more thoroughgoing scheme of executive devolution for Scotland, Wales and five English regions.

This dissonance of voices could only weaken the effect of the Royal Commission's Report. Moreover the whole exercise was flawed by the defensive political motives of the Government, which had set up the Royal Commission in order to ward off the nationalist challenge, and had directed it, in the widest terms, to find a solution to unspecified problems. Even so, both the Report and the Memorandum of Dissent contain much compelling analysis.

While the Kilbrandon Commission deliberated, the Government proceeded with reforms of local government in England and Wales and in Scotland – even though the introduction of any devolutionary scheme would require a review and readjustment of the local government system. The publication of the Report in 1973 was coolly received by Government and Opposition. But within weeks of its appearance a Labour MP was unseated by the SNP in a by-election at Govan; and in the February 1974 general election the SNP won seven seats and Plaid Cymru two, rising to 11 and three seats respectively in October 1974. These events were a stimulus to action.

In September 1974 the White Paper *Democracy and Devolution: Proposals for Scotland and Wales* (Cmnd 5732) announced the Labour Government's 'decisions of principle' to establish elected assemblies in Scotland and Wales, the former with legislative and the latter with executive powers. The difference of treatment was justified by the Government as resting on the need for distinctive legislation in Scotland, with its separate legal system, and the lack of public demand in Wales for a legislative assembly. These proposals were followed by a more detailed scheme in the 1975 White Paper, *Our Changing Democracy: Devolution to Scotland and Wales* (Cmnd 6348), and in a *Supplementary Statement* published in 1976 (Cmnd 6585). The Government's scheme was outlined in the following paragraphs.

> *Our Changing Democracy: Devolution to Scotland and Wales,*
> Cmnd 6348/1975

16. Under the Government's proposals, the [Scottish and Welsh] Assemblies will control policies and spending priorities over a very wide field, including for example most aspects of local government, health, personal social services, education, housing, physical planning, the environment and roads, and many aspects of transport. They will have a very large block grant from the Exchequer and some power to supplement it from local taxation, and they will have the fullest possible freedom to decide how the money should be spent among the services they control. The Scottish Assembly will also be able to make new laws or amend present ones in these matters, and it will be responsible for most aspects of the distinctive private and criminal law of Scotland.

17. All these powers will enable the new Scottish and Welsh administrations to bring far-reaching influence to bear on the whole physical and social environment of their countries. That influence, together with the huge spending power which they will control, will enable them to have a very marked effect also on their economic environment.

18. The new powers will not however be conferred at the expense of the benefits which flow from the political and economic unity of the United Kingdom.

19. Political unity means that The Queen in Parliament, representing all the people, must remain sovereign over their affairs; and that the Government of the day must bear the main responsibility to Parliament for protecting and furthering the interests of all.

In particular, the Government must be able to do whatever is needed for national security; they must conduct international relations, including those flowing from our membership of the European Community; and they must maintain the national framework of law and order, guaranteeing the basic rights of the citizen throughout the United Kingdom.

20. Economic unity plainly means that the Government must manage the nation's external economic relations – the balance of payments, the exchange rate, external assets and liabilities, and economic, trading and other arrangements with other countries. But the principle reaches much further. The Government must be able to manage demand in the economy as a whole – to control national taxation, total public expenditure and the supply of money and credit. The Government must be able to regulate the framework of trade, so as to maintain a fair competitive balance for industry and commerce everywhere. Within the wider common market which the European Community is developing we already enjoy a common market throughout the United Kingdom, and any new and artificial barriers within that long-established market could be seriously damaging. And the Government must also keep the task of devising national policies to benefit particular parts of the United Kingdom, and of distributing resources among them according to relative need. This last point is the cardinal fact about our whole system of allocating public expenditure. Resources are distributed not according to where they come from but according to where they are needed. This applies between geographical areas just as much as between individuals.

In a subsequent Green Paper (*Devolution: The English Dimension*, 1976) the Government ruled out the creation of an English assembly or regional assemblies in England with legislative powers, but canvassed the possibility of executive devolution to new regional authorities. A year later the Government announced that it had found no 'broad consensus of popular support' for devolution in England, and the matter was dropped. (HC Deb. vol. 939, col. *108*w, 15 November 1977.)

A Scotland and Wales Bill introduced in the House of Commons in 1976 incorporated the essential features of the scheme of the White Papers. It provided for directly elected assemblies in Scotland and Wales: the Scottish Assembly would have legislative powers, while the Welsh Assembly would have executive powers only, to be exercised within a framework of Westminster legislation.

The aims and structure of the bill were outlined by the Prime Minister in the second reading debate.

House of Commons, 13 December 1976 (HC Deb. vol. 922, cols. 982–93)

The Prime Minister (MR JAMES CALLAGHAN): . . . There are four guiding principles which underlie the present Bill. They are: a respect for the diversity and distinctive tradition of Scotland and Wales; political and economic unity of the Kingdom; the sovereignty of Parliament; and fairness to the whole of the United Kingdom. Let me elaborate briefly on each of these.

The first is a respect for diversity and distinctive tradition. The unity of the United

Kingdom should not mean uniformity. . . . Otherwise the possibility of a divergence in aim or method embraced in the devolution idea would have no point. In essence, therefore, the Bill leaves domestic decisions to the new Assemblies, which will answer for them to their electors and not to Westminster or Whitehall. The kind of issue for which the Assemblies will have responsibility include such important matters as housing, health, and education, economic issues such as industrial development and factory building, aspects of local government, the social services, forestry and fisheries and, in the case of Scotland, many law functions. But, at the same time, the Bill provides reserve safeguards to enable the Government and Parliament to restrain divergence where its practice could harm other parts of the United Kingdom and thus damage our unity.

The next principle is political and economic unity. The components of the United Kingdom have an immense bond of shared history and friendship. . . . Working in union over the years, the component parts of the United Kingdom have achieved far more than any of us could have done separately. This Bill reflects the overwhelming desire of the country to preserve and maintain the unity of the kingdom.

The third principle is the continuing sovereignty of Parliament. Devolution as expressed in this Bill is the delegation of part of Parliament's powers and not the surrender of them. The expression and guarantee of our political unity under the Crown is the common authority of Parliament and particularly of this House. That theme runs through the Bill.

The fourth guiding principle is fairness throughout the United Kingdom. Devolution is not an instrument for conferring advantages on Scotland and Wales that will not be available to England. . . . Devolution is a concept for the improvement of democratic government. It is not a device for the redeployment of the resources of the United Kingdom in a different way, or for changing the economic balance within the United Kingdom to the detriment of one of its parts. This Parliament will remain the guardian of fairness and equity between the different parts of the United Kingdom. . . .

The arrangements in the Bill for sharing resources are specifically designed to ensure fairness. The people of Scotland and Wales, like some of the English regions, will continue to receive shares of public expenditure above the national average for so long as their needs justify this, without having to pay higher taxes. The final decisions on these matters will properly rest with Parliament, where all parts of the Kingdom are represented.

Overall industrial and regional policies will continue to be settled by Parliament. There are safeguards where powers affecting industry are devolved, such as the guidelines within which the industrial investment powers of the Scottish and Welsh Development Agencies will operate. These safeguards ensure fairness between all partners in the United Kingdom. . . .

Part 1 is brief. Within this single brief clause there are three vital propositions. The first is that changes shall be made:

'in the government of Scotland and Wales as parts of the United Kingdom.'

The second sentence of the clause does two things. It rejects separatism and federalism. No doubt there will be much argument about these two concepts during the passage of the Bill. I have made some references to separatism already and I shall spend no more time on it today. . . .

The other proposition, federalism, which is rejected in Clause 1, has a more superficial attraction because it has been widely applied in successful States which share with us the Western tradition of democracy. . . . We looked realistically at the characteristics of federalism and at the conditions in the United Kingdom, and we concluded that they simply did not match. Federalism is an excellent system, but it is not for us. . . .

Part II of the Bill provides for the establishment of the Scottish Assembly and the Welsh Assembly and provides that initially each parliamentary constituency shall elect two Members to the Assembly, except in the case of large constituencies, where there will be three Members. This will mean that there will be about 150 Assembly Members in Scotland and 80 in Wales.

They will serve for a fixed term of four years . . . and will be elected by the same system as the House of Commons. . . .

Clause 16 provides for full freedom of speech in the conduct and reporting of Assembly business.

Clauses 18 and 19 provide that the Scottish Assembly shall have powers of legislation. Schedule 2 sets out the general principles governing the extent of these powers, including a bar on amending the Scotland and Wales Act itself.

Clause 20 is an important clause that has been inserted following debates in the House of Commons last January. It relates to the scrutiny of Scottish Assembly Bills and provides that, if the Government think a Bill exceeds the legal powers of the Assembly, the Government themselves cannot reject it, but can submit it to the Judicial Committee of the Privy Council, by whose finding they and the Assembly must then abide. The clause also provides that if the Government regard a Bill as contrary to the international obligations of the United Kingdom the Government can reject it, for international obligations must remain the responsibility of the central Government.

Clauses 21 to 25 are about the main functions of the Assemblies, providing for the setting up of a Scottish Executive, headed by a Chief Executive, with assistants who would be like Parliamentary Secretaries. The appointment of the Executive is formally in the hands of the Secretary of State, but he will be bound by the Assembly's and the Chief Executive's wishes. In the case of Wales, Clause 22 provides for the Welsh Assembly itself to exercise executive powers in devolved matters. These administrations will have wide and real executive powers. . . .

Clause 25 and its related Schedules 6 and 7 set out the main subject powers of the devolved administrations. The schedules are long, 44 pages in all, and formidably complex. This is the price of precision and we regard it as fundamental that there should be the most exact possible definition of the line marking the powers of the devolved legislative and executive bodies which is compatible with flexible and efficient administration. . . .

Part III of the Bill is about relations between the Welsh and Scottish Assemblies and the Government. The main features here are central and reserve powers: general powers in Clauses 45 to 48 and a variety of particular ones, including guidelines to the Scottish and Welsh Development Agencies and powers to limit rent increases and so on, in Clauses 49 to 57. . . .

Part IV contains a number of clauses concerned with the financial arrangements that will be required. The most important clause is Clause 62, which provides for each devolved administration to be financed by an annual block fund approved by Parliament. Within the total they can thereafter allocate resources between services as they choose in the light of their own judgment of priorities, and neither Ministers nor the Treasury will have a role in their decisions. . . .

The Bill does not give the Assemblies power to raise extra taxes. . . .

In addition to providing for a large measure of self-government, the Bill also defines as clearly as possible the line separating the powers of the Assemblies from Parliament. It provides for minimum intervention by the United Kingdom Government and by Parliament in the affairs of the Assemblies. It provides a method for settling disputes when they arise, and it ensures that matters that concern the United Kingdom as a whole remain under the control of the United Kingdom Government so that no other part of the kingdom is disadvantaged by these proposals. . . .

The long debates that begin today mark a great constitutional change. None of us in this House underestimates the significance of what we propose. If this Bill becomes law, as I believe it must, there will be a new settlement among the nations that constitute the United Kingdom. We shall be moving away from the highly centralised State that has characterised our system for over two and a half centuries. . . .

When enacted, the Bill can ensure a more democratic Government, more truly accepted by the people within the unity of the United Kingdom. It will not weaken our unity. On the contrary, it will provide an enduring constitutional framework for reconciling legitimate demands for Scottish and Welsh control over their own affairs within the unity of the United Kingdom Government.

From the first the Government found itself in political trouble in the House of Commons. The Conservative Opposition opposed the bill, many Labour MPs were apathetic or hostile, the Liberals and the nationalist parties supported the bill in principle but undertook to attack it in detail. At risk of losing the bill, the Government sought to placate rebellious backbenchers with a promise that the bill would, after royal assent, be submitted to referendums in Scotland and Wales before being put into effect. Even so the bill made little progress and an attempt by the Government to invoke the guillotine, timetabling its further stages, was defeated. Doomed to interminable delay, the bill was withdrawn.

In this impasse and under threat of losing a vote of confidence, the Government found safety in a bargain with the Liberal Party. In pursuance of the 'Lib-Lab' pact the Government made a fresh start with devolution, introducing separate bills for Scotland and Wales in November 1977 which retained the main principles of the previous bill, but with some important modifications. The bills were passed with the aid of the Liberals and a guillotine, and became the Scotland Act 1978 and the Wales Act 1978.

Some of the amendments made to the bills in the course of their passage may be noticed.

Clause 1 of each bill had affirmed the unity of the United Kingdom and the supremacy of Parliament: this was deleted by a combination of Conservatives, Liberals, nationalists and others who objected to it from different points of view. The clause was merely declaratory and its deletion had no practical effect.

A Labour backbencher's amendment to the provision for a referendum in Scotland introduced a threshold requirement of approval by 40 per cent of the Scottish electorate. This was carried against the Government, and section

85(2) of the Scotland Act accordingly provided:

> If it appears to the Secretary of State that less than 40 per cent of the persons entitled to vote in the referendum have voted 'Yes' in reply to the question posed in the Appendix to Schedule 17 to this Act ['Do you want the provisions of the Scotland Act 1978 to be put into effect?'] or that a majority of the answers given in the referendum have been 'No' he shall lay before Parliament the draft of an Order in Council for the repeal of this Act.

An equivalent amendment was made to the Wales Bill.

A further amendment to the Scotland Bill was designed to deal with the 'West Lothian question'. The Labour MP for West Lothian, Mr Tam Dalyell, had repeatedly protested that, since the Scotland Bill maintained the representation of Scotland in Parliament, Scottish MPs might have a decisive voice in legislation on a matter concerned only with England, whereas English MPs would have forfeited their right to take part in legislation devolved to the Scottish Assembly. (A similar objection had troubled the attempts to enact home rule for Ireland in 1886–1914.) The amendment, deplored by the government as a 'constitutional imbecility', provided that if the second reading of an 'English' bill was approved only with the support of MPs for Scottish constituencies, there would have to be a second vote after an interval of 14 days. (It was contemplated that the Scottish MPs would be induced to abstain in the second vote.)

After the bills had received the royal assent they were duly submitted to referendums in Scotland and Wales. In Scotland 52 per cent of those who voted were in favour of devolution and the Scotland Act, but they constituted only 33 per cent of the Scottish electorate. In Wales a mere 20 per cent of those who voted, or 12 per cent of the Welsh electorate, voted 'Yes'. Since the 40 per cent threshold had not been reached in either country, Orders were laid before Parliament (by the new Conservative Government) for the repeal of the two Acts and were duly approved. See further Vernon Bogdanor, 'The 40 per cent Rule' (1980) 33 *Parliamentary Affairs* 249.

The Labour Party election manifesto in 1983 included proposals for legislative devolution to Scotland, and a statement approved by the 1983 Annual Conference of the Labour Party reaffirmed that 'legislation aimed at the establishment of a directly elected Scottish Assembly will be a priority for the next Labour government'. The Liberal/SDP Alliance supports immediate devolution for Scotland, with devolved government for Wales and English regions 'as demand develops'.

Although the Scotland and Wales Acts were lost, they may provide a basis for renewed schemes of devolution in the future. The following were some of the main features of the legislation.

(1) The Acts did not purport to limit in any way the sovereignty of Parliament over the whole of the United Kingdom, although it was expected that convention would restrain Parliament from intervening in matters within

the legislative competence of the Scottish Assembly. In this as in other respects the essence of the devolution settlement would only have become apparent with the passage of time.

(2) Scottish and Welsh representation in Parliament was not altered. The 'West Lothian question' was not satisfactorily resolved. (See above.)

(3) The Secretaries of State for Scotland and Wales were to remain, as Cabinet ministers in the central government. What their role would have been was not entirely clear.

(4) In devolving powers to the Scottish and Welsh Assemblies the Acts adopted a complicated method. They might have defined the subjects to be devolved, leaving the residue to the centre, or have defined the subjects to be retained, all others being devolved. In fact the Acts listed the devolved matters in general terms, while specifying subjects within the devolved categories which would remain at the centre. Difficulties would certainly have arisen in determining whether particular functions had been devolved, and subject to what limits.

(5) The government kept in its own hands powers of economic management and industrial policy for the whole United Kingdom. The Scottish and Welsh Assemblies would have lacked the means of controlling the economic development of their countries.

(6) Revenue-raising powers were not devolved: finance for the devolved administrations was to be provided by a block grant voted by Parliament. This system maintained the hegemony of the Treasury and would have been a considerable limitation of the autonomy of the Assemblies.

(7) The Secretary of State for Scotland could reserve for consideration by Parliament any bill passed by the Scottish Assembly which, in his view, might affect a non-devolved matter (e.g. defence or the economy) and was not in the public interest. Parliament could by resolution prevent submission of the bill for the royal assent. This power might have proved a source of conflict between the central government and the Scottish Executive – especially when the majority party in the Scottish Assembly was not the same as that at Westminster.

(8) The Secretaries of State were given powers of veto and direction, subject to parliamentary approval, in respect of executive actions of the Scottish Executive and the Welsh Assembly affecting non-devolved matters. Here too conflict might have arisen.

(9) If there was doubt whether a Scottish Assembly bill was within the competence of the Assembly, the question would be referred by the Secretary of State for decision by the Judicial Committee of the Privy Council. If ruled to be ultra vires it would not be submitted for the royal assent. The Scottish Law Commission had drawn attention to the difficulty of answering questions of legal vires 'in the abstract rather than in the context of concrete cases' (Memorandum No. 32 (1976), para. 20).

(10) After enactment the validity of a Scottish Assembly Act would have

been open to challenge in the courts, with final appeal to the Judicial Committee of the Privy Council. The courts would doubtless have played a significant part in the demarcation of the powers of the Assembly. Judges would have had a new, 'constitutional' role to perform.

4 Local government

Every modern state, unless of minute size, needs a system of local administration. Even if all important decisions were taken at the centre there would need to be local agencies to implement them, issuing commands and services to local populations, and some subsidiary decision-making would have to be delegated to these agencies. Of course there are many possible kinds of arrangement for local administration. In the United Kingdom, part of this task is performed by local branches of central government, such as the outposts of the Inland Revenue and the Department of the Environment, but the major share falls to elected local government.

It would be generally agreed that local government in the United Kingdom has the following main objectives.

The first is to reduce the load on the centre. Central government in the modern state would be greatly overloaded if the burden of administration were not shared with local institutions.

A second objective is to provide opportunities for democratic choice and popular participation in the government of local areas. In this way government can be made more accountable to local communities, and ordinary citizens can take a fuller part in the democratic process and in public life.

A third objective is to achieve more responsive and rational decision-making through institutions which are well informed about local conditions and aware of local needs and demands. Specific policies can be developed to match local circumstances, and national policies can be adapted to the needs of different areas and communities.

> *Report of the Royal Commission on Local Government in England*
> (Redcliffe-Maud Report), vol. 1, Cmnd 4040/1969

27. The questions that have dominated all our work are these. What is, and what ought to be, the purpose which local government serves; and what, at the present day, is its scope? Our terms of reference require us to consider the structure of local government in England (outside Greater London) in relation to its existing functions; and it was therefore on existing functions that we concentrated our attention. These are of immense scope and significance, covering as they do responsibility for the police, for the fire service, for almost all education other than university, for the health and welfare of mothers and infants, the old and the sick, for children in need of care, for public health, for housing, for sport and recreation, for museums, art galleries and libraries, for the physical environment and the use of land, for highways, traffic and transport, and for

many other matters too numerous to mention. . . . But in considering the structure which will best enable local authorities to discharge these responsibilities, we have kept in mind the whole potential of local government, given the existing functions as the substance of what it does. This substance we see as an all-round responsibility for the safety, health and well-being, both material and cultural, of people in different localities, in so far as these objectives can be achieved by local action and local initiative, within a framework of national policies. . . .

28. Our terms of reference also require us to bear in mind the need to sustain a viable system of local democracy: that is, a system under which government by the people is a reality. This we take to be of importance at least equal to the importance of securing efficiency in the provision of services. Local government is not to be seen merely as a provider of services. If that were all, it would be right to consider whether some of the services could not be more efficiently provided by other means. The importance of local government lies in the fact that it is the means by which people can provide services for themselves; can take an active and constructive part in the business of government; and can decide for themselves, within the limits of what national policies and local resources allow, what kind of services they want and what kind of environment they prefer. More than this, through their local representatives people throughout the country can, and in practice do, build up the policies which national government adopts – by focussing attention on local problems, by their various ideas of what government should seek to do, by local initiatives and local reactions. Many of the powers and responsibilities which local authorities now possess, many of the methods now in general use, owe their existence to pioneering by individual local authorities. Local government is the only representative political institution in the country outside Parliament; and being, by its nature, in closer touch than Parliament or Ministers can be with local conditions, local needs, local opinions, it is an essential part of the fabric of democratic government. Central government tends, by its nature, to be bureaucratic. It is only by the combination of local representative institutions with the central institutions of Parliament, Ministers and Departments, that a genuine national democracy can be sustained.

29. We recognise that some services are best provided by the national government: where the provision is or ought to be standardised throughout the country, or where the decisions involved can be taken only at the national level, or where a service requires an exceptional degree of technical expertise and allows little scope for local choice. Even here, however, there is a role for local government in assessing the impact of national policies on places and on people, and in bringing pressure to bear on the national government for changes in policy or in administration, or for particular decisions. And wherever local choice, local opinion and intimate knowledge of the effects of government action or inaction are important, a service is best provided by local government, however much it may have to be influenced by national decisions about the level of service to be provided and the order of priorities to be observed.

30. We conclude then that the purpose of local government is to provide a democratic means both of focussing national attention on local problems affecting the safety, health and well-being of the people, and of discharging, in relation to these things, all the responsibilities of government which can be discharged at a level below that of the national government. But in discharging these responsibilities local government must, of course, act in agreement with the national government when national interests are involved.

Structure of local government

Until well into the nineteenth century the local government of England and Wales was a Byzantine structure of borough corporations, parishes, justices of the peace and *ad hoc* authorities of various kinds – 'a chaos of institutions, areas and rates' (Peter G. Richards, *The Reformed Local Government System*, 4th edn 1980, p. 15). The Local Government Acts of 1888 and 1894 created a more rational system, which was to endure in essentials until the reorganization effected by the Local Government Act 1972.

The structure of local government established by the Acts of 1888 and 1894 was based on democratically elected local authorities. County councils were the upper-tier authorities in the counties; below them were rural district councils and, for the smaller towns, urban district councils or non-county borough councils. Within the rural districts some minor functions were given to parishes.

Larger towns were separately administered as 'county boroughs' by all-purpose authorities independent of the counties. London was given its own county government – the London County Council – in 1888, and the London Government Act 1899 created 28 metropolitan borough councils within the area of the LCC. (The City of London kept its own ancient institutions.)

The system created by these enactments assumed a separation between town and country which was to become ever more unreal. Suburban development, population growth and mobility, and the increasing scale of local government activity (including such new services as education, health, housing, environmental planning and social welfare) demanded a radical reorganization of the structure and working of local government. The groundwork for reform was done by two Royal Commissions, one on Local Government in Greater London which reported in 1960 (Herbert Report, Cmnd 1164), and the other on Local Government in England, which reported in 1969 (Redcliffe-Maud Report, Cmnd 4040).

The Herbert Commission's proposals were implemented by the London Government Act 1963. The LCC was replaced by the Greater London Council (GLC), with jurisdiction extending over a much larger built-up area, and responsibilities in such matters as strategic planning, transport (from 1970), main roads, fire protection, etc. The bulk of local services, including education, local planning, housing, health and social welfare, were to be discharged by 32 London borough councils. In a central area of London, education was to be administered by the Inner London Education Authority, a committee of the GLC including representatives of the inner London boroughs. The City of London kept its separate institutions.

The Redcliffe-Maud Commission's proposals for the rest of England were criticized on their merits and generated political contention. In the result the Local Government Act 1972 departed in some important respects from the Redcliffe-Maud scheme, in particular in adopting a two-tier structure of local government instead of the Redcliffe-Maud proposal of all-purpose unitary authorities. The Act reorganized local government in both England and Wales, replacing the 1,391 existing counties, boroughs, and urban and rural district councils with 422 new authorities.

The Act abolished the all-purpose county boroughs, incorporating all towns into the two-tier county structure. English county boundaries were redrawn to constitute 45 counties, of which six are the *metropolitan counties* of Greater Manchester, Merseyside, South Yorkshire, Tyne and Wear, West Midlands, and West Yorkshire. In these densely populated conurbations the division of responsibilities between counties and districts is similar to that between the Greater London Council and the London boroughs: the *metropolitan district councils* have the major functions, including education, housing and personal social services.

Outside the metropolitan areas, 39 *county councils* have a wide range of functions, including education, personal social services, strategic planning, roads, transport policy and police. The 296 *district councils* provide the remaining local government services (public health, housing, local planning etc.) and are responsible for collecting the rates. Some services (such as planning and transport) are shared between the two tiers, and county councils may entrust some of their functions to district councils under 'agency' arrangements (e.g. highway maintenance).

District councils in both metropolitan and non-metropolitan areas may petition the Crown for a charter conferring borough status: this is a matter of tradition and formality rather than of legal powers. Parish councils (mainly in rural areas) have limited powers relating to local amenities such as allotments, footpaths and recreation grounds, and are consulted on planning matters. Some parishes are designated as towns.

The structure of local government established in England by the 1963 and 1972 Acts can be represented as follows:

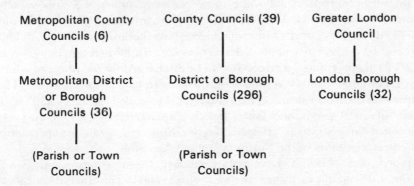

Metropolitan County Councils (6)

County Councils (39)

Greater London Council

Metropolitan District or Borough Councils (36)

District or Borough Councils (296)

London Borough Councils (32)

(Parish or Town Councils)

(Parish or Town Councils)

The Conservative Party manifesto for the 1983 general election declared:

The Metropolitan Councils and the Greater London Council have been shown to be a wasteful and unnecessary tier of government. We shall abolish them and return most of their functions to the boroughs and districts. Services which need to be administered over a wider area – such as police and fire, and education in inner London – will be run by joint boards of borough or district representatives.

The alleged deficiencies of the GLC and the metropolitan county councils and the need for a further reorganization of local government had not in this instance been demonstrated by the impartial investigation of a Royal Commission. A White Paper published in October 1983 set out the Government's arguments for abolition of the GLC and metropolitan councils and described the proposed arrangements for the exercise of their functions by borough and district councils, new joint boards and special-purpose authorities (*Streamlining the Cities*, Cmnd 9063/1983). The proposals were subsequently modified in some respects (for example, there is to be a directly elected Inner London Education Authority instead of a joint board of borough nominees) and a Local Government Bill was introduced at the end of 1984 to implement the Government's scheme. The proposed reallocation of powers in the 'local state' is not only politically contentious but is a constitutional change of considerable importance, raising issues of efficiency, responsiveness and accountability in local government which have not been sufficiently considered.

The structure and functions of local government in Wales are organized on the same lines as the non-metropolitan areas in England. Wales has eight county councils and 37 district councils, and there is a lower tier of community councils equivalent to the parish councils in England.

Scotland has a separate system of local government created by the Local Government (Scotland) Act 1973. On the mainland there is a two-tier structure of nine regional and 53 district councils. The island areas of Orkney, Shetland and the Western Isles are governed by virtually all-purpose island councils.

In Northern Ireland, following the recommendations of a review body chaired by Sir Patrick Macrory (Cmd 546/1970), local government was reformed by the Local Government Act (Northern Ireland) 1972. This established a lower tier of 26 district councils with limited functions, while many local government services were to be discharged for the whole province by the Parliament and Government of Northern Ireland as the upper tier. The imposition of direct rule in 1972 resulted in the so-called 'Macrory gap', with upper-tier local government functions being discharged by civil servants and appointed boards instead of elected bodies. Supervision of the upper tier is now a responsibility of the Northern Ireland Assembly.

Independent Local Government Boundary Commissions for England, Wales and Scotland keep under review the areas and electoral arrangements of local authorities. (See Part IV of the Local Government Act 1972 and Part II of the Local Government (Scotland) Act 1973.) Their proposals for the alteration of local government areas and electoral divisions or wards may be implemented by ministerial order, subject to negative resolution of either House of Parliament.

Central–local government relations

Part of the constitutional importance of local government is that power in the state is dispersed: the autonomy of local authorities, answerable to their own electorates, is a counterweight to the authority of Whitehall. On the other hand central government, ever since it assumed a responsibility for economic progress and social welfare, has laid claim to the support of local government for national policies, and has intervened to maintain uniform standards in services supplied by local authorities.

Since we have no written constitution which fixes the boundary between central and local government, it can be shifted by the actions of successive governments so that, as George Jones and John Stewart say (*The Case for Local Government* (1983), pp. 110–11), 'Apparently minor and administrative changes can accumulate into a fundamental constitutional change, unnoticed until too late'. In recent years both Labour and Conservative governments have extended central control over local authorities, whose autonomy has been significantly reduced.

Several means are available to central government to influence, direct or coerce local authorities into compliance with national policies or standards.

Statutory powers

By statute many acts of local authorities are subject to ministerial approval (and sometimes modification) – for example, capital expenditure projects, 'structure plans' for land use, compulsory purchase orders, and appointments of some local government officers. Various statutes empower ministers to give directions to local authorities – for example section 98 of the Local Government, Planning and Land Act 1980 authorizes the Secretary of State for the Environment to require an authority to dispose of land which in his opinion is not being used for the authority's purposes. There are also certain statutory 'default powers', by which a minister may issue directions to a local authority which has failed to perform its duty, or may transfer its responsibilities to another authority, or assume them himself. This is a radical kind of power and its use may raise in critical and dramatic form the constitutional issue of the respective roles of central and local government. In the following two cases the minister's exercise of a default or analogous power, in circumstances of political controversy, was challenged in the courts.

Secretary of State for Education and Science v. *Tameside Metropolitan Borough Council* [1977] AC 1014 (HL)

The Tameside Borough Council, while under Labour Party control, had prepared plans for a change to comprehensive education in the borough's secondary schools. The plans were approved by the Secretary of State for Education in 1975, and were set in hand so as to take effect from September 1976. Then in local elections held in May 1976 the Conservative Party won power in Tameside, having campaigned on a programme which included abandonment of the comprehensive scheme and retention of the grammar schools in the borough. The new council proposed to make a selection of children for grammar-school places for the school year beginning in September, even though teachers' unions had refused to cooperate in the selection process. The Secretary of State in the Labour Government took the view that a change of plans, so short a time before the new school year, would be disruptive and unworkable, and that the council were acting unreasonably. He therefore decided to exercise his powers under section 68 of the Education Act 1944 which, so far as relevant, reads as follows:

If the Secretary of State is satisfied . . . that any local education authority . . . have acted or are proposing to act unreasonably with respect to the exercise of any power conferred or the performance of any duty imposed by or under this Act, he may . . . give such directions as to the exercise of the power or the performance of the duty as appear to him to be expedient.

The minister accordingly directed the Tameside Council to implement the comprehensive scheme approved in 1975, and as the council were unwilling to comply, applied to the Divisional Court for an order of mandamus to compel them to do so. The order was granted, but the council were successful in the subsequent appeals to the Court of Appeal and the House of Lords.

LORD WILBERFORCE: . . . The direction of June 11, 1976, was given under section 68 of the Education Act 1944. Education is still governed by this notable statute, as amended, and it is necessary to understand its structure. Under the Act responsibility for secondary education rests upon a fourfold foundation: the Minister (as he was then called); local authorities; parental wishes; and school managers and governors. All have their part to play. The primary responsibility rests on the Minister. He has to promote the education of the people of England and

'. . . to secure the effective execution by local authorities, under his control and direction, of the national policy for providing a varied and comprehensive' (old meaning) 'educational service in every area'. (section 1.)

But local education authorities, which are elected, have their place defined. It is they who are responsible for 'providing secondary education' in schools

'. . . sufficient in number, character, and equipment to afford for all pupils opportunities for education offering such variety of instruction and training as may be desirable in view of their different ages, abilities, and aptitudes . . . .' (section 8.)

Analysis of [section 68] brings out three cardinal points.

(1) The matters with which the section is concerned are primarily matters of educational administration. The action which the Secretary of State is entitled to stop is unreasonable action with respect to the exercise of a power or the performance of a duty

– the power and the duty of the authority are presupposed and cannot be interfered with. Local education authorities are entitled under the Act to have a policy, and this section does not enable the Secretary of State to require them to abandon or reverse a policy just because the Secretary of State disagrees with it. Specifically, the Secretary of State cannot use power under this section to impose a general policy of comprehensive education upon a local education authority which does not agree with the policy. He cannot direct them to bring in a scheme for total comprehensive education in their area, and if they have done so he cannot direct them to implement it. If he tries to use a direction under section 68 for this purpose, his direction would be clearly invalid. A direction under section 68 must be justified on the ground of unreasonable action in doing what under the Act the local authority is entitled to do, and under the Act it has a freedom of choice. I do not think that there is any controversy upon these propositions.

The critical question in this case, and it is not an easy one, is whether, on a matter which appears to be one of educational administration, namely whether the change of course proposed by the council in May 1976 would lead to educational chaos or undue disruption, the Secretary of State's judgment can be challenged.

(2) The section is framed in a 'subjective' form – if the Secretary of State 'is satisfied'. This form of section is quite well known, and at first sight might seem to exclude judicial review. Sections in this form may, no doubt, exclude judicial review on what is or has become a matter of pure judgment. But I do not think that they go further than that. If a judgment requires, before it can be made, the existence of some facts, then, although the evaluation of those facts is for the Secretary of State alone, the court must inquire whether those facts exist, and have been taken into account, whether the judgment has been made upon a proper self-direction as to those facts, whether the judgment has not been made upon other facts which ought not to have been taken into account. If these requirements are not met, then the exercise of judgment, however bona fide it may be, becomes capable of challenge: see *Secretary of State for Employment* v. *ASLEF (No. 2)* [1972] 2 QB 455, *per* Lord Denning MR, at p. 493.

(3) The section has to be considered within the structure of the Act. In many statutes a minister or other authority is given a discretionary power and in these cases the court's power to review any exercise of the discretion, though still real, is limited. In these cases it is said that the courts cannot substitute their opinion for that of the minister: they can interfere on such grounds as that the minister has acted right outside his powers or outside the purpose of the Act, or unfairly, or upon an incorrect basis of fact. But there is no universal rule as to the principles on which the exercise of a discretion may be reviewed: each statute or type of statute must be individually looked at. This Act, of 1944, is quite different from those which simply create a ministerial discretion. The Secretary of State, under section 68, is not merely exercising a discretion: he is reviewing the action of another public body which itself has discretionary powers and duties. He, by contrast with the courts in the normal case, may substitute his opinion for that of the authority: this is what the section allows, but he must take account of what the authority, under the statute, is entitled to do. The authority – this is vital – is itself elected, and is given specific powers as to the kind of schools it wants in its area. Therefore two situations may arise. One is that there may be a difference of policy between the Secretary of State (under Parliament) and the local authority: the section gives no power to the Secretary of State to make his policy prevail. The other is that, owing to the democratic process involving periodic elections, abrupt reversals of policy may take place, particularly where there are only two parties and the

winner takes all. Any reversal of policy if at all substantial must cause some administrative disruption – this was as true of the 1975 proposals as of those of the respondents. So the mere possibility, or probability, of disruption cannot be a ground for issuing a direction to abandon the policy. What the Secretary of State is entitled, by a direction if necessary, to ensure is that such disruptions are not 'unreasonable', i.e., greater than a body, elected to carry out a new programme, with which the Secretary of State may disagree, ought to impose upon those for whom it is responsible. After all, those who voted for the new programme, involving a change of course, must also be taken to have accepted some degree of disruption in implementing it.

The ultimate question in this case, in my opinion, is whether the Secretary of State has given sufficient, or any, weight to this particular factor in the exercise of his judgment.

I must now inquire what were the facts upon which the Secretary of State expressed himself as satisfied that the council were acting or proposing to act unreasonably. The Secretary of State did not give oral evidence in the courts, and the facts on which he acted must be taken from the department's letters at the relevant time – i.e., on or about June 11, 1976 – and from affidavits sworn by its officers. These documents are to be read fairly and in bonam partem. If reasons are given in general terms, the court should not exclude reasons which fairly fall within them: allowance must be fairly made for difficulties in expression. The Secretary of State must be given credit for having the background to this actual situation well in mind, and must be taken to be properly and professionally informed as to educational practices used in the area, and as to resources available to the local education authority. His opinion, based, as it must be, upon that of a strong and expert department, is not to be lightly overriden.

The first letter from the department to the local education authority was dated May 26, 1976. This refers to 'a great deal of educational and administrative planning' which had taken place since approval of the 'comprehensive' plan in November 1975. Particular matters mentioned without details were (i) allocation of children to schools; (ii) progress in staffing arrangements including the offer and acceptance of contracts; (iii) planning of curricula and courses; (iv) some building work. Reference is also made to the 'continuing absence of any precise alternative plans'. Tameside answered this on June 7, 1976, in a long letter. I must summarise it at some length because argument has tended to become concentrated on one or two narrow points rather than upon a balanced overall view of the council's plans. I have already commented on the general character and tone of this letter, which is moderate and appreciative of the difficulties, and which shows at least an intention and purpose to reduce them to the minimum.

The letter begins with a narrative section stating that no comprehensive reorganisation in Tameside had yet taken place. The schools were not ready for their changed roles; building works were not completed, and not in most cases begun. Implementation (sc. of the 1975 proposals) in September 1976 would have caused grave disruption to the children's education. A particular case of this would be disruption of the education of 16-year-old pupils, who under the 1975 proposals would have been turned out of the sixth forms of three grammar schools and transferred to two non-selective sixth form colleges. I do not think that any of this is disputed. The authority's own plans were set out under 10 points, which involved continuation of the five grammar schools, continuation and completion of the three new purpose-built comprehensives and continuation of the remaining secondary schools. Their policy as regards allocation to schools is spelt out in five paragraphs. All allocations of pupils for the forthcoming year – about 3,000 in all – made by the old council would be honoured subject to agreement by the parents concerned. Ashton and Hyde grammar schools – by the old council destined to become sixth form colleges – would remain grammar schools and would be open to 11-year-old entry, thus making 240 selective places available. All parents of 11-year-olds were to be given the right to apply for reallocation of their children, but if they were satisfied with the existing allocations those allocations would stand. Then it is said (paragraph 7):

> 'If the number of applicants to the grammar schools exceeds the number of places available, as is likely, then those pupils most suitable and most likely to benefit from that type of education will be selected by a combination of reports, records and interviews. There will be no formal 11-plus examination'.

Finally, it was said that there would be a review of the first year entries, and a very flexible transfer system would be operated at the end of the first year, or earlier if required. I do not think that we need to consider this proposal since there is plenty of time for it to be reconsidered. . . .

On June 11, the direction under section 68 was given in a letter of that date. The letter stated that the Secretary of State was satisfied that the authority was proposing to act unreasonably according to the formula used in section 68 of the Act. A change of plan designed to come into effect in less than three months must, in the opinion of the Secretary of State, give rise to 'considerable difficulties'. It pointed out that over 3,000 pupils transferring from primary schools had already been allocated and allotted places. Then followed this paragraph (which I shall call 'paragraph A').

> 'The authority's revised proposals *confront* the parents of children due to transfer in September *with the dilemma* of either adhering to secondary school allocations for their children which they may no longer regard as appropriate, or else *submitting* to an improvised selection procedure (the precise form of which, the Secretary of State understands, has even now not been settled) carried out in circumstances and under a timetable which raise substantial doubts about its educational validity.' (My emphasis.)

A further objection was taken to the proposed possible reallocation during or after the first year – I have commented on this above. The change of plan at this time in the educational year threatened to give rise to practical difficulties in relation to the appointments of staff already made and the construction of buildings for the new comprehensive schools and to create a degree of confusion and uncertainty which could impair the efficient working of the schools.

These arguments were restated and expanded in the affidavit sworn on behalf of the Secretary of State in support of the application for mandamus. The affidavit stated three points.

Point (i): that 653 of the 802 transfers, promotions and other appointments (of teachers) required to implement the reorganisation had been made.

Point (ii): that contracts had been entered into for building work directly related to the change in character of two of the schools and work had started under the contracts. In the case of a third school, the authority had entered into commitments for such building work.

Point (iii): that preparations had been made for courses on the basis that the proposals communicated to the Secretary of State would be put into effect.

These points (i), (ii) and (iii) were dealt with fully by the authority and I need say no more about them than that they were completely exploded. They were held to have no substance in them by five of the six learned judges who have considered this matter: the sixth indicated general agreement without specific discussion. . . .

Some attempt was made to rehabilitate these points in this House, but learned counsel decided, no doubt wisely, to concentrate on the allocation issue. But these three points cannot just be discarded as if they had never been made. They form part of a composite set of facts relied upon as showing unreasonable conduct, and I am not at all sure that the disappearance of so many planks does not fatally weaken the stability of the platform. At the least – and I will give the department the benefit of this assumption – the remaining factual basis would need to be strong and clear if it alone were to be the basis for the Secretary of State's 'satisfaction' as to unreasonable conduct.

So I come to the question of allocation, which was at the centre of the case as argued, and it can best be approached via 'paragraph A' above, a paragraph which I regard as revealing. It shows a very strange attitude toward the decision taken by the authority. After the electorate, including no doubt a large number of parents, had voted the new council into office on the platform that some selective basis would be preserved, to say that this created 'a dilemma' for the parents, with the undertone that this was something unreasonable, appears to me curious and paradoxical. Parents desired to have a chance of selective places. The new council was giving it to them. If they did not want selective places, they had no need and no obligation to apply for them. Unless the creation of freedom of choice, where no such freedom existed previously, is intrinsically an evil, it seems hard to understand how this so-called dilemma could be something unreasonably created. The impression which it gives of upsetting 3,000 places is entirely a false one since over 90 per cent of these would remain unaltered. Then, to refer to 'submitting to an improvised selection procedure' hardly does justice to the authority's plan. Some selection procedure was inherent in what the electorate had voted for, a choice which, if it meant anything, must involve some change in allocations for the forthcoming school year and, unless exactly 240 parents applied for the 240 places, some selection. It would seem likely that in voting for this change in May 1976 the electors must have accepted, if not favoured, some degree of improvisation. The whole paragraph forces the conclusion that the Secretary of State was operating under a misconception as to what would be reasonable for a newly elected council to do, and that he failed to take into account that it was entitled – indeed in a sense bound – to carry out the policy on which it was elected, and failed to give weight to the fact that the limited degree of selection (for 240 places out of some 3,000) which was involved, though less than perfect, was something which a reasonable authority might accept and which the parents concerned clearly did accept.

What the Secretary of State was entitled to do, under his residual powers, was to say something to the effect: 'the election has taken place; the new authority may be entitled to postpone the comprehensive scheme: this may involve some degree of selection and apparently the parents desire it. Nevertheless from an educational point of view, whatever some parents may think, I am satisfied that in the time available this, or some part of it, cannot be carried out, and that no reasonable authority would attempt to carry it out.' Let us judge him by this test – though I do not think that this was the test he himself applied. Was the procedure to be followed for choosing which of the applicants were to be allotted the 240 selective places such that no reasonable authority could adopt it? The authority's letter of June 7 said that selection would be by 'a combination of reports, records and interviews'. They had about three months in which to carry it out. The plan was lacking in specification, but it must have conveyed sufficient to the experts at the department to enable them to understand what was proposed. Selection by 11-plus examination was not the only selection procedure available. Lancashire, part of which was taken over by Tameside, had evolved and operated a method of selection by head teacher recommendation, ranking of pupils, reports and records and standardised verbal reasoning tests. The Tameside authority had set up in May a panel of selection to operate a procedure of this kind, the chairman of which was experienced in the Lancashire method. He, as he deposed in an affidavit before the Court of Appeal, was of opinion that even though a verbal reasoning test might not be practicable in the time there would be no difficulty in selecting the number of pupils required. There were other opinions, expressed with varying degrees of confidence by experts, and no doubt the procedure could not be said to be perfect, but I do not think that such defects as there were could possibly, in the circumstances, having regard to the comparatively small number of places involved, enable it to be said that the whole of the authority's programme of which this was a part was such that no reasonable authority would carry it out.

But there is a further complication. The authority's selection plans were opposed by a number of the teachers' unions, and there was the likelihood of non-cooperation by some of the head teachers in the primary schools in production of records and reports. The department letters and affidavits do not rely upon this matter, for understandable reasons, but they must be assumed to have had it in mind. Is this a fact upon which the Secretary of State might legitimately form the judgment that the authority was acting unreasonably?

To rephrase the question: on June 11, 1976 (this is the date of the direction, and we are not entitled to see what happened thereafter), could it be said that the authority was acting unreasonably in proceeding with a selection procedure which was otherwise workable in face of the possibility of persistent opposition by teachers' unions and individual teachers, or would *the only* (not 'the more') reasonable course have been for the authority to abandon its plans? This is, I think, the ultimate factual question in the case. And I think that it must be answered in the negative – i.e., that it could not be unreasonable, in June 1976, and assuming that the Secretary of State did not interfere, for the authority to put forward a plan to act on its approved procedure. The teachers, after all, are public servants, with responsibility for their pupils. They were under a duty to produce reports. These reports and the records in the primary schools are public property. I do not think that it could be unreasonable (not 'was unreasonable') for the authority to take the view that if the Secretary of State did not intervene under his statutory powers the teachers would cooperate in working the authority's procedure – a procedure which had, in similar form, been operated in part of this very area.

On the whole case, I come to the conclusion that the Secretary of State, real though his difficulties were, fundamentally misconceived and misdirected himself as to the proper manner in which to regard the proposed action of the Tameside authority after the local election of May 1976: that if he had exercised his judgment on the basis of the factual situation in which this newly elected authority was placed – with a policy approved by its electorate, and massively supported by the parents – there was no ground – however much he might disagree with the new policy, and regret such administrative dislocation as was brought about by the change – upon which he could find that the authority was acting or proposing to act unreasonably. In my opinion the judgments in the Court of Appeal were right and the appeal must be dismissed.

LORD SALMON: . . . In my opinion, section 68, on its true construction, means that before the Secretary of State can lawfully issue directions under it he must satisfy himself not only that he does not agree with the way in which the authority have acted or are proposing to act nor even that the authority is mistaken or wrong. The question he must ask himself is: 'Could any reasonable local authority act in the way in which this authority has acted or is proposing to act?' If, but only if, he is satisfied on any material capable of satisfying a reasonable man that the answer to the crucial question is 'No,' he may lawfully issue directions under section 68. I would adopt what Lord Hailsham of St Marylebone LC said in *In re W. (An Infant)* [1971] AC 682, 700:

> 'Two reasonable [persons] can perfectly reasonably come to opposite conclusions on the same set of facts without forfeiting their title to be regarded as reasonable. . . . Not every reasonable exercise of judgment is right, and not every mistaken exercise of judgment is unreasonable.'

There is certainly no evidence as to how the Secretary of State construed section 68 nor as to the questions he asked himself before deciding to issue his directions set out in the letter of June 11. . . . It may be that the Secretary of State misconstrued section 68, asked himself the wrong question (e.g. 'do I agree with the action proposed by the authority?') and therefore misdirected himself in law. On that assumption, the Secretary of State's directions to the authority on June 11, 1976, would have to be overruled on the grounds of their illegality. Assuming however that he asked himself the right questions and decided that no reasonable authority would act as this authority now proposed to act, I cannot discern any valid ground upon which such a decision could be justified. The grounds upon which the Secretary of State purported to act under section 68 are set out in the letter of June 11; there were five of them. Four of these . . . appeared to the Divisional Court and to the Court of Appeal to have no substance in them. They were not pressed in this House and I do not consider that they lend any support to the Secretary of State's case. Nor am I any more impressed by the fifth ground upon which the Secretary of State succeeded in the Divisional Court and upon which he chiefly relied thereafter. It was only hinted at in the letter of June 11. This was that no reasonable authority in the position of the Tameside authority could have concluded that it had time between June 11 and September 1, 1976, to make a fair and efficient selection on merit of 240 pupils out of the 783 applicants for the 240 places which would be available in the grammar schools on September 1, 1976. The Divisional Court with considerable hesitation decided this question in favour of the Secretary of State only, I think, because of an uncontradicted affidavit by a former chief education officer of Gloucestershire . . . stating that the whole process of selection normally takes a full term of 12 weeks to complete and therefore there was no chance of the test being completed before September 1.

The authority's letter of June 7 had pointed out . . . that pupils most suitable and likely to benefit from the type of education would be selected by a combination of reports, records and interviews instead of by an 11-plus examination. The evidence of a number of distinguished educationalists, produced without objection before the Court of Appeal, showed that this alternative method of selection had been widely used since the 1960s . . . and that it had proved entirely satisfactory. With a selection panel of 20 teachers (10 couples) the whole operation of making a fair and accurate selection of 240 from 783 applications could have been comfortably carried out in Tameside within one week. In the London Borough of Barnet for the period 1965 to 1970 eight panels – each consisting of three teachers – yearly completed a fair selection of 850 pupils from about 3,000 in 10 working days.

It seems incredible to me that these facts were unknown to the Department of Education and not available to the Secretary of State on June 11, 1976. It follows that if the Secretary of State before making his decision had asked himself the right question – 'could any reasonable authority in the position of Tameside have reasonably come to the conclusion that a fair selection could have been made to fill the 240 vacancies before September 1, 1976?' – the answer could only have been 'yes.' It may be that some authorities might have preferred the views of the expert witness upon whose evidence the Secretary of State relied in the Divisional Court to the views of the witnesses upon whose evidence the Tameside authority relied in the Court of Appeal. I find it impossible however to accept that any reasonable man could have been satisfied that no reasonable authority on the evidence could take the view that a satisfactory selection of candidates for the 240 places in the grammar schools could have been made between June 11 and September 1, 1976. Therefore either the Secretary of State must have erred in law by misconstruing section 68 and failing to ask himself the right question or he asked himself that question and answered it 'no' without any valid ground for doing so. . . .

I am convinced that there are no valid grounds for holding that the authority acted or were proposing to act unreasonably within the meaning of section 68. The directions given by the Secretary of State on June 11, 1976, were in my view unlawful. . . .

My Lords, I would dismiss the appeal.

[Viscount Dilhorne, Lord Diplock and Lord Russell of Killowen delivered concurring speeches.]

Professor Anthony Bradley, in commenting on this decision in *The Listener*, 5 May 1977, said:

There is nothing in the judgments to suggest that the judges had any bias against the government or against comprehensive schools. It was, indeed, admitted by the minister that he had no power to compel a council to adopt a scheme of comprehensive schools. But there are some indications in the judgments that sensitive educational issues were not always appreciated by some of the judges. More than one judge emphasised that only 240 grammar school places were in question and that this did not seriously affect the comprehensive scheme for the remainder of the children. This attitude does not appear to grasp the argument against 'creaming off' the brightest children.

In legal terms, the outcome of the Tameside case was clear-cut. It reinforced the trend in recent case law by which the courts are more willing than in the past to review the exercise of discretionary powers. It protected the right of local education authorities to make decisions in accordance with their own policies and it is thereby unlikely that the secretary of state will again act under section 68 in any future situation of political controversy. Whether or not the secretary of state should have a power of intervention which can be more easily exercised is, of course, a matter for Parliament to decide.

Was this, nonetheless, a case in which the courts may be criticised for having taken upon themselves the task of seeking to govern the country, of having usurped the powers of the executive? . . . . [T]he logic of the judges' approach to the Education Act led them to examine closely the detailed issues in the controversy. The legal process thereby had the effect of re-examining the merits of the minister's decision. Paradoxically, the judges were seeking to apply to the minister's power of intervention the same standard of unreasonableness which they would have considered appropriate if, for example, a parent from Tameside had come directly to the courts alleging that the Conservative council's scheme was unreasonable. This test of unreasonableness seems to take no account of the fact that the decision to intervene was entrusted by Parliament in 1944 to a minister, and not to a judge.

See further D. G. T. Williams [1977] *CLJ* 1, and H. W. R. Wade (1977) 93 *LQR* 4.

R. v. Secretary of State for the Environment, ex p. Norwich City Council
[1982] QB 808 (CA)

Section 5 of the Housing Act 1980 gave council tenants the right to buy their houses from the council at a discount. If a tenant applied to buy his house the council was required to admit or deny his right to buy within four weeks: section 5(1). The right admitted, the council was bound 'as soon as practicable' to notify the tenant of the price demanded: section 10(1). Any disagreement about the price was to be resolved by the district valuer: section 11. As soon as all matters relating to the sale and mortgage were settled, the council was bound to convey the house to the tenant: section 16(1).

Council house sales were politically contentious and were unwelcome to many local authorities which feared the depletion of their housing stocks and disruption of their housing policies. Resistance by some local authorities was foreseen. Section 23 of the Housing Act empowered the Secretary of State to intervene if it appeared to him that tenants were having difficulty in exercising their right to buy 'effectively and expeditiously': he might in that event himself assume the council's responsibility of selling to tenants and charge the cost to the council.

Tenants of the Norwich City Council who had applied to buy their houses complained of long delays by the council in processing the sales. After fruitless meetings between the Department of the Environment and the council, the Secretary of State gave notice to exercise his powers under section 23. The council applied to the Divisional Court for an order of certiorari to quash the Minister's decision. The application failed, and the council's appeal was dismissed by the Court of Appeal.

Among the Minister's stated reasons for intervening were the fixing of over-high prices by the council, delay caused by insistence on 'counselling interviews' with tenants, onerous covenants to be imposed in conveyances, delay in making valuations coupled with a refusal to employ the district valuer in this task, and poor performance in comparison with other local authorities.

KERR LJ: The unfortunate but inescapable feature of section 23 of the Housing Act 1980 is that it envisages a direct confrontation between the central government and local authorities in relation to the administration of Part I, chapter 1, of the Act, whereby local authorities are compelled to sell off large parts of their stock of council houses and flats to their existing tenants if they wish to buy them. Many tenants are inevitably likely to wish to do so, since the Act provides powerful incentives in the form of a large discount from the open market value and a right to a mortgage. Given these incentives, it is also highly likely that differences will arise in many cases between those tenants who wish to buy and their local authority. The tenants will want to see the procedure completed as soon as possible, so that they can start making mortgage repayments instead of continuing to pay rent; and in the case of tenants who are near retiring age, delay may also affect the mortgage which they are able to obtain. On the other hand, their landlord, the local authority, may reasonably consider that its many other duties and functions deserve a higher priority in the use of its resources than expediting the sale of council properties to that proportion of the tenants who wish to buy.

Such a confrontation has now unfortunately occurred in Norwich. It is therefore the duty of the court to rule on the legality of the minister's intervention in this case. This duty, it should be stressed, in no way involves any judgment of a political nature; either in favour of an elected central government of one political colour; nor in favour of an elected local authority of another political colour; nor in favour of tenants as against their landlords, or vice versa, when their views differ as to how the scheme of the Act should be implemented. The court's duty is solely to construe the relevant provisions of the Act and to determine whether the minister's exercise of his powers under section 23 was lawful or not.

It is necessary at the outset to consider the wording of section 23 against the background of the scheme as a whole. Whether or not it is right to describe it as a 'penal' section, as contended on behalf of the council, it is certainly Draconian in its terms, since its application in relation to any local authority is liable to have substantial consequences for the authority's funds in the housing sector, and therefore also for the general body of ratepayers. I therefore agree that a provision of this kind requires a strict construction in so far as its terms permit. On the other hand, short of seeking to exclude altogether any power of review by the courts, the wording of section 23 has clearly been framed by Parliament in such a way as to maximise the power of the Secretary of State and to minimise any power of review by the court. The governing words are 'Where it appears to the Secretary of State. . . .' These words make it clear that the determinative factor is the view of the Secretary of State; not the view of the local authority in question; nor any abstract standard of reasonableness to be determined by the court.

Among the authorities cited to us, I think that the following two passages provide the most useful guidance to the way in which the court must approach the interpretation of section 23 and its application to the facts of any particular case.

First, in *Secretary of State for Employment* v. *ASLEF (No. 2)* [1972] 2 QB 455, 492–493, Lord Denning MR said:

'This brings me to the important question: What is the effect of the words "If it appears to the Secretary of State"? This, in my opinion, does not mean that the minister's decision is put beyond challenge. The scope available to the challenger depends very much on the subject matter with which the minister is dealing. In this case I would think that, if the minister does not act in good faith, or if he acts on extraneous considerations which ought not to influence him, or if he plainly misdirects himself in fact or in law, it may well be that a court would interfere; but when he honestly takes a view of the facts or the law which could reasonably be entertained, then his decision is not to be set aside simply because thereafter someone thinks that his view was wrong. After all, this is an emergency procedure. It has to be set in motion quickly, when there is no time for minute analysis of facts or of law.'

The last two sentences in that passage must be confined to the issue in that case, which concerned an urgent intervention by the minister in an industrial dispute pursuant to the Industrial Relations Act 1971 which has since been repealed. They have no application here. However, the passage as a whole was expressly approved, and the same test reiterated in substance, by Lord Wilberforce in *Secretary of State for Education and Science* v. *Tameside Metropolitan Borough Council* [see p. 213 above]. . . .

In the *Tameside* case the minister's power to intervene turned on section 68 of the Education Act 1944. . . . In the upshot it was . . . held that the power under that section only arose if the minister, directing himself properly, could reasonably conclude that the local authority had acted, or was proposing to act, unreasonably in what is often referred to as the *Wednesbury* sense (based upon the judgment of Lord Greene MR in *Associated Provincial Picture Houses Ltd* v. *Wednesbury Corporation* [1948] 1 KB 223, 229), i.e. in the sense that no reasonable local authority could have acted in the manner in question. The position under section 23 of the Housing Act 1980 is somewhat different, and I think that it confers greater power on the minister than the power under section 68, and that to this extent it may well be without precedent in legislation of this nature. Section 23 applies when it appears to the minister that a certain state of fact exists, viz. that tenants 'have or may have difficulty in exercising the right to buy effectively and expeditiously'. These words are not qualified by any reference to the consideration whether that state of fact was due to any unreasonable conduct on the part of the local authority. I cannot see any basis for reading any words to this effect into the section without re-writing it, which would not be permissible. I am therefore driven to the conclusion that the question which the court must ask itself, and answer, in this case is simply as follows:

'Provided that the minister had properly directed himself in accordance with the passages which I have cited above, could he reasonably conclude on December 3, 1981, that council tenants in Norwich in fact had, or might have, difficulty in exercising their right to buy effectively and expeditiously?'

It follows that in my judgment all the submissions put forward on behalf of the council, to the effect that its approach to its obligations under the Act was reasonable or not unreasonable are of no direct relevance. The question of reasonableness only enters into the construction of section 23 in relation to the minister's decision to invoke his powers under the section on the basis of the facts which, upon a proper self-direction, appear to him to exist by reference to the words of the section. A striking illustration of the profound difference of approach as between the council and the minister is provided by a key-passage in the correspondence which passed between them. It is taken from the council's letter of November 11, 1981 . . . and it was quoted back to the council by the minister in his decision letter of December 3, 1981, as illustrative of the council's approach, which the minister regarded as unacceptable when he decided to exercise his power under section 23. The chief executive of the council wrote as follows:

'It simply will not do, in our judgment, to neglect the problems of the homeless, and other statutory housing obligations – and the work we are doing to create employment – and combat other problems – just to enable a relatively small number of people, who are already comfortably housed, to buy a property a few months earlier than they themselves could, when they will lose nothing by waiting.'

The words 'when they will lose nothing by waiting' are in my view clearly an overstatement, for the reasons already mentioned. However, this is not the point. The point for present purposes is that in my view the council could not possibly be regarded as having acted unreasonably in approaching its obligations under the Act on this basis. Indeed, many would wholly agree with this policy. But this is not the relevant question under section 23. The relevant question is whether the minister could reasonably conclude that in consequence of the policy of the council, as illustrated by this passage, its tenants had or might have difficulty in exercising their right to buy effectively or expeditiously. In this connection I do not think that the position can be put more clearly and succinctly than in the following passage from the judgment of the Divisional Court in the present case:

'If it (the local authority) decides, as this council has done, that giving effect to the tenants' rights to buy their homes should have a relatively low priority, so be it. But the consequence may well be that the tenants will have difficulty in exercising the right to buy effectively and expeditiously. If it appears to the Secretary of State that this is the result, the right to intervene will arise.'

Before considering the submissions on behalf of the council that the minister misdirected himself in various respects because of matters which he should reasonably have taken into account or which he unreasonably took into account, I must shortly deal with the primary submission made on behalf of the council. This concerned the construction of section 23 in the context of section 10. The relevance of section 10 is that the minister's decision to intervene under section 23 was mainly influenced by the fact that the notices required to be served on tenants under section 10 were in his view unduly delayed. . . . In effect, the submission was, since the notices under section 10 had to be served on the tenants 'as soon as practicable,' that in so far as the minister decided to intervene under section 23 because of delays in the service of these notices, he could only do so if these had in fact not been served 'as soon as practicable'.

I cannot accept this submission. I have already repeatedly quoted the relevant words of section 23, which are entirely general and not related to any timetable in any other section. In substance the argument is that the minister was not entitled to conclude under section 23 that the tenants in Norwich were having, or might have, difficulty in exercising their right to buy 'expeditiously' unless the local authority was, or at any rate appeared to him to be, in breach of its statutory obligations. However, if this had been the intention of Parliament it would have been easy to say so in section 23, but it is not said. Further, the word 'expeditiously' has no counterpart in any other provision of the Act: it is simply geared to the view of the minister. Thus, take an example which I mentioned during the argument. Suppose that a local authority had adopted a settled policy of never serving the notices under section 5, admitting or denying the tenants' right to buy (known as 'RTB 2 notices'), until the last day of the periods of four and eight weeks respectively, as prescribed by this section, and that it then appeared to the minister that this policy was causing a bottleneck and avoidable delay. In my view it would then have been open to the minister to conclude under section 23 that the tenants had difficulty in exercising their right to buy expeditiously, even though the authority was not in breach of section 5.

I then turn to the facts, but I need not set them out in detail. . . . However, I feel bound to make two general observations at the outset about the minister's decision to intervene under section 23 on December 3, 1981, after much correspondence and several meetings with representatives of the council.

First, it seems to me, looking at the history as a whole, that there was overwhelming evidence in this case that the council's policy in relation to the implementation of the Act was not merely one of lack of enthusiasm, but what might more appropriately be described as passive resistance. A striking example were the instructions for the obligatory 'counselling' interviews of those tenants who were entitled to buy, which included a warning (expressly imposed by the housing committee in capital letters) that the right to resell after five years might well disappear with a change of government. However, as I have already said, the council was in my view entitled to form its own view as to what it regarded to be 'as soon as practicable' under section 10. Further, I have no doubt that the council throughout took the understandable view that its approach to the Act was in accordance with its overall duties to the local electorate and to the ratepayers as a whole. But, as I have also already explained, in deciding to take the line which it did, the council courted the risk that the minister would ultimately act under section 23, since he was then entitled to conclude that this had become applicable to the situation.

The second matter which it is right to mention for completeness, in passing judgment on whether the view taken by the minister was one which he could reasonably take in all the circumstances, is that one cannot close one's eyes to the fact that, throughout the whole history, the policy of the council was only that of a majority of the councillors, and that a minority substantially agreed throughout with the complaints of the tenants and with the substance of the views expressed by the department and ultimately by the minister himself. What happened, as we were told, is – not surprisingly – that the council and the housing committee divided on these issues on party lines. This is only to be expected in relation to a highly political piece of legislation such as this. However, it does have the consequence that a minority of councillors, who were fully familiar with the local situation and the practicalities, clearly appear themselves to have taken the view that council tenants in Norwich were having difficulty in exercising their right to buy effectively and expeditiously. Given this fact, it is a priori difficult to see why the minister could not reasonably have reached the same conclusion.

However, there still remains the question whether the minister in some way misdirected himself in fact or in law, on the lines of the two passages cited at the beginning of this judgment, since the court would not only be entitled, but bound, to set aside his decision if he did so. In this connection a number of submissions were made with which I must deal in so far as these are not already covered by the foregoing analysis of section 23 in the context of the Act. They were all concerned with matters which it is contended the minister unreasonably failed to take into account, or unreasonably took into account, in arriving at his decision. However, with the exception of the submission concerning the district valuer, I can do so fairly briefly.

First, it was submitted that the minister acted unreasonably in failing to take into account the council's overall duties, other than those relating to the tenants' right to buy. In effect, I have already dealt with this: although the council was entitled to decide what the priorities should be, the minister was entitled to intervene if the effect of the council's decision on priorities was that its tenants had, or might have, difficulty in exercising their right to buy effectively or expeditiously.

Secondly, it was said that the minister acted unreasonably in failing to take into account that by December 3, 1981, there was relatively little difference in the timetable for serving the outstanding section 10 notices between the view of the minister and that of the council. The minister's view was that this operation could and should be completed by about the middle of February 1982 whereas the council envisaged completion by about the end of June. However, the difference is not de minimis in relation to the word 'expeditiously'. Furthermore, the council made it clear that about 100 'difficult cases', mostly involving flats, would not be completed by then, and felt unable to give any assurance as to the time by which these would be dealt with.

Next, it was said that the minister acted unreasonably in taking into account matters which neither his department nor he had 'taken up with the council or given them a fair opportunity to deal with', viz. the council's insistence on the inclusion of 'onerous', i.e. unreasonable, covenants in the conveyances, improper bases of valuation, and over-valuations which necessitated resort to the district valuer under section 11. However, in my view the department and the minister were not obliged to become involved in argument with the council on every point which cumulatively led the minister to the conclusion that tenants were having difficulty in exercising their right to buy. Indeed, one of the Draconian aspects of section 23 is that it does not require any prior process of consultation or warning before the notice which brings it into effect. No doubt, however, the minister must act fairly, and the long history of correspondence and meetings clearly shows that he did not act unfairly in any way in this case. Moreover, all these matters were well known to the council as being matters of complaint by the tenants, and in this connection it is striking that the council was ultimately persuaded to drop the onerous covenants, to reconsider its bases of valuation (which took no account of the fact that many of the properties were situated on housing estates, since this was considered to be already covered by the statutory discount, which was clearly untenable), and that in every single determination by the district valuer in Norwich under section 11 (of which there were no less than 133 by November 30, 1981), the price put forward by the council was reduced substantially.

Then it was submitted that the minister acted unreasonably in taking into account the performance of other local authorities in completing the service of section 10 notices 'when circumstances would vary from one authority to another'. However, I can see nothing wrong in this, having regard to the way in which it was in fact done. Inevitably, authorities with a larger stock of council properties and a larger housing department would be expected to serve a greater number of section 10 notices in a given time; and there was also the factor that Norwich had had no previous experience of selling council properties whereas other authorities had. However, the comparison was in fact made on the basis of the ratio between the number of RTB 2 notices and section 10 notices within the same period, and the comparison only extended to other authorities to which similar warnings had also already been given, including authorities with no previous experience of selling, i.e. those whose performance was at the bottom end of the scale. In these circumstances, and on this basis, I cannot see anything unfair in relying on comparisons to some extent as one of the ingredients leading to the decision to invoke section 23. Indeed, I do not think that the minister could reasonably have been expected to approach the situation in Norwich in isolation, without some attempt to evaluate it in relation to what was happening elsewhere. He would certainly have been criticised if he had not done so.

I then come finally to the issue concerning the district valuer, which caused me the greatest anxiety. It is said that the minister was not entitled to take into account the availability of the district valuer to assist in the preparation of section 10 notices because, due to what were submitted to be 'the appellate or arbitration duties' of the district valuer under section 11, it would have been unlawful for the council to make use of his assistance.

This raises an issue of law, but for the sake of completeness it should be mentioned that this was not in fact the only reason why the council declined to ask the district valuer to assist. It took the view, which the minister could reasonably regard as causing unnecessary delay, that the conveyances must incorporate plans to a scale of 1:500, whereas it was known that the district valuer could only work on the basis of the 1:1250 ordnance sheets which, as we were told, are normally used in conveyancing and are in fact recommended by the Land Registry. Above all, however, it is clear that an important reason for the decision not to use the district valuer was that his office would have produced valuations, which could have been used in connection with the section 10 notices, at a rate which could not have been dealt with by such of the council's resources as the council was prepared to allocate for this purpose; and which could also not have been dealt with by the housing committee on the basis of the frequency of its meetings which were considered to be sufficient, bearing in mind that the council took the view – as it was clearly entitled – that each individual valuation required the approval of the whole committee.

However, none of these facts – though they cannot be doubted as facts on the evidence before us – can affect the ultimate issue whether it would have been unlawful for the council to have resorted to the district valuer. If it would have been unlawful, and if the minister in fact based his decision on the council's refusal to make use of the district valuer, then it cannot be doubted that his decision would have to be set aside.

In my view, however, neither of these considerations apply. I do not think that resort to the district valuer at the section 10 stage would have been unlawful because of his statutory function under section 11. Since the statute does not prohibit such resort, it could only be unlawful if this would infringe the rules of natural justice. What was said in this connection was that it would have this effect, because justice might not appear to be done, and because tenants might be deterred from resorting to a determination under section 11 if the district valuer's office had already been involved at the stage of section 10. In my view, however, this argument goes much too far in relation to the rules of natural justice. At the section 10 stage the price put forward by the council depends solely upon the council's opinion as to the value of each property. It is free to disregard any view expressed by someone in the district valuer's office. The experience of the (about) 250 other authorities which in fact used the district valuer at the section 10 stage for some 168,000 cases, of which about 50 per cent were subsequently reduced upon a determination under section 11, in no way suggests that any unfairness resulted . . . . Moreover, the department took steps to ensure that the persons involved at the section 10 stage, if the district valuer's office was requested to assist, would not be the senior valuation officer or his deputy, who were expressly instructed to reserve themselves for section 11 determinations whenever these might arise.

Although I am accordingly of the opinion that resort to the district valuer's office at the section 10 stage was not, and would in this case not have been, unlawful, I think that I might well have been driven to the conclusion that the minister's decision should nevertheless be set aside if he had *insisted* on the council using the district valuer at the section 10 stage and had then based his decision to intervene under section 23 on the ground that the council refused to do so. If this had happened, then – in view of the understandable doubt about the legal position – I might well have concluded that the basis of the minister's decision was sufficiently unreasonable to entitle the court to set it aside. But this was in fact not the case. The affidavit sworn on behalf of the minister states expressly that 'his decision to intervene in the case of the applicant was in no way based on their reluctance to use the services of the district valuer for section 10 purposes'. Any challenge to the good faith of the minister, or to the truthfulness of the contents of the affidavit, was expressly disclaimed before us. Moreover, the correspond-ence and the record of the various meetings bear this out. Thus, at the final meeting on November 5, 1981 . . . the Secretary of State and the Minister of State for Housing and Construction . . . said . . . that it was for the council to decide whether or not to invoke the assistance of the district valuer in order to achieve a rate of progress which the Secretary of State regarded as acceptable against the background of section 23. . . .

In the result, and in agreement with the Divisional Court, I cannot see any basis which would entitle the court to interfere with the minister's decision to invoke his power under section 23 in this case, and I accordingly agree that this appeal must be dismissed.

May LJ in his concurring judgment agreed that, while the Minister must act fairly and 'reasonably' (in the *Wednesbury* sense) in exercising his power under section 23, it was irrelevant whether the council had acted unreasonably: it was enough that tenants were in fact encountering delay in exercising their right to buy.

Lord Denning, on the other hand, was of the opinion that the Minister could intervene only if the delay was caused by unreasonable conduct of the council: 'Any other view would give the central government too much power over the elected representatives of the people' (p. 825). But his Lordship concluded that the council had in the circumstances acted unreasonably.

After the judgment in this case the Norwich City Council agreed to expedite council house sales, and the Minister stayed his hand. The effect of the case was to strengthen ministerial powers of intervention in a politically contentious area of policy. (See further S. H. Bailey [1983] *PL* 8.)

Other techniques of control

Another means available to ministers for the control of local authorities is the making of regulations, where this is authorized by statute. Ministerial regulations or orders apply to many local government services, such as education, housing and planning.

A potent and varied instrument of control is the circular. Some circulars, issued under statutory powers, are mandatory, but even those which merely advise, exhort or give guidance are generally acted upon by local authorities, and statutory powers often lie in reserve. A well known instance was Department of Education and Science Circular 10/65 issued to local authorities by the Secretary of State for Education in 1965, requesting them to submit plans for the reorganization of secondary schools in their areas on comprehensive lines. The Circular met some resistance from Conservative councils, and was followed the next year by a Circular (10/66) which declared that no building grants would be allocated to schools that were not included in reorganization plans. Eventually the 1974–9 Labour Government resorted to legislation (the Education Act 1976) to implement its policy on comprehensive schools. (See now the Education Act 1979, s.1.)

Finally, since local authorities are to a great extent dependent on funds provided by central government, finance provides another and far-reaching means of central control. About half local government expenditure is met from the general rate support grant and various specific grants (such as the housing subsidy, police grant and student grant) made by the Exchequer. There is considerable scope for ministerial discretion in the working of the grant system, and a local authority which insists on policies disapproved by central government may be threatened with the reduction or withholding of grant.

In recent years central government has tightened its control of local authority expenditure by both statutory and informal means. While the Local Government, Planning and Land Act 1980 removed some detailed central controls, its revision of the rate support grant system and provisions for control of local authority capital expenditure reduced local government autonomy in England and Wales. The Local Government Finance Act 1982 introduced new controls over rates and an enlarged ministerial power to withhold grant. This was followed by the Rates Act 1984 which empowers the Secretary of State for the Environment to set rate limits for selected local authorities identified as 'over-spenders', and includes a reserve power of general rate limitation, exercisable subject to parliamentary approval. (Control of local government expenditure and rate levels in Scotland has also been extended in recent years: see the Local Government (Miscellaneous Provisions) (Scotland) Act 1981, Part II, the Local Government and Planning (Scotland) Act 1982 and the Rating and Valuation (Amendment) (Scotland) Act 1984.)

The Redcliffe-Maud Report declared (Cmnd 4040/1969, vol. 1, para. 28): 'It is only by the combination of local representative institutions with the central institutions of Parliament, Ministers and Departments, that a genuine national democracy can be sustained.' The authors of a recent study (Murray Stewart et'al., 'The Future of Local Democracy' (1984) 10(2) *Local Government Studies* 1 at 2) see in the present Government's measures an intention

to alter fundamentally the balance between centralized power and local discretion. This we believe will severely impair the ability of local government to respond to changing economic and social circumstances. Such measures will seriously dilute the legitimacy of local authorities, their institutional, administrative and political capacity and their ability to offer effective local services. They will also seriously diminish the accountability and responsiveness of government to the community at a time of growing economic and social stress.

See also Richard Jackman, 'The Rates Bill: A Measure of Desparation' (1984) 55 *Political Quarterly* 161.

Some now fear a gradual transformation of local authorities into mere agencies of central government. The authors of the following passage are more sanguine.

Patrick Dunleavy and R. A. W. Rhodes, 'Beyond Whitehall', in Henry Drucker *et al* (eds.), *Developments in British Politics* (1983), pp. 114–15

Central government's powers are considerable. Ministers can usually change the law to require councils to do what they want. They can acquire extensive powers to regulate what local authorities do under legislation, set service standards, and maintain an overall 'quality control' over councils' outputs. And, of course, central grants provide much of the money for local services. But the limits on what Whitehall can do are also considerable. Most obviously, central departments do not have the staff or the operational knowledge to run local services themselves (nor do they want to). Indeed, central departments do not have enough staff to police the full range of controls they formally have over local government. Consequently they have to be selective, concentrating only on the most serious departures in local-authority policies from the goals they would like to see met. Nor can central government easily manipulate much of its funding to control local authorities. Over four-fifths of central finance is paid over in a general or block grant which is not directly linked to particular services. Within their grant total, local authorities may distribute money between services as they wish, even in a way that will frustrate central objectives. For example, councils may protect one service from centrally imposed cuts by reducing spending elsewhere in their budgets and using these savings to preserve the threatened service's funding.

Local authorities' powers are less decisive but equally real. Most important, they have the power either to do nothing, or to delay implementing government policies for a considerable period, or simply to be half-hearted about doing something they dislike. Even when a government builds into new laws draconian powers to compel councils to do things . . . it can only use these powers very sparingly; and threatening their use cannot force councils who drag their feet without obviously breaking the law, to change their ways. Council-house sales in the period 1979–81 were considerably reduced because large numbers of Labour councils claimed that they had not the staff to process sales quickly, and generally made it as difficult and slow as they could within the law for tenants to buy property. [Cf. *R.* v. *Secretary of State for the Environment, ex p. Norwich CC*, above.] Above all, central government cannot force local councils to do something *well*. They need to encourage them to behave as they wish, and this encouragement can only be very successful if local authorities feel free to take the initiative and guide their own affairs.

All these points tend to mean that central-local relations take on the aspects of a 'game' in which both sides manoeuvre for advantage, deploying the resources they control to maximise their influence over outcomes, and trying to avoid (where they can) becoming dependent on the other 'player'. This is not, of course, to suggest that central and local government are always in conflict, merely that their interests are by no means identical and that both sides are vigilant in defence of their interests.

While the relationship between central and local government is often (perhaps typically) one of cooperation or partnership, conflicts of interest frequently arise, especially when different parties rule at the centre and in the locality. A local authority may see it as its duty to defend the local community by which it was elected against what it regards as harmful government policies. In recent years the political conflict has contributed to a deepening crisis in the relations between central and local government. Tony Byrne remarks (*Local Government in Britain*, 2nd edn 1983, p. 282):

Central-local government relations should be seen as *the* constitutional issue of the 1980s. It raises fundamental questions about the place of local government in Britain, accountability and the clash of mandates, and the future of Britain as a liberal-democratic state.

Powers of local government

Local authorities owe their existence to statute, and their powers are conferred on them (and can be taken away) by Parliament. All local government expenditure requires statutory authorization.

Among the numerous statutes that give powers to (or impose duties on) local authorities are the Public Health Act 1936, the Education Act 1944, the Housing Act 1957, the Town and Country Planning Act 1971, the Highways Act 1980, and the Child Care Act 1980. If a local authority needs additional powers, for example to undertake some new activity – say to operate a municipal caravan park or yachting marina – it may promote a private bill in Parliament to obtain the necessary power. (Authority to do this is given by the Local Government Act 1972, s.239.) This is a rather troublesome and costly process, and sometimes the required power can be more easily obtained from the Secretary of State, who is authorized by statute to make orders, subject to a special parliamentary procedure, conferring certain powers (e.g. for the compulsory acquisition of common land) on local authorities. (See the Statutory Orders (Special Procedure) Acts 1945 and 1965.) In recent years a programme has been under way of repealing outdated local Acts (see the Local Government Act 1972, s.262) and of consolidating necessary local powers in new private Acts and in public legislation such as the Local Government (Miscellaneous Provisions) Acts 1976 and 1982.

The statutory powers of local authorities are marginally extended by section 111(1) of the Local Government Act 1972, which provides that a local authority 'shall have power to do any thing . . . which is calculated to facilitate, or is conducive or incidental to, the discharge of any of their functions'. The Act (section 137) also permits local authorities to incur expenditure up to the sum realized by a rate of 2p in the pound for any purpose which, in their opinion, is in the interests of the area or its inhabitants. (See Colin Crawford and Victor Moore, 'A 2p Rate – in the Interests of the Community' (1983) 133 *NLJ* 200.)

Beyond its statutory powers a local authority cannot go: any unauthorized action is ultra vires and illegal. If the action involves expenditure, the auditor appointed (by the Audit Commission for Local Authorities) to audit local authority accounts may apply to court for a declaration that the expenditure is unlawful: Local Government Finance Act 1982, s.19(1). Moreover any individual may bring proceedings to challenge ultra vires action of a local authority, either if he has a 'sufficient interest' to take proceedings on his own account, or if he is assisted by the Attorney-General in a 'relator' action. (See Hartley and Griffith, *Government and Law*, pp. 369–73.)

The act of a local authority is ultra vires not only if it goes beyond the powers conferred (as in *Attorney-General* v. *Fulham Corporation* [1921] 1 Ch. 440) but also if, although apparently covered by statutory authority, it is vitiated by any of the following factors (which may overlap): (1) bad faith (*Cannock Chase District Council* v. *Kelly* [1978] 1 WLR 1); (2) unreasonableness, or something that no reasonable authority would have done (*Associated Provincial Picture Houses Ltd* v. *Wednesbury Corporation* [1948] 1 KB 223); (3) misuse of the power for an improper purpose (*Sydney Municipal Council* v. *Campbell* [1925] AC 338); (4) reliance upon extraneous or irrelevant considerations, or failure to take account of relevant considerations (*Roberts* v. *Hopwood* [1925] AC 578; (5) failure to proceed fairly or in accordance with natural justice in relation to individuals affected by the action (*R.* v. *Liverpool Corporation, ex p. Liverpool Taxi Fleet Operators' Association* [1972] 2 QB 299); (6) disregard of the fiduciary duty owed in law to ratepayers.

All these factors except the last are relevant to the exercise of discretionary powers by public authorities in general, and together they provide a formidable array of weapons for challenging official action. The courts have, however, often said that it is not their function to substitute their own view of what is good policy or sound administration for that of an elected local authority (See, e.g., *Pickwell* v. *Camden London Borough Council* [1983] QB 962.)

Fiduciary duty

The fiduciary duty owed by a local authority to its ratepayers was the basis of the decision in the following case.

Prescott v. *Birmingham Corporation* [1955] Ch. 210 (CA)

The Birmingham Corporation operated a passenger transport service under powers given by its private Acts of Parliament, which authorized it to charge such fares as it thought fit. The Corporation adopted a scheme of free travel facilities for old people in the city. A ratepayer brought proceedings for a declaration that the scheme was ultra vires and illegal. Vaisey J gave judgment for the plaintiff, and the Corporation appealed. Jenkins LJ read the judgment of the Court of Appeal.

JENKINS LJ: . . . Mr Rowe's argument for the defendants [the corporation] has all the attractions of simplicity. It is to this effect: (1) Under the relevant statutory provisions the defendants are empowered (not enjoined) to charge fares, and are, moreover, empowered to charge such fares as they think fit, provided that they do not exceed any prescribed statutory maxima for the time being in force. The legislation contains no equality clause. Therefore the defendants are not obliged to charge at the same rate for every passenger, but can charge different rates for different passengers, or, indeed, allow some passengers to travel free while charging others. For that matter, as the provisions in regard to the charging of fares are permissive and not imperative, the defendants could, if so minded, allow everyone to travel free of charge and defray the entire cost of their transport undertaking out of the rates. . . .

(2) Mr Rowe admits that acceptance of the proposition that the defendants have power to discriminate in this way does not conclude the case in his favour, for it still remains to consider whether the adoption of the discriminatory scheme now in question would be a proper exercise of the power. He does not contend that a purely arbitrary or capricious course of discrimination would be permissible, but he says that, given the power, the question whether a particular mode of exercising it is a proper one is primarily a matter for the discretion of the defendants, and submits that the court should not override a decision reached by the defendants in exercise of that discretion (apart from mala fides, of which, of course, there is no suggestion here), unless satisfied that the defendants, in exercising it, failed to take into account relevant matters, or took into account irrelevant matters, or exercised it, in short in such an unreasonable or irrational fashion that there was in truth no real exercise of it at all. . . .

(3) Mr Rowe finally submits that, given that the defendants did have a discretionary power of discrimination, there is no ground for holding that the defendants have exercised their discretion improperly in using the power for the purpose of introducing the scheme now under consideration. He says it appears from the report of the general purposes committee that all relevant matters such as hours, routes and so forth were considered. He says, further, that the age, means and health of potential passengers are all matters relevant to be taken into account in deciding whether any, and if so what, discrimination should be made in their favour. He adds that the transport undertaking is not to be regarded purely as a business enterprise, and that the function of the defendants in relation to it is to provide a transport service (whether remunerative or not) for the benefit of the inhabitants of their city, and says that any scheme of discrimination calculated to make the service more useful to those inhabitants is intra vires the defendants. . . .

We cannot accept Mr Rowe's argument. We do not doubt his proposition (for which there appears to be clear authority) that in the absence of an equality clause, or some necessary implication to the like effect, a person or body, having statutory power to charge tolls or rates, or, for that matter, fares, is entitled to discriminate in the charges made to different people. But this, as a general proposition, only means that the person discriminated against cannot object merely on the ground that he is charged more than the other man. It does not necessarily follow that nobody else can object. No doubt that might be the position, if the power was exercisable simply and solely for the benefit of the person or body on whom it was conferred. But take the case of a trustee running an omnibus service with a statutory power to charge fares to passengers, and no equality clause. If such a trustee chose, from motives of philanthropy, to allow some person or class of persons, considered by him to be badly off, to travel free or at reduced fares, it may be that passengers charged the full fare could not object on that account. But we apprehend that the cestuis que trustent [i.e. the beneficiaries of the trust] certainly could. A similar situation might arise as between a company, or the directors of a company, running an omnibus undertaking with a similar right to charge fares, and the shareholders of such company. . . .

Local authorities are not, of course, trustees for their ratepayers, but they do, we think, owe an analogous fiduciary duty to their ratepayers in relation to the application of funds contributed by the latter. Thus local authorities running an omnibus undertaking at the risk of their ratepayers, in the sense that any deficiencies must be met by an addition to the rates, are not, in our view, entitled, merely on the strength of a general power, to charge different fares to different passengers or classes of passengers, to make a gift to a particular class of persons of rights of free travel on their vehicles, simply because the local authority concerned are of opinion that the favoured class of persons ought, on benevolent or philanthropic grounds, to be accorded that benefit. In other words, they are not, in our view, entitled to use their discriminatory power as proprietors of the transport undertaking in order to confer out of rates a special benefit on some particular class of inhabitants whom they, as the local authority for the town or district in question, may think deserving of such assistance. In the absence of clear statutory authority for such a proceeding (which to our mind a mere general power to charge differential fares certainly is not) we would, for our part, regard it as illegal, on the ground that, to put the matter bluntly, it would amount simply to the making of a gift or present in money's worth to a particular section of the local community at the expense of the general body of ratepayers. . . .

We are not persuaded by Mr Rowe's argument to the effect that the relevant legislation would allow the defendants to charge no fares at all to anyone and to finance their transport undertaking entirely out of the rates. We think it is clearly implicit in the legislation, that while it was left to the defendants to decide what fares should be charged within any prescribed statutory maxima for the time being in force, the undertaking was to be run as a business venture, or, in other words, that fares fixed by the defendants at their discretion, in accordance with ordinary business principles, were to be charged. That is not to say that in operating their transport undertaking the defendants should be guided by considerations of profit to the exclusion of all other considerations. They should, no doubt, aim at providing an efficient service of omnibuses at reasonable cost, and it may be that this objective is impossible of attainment without some degree of loss. But it by no means follows that they should go out of their way to make losses by giving away rights of free travel. . . .

In our opinion the scheme now in question goes beyond anything which can reasonably be regarded as authorized by the discretionary power of fixing fares and differentiation in the fares charged to different passengers or classes of passengers possessed by the defendants under the relevant legislation, and is, accordingly, ultra vires the defendants.

. . . But, in our view, the scheme fares no better if its adoption is considered as a purported exercise by the defendants of their discretion in a matter not, on the face of it, necessarily outside the general ambit of the discretionary power of differentiation of fares conferred on them by the relevant legislation. What the defendants did was simply to form the opinion that women of or over the age of 65 and men of or over the age of 70, fulfilling one or other of the conditions as regards means referred to in the scheme, ought to be allowed free travel facilities, and then call for and adopt a scheme giving effect to that opinion. If we are right in thinking that, after all allowance is made for their special position as a local authority, the defendants owe a duty to their ratepayers to operate their transport undertaking substantially on business lines, we think it must necessarily follow that, in adopting the scheme, the defendants misapprehended the nature and scope of the discretion conferred on them, and mistakenly supposed that it enabled them to confer benefits, in the shape of rights of free travel, on any class or classes of the local inhabitants appearing to them to be deserving of such benefits by reason of their advanced age and limited means. Accordingly, if the case is to be regarded as turning upon the question whether the decision to adopt the scheme was a proper exercise of a discretion conferred on the defendants with respect to the differential treatment of passengers in the matter of fares, the answer, in our opinion, must be that it was not a proper exercise of such discretion. . . .

For these reasons we are of opinion that the judge came to a right conclusion in this case, and we would accordingly dismiss the appeal.

Wolfgang Friedmann (*Law in a Changing Society*, 2nd edn 1972, pp. 394–5) says of this case that the Court of Appeal

read 'ordinary business principles' into the statutory power to charge fares as the local authority, with the consent of the licensing authority thought fit. It would be difficult to find any guidance in the court's judgement on the meaning of 'ordinary business principles' and, in particular, on the point at which differential fares would cease to be permissible as 'giving away rights of free travel'.

(See also *Roberts* v. *Hopwood* [1925] AC 578.)

In *Bromley London Borough Council* v. *Greater London Council* [1983] 1 AC 768 the GLC, in implementing an election manifesto promise of its Labour majority to cut London transport fares by 25 per cent, paid a subsidy to the London Transport Executive (LTE), which then ran London's buses and tubes, to enable it to make the reduction. To raise money for the subsidy the GLC issued a supplementary rate precept to the London boroughs, to be met from additional rates. The House of Lords ruled unanimously that the GLC, in exercising in this way its discretionary power under the Transport (London) Act 1969 to make grants to the LTE, had acted ultra vires and unlawfully. Their Lordships held that the Act required the GLC to strike a fair balance between users of London transport and the ratepayers from whose resources any subsidy would be supplied. The GLC, in the view of the House, had failed properly to strike this balance in introducing low fares without due regard to ratepayers' interests or the requirement that the LTE should, so far as practicable, break even in its operations. In reaching this conclusion their Lordships interpreted the Act as requiring that London transport should be run on business principles, not for objects of social policy, and placed a strong emphasis on the GLC's fiduciary duty to ratepayers, interpreting provisions of the Act as being implicitly qualified by this duty.

The reasoning of the five Law Lords in the *Bromley* case differed markedly in detail, in interpreting a statute which was by no means explicit as to the extent of the GLC's power to pay revenue subsidies to the LTE. 'It is very remarkable', says one commentator, 'that there is such a range of interpretation from a court from which there is no appeal' (C. D. Foster, 'Urban

Transport Policy after the House of Lords' Decision' (1982) 8(3) *Local Government Studies* 105 at 111). Moreover it would seem that the concept of a fiduciary duty to ratepayers is more problematic than was realized in this and other cases in which it has been pressed into service. (See further C. D. Foster, op. cit., P. P. Craig, *Administrative Law* (1983), pp. 367–8, and J. Dignan, 'Policy-Making, Local Authorities and the Courts: the "GLC Fares" Case' (1983) 99 *LQR* 605.) The courts acknowledge that local authorities also owe duties to other classes of residents – for example to transport users – and must themselves balance one duty against the other. But this discretionary judgement is subject to judicial control, and a policy which may appear to a local authority to contribute to social welfare and an improved urban environment (and to be justified by an election manifesto commitment) may seem to a judge to be 'a hasty, ill-considered, unlawful and arbitrary use of power' (*per* Watkins LJ in the *Bromley* case at p. 796.)

(Cf. the view taken of the supervisory jurisdiction of the courts over the exercise of discretionary powers by local authorities in *Pickwell* v. *Camden London Borough Council* [1983] QB 962, and see, too, *R.* v. *London Transport Executive, ex p. GLC* [1983] QB 484.)

By-laws

District councils and London borough councils have a general power under section 235 of the Local Government Act 1972 to make by-laws 'for the good rule and government of the whole or any part of the district or borough, as the case may be, and for the prevention and suppression of nuisances therein'. In addition, specific powers to make by-laws are given to local authorities by a variety of other statutes. By-laws have to be confirmed by the Home Secretary or other appropriate minister. Government departments issue model by-laws for the guidance of local authorities, and since these are widely followed they constitute in effect a body of common local government law. By-laws are subject, like other acts of local authorities, to the doctrine of ultra vires. They must be consistent with the general law, and must not be unreasonable or uncertain. (For examples of by-laws held to be invalid because unreasonable see *Arlidge* v. *Islington Corporation* [1909] 2 KB 127 and *Nicholls* v. *Tavistock Urban District Council* [1923] 2 Ch. 18. Cf. *Kruse* v. *Johnson* [1898] 2 QB 91.)

Maladministration

Complaints by members of the public that they have suffered 'injustice in consequence of maladministration' by local authorities in England or Wales may be referred to a Local Commissioner for Administration ('local Ombuds-man') in terms of Part III of the Local Government Act 1974. (For Scotland similar provision is made by the Local Government (Scotland) Act 1975, Part II. In Northern Ireland complaints of maladministration by local authorities are investigated by the Commissioner for Complaints: see the Commissioner for Complaints Act (Northern Ireland) 1969). 'Maladministration' refers to the manner in which a decision was taken and not to the merits of the decision itself: see section 34(3) of the Local Government Act 1974 and *R. v. Local Commissioner for Administration for the North and East Area of England, ex p. Bradford Metropolitan City Council* [1979] QB 287. Most complaints of maladministration by local authorities relate to planning and housing decisions. If a complaint is upheld by a Commissioner it is for the local authority to decide on any remedial action, which may take the form of monetary compensation (authorized by the Local Government Act 1978). If a local authority refuses to accept or act upon an adverse finding by a Commissioner he may review the matter and issue a second report, but can take no further action. Some authorities have been criticized for unwillingness to cooperate with the Commissioners or respond positively to their reports. Such criticisms may be justified, but an authority is sometimes placed in difficulty by the need to have regard to wider considerations when taking decisions in individual cases. (See Harlow and Rawlings, *Law and Administration*, pp. 221–2 and generally pp. 210–26.)

Should a finding of injustice caused by maladministration give rise to a legal remedy? (Cf. the Commissioner for Complaints Act (Northern Ireland) 1969, s.7 and the Report by JUSTICE, *The Local Ombudsmen*, 1980, ch. 7.)

5
The European dimension

1 New legal orders

We have already met with Dicey's aphorism that 'the constitution is the result of the ordinary law of the land' – a sharp perception of a partial truth (see p. 60 above). Until very recently an account of the legal part of the constitution would have been limited to the municipal (domestic) law – an essentially unitary public law of the United Kingdom. Relations with other countries of the Commonwealth were governed by a body of conventions and law – the 'constitutional' law of the Commonwealth – which was gradually dissolving as these relations became less differentiated from the pattern of relations between the United Kingdom and non-Commonwealth countries. (The few remaining *colonies* are still governed, in their relation to the United Kingdom, by special instruments and rules.)

The international obligations undertaken by the United Kingdom in concluding treaties with other countries sometimes necessitated changes in the domestic law, but even in this indirect manner treaties did not significantly influence the course of constitutional development in the United Kingdom (leaving aside the Treaty of Union with Scotland of 1706: see chapter 4 above.) In recent times, however, the United Kingdom has concluded treaties which are having far-reaching effects on the domestic law and the rights and obligations of both private persons and public authorities. The treaties in question are the Treaty of Accession of the United Kingdom to the European Communities, concluded in 1972 (amended text: Cmnd 7463/1979), and the European Convention for the Protection of Human Rights and Fundamental Freedoms, agreed in 1950 (Cmd 8969/1953). By the former treaty the United Kingdom became a party to the treaties establishing the European Communities, and in particular the Treaty of Rome which is the main governing instrument of the European Economic Community.

Accession to the Treaty of Rome has had an unprecedented impact on law and administration in the United Kingdom, and has raised issues concerning such fundamentals of the constitution as parliamentary sovereignty and ministerial responsibility. This is because the Treaty of Rome has given rise to a new kind of legal order. The legal product of the treaty and of the institutions created by it is something more than international law governing the relations between sovereign states. From the treaty there has evolved a common European law which has a dynamic or developing character, is implemented both by institutions set up by the treaty and by agencies (law-making and law-enforcing) of the member states, and is capable of being invoked by individuals in those states. As the European Court of Justice has declared, the member states have, in creating the European Community, 'limited their sovereign rights, albeit within limited fields, and have . . . created a body of law which binds both their nationals and themselves' (*Costa* v. *Ente Nazionale Per L'Energia Elettrica* (ENEL), p. 256 below).

In this chapter we shall consider the impact of Community law on the United Kingdom. The European Convention on Human Rights has had a much less profound effect on law and administration in the United Kingdom, but it provides an important avenue of redress for infringements of individual rights. The following outline is given of some principal features of the Convention.

The European Convention on Human Rights and Fundamental Freedoms

The Convention, to which all 21 member states of the Council of Europe (including the ten member states of the European Communities) are parties, is a 'law-making treaty' (see *Wemhoff* v. *Federal Republic of Germany* ECHR 1968, Series A, No.7, p. 23). It establishes a system of rules for the protection of human rights which are interpreted, applied and developed by the Convention's institutions – the European Commission of Human Rights and the European Court of Human Rights – and by the Committee of Ministers of the Council of Europe (consisting of the Foreign ministers of the member states or their deputies).

It has been said that the Convention 'establishes, in the field of civil liberties, a new legal order designed to substitute for the particular systems of individual States a common European system' (A. H. Robertson, *Human Rights in Europe*, 2nd edn 1977, p. 231). The application of the Convention in the United Kingdom, is, however, qualified by the principle that the conclusion of a treaty by the Crown does not itself have any effects in the domestic law of the United Kingdom. (See further p. 271 below.) Since the Convention came into force on 3 September 1953 its provisions have been binding on the United Kingdom in international law, but they have not been given internal effect by Act of Parliament and are not enforceable by the courts of this country. The Courts do, however, adopt 'a prima facie presumption that Parliament does not intend to act in breach of international law, including therein specific treaty obligations' (*Salomon* v. *Commissioners of Customs and Excise* [1967] 2 QB 116, 143, *per* Diplock LJ). Accordingly if a statutory provision is ambiguous or unclear, the courts will interpret it in the sense that is more consonant with the provisions of the Convention. In *R*. v. *Secretary of State for the Home Department, ex p. Phansopkar* [1976] QB 606, 626, Scarman LJ expressed this principle more ardently in saying, with reference to the rights to respect for private and family life protected by the Convention, that 'it is the duty of the courts, so long as they do not defy or disregard clear unequivocal provision, to construe statutes in a manner which promotes, not endangers, those rights'. (See further *R*. v. *Secretary of State for the Home Department, ex p. Bhajan Singh* [1976] QB 198; *R*. v. *Chief Immigration Officer, Heathrow, ex p. Salamat Bibi* [1976] 1 WLR 979; *Ahmad* v. *Inner London Education Authority* [1978] QB 36; *R*. v. *Secretary of State for the Home Department, ex p. Kirkwood* [1984] 2 All ER 390.)

Complaints of breaches of the Convention are made to the European Commission of Human Rights, either by a state party or, much more often in practice, by an individual – if the state complained against has expressly recognized the right of individual petition. (The United Kingdom renewed its acceptance of the right of individual petition in January 1981 for a period of five years.) Applications found to be admissible may then be the subject of a friendly settlement, which may include a compensatory payment or other redress for an individual complainant. Otherwise the proceedings may conclude with a determination by the Committee of Ministers or – if a reference is made to the European Court of Human Rights by the Commission or by the state party to the proceedings – a judgment by the court. (For details of the procedure see Ralph Beddard, *Human Rights and Europe*, 2nd edn 1980, ch. 3.)

Decisions of the Committee of Ministers and judgments of the court are binding on the state concerned and may oblige it to make changes in the domestic law. A number of changes in the law of the United Kingdom have been made in consequence (or in anticipation) of findings that the United Kingdom was in breach of the Convention. For example, the judgment of the European Court of Human Rights in the *Sunday Times* case, ECHR 1979, Series A, No.30, resulted in a corrective provision in the Contempt of Court Act 1981, s.2, and the judgment in *Campbell and Cosans* v. *United Kingdom*, ECHR 1982, Series A, No. 48, led to the enactment of the Education (Corporal Punishment) Act 1985. See further P. J. Duffy, 'English Law and the European Convention on Human Rights' (1980) 29 *ICLQ* 585.

2 Objectives of the European Community

There are not one but three European Communities. The European Coal and Steel Community was set up in 1951 by the Treaty of Paris; the European Economic Community (EEC) and the Atomic Energy Community were established by two Treaties of Rome in 1957. Our main concern is with the

Economic Community, which is the most important, and in its operations the most ramified and diverse, of the three Communities. We can refer to it as 'the European Community' or simply as 'the Community'. The Communities have in any event certain major institutions in common. There are but one Court of Justice and one parliamentary Assembly, and a single Commission and Council, for all three Communities.

The original members of the Communities were France, West Germany, Italy, Belgium, the Netherlands and Luxembourg. The United Kingdom, Denmark and Ireland acceded to the Communities in 1972 (with effect from 1 January 1973), and Greece became a member at the beginning of 1981. Portugal and Spain have applied for membership of the Communities and negotiations are taking place for their admission to what will then be a Community of twelve nations.

Article 240 of the EEC Treaty provides: 'This Treaty is concluded for an unlimited period.' The Treaty makes no provision for withdrawal by a member state, and it is arguable that unilateral withdrawal would be a breach of international law. (See Dagtoglou, 'How Indissoluble is the Community?' in P. D. Dagtoglou (ed.), *Basic Problems of the European Community*, 1975, p. 258, and Akehurst, 'Withdrawal from International Organizations' (1979) 32 *CLP* 143.) Withdrawal could, however, be lawfully effected with the agreement of all parties to the Treaty. (Greenland, which entered the Communities as part of the Kingdom of Denmark, having gained home rule withdrew from membership at the beginning of 1985 upon ratification of an amending treaty by all the member states.) The Labour Party's 1983 general election manifesto included a commitment to open negotiations for withdrawal from the Community, and its manifesto for the 1984 elections to the European Parliament declared that Britain must 'retain the option of withdrawal from the EEC'. Withdrawal will, however, become increasingly difficult as the United Kingdom becomes further locked in economic and political relations with the other member states of the Community.

The preamble to the EEC Treaty includes a general and somewhat rhetorical declaration of principles, the first being 'to lay the foundations of an ever closer union among the peoples of Europe'. This is followed by a statement of the objectives of the Community in Article 2:

The Community shall have as its task, by establishing a common market and progressively approximating the economic policies of Member States, to promote throughout the Community a harmonious development of economic activities, a continuous and balanced expansion, an increase in stability, an accelerated raising of the standard of living and closer relations between the States belonging to it.

From this it appears that the goals of the Community are to be attained by the two mechanisms of a 'common market' and the 'approximation of economic policies'. Article 3 of the Treaty gives further particulars of the means to be adopted:

For the purposes set out in Article 2, the activities of the Community shall include, as provided in this Treaty and in accordance with the timetable set out therein:

(a) the elimination, as between Member States, of customs duties and of quantitative restrictions on the import and export of goods, and of all other measures having equivalent effect;

(b) the establishment of a common customs tariff and of a common commercial policy towards third countries;

(c) the abolition, as between Member States, of obstacles to freedom of movement for persons, services and capital;

(d) the adoption of a common policy in the sphere of agriculture;

(e) the adoption of a common policy in the sphere of transport;

(f) the institution of a system ensuring that competition in the common market is not distorted;

(g) the application of procedures by which the economic policies of Member States can be coordinated and disequilibria in their balances of payments remedied;

(h) the approximation of the laws of Member States to the extent required for the proper functioning of the common market;

(i) the creation of a European Social Fund in order to improve employment opportunities for workers and to contribute to the raising of their standard of living;

(j) the establishment of a European Investment Bank to facilitate the economic expansion of the Community by opening up fresh resources;

(k) the association of the overseas countries and territories in order to increase trade and to promote jointly economic and social development.

The customs union which was an essential preliminary goal of the Community has been achieved, and member states are accordingly not at liberty to act independently in imposing customs duties or equivalent charges. Much has also been done to remove restrictions upon the 'four freedoms' – the free movement of goods, persons, services, and capital. A common agricultural policy has been developed which is a main preoccupation of the Community and results in a continuous activity of rule-making. Provision is made in the Treaty for the coordination of economic policies (Articles 6, 103–5) and halting steps have been taken in this direction.

Article 3(i) above shows that the Community has also undertaken certain social objectives. These are more fully developed in Title III of the Treaty. They include the principle of equal pay without discrimination based on sex, a common vocational training policy, and the maintenance of a European Social Fund which provides assistance for such schemes as the retraining and resettlement of workers.

The Community has developed its own policies and action programmes on consumer protection, energy, and the environment.

The Community established by the EEC Treaty does not merely possess an independent legal personality (Article 210) but has also, one might say, its own organic life, is driven by its own machinery and personnel, and is capable of developing new or refined objectives which are not expressed in the Treaty.

The makers of the Treaty of Rome were inspired by the ideal of a United Europe – although this vision did not encompass the *whole* of Europe. The Treaty itself refers only vaguely to this aspiration in its preamble ('. . . an ever closer union among the peoples of Europe'), and its substantive provisions are directed to economic, not political, integration. But there were those who envisaged the progress of the Community towards a federation (or looser 'confederation') of European states, and although this prospect is now realized to be a distant one, political union in some form is a frequently reiterated goal of Community policy. In 1971 the Community set itself the interim objective of economic and monetary union (EMU), which would have transferred major economic policy-making to Community institutions. This plan foundered, however, and the present objective is to achieve a more effective *coordination* of national economic policies.

The Community is unlikely in the near future to make great advances in economic or political integration. The economic climate is unfavourable, and new member states will have to be accommodated to existing structures and policies. In time, however, the momentum of integration may be recovered, and we may then see the Community institutions take over more powers from the member states.

3 Institutions and law of the European Community

(a) Community institutions

The institutions of the Community were set up by the Treaty of Rome and the Merger Treaty of 1965 (Treaty Establishing a Single Council and a Single Commission of the European Communities).

Four institutions carry out the tasks and exercise the powers of the Community: the Commission, the Council, the European Parliament, and the Court of Justice.

The Commission

The 'Commission of the European Communities' consists of 14 members, of whom no more than two may be nationals of the same member state. Commissioners are appointed by the governments of the member states, and the practice is for the largest countries, France, Germany, Italy and the United Kingdom, each to have two Commissioners, while the other six countries each have one. Commissioners hold office for four years. One of the Commissioners is appointed as President, by agreement of the member states, and holds office for an initial term of two years, which is normally renewed for a second term.

The Commissioners are appointed to work for the interests of the Communities, and are not the representatives of their own governments.

Article 10(2) of the Merger Treaty provides:

The members of the Commission shall, in the general interest of the Communities, be completely independent in the performance of their duties. In the performance of these duties, they shall neither seek nor take instructions from any Government or from any other body. They shall refrain from any action incompatible with their duties. Each Member State undertakes to respect this principle and not to seek to influence the members of the Commission in the performance of their tasks.

The Commission has many duties under the EEC Treaty. In broad terms it acts as guardian of the Treaty (Article 155), initiates Community policies, and executes decisions. The Commissioners are collectively responsible for the work of the Commission, but each has a 'portfolio' related to one or more of the 20 Directorates-General of the Commission which together cover the whole range of Community activity.

As guardian of the Treaty the Commission watches to see that Treaty obligations are carried out by the member states. If after investigation the Commission concludes that there has been an infringement of the Treaties, or of the acts (secondary legislation) of Community institutions under the Treaties, it is empowered to take steps to ensure compliance. Article 169 of the EEC Treaty provides:

If the Commission considers that a Member State has failed to fulfil an obligation under this Treaty, it shall deliver a reasoned opinion on the matter after giving the State concerned the opportunity to submit its observations.

If the State concerned does not comply with the opinion within the period laid down by the Commission, the latter may bring the matter before the Court of Justice.

Enforcement proceedings were taken by the Commission against the United Kingdom in the following case.

> Case 61/81 *Commission of the European Communities v. United Kingdom of Great Britain and Northern Ireland* [1982] ECR 2601
> (Court of Justice of the European Communities)

Article 119 of the EEC Treaty requires member states to ensure the application of the principle 'that men and women should receive equal pay for equal work'. To reinforce and clarify this provision the Council of the European Communities in 1975 adopted Directive 75/117, the equal pay Directive, with which member states were bound to comply. Article 1 of the Directive provided:

The principle of equal pay for men and women outlined in Article 119 of the Treaty . . . means, for the same work *or for work to which equal value is attributed*, the elimination of all discrimination on grounds of sex with regard to all aspects and conditions of remuneration. In particular, where a job classification system is used for determining pay, it must be based on the same criteria for both men and women and so drawn up as to exclude any discrimination on grounds of sex. [Italics added.]

The Sex Discrimination Act enacted by Parliament in 1975 was intended to fulfil the United Kingdom's obligations under Article 119 and the equal pay Directive; it included amendments to the Equal Pay Act 1970. In terms of the Equal Pay Act as amended, a woman was entitled to equal pay if she was doing 'like work' to that of a man in the same employment, or if her work was 'rated as equivalent' with that of a male employee. By section 1(5) a woman was to be regarded as employed on work rated as equivalent with that of a man, only if their jobs had been given equal value on a job evaluation study. However an employer was under no obligation to introduce a job evaluation scheme, and his failure to do so would prevent a woman from claiming equal pay under the Act on the basis that her work was equivalent with that of a male employee.

The European Commission took the view that the United Kingdom had not fully implemented the equal pay Directive. It duly delivered to the United Kingdom Government its 'reasoned opinion' that Article 1 of the Directive had been 'incorrectly applied' in the Equal Pay Act, and invited the United Kingdom to adopt appropriate measures of compliance within two months. The Government replied that it considered the United Kingdom legislation to be in conformity with the Directive, whereupon the Commission took proceedings in the Court of Justice under Article 169 (above), claiming a declaration that the United Kingdom had failed to fulfil its obligations under the Directive.

Decision of the Court

By application lodged at the Court Registry on 18 March 1981 the Commission of the European Communities brought an action under Article 169 of the EEC Treaty for a declaration that the United Kingdom had failed to fulfil its obligations under the Treaty by failing to adopt the laws, regulations or administrative provisions needed to comply with Council Directive 75/117/EEC of 10 February 1975 on the approximation of the laws of the Member States relating to the application of the principle of equal pay for men and women . . . as regards the elimination of discrimination for work to which equal value is attributed. . . .

Comparison of [Article 1 of the directive and section 1(5) of the Equal Pay Act 1970, as amended] reveals that the job classification system is, under the directive, merely one of several methods for determining pay for work to which equal value is attributed, whereas under the provision in the Equal Pay Act . . . the introduction of such a system is the sole method of achieving such a result.

It is also noteworthy that, as the United Kingdom concedes, British legislation does not permit the introduction of a job classification system without the employer's consent. Workers in the United Kingdom are therefore unable to have their work rated as being of equal value with comparable work if their employer refuses to introduce a classification system.

The United Kingdom attempts to justify that state of affairs by pointing out that Article 1 of the directive says nothing about the right of an employee to insist on having pay determined by a job classification system. On that basis it concludes that the worker may not insist on a comparative evaluation of different work by the job classification method, the introduction of which is at the employer's discretion.

The United Kingdom's interpretation amounts to a denial of the very existence of a right to equal pay for work of equal value where no classification has been made. Such a position is not consonant with the general scheme and provisions of Directive 75/117. The recitals in the preamble to that directive indicate that its essential purpose is to implement the principle that men and women should receive equal pay contained in Article 119 of the Treaty and that it is primarily the responsibility of the Member States to ensure the application of this principle by means of appropriate laws, regulations and administrative provisions in such a way that all employees in the Community can be protected in these matters.

To achieve that end the principle is defined in the first paragraph of Article 1 so as to include under the term 'the same work', the case of 'work to which equal value is attributed', and the second paragraph emphasizes merely that where a job classification system is used for determining pay it is necessary to ensure that it is based on the same criteria for both men and women and so drawn up as to exclude any discrimination on grounds of sex.

It follows that where there is disagreement as to the application of that concept a worker must be entitled to claim before an appropriate authority that his work has the same value as other work and, if that is found to be the case, to have his rights under the Treaty and the directive acknowledged by a binding decision. Any method which excludes that option prevents the aims of the directive from being achieved.

That is borne out by the terms of Article 6 of the directive which provides that Member States are, in accordance with their national circumstances and legal systems, to take the measures necessary to ensure that the principle of equal pay is applied. They are to see that effective means are available to take care that this principle is observed.

In this instance, however, the United Kingdom has not adopted the necessary measures and there is at present no means whereby a worker who considers that his post is of equal value to another may pursue his claims if the employer refuses to introduce a job classification system.

The United Kingdom has emphasized ... the practical difficulties which would stand in the way of implementing the concept of work to which equal value has been attributed if the use of a system laid down by consensus were abandoned. The United Kingdom believes that the criterion of work of equal value is too abstract to be applied by the courts.

The Court cannot endorse that view. The implementation of the directive implies that the assessment of the 'equal value' to be 'attributed' to particular work, may be effected notwithstanding the employer's wishes, if necessary in the context of adversary proceedings. The Member States must endow an authority with the requisite jurisdiction to decide whether work has the same value as other work, after obtaining such information as may be required.

Accordingly, by failing to introduce into its national legal system in implementation of the provisions of Council Directive 75/117/EEC of 10 February 1975 such measures as are necessary to enable all employees who consider themselves wronged by failure to apply the principle of equal pay for men and women for work to which equal value is attributed and for which no system of job classification exists to obtain recognition of such equivalence, the United Kingdom has failed to fulfil its obligations under the Treaty. . . .

On those grounds, THE COURT hereby:

1. Declares that, by failing to introduce into its national legal system in implementation of the provisions of Council Directive 75/117/EEC of 10 February 1975 such measures as are necessary to enable all employees who consider themselves wronged by failure to apply the principle of equal pay for men and women for work to which equal value is attributed and for which no system of job classification exists to obtain recognition of such equivalence, the United Kingdom has failed to fulfil its obligations under the Treaty;

2. Orders the United Kingdom to pay the costs.

(See the note by Susan Atkins, (1983) 8 *EL Rev.*48.)

As a result of this judgment the United Kingdom Government was bound to introduce new legislation to give full effect to the equal pay Directive. The Equal Pay Act 1970 was accordingly amended by the Equal Pay (Amendment) Regulations 1983 (SI 1983 No. 1794), allowing claims for equal pay whether or not a job evaluation scheme has been carried out. Unfortunately the new regulations (and the associated procedural regulations, SI 1983 No. 1807) are extremely complex and, at best, a grudging and minimal compliance with the ruling of the European court. Indeed it is doubtful whether the equal pay Directive has been fully implemented. (See further Christopher McCrudden, 'Equal Pay for Work of Equal Value: the Equal Pay (Amendment) Regulations 1983' (1983) 12 *Industrial Law Journal* 197; Richard Townshend-Smith (1984) 47 *MLR* 201.) (The United Kingdom has also been held to be in breach of the 'equal treatment' Directive, 76/207: Case 165/82 *Commission* v. *United Kingdom* [1984] 1 CMLR 44.)

The principal function of the Commission is to initiate Community policies. The Treaty of Rome in the main declares only the general outlines of policy, and it is left to the institutions to work out detailed policies and rules for implementing the objectives of the Treaty. The Commission takes the initiative in this, acting in conjunction with the Council. The most important Community decisions are taken by the Council, but in the great majority of cases the Council can act only on a proposal by the Commission. In formulating its proposals the Commission consults outside interests and has discussions with working groups of national experts. After submission of a proposal, dialogue continues between Commission and Council, and the Commission may modify its proposal before the Council has acted on it. The Council can amend a Commission proposal only by a unanimous vote (EEC Treaty, Article 149).

The Commission is also the executive of the Community. It exercises a wide range of rule-making powers in implementing provisions of the EEC Treaty and giving detailed effect to legislation of the Council.

In carrying out its work the Commission issues a flood of regulations, directives, decisions, recommendations, opinions, and proposals for Council legislation. Conceived as the main driving force of the Community, its role in practice is secondary to that of the Council.

The Council

The Council of the European Communities, usually known simply as the Council of Ministers or the Council, consists of representatives of the governments of the member states. Its membership varies according to the subject under consideration – Ministers of Agriculture, for example, meeting as the Council when issues of the common agricultural policy are to be discussed. A 'General Council' of Foreign Ministers deals with the widest range of matters. The office of President of the Council is held in rotation among the member states for terms of six months.

The role of the Council is both to represent the interests of the member states and to concert national policies in realizing the objectives of the Treaty. It is responsible for the major decisions in Community matters and is the principal legislative authority of the Community.

Under the Treaty most Council decisions are to be taken by a qualified majority with weighted votes. The largest countries, the United Kingdom, France, Germany and Italy, have ten votes each; Belgium, Greece and the Netherlands have five each; Denmark and Ireland have three each; Luxembourg has two votes. In the normal case a decision can be taken only if at least 45 votes are cast in favour of it. This means that any two of the four largest states, or a combination of the smaller ones, can block a decision.

A small number of decisions under the Treaty can be taken by a simple majority of member states, and in a few instances – e.g. for the admission of a new member state – the Treaty requires a unanimous vote.

The preference for majority voting expressed in the Treaty reflected a perception of the Council as a Community body pursuing Community goals, and not a mere inter-governmental forum for representing national interests. But the majority principle was challenged (and the Community thrown into crisis) by France in 1965 and the result was a political compromise recorded in the Luxembourg Agreement (or Accords) of 1966.

The Luxembourg Accords: Extraordinary Session of the
Council, January 1966

Statement on Majority Voting Procedure
I. Where, in the case of decisions which may be taken by majority vote on a proposal of the Commission, very important interests of one or more partners are at stake, the Members of the Council will endeavour, within a reasonable time, to reach solutions which can be adopted by all the Members of the Council while respecting their mutual interests and those of the Community, in accordance with Article 2 of the Treaty.
II. With regard to the preceding paragraph, the French delegation considers that where very important interests are at stake the discussion must be continued until unanimous agreement is reached.
III. The six delegations note that there is a divergence of views on what should be done in the event of a failure to reach complete agreement.
IV. The six delegations nevertheless consider that this divergence does not prevent the

Community's work being resumed in accordance with the normal procedure.

This declaration left the issue of persisting disagreement in the Council unresolved. However the general practice after 1966 was to continue the discussion of important matters until unanimity was reached, even where the Treaty provided for majority decision.

The convention of unanimity established by the Luxembourg Accords and subsequent practice received a check in 1982. The annual farm price review had been under discussion in the Council, and ministers representing nine member states were prepared to adopt new regulations on farm prices. The United Kingdom Minister of Agriculture withheld his agreement to the regulations, not because his Government was opposed to the regulations themselves, but as a means of putting pressure on the other member states to agree to a reduction in the United Kingdom's contribution to the Community budget. The response to this was that the Council overrode the United Kingdom veto, adopting the farm price regulations by a qualified majority as allowed by the letter of the Treaty.

> Statement in the House of Commons by the Minister of
> Agriculture, Fisheries and Food, Mr Peter Walker
> (HC Deb. vol. 24, col. 352, 19 May 1982)

Together with my right hon. Friend the Minister of State I attended a meeting of the Agriculture Council which met in Brussels on 17 and 18 May.

Since January, at eight meetings of the Council of Agriculture Ministers we have been negotiating this year's price-fixing arrangements. During these meetings member States had by negotiation obtained unanimity on many of the questions involved. Britain had retained specific reserves on a number of agricultural issues and a general reserve on the entire package. The purpose of the general reserve was to ensure that the position adopted at last November's European Council meeting in London by all member States in considering the 30 May mandate, that the budget and agricultural matters should be dealt with in parallel, should be complied with.

We therefore expected that at the meeting this week we would continue to negotiate on those remaining questions where unanimity had not been obtained. If by the time of the completion of our meeting there was no agreement upon the budget measures we would retain our general reserve.

Together with Denmark and Greece we strongly protested when the Presidency, encouraged by the Commission, announced that for the first time since 1966 the principle of obtaining unanimity where a very important national interest had been invoked was to be violated – [HON. MEMBERS: 'Shame.'] – and that a decision was to be taken in accordance with the treaty arrangements for majority voting.

I made a firm statement to the Council contesting the procedure and declaring that the Council had violated an accepted convention under which all previous price-fixings had been adopted. I stated that the Government considered that, as important national interests were involved, in accordance with the established practice of the Community, discussions should have continued in this Council until a unanimous agreement had been reached. I pointed out that the decisions that were being taken would place a further financial burden on the United Kingdom, that there was clearly a direct and organic link between the price-fixing decision and the budget negotiations and that this link had been recognised by all member States in their agreement that the three chapters of the 30 May mandate should proceed in parallel. I placed it on record that I considered that the conduct of the Presidency of the Commission and the member States which had joined in this procedure had created a very sad and damaging day in the Community's history – [HON. MEMBERS: 'Hear, hear.'] – and that the Council had quite unjustifiably chosen to depart from the established working practices based on the agreement reached in 1966.

A majority decision was, therefore, taken on all of the regulations in accordance with what had been negotiated and agreed by nine member States in the meetings prior to this week's Council. Under the treaty these regulations become Community law with effect from tomorrow. . . .

Statement in the House of Commons by the Secretary of State
for Foreign and Commonwealth Affairs, Mr Francis Pym (HC
Deb. vol. 26, col. 155, 22 June 1982)

With permission, Mr Speaker, I will make a statement on the visit which I paid to Luxembourg on 20 and 21 June, during which I attended a meeting of the Foreign Ministers of the Ten and the first part of the Foreign Affairs Council, which continues today, and on which there will be a report to the House.

At my request there was, first, a discussion of the Community's decision-making procedures. I left our partners in no doubt about the British Government's position that where a member State considers that very important interests are at stake discussions must be continued until unanimous agreement is reached, and that Community business should continue to be governed by this principle, in accordance with the Luxembourg compromise. This position was supported unreservedly by two member States and by two others with minor qualifications.

The position is, therefore, that five member States support the principle that decisions must be deferred where a member State considers that its major national interests are at stake. It was not to be expected that the five members which declined to endorse this principle in 1966 would do so now, but they made it clear that they were not seeking to reopen the Luxembourg compromise. The Community's practice since 1966 was based on an agreement to disagree, and this remains the position.

In view of what happened at the Agriculture Council on 18 May, I would obviously have preferred a clear-cut result. Although there is now a better understanding in the Community of our position and of the principles involved, we may have to return to the subject. The crucial point is what will happen in practice when our very important national interests are at stake. We shall continue to defend them on the basis we have made clear to our partners. . . .

It remains a matter of controversy whether the Luxembourg compromise was properly invoked by the United Kingdom in the particular circumstances of this case. Uncertainty persists as to the scope of the convention of unanimity and as to when an important national interest can be said to be involved. The convention has not been repudiated, but reliance upon it has become more problematic as a result of this case. (See further Evans, 'The "Veto" in EEC

Law' [1982] *PL* 366.)

The Council is assisted by a Committee of Permanent Representatives (COREPER) which consists of officials of the member states with ambassadorial rank. This Committee, which sets up its own specialized working groups of national officials, examines proposals that have been submitted to the Council and tries to reach an accommodation of national viewpoints. COREPER and its working groups take no decisions themselves but exercise an important influence in settling and defining the issues for Council decision. These official bodies operate beyond the reach of democratic control and accountability. Proposals on which COREPER has reached agreement are generally adopted without debate by the Council.

Decisions of the Council on more contentious matters are the product of inter-governmental bargaining and compromise. Ministers are often compelled to make concessions on one issue in return for support on another.

The Economic and Social Committee

This is not one of the 'institutions' of the Community but an advisory body established by the Treaty (Articles 4 and 193) to assist the Commission and the Council. It consists of representatives, appointed by the Council, of 'the various categories of economic and social activity': its members are chosen as representing employers, trade unions, and a variety of other interest groups including the professions, farmers, shopkeepers and consumers. The Council and the Commission are obliged by a number of Treaty provisions to consult the Committee on proposed action, and may do so at their discretion in other cases.

The European Council

This body, for which no provision is made in the Treaty, is to be distinguished from the Council of Ministers considered above. Informal 'summit' meetings of the heads of government of Community countries have become institutionalized as the supreme policy-making organ of the Community. The European Council of nine Prime Ministers and the President of France (accompanied by their Foreign Ministers) meets about three times a year and 'provides a forum for free and informal exchanges of view between heads of government, where they can range across the whole field of Community activity, generate the impetus for action, and resolve matters unsolved at lower levels' (Commission Background Report ISEC/B13/80: see also the *Report on European Institutions* presented by the Committee of Three to the European Council, 1979, pp. 16–17). The European Council is a hybrid body for it does not confine its deliberations to matters within the scope of the Treaty. When dealing with Community affairs it is an *alter ego* of the Council of Ministers, but as such it concerns itself mainly with matters of general policy, and its conclusions are left to be put into effect by the Commission and Council through the ordinary processes of Community action.

The European Parliament

The Treaties established an Assembly to represent the peoples of the Community; since 1962 it has been known as the European Parliament. It has 434 members, elected for a term of five years by the electorates of the member states. The number of representatives of each state is as follows:

Belgium	24
Denmark	16
France	81
Germany	81
Greece	24
Ireland	15
Italy	81
Luxembourg	6
Netherlands	25
United Kingdom	81

For an initial period the members were nominated by their national Parliaments, but Article 138(3) of the EEC Treaty provided:

The Assembly shall draw up proposals for elections by direct universal suffrage in accordance with a uniform procedure in all Member States.

The Council shall, acting unanimously, lay down the appropriate provisions which it shall recommend to Member States for adoption in accordance with their respective constitutional requirements.

Acting under this provision the Council of Ministers agreed in 1976 to institute direct elections to the European Parliament, but there was no agreement on a uniform electoral system and it was decided that the member states should be free for the time being to use the systems of their choice. For the first two elections, of 1979 and 1984, the United Kingdom adopted the plurality or 'first past the post' system for the elections in England, Scotland and Wales and proportional representation (the single transferable vote) for Northern Ireland. (See the European Assembly Elections Act 1978.) The other member states used one or other system of proportional representation. In 1982 the European Parliament proposed to the Council that it should adopt a uniform electoral procedure based on the regional list system of proportional representation, but the Council failed to reach agreement on this proposal.

Members of the European Parliament are not debarred from being members also of their national Parliaments. It is provided that they shall vote 'on an individual and personal basis' and 'shall not be bound by any instructions and shall not receive a binding mandate' (Article 4(1) of the Act annexed to the Council Decision on direct elections, OJ 1976, L278.)

The European Parliament has no legislative power. Its functions are mainly 'advisory and supervisory' (EEC Treaty Article 137). Many Treaty provisions conferring powers on the Council require it to consult the Parliament, and if it fails to do so or acts before the Parliament has given its opinion, the act of the Council is liable to be annulled: see the *Isoglucose* cases, 138/79 and 139/79, [1980] ECR 3333, 3393. In practice the Commission also frequently consults the Parliament, but neither Council nor Commission is obliged to accept the Parliament's advice. Its suggested amendments to less contentious legislative proposals are often accepted, but a proposal submitted to the Parliament for its opinion may already have been firmly settled in the process of political bargaining, so that little room is left for parliamentary influence.

In its supervisory function the Parliament receives and debates an annual General Report from the Commission, and can put written and oral questions to the Commission and the Council. It possesses a power of last resort, never yet exercised, to dismiss the Commission by a motion of censure carried by a two-thirds majority (EEC Treaty, Article 144). Against the Council of Ministers the Parliament has no coercive power.

An important role is performed by the Parliament's specialized standing committees (e.g. on agriculture, economic and monetary affairs, legal affairs) which examine and report to the Parliament on the legislative proposals submitted for its opinion. The committees maintain the parliamentary dialogues with Commission and Council when the Parliament is not sitting.

It is in relation to the Community budget that the Parliament exercises a measure of real power. It can propose modifications to budget provisions for 'compulsory expenditure' (necessarily resulting from the Treaties or from Community legislation), but here the Council has the last word and may reject the modifications. On the other hand, amendments made by the Parliament to 'non-compulsory expenditure' (e.g. on regional development), if rejected by the Council, may be reinstated in the Parliament by a three-fifths majority vote. The Parliament has also the power to reject the whole budget by a two-thirds majority vote, thereby freezing expenditure, until a new budget is adopted, at the previous year's level. (This power was used in 1979 and 1984.) Its budgetary powers, which have been gradually augmented, provide the Parliament with the means, which it has begun to exploit, of taking a weightier part in the Community's bargaining processes. (It has twice blocked the payment of agreed budgetary rebates to the United Kingdom in attempts to extend its control over Community spending.)

Any formal addition to the powers of the Parliament would require the agreement of all the member states. In the United Kingdom the Government was persuaded to introduce an amendment to the European Assembly Elections Bill which provided for an unusual restraint upon the treaty-making power of the Crown. This became section 6(1) of the European Assembly Elections Act 1978:

No treaty which provides for any increase in the powers of the Assembly shall be ratified by the United Kingdom unless it has been approved by an Act of Parliament.

The Court of Justice

The Court of Justice of the European Communities, which has its seat in Luxembourg, consists of 11 judges who are appointed by agreement of the governments of the member states. The practice is for there to be a judge from each of the ten member states, and for the eleventh judge to be chosen from the four larger countries in turn. A judge holds office for six years and may be reappointed; he can be dismissed only by the unanimous decision of the other judges and the advocates general of the court. Most cases are heard not by the full court but by a Chamber of three or five judges.

The judges are assisted by five advocates general, themselves members of the court, also appointed by agreement of the governments of the member states for renewable terms of six years and enjoying the same status and security of tenure as the judges. The office of advocate general is similar to that of the *commissaire du gouvernement* of the French *Conseil d'Etat*. His role is defined by Article 166 of the EEC Treaty:

> It shall be the duty of the Advocate-General, acting with complete impartiality and independence, to make, in open court, reasoned submissions on cases brought before the Court of Justice, in order to assist the Court in the performance of the task assigned to it. . . .

When the arguments in a case have been concluded, the advocate general gives his opinion to the court in an oral statement which reviews the facts and the law and suggests how the case should be decided. The Court is not bound to adopt the advocate general's conclusions but commonly does so, and his opinion is therefore often a valuable exposition of the reasoning on which a decision is based – more so because the judgments themselves are expressed in a formal style of particular succinctness. The opinions of advocates general, whether or not adopted in the cases for which they were given, may be cited for the reasoning they contain and have weight as authority when similar issues arise in subsequent cases.

'The Court of Justice', says Article 164 of the EEC Treaty, 'shall ensure that in the interpretation and application of this Treaty the law is observed.' Other Articles of the Treaty provide in detail for the Court's manifold jurisdiction, of which the following are the main categories.

(1) *Judicial review*: the Court's jurisdiction, in proceedings brought by a Community institution or a member state – or exceptionally by a private person – to determine the legality of an act, or failure to act, of a Community institution.

(2) *Enforcement proceedings*: the Court's jurisdiction in proceedings brought against a member state by the Commission or another member state for a

breach of Community obligations. (See, e.g., Case 61/81 *Commission* v. *United Kingdom*, p. 243 above.)

(3) *Plenary jurisdiction* of the Court in claims for damages against the Community, appeals against penalties imposed by Community institutions, and disputes between the Community and its employees. ('Plenary jurisdiction' is a category derived from continental systems of administrative law.)

(4) *Preliminary rulings*: the Court's jurisdiction to rule on questions of Community law arising in national courts and tribunals.

Proceedings in the first three jurisdictional categories are brought and concluded in the European Court of Justice itself, but preliminary rulings arise from a reference to the Court of Justice made in the course of proceedings in a national court.

A judgment or ruling of the Court of Justice is not subject to appeal. Its decisions on the interpretation of the Treaty cannot be reversed by legislation but only by the more difficult process of amendment of the Treaty.

References for a preliminary ruling, which are the largest class of cases heard by the Court, are made under Article 177 of the EEC Treaty, which provides:

> The Court of Justice shall have jurisdiction to give preliminary rulings concerning:
> (a) the interpretation of this Treaty;
> (b) the validity and interpretation of acts of the institutions of the Community;
> (c) the interpretation of the statutes of bodies established by an act of the Council, where those statutes so provide.
>
> Where such a question is raised before any court or tribunal of a Member State, that court or tribunal may, if it considers that a decision on the question is necessary to enable it to give judgment, request the Court of Justice to give a ruling thereon.
>
> Where any such question is raised in a case pending before a court or tribunal of a Member State, against whose decisions there is no judicial remedy under national law, that court or tribunal shall bring the matter before the Court of Justice.

This provision emphasizes and is designed to preserve the uniformity of Community law as an independent legal order with the same force and meaning throughout the Community. Without the discipline of Article 177 national courts might develop Community law in divergent ways and the result would be a fragmented system which failed to sustain the common objectives of the Community.

A reference under Article 177 can be made only by the national court or tribunal itself: the article does not provide an avenue of recourse to the European Court for the parties to litigation. What is referred to the Court is not the case as a whole but a specific question of Community law which is relevant to the decision of the case. When the European Court has given its ruling on the question the proceedings continue in the national court, which is bound to adopt the European Court's ruling but retains its independence of decision on all other aspects of the case.

A national court is always *entitled* to refer to the European Court a question of Community law which it considers relevant to the case before it, but a court from which there is no appeal is *bound* to refer such a question. A final court of appeal like the House of Lords is therefore obliged by Article 177 to refer to the European Court, and the better view is that any other court or tribunal is also bound to refer if there can be no appeal from its decision in the particular case. (On this view the Court of Appeal in England is a final court of appeal when leave for a further appeal to the House of Lords is not given. Against this is a dictum of Lord Denning in *Bulmer Ltd* v. *Bollinger SA* [1974] Ch. 401 at 420.) A court of final appeal is only bound to refer, however, if it considers that a decision on the question is necessary to enable it to give judgment. (See Article 177 above, the discussion by T. C. Hartley, *The Foundations of European Community Law*, 1981, pp. 266–7, and the *Srl CILFIT* case below.) Moreover no reference need be made if the question has already been resolved by the European Court, or if the national court is convinced that the Community law on the question is clear beyond reasonable doubt. The latter qualification, known as the doctrine of *acte clair*, was accepted by the European Court in Case 283/81 *Srl CILFIT* v. *Ministry of Health* [1982] ECR 3415. The doctrine has to be applied with caution, however, for it depends upon a degree of clarity in the relevant legal provisions which is not often present. In *R.* v. *Henn* [1978] 1 WLR 1031 (CA), [1981] AC 850 (ECJ and HL), while the Court of Appeal had no doubt at all about the right solutions to the questions of Community law that arose before it, the House of Lords, having given leave to appeal, decided that there was sufficient doubt to require a reference to be made to the European Court. The judgment of that court showed that the Court of Appeal had indeed misconstrued the relevant provisions of the EEC Treaty.

A court which is not sitting as a final court of appeal has a discretion whether or not to refer a relevant question of Community law for decision by the European Court. In regard to the exercise of this discretion an English judge, Bingham J, said in *Customs and Excise Commissioners* v. *ApS Samex* [1983] 1 All ER 1042, 1055–6:

Sitting as a judge in a national court, asked to decide questions of Community law, I am very conscious of the advantages enjoyed by the Court of Justice. It has a panoramic view of the Community and its institutions, a detailed knowledge of the treaties and of much subordinate legislation made under them, and an intimate familiarity with the functioning of the Community market which no national judge denied the collective experience of the Court of Justice could hope to achieve. Where questions of administrative intention and practice arise the Court of Justice can receive submissions from the Community institutions, as also where relations between the Community and non-member states are in issue. Where the interests of member states are affected they can intervene to make their views known. . . . Where comparison falls to be made between Community texts in different languages, all texts being equally authentic, the multinational Court of Justice is equipped to carry out the task in a way which no national judge, whatever his linguistic skills, could rival. The interpretation of Community instruments involves very often not the process familiar to common lawyers of laboriously extracting the meaning from words used but the more creative process of supplying flesh to a spare and loosely constructed skeleton. The choice between alternative submissions may turn not on purely legal considerations, but on a broader view of what the orderly development of the Community requires. These are matters which the Court of Justice is very much better placed to assess and determine than a national court.

More specific guidelines for the exercise of the discretion to refer were given by Lord Denning in *Bulmer Ltd* v. *Bollinger SA* [1974] Ch. 401, and by Neill J in *An Bord Bainne* v. *Milk Marketing Board* [1985] 1 CMLR 6.

A judgment of the European Court, whether as a preliminary ruling or in enforcement proceedings against a member state, is of course binding, but it is for the agencies of the member state to give effect to it. A preliminary ruling has to be adopted and applied by the national court; an adverse judgment in enforcement proceedings requires corrective action by the executive or legislative authorities of the member state. Compliance with the judgments of the European Court is normal, but some judgments in enforcement proceedings have met with delay or defiance. For this a remedy has to be sought in a political accommodation rather than in legal sanctions.

(b) Community law

In Case 6/64 *Costa* v. *ENEL* [1964] ECR 585, 593, the European Court of Justice declared:

> By contrast with ordinary international treaties, the EEC Treaty has created its own legal system which, on the entry into force of the Treaty, became an integral part of the legal systems of the Member States and which their courts are bound to apply.
>
> By creating a Community of unlimited duration, having its own institutions, its own personality, its own legal capacity and capacity of representation on the international plane and, more particularly, real powers stemming from a limitation of sovereignty or a transfer of powers from the States to the Community, the Member States have limited their sovereign rights, albeit within limited fields, and have thus created a body of law which binds both their nationals and themselves.

In becoming parties to the Treaty of Rome the member states not only undertook mutual obligations which would be binding in international law, but laid the foundations of a system of Community law which would create rights and duties between the Community and its 'subjects', both member states and their nationals, while also regulating relationships between those subjects themselves. Community law was not conceived simply as a supranational body of law but was to enter the legal orders of the member states and be enforced by the national courts as well as by the European Court of Justice. Lord Denning gave vivid expression to some of these features of Community law in *Bulmer Ltd* v. *Bollinger SA* [1974] Ch. 401, 418–9, a case decided soon after the United Kingdom's accession to the Communities:

[W]hen we come to matters with a European element, the Treaty is like an incoming tide. It flows into the estuaries and up the rivers. It cannot be held back. Parliament has decreed that the Treaty is henceforward to be part of our law. It is equal in force to any statute. . . . Any rights or obligations created by the Treaty are to be given legal effect in England without more ado. Any remedies or procedures provided by the Treaty are to be made available here without being open to question. In future, in transactions which cross the frontiers, we must no longer speak or think of English law as something on its own. We must speak and think of community law, of community rights and obligations, and we must give effect to them.

While Community law has its main application in the economic sphere, its rules also extend to many branches of social and environmental affairs, such as consumer protection, social security, working conditions, sex discrimination, pollution, and wildlife conservation.

The law embodied in the Treaties (in particular the EEC Treaty) is described as *primary* Community law, while the legislative acts of Community institutions – the Council and the Commission – constitute the *secondary legislation* of the Community. Community law can be amended and added to by subsequent treaties between the member states, but is mainly developed by secondary legislation and the decisions of the European Court of Justice.

Secondary legislation

Both the Council of Ministers and the Commission have a role in Community legislation. The Commission acts as an independent legislative body under certain Treaty provisions and in exercising powers conferred upon it by the Council, but it is the Council that has the principal task of legislating to achieve the broader objectives of the Treaty. As we have seen, the Commission participates in Council legislation through its power of initiative: generally speaking the Council can legislate only on a proposal from the Commission.

The process of law-making has already been indicated in the account of the Community institutions. The figure on page 258 gives a simplified representation of legislation by the Council.

The legislative acts of the Council and the Commission are *regulations* and *directives*. Both bodies also take 'decisions' which have rather the character of administrative action than of general legislation, although decisions give rise to legal obligations and are sometimes quasi-legislative in effect. Article 189 of the EEC Treaty provides:

In order to carry out their task the Council and the Commission shall, in accordance with the provisions of this Treaty, make regulations, issue directives, take decisions, make recommendations or deliver opinions.

A regulation shall have general application. It shall be binding in its entirety and directly applicable in all Member States.

A directive shall be binding, as to the result to be achieved, upon each Member State to which it is addressed, but shall leave to the national authorities the choice of form and methods.

A decision shall be binding in its entirety upon those to whom it is addressed. Recommendations and opinions shall have no binding force.

In 1983 the Council of Ministers adopted 41 directives, 395 regulations, and 108 decisions.

LEGISLATION BY THE COUNCIL OF MINISTERS

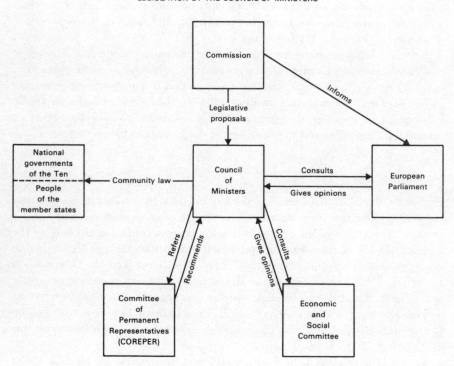

Regulations

A regulation, being 'directly applicable', has automatic effect as law in all the member states without any intervention by the national authorities. This form of legislation avoids the possibility that the law might be distorted or delayed in being re-enacted by agencies of the member states, and is especially apt when what is wanted is a prompt, precise and uniform application of rules throughout the Community. Any necessary implementing action by a member state must not qualify the scope or effectiveness of the regulation.

Case 128/78 *Commission of the European Communities* v. *United Kingdom of Great Britain and Northern Ireland* [1979] ECR 419
(Court of Justice of the European Communities)

A Council Regulation, no. 1463/70, provided that tachographs, for recording driving periods and speeds, should be installed and used in road transport vehicles registered in member states, with effect from 1 January 1975 (extended to 1 January 1976 for the United Kingdom). The Regulation said:

Member States shall . . . adopt such laws, regulations or administrative provisions as may be necessary for the implementation of this regulation.
Such measures shall cover, *inter alia* . . . checks on compliance and the penalties to be imposed in case of breach.

The United Kingdom Government objected to carrying out the Regulation fully for reasons based on economic, industrial and practical considerations, and proposed to introduce a voluntary instead of a compulsory scheme for the use of tachographs. The United Kingdom having failed to act upon the Commission's reasoned opinon inviting it to comply fully with the Regulation, the Commission brought this action for enforcement. The following is part of the Court's judgment.

It is not denied that provision for the installation and use of the recording equipment has been made by the British legislation only on an optional and voluntary basis as regards both vehicles engaged in intra-Community transport and those engaged in national transport. On the other hand, the British legislation has maintained in force the obligations relating to the keeping of an individual control book which were abolished by the . . . regulation.

The defendant claims that this arrangement is sufficient to meet the objectives of promoting road safety, of social progress for workers and of the harmonization of conditions of competition. It maintains that the implementation of Regulation No 1463/70 on its territory is best achieved by the installation and use of the recording equipment on a voluntary basis, though this may be made compulsory at an appropriate time. It adds that implementation of the regulation involving compulsory measures would meet with active resistance from the sectors concerned, in particular the trade unions, which would result in strikes in the transport sector and would therefore seriously damage the whole economy of the country.

It contends that since, in the case of the United Kingdom, the objectives of the Community policy in this field can be achieved just as satisfactorily by the maintenance of the system of the individual control book as by the compulsory introduction of recording equipment, the alleged failure to fulfil an obligation is of a purely technical nature and, in view of the difficulties referred to, should not be taken into account. Moreover the installation and use of recording equipment is in practice already guaranteed in respect of intra-Community transport by the fact that the other Member States have made it compulsory.

Article 189 of the Treaty provides that a regulation shall be binding 'in its entirety' in the Member States. As the Court has already stated in its judgment of 7 February 1973 (Case 39/72 *Commission* v. *Italian Republic* [1973] ECR 101) it cannot therefore be accepted that a Member State should apply in an incomplete or selective manner provisions of a Community regulation so as to render abortive certain aspects of Community legislation which it has opposed or which it considers contrary to its national interests. In particular, as regards the putting into effect of a general rule intended to eliminate certain abuses to which workers are subject and which in addition involve a threat to road safety, a Member State which omits to take, within the requisite period and simultaneously with the other Member States, the measures which it ought to take, undermines Community solidarity by imposing, in particular as regards intra-Community transport, on the other Member States the necessity of remedying the effects of its own omissions, while at the same time taking an undue advantage to the detriment of its partners.

As the Court said in the same judgment, practical difficulties which appear at the stage when a Community measure is put into effect cannot permit a Member State unilaterally to opt out of fulfilling its obligations. . . .

In these circumstances, the possible difficulties of implementation alleged by the defendant cannot be accepted as a justification.

Further, as the Court said in the case mentioned above, in permitting Member States to profit from the advantages of the Community, the Treaty imposes on them also the obligation to respect its rules. For a State unilaterally to break, according to its own conception of national interest, the equilibrium between the advantages and obligations flowing from its adherence to the Community brings into question the equality of Member States before Community law and creates discrimination at the expense of their nationals. This failure in the duty of solidarity accepted by Member States by the fact of their adherence to the Community strikes at the very root of the Community legal order. . . .

The court ruled accordingly that in refusing to implement Regulation No. 1463/70 the United Kingdom was in breach of its obligations under the Treaty.

Regulations are much more numerous than directives. The great majority are made by the Commission and most have to do with the detailed operation of the common agricultural policy: as such they are often of narrow compass and short duration. But some regulations (especially of the Council) are of much wider importance. The following Council Regulation was unusual in being a response to military conflict between a member state and another country.

Council Regulation (EEC) No. 877/82 of 16 April 1982

THE COUNCIL OF THE EUROPEAN COMMUNITIES

Whereas the serious situation resulting from the invasion of the Falkland Islands by Argentina, which was the subject of Resolution 502 of the Security Council at the United Nations has given rise to discussions in the context of European political cooperation which have led in particular to the decision that economic measures will be taken with regard to Argentina in accordance with the relevant provisions of the Community Treaties;

Whereas, following the measures already taken by the United Kingdom, the Member States have consulted one another pursuant to Article 224 of the Treaty establishing the European Economic Community;

Whereas in the context of these consultations it has proved important to take urgent and uniform measures; whereas the Member States have therefore decided to adopt a Council Regulation pursuant to the Treaty;

Whereas, in these circumstances, the interests of the Community and the Member States demand the temporary suspension of imports of all products originating in Argentina;

Whereas import documents issued and contracts concluded before the entry into force of this Regulation should not be affected by it; whereas, however, transitional provisions should not be applied to imports into the United Kingdom which were the subject of United Kingdom measures with effect from 7 April;

Having regard to the Treaty establishing the European Economic Community, and in particular Article 113 thereof,

Having regard to the proposal from the Commission,

HAS ADOPTED THIS REGULATION:

Article 1

Imports of all products originating in Argentina for the purpose of putting them into free circulation in the Community are hereby suspended.

Article 2

1. This Regulation shall not preclude the putting into free circulation of products originating in Argentina:
   - accompanied by import documents issued before the date of its entry into force which mention Argentina as the country of origin, or
   - to be imported in execution of contracts concluded before that date, or
   - in course of shipment to the Community at that date. . . .

Article 3

This regulation shall enter into force on the day of its publication in the *Official Journal of the European Communities*.

It shall apply until 17 May 1982.

Before that date, the Council, acting on a proposal from the Commission, shall examine whether it is appropriate to extend, amend, or, if necessary, repeal this Regulation.

This Regulation shall be binding in its entirety and directly applicable in all Member States.

Done at Brussels, 16 April 1982.

For the Council

The President
L. TINDEMANS

Much more typical of everyday Community legislation is Commission Regulation (EEC) No. 2124/83 of 26 July 1983 on crop and stock declarations for rice, which requires agricultural producers and rice mills in the member states to provide annual statements giving specified information about rice crops and holdings of rice stocks, for the assistance of the Commission in managing the market in rice.

Directives

Directives are binding 'as to the result to be achieved': the member states are obliged to implement them but use their own legislative or administrative techniques in doing so. Directives, as instruments of *Community* law, accordingly produce effects in the *national* laws of the member states. The directive is an appropriate legislative instrument when a precisely uniform implementation is not necessary or would be difficult to realize because of differing legal, administrative or economic structures in the member states. It is particularly suitable for achieving a harmonization of national laws, when that is required for the operation of the common market, and its use for this purpose is expressly indicated by Article 100 of the EEC Treaty:

The Council shall, acting unanimously on a proposal from the Commission, issue directives for the approximation of such provisions laid down by law, regulation or administrative action in Member States as directly affect the establishment or functioning of the common market. . . .

Here follows an example of a Council directive made under Article 100.

Second Council Directive of 10 June 1982 on summertime
arrangements 82/399/EEC

THE COUNCIL OF THE EUROPEAN COMMUNITIES,
Having regard to the Treaty establishing the European Economic Community, and in particular Article 100 thereof,
Having regard to the proposal from the Commission,
Having regard to the opinion of the European Parliament,
Having regard to the opinion of the Economic and Social Committee,
Whereas Council Directive 80/737/EEC of 22 July 1980 on summertime arrangements introduced a common date and time for the beginning of the summertime period in the Community for the years 1981 and 1982;
Whereas Article 4 of that Directive states that the Council, acting on a proposal from the Commission and as soon as possible, will adopt more comprehensive measures for the harmonization of summertime;
Whereas such measures are highly desirable, in particular in the interests of facilitating and reducing the costs of transport and telecommunications between Member States;
Whereas a common date and time for the beginning of the summertime period in the Community should now be fixed for the years 1983, 1984 and 1985;
Whereas, as an experiment during those three years, two different dates for the end of the summertime period should be fixed for the Member States belonging to the zero time zone and the other Member States. . . .
HAS ADOPTED THIS DIRECTIVE:

Article 1

For the purposes of this Directive the expression 'summertime period' means the period of the year during which the time is advanced by 60 minutes in relation to the time for the rest of the year.

Article 2

Member States shall take the measures necessary to ensure that in each Member State the summertime period for 1983, 1984 and 1985 begins at 1 a.m. Greenwich Mean Time on the last Sunday in March.

Article 3

Member States other than those in the zero (Greenwich) time zone shall take the measures necessary to ensure that the summertime period ends at 1 a.m. Greenwich Mean Time:
- in 1983: on 25 September,
- in 1984: on 30 September,
- in 1985: on 29 September.

Article 4

Member States belonging to the zero (Greenwich) time zone, namely Ireland and the United Kingdom, shall take the measures necessary to ensure that the summertime period ends at 1 a.m. Greenwich Mean Time:
- in 1983: on 23 October,
- in 1984: on 28 October,
- in 1985: on 27 October.

Article 5

The Council, acting on a proposal from the Commission, shall adopt by 1 January 1985 the arrangements to apply from 1986 onwards. . . .

Article 7

This Directive is addressed to the Member States.
  Done at Luxembourg, 10 June 1982.

For the Council

The President
H. DE CROO

A directive usually leaves to the member states a margin of discretion in carrying out its objectives. Discretion in implementation means a less consistent application of Community policies, and Community institutions show a preference for regulations (when free to choose between these and directives) or may formulate directives in precise terms which leave little freedom of action to the member states. Such a directive may not differ much in effect from a regulation, even though national measures of implementation are called for.

Directives usually set time-limits for their implementation. Often these are not observed by the member states. The European Court of Justice is frequently seized of actions brought against member states for failing to implement directives or for implementing them incorrectly.

Direct effect

A Community regulation, since it automatically acquires the force of law in the member states, may at once give rise to rights and obligations that can be enforced by individuals or firms in the national courts. This 'direct effect' is not an exclusive characteristic of regulations: the European Court, in developing the doctrine of direct effect, has attributed it to other kinds of Community law. In Case 26/62 *Van Gend en Loos* v. *Nederlandse Administratie der Belastingen* [1963] ECR 1, it was decided that a provision of the EEC Treaty could have direct effect. A more recent example is Case 43/75 *Defrenne* v. *SABENA* [1976] ECR 455, in which the European Court held that Article 119 of the Treaty, in laying down the principle that men and women should receive equal pay for equal work, had direct effect so that individuals could rely upon it in the national courts, irrespective of any measures taken by Community institutions or member states to implement the Article. It is now also established that a *directive* may have direct effect if certain conditions are present. This is shown by the following case.

Case 41/74 *Van Duyn* v. *The Home Office* [1974] ECR 1337 (Court of Justice of the European Communities)

Yvonne Van Duyn, a Dutch national and a Scientologist, came to the United Kingdom to take up employment with the Church of Scientology. She was refused entry by the immigration authorities in accordance with the government's policy of not admitting foreign nationals coming to work for the Church of Scientology, which was believed to be a socially harmful organization. Miss Van Duyn brought proceedings in the High Court in England for a declaration that she was entitled to enter the country. She relied on Article 48 of the EEC Treaty, which assures freedom of movement for workers within the Community. The Article allows restrictions to be imposed on grounds of 'public policy, public security or public health', but Council Directive 64/221, Article 3(1), provides that 'measures taken on grounds of public policy or of public security shall be based exclusively on the personal conduct of the individual concerned'. Miss Van Duyn argued that her membership of the Church of Scientology could not amount to 'personal conduct'.

The judge referred a number of questions to the European Court of Justice under Article 177 of the EEC Treaty. (See p. 254 above.) One of these was whether Directive 64/221 was 'directly applicable so as to confer on individuals rights enforceable by them in the courts of the United Kingdom'. Only if the Directive had this kind of direct effect could Miss Van Duyn rely on it in the English court as limiting the 'public policy' grounds upon which she could properly be excluded from the United Kingdom.

The advocate general, in his opinion, drew the attention of the European Court to previous cases in which directives had been found to have direct effect. In each case the directive must be examined to see if its provisions were capable of producing direct effects between member states and their subjects: this would be so only if the obligations imposed were precise and unconditional. He concluded:

What other aim could the Council have had in enacting this provision than to limit discretionary power of Member States and subject restrictions on freedom of movement, such as refusal of leave to enter, exclusion or expulsion, to the condition that these measures should be based *exclusively* on the personal conduct of the persons concerned?

It seems that the Council thereby wished to prevent Member States from taking general measures relating to whole categories of persons and were seeking, in particular, to prohibit collective exclusions and expulsions.

The Council has, in any case, imposed on Member States a clear and precise obligation. The first condition for direct effect is satisfied.

The second is also. The rule is sufficient in itself. It is not subject either to the adoption of subsequent acts on the part either of the Community authorities or of Member States. The fact that the latter have, in accordance with the principle relating to directives, the choice of form and methods which accord with their national law does not imply that the Community rule is not directly applicable. On the contrary, it is so closely linked to the implementation of Article 48, as regards employed persons, that it seems to me to be inseparable from and is of the same nature as that provision of the Treaty. [The advocate general had argued that it was not open to doubt that Article 48 had direct effect.]

Finally, it is clear that even though the States have retained their competence in the field of public security, Article 3(1) of the Directive imposes a specific limitation on that competence, in the exercise of which they cannot act in a discretionary manner towards Community nationals.

These considerations lead me to conclude that the provision in question confers on Community nationals rights which are enforceable by them in the national courts and which the latter must protect.

In giving judgment on the question of the direct effect of Article 3(1) of the Directive, the Court said:

The United Kingdom observes that, since Article 189 of the Treaty distinguishes between the effects ascribed to regulations, directives and decisions, it must therefore be presumed that the Council, in issuing a directive rather than making a regulation, must have intended that the directive should have an effect other than that of a regulation and accordingly that the former should not be directly applicable.

If, however, by virtue of the provisions of Article 189 regulations are directly applicable and, consequently, may by their very nature have direct effects, it does not follow from this that other categories of acts mentioned in that Article can never have similar effects. It would be incompatible with the binding effect attributed to a directive by Article 189 to exclude, in principle, the possibility that the obligation which it imposes may be invoked by those concerned. In particular, where the Community authorities have, by directive, imposed on Member States the obligation to pursue a particular course of conduct, the useful effect of such an act would be weakened if individuals were prevented from relying on it before their national courts and if the latter were prevented from taking it into consideration as an element of Community law. Article 177, which empowers national courts to refer to the Court questions concerning the validity and interpretation of all acts of the Community institutions, without distinction, implies furthermore that these acts may be invoked by individuals in the national courts. It is necessary to examine, in every case, whether the nature, general scheme and wording of the provision in question are capable of having direct effects on the relations between Member States and individuals.

By providing that measures taken on grounds of public policy shall be based exclusively on the personal conduct of the individual concerned, Article 3(1) of Directive No 64/221 is intended to limit the discretionary power which national laws generally confer on the authorities responsible for the entry and expulsion of foreign nationals. First, the provision lays down an obligation which is not subject to any exception or condition and which, by its very nature, does not require the intervention of any act on the part either of the institutions of the Community or of Member States. Secondly, because Member States are thereby obliged, in implementing a clause which derogates from one of the fundamental principles of the Treaty in favour of individuals, not to take account of factors extraneous to personal conduct, legal certainty for the persons concerned requires that they should be able to rely on this obligation even though it has been laid down in a legislative act which has no automatic direct effect in its entirety. . . .

Accordingly the Court of Justice ruled that Article 3(1) of Directive No. 64/221 conferred on individuals rights which were enforceable by them in the courts of a member state and which the national courts must protect. (The Court ruled further, however, that a person's voluntary association with a particular organization *could* be considered as 'personal conduct': it followed that the United Kingdom had not acted in breach of the directive.)

On this case see Simmonds (1975) 24 *ICLQ* 419, and see further the opinion of the advocate general in Case 131/79 *R.* v. *Secretary of State for Home Affairs, ex p. Santillo* [1980] ECR 1585.

Is there a difference between 'direct applicability' and 'direct effect'? See Steiner, 'Direct Applicability in EEC Law – A Chameleon Concept' (1982) 98 *LQR* 229. See also Case 8/81 *Becker* v. *Finanzamt Münster-Innenstadt* [1982] ECR 53. It is not yet certain whether a directive may be directly enforceable against individuals as well as against member states (the so-called 'horizontal' direct effect): see Steiner, op. cit., at 244–6.

May we see in the doctrine of direct effect, in conjunction with a more precise formulation of directives, an appropriation of power by the Community institutions from the member states?

Case law

Community law is also developed in the judgments of the European Court of Justice. This court is not bound by a doctrine of precedent and is free to depart from its own previous decisions. In practice, however, it attempts to decide cases consistently and generally follows its previous decisions unless there are compelling reasons for a change of course. In the result its decisions constitute a body of case law which interprets and supplements the primary law of the Treaties and the secondary legislation of Community institutions.

The Court of Justice is a strong and innovative court which has formulated original doctrines of great importance in the evolution of Community law – for example that of 'direct effect' already considered, and the doctrine of primacy (below). Without express justification in the Treaties (but cf. Article 215(2) of the EEC Treaty) the court has developed certain general principles by derivation from Treaty provisions or from elements common to the legal systems of a number of member states. For example the court has declared it to be a principle of Community law that a public authority (such as the Commission of the Communities) should not take action which is detrimental to the interests of an individual without first giving him a hearing (*audi alteram partem*): see Case 17/74 *Transocean Marine Paint Association* v. *Commission* [1974] ECR 1063. The Court has gone further in affirming in a number of cases that the general principles of Community law include protection for those fundamental human rights that are part of a common legal tradition of the member states and are enshrined in the European Convention on Human Rights to which all member states of the Community are parties. (See M. H. Mendelson, 'The European Court of Justice and Human Rights' (1981) 1 *Yearbook of European Law* 125.)

Community law and national law

Community law is transformed into national law when (as in the case of directives) it is implemented by national legislation. But Community law has an autonomous legal force in the member states when it is made directly applicable to them by the Treaty (as regulations are made directly applicable by Article 189) or when, in accordance with the jurisprudence of the European Court, it has direct effect in the member states. Even when Community law is applied by the courts of the member states it retains its independent character and does not simply merge with the national law.

Moreover the European Court has consistently held that Community law takes precedence over the laws of the member states. This doctrine of the 'primacy' or supremacy of Community law was first clearly formulated in Case 6/64 *Costa* v. *ENEL* [1964] ECR 585 as a necessary condition of the uniformity and effectiveness of the Community legal order. The court said (pp. 593-4):

The integration into the laws of each member State of provisions which derive from the Community, and more generally the terms and the spirit of the Treaty, make it impossible for the States, as a corollary, to accord precedence to a unilateral and subsequent measure over a legal system accepted by them on a basis of reciprocity. Such a measure cannot therefore be inconsistent with that legal system. The executive force of community law cannot vary from one State to another in deference to subsequent domestic laws, without jeopardizing the attainment of the objectives of the Treaty. . . . [T]he law stemming from the Treaty, an independent source of law, could not, because of its special and original nature, be overriden by domestic legal provisions, however framed, without being deprived of its character as Community law and without the legal basis of the Community itself being called into question. The transfer by the States from their domestic legal system to the Community legal system of the rights and obligations arising under the Treaty carries with it a permanent limitation of their sovereign rights, against which a subsequent unilateral act incompatible with the concept of the Community cannot prevail.

The doctrine of primacy has been many times reaffirmed by the European Court and with no mitigation of its rigour. National legal provisions of whatever order (even if part of the constitution of a member state) must yield precedence to Community law and, to the extent of any conflict with it, must be treated as inapplicable. This is so even if the national law is of more recent date than the Community rule with which if conflicts. The *Simmenthal* case was another landmark in the evolution of this doctrine.

Case 106/77 *Amministrazione delle Finanze dello Stato* v. *Simmenthal SpA* [1978] ECR 629 (Court of Justice of the European Communities)

The Simmenthal Company had been charged a fee for a public health inspection of beef which it had imported into Italy from France. The company reclaimed the fee in an Italian magistrate's court on the ground that its imposition was contrary to provisions of Community law on the free movement of goods. This contention was upheld by the European Court of Justice on a reference made to it by the Italian court. The Italian authorities then raised a new argument: the Italian law providing for the fee had been enacted *after* the relevant Community provisions, and although under Italian law an enactment could be held invalid if it conflicted with prior Treaty obligations, only the Italian Constitutional Court had jurisdiction to give such a ruling; in the meantime other courts must give effect to the enactment. The Italian magistrate then made a second reference to the European Court, for a ruling on this question. In the course of its judgment the Court of Justice restated the principle of the primacy of Community law as follows (italics added):

The main purpose of the first question is to ascertain what consequences flow from the direct applicability of a provision of Community law in the event of incompatibility with a subsequent legislative provision of a Member State.

Direct applicability in such circumstances means that rules of Community law must be fully and uniformly applied in all the Member States from the date of their entry into force and for so long as they continue in force.

These provisions are therefore a direct source of rights and duties for all those affected thereby, whether Member States or individuals, who are parties to legal relationships under Community law.

This consequence also concerns any national court whose task it is as an organ of a Member State to protect, in a case within its jurisdiction, the rights conferred upon individuals by Community law.

Furthermore, in accordance with the principle of the precedence of Community law, the relationship between provisions of the Treaty and directly applicable measures of the institutions on the one hand and the national law of the Member States on the other is such that those provisions and measures *not only by their entry into force render automatically inapplicable any conflicting provision of current national law but* – in so far as they are an integral part of, and take precedence in, the legal order applicable in the territory of each of the Member States – *also preclude the valid adoption of new national legislative measures to the extent to which they would be incompatible with Community provisions.*

Indeed any recognition that national legislative measures which encroach upon the field within which the Community exercises its legislative power or which are otherwise incompatible with the provisions of Community law had any legal effect would amount to a corresponding denial of the effectiveness of obligations undertaken unconditionally and irrevocably by Member States pursuant to the Treaty and would thus imperil the very foundations of the Community.

The same conclusion emerges from the structure of Article 177 of the Treaty which provides that any court or tribunal of a Member State is entitled to make a reference to the Court whenever it considers that a preliminary ruling on a question of interpretation or validity relating to Community law is necessary to enable it to give judgment.

The effectiveness of that provision would be impaired if the national court were prevented from forthwith applying Community law in accordance with the decision or the case-law of the Court.

It follows from the foregoing that every national court must, in a case within its jurisdiction, apply Community law in its entirety and protect rights which the latter confers on individuals and must accordingly set aside any provision of national law which may conflict with it, *whether prior or subsequent to the Community rule.*

Accordingly any provision of a national legal system and any legislative, administrative or judicial practice which might impair the effectiveness of Community law by withholding from the national court having jurisdiction to apply such law the power to do everything necessary at the moment of its application to set aside national legislative provisions which might prevent Community rules from having full force and effect are incompatible with those requirements which are the very essence of Community law.

This would be the case in the event of a conflict between a provision of Community law and a subsequent national law if the solution of the conflict were to be reserved for an authority with a discretion of its own, other than the court called upon to apply Community law, even if such an impediment to the full effectiveness of Community law were only temporary.

The first question should therefore be answered to the effect that a national court which is called upon, within the limits of its jurisdiction, to apply provisions of Community law is under a duty to give full effect to those provisions, if necessary refusing of its own motion to apply any conflicting provision of national legislation, even if adopted subsequently, and it is not necessary for the court to request or await the prior setting aside of such provision by legislative or other constitutional means. . . .

See the note on this case by Freestone, (1979) 42 *MLR* 220.

It is evident that the doctrine of primacy puts in question the authority of the national law of a member state and the sovereignty of its lawgiver. Nevertheless the courts of the member states have in general, if with occasional deviation, acknowledged the supremacy of Community law. (See, e.g.,

Warner, 'The Relationship between European Community Law and the National Laws of Member States' (1977) 93 *LQR* 349; Simon and Dowrick, 'Effect of EEC Directives in France' (1979) 95 *LQR* 376.)

4 The United Kingdom in the Community

(a) Accession and integration

While negotiations were taking place for British accession to the European Communities an unsuccessful attempt was made in the courts to prevent the Government from acceding to the Treaty of Rome.

Blackburn v. *Attorney-General* [1971] 1 WLR 1037 (CA)

Mr Raymond Blackburn brought proceedings against the Attorney-General for declarations that it would be unlawful for her Majesty's Government to sign the Treaty of Rome because by so doing they would irreversibly surrender part of the sovereignty of the Crown in Parliament. Eveleigh J dismissed the action on the ground that the statement of claim disclosed no reasonable cause of action. Mr Blackburn appealed.

LORD DENNING MR: . . . Much of what Mr Blackburn says is quite correct. It does appear that if this country should go into the Common Market and sign the Treaty of Rome, it means that we will have taken a step which is irreversible. The sovereignty of these islands will thenceforward be limited. It will not be ours alone but will be shared with others. Mr Blackburn referred us to a decision by the Court of Justice of the European Communities, *Costa* v. *Ente Nazionale Per L'Energia Elettrica* (ENEL) [see p. 256 above] in which the European court in its judgment said:

'. . . the member-states, albeit within limited spheres, have restricted their sovereign rights and created a body of law applicable both to their nationals and to themselves.'

Mr Blackburn points out that many regulations made by the European Economic Community will become automatically binding on the people of this country: and that all the courts of this country, including the House of Lords, will have to follow the decisions of the European court in certain defined respects, such as the construction of the treaty.

I will assume that Mr Blackburn is right in what he says on those matters. Nevertheless, I do not think these courts can entertain these actions. Negotiations are still in progress for us to join the Common Market. No agreement has been reached. No treaty has been signed. Even if a treaty is signed, it is elementary that these courts take no notice of treaties as such. We take no notice of treaties until they are embodied in laws enacted by Parliament, and then only to the extent that Parliament tells us. That was settled in a case about a treaty between the Queen of England and the Emperor of China. It is *Rustomjee* v. *The Queen* (1876) 2 QBD 69. Lord Coleridge CJ said, at p. 74:

'She' – that is the Queen – 'acted throughout the making of the treaty and in relation to each and every of its stipulations in her sovereign character, and by her own inherent authority; and, as in making the treaty, so in performing the treaty, she is beyond the control of municipal law, and her acts are not to be examined in her own courts.'

Mr Blackburn acknowledged the general principle, but he urged that this proposed treaty is in a category by itself, in that it diminishes the sovereignty of Parliament over the people of this country. I cannot accept the distinction. The general principle applies to this treaty as to any other. The treaty-making power of this country rests not in the courts, but in the Crown; that is, Her Majesty acting upon the advice of her Ministers. When her Ministers negotiate and sign a treaty, even a treaty of such paramount importance as this proposed one, they act on behalf of the country as a whole. They exercise the prerogative of the Crown. Their action in so doing cannot be challenged or questioned in these courts.

Mr Blackburn had also argued that if Parliament should pass an Act to give effect to the United Kingdom's accession to the Community it would be seeking to bind its successors, which no Parliament was capable of doing. Lord Denning declined to decide this hypothetical point: 'if Parliament should do so, then I say we will consider that event when it happens. We will then say whether Parliament can lawfully do it or not.'

Salmon and Stamp LJJ agreed with Lord Denning that the appeal should be dismissed.

When Ministers of the Crown exercised the royal prerogative in concluding the Treaty of Accession of the United Kingdom to the European Communities in 1972, this act produced no effects in the law of the United Kingdom. Our courts act upon a dualist theory of the relation between international law and municipal (national) law, in holding that treaties can bring about changes in the law of the United Kingdom only through the intervention of Parliament. (See *Blackburn* v. *Attorney-General*, above, and *Attorney-General for Canada* v. *Attorney-General for Ontario* [1937] AC 326, 347.) It was therefore necessary for Parliament to enact a statute which would make the changes in the law required by United Kingdom membership of the European Communities. Not only would existing Community law have to be incorporated as a whole but provision would have to be made for future Community legislation to take effect in the United Kingdom in accordance with the Treaties.

Both these commitments were implemented by a single enactment effecting a radical transformation of the legal system of the United Kingdom. The European Communities Bill introduced in Parliament in 1972 was given a second reading in the House of Commons by a majority of eight votes after the Prime Minister had announced that the vote would be regarded as one of confidence in the Government. Although strongly contested, the bill was passed by both Houses with a single amendment. So Parliament exercised its sovereignty, and the European Communities Act 1972 came into force on 1 January 1973.

A few institutional changes have been made in the United Kingdom in consequence of accession to the Communities. No new government department was created to handle Community affairs, for these affect the work of most departments – principally the Foreign and Commonwealth Office, the Treasury, and the departments concerned with agriculture, industry and trade. The Foreign and Commonwealth Secretary has the main responsibility for Community policy, assisted in this by a minister of state. The Cabinet has a standing committee on the European Communities and there is a parallel inter-departmental committee of officials. A small European Secretariat in the Cabinet Office provides the machinery for coordinating departmental policies on community matters. A senior Foreign Office official acts as the United Kingdom's Permanent Representative to the European Communities and as such takes part in the work of the Committee of Permanent Representatives (see p. 250 above). He has his staff of British civil servants in Brussels.

Parliament has undertaken a scrutinizing role in respect of Community legislation, setting up for this purpose a new committee of each House. (See chapter 7 below.)

After a renegotiation by a Labour Government of some of the terms of British membership of the Communities in 1974–5, a referendum was held in the United Kingdom in 1975 in which the electorate voted in favour of continued membership. (On the referendum see further pp. 449–50 below.)

Since 1972 the process of integration of the United Kingdom into the Communities has continued, the 'incoming tide' of Community law flowing strongly up our rivers.

(b) **The European Communities Act 1972**

The provisions of the European Communities Act to be discussed below are set out here for reference:

2.–(1) All such rights, powers, liabilities, obligations and restrictions from time to time created or arising by or under the Treaties, and all such remedies and procedures from time to time provided for by or under the Treaties, as in accordance with the Treaties are without further enactment to be given legal effect or used in the United Kingdom shall be recognised and available in law, and be enforced, allowed and followed accordingly; and the expression 'enforceable Community right' and similar expressions shall be read as referring to one to which this subsection applies.

(2) Subject to Schedule 2 to this Act, at any time after its passing Her Majesty may by Order in Council, and any designated Minister or department may by regulations, make provision–

(a) for the purpose of implementing any Community obligation of the United Kingdom, or enabling any such obligation to be implemented, or of enabling any rights enjoyed or to be enjoyed by the United Kingdom under or by virtue of the Treaties to be exercised; or

(b) for the purpose of dealing with matters arising out of or related to any such obligation or rights or the coming into force, or the operation from time to time, of subsection (1) above;

and in the exercise of any statutory power or duty, including any power to give directions or to legislate by means of orders, rules, regulations or other subordinate instrument, the person entrusted with the power or duty may have regard to the objects of the Communities and to any such obligation or rights as aforesaid.

In this subsection 'designated Minister or department' means such Minister of the Crown or government department as may from time to time be designated by Order in Council in relation to any matter or for any purpose, but subject to such restrictions or conditions (if any) as may be specified by the Order in Council.

. . . .

(4) The provision that may be made under subsection (2) above includes, subject to Schedule 2 to this Act, any such provision (of any such extent) as might be made by Act of Parliament, and any enactment passed or to be passed, other than one contained in this Part of this Act, shall be construed and have effect subject to the foregoing provisions of this section; but, except as may be provided by any Act passed after this Act, Schedule 2 shall have effect in connection with the powers conferred by this and the following sections of this Act to make Orders in Council and regulations.

3.–(1) For the purposes of all legal proceedings any question as to the meaning or effect of any of the Treaties, or as to the validity, meaning or effect of any Community instrument, shall be treated as a question of law (and, if not referred to the European Court, be for determination as such in accordance with the principles laid down by and any relevant decision of the European Court).

We have seen that the European Communities Act had to provide for the application in the United Kingdom of Community law – both the law already existing and that to be enacted in the future by the Community institutions. Some specific alterations of United Kingdom law were immediately necessary and these were made by sections 4–12 of the Act; for example, section 9(1) modified the doctrine of ultra vires in company law to conform to a Community directive of 1968. For the rest, the existing Community law to be given effect in the United Kingdom was incorporated *en bloc* by section 2(1) of the Act (set out above).

The rights and remedies etc. to which section 2(1) refers are those that by Community law are to be given legal effect 'without further enactment' – that is, are to be directly effective and enforceable in the courts of the member states. The sub-section means that all directly effective Community law is to be recognized and enforced in the United Kingdom; by this provision the Act adopted at a stroke almost the entire existing corpus of Community regulations (which only exceptionally do not have direct effect) together with the directly effective provisions of directives, decisions and the Treaties. As a result some 1,500 Community instruments came into force in the United Kingdom on 1 January 1983.

It will be noticed that the law made applicable by sub-section (1) keeps its separate identity as Community law: it is not made a part of English (or Scottish) law but is to be enforced together with that law in the courts of the United Kingdom.

What was to be done about *future* Community legislation that was to be given direct effect in the United Kingdom? A Government White Paper of 1967 had drawn attention to the 'constitutional innovation' which would be necessary for 'the acceptance in advance as part of the law of the United Kingdom of provisions to be made in the future by instruments issued by the Community institutions – a situation for which there is no precedent in this country' (*Legal and Constitutional Implications of United Kingdom Membership of the European Communities*, Cmnd 3301, para. 22). The situation was the more unprecedented in that future Community legislation was not only to be accepted in advance, but was to be given that primacy over domestic law which is a keystone of the Community's legal order.

The way was not taken of attempting to make an express transfer of legislative power from Parliament to the Community institutions. (On one view this has indeed been the *effect* of the Act: see John Usher, *European Community Law and National Law*, 1981, pp. 35–8.) Rather, the subtle mechanism of section 2(1) was made to serve a dual purpose. For the sub-section gives effect in the United Kingdom to what it terms 'enforceable Community rights' as *'from time to time'* arising under the Treaties, and so covers prospective Community law as well as the law in existence when the Act came into force.

Neither was it thought right (or politic?) to make an express declaration in the Act of the primacy or supremacy of Community law over the laws of the United Kingdom. The words designed to achieve this are to be found oddly sandwiched in the middle of section 2(4), and read as follows:

any enactment passed or to be passed . . . shall be construed and have effect subject to the foregoing provisions of this section. . . .

Among the foregoing provisions are those in sub-section (1) giving the force of law in the United Kingdom to the 'enforceable Community rights' there defined. It is therefore intended that any enactment (including any Act of Parliament) is to be construed and have effect *subject to* Community law applied in the United Kingdom.

The same principle is impressed upon the judges by some bracketed words in section 3(1): it is there provided that any question of the validity, meaning or effect of Community law is to be decided by our courts 'in accordance with the principles laid down by and any relevant decision of the European Court'. That court has, as we have seen, consistently upheld the precedence of Community law over national law.

The provisions we have considered are apt to ensure that Community law, of whatever date, that has direct effect in the United Kingdom will override any inconsistent provisions in United Kingdom legislation enacted before 1 January 1973, when the European Communities Act came into force. This follows from the simple rule that the later Act (the European Communities Act) must prevail over any earlier enactment.

A more difficult problem arises if an Act of Parliament passed *after* 1 January

1973 should conflict with Community law (of whatever date). Here the simple rule mentioned above gives precedence to the Act of Parliament as the latest expression of Parliament's will, but the Community doctrine of primacy and the apparent intention of section 2(4) of the European Communities Act require the Community law to prevail. This conflict raises the question of the continuing sovereignty of Parliament. We shall see in the next section how the English courts have so far responded to it.

Some Community enactments (in particular directives) call for implementing action by the national authorities. This may be done, especially in important matters, by Act of Parliament, but often subordinate legislation will suffice. Section 2(2) of the European Communities Act authorizes the making of Orders in Council or departmental regulations for this purpose. The power given is a wide one, for it is amplified by section 2(4) to include 'any such provision (of any such extent) as might be made by Act of Parliament', subject only to certain limitations in Schedule 2 to the Act. (These relate to taxation, retrospective legislation, sub-delegated legislation and the creation of new criminal offences.) An Order in Council or regulation made under section 2(2) can repeal or amend an Act of Parliament passed before 1 January 1973.

Some Community directives can be implemented without legislation by changes in administrative practice or procedure. For example, directives on public sector contracts have been acted on by making changes in the administrative procedures for advertising and awarding contracts.

Among the provisions which have effect in the United Kingdom by virtue of section 2(1) of the European Communities Act is Article 177 of the EEC Treaty, providing for reference of questions of Community law to the European Court of Justice. (See p. 254 above.) See also section 3(1) of the Act, above.

(c) **Community law in the courts**

The courts regularly act upon section 2(1) of the European Communities Act in giving effect to Community law. Once it is established – it may be by reference to the case law of the European Court, in accordance with section 3(1) – that the Community provision in question is of the kind that produces direct effects, it is enforced accordingly. In *Bulmer Ltd* v. *Bollinger SA* [1974] Ch. 401, 419, Lord Denning, having referred to section 2(1), said:

The statute is expressed in forthright terms which are absolute and all-embracing. Any rights or obligations created by the Treaty are to be given legal effect in England without more ado.

Section 2(1) was applied, for example, in *Application des Gaz SA* v. *Falks Veritas Ltd* [1974] Ch. 381, where the Court of Appeal held that Articles 85 and 86 of the EEC Treaty (on competition) could be relied upon in the English courts. These articles had previously been held by the European Court to have direct effect. (See also *Garden Cottage Foods Ltd* v. *Milk Marketing Board* [1984] AC 130.)

Community law is applied by English courts so as to override contrary provisions in laws made before the European Communities Act came into force on 1 January 1973. This is clearly recognized in decisions of the Court of Appeal and House of Lords: see *Polydor Ltd* v. *Harlequin Record Shops Ltd* [1980] 2 CMLR 413 (CA), *R.* v. *Henn* [1981] AC 850 and *R.* v. *Goldstein* [1983] 1 All ER 434. This aspect of the primacy of Community law is consistent with the normal operation of United Kingdom statutes and is uncontroversial.

When a statute enacted after 1 January 1973 is in question the court will attempt to interpret the statute in such a way as to reconcile it with any relevant Community law. As Lord Diplock observed in *Garland* v. *British Rail Engineering Ltd* [1983] 2 AC 751, 771, when the United Kingdom has assumed an obligation under any international treaty or convention

it is a principle of construction of United Kingdom statutes, now too well established to call for citation of authority, that the words of a statute passed after the Treaty has been signed and dealing with the subject matter of the international obligation of the United Kingdom, are to be construed, if they are reasonably capable of bearing such a meaning, as intended to carry out the obligation, and not to be inconsistent with it.

This approach is in any event demanded by section 2(4) of the European Communities Act, by which enactments must be 'construed and have effect' subject to the application in the United Kingdom of directly effective Community law.

Interpretation in accordance with this principle will often resolve an apparent inconsistency, but if a court is faced with an irreconcilable conflict between Community law and a post–1972 statute the issue of primacy has to be confronted.

The primacy of Community law has been acknowledged in general terms in dicta of English judges. For example, Lord Hailsham said in the *Siskina* [1979] AC 210, 262:

It is the duty of the courts here and in other member states to give effect to community law as they interpret it in preference to the municipal law of their own country over which ex hypothesi community law prevails.

(What comment may be made upon the words, 'as they interpret it'?)

In *Shields* v. *Coomes (Holdings) Ltd* [1978] 1 WLR 1408, the question for the Court of Appeal was whether a female employee was entitled under provisions of the Equal Pay Act 1970, re-enacted with amendments by the Sex Discrimination Act 1975, to equal pay with male employees of the same firm on the ground that she was employed in 'like work' with the men. The majority of the court (Orr and Bridge LJJ) thought that there was no ambiguity in the provisions of the Equal Pay Act and found it unnecessary to consider the Community directives which these provisions were intended to implement. The woman was doing like work and was entitled to equal pay. Lord Denning, while agreeing in the result, was uncertain whether the woman could be said to be employed in like work with the men in terms of the Equal Pay Act considered alone. Having examined the EEC Treaty and the directives, he concluded (p. 1419):

my difficulties on this score have been resolved by giving supremacy to Community law.

While acknowledging the primacy of Community law in these words, Lord Denning was here invoking Community law to interpret and not to override an English statute. However he also observed, obiter, that Parliament had by section 3(1) of the European Communities Act accepted the principle of primacy, by which Community law must prevail over inconsistent provisions in the internal law of a member state 'whether passed before or after joining the Community'.

In the following case the question again arose of the relation between the Equal Pay Act – as re-enacted by the Sex Discrimination Act 1975 *after* the European Communities Act had come into force – and Community law.

Macarthys Ltd v. *Smith* [1979] 3 All ER 325 (CA)

Macarthys Ltd had employed a Mr McCullough as their stockroom manager. Some time after he left, Mrs Smith was employed in the same position, with similar duties, at lower pay. An industrial tribunal held that she was entitled to be paid at the same rate as Mr McCullough, and the Employment Appeal Tribunal, with Phillips J presiding, affirmed that decision. Macarthys Ltd appealed.

LORD DENNING MR: . . . The employers say that this case is not within the Equal Pay Act 1970. In order to be covered by that Act, the employers say that the woman and the man must be employed by the same employer on like work *at the same time*: whereas here Mrs Smith was employed on like work *in succession* to Mr McCullough and not at the same time as he.

To solve this problem I propose to turn first to the principle of equal pay contained in the EEC Treaty, for that takes priority even over our own statute.
The EEC Treaty
Article 119 of the EEC Treaty says:

'Each Member State shall during the first stage ensure and subsequently maintain the application of the principle that men and women should receive equal pay for equal work. . . .'

That principle is part of our English law. It is directly applicable in England. So much so that, even if we had not passed any legislation on the point, our courts would have been bound to give effect to art. 119. If a woman had complained to an industrial tribunal or to the High Court and proved that she was not receiving equal pay with a man for equal work, both the industrial tribunal and the court would have been bound to give her redress. . . .

In point of fact, however, the United Kingdom has passed legislation with the intention of giving effect to the principle of equal pay. It has done it by the Sex Discrimination Act 1975 and in particular by s.8 of that Act amending s.1 of the Equal Pay Act 1970. No doubt the Parliament of the United Kingdom thinks that it has fulfilled its obligations under the Treaty. But the European Commission take a different view. They think that our statutes do not go far enough.

What then is the position? Suppose that England passes legislation which contravenes the principle contained in the Treaty, or which is inconsistent with it, or fails properly to implement it. There is no doubt that the European Commission can report the United Kingdom to the European Court of Justice; and that court can require the United Kingdom to take the necessary measures to implement art. 119. . . .

It is unnecessary, however, for these courts to wait until all that procedure has been gone through. Under s.2(1) and (4) of the European Communities Act 1972 the principles laid down in the Treaty are 'without further enactment' to be given legal effect in the United Kingdom; and have priority over 'any enactment passed or to be passed' by our Parliament. So we are entitled and I think bound to look at art. 119 of the EEC Treaty because it is directly applicable here; and also any directive which is directly applicable here: see *Van Duyn* v. *Home Office (No. 2)* [p. 264 above]. We should, I think, look to see what those provisions require about equal pay for men and women. Then we should look at our own legislation on the point, giving it, of course, full faith and credit, assuming that it does fully comply with the obligations under the Treaty. In construing our statute, we are entitled to look to the Treaty as an aid to its construction; but not only as an aid but as an overriding force. If on close investigation it should appear that our legislation is deficient or is inconsistent with Community law by some oversight of our draftsmen then it is our bounden duty to give priority to Community law. Such is the result of s.2(1) and (4) of the European Communities Act 1972.

I pause here, however, to make one observation on a constitutional point. Thus far I have assumed that our Parliament, whenever it passes legislation, intends to fulfil its obligations under the Treaty. If the time should come when our Parliament deliberately passes an Act with the intention of repudiating the Treaty or any provision in it or intentionally of acting inconsistently with it and says so in express terms then I should have thought that it would be the duty of our courts to follow the statute of our Parliament. I do not however envisage any such situation. As I said in *Blackburn* v. *Attorney-General* [above]: 'But if Parliament should do so, then I say we will consider that event when it happens.' Unless there is such an intentional and express repudiation of the Treaty, it is our duty to give priority to the Treaty. In the present case I assume that the United Kingdom intended to fulfil its obligations under art. 119. Has it done so?

Article 119

Article 119 is framed in European fashion. It enunciates a broad general principle and leaves the judges to work out the details. In contrast the Equal Pay Act is framed in English fashion. It states no general principle but lays down detailed specific rules for the courts to apply (which, so some hold, the courts must interpret according to the actual language used) without resort to considerations of policy or principle.

Now consider art. 119 in the context of our present problem. Take the simple case envisaged by Phillips J. A man who is a skilled technician working single-handed for a firm receives £1.50 an hour for his work. He leaves the employment. On the very next day he is replaced by a woman who is equally capable and who does exactly the same work as the man but, because she is a woman, she is only paid £1.25 an hour. That would be a clear case of discrimination on the ground of sex. It would, I think, be an infringement of the principle in art. 119 which says 'that men and women should receive equal pay for equal work'. All the more so when you take into account the explanatory sentence in art. 119 itself which says:

'Equal pay without discrimination based on sex means . . . that pay for work at time rates shall be the same for the same job.'

If you go further and consider the Council directive of 10th February 1975, it becomes plain beyond question:

'The principle of equal pay for men and women outlined in Article 119 of the Treaty, hereinafter called "principle of equal pay", means, for the same work or for work to which equal value is attributed, the elimination of all discrimination on ground of sex with regard to all aspects and conditions of remuneration.'

That directive may be directly applicable in England; but, even if it be not, it is relevant as showing the scope of the principle contained in art. 119. It shows that it applies to the case of the skilled technician (which I have put) and that the difference between the woman and the man should be eliminated by paying her £1.50 an hour just like the man.

In my opinion therefore art. 119 is reasonably clear on the point; it applies not only to cases where the woman is employed on like work *at the same time* with a man in the same employment, but also when she is employed on like work in succession to a man, that is, in such close succession that it is just and reasonable to make a comparison between them. So much for art. 119.

The Equal Pay Act 1970

Now I turn to our Act to see if that principle has been carried forward into our legislation. The relevant part of this Act was passed not in 1970 but in 1975 by s.8 of the Sex Discrimination Act 1975.

Section 1(2)(a)(i) of the Equal Pay Act 1970 introduces an 'equality clause' so as to put a woman on an equality with a man 'where the woman is employed on like work with a man in the same employment'. The question is whether the words 'at the same time' are to be read into that subsection so that it is confined to cases where the woman and the man are employed *at the same time* in the same employment.

After considering this and related provisions Lord Denning concluded that section 1(2)(a)(i) of the Equal Pay Act should *not* be read as if it included the words 'at the same time', but should be interpreted so as to apply to cases where a woman was employed on like work *in succession* to a man. He continued:

So I would hold, in agreement with Phillips J, that both under the Treaty and under the statutes a woman should receive equal pay for equal work, not only when she is employed *at the same time* as the man, but also when she is employed at the same job *in succession* to him, that is, in such close succession that it is just and reasonable to make a comparison between them.

If I am wrong

Now my colleagues take a different view. They are of opinion that s. 1(2)(a)(i) of the

Equal Pay Act should be given its natural and ordinary meaning, and that is, they think, that it is confined to cases where the woman is employed *at the same time* as a man.

So on our statute, taken alone, they would allow the appeal and reject Mrs Smith's claim. My colleagues realise, however, that in this interpretation there may be a conflict between our statute and the EEC Treaty. As I understand their judgments, they would hold that if art. 119 was clearly in favour of Mrs Smith it should be given priority over our own statute and Mrs Smith should succeed. But they feel that art. 119 is not clear, and, being not clear, it is necessary to refer it to the European Court at Luxembourg for determination under art. 177 of the Treaty . . . .

Conclusion

For myself I would be in favour of dismissing the appeal, because I agree with the decision of the Employment Appeal Tribunal. I have no doubt about the true interpretation of art. 119.

But, as my colleagues think that art. 119 is not clear on the point, I agree that reference should be made to the European Court at Luxembourg to resolve the uncertainty in that article.

Pending the decision of the European court, all further proceedings in the case will be stayed . . . .

LAWTON LJ: . . . In my judgment the grammatical construction of s.1(2) [of the Equal Pay Act] is consistent only with a comparison between a woman and a man in the same employment at the same time. The words, by the tenses used, look to the present and the future but not to the past. They are inconsistent with a comparison between a woman and a man, no longer in the same employment, who was doing her job before she got it.

I find in the words used a clear indication of policy, namely that men and women in the same employment doing like work, or work of a broadly similar nature, should be paid the same. . . .

As the meaning of the words used in s.1(2) and (4) is clear, and no ambiguity, whether patent or latent, lurks within them, under our rules for the construction of Acts of Parliament the statutory intention must be found within those words. It is not permissible to read into the statute words which are not there or to look outside the Act, as counsel for Mrs Smith invited us to do and Phillips J did, to read the words used in a sense other than that of their ordinary meaning. . . .

What led Phillips J to construe s.1(2) and (4) of the Act so as to allow such a comparison were the provisions of art. 119 of the EEC Treaty to which Lord Denning MR has referred for its full terms. In this court counsel on both sides have submitted that the meaning of this article is clear; but they have differed as to what that meaning is. Counsel for Mrs Smith has submitted that under art. 119 a woman should receive the same pay as a man she follows in a job, unless there are factors, other than sex discrimination, which justify the difference. If this be right, art. 119 says something different from what I adjudge to be the plain, unambiguous meaning of s.1(2) and (4) of the Act. When an Act and an article of the EEC Treaty are in conflict, which should this court follow? Counsel for Mrs Smith says the article, because s.2 of the European Communities Act 1972 so provides, as does European Community law.

. . . Counsel for the employers submission as to the meaning of art. 119 did not . . . convince me that when construed in accordance with the canons of construction as used in our court for finding out the meaning of statutes and deeds, its ambit was confined to men and women doing like or broadly similar work side by side at the same time. The part of the article which begins with the words 'Equal pay without discrimination based on sex' takes in para (*a*) 'the same work' and in para (*b*) 'the same job' as the bases of comparison. A woman may do 'the same work' or 'the same job' after a man as well as alongside a man. In my opinion there is some doubt whether art. 119 applies to the facts of this case.

We cannot, as counsel for the employers submitted, ignore art. 119 and apply what I consider to be the plain meaning of the Act. The problem of the implementation of art. 119 is not one for the EEC Commission to take up with the government of the United Kingdom and Northern Ireland, as counsel for the employers submitted it was. Article 119 gives rise to individual rights which our courts must protect. . . .

Being in doubt as to the ambit of art. 119 and being under an obligation arising both from the decisions of the European Court of Justice . . . and s.2 of the European Communities Act 1972 to apply that article in our courts, it seems to me that this is a situation to which art. 177 of the EEC Treaty applies. I consider that a decision is necessary as to the construction of art. 119 and I would request the European Court of Justice to give a ruling on it. . . .

Before saying au revoir, if not adieu, to this appeal, I would like to set out my reasons for deciding as I have that there should be a reference to the European Court of Justice. First, counsel on both sides persuaded me that it would be more convenient and less expensive to the parties for this court to request the European Court of Justice to give a ruling on the application of art. 119 than for the House of Lord to do so. The issue in the appeal is clear, even if by English concepts the construction of art. 119 is not. The ruling when given may decide the case; and when the ruling is given, there can be no appeal from it. There seems to be nothing else which would justify an appeal to the House of Lords. Further, I can see nothing in this case which infringes the sovereignty of Parliament. If I thought there were, I should not presume to take any judicial step which it would be more appropriate for the House of Lords, as part of Parliament, to take. Parliament by its own act in the exercise of its sovereign powers has enacted that European Community law shall 'be enforced, allowed and followed' in the United Kingdom of Great Britain and Northern Ireland (see s.2(1) of the European Communities Act 1972) and that 'any enactment passed or to be passed . . . shall be construed and have effect subject to [s.2]' (see s.2(4) of that Act). Parliament's recognition of European Community law and of the jurisdiction of the European Court of Justice by one enactment can be withdrawn by another. There is nothing in the Equal Pay Act 1970 as amended by the Sex Discrimination Act 1975, to indicate that Parliament intended to amend the European Communities Act 1972, or to limit its application. Secondly, as I am in doubt as to what is the right construction of art. 119 when our canons of construction are applied and in ignorance as to how the European Court of Justice would construe that article when it applies its own rules of construction, I consider myself under a judicial duty not to guess how that court would construe it but to find out how it does.

Cumming-Bruce LJ agreed with the reasoning and conclusion of Lawton LJ. In the course of his judgment he said:

If the terms of the Treaty are adjudged in Luxembourg to be inconsistent with the provisions of the Equal Pay Act 1970, European law will prevail over that municipal legislation.

The case duly came before the European Court of Justice for a preliminary ruling under Article 177 of the EEC Treaty. The European Court ruled that the principle of equal pay enshrined in Article 119 of the Treaty is not confined to situations in which men and women are employed contemporaneously by the same employer: see case 129/79 *Macarthys Ltd* v. *Smith* [1980] ECR 1275. In the light of this answer the employers conceded defeat when the case returned to the Court of Appeal: *Macarthys Ltd* v. *Smith* [1981] QB 199. Lord Denning took the opportunity of saying (at p. 200):

> The majority of this court felt that article 119 was uncertain. So this court referred the problem to the European Court at Luxembourg. We have now been provided with the decision of that court. It is important now to declare – and it must be made plain – that the provisions of article 119 of the EEC Treaty take priority over anything in our English statute on equal pay which is inconsistent with article 119. That priority is given by our own law. It is given by the European Communities Act 1972 itself. Community law is now part of our law: and, whenever there is any inconsistency, Community law has priority. It is not supplanting English law. It is part of our law which overrides any other part which is inconsistent with it.

Macarthys Ltd v. *Smith* was not a case in which an English statutory provision was deprived of its effect by an overriding Community law: rather the Community law extended to employees a right to equal pay in circumstances which fell outside the scope of the English statute. Nevertheless, as the Court of Appeal recognized, there was an inconsistency between the English statute and Community law, and the court held unequivocally that the Community law had 'priority'. T. R. S. Allan comments ('Parliamentary Sovereignty: Lord Denning's Dexterous Revolution' (1983) 3 *Oxford J. Legal Stud.* 22 at 25):

> The attempt to entrench section 2(1) of the European Communities Act by means of section 2(4) has to some extent succeeded: the effect of the decision seems to be to impose a requirement of form (express wording) on future legislation designed to override Community law. In short, Parliament in 1972 accomplished the impossible and (to a degree) bound its successors.

In *Garland* v. *British Rail Engineering Ltd* [1983] 2 AC 751, the House of Lords was able to reconcile a provision of the Sex Discrimination Act 1975 with Community law as declared by the European Court in a preliminary ruling, by interpreting the English provision in a sense consistent with the Community law. Lord Diplock said, in the course of a speech with which the other Law Lords concurred (p. 771):

> The instant appeal does not present an appropriate occasion to consider whether, having regard to the express direction as to the construction of enactments 'to be passed' which is contained in section 2(4) [of the European Communities Act], anything short of an express positive statement in an Act of Parliament passed after January 1, 1973, that a particular provision is intended to be made in breach of an obligation assumed by the United Kingdom under a Community treaty, would justify an English court in construing that provision in a manner inconsistent with a

Community treaty obligation of the United Kingdom, however wide a departure from the prima facie meaning of the language of the provision might be needed in order to achieve consistency.

(d) **Sovereignty**

The cases considered in the last section show a willingness on the part of the English courts to accept the primacy of Community law. Has their recognition of this doctrine – and, more generally, their submission to the authority of Community law – undermined the sovereignty of Parliament?

Parliamentary sovereignty and the sovereignty of the United Kingdom as a state are different things, although they are not unrelated. In case 6/64 *Costa* v. *ENEL* [1964] ECR 585 (p. 267 above) the European Court of Justice adverted to the impact of the EEC Treaty upon national sovereignty (at p. 594):

The transfer by the States from their domestic legal system to the Community legal system of the rights and obligations arising under the Treaty carries with it a permanent limitation of their sovereign rights. . . .

But the permanence of any such limitation of national sovereignty may depend upon a continued assent to the terms of membership of the Community. (See p. 240 above.)

Parliament retains its ultimate sovereignty as long as it has the power to terminate the application of Community law in the United Kingdom (and its overriding force) by repealing or amending the European Communities Act. At least while our membership of the Community remains contentious such action by Parliament is conceivable, and it is hardly open to doubt that the Queen's courts would give effect to an Act of Parliament which was passed in the process of withdrawal from the Community. While membership continues it is possible although unlikely that Parliament might legislate with the express purpose of negating the effect in the United Kingdom of a rule of Community law. The courts could not refuse to apply such an Act without asserting a power which our constitution has not hitherto accorded to them and to which no English court has yet laid claim. In time this may change, as de Smith observed in (1971) 34 *MLR* 597 at 614:

If, however, with the passage of time, the Community develops characteristics of a political federation, and if the incongruity of the orthodox doctrine of parliamentary sovereignty becomes increasingly apparent in a context of expanding Community law, then a climate of opinion will doubtless develop in which heterodoxy will thrive and eventually prevail. The legal concept of parliamentary sovereignty may then drift away into the shadowy background from which it emerged.

Meanwhile Parliament in practice refrains from any deliberate exercise of its legislative power that would contradict or forestall the application of Community law. If this should happen inadvertently corrective action would be taken – if not by the courts in giving primacy to Community law, then by amending legislation. To this extent, and in the area occupied by Community law, parliamentary sovereignty may be said to be in abeyance.

6

The powers of government

No one in the modern state is untouched by the power of government. Even in the first half of the nineteenth century the condition of working people in Britain was relieved or exacerbated by acts of government – by Corn Laws, Enclosure Acts, Poor Laws, Public Health Acts and Factory Acts. But the increase since that time in the activity of government and its impact on the daily life and work of the community has been immeasurable. Nineteenth-century governments were not called upon to regulate a welfare state or town and country planning, and did not attempt to manage the economy, foster industrial development or protect the environment. They concerned themselves little or not at all with consumer protection, fair rents, restrictive trade practices or equal pay for men and women. They had no need to be troubled with the construction and use of motor vehicles, the location of airports, or the disposal of nuclear wastes. All these and many other new activities and concerns have made enormous claims upon the resources of government in our time.

Report of the Royal Commission on the Constitution, vol. 1, Cmnd 5460/1973

THE SCOPE OF GOVERNMENT

The subject matter of government
227. Throughout most of the nineteenth century government was concerned mainly with law and order, external affairs and defence, the regulation of overseas trade and the raising of revenue; it exercised a narrow range of regulatory functions, but its attitude in domestic affairs was mostly passive and non-interventionist.... The situation today is quite different; there are now very few areas of public and even personal life with which government can be said to have no concern at all.
228. This expansion of government, while a constant feature of modern history, has markedly quickened its pace at certain times. In this century two periods stand out, both associated with the world wars.
229. The first period extended from 1908 to 1919. It began with the extensive social reforms which were embodied in the Old Age Pensions Act 1908, the Labour Exchanges Act 1909 and the National Insurance Act 1911. There followed in war-time

the imposition of a widening range of administrative and economic controls. After the war those controls were quickly wound up, but many of the new government departments, including those established for Pensions, Labour, Air and Scientific and Industrial Research, remained in being, and two additional departments, for Transport and Health, were set up. Each of these new departments represented an enlarged area of government intervention.

230. The second period of rapid expansion was the decade from 1940. Apart again from the complex apparatus of war-time controls, finally dismantled in the 1950s, there were major developments in the social services and in the economic and environmental fields. Legislation was passed to bring about major changes in the arrangements for education, social security, health, agriculture, and town and country planning, and the Government's direct involvement in industry and the economy was increased through a series of Acts providing for the nationalisation of basic industries. Changes in the character of economic intervention were also implicit in the acceptance by the war-time Government of responsibility for maintaining full employment.

231. In these and other ways government responsibilities have, within the lifetime of many people now living, widened immensely. The range of subjects that may now be raised in Parliament provides some illustration of this. We have examined a recent series of Parliamentary Questions to see how far it would have been appropriate to put them at the beginning of the century. Our analysis covered Questions receiving both oral and written reply in the House of Commons in one week in June 1971. There were 718 Questions in all, and we estimate that between 80 and 90 per cent of them could not have been tabled in 1900 since they related to matters which were not then of government concern. . . .

The system of government which has charge of the welfare state and managed economy of the 1980s is fundamentally the same as that with which Britain entered the First World War, after the nineteenth-century Reform Acts had laid the foundations of parliamentary democracy and the Parliament Act 1911 had curbed the powers of the House of Lords. In carrying out their increased commitments British Governments have been able to use the powers available to the Crown under the traditional constitution, and have also captured powers from other institutions – from Parliament and from local government – although it might be without any change in the formal location of the power. Governments have often tried to remove restraints upon the exercise of their powers and have invented new techniques for putting their policies into effect. But far from being something malign, the growth of governmental power has followed inevitably from the increase in the tasks of government and has been stimulated, at least in part, by the demands of social justice and public welfare. In this chapter we shall consider the tasks of modern government and the powers available to governments for carrying them out.

1 The tasks of government

Governments decide upon their objectives and policies in response to innumerable and varied – often overlapping – influences, among which are party policies, group pressures, departmental studies, parliamentary opinion, perceptions of public demand, NATO, the International Monetary Fund and the European Communities. It may be helpful to distinguish ultimate objectives – such as a healthy or well-educated or socially and economically unstratified society, if these should be the benign goals of government – from the policies designed to achieve such ends.

Brian Smith, *Policy-Making in British Government* (1976),
pp. 13–15

Policy can be distinguished from objectives as means from ends. It may be of course that what appear to be ends are in fact means to other ends; and that a means may become an end in itself, regardless of its effectiveness in reaching the objectives for which it was originally designed. All this, however, tells us more about the importance of evaluating the effects of policies in the decision-making process than about the nature of policies themselves which are analytically distinct from the goals which the policy-maker might be pursuing.

If policies are distinct from goals and objectives they nevertheless involve a deliberate choice of actions designed to reach those objectives. The actions referred to can take the form of directives to perform certain actions (for example, pay tax at a certain rate or register a marriage, birth or death), or refrain from certain actions (parking on the wrong side of the street at night or engaging in commercial dealings with Rhodesia). They may take the form of publicly financed services, such as education, health care or housing, or publicly financed projects, such as missiles, power stations or motorways. Policies create obligations for both the citizen (for example, not to develop his land without planning permission) and the state (to provide unemployment benefit to a person who is unemployed, capable of work and available to take a job).

It is clear that within any one policy area (for example, defence or social welfare) there is a hierarchy of policies and a range of different policies. There is, for example, a wide range of benefits paid under social security legislation. Family allowances, welfare milk and foods, retirement pensions and industrial injuries benefits are all policies designed to provide social security. Each has been designated to meet some second-level objective within the very broad goal of 'social security'. The hierarchy of policies develops as rules have to be formulated to govern the various activities which contribute to the implementation of policy. Each policy in the hierarchy corresponds to some value or objective existing at that level. For example, one aim of housing policy is slum clearance. The policy is to give local authorities power to demolish property unfit for human habitation. Within this it is policy to use either clearance orders or compulsory purchase orders. In either case it is policy to require ministerial confirmation. Within the central department there needs to be a policy on what constitutes 'unfitness'. To determine this it is policy to have every house alleged by a local authority to be unfit examined by a housing inspector. In any case of doubt, it is policy to give the owner the benefit. Doubtless there are further rules governing how the inspectors conduct themselves, each reflecting departmental policy on procedures.

Policies thus range from the choice of priorities, through plans, to decision rules.

Hence the difficulty in distinguishing policy from administration or policy implementation. What appears to be 'execution by subdecisions' from the level of policy defined as
'general directives on the main lines of action to be followed', may be policy-making
itself at a lower level in the organisation, where general policy has to be translated into
the more concrete forms needed for administration.

. . . [P]olicies as much as objectives are chosen under the influence of values. Indeed
an objective (such as a properly housed community) may be shared by different
political groups; but the means or policies chosen will be dependent on the values of
those making the choice. One housing programme will be constrained by an
inegalitarian ideology which involves, say, reducing mortgage rates for all, including
the wealthy, and the selling of council houses. Another strategy will be equally
conditioned by a different evaluation of the side effects of different policy options.
Similarly the eradication of poverty may be a widely shared objective, but the policies
adopted will be determined by the protagonists' views on the desirability of
redistributing wealth.

Once a policy has been decided upon, the means must be found to
implement it – to perform the governmental task assumed. The performance of
tasks depends both on the availability of the necessary resources of manpower
and money, and on the authority and powers of government.

2 The basis of governmental authority

Specific actions of the government generally rest upon legal powers conferred
on it by statute or common law, or otherwise can be supported on the broad
principle that an act is lawfully done if 'there is nothing to make it unlawful'
(*per* Sir Robert Megarry v–c in *Malone* v. *Metropolitan Police Commissioner* [1979]
Ch. 344, 367: see p. 51 above). From an exclusively legal perspective no other
justification of governmental action is called for. A government armed with
law and (consequently) supported by the courts can and does take measures
that are damaging to sectional or individual interests, or are strongly
disapproved by opposition parties, or are widely unpopular. But there are
limits to what it can do in this way without provoking non-cooperation,
disobedience or disorder. Dicey recognized this in saying that the legal
sovereignty of Parliament 'is limited on every side by the possibility of popular
resistance' (*The Law of the Constitution*, p. 79); he added that this external limit
to the exercise of sovereign power was marked by no definite boundary.

Nevertheless British governments have generally been able to rely, within
wide limits, upon the compliance of those to whom their actions have been
directed. This compliance has been assured, not only by the government's
possession of the means of coercion, but as much or more by public recognition
that governments exercise a legitimate authority.

Legitimacy is primarily a feature of constitutional systems. They possess
this quality by virtue of a general public support for their authority, and may
have it in greater or lesser degree. Successive governments, even unpopular

ones, benefit from the legitimacy attaching to the constitutional order, so that their own actions are perceived as 'legitimate'. It will be evident that this is not the same thing as 'lawful', although legality is normally a condition of legitimacy, in that a government which disregards the law is seen to be acting discordantly with the constitutional system from which its legitimacy is derived.

The effectiveness of government will to a great extent depend on whether it is accepted as legitimate by people generally and by those particularly affected by its acts. Not only is obedience to law more easily secured by a government of acknowledged legitimacy, but organized interests or groups whose co-operation is necessary for the success of a policy will be more willing to give it if they recognize the government's legitimacy and its right to have its policies carried out. Legitimacy is of no less importance in the constitution and government than law itself. It is, however, an elusive concept, springing from public attitudes and the 'political culture' (pp. 6–7 above), and the legitimacy accorded to a regime is not necessarily something constant.

British governments have generally been said to enjoy a high degree of legitimacy, and surveys have confirmed a strong allegiance among the British people to established political authority. (See, e.g., Richard Rose, *Politics in England*, 3rd edn 1980, ch. iv.) Various factors have contributed to popular acceptance of the authority of government. A respect for British political institutions has doubtless been instilled in many people by parents, the educational system and the media. The main political parties have been in agreement, as Samuel Beer observes, on 'the basic legal structures, the basic parliamentary conventions, and the main contemporary practices of party government' (*Modern British Politics*, 3rd edn 1982, p. 387). This must have contributed to public acceptance of the political structure and the laws that issue from it. A faculty of deference to authority has been discerned by some writers as a British social phenomenon making for trust in the political leadership. (See, e.g., Gabriel Almond and Sidney Verba, *The Civic Culture*, 1963.)

Factors like these, of tradition, party-political consensus on the 'rules of the game', and deference, may have helped to sustain the legitimacy of govern-ment in the United Kingdom. More fundamentally, the democratic system itself provides for many people the strongest justification of the legitimacy of British governments. In the long run, as Vivien Hart says, the 'legitimacy of the polity' depends on 'assent to the forms of institutions and the principles which guide them; people will accept policies with which they disagree and the neglect of their own priorities, provided that they believe decisions have been reached by democratic processes' (*Distrust and Democracy*, 1978, p. 1).

But in recent years a change has been observed in the political culture, with surveys showing markedly less confidence in British government than formerly. One of the props of the legitimacy of government is said to have been knocked away with the 'collapse of deference'. (See Samuel Beer, *Britain*

Against Itself, 1982, pp. 114–20.) A survey carried out for the Royal Commission on the Constitution in 1970 discovered a general feeling of dissatisfaction with the system of government (Research Paper 7, *Devolution and Other Aspects of Government: An Attitudes Survey*, HMSO 1973, p. 10) and there are indications of alienation from the political system among disadvantaged or vulnerable groups such as immigrant communities, the unemployed and those whose jobs are at risk. Some have rejected the authority of Acts of Parliament perceived as instruments of an antipathetic political ideology. In Scotland a majority has claimed, and been refused, devolution of power (see chapter 4 above). In the extremest case, allegiance has been renounced by those waging guerrilla warfare in Northern Ireland. These diverse dissatisfactions spring from a variety of causes. Some discontents may be attributable to the relative economic decline of the United Kingdom, others to prejudice or oppression suffered by particular social groups. But there are those who would include among the precipitating factors of a 'crisis of legitimacy' already arrived or imminent, misgovernment and failures of policy, and defects in the constitutional system itself. None other than the present Lord Chancellor has castigated the system of government as one of 'elective dictatorship' (Lord Hailsham, *Elective Dictatorship*, 1976); many have called for the restraints of a bill of rights; the electoral system is denounced as undemocratic.

The consequences for government and the state may be serious if legitimacy is denied to the regime by numerically significant groups, parties or interests in society. Clear proof of this is given by the experience of the Stormont Government of Northern Ireland, which forfeited the allegiance of a substantial minority in the community and ceased to be an effective government of the province.

Majority rule under a system of parliamentary democracy is not a sufficient guarantee of legitimacy. Among the conditions of full legitimacy would seem to be, that governments attain power by processes recognized as being fair, that the public is not denied information necessary for evaluating government policies, and that in exercising their authority governments respect the rights of opposition parties and are responsive to the claims of minorities and the views of organized interests. Those excluded from power must be assured, at least, the right to be heard, fair dealing, and sufficient explanations of decisions taken. Can it be said that our present constitutional system and practice fully meet these conditions?

Even if a regime enjoys legitimacy, or a substantial measure of it, in general, this is not to say that it is given *carte blanche* to act as it chooses. Some kinds of governmental action would be generally regarded as going beyond the limits of a legitimate exercise of authority – for example if a government were to prolong its rule by securing the passage of legislation to extend the life of Parliament, otherwise than in circumstances of national emergency. Again, governmental action might have majority support both in Parliament and in the community but be rejected by groups in society which considered it to be, not merely ill-advised, but an illegitimate exercise of authority: disobedience to law might result. British society is not now, if ever it was, in full agreement on the 'rules of the game'. As Brian Smith remarks, 'Society is divided in the way in which it evaluates the legitimacy of the state's territorial jurisdiction, the rightful access of certain types of people to political roles or the extent of state intervention in social and economic affairs' (*Policy-Making in British Government*, 1976, p. 27). (Think if you can of incidents in recent years which have raised questions of the legitimacy of governmental action.)

As we consider the different means by which governmental powers are exercised and policies are implemented, our attention is focused primarily on the rules – laws and conventions – of the constitution. But there is an ever-present restraint upon the effective exercise of power in the degree of legitimacy extended to the political institutions, to the government that for the time being inhabits them, and to specific actions of that government. Doubtless a government can, at least in the short term, overcome a want of legitimacy by reliance upon coercion. This raises the great danger, of which Ralf Dahrendorf has warned, that 'the response to a crisis of legitimacy will be authoritarianism and illiberty' ('Effectiveness and Legitimacy' (1980) 51 *Political Quarterly* 393 at 409). A persisting and widespread loss of legitimacy would threaten not only the survival of governments but the democratic constitutional system itself.

3 The powers of government

(a) General

Among the power-resources available to government for implementing its policies, Professor Daintith makes a useful distinction between the coercive power or the resource of force, which he terms *imperium*, and the power to employ the government's material resources of wealth or property, which he terms *dominium* ('Legal Analysis of Economic Policy' (1982) 9 *Journal of Law and Society* 191). The use of coercion by government requires express legal authority, to be found in a body of 'imperium-law' which consists almost entirely of statutes and delegated legislation, but includes some remaining prerogative powers. The use by the government of its dominium must be covered by parliamentary authorization of expenditure – the annual Appropriation Act or specific legislation. Daintith includes in 'dominium-law', 'those legal devices of the common law, such as contracts, gifts and other transfers, through which the wealth of government may be deployed' (op. cit., p. 215).

When the government requires an extension of its coercive powers, primary legislation by Parliament will be necessary unless statutory authority already exists for recourse to delegated legislation, or unless the exceptional power to legislate under the prerogative is available. Again, if the government needs to make provision for expenditure on a continuing basis, for which annual parliamentary appropriation is considered constitutionally insufficient, it is obliged to resort to parliamentary legislation.

Imperium-law and dominium-law invest the government with a host of executive powers by which policies are carried out in detail. Such powers generally include some (often considerable) degree of discretion as to the way in which they are exercised.

The exercise of governmental power in modern conditions frequently necessitates an informal, administrative rule-making which is a kind of self-regulation by the government. This 'quasi-legislation' does not (indeed cannot) effect alterations in statute or common law but, as we shall see, it can affect private interests and may have legal consequences.

In some instances the government seeks to achieve its objects by the use of guidance – a hybrid technique which sometimes includes an element of legal authority and sometimes depends simply on the government's persuasive power.

Increasingly in modern times the government implements policies by making agreements – which may or may not have the binding force of contract – with other organizations.

All the powers of government are subject to constraints. Some of these are inherent in the specific powers themselves: for example, the power to legislate depends on parliamentary consent, and the exercise of discretionary powers under statute or common law is subject to legal limits supervised by the courts. Other constraints stem from the European context in which British governments must function (chapter 5 above). Then there are the countervailing powers possessed in various measure by opposition parties, organized groups, local authorities, multi-national corporations and international organizations. At times these forces of limitation may be so powerful, especially in combination, that the government is impotent. Or again the government may be driven to use one form of power instead of another, to request or bargain rather than to command. Some goals are in any event beyond the capacity of government to achieve, whatever the outpouring of laws, guidance or admonition.

But this is not to say that government in the United Kingdom is feeble and constricted. We have a central executive which is unconfined by a written constitution or a federal structure and unchecked by the balancing arrangements of a separation of powers. It has established a firm ascendancy over the House of Commons and can dominate local government. In what the Memorandum of Dissent to the Kilbrandon Report described as 'the largest and most centralised unitary state in Western Europe' (Cmnd 5460-1/1973, para. 34), the government has at its disposal great and far-reaching powers for putting its policies into effect.

(b) **Parliamentary legislation**

For many of its purposes the government needs to obtain an Act of Parliament. In particular, an Act is necessary for implementing government policies that require changes in the law, the imposition of charges on the public, or the assumption of new legal powers.

Putting aside the Consolidated Fund and Appropriation Acts (which formally authorize expenditure), the annual Finance Act (for the raising of taxes) and Acts to consolidate existing legislation, public Acts can be categorized as 'policy' or 'administration' Acts, as proposed by the authors of the following passage.

Ivor Burton and Gavin Drewry, *Legislation and Public Policy* (1981), pp. 36–40

Policy bills are intended to change public policy. They may do this by making alterations in the civil or the criminal law, by establishing rights to benefits or obligations to pay charges, by setting up new official agencies charged with a duty to provide services for the public or by imposing such a duty upon existing agencies, by bringing undertakings under public ownership, by making constitutional changes (including changes in the structure of the Commonwealth), or by a combination of such means. Policy bills usually result from extensive discussions with interested parties and may follow the report of a royal commission or departmental committee of enquiry. There may have been extensive research – official, semi-official or private – and considerable party political activity, perhaps reflected in conference resolutions and, ultimately, in a commitment in an election manifesto. The government's proposals are likely to have been preceded by a white paper or by a more flexible consultative document. In all probability, therefore, the bill will presage the final stages of a protracted public debate, the description 'public' referring here to the active involvement of specialised and informed groups rather than to the diffuse manifestations of a Rousseauvian general will.

By contrast, administration bills are designed to effect changes in the law that are needed to *maintain* existing public policies. Such a need will arise when, for example, borrowing limits placed upon nationalised industries become out of date through inflation, when defects are discovered in the drafting of the original legislation or are invented by the courts, when eventualities arise that were not foreseen by the original draftsmen, when legislation passed in another area of public policy has unintended consequences for the policy enshrined in the original legislation, when existing machinery proves cumbersome or inefficient, when existing provisions need to be brought into line with changed social facts or administrative structures, or generally when existing legislation needs to be brought up to date. Administration bills can be regarded as providing running repairs to the machinery that has been established for securing policy objectives but without any intention of altering those objectives. . . . [I]n the final analysis, much of the explanation for the incidence of administration bills lies, quite simply, in the unpredictability of life and the fallible foresight of policy makers.

The categories just described are of course ideal types and not every bill is readily classed as either policy or administration. In the first place, governments sometimes abuse the legislative process by tacking clauses onto a bill that are out of character with the main purpose of the bill or even tying two quite different measures together into one bill. To describe these practices as abuses is justified by the fact that they make it impossible for parliament properly to consider the bill in principle, which they are expected to do at second reading, when they must accept or reject the bill as a whole, something that may be quite impossible when it comprises two distinct elements, one supporting existing policy and the other changing it. The existence of a small handful of such bills, motivated by a desire to save parliamentary time and often originating either in circumstances whereby a bill prepared by the department for one government is after a general election modified to make it acceptable to a new government, or where a department, having secured cabinet approval for the inclusion of an item in a crowded timetable, tries to get two acts for the price of one, does not affect the validity of the distinction between policy and administration bills (or in these cases parts of bills). . . .

The second difficulty arises from the problem of defining a self-contained area of public policy. For example, of these three policy areas, social policy, social security policy and one-parent-family policy, is the first the only true self-contained area, with the last two merely sub-areas, or administrative supports for the basic policy of maintaining a welfare state? Common sense rejects this view and would regard all three as areas of public policy while regarding, say, the rule that requires co-habitees to be treated as husbands when women claim social security benefit, as a matter of departmental policy, albeit elevated from time to time to a high level of political controversy. There are therefore various levels of comprehensiveness in policy making, even excluding the very top level where the issues become matters of unchallengeable principle – including possibly the establishment and preservation of a welfare state. In practice, the confusion is not as bad as might be expected and the number of levels at which policy comes before parliament proves to be basically two. The first is where the area is identical with that of a major government department or, in the case of a giant department, that of a major responsibility of that department. Bills dealing with policy at this level resemble very closely the ideal type of policy bill. The second level is where the policy area represents an aspect of a major policy area, for example the provision of free milk within the state education system. Bills at this level may be regarded, like administration bills, as being designed to reinforce the major policy but unlike administration bills they do it by innovating, for however restricted the area with which it is concerned, a bill is not a policy bill unless it seeks to change public policy.

Minor policy bills, the name proposed for measures which are concerned only with an aspect of an area of public policy which otherwise they leave unchanged, amount to about a quarter of all policy bills. They have the same structure as a policy bill but are obviously less complex and are not likely to be preceded by much public debate beyond consultation with an interested group.

Administration bills similarly fall into two different types according to whether they deal only with the correction of anomalies discovered in the original drafting or resulting from subsequent developments or from the effects of inflation upon financial constraints, or whether instead they are designed to effect a substantial reorganisation of the administrative machinery and procedures that support a policy, which might include an extension of administrative provisions to meet new developments. It is the first type of bill designed only to correct anomalies that constitutes the ideal type of administration bill. What we shall call administrative reform bills make up about a quarter of the total and being less straightforward demand more consideration from parliament. . . .

The relationship between the four species of policy and administration bills now identified . . . can be further explained by considering what may happen when a particular public policy is not working. If it is basically sound but is failing in some particular, then if this failure is due to some anomaly in existing provisions, the remedy is an administration bill. If it is due to some defect in the policy, then the remedy is a minor policy bill. If, however, the policy is generally failing to work properly then the remedy is either comprehensive reorganisation of the administrative machinery through an administrative reform bill or, if the cause of the failure lies in the fact that the basic policy is defective, then a new policy is required through the medium of a policy bill.

Of course these are ideal situations and in practice the circumstances set out above overlap.

No distinction is made in parliamentary procedures between 'administration' and 'policy' bills although, as Gavin Drewry remarks, the former bills should in principle be dealt with more quickly, whereas 'all too often a great deal of time is taken reopening long settled issues of principle: the bulk of legislative scrutiny should be directed at policy bills, but this does not always happen' (S. A. Walkland and Michael Ryle (eds.), *The Commons Today*, rev. edn 1981, p. 112).

From the government's point of view Parliament is part of the machinery by which its policies are implemented. The approving and legitimizing function of Parliament dominates the perspective not only of the government front bench but also, in general, that of backbenchers on the government side. The improvement of a bill as an instrument of the government's policy is part of this function, and is carried out chiefly on the initiative of the government itself. Opposition members may cooperate in the work of improvement of an uncontroversial bill, but if they oppose a bill will fight for concessions or – wholly rejecting the policy on which a bill is based – will set to work to defeat, weaken or delay it if they can. In short government and opposition act, with respect to many bills, upon different conceptions of the parliamentary function. But Parliament as an institution normally acts in accordance with the government's conception of its role, which is to support, perfect and enact the government's bills. For this reason it is commonly said that parliamentary legislation is in reality a function of government.

When a government bill is introduced in Parliament it has usually already been firmly shaped in a process of consultation in which Parliament will not ordinarily have participated. The House receives, as John P. Mackintosh observes, 'what is, to all intents and purposes, a finished product' (*The Government and Politics of Britain*, 5th edn 1982, pp. 144–5). The bill's passage through Parliament is generally assured by the government's disciplined majority, its control of the parliamentary timetable, and its command of procedural techniques such as the closure and the guillotine.

J. A. G. Griffith, 'The Place of Parliament in the Legislative
Process' (1951) 14 *MLR* 279 at 286–8

The Legislative Process Today

The legislative process embraces the whole train of events which take place from the
conceiving of a measure to its final enactment by the King in Parliament. A proposal for
legislation springs from some real or supposed defect in the existing statutory or
common law or in the administration of the State. While this description covers all
forms of legislation we are here concerned solely with those proposals which become
public Bills put forward on behalf of the Government. . . . The original suggestion may
come from one of a number of sources. It may be a part of declared Government policy;
it may be departmental policy; it may be advanced by a group to which the
Government is linked and on whom it depends for support; it may be the result of a
Royal Commission or of an *ad hoc* committee. Whatever its source . . . the general
principles which lie behind it are likely to have been debated at considerable length
before the first clause is drafted. If it is a matter of governmental policy, the idea has
probably been thrashed out by every type of important and unimportant member of the
political party for many years; it will have been the subject of articles and papers, of
conferences and public meetings. The proposal may well take the form of an amending
Bill; if so, the practical shortcomings of its predecessor will form the basis of
examination. Almost certainly some organisation will, for some time, have been
pressing on the department concerned the urgency and desirability of the measure. A
department which decides to press for legislation on a particular subject must persuade
the Cabinet that it is desirable. Having done so, the department must obtain a place in
the legislative programme of the Cabinet. Later, the Cabinet will examine the final
draft of the Bill and further alterations may be made. For all these purposes the Cabinet
normally operates through committees. . . . The composition of these committees
varies according to the subject-matter of the Bill (as to which departments other than
the sponsoring department will attend) and according to the stage which the
negotiations have reached (thus the Chief Whip will always be present when the
legislative programme is being discussed and the draftsman will be present when an
actual draft is under consideration). These negotiations will start many months before
the beginning of the session in which, it is hoped, the Bill will be introduced. . . .

The drafting of the Bill commences after policy approval and a place in the legislative
programme have been obtained. The division of the department will normally give full
details to the legal officers of the department who will then instruct Parliamentary
Counsel. The next stage does not seem to have altered since Ilbert wrote in 1901: 'The
first crude sketch will be gradually elaborated. There will be daily conferences with the
Minister or with the permanent head of the department, or with both. There will be
interviews and correspondence with experts in various branches of the subject with
which the measure deals. Notes will have to be written tracing the history of previous
legislation or attempts at legislation, and explaining the reasons for and effect of the
several proposals embodied in the draft Bill, and stating the arguments which may be
advanced for and against them, and these will soon grow into a formidable literature of
commentaries.' [*Legislative Methods and Forms*, 1901, p. 228.] Nor will consultation and
discussion be confined to those employed in an official or advisory capacity by the
department. The opinions, arguments and view-points of those who are to be directly
affected by the measure will no doubt have already been made known to the

department. And now, while the Bill is being drafted these affected persons are likely to be drawn into consultation once more. Probably the amount of detailed information on the nature of the departmental proposal which is given to such persons is not great; but particular points are raised and reactions ascertained. The more matters of dispute which can be settled outside Parliament the better for the department and the more speedy the passage of those parts of the Bill particularly in Committee.

'Those who are familiar with Parliamentary procedure', writes Ilbert, 'are well aware of the difficulties with which the promoter of any important measure has necessarily to contend. The measure may have gone through a long period of gestation before its introduction to Parliament. Information and opinions on different points will have been confidentially obtained from various quarters; the provisions of the measure will have assumed many varying forms; and the alternatives will have been carefully discussed and compared. Yet, in spite of all these precautions, as soon as the measure has been printed and circulated, swarms of amendments will begin to settle down on the notice paper, like clouds of mosquitoes.' [id., p. 230.] The procedure in Parliament which follows is so well-known that no detailed comment is called for. It is worth noting, however, that the opposition to the Bill in Parliament both in principle and on points of detail is to a large extent inspired by those sections of the community who, as affected interests, will already have had some opportunity of making their opinions known. Discussion and consideration at Westminster are not confined to the recognised stages of a Bill. Often the informal meetings are more important. These are of two kinds: those which take place within each Parliamentary party and those which take place between the parties. Of the first kind, are the regular meetings of the leaders of the parties with their Parliamentary members in the House of Commons. In these private meetings, matters of policy and detail are discussed at length and amendments to be urged (in the case of the Opposition) or made (in the case of the Government) are agreed. This is part of the planning stage for the Parliamentary battle and gives an opportunity for the opinions of backbenchers to be heard once again. The second kind comprises all the negotiations on a Bill which take place 'through the usual channels' or 'behind the Speaker's chair'. In the House of Lords in particular, informal negotiations between parties may involve discussion on the merits of different parts of the Bill. Short of this, the negotiations will do much to settle the course of the battle in the Chamber and in Committee. The whole of the Bill may not be discussed in detail due to the shortage of time and the use of the kangaroo and the guillotine procedures. But eventually, on receiving the threefold assent, the Bill becomes law.

The government's legislative programme is managed by the Cabinet through its committee structure, under arrangements which have varied with different administrations. In the present Government it appears that one committee is responsible for the programme of future legislation and the contents of the Queen's speech, while another, the Legislation Committee, is responsible for the implementation of the programme in the current session. (See Miers and Page, op cit. below, pp. 27–8.)

David R. Miers and Alan C. Page, *Legislation* (1982), pp. 28–9

The task of shaping the programme usually begins during the previous session. This is so firstly because all legislative proposals must be considered and approved by the appropriate policy committee of Cabinet before a Minister can seek a place in the programme, and secondly because it takes time to agree the content of the programme, to prepare and issue instructions to the draftsman, and to draft and approve Bills. These tasks have to be performed in the context of the allocation of all the other government and non-government business which occupies the parliamentary time-table. In a normal parliamentary session there are about 160 working days for this business. Just under half of that is taken up with government legislation; the other half is taken up with such items as the debate on the Address in reply to the Queen's Speech, debates on government expenditure and executive actions, private Members' time, question time, debates on the adjournment and so on.

All attempts to devise criteria for determining what Bills shall be included in the programme begin by making an allocation for annual financial legislation; principally the Finance Bill which incorporates the Budget proposals and requires about 20 days to complete its stages – the single largest allocation – and the Consolidated Fund and Consolidated Fund (Appropriation) Bills. There remain fifty-sixty working days to be allocated between major government commitments (representing its manifesto and campaign promises) and departmental interests. As room will usually be found for the former (though this may lead to congestion and unusually long sessions such as in 1967 and 1979–1980), the allocation of the rest of the programme is devoted to departmental proposals promoted by Ministers in competition with one another. In an attempt to reduce this element of competition, the Home Affairs Committee [a Cabinet committee formerly responsible for the legislative programme] devised a classification for the purposes of its recommendations to Cabinet. After annual Bills, this basically distinguished between urgent or essential Bills representing major government policies and useful Bills representing departmental proposals of no great political importance. This classification was adopted by the Future Legislation Committee, but . . . the programme is as likely to be determined by arguments based on political expediency as anything else.

By whatever means the appropriate committee employs, a list of Bills is prepared in order of priority having regard to dates when instructions to the draftsman can be ready, the time the drafting will take, and to the Chief Whip's estimate of the approximate dates on which the Bills must be introduced to pass through their parliamentary stages. This list is then presented to the Cabinet for formal approval; this occurs in a normal session during the Easter recess. Once approved, the main features of the programme are incorporated into the Queen's Speech for the opening of the new session.

Most bills, and in particular those of substantial political importance, are introduced in the House of Commons. (Bills whose main purpose is financial cannot begin in the House of Lords.) The first reading of a bill is purely formal. The second reading provides the government with an opportunity to explain the aims and principles of the bill and to outline its main provisions. This is also an opportunity for opposition parties to deliver their challenge to the policy of the bill. It is extremely rare for a government bill to be defeated on the motion for second reading. The only instance since 1924 was the defeat by one vote of the Reduction of Redundancy Rebates Bill in 1977.

For the committee stage in the House of Commons most bills are referred to a standing committee, where the government will normally have a majority. Among the members is a government Whip, with responsibility for ensuring the attendance and support of government backbenchers on the committee. From the government's point of view the committee stage provides it with an opportunity of making improvements to its bill. J. A. G. Griffith observes (*Parliamentary Scrutiny of Government Bills*, 1974, p. 38):

> If moved by the Government, the purpose of an amendment is most likely to be to correct a drafting error or to make minor consequential changes, to record agreements made with outside bodies which were uncompleted when the bill was introduced, to introduce new matter, or occasionally to meet a criticism made by a Member either during the second reading debate or at an earlier part of the committee stage, or informally.

A minority government, or one with a slender majority, may have difficulty in managing the proceedings of standing committees and, like the Labour Government of 1974–9, may be unable to avoid numerous defeats there. If it resorts to taking the committee stage on the floor of the House, this may hold up other items of its legislative programme.

The report stage of a bill gives the government an opportunity to reverse defeats suffered in committee, and also to introduce new amendments embodying promised concessions or the results of its further reflections on the bill. The third reading is taken without debate unless six members table an amendment or motion.

The subsequent passage of the bill through the House of Lords enables the government to continue the process of refinement of the bill in response to arguments and pressures brought to bear on it. Here too amendments may be carried against the government, and the difficulty that can be occasioned by the Upper House to the legislative programme of a Labour Government, in particular, is far from negligible. In the last resort, however, the government can overcome the resistance of the House of Lords by invoking the Parliament Acts 1911 and 1949.

The procedure for the enactment of a public bill is not without its hazards for the government. Even if it has a sufficient majority to overwhelm opposition parties they may by exploiting the procedures of Parliament cause trouble for the government in its efforts to get a bill enacted, intact and on time. The government's own backbenchers cannot always be coerced by the Whips, and in recent years numbers of them have shown a robust willingness to vote in the Opposition Lobby. Minority governments are especially vulnerable, as was shown in the 1976–7 session when a minority Labour Government failed to secure the passage of eight of its bills.

But in ordinary circumstances the obstacles of the parliamentary process can be overcome. Governments have normally enjoyed the support of mainly loyal majorities in the House of Commons; opposition parties are usually open to bargaining, and if persistently obstructive can be curbed by use of the closure or the guillotine. In a full session the government can generally achieve the passage of between 50 and 70 bills, substantially or entirely in the form in which they are wanted. In urgent cases a public bill can be passed in a few days or even hours: for example the Northern Ireland Bill 1972, retrospectively validating certain ultra vires actions of the armed forces, was presented to the House of Commons at 7 p.m. on 23 February 1972, and had been passed by both Houses and given the royal assent by 2.10 the next morning.

Governments must govern, and they have a proper interest in getting their bills enacted. Procedural innovations have often been designed to protect this interest rather than to improve the effectiveness of parliamentary scrutiny. There is, indeed, a tension between these aims, and its balanced resolution should be the constant concern of parliamentary reformers. For example, there are arguments of efficiency for the timetabling of all public bills and for 'framework' bills restricted to broad principles, the substance to be supplied by subordinate legislation; but there is a risk that changes of this kind would weaken opposition and further diminish the role of Parliament. (See *First Report from the Select Committee on Procedure*, vol. 1, HC 588–1 of 1977–8, paras. 2.29–2.37.)

Legislative effectiveness

The need for Parliament's consent is not the only limitation of the government's power to realize its objectives by legislation. Public or group consent is another limiting factor (one that is related to the *legitimacy* of the government and its measures – see above), in so far as the efficacy of an Act may depend on the cooperation or acquiescence of those affected by it. The Industrial Relations Act 1971 failed to accomplish its main purposes when it encountered intense opposition from the trade union movement and only limited and equivocal support among employers. (See Michael Moran, *The Politics of Industrial Relations*, 1977, ch. 8.)

Richard Rose, *The Problem of Party Government* (1974), p. 385

In some policies both legislative and co-operative elements are important. For example, an Act of Parliament can authorize subsidies to industries expanding in depressed regions. Success requires that firms will respond by altering their investment decisions to take up the subsidies authorized by Act of Parliament.

In the British system of government, the party in office usually can expect that any proposal it puts to Parliament will become law. The test of the legislative element in a policy is simple: does the government of the day wish to realize its intentions and are they draftable, that is capable of expression in a form suitable for an Act of Parliament? By contrast, the co-operative elements of policy cannot be realized by legislation alone; co-operation results from complex negotiations, in which participants outside Whitehall are free to agree or disagree with the government's intentions. The test of a co-operative policy thus becomes: Is it agreeable, that is acceptable, to organizations taking decisions independently of Parliament? The co-operative elements of any policy involve many more contingencies than the legislative elements. When policies involve both legislative and co-operative elements the government can be certain of realizing its legislative intentions, but it cannot be certain of the response of those whose co-operation it needs for success.

The courts recognize Acts of Parliament as the highest law, to which unqualified obedience is due. But 'Parliament, under our constitution, is sovereign only in respect of what it expresses by the words used in the legislation it has passed' (*per* Lord Diplock in *Black-Clawson International Ltd* v. *Papierwerke Waldhof-Aschaffenburg A G* [1975] 1 All ER 810, 836). The courts in the exercise of their power of interpretation, aided by recourse to a fund of common law principles, may give to an Act a meaning and effect contrary to what the government had in view. A striking instance was the decision of the House of Lords in *Anisminic Ltd* v. *Foreign Compensation Commission* [1969] 2 AC 147. In this case a statutory provision that a determination by the Foreign Compensation Commission should 'not be called in question by any court of law' was held ineffective to prevent a court from setting aside a 'determination' that went beyond the legal powers of the Commission. As J. A. G. Griffith remarks, the decision 'shows how, on occasions, the courts will resist the strongest efforts of the Government to exclude them from reviewing executive discretion' (*The Politics of the Judiciary*, 1977, p. 123.)

There are many other circumstances which can frustrate the implement-ation of government policies even when these are clothed in the forms of sovereign legislation. Sometimes the techniques of control or enforcement adopted in the Act are inappropriate to the ends desired. One example is the failure of the attempt to deal by statute with speeches and publications that stir up racial antagonism. Conduct of this sort was made an offence, on certain conditions, by section 6 of the Race Relations Act 1965. In his *Report on the Red Lion Square Disorders of 15 June, 1974* (Cmnd 5919/1975, para. 125), Sir Leslie (now Lord) Scarman observed:

Section 6 of the Race Relations Act is merely an embarrassment to the police. Hedged about with restrictions (proof of intent, requirement of the Attorney-General's consent) it is useless to a policeman on the street.... The section needs radical amendment to make it an effective sanction, particularly, I think, in relation to its formulation of the intent to be proved before an offence can be established.

Section 6 was replaced by section 70 of the Race Relations Act 1976 (enacting a new section 5A of the Public Order Act 1936) which redefined the offence, deleting the requirement of an intent to stir up racial hatred. But a few years later the Commission for Racial Equality said that the new section had not proved very effective: there had been relatively few prosecutions although a large amount of very objectionable literature was circulating. Possible explanations were the lack of a power of arrest without warrant, constraints flowing from the requirement of the Attorney-General's consent to prosecutions, and the difficulty of proving that racial hatred was likely to be stirred up against a racial group. (See Memorandum by the Commission for Racial Equality to the Home Affairs Committee, HC 384–iv of 1979–80, paras. 21–8.)

Another example of failure of legislation to achieve its object is the Obscene Publications Act 1959 – at all events for a period of some 20 years after its enactment. In *R.* v. *Metropolitan Police Commissioner, ex p. Blackburn (No. 3)* [1973] QB 241, Lord Denning MR observed that the Act had 'misfired', and found the reason 'in the wording of the statute and in the way the courts have applied it' (p. 250). The Court of Appeal was of the opinion that the test of obscenity in the Act was unsatisfactory and had been too narrowly interpreted by the courts; penalties were inadequate; there was uncertainty as to the powers and duties of the police. (Another factor mentioned by the court was the relative lack of public concern about the enforcement of this branch of the criminal law.) More recent decisions of the courts have closed some of the avenues of defence to charges under the Obscene Publications Acts: see *R.* v. *Jordan* [1977] AC 699 and *Attorney-General's Reference (No. 3 of 1977)* [1978] 1 WLR 1123. (See further chapters 2 and 4 of the *Report of the Committee on Obscenity and Film Censorship*, Cmnd 7772/1979.)

Deficiencies in a statute are exacerbated if insufficient resources of money, administrative machinery, personnel or publicity are committed to its implementation.

The Supplementary Benefit Act 1966 (consolidated in the Supplementary Benefits Act 1976) was hampered by an outmoded legal structure and complexity of administration. A departmental review of 1978 found

voluminous instructions which cannot be fully assimilated or applied; a scheme too complex for claimants or staff to understand fully or operate with anything like the accuracy of the national insurance system; growing dissatisfaction among claimants and staff alike with the struggle to maintain an acceptable standard of service; problems of communication and take-up; allegations of secrecy and unfairness. . . . [*Social Assistance*, DHSS 1978, para. 1.10.]

The Social Security Act 1980 introduced reforms, but it has been said of new sets of regulations that some 'are difficult for lawyers to understand and almost all . . . are wholly incomprehensible to laymen' (A. I. Ogus and E. M. Barendt, *The Law of Social Security*, 2nd edn 1982, p. 454). It has been reported that in 1981 the sum of £760 million was unclaimed by persons entitled under the Act. (See Frank Field, *The Times*, 19 December 1983, p. 12.)

Despite these shortcomings the Supplementary Benefits Act has mitigated poverty and cannot be described as a failure. But an earlier major enactment, the Rent Act 1957, signally failed to achieve its objectives: see Malcolm Barnett, *The Politics of Legislation* (1969).

There is more that can be demanded of legislation than that it should effectively implement the government's policy. A requirement of principle was expressed as follows by Sir John Donaldson MR in *Merkur Island Shipping Corp.* v. *Laughton* [1983] 2AC 570, 594–5 (with particular reference to the Trade Union and Labour Relations Act 1974, the Trade Union and Labour Relations (Amendment) Act 1976, and the Employment Act 1980):

At the beginning of this judgment I said that whilst I had reached the conclusion that the law was tolerably clear, the same could not be said of the way in which it was expressed. The efficacy and maintenance of the rule of law, which is the foundation of any parliamentary democracy, has at least two pre-requisites. First, people must understand that it is in their interests, as well as in that of the community as a whole, that they should live their lives in accordance with the rules and all the rules. Second, they must know what those rules are. Both are equally important and it is the second aspect of the rule of law which has caused me concern in the present case. . . .

In industrial relations it is of vital importance that the worker on the shop floor, the shop steward, the local union official, the district officer and the equivalent levels in management should know what is and what is not 'offside'. And they must be able to find this out for themselves by reading plain and simple words of guidance. The judges of this court are all skilled lawyers of very considerable experience, yet it has taken us hours to ascertain what is and what is not 'offside', even with the assistance of highly experienced counsel. This cannot be right.

We have had to look at three Acts of Parliament, none intelligible without the other. We have had to consider section 17 of the Act of 1980, which adopts the 'flow' method of Parliamentary draftsmanship, without the benefit of a flow diagram. We have furthermore been faced with the additional complication that subsection (6) of section 17 contains definitions which distort the natural meaning of the words in the operative subsections. . . . But I do not criticise the draftsman. His instructions may well have left him no option. My plea is that Parliament, when legislating in respect of circumstances which directly affect the 'man or woman in the street' or the 'man or woman on the shop floor' should give as high a priority to clarity and simplicity of expression as to refinements of policy. Where possible, statutes, or complete parts of statutes, should not be amended but re-enacted in an amended form so that those concerned can read the rules in a single document. When formulating policy, ministers, of whatever political persuasion, should at all times be asking themselves and asking parliamentary counsel: 'Is this concept too refined to be capable of expression in basic English? If so, is there some way in which we can modify the policy so that it can be so expressed?' Having to ask such questions would no doubt be frustrating for ministers and the legislature generally, but in my judgment this is part of the price which has to be paid if the rule of law is to be maintained.

(See also the remarks of Lord Diplock in the House of Lords: [1983] 2 AC 570, 612.)

(c) **Delegated legislation**

Many Acts of Parliament confer power upon the administration to legislate for specified purposes. In formal constitutional terms Parliament as supreme lawgiver delegates a circumscribed portion of legislative competence to a subordinate minister of the Crown or other public authority. The reality is that the government, in drawing up a bill for enactment by Parliament, decides how much detailed regulation of the subject-matter to include in the bill itself, and what powers to keep in its own hands for carrying out the principles of the bill.

The delegation of legislative power by Parliament to the King or to *ad hoc* authorities occurred as long ago as Tudor times, but the expansion of governmental activity in the nineteenth and twentieth centuries brought about a great increase in delegated legislation. By the 1930s the number of departmental regulations issued annually was 15 or 20 times that of Acts passed by Parliament. This abundant production of law by agencies other than Parliament was viewed by some with an exaggerated alarm as a triumph of bureaucracy over the constitution (e.g. Lord Hewart, *The New Despotism*, 1929). Others, like Harold Laski (*Parliamentary Government in England*, 1938, p. 216), recognized that

It would be foolish for Parliament to waste its time legislating separately upon applications or extensions of general principles about which it has already legislated. To say, for example, that a poison is a substance declared to be such by the Home Office in consultation with the Pharmaceutical Society is, under proper safeguards, infinitely more sensible than for the Cabinet to ask Parliament for a separate statute on each occasion when it is desirable to restrict the sale of some chemical substance on the ground of its poisonous nature.

The government responded to criticism of the practice of delegated legislation (and of the vesting of judicial and quasi-judicial powers in ministers) by setting up the Committee on Ministers' Powers (Donoughmore Committee) which reported in 1932. (See pp. 39–40 above.) The Committee expressed its general conclusion on the subject of delegated powers in saying (Cmd 4060, pp. 4–5):

We do not agree with those critics who think that the practice is wholly bad. We see in it definite advantages, provided that the statutory powers are exercised and the statutory functions performed in the right way. But risks of abuse are incidental to it, and we believe that safeguards are required, if the country is to continue to enjoy the advantages of the practice without suffering from its inherent dangers.

The Committee added:

But in truth whether good or bad the development of the practice is inevitable.

It went on to give reasons why the delegation of legislative powers was necessary (pp. 51–2). The reasons were restated, as follows, in 1967.

> Sixth Report from the Select Committee on Procedure, HC 539
> of 1966–7, Appendix 8: Memorandum by Mr Speaker's
> Counsel, para. 6

The advantages and justifications of delegated legislation may be summarised as follows:-

(a) The normal justification is its value in relieving Parliament of the minor details of law making. The province of Parliament is to decide material questions affecting the public interest; and the more procedure and subordinate matters can be withdrawn from their cognizance the greater will be the time afforded for the consideration of more serious questions involved in legislation.
(b) Another advantage is *speed of action*. Action can be taken at once in a crisis without public notice which might prejudice the object of the exercise. For instance an increase in import duties would lose some of its effect if prior notice was given and importers were able to import large quantities of goods at the old lower rate of duty.
(c) Another advantage is in dealing with *technical* subjects. Ministers and Members of Parliament are not experts in the variety of subjects on which legislation is passed e.g. trade marks, patents, designs, diseases, poison, legal procedure and so on. The details of such technical legislation need the assistance of experts and can be regulated after a Bill passes into an Act by delegated legislation with greater care and minuteness and with better adaptation to local and other special circumstances than they can be in the passage of a Bill through Parliament.
(d) Another is that it enables the Department to deal with *unforeseen circumstances* that may arise during the introduction of large and complicated schemes of reform. It is not possible when drafting legislation on a new subject, to forecast every eventuality and it is very convenient to have power to adjust matters of detail by Statutory Instrument without of course going beyond the general principles laid down in the Bill.
(e) Another is that it provides *flexibility*. Circumstances change and it may be desirable to take power to deal quickly with changing circumstances rather than wait for an amending Bill. This is particularly convenient in regard to economic controls, for instance exchange control and hire purchase.
(f) Finally, there is the question of emergency; and in time of war it is essential to have wide powers of delegated legislation.

The complex activity of a modern industrial society necessitates a far-reaching governmental regulation in the interests of public safety, health and welfare. Much of this regulation is carried out by means of the numerous powers of delegated legislation committed to the executive. Although delegated legislation is an executive function, it is subject to a measure of parliamentary supervision and to a check of another sort in the processes of consultation with outside interests. (See further below.) A balanced modern view of delegated legislation is given in the following passage.

S. A. Walkland, *The Legislative Process in Great Britain* (1968), pp. 16–18

[A]lthough there have been many encomiums on the Public General Act as a legislative device, there has been a curious reluctance to recognize the legitimacy and permanence of Departmental legislation as the main twentieth-century vehicle of legislative regulation. Partly because the Public General Act was identified with the 'rule of law' (although much that has been done by its agency would not have met with

Dicey's approval), and, to the same extent, supported formal-legal concepts of the legislative sovereignty of Parliament, it has been regarded as the normal end-product of the legislative process, from which Ministerial legislation is a distinctly inferior, temporary derogation suspected, by right-wing lawyers, at least, of containing the seeds of the overthrow of responsible government in Britain. . . .

. . . [D]espite the rapid growth in the volume of subordinate legislation and its importance in the regulatory roles of government, official enquiries into the place of statutory powers to make regulations in the legislative process have never directly recognized their potential. Instead the investigations have been almost entirely negatively conceived, concerned mainly with confining the scope of the process and improving judicial and Parliamentary controls over it. This was particularly true of the 1932 Committee on Ministers' Powers, whose attempts at a formal and outdated analysis of governmental processes led it into semantic confusion, which together with its suspicious approach to the subject-matter of the enquiry, set the pattern for much subsequent discussion of delegated legislation. . . .

Much of the suspicion of delegated legislation is aroused by the fact that civil servants are intimately associated with its procedures, and that the opportunities for participation in the process by representative and politically responsible members of the House of Commons are necessarily limited. . . . It may be that the civil service, with its ability to evade immediate political responsibility, is unfitted to carry the sole weight of public policies which are matters of political dispute, or which are likely to bear very heavily on sections of the public. But charges of remoteness from some sections of public opinion and of inaccessibility must give way when the extent of consultation by the civil service with organized groups and its ability to have recourse to a vast network of advisory committees is taken into account.

As a result, whilst legislative procedure in Parliament has been relatively static for some time, the Departmental phase of the modern legislative process has seen considerable technical advances, which have had the result of introducing a marked degree of procedural flexibility and sensitivity into legislative rule-making by administrative agencies. Of these, the most widespread and influential procedure is the informal consultation with interests in the making of subordinate legislation.

Doubtless the greater flexibility of delegated legislation leads governments sometimes to obtain delegated powers when the subject-matter is of an importance that demands the fuller parliamentary scrutiny applied to primary legislation.

If the subject-matter of delegation is of a constitutional character or is otherwise of particular importance, the power to legislate may be conferred on the Queen in Council. Orders in Council are drawn up in the department principally concerned and are formally ratified by the Sovereign and a small group of ministers meeting as the Privy Council. Among many enabling Acts which make this kind of provision are the Emergency Powers Acts 1920 and 1964, which invest the government with a wide power to legislate by Order in Council, after the proclamation of an emergency, 'for securing the essentials of life to the community'. Under the present system of direct rule of Northern Ireland, Orders in Council made under the Northern Ireland Act 1974 are the normal mode of legislation for the province: these Orders in Council often have the same scope as Acts of Parliament applicable to the rest of the United Kingdom.

Orders in Council made under statutory authority are to be distinguished from *prerogative* Orders in Council (see below) which are a type of primary, not delegated, legislation.

Other statutes give powers to ministers of the Crown to legislate by means of instruments variously named as regulations, directives, rules, orders, etc.; we may refer to them generally as regulations. Law-making powers are also delegated to local authorities and to certain other public bodies (e.g. the British Airports Authority and the Nature Conservancy Council) but our present concern is with powers conferred on ministers of the Crown. These powers are the means to a comprehensive ministerial regulation (within the statutory framework) of many public services and other activities, including the National Health Service, social security, industrial training, town and country planning, merchant shipping, health and safety at work, road traffic, and so on.

Statutory instruments

The legislative powers delegated to ministers or to the Queen in Council are exercised, for the most part, in the form of statutory instruments, which are defined in the following terms by section 1 of the Statutory Instruments Act 1946:

1(1) Where by this Act or any Act passed after the commencemnet of this Act [on 1 January 1948] power to make, confirm or approve orders, rules, regulations or other subordinate legislation is conferred on His Majesty in Council or on any Minister of the Crown then, if the power is expressed –

(*a*) in the case of a power conferred on His Majesty, to be exercisable by Order in Council;

(*b*) in the case of a power conferred on a Minister of the Crown, to be exercisable by statutory instrument,

any document by which that power is exercised shall be known as a 'statutory instrument' and the provisions of this Act shall apply thereto accordingly.

(2) Where by any Act passed before the commencement of this Act power to make statutory rules within the meaning of the Rules Publication Act 1893, was conferred on any rule-making authority within the meaning of that Act, any document by which that power is exercised after the commencement of this Act shall, save as is otherwise provided by regulations made under this Act, be known as a 'statutory instrument' and the provisions of this Act shall apply thereto accordingly.

The regulations referred to in section 1(2) are the Statutory Instruments Regulations 1947 (SI 1948 No. 1).

In broad terms the effect of the section is as follows:

By section 1(1) an instrument made under a post-1947 Act is a statutory instrument either if it is an Order in Council or if it is made by a minister of the

Crown and the empowering Act expressly provides that the power is to be exercised by statutory instrument.

Section 1(2) deals with instruments made under pre-1948 Acts. All such instruments made by ministers or by Her Majesty in Council are statutory instruments unless excepted by the Statutory Instruments Regulations: instruments so excepted are those having an executive and not a legislative character.

Statutory instruments are subject to the provisions of the Statutory Instruments Act relating to publication and the procedure for laying before Parliament. (See below.)

The exercise by the government of powers of delegated legislation may be subject to certain conditions.

Consultation. In the first place some enabling Acts oblige the minister concerned to consult organized interests or other bodies before making regulations. The particular organizations to be consulted may be specified by the Act, or may be left to the judgement of the minister in accordance with some general formula. A typical example of the latter kind occurs in the Medicines Act 1968. The Act empowers the Health and Agriculture Ministers to make regulations and orders for certain purposes, and section 129(6) provides:

Before making any regulations under this Act and before making any order under this Act . . . the Ministers proposing to make the regulations or order shall consult such organisations as appear to them to be representative of interests likely to be substantially affected by the regulations or order.

(Does a provision of this kind give the Minister an unfettered discretion as to the organizations to be consulted? See the *Aylesbury Mushrooms* case below.) In April 1980, before making an order under this Act, the departments concerned acted upon section 129(6) by sending 'consultation letters' inviting comments from 56 organizations. (See HC Deb. vol. 984, cols. *155–9*w, 7 May 1980.)

Some enabling Acts combine a general formula with a direction to consult named organizations. Section 9(3) of the Public Health Act 1961 provides:

Before making any building regulations, the Minister shall consult the Building Regulations Advisory Committee and such other bodies as appear to him to be representative of the interests concerned.

A statutory duty of consultation was in issue in the following case.

Agricultural, Horticultural and Forestry Industry Training Board
v. *Aylesbury Mushrooms Ltd* [1972] 1 WLR 190 (Donaldson J)

The Industrial Training Act 1964 authorized the Minister of Labour to make Orders setting up industrial training boards which would arrange for the training of employees in the industries concerned. The expenses of a board would be met by a levy imposed on employers in the industry, subject to exceptions specified in the Order. Section 1(4) of the Act required the minister, before making an Order, to consult 'any organisation or association of organisations appearing to him to be representative of substantial numbers of employers engaging in the activities concerned'.

The Ministry was minded to set up the plaintiff board, and after preliminary consultations with the National Farmers' Union, the largest representative body concerned, with 150,000 members, a draft order was prepared. Copies of a draft schedule, defining the industry to which the Order would relate, were sent to the National Farmers' Union and afterwards, on 26 April, 1966, to many other organizations, among them the Mushroom Growers' Association, inviting their comments. The Mushroom Growers' Association was an autonomous, specialist branch of the National Farmers' Union with 180 full members, representing about 85 per cent of all mushroom growers in England and Wales. The Association never received the draft schedule sent to it and had no knowledge of the consultations between the Ministry and the National Farmers' Union. It was also unaware of a press notice issued by the Ministry inviting interested organizations to apply for copies of the schedule.

Some time after the Order had been made and come into force, the Mushroom Growers' Association became aware of its existence and applied to be excluded from its operation. The Board then brought proceedings to determine whether the Order applied to mushroom growers; Aylesbury Mushrooms Ltd were the nominal defendants, representing the membership of the Association.

DONALDSON J: . . . Both parties are agreed that under the terms of section 1(4) of the Act, some consultation by the Minister is mandatory and that in the absence of any particular consultation which is so required, the persons who should have been but were not consulted are not bound by the Order, although the Order remains effective in relation to all others who were in fact consulted or whom there was no need to consult. Both parties are further agreed that if consultation with the Mushroom Growers' Association was mandatory and there was no or no sufficient consultation the Order takes effect according to its terms subject to a rider that it does not apply to the growing of mushrooms or to persons engaged in this activity. . . .

Both parties are also agreed that the organisations required to be consulted are those which appear to the Minister, or to his alter ego who in this case was a Mr Devey, to be representative of substantial numbers of employers engaging in the activities concerned. . . . Thus whether any particular organisation has to be consulted depends upon a subjective test, subject always to bona fides and reasonableness which are not in question.

Against this background Mr Bradburn, for the association, submits that the court must see what organisations appeared to the Minister to fall into the specified categories, and that the Minister clearly sought to consult the Mushroom Growers' Association thereby showing that he regarded it as being within the class of organisation which had to be consulted. It follows, as he submits, that neither the board nor the Minister can now turn round and say that consultation with the National

Farmers' Union constituted a sufficient discharge of his duties. Mr Bradburn goes on to submit that there can be no consultation without at least unilateral communication and that no such communication occurred.

Mr Gettleson for the board submitted that 'any' in the phrase 'the Minister shall consult any organisation' imposed a duty to consult not more than one organisation, that posting the letter of April 26, 1966, constituted consultation with the Mushroom Growers' Association despite the fact that it was never received, that the Mushroom Growers' Association was not an organisation which had to be consulted and that consultation with the National Farmers' Union involved consultation with all its branches including the Mushroom Growers' Association.

I have no doubt that Mr Gettleson's first point is without foundation. 'Any' must mean 'every' in the context of section 1(4). There is a little more to be said for his submission that the mere sending of the letter of April 26, 1966, constituted consultation in that the Shorter Oxford English Dictionary gives as one definition of the verb 'to consult' 'to ask advice of, seek counsel from; to have recourse to for instruction or professional advice'. However, in truth the mere sending of a letter constitutes but an attempt to consult and this does not suffice. The essence of consultation is the communication of a genuine invitation, extended with a receptive mind, to give advice: see *per* Bucknill LJ approving a dictum of Morris J in *Rollo* v. *Minister of Town and Country Planning* [1948] 1 All ER 13, 17. If the invitation is once received, it matters not that it is not accepted and no advice is proffered. . . . But without communication and the consequent opportunity of responding, there can be no consultation.

This leaves only the related questions of whether the Mushroom Growers' Association did in fact appear to the Minister to be an organisation falling within . . . section 1(4) with the consequence that he was under an obligation to consult them and whether in any event his consultations with the National Farmers' Union constituted consultation with the Mushroom Growers' Association as a branch of the NFU. This is the heart of the problem.

Mr Devey has deposed in paragraph 5 of his affidavit:

'In accordance with practice the circulation of the draft schedule was not restricted to organisations that appeared to me to be representative of substantial numbers of employers engaging in activities specified in the draft schedule. This will appear sufficiently from a perusal of the document. In particular the Mushroom Growers' Association was listed, although it was, and remains, a specialist branch of the National Farmers' Union. The listed address of the association is the same as that of the union which is Agriculture House, Knightsbridge, London, S.W.1.'

In each case he sent a covering letter in one of three forms. The addressees on the first list, such as the National Farmers' Union, the Trades Union Congress, the Confederation of British Industry, and major government departments received special letters from Mr Devey. Those on the second list received letters which were in standard form but were sent personally to named officials of the organisations concerned. These included the Local Government Examinations Board which clearly is an organisation which should have been consulted, but not one which in the terms of the Act had to be consulted. Those on the third list, including the Mushroom Growers' Association, received or should have received letters in standard form addressed to the organisation impersonally. I can find no clue in the form of the covering letter to whether any particular addressee appeared to the Minister to be a section 1(4) organisation and examples can be found in each list of organisations which plainly fall outside this category. I am thus thrown back on Mr Devey's affidavit coupled with a letter dated January 20, 1969, signed by a Mr Thomson of the Department of Employment and Productivity which states that a copy of the draft schedule was sent to the National Farmers' Union of which it is understood that the Mushroom Growers' Association is a specialist branch 'and also as a matter of courtesy to that association'. Bearing in mind the importance which attaches to consultation in the scheme of the Industrial Training Act 1964, which seems to be based upon the healthy principle of 'no taxation without consultation', and the fact that Mr Devey has not in terms said that the association did not appear to him to fall within the scope of section 1(4), I feel obliged to conclude that it was an organisation which had to be consulted, although its small membership in the context of the number of persons employed in agriculture, horticulture and forestry, and the specialised nature of their activities could well have led the Minister to take a different view.

This only leaves the question of whether it was consulted vicariously, and it may be accidentally, by means of the consultations with the National Farmers' Union. This is a nice point. Prima facie consultation with the parent body undoubtedly constitutes consultation with its constituent parts, but I think that this general rule is subject to an exception where, as here, the Minister has also attempted and intended direct consultation with a branch. The association's complaint has very little merit, because it seems to have been completely blind to all that was going on around it. Nevertheless it is important that statutory powers which involve taxation shall be strictly construed and, so construed, I consider that the association should have been consulted and was not consulted.

I therefore answer the questions in the originating summons as follows: 'Whether before making an order establishing a training board for the agricultural, horticultural and forestry industry, the Minister was under a duty to consult the Mushroom Growers' Association' – yes.

'Whether the consultations held by the Minister with the National Farmers' Union constituted a sufficient consultation with an organisation or association of organisations representative of those engaged in the activity of horticulture' – no.

'If it be held that the Minister was under a duty to consult the Mushroom Growers' Association, whether on the facts such consultation took place' – no.

'If it be held that the Minister was under a duty to consult the Mushroom Growers' Association and failed to do so, what effect such failure had upon the provisions of the Industrial Training (Agricultural, Horticultural and Forestry Board) Order 1966 (SI 1966 No. 969)' – the Order has no application to mushroom growers as such.

See the note on this case by David Foulkes, (1972) 35 *MLR* 647.

Donaldson J accepted that the 'subjective test' of the Minister's judgement determined whether a particular organization had to be consulted, 'subject always to bona fides and reasonableness'. How should a minister act on a provision like section 1(4) of the Industrial Training Act 1964 if he is to conform to these limits upon his discretion?

Is there any limitation at all upon the discretion of a minister who is empowered to make regulations 'after such consultations as he thinks proper' (cf. the Local Government Act 1972, s. 27(4))? See *R.* v. *Post Office, ex p.*

Association of Scientific, Technical and Managerial Staffs [1981] 1 All ER 139 at 141–2.

See generally Allan D. Jergesen, 'The Legal Requirements of Consultation' [1978] *PL* 290.

Even when no duty to consult is imposed by the enabling Act, it is the regular practice of government departments to consult affected interests before regulations are made. Consultation is often essential if the regulations are to be properly tailored to the objectives sought and if the support is to be won of interests whose cooperation is needed for them to work effectively. It was typical of departmental practice that before the making of the Public Health (Ships) (Amendment) Regulations 1978,

proposals were put to the Association of Sea and Airport Health Authorities, the Environmental Health Officers' Association, the General Council of British Shipping and interested Government Departments in December 1976. Draft regulations were circulated on the same basis in August 1977, and a final revision was circulated in January 1978. [HC Deb. vol. 958, col. 1613, 23 November 1978.]

However, ministers are under no legal duty to consult affected persons or organizations if the enabling Act imposes no such requirement: see *Bates* v. *Lord Hailsham* [1972] 1 WLR 1373.

Consideration of specified matters.   The enabling Act may direct the minister to 'have regard to' specified matters in making regulations. For example, section 1(3) of the Industrial Development Act 1982 provides that the Secretary of State, in exercising his powers to make orders specifying areas of Great Britain as 'development areas',

shall have regard to all the circumstances actual and expected, including the state of employment and unemployment, population changes, migration and the objectives of regional policies.

Even in the absence of an express requirement of this kind, there is an implied obligation to have regard to relevant factors, to be gathered from the provisions and objects of the Act, and to disregard irrelevant factors, in exercising a statutory power. Moreover the delegated power must be used for the purposes for which it was conferred by the Act, and not for unauthorized purposes. (See *Attorney-General for Canada* v. *Hallet & Carey Ltd* [1952] AC 427 and *Commissioners of Customs and Excise* v. *Cure & Deeley Ltd* [1962] 1 QB 340.) Failure to observe these conditions may result in the invalidity of the regulations.

Public inquiry.   Some enabling Acts require the minister, before making regulations, to publish his proposals and cause an inquiry to be held for the hearing of objections. The minister must consider the objections and the report of the person appointed to hold the inquiry before deciding whether to make the regulations (with or without modifications). This requirement applies, for example, to regulations made under section 31(5) of the Control of Pollution Act 1974 to prohibit or restrict activities likely to result in the pollution of waters. (See section 104(3).)

Sometimes an Act makes provision for objections to be considered without the holding of a public inquiry.

Publication. Section 2(1) of the Statutory Instruments Act 1946 provides for the publication of statutory instruments:

Immediately after the making of any statutory instrument, it shall be sent to the King's printer of Acts of Parliament and numbered in accordance with regulations made under this Act, and except in such cases as may be provided by any Act passed after the commencement of this Act or prescribed by regulations made under this Act, copies thereof shall as soon as possible be printed and sold by the King's printer of Acts of Parliament.

The Statutory Instruments Regulations 1947, SI 1948 No. 1, except certain instruments from the requirement of publication. For example, instruments classified as local by reason of their restricted application (and by analogy with local and personal or private Acts), those of which it is certified that their publication would be contrary to the public interest, temporary instruments, and bulky schedules to instruments, need not be published. Regulations that are not statutory instruments as defined by the 1946 Act escape the Act's requirements for publication. It may be too – the matter is not free from doubt – that sub-delegated legislation, authorized by an instrument itself made under delegated power (or by virtue of the prerogative), is not covered by the 1946 Act. (See P. P. Craig, *Administrative Law*, 1983, pp. 200–1.)

The requirement of publication of an instrument after it has been made is generally considered to be directory only and not mandatory, so that failure to publish does not invalidate the instrument: see *R.* v. *Sheer Metalcraft Ltd* [1954] 1 QB 586. (For discussion of this question see D. J. Lanham (1974) 37 *MLR* 510, [1983] *PL* 395, and A. I. L. Campbell [1982] *PL* 569.) Section 3(2) of the 1946 Act allows a qualified defence to a person charged with an offence against an instrument that has not been published in accordance with the Act.

Parliamentary procedure. When a government bill is being prepared which confers a power of delegated legislation, a decision has to be made on the appropriate form of parliamentary control.

For some instruments no parliamentary control is thought necessary and these are not required even to be laid before Parliament: they include, for example, commencement orders bringing Acts of Parliament into operation and orders prescribing forms. A few instruments have simply to be laid before Parliament so that members may be informed of them, without any further parliamentary procedure being prescribed. An example is section 2(4) of the Stock Transfer Act 1982 which provides that the power conferred by the Act upon the Treasury to make orders amending the Act's schedule of 'specified securities'

shall be exercisable by statutory instrument which shall be laid before Parliament after being made.

To comply with such a provision, copies of the instrument must be delivered to the Votes and Proceedings Office of the House of Commons and to the Office of the Clerk of the Parliaments in the House of Lords. (Instruments of a financial nature are laid before the Commons only.) Section 4(1) of the Statutory Instruments Act 1946 provides that statutory instruments required to be laid before Parliament after being made 'shall be so laid before the instrument comes into operation'. But in urgent cases an instrument may be brought into operation before being laid, if an explanation of the reasons is sent to the Lord Chancellor and the Speaker of the House of Commons. The government has given an undertaking to Parliament that there will normally be an interval of 21 days between the laying of an instrument and its coming into operation. (HC Deb. vol. 825, col. 649, 8 November 1971.)

Departments have sometimes accidentally neglected to lay an instrument before Parliament as required by the enabling Act, and have taken corrective action when the failure has come to light. The effect of such a failure upon the validity of the instrument has not been definitely determined. (See A. I. L. Campbell [1983] *PL* 43.)

Most statutory instruments have not only to be laid before Parliament but are subject to a further procedure for enabling Parliament to exercise a degree of control. In practice the choice between the available procedures is made by the department responsible for the enabling bill. A basic distinction can be made between 'affirmative' and 'negative' control procedures, although there are sub-varieties of each class. Under the affirmative procedure the instrument or a draft of it has to be approved by resolutions of both Houses (exceptionally of the Commons only). Under the negative procedure the instrument or a draft of it may be disapproved by a resolution, usually of either House. Examples follow of provisions for each kind of procedure.

The Airports Authority Act 1975 (as amended) empowers the Secretary of State to increase the British Airports Authority's borrowing limit by order. Section 5(4)(A) provides that the power to make such an order 'shall be exercisable by statutory instrument and no such order shall be made unless a draft of it has been approved by resolution of the House of Commons.

The Mineral Workings (Offshore Installations) Act 1971, section 7(8), provides:

Regulations made under this Act shall be contained in a statutory instrument subject to annulment in pursuance of a resolution of either House of Parliament.

To a great extent departments follow precedent in choosing between the affirmative and negative procedures or in providing only for the laying of an instrument before Parliament for its information, but there are no firm rules or criteria governing the matter. A Memorandum by the Civil Service Department in 1972 (*Report from the Joint Committee on Delegated Legislation*, HC 475 of 1971–2, Appendix 8) concluded that:

This is an area of legislation where criteria have not been considered desirable. Ministers and Parliament have instead preferred to maintain flexibility as to the choice of Parliamentary procedure, so that the procedure adopted has been determined by reference to the circumstances of each particular case, rather than by the application of a set of rules.

In practice the negative procedure is most often chosen. The affirmative procedure obliges the government to move for approval of the instrument and allow a debate (which can, however, be held in a standing committee, so saving government time on the floor of the House) and is generally reserved for instruments that raise issues of principle or are of some special importance. For example, the affirmative procedure is usually preferred for powers whose exercise will substantially qualify the operation of Acts of Parliament, powers to impose financial charges, and powers to create new offences of a serious nature.

The enabling Act may exceptionally incorporate a formula allowing the government to apply either the affirmative or the negative procedure in its discretion. The European Communities Act 1972, Schedule 2, para. 2(2), provides:

Any statutory instrument containing an Order in Council or regulations made in the exercise of a power so conferred [by this Act], if made without a draft having been approved by resolution of each House of Parliament, shall be subject to annulment in pursuance of a resolution of either House.

The legislative powers assumed by the government are sometimes very great, and the scrutiny and control applied by Parliament to their exercise is of a weak kind. (Parliamentary control of delegated legislation is more fully considered in chapter 7.) One kind of enabling provision, known as a 'Henry VIII clause', allows ministers to repeal or amend Acts of Parliament. The Donoughmore Committee recommended in 1932 that this kind of clause should be adopted only rarely, when it could be justified 'up to the hilt', and used for strictly limited purposes (Cmd 4060/1932, p. 61), but it still makes a not infrequent appearance in modern statutes. (Examples are the European Communities Act 1972, s.2(4) – see p. 275 above – and the Health and Safety at Work etc. Act 1974, s.15(3).)

(d) **Prerogative legislation**

The *Case of Proclamations* (1611) 12 Co. Rep. 74 established that the Crown has no power, by virtue of the prerogative, to alter the general law. Only in certain limited fields does the Crown retain a prerogative power to legislate, usually by Order in Council.

Prerogative Orders in Council can be used to regulate the civil service, so far as it is not governed by statutes. The principal Order is the Civil Service Order in Council 1982, which makes provision for certifying the qualifications of persons appointed to the civil service, and empowers the Minister for the Civil Service and the Treasury to make regulations relating to the conduct of the home civil service and the conditions of service of persons employed in it.

Another domain of the prerogative was referred to by Diplock LJ in *Post Office* v. *Estuary Radio Ltd* [1968] 2 QB 740, 753:

It still lies within the prerogative power of the Crown to extend its sovereignty and jurisdiction to areas of land or sea over which it has not previously claimed or exercised sovereignty or jurisdiction. For such extension the authority of Parliament is not required. The Queen's Courts, upon being informed by Order in Council or by the appropriate Minister or Law Officer of the Crown's claim to sovereignty or jurisdiction over any place, must give effect to it and are bound by it. . . .

See, e.g., the Territorial Waters Order in Council 1964 (SI 1965, p. 6452A) which establishes the base line from which the territorial sea adjacent to the United Kingdom is measured.

In the First World War prerogative Orders in Council were among the instruments of economic warfare. (See the Reprisals Orders in Council of 1915 and 1917: SR & O 1915, III, p. 107; SR & O 1917, pp. 951, 952.) When the Falklands conflict of 1982 necessitated the requisitioning of ships, the Government was able to invoke the prerogative of the Crown:

At the Court at Windsor Castle

THE 4TH DAY OF APRIL 1982

PRESENT,

THE QUEEN'S MOST EXCELLENT MAJESTY IN COUNCIL

Whereas it is expedient in view of the situation now existing in relation to the Falkland Islands that Her Majesty should be enabled to exercise in the most effectual manner the powers at law vested in Her for the defence of the realm including Her Majesty's dependent territories:

Now, therefore, Her Majesty is pleased, by and with the advice of Her Privy Council, to order, and it is hereby ordered, as follows:–

1. This Order may be cited as the Requisitioning of Ships Order 1982.

2. A Secretary of State or the Minister of Transport . . . or the Lords Commissioners of the Admiralty may requisition for Her Majesty's service any British ship and anything on board such ship wherever the ship may be.

3. [Power to delegate functions under Article 2.]

4. The owner of any ship or thing requisitioned under this Order shall receive such payment for the use thereof during its employment in Her Majesty's service and such compensation for loss or damage to the ship or thing occasioned by such employment as may be provided by any enactment relating to payment or compensation in respect of the exercise of powers conferred by this Order and, in the absence of such an enactment, such payment or compensation as may be agreed between a Secretary of

State [or the Minister or the Lords Commissioners] and the owner or, failing such agreement, as may be determined by arbitration.

5. In this Order:

'Secretary of State' means any of Her Majesty's Secretaries of State;

'Requisition' in relation to any ship or thing means take possession of the ship or thing or require the ship or thing to be placed at the disposal of the requisitioning authority;

'British ship' means a ship registered in the United Kingdom or any of the following countries –

(a) the Isle of Man;

(b) any of the Channel Islands;

(c) any colony;

(d) any country outside Her Majesty's dominions in which Her Majesty has jurisdiction in right of the Government of the United Kingdom.

The government can also legislate under the prerogative to amend the constitutions of a few remaining colonies (only those once conquered or ceded), to create new courts of common law (see *Re Lord Bishop of Natal* (1864) 3 Moo. PCC (NS) 115), and for a few other purposes.

(e) Executive powers

The government possesses a considerable number of executive powers – powers which do not extend to alteration of the law but may affect the rights or obligations of those with respect to whom they are exercised. (A distinction between legislative and executive powers cannot be very exactly made: see J. A. G. Griffith and H. Street, *Principles of Administrative Law*, 5th edn 1973, pp. 48, 60–66.)

Most executive powers of government derive from statute and are vested in particular ministers, the 'Secretary of State' (see p. 66 above), or (less often) in government departments.

When power is conferred upon a minister it does not necessarily follow that he must personally decide whether to exercise the power. In practice the decision is often taken by officials on the minister's behalf.

Carltona Ltd v. *Commissioners of Works* [1943] 2 All ER 560 (CA)

Under the Defence (General) Regulations 1939 the Commissioners of Works were authorized to requisition land if it appeared to them to be necessary to do so in the national interest. The powers of the Commissioners were by statute exercisable by the Minister of Works and Planning. An official of the Ministry of Works and Planning signed on behalf of the Commissioners of Works a notice to the owners of a factory stating that possession would be taken of the factory premises. The owners argued unsuccessfully that the requisition was invalid because the Minister had not personally directed his mind to the question.

LORD GREENE MR: . . . In the administration of government in this country the functions which are given to ministers (and constitutionally properly given to ministers because they are constitutionally responsible) are functions so multifarious that no minister could ever personally attend to them. To take the example of the present case no doubt there have been thousands of requisitions in this country by individual ministries. It cannot be supposed that this regulation meant that, in each case, the minister in person should direct his mind to the matter. The duties imposed upon ministers and the powers given to ministers are normally exercised under the authority of the ministers by responsible officials of the department. Public business could not be carried on if that were not the case. Constitutionally, the decision of such an official is, of course, the decision of the minister. The minister is responsible. It is he who must answer before Parliament for anything that his officials have done under his authority, and, if for an important matter he selected an official of such junior standing that he could not be expected competently to perform the work, the minister would have to answer for that in Parliament. The whole system of departmental organisation and administration is based on the view that ministers, being responsible to Parliament, will see that important duties are committed to experienced officials. If they do not do that, Parliament is the place where complaint must be made against them.

Acts properly done by departmental officials on the minister's behalf are in law considered to be the acts of the minister himself. (See also *In re Golden Chemical Products Ltd* [1976] Ch. 300.) It is possible, but not yet definitely settled, that certain powers affecting personal liberty, such as orders of deportation or for the return of fugitive offenders, must be exercised by the minister personally. (See S. A. de Smith, *Judicial Review of Administrative Action*, 4th edn 1980, pp. 307–9. See too the Immigration Act 1971, s.13(5).) Certain matters are reserved by departmental rules or practice for personal decision by the minister. (See, e.g., p. 327 below.)

The executive powers of government are of great variety. They include powers to allocate licences, authorize certain kinds of business, make appointments to public offices, approve by-laws of public bodies, make compulsory purchase orders, give directions, require information, and award contracts, loans and subsidies. Under various 'default' powers ministers may take over the functions of other public authorities. (See p. 211 above.)

Powers conferred upon ministers nearly always involve an element of discretion as to their exercise. The nature and limits of the discretion must be looked for in the empowering Act, which may qualify the minister's discretion in a number of ways. In particular it may appear that the minister (i) may exercise the power only if a certain state of affairs exists, or if he believes it to exist; (ii) must consult or receive representations from certain persons (or even obtain another's consent) before exercising the power; (iii) must have regard to specified factors in deciding whether, or how, to exercise the power; (iv) may exercise the power only for specified purposes. An example is section 7 of the Industrial Development Act 1982, which confers a discretionary power ('the Secretary of State may . . . ') qualified by a number of conditions which impose duties upon the Minister, while leaving considerable scope for his subjective judgement. The section reads as follows:

Selective financial assistance for industry in assisted areas

7. (1) For the purposes set out in the following provisions of this section the Secretary of State may, with the consent of the Treasury, provide financial assistance where, in his opinion –

> (a) the financial assistance is likely to provide, maintain or safeguard employment in any part of the assisted areas; and
> (b) the undertakings for which the assistance is provided are or will be wholly or mainly in the assisted areas.

(2) The purposes mentioned in subsection (1) above are –

> (a) to promote the development or modernisation of an industry;
> (b) to promote the efficiency of an industry;
> (c) to create, expand or sustain productive capacity in an industry, or in undertakings in an industry;
> (d) to promote the reconstruction, reorganisation or conversion of an industry or of undertakings in an industry;
> (e) to encourage the growth of, or the proper distribution of undertakings in, an industry;
> (f) to encourage arrangements for ensuring that any contraction of an industry proceeds in an orderly way.

(3) Subject to the following provisions of this section, financial assistance under this section may be given on any terms or conditions, and by any description of investment or lending or guarantee, or by making grants, and may, in particular, be –

> (a) investment by acquisition of loan or share capital in any company . . .
> (b) investment by the acquisition of any undertaking or of any assets,
> (c) a loan . . .
> (d) any form of insurance or guarantee to meet any contingency. . . .

(4) Financial assistance shall not be given under this section in the way described in subsection (3)(a) above unless the Secretary of State is satisfied that it cannot, or cannot appropriately, be so given in any other way; and the Secretary of State, in giving financial assistance in the way so described, shall not acquire any shares or stock in a company without the consent of that company.

(5) In this section 'industry', unless the context otherwise requires, includes any description of commercial activity, and references to an industry include references to any section of an industry.

(6) In this section 'the assisted areas' means the development areas, the intermediate areas and Northern Ireland.

A requirement to 'have regard to' specified factors (which we have already met in relation to delegated legislation) appears, for example, in section 11 of the Countryside Act 1968:

> In the exercise of their functions relating to land under any enactment every Minister, government department and public body shall have regard to the desirability of conserving the natural beauty and amenity of the countryside.

This is a rather weak kind of limitation upon a minister's power, for it leaves him free to have regard, and give greater weight, to other considerations in reaching a decision.

Often indeed a minister's power appears to be virtually unfettered, for example if he is authorized to act 'if it appears to him to be desirable in the public interest' that he should do so, or simply 'if he thinks fit'. But even in these cases the minister must exercise his discretion in accordance with the policy or objectives of the Act: see *Attorney-General for Canada* v. *Hallett & Carey Ltd* [1952] AC 427, 450; *Padfield* v. *Minister of Agriculture, Fisheries and Food* [1968] AC 997.

Prerogative powers

Some executive powers depend not on statute but on the prerogative. When the government – or the responsible minister – grants a royal pardon (through submission of advice to the Sovereign), terminates a prosecution by entering a *nolle prosequi*, or sends armed forces to quell a disturbance in a British city or a distant colony, it exercises the prerogative of the Crown. Foreign relations are conducted under the prerogative. In 1982 while negotiations were taking place for a settlement of the Falklands conflict, the Leader of the Opposition urged that 'the House of Commons has the right to make a judgment on this matter before any decision is taken by the government that would enlarge the conflict'. Refusing to accede to this demand, the Prime Minister said, 'it is an inherent jurisdiction of the government to negotiate and to reach decisions. Afterwards, the House of Commons can pass judgment on the government.' (HC Deb. vol. 23, cols. 597–8, 11 May 1982.)

It is disputed whether the prerogative covers all executive acts of the Crown that are not based on statute. Two classic definitions of the prerogative may be compared. Blackstone, in his *Commentaries on the Laws of England* (8th edn 1778, Book 1, ch.7, p. 239), wrote:

By the word prerogative we usually understand that special pre-eminence, which the king hath, over and above all other persons, and out of the ordinary course of the common law, in right of his regal dignity. It signifies, in its etymology, (from *prae* and *rogo*) something that is required or demanded before, or in preference to, all others. And hence it follows, that it must be in it's nature singular and eccentrical; that it can only be applied to those rights and capacities which the king enjoys alone, in contradistinction to others, and not to those which he enjoys in common with any of his subjects: for if once any one prerogative of the crown could be held in common with the subject, it would cease to be prerogative any longer. And therefore Finch [*Law*, 1627, p. 85] lays it down as a maxim, that the prerogative is that law in case of the king, which is law in no case of the subject.

This definition of the prerogative limits it to those common law powers that are possessed by the Sovereign alone. Dicey has a different definition in *The Law of the Constitution*, pp. 424–5:

The prerogative appears to be both historically and as a matter of actual fact nothing else than the residue of discretionary or arbitrary authority, which at any given time is legally left in the hands of the Crown . . . . From the time of the Norman Conquest down to the Revolution of 1688, the Crown possessed in reality many of the attributes of sovereignty. The prerogative is the name for the remaining portion of the Crown's original authority. . . . Every act which the executive government can lawfully do without the authority of the Act of Parliament is done in virtue of this prerogative.

Notwithstanding the initial references to 'authority' and 'sovereignty', the concluding words of this passage express a comprehensive view of the prerogative.

Blackstone's and Dicey's views have both received judicial and academic approval. It is therefore debatable whether the government can be said to exercise the prerogative of the Crown when, for example, it engages an employee or purchases goods or makes grants of money, these being acts that any other person may perform. Perhaps these are simply things that the Crown can do by virtue of its corporate capacity at common law – although in making payments of money it must act within the limits of parliamentary authorization of expenditure. It is also questionable whether the prerogative label should be attached to governmental acts that have no effect on the rights or duties of persons under English law, as when the government publishes official information, or issues a passport. But these actions too have been said to involve the prerogative: see *Jenkins* v. *Attorney-General*, *The Times*, 14 August 1971; *Secretary of State* v. *Lakdawalla* [1972] Imm. AR 26. (On the whole question see H. W. R. Wade, *Constitutional Fundamentals*, 1980, pp. 46–53.)

In using either prerogative or other common law powers, the government is free of the constraints of an enabling statute; neither is it fully subject to the supervisory jurisdiction of the courts. (See pp. 343–4 below.) The government may therefore prefer to take this course when it is open to it, rather than obtain statutory authority for its actions. But there is an important limitation upon the government's freedom to act in this way. If statutory powers already exist which cover the same ground as a prerogative power, the government is not free to choose between them, but must act under the statute.

Attorney-General v. *De Keyser's Royal Hotel Ltd* [1920] AC 508
(HL)

During the First World War the Government took possession of De Keyser's Royal Hotel in London for the accommodation of staff officers. Afterwards the owners of the hotel sued the Crown (by the procedure known as petition of right, which has since been superseded) for compensation for the use and occupation of the hotel. The main ground of their claim was that the hotel had been taken under the Defence Act 1842, which provided for compensation. The Government's reply was that the hotel had been occupied under the prerogative power to take property for the defence of the realm, which (it was contended) imported no duty to pay compensation. The House of Lords held that the Government could not lawfully act on the prerogative power when there was a statute which authorized it to take the property and prescribed the conditions on which that could be done. The taking could only be justified by the statute, and its provisions as to compensation must be observed. The reasoning of their Lordships is indicated by the following passages.

LORD ATKINSON: . . . It is quite obvious that it would be useless and meaningless for the Legislature to impose restrictions and limitations upon, and to attach conditions to, the exercise by the Crown of the powers conferred by a statute, if the Crown were free at its pleasure to disregard these provisions, and by virtue of its prerogative do the very thing the statutes empowered it to do. One cannot in the construction of a statute attribute to the Legislature (in the absence of compelling words) an intention so absurd. It was suggested that when a statute is passed empowering the Crown to do a certain thing which it might theretofore have done by virtue of its prerogative, the prerogative is merged in the statute. I confess I do not think the word 'merged' is happily chosen. I should prefer to say that when such a statute, expressing the will and intention of the King and of the three estates of the realm, is passed, it abridges the Royal Prerogative while it is in force to this extent: that the Crown can only do the particular thing under and in accordance with the statutory provisions, and that its prerogative power to do that thing is in abeyance. Whichever mode of expression be used, the result intended to be indicated is, I think, the same – namely, that after the statute has been passed, and while it is in force, the thing it empowers the Crown to do can thenceforth only be done by and under the statute, and subject to all the limitations, restrictions and conditions by it imposed, however unrestricted the Royal Prerogative may theretofore have been.

Lord Moulton, after discussing the legislation culminating in the Defence Act 1842, said:

What effect has this course of legislation upon the Royal Prerogative? I do not think that it can be said to have abrogated that prerogative in any way, but it has given to the Crown statutory powers which render the exercise of that prerogative unnecessary, because the statutory powers that have been conferred upon it are wider and more comprehensive than those of the prerogative itself. But it has done more than this. It has indicated unmistakably that it is the intention of the nation that the powers of the Crown in these respects should be exercised in the equitable manner set forth in the statute, so that the burden shall not fall on the individual, but shall be borne by the community.

   This being so, when powers covered by this statute are exercised by the Crown it must be presumed that they are so exercised under the statute, and therefore subject to the equitable provision for compensation which is to be found in it. There can be no excuse for reverting to prerogative powers simpliciter – if indeed they ever did exist in such a form as would cover the proposed acquisition, a matter which is far from clear in such a case as the present – when the Legislature has given to the Crown statutory powers which are wider even than anyone pretends that it possessed under the prerogative, and which cover all that can be necessary for the defence of the nation, and which are moreover accompanied by safeguards to the individual which are in agreement with the demands of justice.

Whether the prerogative power, had it been available to the government in this case, would have permitted the taking of property without compensation, did not fall to be decided. On this question see *Burmah Oil Co. Ltd* v. *Lord Advocate* [1965] AC 75 (p. 56 above).

It is a question of construction of the relevant statute whether it has displaced, in whole or in part, a pre-existing prerogative power. (See, e.g., *In re M. (An Infant)* [1961] Ch. 328.) Some statutes expressly *preserve* the prerogative: e.g. the Immigration Act 1971, s.33(5). It may be clear from the statute that a prerogative power is left in being, but be open to question how far its exercise is fettered by the statute. This was one of the questions in the following case.

Laker Airways Ltd v. *Department of Trade* [1977] QB 643 (CA)

In 1972 Laker Airways were given a licence by the Civil Aviation Authority (CAA) to operate their Skytrain air transport service from London to New York. In the following year the Government 'designated' Laker Airways for the London-New York route in terms of the Bermuda Agreement of 1946 between the United Kingdom and the United States: the United States authorities were then bound by the Agreement to grant Laker Airways an operating permit, giving landing rights in New York. Before the permit had been issued there was a change of government in the United Kingdom and a new civil aviation policy was announced, by which the state-owned airline, British Airways, was to be protected from competition on the London–New York route. The new Secretary of State for Trade accordingly took steps to have Laker Airways' licence revoked by the CAA, and also withdrew the designation of Laker Airways under the Bermuda Agreement. Both actions were challenged by the airline.

The Court of Appeal held that the Minister's attempt to get the licence revoked by issuing 'guidance' to the CAA under the Civil Aviation Act 1971 was ineffective, since the guidance was contrary to the policy of the Act itself, which was to encourage competition with the state-owned airline.

The Minister sought to justify the withdrawal of designation as an exercise of the prerogative which could not be examined in the courts.

LAWTON LJ: . . . The next problem to be considered is whether the Secretary of State by the exercise of the Crown's prerogative rights in the sphere of international relations can stop Laker Airways Ltd from doing what the Authority has licensed them to do, namely, to operate a scheduled route to the USA. He can only take a step towards this end by withdrawing their designation as carriers for the purposes of the Bermuda Agreement made between the United Kingdom and the USA in 1946. The act of withdrawing designation by itself has no effect in our municipal law. A licensee from whom designation has been withdrawn cannot be restrained from flying planes out of the United Kingdom and commits no criminal offence in doing so. If the USA government saw fit to disregard the withdrawal of designation the licensee could continue to operate the scheduled route. These are, however, theoretical possibilities. When the Secretary of State issued his 'guidance' Laker Airways Ltd were about to be given by the USA government permission to operate a scheduled route to that country. The permit had been sent to the President for his signature. When the Secretary of State's decision about Laker Airways Ltd became known the draft permit was withdrawn from the White House. They have no permit to operate in the USA and are not likely to get one if they are no longer British designated carriers. That which the Secretary of State could not lawfully do in the way he purported to do it, the Attorney-General submitted he could do through the prerogative powers and that when he had done so his act was not cognizable by the courts. Put in other words, the Attorney-General was submitting that a licence to operate a scheduled route, which had been granted under statute and after full inquiry by the Authority and which had been made effective internationally by designation, could be rendered useless by a decision of the Secretary of State made without the holder being given any opportunity of being heard or appealing to the courts. Now getting a licence takes time and is an expensive process. Once an applicant for a licence has been granted one and been designated a British carrier for the purpose of the Bermuda Agreement he is entitled to expect the USA government to grant a permit in that country without delay. The agreement says this should be so. When Laker Airways Ltd were in this position they spent large sums in getting ready to operate the scheduled route. The Secretary of State must have expected them to do so and knew they had. Yet, submitted the Attorney-General, the Secretary of State could still withdraw the designation.

The Attorney-General based his submission on the well known and well-founded proposition that the courts cannot take cognizance of Her Majesty's Government's conduct of international relations. Laker Airways' designation as a British carrier for the purpose of the Bermuda Agreement was an act done in the course of conducting international relations. The Civil Aviation Act 1971 did not apply. That Act nowhere refers to designated carriers. An airline might be granted a licence to operate a scheduled route but not become a designated carrier. It could not by any legal process compel the Secretary of State to designate it as a British carrier. It followed, submitted the Attorney-General, that the withdrawal of designation must be within the prerogative powers exercisable by the Secretary of State on behalf of the Crown. Although the Bermuda Agreement does not provide in terms for the withdrawal of designation, both high contracting parties to it must by necessary implication have power to do so. The agreement might not be effective if this were not so. For example, the Secretary of State might have designated as a British carrier an airline which had a licence to operate a scheduled route but which for reasons of its own decided not to do so. . . . The withdrawal of designation and the designating of another carrier would be the sensible course for the Secretary of State to take. The act of withdrawing designation must come within the prerogative powers exercisable by the Secretary of State on behalf of the Crown. The problem, however, is whether the power to withdraw the designation can be exercised when the carrier still has a licence to operate granted in accordance with statute. Should not such a licence first be revoked in the way provided by the Act and the regulations made under it? . . . . If the Authority revoked the licence, the Secretary of State could at once withdraw the designation; but if after full investigation the Authority was not satisfied that the reason for revocation put forward by the Secretary of State was a good one, why should he be allowed, by withdrawing the designation, to stop the licence holder from using a licence which the statutory body entrusted by Parliament to control the grant of licences had decided he should continue to have?

The Attorney-General's answer to that question was that the Secretary of State was empowered to act in this way because there was nothing in the Act of 1971 which curbed the prerogative rights of the Crown in the sphere of international relations. Far from curbing these powers, by section 19 (2) (*b*) Parliament recognised that the Crown had them. This is so; but the Secretary of State cannot use the Crown's powers in this sphere in such a way as to take away the rights of citizens: see *Walker* v. *Baird* [1892] AC 491. By withdrawing designation this is what in reality, if not in form, he is doing. A licence to operate a scheduled route is useless without designation. In my judgment the Act of 1971 was intended by Parliament to govern the rights and duties of British citizens in all aspects of civil aviation and to indicate what the Secretary of State could and should do. An applicant for a licence to operate a scheduled route has to satisfy the Authority that he is experienced and has the financial resources to do what he wants to do: see section 22(2). Even then the Authority in its discretion can refuse a licence: see section 22(4). Licences are hard to get; and, when granted, easy to lose if the attached conditions are not met: see section 23. The Act made provision for revocation by the Authority under section 23 and by the Secretary of State under section 4. These provisions regulate all aspects of the revocation of licences. By necessary implication, the Act, in my judgment, should be construed so as to prevent the Secretary of State from rendering licences useless by the withdrawal of designation when he could not procure the Authority to revoke them nor lawfully do so himself. . . .

[Lord Denning MR and Roskill LJ agreed that the power to withdraw designation had been unlawfully exercised.]

Was the power of designation (and its withdrawal) correctly regarded as a *prerogative* power? See p. 321 above. The issues raised by this controversial decision are analysed by H. W. R. Wade, *Constitutional Fundamentals* (1980), pp. 45–7, and Harlow and Rawlings, *Law and Administration*, pp. 52–9.

If a prerogative power is displaced or abridged by statute, it seems that the repeal of the statute does not revive the prerogative unless an intention to revive it appears from the repealing Act: see the Interpretation Act 1978, s.16(1)(*a*) and *R.* v. *Secretary of State for Foreign and Commonwealth Affairs, ex p. Council of Civil Service Unions* [1984] IRLR 309, 320–2, 358. If the prerogative in question embodied an essential power of government, a court would doubtless readily infer an intention that it should be revived. (See de Smith, *Constitutional and Administrative Law*, 4th edn 1981, pp. 139–40.)

(f) Quasi-legislation

Administrative authorities, in particular government departments acting in the name of ministers, frequently make rules, without statutory authority, which are intended to regulate the way in which statutory or other discretionary powers will be exercised. These are rules of administrative practice, not of law, and rule-making of this kind is commonly described as administrative quasi-legislation. (See R. E. Megarry, 'Administrative Quasi-Legislation' (1944) 60 *LQR* 125.)

Quasi-legislative rules are a means by which the administration injects specific policies into the exercise of its discretionary powers. The courts have recognized that administrative authorities are entitled to adopt policies or rules for their own guidance in exercising discretions conferred upon them. (See *British Oxygen Co. Ltd* v. *Board of Trade* [1971] AC 610.) Rules ensure consistent decisions which further the administration's objectives and, applied reasonably, make for public confidence in the integrity and fairness of official conduct. It is therefore unsurprising that much administrative activity is regulated by such self-imposed rules. They may be expressed as broad principles, standards or guidelines, or may prescribe in specific detail the terms upon which action will be taken. In speaking generally of 'rules' we should keep in mind that they may differ in this way. Let us look at some examples.

Naturalization

The Home Secretary, in deciding on an application for naturalization as a British citizen, has to be satisfied that the applicant fulfils certain requirements, among them that he is 'of good character': British Nationality Act 1981, s.6(1) and Sched.1. For the assessment of this element (which has existed in the law since 1844) a number of rules or criteria have been evolved, stated as follows in 1981.

> House of Commons Standing Committee F (British Nationality
> Bill), 19 March 1981, cols. 692–3

MR TIMOTHY RAISON (Minister of State, Home Office): Perhaps I might give some indication of how the good character requirement is currently interpreted. A person with a serious criminal record cannot be regarded as a person of good character. Equally, it is normal to refuse applicants with few or no convictions who are strongly suspected of being engaged in crime or are known associates of serious criminals. Sexual morality, however, is not normally taken into account, nor are, for instance, homosexual activities within the law. Scandalous sexual misbehaviour might, however, when combined with other personal characteristics, be a factor in a very few cases. Applicants are expected to meet their financial responsibilities. Financial irresponsibility, serious insolvency or bankruptcy invariably leads to refusal. But mere financial incompetence is not necessarily a bar, and neither is unemployment or receipt of social security benefits. Where a person is in debt but is making efforts to repay what he owes, it is usual to postpone a decision on his application for a year or two to give him time to put matters right. Commercial malpractices are taken seriously. They are usually calculated and sustained acts which reflect adversely on the applicant's general character.

Defects of temperament on their own are not normally held to bar an applicant on grounds of character. Heavy drinking, gambling or a disinclination to work are not in themselves sufficient to warrant refusal. There comes a point in a very few cases, however, where failings of this type become so pronounced, or notorious in the locality, that it would be unwise to grant naturalisation.

Honesty and integrity are essential elements in any definition of good character, and it follows, therefore, that applicants are required to be frank with the Home Office in the statements made on their application forms, which have to be declared before a magistrate or Commissioner for oaths. They must also tell the truth to the interviewing officer. False statements made to improve an applicant's chance of naturalisation obviously throw doubts on his fitness.

In a few cases, there are doubts about the nature of the applicant's loyalties to this country. These are not on security grounds but where, for instance, people clearly want citizenship for its convenience, particularly for the purpose of having a British passport.

Is a requirement of 'good character' best left to ministerial discretion, subject to self-imposed criteria, or would it be better if precise, objective rules were formulated in legislation?

Passports

The Home Secretary's discretionary power to grant and withdraw passports is wholly unregulated by law. In practice the withholding of passports is governed by rules formerly applied by the Foreign and Commonwealth Office. (See the JUSTICE Report on Passports, *Going Abroad* (1975).) The rules were stated as follows in 1982 (*Third Report from the Foreign Affairs Committee*, HC 406 of 1981–2, Memorandum by the Foreign and Commonwealth Office, p. 71, para. 20):

[R]efusal of passport facilities to United Kingdom nationals is confined to the following clearly defined categories:
  (a) Minors whose journey is known to be contrary to a Court Order; or to the wishes of a parent or other person or authority awarded custody or care and control; or to legislation regulating the employment of young persons abroad and the removal of children from the United Kingdom for adoption overseas.
  (b) Persons for whose arrest a warrant has been issued in the United Kingdom or persons who are wanted by the United Kingdom police on suspicion of a serious crime.
  (c) In very rare instances persons whose past or proposed activities are so demonstrably undesirable that the grant or continuation of passport facilities would be contrary to the public interest. Decisions in these cases are always taken personally by the Secretary of State.
  (d) United Kingdom nationals repatriated from abroad at public expense until they have repaid their debt.
Cases are decided on their individual merits and not everyone in these four categories is denied passport facilities.

The rules can be varied at any time, as occurred in 1968 when the Government decided to declare invalid all then existing Rhodesian passports, and to issue British passports to certain specified categories of Rhodesians. (See HC Deb. vol. 766, cols. 738–9, 17 June 1968.)

Interception of communications

The interception of postal and telephonic communications was for many years carried out without statutory authority under rules laid down by the Home Office. The rules were published for the first time in the *Report of a Committee of Privy Councillors* in 1957 (Birkett Report, Cmnd 283), whose recommendations led to the adoption of new rules, published in 1980 (*The Interception of Communications in Great Britain*, Cmnd 7873). It is questionable whether the rules were ever fully disclosed.

Following the judgment of the European Court of Human Rights against the United Kingdom in the *Malone* case (p. 52 above), the power of interception was put on a statutory footing by the Interception of Communications Act 1985.

Financial assistance

Government departments adopt policies, principles or guidelines for dealing with applications for discretionary financial assistance. Examples are the 'criteria for assistance to industry' under section 7 of the Industrial Development Act 1982 (which are notified to Parliament) and the Department of the Environment's guidelines for grant-aid under section 11 of the Local Government Act 1966 (towards expenditure related to immigrant communities).

Planning

Department of the Environment circulars to local planning authorities set out departmental policies for different kinds of proposed development, by which the department (and its inspectors) will be guided in the determination of planning appeals.

Quasi-legislative rules of these kinds may or may not be published. Some are kept secret within the administration; some are privately notified to bodies primarily concerned; others are publicly announced, with or without full details, in published circulars, government White Papers, departmental publications, or ministerial statements or answers in Parliament. Even the published rules are sometimes not easily accessible. Some rules, like those for the interception of communications, raise important issues of public concern; many others affect the interests of individuals or organizations. In general the question whether rules should be published, and in what detail, is something the government decides for itself. In 1971 the government agreed to 'bear in mind' the need for publicity when significant changes affecting the public were made in administrative rules, and in particular undertook that where a rule had been announced in Parliament, subsequent changes of significance would also be announced there. (*First Report from the Parliamentary Commissioner for*

Administration , Cmnd 4729/1971, para. 2.) Does this sufficiently dispose of the problem? Do you agree that, in principle, rules affecting private interests should be made known unless there are compelling reasons to the contrary? Could this objective be secured by law?

Exceptionally non-statutory rules are made subject to a parliamentary procedure. The Immigration Rules made by the Home Secretary are not expressly authorized by the Immigration Act 1971 but the Act assumes or acknowledges the fact that the Minister may make rules. Section 3(2) provides:

> The Secretary of State shall from time to time (and as soon as may be) lay before Parliament statements of the rules, or of any changes in the rules, laid down by him as to the practice to be followed in the administration of this Act for regulating the entry into and stay in the United Kingdom of persons required by this Act to have leave to enter, including any rules as to the period for which leave is to be given and the conditions to be attached in different circumstances. . . .
>
> If a statement laid before either House of Parliament under this subsection is disapproved by a resolution of that House passed within the period of forty days beginning with the date of laying (and exclusive of any period during which Parliament is dissolved or prorogued or during which both Houses are adjourned for more than four days), then the Secretary of State shall as soon as may be make such changes or further changes in the rules as appear to him to be required in the circumstances, so that the statement of those changes be laid before Parliament at latest by the end of the period of forty days beginning with the date of the resolution (but exclusive as aforesaid).

If disapproved by Parliament the rules do not cease to apply, but the Minister is obliged to make whatever changes in the rules he thinks necessary and lay a statement of the revised rules before Parliament.

The Immigration Rules are a peculiar amalgam of explanations of statutory provisions, information about administrative practice and procedures, and directions to be followed by officials in carrying out their duties. Their hybrid character has troubled the courts, which were at first disposed to regard them as delegated legislation: see *R.* v. *Chief Immigration Officer, Heathrow, ex p. Salamat Bibi* [1976] 1 WLR 979, 985 (*per* Roskill LJ). Subsequently the Court of Appeal in *R.* v. *Secretary of State for Home Affairs, ex. p. Hosenball* [1977] 1 WLR 766 took the view that they are not delegated legislation or rules of law in the strict sense but 'rules of practice laid down for the guidance of immigration officers and tribunals who are entrusted with the administration of the Act' (*per* Lord Denning at p. 780).

Rules of the kind we are considering cannot alter the law or abridge rights conferred by law. But such rules may supplement the law in allowing concessions to which there is no legal entitlement or in laying down the conditions on which discretionary benefits will be granted. A statement of the relevant legal rules will therefore often give an incomplete account of the circumstances in which claims are admitted by the administration. An example can be found in the practice of immigration control. When Pakistan withdrew from the Commonwealth in 1972 its citizens ceased to be 'Commonwealth citizens' under the law of the United Kingdom (Pakistan Act 1973). Nevertheless the Home Office adopted the rule that Pakistani 'overstayers' in the United Kingdom would normally be allowed, on similar conditions, the immunity from deportation extended to resident Commonwealth citizens by section 7(1) (b) of the Immigration Act 1971. (HC Deb. vol. 973, cols. 511–2w, 13 November 1979.) An example from another government department is provided by the set of rules adopted by the Inland Revenue in 1971 for the remission of arrears of tax when the arrears resulted from a failure of the department to act on information supplied by the taxpayer. (The rules were published in the Government's reply to a *Report from the Select Committee on the Parliamentary Commissioner for Administration*, Cmnd 4729/1971; subsequent amendments have been announced in Parliament by the Chancellor of the Exchequer.) For a third example reference may be made to the 'Crichel Down' rules for the disposal of surplus land by government departments (see pp. 77–8 above.) Under these rules a former landowner may have the 'right' to buy back the land from the government.

The government cannot lawfully apply a rule by which benefits of any kind are *withheld* from those who are legally entitled to them. However government departments do adopt and act upon their own interpretations of statutory provisions under which entitlements may arise, and these may be less favourable to claimants than other, perhaps equally tenable interpretations. Unless and until the government's view is successfully challenged in the courts, it will effectively determine the question of entitlement.

Non-statutory rules may have legal consequences in so far as they are taken into consideration by courts or tribunals in reaching decisions. In the case of the Immigration Rules, an adjudicator hearing an appeal under the Immigration Act 1971 is expressly directed (section 19(1)) to allow the appeal if he considers that a decision 'was not in accordance with the law or with any immigration rules applicable to the case'. But even in the absence of a provision of this sort a court may take account of non-statutory rules and can intervene if the administration disregards rules of its own making: see *R. v Criminal Injuries Compensation Board, ex p. Lain* [1967] 2 QB 864; *R. v. Chief Immigration Officer, Gatwick, ex p. Kharrazi* [1980] 1 WLR 1396; *R. v. Secretary of State for the Home Department, ex p. Khan, The Times*, 11 April 1984.

Is the practice of administrative quasi-legislation not open to abuse? How might it be brought under proper control? (See further P. P. Craig, *Administrative Law*, 1983, pp. 210–20.)

(g) Guidance

Guidance is a means by which the government seeks to influence the conduct of public authorities (such as local authorities, nationalized industries, health and water authorities, the police and magistrates), or of private individuals or organizations (such as employers or farmers). Non-departmental or fringe bodies are also sometimes authorized to issue guidance to their 'clients': for example, the Commission for Racial Equality is empowered by the Race Relations Act 1976, s.47, to issue codes of practice containing guidance for the elimination of racial discrimination and the promotion of equal opportunity in employment. (See also the Sex Discrimination Act 1975, s.56A.)

Guidance may be used in preference to coercive powers because it is believed that existing, perhaps long-established, practices are better modified through persuasion and cooperation than by a machinery of legal duties and sanctions. Guidance is also preferred when it is thought that the body concerned should have freedom to use its own discretion rather than be subject to governmental regulation in the performance of its tasks. This may be because it possesses an expertise which the government lacks, or because it is an elected body answerable primarily to its own electors rather than to the government, or for other reasons of principle or policy.

Guidance ranges from the formal, published and explicit to informal pressures, inducements and advice where 'much is likely to happen behind the scenes, in committees or even in private discussions' (Jean Blondel *et al.*, (1969–70) 5 *Government and Opposition* 67 at 71).

Some forms of guidance have a statutory basis. A statute may both empower a minister to give guidance to a public body and prescribe the duty of that body with respect to any guidance given. The strongest form of guidance gives rise to a duty to act in accordance with it. Such was the duty of the Civil Aviation Authority under section 3(2) (since repealed) of the Civil Aviation Act 1971, which provided that

the Secretary of State may from time to time, after consultation with the Authority, give guidance to the Authority in writing with respect to the performance of the functions conferred on it . . . and it shall be the duty of the Authority to perform those functions in such a manner as it considers is in accordance with the guidance for the time being given to it. . . .

In *Laker Airways Ltd* v. *Department of Trade* [1977] QB 643 (above), the Court of Appeal held that guidance given under this sub-section could not override the express provisions or the policy of the Act. Lord Denning MR said (pp. 699–700):

. . . the word 'guidance' in section 3 does not denote an order or command. It cannot be used so as to reverse or contradict the general objectives or provisions of the statute. It can only be used so as to explain, amplify or supplement them. So long as the 'guidance' given by the Secretary of State keeps within the due bounds of guidance, the Authority is under a duty to follow his guidance. Even so, the Authority is allowed some degree of flexibility. It is to perform its function 'in such a manner as it considers is in accordance with the guidance'. So, while it is obliged to follow the guidance, the manner of doing so is for the Authority itself.

Lawton LJ in the same case emphasized the difference in the meaning of the words 'guidance' and 'direction': 'The word "guidance" has the implication of leading, pointing the way, whereas "direction" even today echoes its Latin root of regere, to rule' (p. 725). Yet a power to give guidance that must be followed (even with a degree of discretion as to the mode of compliance) evidently approximates to a rule-making power. The distinction between 'guidance' and 'rules' (which may in reality be broad 'principles') is not always clear-cut.

A less stringent obligation is imposed by some statutes which require those to whom guidance is issued to 'have regard' to the guidance. The Housing (Homeless Persons) Act 1977 is an example. Section 12(1) provides:

In relation to homeless persons and persons threatened with homelessness a relevant authority shall have regard in the exercise of their functions to such guidance as may from time to time be given by the Secretary of State.

The Code of Guidance issued under this provision (*Housing (Homeless Persons) Act 1977 Code of Guidance* , 2nd edn 1983) urges local authorities 'to do their utmost to implement the Code'; but they are not legally bound to comply with it. (See *De Falco* v. *Crawley BC* [1980] QB 460, 478, 482; and cf. *R.* v. *Police Complaints Board, ex p. Madden* [1983] 1 WLR 447.) They are, however, obliged to take account of the Code and give fair consideration to its provisions before reaching a decision.

Another kind of legal effect is sometimes given by statute to forms of guidance or codes of practice. Section 3(1) of the Employment Act 1980 authorizes the Secretary of State to issue codes of practice 'containing such practical guidance as he thinks fit for the purpose of promoting the improvement of industrial relations'. Section 3(8) provides that:

in any proceedings before a court or industrial tribunal or the Central Arbitration Committee –
  (a) any such Code shall be admissible in evidence, and
  (b) any provision of the Code which appears to the court, tribunal or Committee to be relevant to any question arising in the proceedings shall be taken into account in determining that question.

(See also the Race Relations Act 1976, s.47(10), the Sex Discrimination Act 1975, s.56A (10) and the Police and Criminal Evidence Act 1984, s.67(11).)

It is common for statutes to provide that codes of guidance (especially if they have legal effects of the sorts mentioned above) shall be subject to parliamentary procedures similar to those applied to delegated legislation. For example, drafts of codes prepared under the Employment Act 1980 must be laid before Parliament and may be issued only after approval by both Houses (section 3(4)).

A great deal of ministerial guidance has, however, no statutory basis and is without any legislative element. It may nevertheless be effective in influencing

the conduct of those to whom it is directed, especially when it is based on clear constitutional understandings or if the means of compulsion are available in reserve.

Local authorities

Local authorities are the recipients of much guidance from central government. Conscious of their own powers and their democratic base, they do not always respond favourably to the government's attempts to influence them in the performance of their functions. But most circulars to local authorities contain guidance of a politically uncontroversial nature which is generally followed. They deal with such matters as the supply of teachers, conservation of old buildings, eviction of gipsies, disclosure of councillors' pecuniary interests, and so on.

Department of the Environment Circular 14/84 to Local Authorities etc.

Green Belts

1. The Government continues to attach great importance to Green Belts, which have a broad and positive planning role in checking the unrestricted sprawl of built-up areas, safeguarding the surrounding countryside from further encroachment, and assisting in urban regeneration. There must continue to be a general presumption against inappropriate development within Green Belts. The government reaffirms the objectives of Green Belt policy and the related development control policies set out in Ministry of Housing and Local Government Circular 42/55.

2. Structure plans have now been approved for most parts of the country and these identify the broad areas of the Green Belt. Detailed Green Belt boundaries are now being defined in local plans and in many cases these are based on Green Belt areas defined in earlier development plans approved prior to the introduction of structure and local plans. This process of local plan preparation is continuing and this circular includes advice on the definition of detailed Green Belt boundaries in local plans.

3. The essential characteristic of Green Belts is their permanence and their protection must be maintained as far as can be seen ahead. It follows from this that:

(a) Once the general extent of a Green Belt has been approved as part of the structure plan for an area it should be altered only in exceptional circumstances. If such an alteration is proposed the Secretary of State will wish to be satisfied that the authority has considered opportunities for development within the urban areas contained by and beyond the Green Belt. Similarly, detailed Green Belt boundaries defined in adopted local plans or earlier approved development plans should be altered only exceptionally.

(b) Where detailed Green Belt boundaries have not yet been defined in earlier approved development plans or in adopted local plans . . . it is necessary to establish boundaries that will endure. It is especially important that these boundaries of Green Belts should be carefully drawn so as not to include land which it is unnecessary to keep permanently open for the purpose of the Green Belt. Otherwise there is a risk that encroachment on the Green Belt may have to be allowed in order to accommodate future development. If Green Belt boundaries are drawn excessively tightly around existing built-up areas it may not be possible to maintain the degree of permanence that Green Belts should have. This would devalue the concept of the Green Belt and also reduce the value of local plans in making proper provision for necessary development in the future.

4. Since the protection of Green Belts must be maintained, planning authorities in defining detailed Green Belt boundaries in local plans will need to relate their proposals to a longer time scale than is normally adopted in plans for new development. While making provision for development in general conformity with the structure plan they should satisfy themselves that Green Belt boundaries will not need to be altered at the end of that period. In some cases this will mean safeguarding land between the urban area and the Green Belt which may be required to meet longer term development needs. The normal process of development control serves this purpose and authorities should state clearly in structure and local plans the policies that they intend to apply in those areas over the period covered by the plan.

5. It is particularly important that full use is made of opportunities for bringing back into use areas of neglected or derelict land and for recycling urban land, including obsolete industrial sites and buildings unlikely to be required in future for their original purpose. . . .

6. Well defined long-term Green Belt boundaries will help to ensure its future agricultural, recreational and amenity value, whereas less secure boundaries would make it more difficult for farmers and other land owners to maintain and improve their land. Local planning authorities can assist in this by working together with land owners and voluntary groups to enhance the countryside, and especially those areas of land within the Green Belt, or adjacent to it, which are suffering from disuse or neglect. This is particularly important in parts of the Green Belt that are close to existing urban development, or between urban areas within conurbations, and which can be especially vulnerable to neglect or damage. Such areas may form an important part of the Green Belt and, if so, need to be protected and maintained. But in considering whether to include such areas within the Green Belt, where detailed boundaries have not yet been established, authorities should also consider carefully whether the land could be better reserved for future development and thus ease the pressure on other land that should have the long-term protection of the Green Belt. . . . The overall aim should be to develop and maintain a positive approach to land-use management which *both* makes adequate provision for necessary development *and* ensures that the Green Belt serves its proper purpose. . . . [Crown copyright: reproduced with the permission of the Controller of HMSO.]

In 1979 the Government decided that the issue of circulars of guidance to local authorities on matters in which the Government had no statutory powers would in future be 'strictly limited' (*The Guardian*, 26 July 1979; see also HC Deb. vol. 9, col. 534w, 30 July 1981).

The police

The Home Secretary has no power to direct chief officers of police as to the performance of their duties, but the Home Office issues many *advisory* circulars to chief constables. An example is Home Office Circular 133/71 which gave guidance to the police on the use of the power to stop and search persons reasonably suspected of being in possession of controlled drugs (Misuse of Drugs Act 1971, s.23). The Circular recommended that modes of dress and hair style should not be regarded as reasonable grounds to stop and search. (See now Annex B to the proposed *code of practice for the exercise of powers of stop and search*.)

Jury vetting

Guidelines to regulate the practice of 'jury vetting', by which potential jurors were checked by reference to police records for 'undue bias or susceptibility to improper pressures', those found wanting being asked to 'stand by for the Crown', were issued by the Attorney-General in 1975 in circulars to chief constables and the staff of the Director of Public Prosecutions. The guidelines were not published until 1978, when the Attorney-General said that they were 'a means of controlling an administrative practice which is inappropriate for legislation' (HC Deb. vol. 959, col. 30w, 27 November 1978). In *R.* v. *Sheffield Crown Court, ex p. Brownlow* [1980] QB 530 at 542, 545–6, the view was expressed that the practice of jury vetting was unconstitutional; but in *R.* v. *Mason* [1981] QB 881 the Court of Appeal declared that it was not unlawful for the police to obtain and supply to prosecuting counsel information about previous convictions of potential jurors, even if these did not disqualify them from jury service. The circumstances in which jury vetting would be appropriate were more strictly defined in new guidelines issued in 1980. (See (1980) 130 *NLJ* 694.) It has been objected that the guidelines, which have no legal force, are academic since police and prosecution are not bound to observe them and have not always done so (Patricia Hewitt, *The Abuse of Power* (1982), p. 55). The question of the legality of jury vetting (and hence of the guidelines) was not wholly resolved by the decision in *R.* v. *Mason* (above), and there is a compelling case for

an intervention by Parliament which would either declare the practice of jury vetting to be unlawful or give it a clear statutory basis and define in precise terms the circumstances in which it could be resorted to in derogation of the provisions of the Juries Act 1974 relating to eligibility for jury service.

(Editorial (1980) 130 *NLJ* 449. See further Harriet Harman and John Griffith, *Justice Deserted*, NCCL 1979.)

When guidance fails to yield results the government may resort to legislation. A 1977 Circular asked local education authorities to provide parents with certain information about schools in their areas. The response was disappointing and the guidance was replaced by a statutory obligation: section 8 of the Education Act 1980 requires local education authorities to publish their arrangements for admission of pupils to maintained schools and such other information about schools in their areas as the Secretary of State may by regulations require. (See also pp. 227–8 above.)

Guidance, even when published, generally attracts less public attention than legislation, and there have doubtless been occasions when governments have hoped to escape criticism by using this less visible means of policy implementation.

There are limits to what can be lawfully achieved by guidance. The government cannot nullify a discretionary power which a public body has under statute by giving it guidance, and the public body cannot abdicate its discretion by treating the guidance as binding on it: see *R. v. Police Complaints Board, ex p. Madden* [1983] 1 WLR 447; *R. v. Worthing BC, ex p. Burch, The Times*, 22 November 1983. Again, the government's interpretations of the law expressed in advisory circulars have no legal authority. While a departmental interpretation may acquire 'vitality and strength' through being accepted and acted upon in practice (see *Coleshill and District Investment Co. Ltd v. Minister of Housing and Local Government* [1969] 2 All ER 525, 538, *per* Lord Wilberforce; Patrick McAuslan, *Land, Law and Planning*, 1975, pp. 92–3), a person whose interests are affected by the department's interpretation may seek a declaration from the courts that it is wrong in law.

> *Royal College of Nursing of the United Kingdom v. Department of Health and Social Security* [1981] AC 800 (CA and HL)

Section 1 of the Abortion Act 1967 provides that a person is not guilty of an offence of abortion when a pregnancy is terminated 'by a registered medical practitioner', if the treatment is carried out in a National Health Service hospital (or approved private clinic) after a certificate has been given by two doctors as to the necessity for the abortion.

The Department of Health and Social Security issued a Circular to health authorities and the medical and nursing professions stating its view that it was lawful for a nurse to administer the drug which induced labour and the termination of pregnancy, provided that a registered medical practitioner personally decided upon and initiated the process of induction (by inserting a catheter into the woman's body) and remained responsible for the subsequent treatment carried out by the nurse. The Circular said:

> [T]he Secretary of State is advised that the termination can properly be said to have been termination by the registered medical practitioner provided it is decided upon by him, initiated by him, and that he remains throughout responsible for its overall conduct and control in the sense that any actions needed to bring it to conclusion are done by appropriately skilled staff acting on his specific instructions but not necessarily in his presence.

The Royal College of Nursing, wishing to have the law clarified, brought proceedings for a declaration that the department's advice was wrong in law. Woolf J held that, although a nurse might play a large part in the procedure approved by the Circular, it was still treatment by a registered medical practitioner, and accordingly was lawful. The Court of Appeal reversed this decision, holding that in these circumstances the pregnancy was in fact terminated by the nurses. Lord Denning MR concluded his judgment by saying (pp. 806–7):

> If the Department of Health want the nurses to terminate a pregnancy, the Minister should go to Parliament and get the statute altered. He should ask them to amend it by adding the words 'or by a suitably qualified person in accordance with the written instructions of a registered medical practitioner'. I doubt whether Parliament would accept the amendment. It is too controversial. At any rate, that is the way to amend the law: and not by means of a departmental circular.

The House of Lords by a majority allowed an appeal by the Department and restored the ruling of Woolf J. The procedure approved by the Circular was held to be in conformity with the requirement of the Abortion Act, which was that a registered medical practioner should accept responsibility for all stages of the treatment. Parts of the treatment could properly be carried out, in accordance with established medical practice, by nursing staff under his instructions.

(See also *Gillick* v. *West Norfolk and Wisbech Area Health Authority* [1985] 1 All ER 533.)

(h) Contract

It is convenient for present purposes to use the term 'contract' to include both legally enforceable agreements (to which the government, like a private individual, may be a party), and agreements not intended to have legal consequences, and perhaps also lacking the element of 'bargain' or consideration necessary for a binding contract, which the government may make with either public bodies or private organizations. Contract in this enlarged sense provides another mechanism for the exercise of the powers of government, and one that is in some circumstances preferable from the government's point of view to legislation. Anthony Barker writes (in D. C. Hague *et al.* (eds.), *Public Policy and Private Interests*, 1975, p. 354):

> In advanced industrial nations, the official and legal systems increasingly interpenetrate with the economic and social systems. So, 'government' is expected to take some kind of 'responsibility' for almost everything that is wanted, or needed, or is thought to have gone wrong.
>
> This has created a vast public demand for 'government responsibility' of some kind in almost every significant walk of the nation's life: protecting the customer, defending the environment and regulating business relationships. Yet even the largest and most interventionist government machine cannot do everything itself. Because it controls the state and can make laws, the government obviously has the means of offering semi-official status to private groups and interests, who are willing and able to enter into a constructive relationship.

If the government wishes to see the adoption of new standards or practices in a trade or industry, it can sometimes achieve this by negotiating a scheme of self-regulation with the appropriate traders' or manufacturers' organization. A code of practice agreed to and supervised by the organization may bring about the desired result, when a legislative scheme would, perhaps, be controversial or difficult to administer.

Codes of practice have been negotiated by government departments with, among others, the Society of Motor Manufacturers and Traders (action on vehicle defects affecting safety), the Association of the British Pharmaceutical Industry (advertising practice), the Brewers' Society (tenancies and rents in the licensed trade), the electricity and gas industries (payment of bills and disconnection of supply), and the British Shooting Sports Council (control of firearms).

A well known instance of regulation by contract is the agreement of 1977, since renegotiated and renewed, between the Health Ministers and the tobacco industry, represented by the Tobacco Advisory Council and the Imported Tobacco Products Advisory Council, on tobacco advertising, tar yields, etc. The conference of medical Royal Colleges, among others, has called for legislative controls, but the Secretary of State for Social Services said in the House of Commons on 9 May 1980 (HC Deb. vol. 984, col. 783):

[I]t has been the view of successive Governments that they should seek to achieve their health objectives by voluntary agreement. . . . In other words, this is a field where our tradition of proceeding by persuasion and consent rather than legislation and compulsion has a great deal to commend it. It would be wrong to force sudden abrupt changes on an industry on which tens of thousands of families depend. So long as progress by agreement is possible, it would be wrong to introduce legislation, for instance on advertising, although no Government could rule that out for all time.

The main provisions of a new agreement were announced by the Minister on 27 October 1982 (HC Deb. vol. 29, cols. 437–8w). It covers such matters as the government health warning on cigarette packets and advertisements, reductions in expenditure on advertising, and the tar ceiling above which cigarette brands are not to be advertised. A separate agreement covers the tobacco industry's sponsorship of sport.

Provision for compensation of the victims of uninsured and untraced drivers is made by the terms of agreements of 1972 between the Secretary of State for the Environment and the Motor Insurers' Bureau. (The original agreement was made in 1946.) Lord Denning has described these agreements as being 'as important as any statute' (*Hardy* v. *Motor Insurers' Bureau* [1964] 2 QB 745, 757).

In some instances there is a statutory basis for the adoption of voluntary codes of practice: an important example is section 124(3) of the Fair Trading Act 1973 which requires the Director General of Fair Trading 'to encourage relevant associations to prepare, and to disseminate to their members, codes of practice for guidance in safeguarding and promoting the interests of consumers in the United Kingdom'. Codes have been issued to cover a variety of consumer goods and services. As the Director General of Fair Trading has observed, the codes 'are intended to *supplement* the requirements of the law by obtaining the agreement of trade associations on behalf of their members to raise their standards of trading' (Gordon Borrie, 'Laws and Codes for Consumers' [1980] *Journal of Business Law* 315 at 322). Here the relationship between the government and the trade associations is an 'arm's length' one, for the Director General, although an officer of the Crown, has an independent responsibility in carrying out his functions.

In the regulation of City institutions the government has often preferred persuasion to compulsion and has fostered the establishment of self-regulatory agencies such as the Panel on Take-overs and Mergers (set up in 1968), while exercising a degree of supervision through the Bank of England. (See L. C. B. Gower, *Review of Investor Protection*, HMSO 1980 and 1982.) The government's preference for 'contract' and self-regulation in dealing with City institutions was shown by events of July 1983. The Director General of Fair Trading had referred the rule book of the Stock Exchange to the Restrictive Practices Court, for a determination of its compatibility with the public interest. The Secretary of State for Trade and Industry intervened, and reached an agreement with the Council of the Stock Exchange. In return for the termination of the proceedings before the court and the exemption of the Stock Exchange from the restrictive trade practices legislation, the Council undertook to make certain changes in its structure and rules. (In particular, minimum scales of commission would be phased out.) The Government performed its side of the bargain by securing the passage of the Restrictive Trade Practices (Stock Exchange) Act 1984, which exempted rules and regulations of the Stock Exchange from the Restrictive Trade Practices Act 1976 and formally terminated the proceedings already begun in the Restrictive Practices Court. Arrangements were made for the Bank of England and the Government to monitor the implementation by the Stock Exchange of the changes to which it had agreed.

Agreed codes of practice and similar arrangements have certain advantages over governmental regulation. Besides relieving the government of administrative costs, they may be more effective in getting the cooperation of the individuals or firms concerned in applying the agreed code according to its spirit, whereas those bound by regulations may be more disposed to look for loopholes in them. Self-administered codes, it is said, are flexible in that they can be continually reviewed by those best informed about their effects and promptly updated as conditions change.

What might be the *disadvantages* of voluntary codes, as against statutory schemes of regulation?

The granting of financial aid by the government is sometimes linked to an agreement with the aided body on a programme of action to be adopted by it. An agreement of 1978 between the Government, the Port of London Authority (a public corporation) and trade unions provided for financial assistance by the Government in return for undertakings on manpower reductions and changes in working practices, and a commitment by the Authority not to proceed with closure of the Royal Docks. (See HC Deb. vol. 955, cols. *169–70*w, 31 July 1978.)

On a broader front, governments have resorted to contract in the attempt to implement incomes policies. The Labour Government's 'social contract' with the Trades Union Congress in 1974 secured, for some years, trade union cooperation on wages, in return for which the Government brought about the repeal of the Industrial Relations Act 1971 and the passage of legislation on job security and redundancy entitlements. In rejecting recourse to law for the control of wages, the Chancellor of the Exchequer (Mr Healey) said in 1978 (HC Deb. vol. 954, col. 1021, 21 July 1978):

I do not believe . . . that to attempt to control wages by law would be either feasible or desirable. It has been tried by previous Governments and in all cases the operation of the law against trade unions has proved ineffective and has been withdrawn. . . .

Secondly, I do not believe that it is possible to define a pay policy with the necessary strictness required to involve the law in its application and still have the degree of flexibility that is needed. . . .

Of an earlier wage restraint bargain between the Government and the two sides of industry in 1948, Samuel Beer has written (*Modern British Politics*, 3rd edn 1982, p. 205):

it achieved a regulation of an important aspect of the British economy that no . . . legislative instrument by itself could have done. Indeed, one may think of it as a kind of extra-governmental legislation.

Contract can of course only be used as a means of carrying out policies when there is willingness on the other side – even if a willingness induced by the threat of statutory coercion – to enter into bargains with the government. The 1974–9 Labour Government's scheme for planning agreements with industrial undertakings was intended as 'the framework within which the decision-taking of Government and management can be improved by sharing information about plans and objectives' (*Survey of Current Affairs*, September 1975, p. 356). But the scheme foundered because private sector firms were unwilling to cooperate.

Procurement and policy

Even when the government enters into ordinary commercial contracts for the procurement of goods or services, it can inject its policies into the contracting process. In awarding contracts and by imposing conditions on the supplying firms it can influence the structure or location of industry, the modernization of plant, employment practices, rates of pay, and other matters. The government's power to further its policies in this way seems great, for it is a massive purchaser from the private sector, and the prosperity of many firms depends on government contracts. (The central contracts organization of the Ministry of Defence alone places 30,000 to 40,000 new contracts each year, involving some 10,000 firms: see HC Deb. vol. 52, col. *81*w, 16 January 1984.) The government does indeed use its purchasing power in a way that will advance its social and economic policies, and has in the past applied 'buy British' policies, given preference to firms considered important to the economy, and imposed a 'fair wages' condition on all government contractors. (This last was based on a House of Commons resolution, which was rescinded in 1983.) But the extent to which these collateral aims can be pursued has always been limited, in particular by the Treasury's insistence on 'value for money' in contracting and the need to justify departures from this principle to the Public Accounts Committee of the House of Commons. Membership of the European Communities and of the General Agreement on Tariffs and Trade (GATT) has brought further constraints. Community rules require open competition and avoidance of national discrimination in the placing of public contracts, and the Agreement on Government Procurement, concluded in 1979 as an instrument of GATT, requires the government parties to refrain from preferential treatment for domestic suppliers and products.

The present policy of the government, coordinated by the Department of Trade and Industry, is that public sector bodies 'should use the influence their purchases give them to help develop the design, technology and competitiveness of their suppliers' (*Third Report from the Public Accounts Committee*, HC 29 of 1981–2, Appendix, p. 6). British suppliers are preferred, subject to their competitiveness and to the extent permitted by international obligations. The government applies a contracts preference scheme, of limited scope, for firms in development areas and in Northern Ireland. Government contracts incorporate a condition that requires the contractor to refrain from unlawful racial discrimination: an extension of the condition to oblige contractors to provide information about the employment of minorities has been considered, but not yet adopted. (See *Annual Report for 1981 of the Commission for Racial Equality*, HC 437 of 1981–2, p. 11). The chairman of the Commission for Racial Equality has urged the government to ensure that its contractors follow the Commission's code of practice for the elimination of discrimination in employment. (*The Times*, 4 July 1984.) In Northern Ireland, tenderers for government contracts must normally hold an equal opportunity certificate issued by the Fair Employment Agency, confirming that they have accepted the principle of equality of employment opportunity between the two religious communities. (See Christopher McCrudden, 'Law Enforcement by Regulatory Agency: the Case of Employment Discrimination in Northern Ireland' (1982) 45 *MLR* 617 at 631–3.)

Between 1975 and 1978 the Government used its contracting power in support of a 'counter-inflation' policy on wages. Contractors who paid wages higher than those approved by the Government were 'blacklisted' and denied the award of government contracts. A new contractual condition required the contractor to observe the Government's pay guidelines during the currency of the contract. These measures were strongly opposed by employers' organizations and were criticized as arbitrary and 'unconstitutional'. The Government's defence was that the pay policy and its extension to government contracts had been approved by resolutions of the House of Commons (although not given statutory authority), and that the Government was only exercising its proper discretion and freedom to buy, as any buyer might do. How persuasive are these justifications? (See further R. B. Ferguson and A. C. Page, 'Pay Restraint: The Legal Constraints' (1978) 127 *NLJ* 515; G. Ganz, 'Comment' [1978] *PL* 333; Terence Daintith, 'Regulation by Contract: The New Prerogative' (1979) 32 *CLP* 41, and p. 52 above.) The application of sanctions against firms breaking the pay guidelines was disapproved by a vote of the Commons on 13 December 1978 (HC Deb. vol. 960, cols. 799–810). The Government accepted this judgement and abandoned the practice.

(i) **Judicial review**

Most but not all of the powers of goverment are subject to judicial control. (On the principle of judicial review see p. 42 above.)

Statutory powers

Statutory powers, whether of an executive or legislative kind, that are conferred on ministers or other public authorities are controllable on the principle of ultra vires: any such power can only be exercised within the limits and for the purposes of the enabling Act. In applying this sort of control the courts insist that they are not asserting an independent overriding power but are acting in deference to Parliament and to implement its will. The remarks of Lord Greene in *Associated Provincial Picture Houses Ltd* v. *Wednesbury Corporation* [1948] 1 KB 223, 234, with reference to the power of the courts to review the actions of a local authority, have a general application and have been many times reaffirmed:

The power of the court to interfere in each case is not as an appellate authority to override a decision of the local authority, but as a judicial authority which is concerned, and concerned only, to see whether the local authority have contravened the law by acting in excess of the powers which Parliament has confined in them.

A court is evidently justified in intervening on the ultra vires principle if a public authority has misinterpreted a statute and has consequently assumed a power which it does not possess. In deciding what the statute permits, a court will interpret it against the background of the common law – for example, in *Raymond* v. *Honey* [1983] 1 AC 1 the House of Lords held that section 47 of the Prison Act 1952, empowering the Secretary of State to make rules for the regulation of prisons, was 'quite insufficient to authorize hindrance or interference with so basic a right' as that of access to the courts. But the courts go much further than this, for they have developed the doctrine of ultra vires so as to allow a far-reaching control of administrative action on the basis of judicial inferences as to what Parliament must have intended to require or disallow in the exercise of a statutory power. Moving forward on this wide front the courts have reviewed the acts of the administration on a variety of grounds, such as that a public authority must not have come to an erroneous conclusion on any question on which its jurisdiction, or power to act, depends; must take account of considerations relevant to its decision and disregard irrelevant considerations; must act for purposes which are consistent with the objects of the empowering statute; and must not act unreasonably – that is, in a way in which no reasonable authority would have acted.

The ultra vires principle and presumed parliamentary intent are also often invoked as justifying the application to administrative authorities of the rules of natural justice. (See pp. 66–7 above.) The obligations embraced in natural justice – to act fairly, hear representations and refrain from bias – are in any event further grounds of review applicable to a wide range of executive acts (but not to legislation or quasi-legislation).

The grounds of judicial review of administrative action have been summed up by Lord Diplock in *Council of Civil Service Unions* v. *Minister for the Civil Service* [1984] 3 All ER 935, 950–1, under the heads of 'illegality', 'irrationality' and 'procedural impropriety'; they do not extend to the *merits* of decisions – the questions of policy or of 'pure judgment' (*per* Lord Wilberforce in *Secretary of State for Education and Science v. Tameside MBC* [1977] AC 1014, 1047) that are committed by the statute to the administrative authority and not to the courts.

Non-statutory powers

In regard to the *prerogative*, it has in the past often been affirmed that while the courts can determine the existence and extent of any prerogative, they may not question or review the grounds on which, in a particular case, a prerogative power has been exercised. Judges have in a number of cases disclaimed competence to review particular prerogative acts, as when Lord Denning MR said in *Blackburn* v. *Attorney-General* [1971] 1 WLR 1037, 1040 that ministers in negotiating and signing a treaty 'exercise the prerogative of the Crown. Their action in so doing cannot be challenged or questioned in these courts.' (See also, e.g., *China Navigation Co. Ltd* v. *Attorney-General* [1932] 2 KB 197: disposition of the armed forces; and *Hanratty* v. *Lord Butler* (1971) 115 SJ 386: prerogative of pardon.) On the other hand there were indications in the case law that judicial review was not wholly excluded, as when Lord Devlin, in *Chandler* v. *Director of Public Prosecutions* [1964] AC 763, 810, equated prerogative with other discretionary powers, saying that the courts could intervene to correct 'excess or abuse'. In the seminal case of *R.* v. *Criminal Injuries Compensation Board, ex p. Lain* [1967] 2 QB 864, it was held by the

Divisional Court that the actions of a public body set up under the prerogative to make awards of compensation to victims of criminal offences could be the subject of judicial review.

The applicability of judicial review to prerogative powers has been authoritatively confirmed in *Council of Civil Service Unions* v. *Minister for the Civil Service* [1984] 3 All ER 935 (p. 159 above), in which the majority of the House of Lords held that the law has now reached the stage where the exercise of prerogative powers is open to judicial review on the same principles as are applied by the courts in reviewing an exercise of statutory power. The limitation of judicial review therefore no longer depends on the source of the power under challenge but on whether the subject-matter of the power, whatever its source, is 'justiciable', or amenable to the judicial process. Some prerogative powers, such as those relating to the making of treaties, the prerogative of mercy and the defence of the realm, may by this criterion still be beyond the scope of judicial review. The presence of considerations of national security may in any event – as in *Council of Civil Service Unions* v. *Minister for the Civil Service* itself – exclude review if there is evidence which satisfies the court that it was on this ground that a governmental decision was taken.

Other kinds of executive action, based neither on statute nor on the prerogative and not considered to be an exercise of powers under public law – as when the Government awards contracts, publishes information, issues (non-statutory) guidance, and so on – appear to be beyond the reach of judicial review, at all events to the extent that action of this kind does not infringe or frustrate any statutory provision. In cases of this sort it is probable that any remedy for an aggrieved person will have to be of a political kind.

PART III
The responsibility of Government

Introduction

Our constitutional system is one of 'responsible government'. The idea of responsibility is wide enough to include a number of values (no fewer than twelve are identified by Charles E. Gilbert, 'The Framework of Administrative Responsibility' (1959) 21 *The Journal of Politics* 373), but in the present context two are of particular importance. The first is indicated by A. H. Birch, *Representative and Responsible Government* (1964), pp. 17–18, in saying that 'the term "responsible" is commonly used to describe a system of government in which the administration is responsive to public demands and movements of public opinion'. The responsibility of government in this sense implies that it is responsive to (takes heed of, defers to) demands, pressure or influence exerted by the public, or on its behalf by institutions or organizations that have an acknowledged place in the constitutional system. We may take the correlative of 'responsiveness' to be 'control', so that a responsive government is one that submits to control by the public or by representative bodies. 'Control' is a central concept of constitutional thought and practice, and it needs some elucidation.

A dictionary definition of control gives as synonyms 'command', 'restraint' and 'a check', and it is evident that the word may be used in strong or weak senses. Even mere influence can be thought of as a relative power, or control in a weak sense, so that control extends in a series from a power of direction at one extreme to inducement or influence at the other. It is helpful for our purposes to retain the full range of meaning. If control were to be restricted to the power of directing the actions of subordinates, the usefulness of this term in describing the working of the constitution would be very limited, and in practice it is not so restricted. The weaker forms of control are of great importance in our system of government. Carl Friedrich has written that, apart from power, 'influence is probably the most important basic concept of political science' (*Constitutional Government and Politics*, 1937, pp. 16–17).

Control in whatever degree is exercised *a priori*, before the relevant action or decision is taken.

The second concept embodied in the idea of responsibility is that of accountability (or 'responsibility' in a narrow sense). Accountability implies obligations: in the first place, an obligation to *give account* – to answer, disclose, explain or justify – which has been called 'explanatory accountability' (Geoffrey Marshall in David Butler and A. H. Halsey (eds.), *Policy and Politics*, 1978, pp. 61–2). Next to it is 'amendatory accountability', the obligation to *account for* action or inaction – to 'answer for' whatever has been revealed of error or misgovernment, and correct or make due reparation for it. (It is this sense of accountability that is meant in phrases such as 'held accountable for', with its connotations of blame and penalty.) Amendatory accountability is evidently retrospective or *a posteriori*.

Like control, accountability (of either kind) may be strong or weak. There may be a strict legal liability to account, or a merely voluntary – and perhaps limited – acceptance of the obligations of accountability.

Accountability complements control. A fully responsible government is responsive, submitting to constitutional controls, and is subject to accountability in both the explanatory and the amendatory forms. In an ideal system the machinery of control prescribes or indicates limits, guidelines or policies for government; explanatory accountability provides a flow of information before, during and after the exercise of control; and amendatory accountability enables blame to be attached to government for its failures, and redress or amendment to be exacted.

To what extent is the ideal of responsible government realized in the constitution of the United Kingdom? Here we must ask, who exercises control over government? To whom is government accountable? We find that these questions lead us to a study of the relationship between government, on the one hand, and Parliament, the general public (or the electorate), political parties, and organized groups on the other.

As we consider the various institutions and structures through which control and accountability are made effective against the government, we need to be aware that these organizations are themselves possessors of power and may have their own interests and objectives. As M. J. C. Vile observes (*Constitutionalism and the Separation of Powers*, 1967, p. 333):

There have grown up new and powerful means of controlling government, but like the earlier mechanisms of control they are not neutral instruments, but organizations which must themselves be subject to control. Indeed, there can *never* be a 'neutral' control system, for we must never lose sight of the fact that these 'controls' are not pieces of machinery in the mechanical sense. The mechanical analogy is a dangerous one. They are all, without exception, patterns of behaviour, they are all procedures operated by human beings, and they can never be neutral.

We should also be aware that control and accountability function as restraints upon government and make demands on public resources. These must be accepted in a system of responsible government under law, and indeed such restraints can contribute to the rationality (prudence, consistency and competence) of government. (Cf. Gilbert, op. cit.) But there is a balance to be struck between their claims and the need for governmental effectiveness, because after all, as L. J. Sharpe tells us (in J. A. G. Griffith (ed.), *From Policy to Administration*, 1976, p. 132),

government in a democracy must possess the capacity to govern; that is to say, it must have that functional effectiveness that makes a reality [of] the choice between alternative policies that democracy claims to offer the electorate.

7
Parliament and government

1 Responsible government

In the description of the British constitutional system as one of responsible government, what is primarily meant is that the government is responsible to Parliament, and more precisely to the House of Commons. In other words ours is a system of parliamentary government in which the government's authority depends upon its having the confidence of the elected House. The aspect of responsibility which is emphasized in this description is the liability of the government to be dismissed by a vote of the Commons (subject to an appeal to the electorate). Dorothy Pickles has written (*Democracy*, 1970, p. 148): 'The essential requirement in a parliamentary democracy is that Parliament shall retain the power to dismiss Governments.' In practice such dismissals have been of an exceptional rarity in Britain. Governments have been defeated on votes of confidence only three times in the present century – in 1924 (twice) and 1979 – but the requirement that the government must retain the confidence of the House of Commons is still a fundamental principle of the constitution. In the last resort it is sustained by the government's dependence on the House of Commons for supply and the passing of legislation.

The most recent vindication of the principle was in 1979. The minority Labour Government headed by Mr Callaghan depended on the support of other parties for its survival; some of this support evaporated on 28 March when a motion of no confidence was carried against the Government by 311 votes to 310. A dissolution of Parliament followed.

In practice the power of Parliament to dismiss the government is a contingent power, which can be asserted only in circumstances of minority government or breakdown of party solidarity. In normal circumstances, as John Mackintosh says, 'the House of Commons is enmeshed with and supports the government of the day' (John P. Mackintosh (ed.), *People and Parliament*, 1978, p. 210). It is, indeed, a paradoxical feature of the modern constitution that for the control and accountability of government we rely mainly upon an elected House in which a majority see it as their principal function to maintain the government in power. But the ultimate, collective responsibility of the government to Parliament is not without meaning. The need to retain the confidence of the House imposes restraints. It compels governments to explain, justify, bargain and concede.

John Stuart Mill, *Considerations on Representative Government* (1861), p. 104

Instead of the function of governing, for which it is radically unfit, the proper office of a representative assembly is to watch and control the government: to throw the light of publicity on its acts; to compel a full exposition and justification of all of them which any one considers questionable; to censure them if found condemnable, and, if the men who compose the government abuse their trust, or fulfil it in a manner which conflicts with the deliberate sense of the nation, to expel them from office, and either expressly or virtually appoint their successors.

Ordinarily a government with an absolute majority in the House of Commons can rely on party cohesion and discipline to assure it of the confidence of the House. Nor are defeats in the House, even on important issues, regarded as compelling resignation or a dissolution unless the House has been expressly invited to treat the issue as one of confidence in the government.

In the Parliament of March–September 1974 a minority Labour Government faced a House of Commons in which supporters of opposition parties outnumbered Labour MPs by over 30. The Prime Minister explained the Government's position to the House:

House of Commons, 12 March 1974 (HC Deb. vol. 870, cols. 70–71)

The Prime Minister (MR HAROLD WILSON): ... The Government intend to treat with suitable respect, but not with exaggerated respect, the results of any snap vote or any snap Division. ...

In case of a Government defeat, either in such circumstances or in a more clear expression of opinion, the Government will consider their position and make a definitive statement after due consideration. But the Government will not be forced to go to the country except in a situation in which every hon. Member in the House was voting knowing the full consequences of his vote.

... I am saying that if there were to be anything put to the House which could have those consequences, every hon. Member would have it explained to him in the House by the Government before he voted.

(A similar statement was made by Ramsay Macdonald as head of a minority government in 1924: see Ivor Jennings, *Cabinet Government*, 3rd edn 1959, p. 494.)

The 1974 Labour Government suffered 17 defeats in the House of Commons in that year. In the 1974–9 Parliament, the Labour Government – again without an overall majority from 1976 – suffered 42 defeats before being obliged to appeal to the electorate. (See Philip Norton, *Dissension in the House of Commons 1974–1979*, 1980, p. 441.)

Philip Norton, 'The House of Commons and the Constitution:
The Challenges of the 1970s' (1981) 34 *Parliamentary Affairs* 253,
254–5, 266–7

As a result of the political developments of the nineteenth century, the House of Commons became the dominant element of the triumvirate of the Queen-in-Parliament, but these very developments (the introduction of near-universal male suffrage and the resulting party government) served to move the House from an important position in the decision-making process to a somewhat ambivalent one related to, yet not part of, the main decision-making machinery. The outputs of the Queen-in-Parliament continued to be legally omnipotent as a result of the judicially self-imposed if not universally revered doctrine of 'parliamentary sovereignty', but those outputs were the results of decisions taken elsewhere. To adapt the House of Commons to the changed political circumstances, and especially to the new relationship between it and the government, its functions were variously redefined. These functions find no delineation in one formal, binding document. There does appear, though, to be some general if at times tenuous agreement on the main functions of the post-1867 House: To provide, by convention, the personnel of government (a function shared with the Lords); to constitute a 'representative' assembly, members being returned to defend and pursue the interest of their constituents and de facto of wider interests (which may be categorised as the specific and general functions of representation); in pursuance of the representative function, to legitimise the actions and the legislative measures advanced by Her Majesty's government, and prior to giving legitimisation to subject the government and its measures to a process of scrutiny and influence. The House fulfils a number of other functions, including a minor shared legislative role, but the foregoing constitute the most important.

In fulfilling the function of scrutiny and influence, MPs found themselves faced with a serious limitation. To be effective, scrutiny rested primarily on the existence of the House's sanction of defeating the government in the division lobbies – its ability to deny legitimisation to a measure or part of it – but the MPs in the government party proved unwilling to utilise this power. Much of this refusal was for political reasons: members of the governing party wanted to support the government and normally approved of its measures. On those occasions when they were inclined to vote with the opposition, they were restrained from doing so by what they perceived to be a constitutional convention: that a government defeat in the division lobbies would necessitate the government either resigning or requesting a dissolution. As Arthur Balfour commented in 1905, it appeared to be assumed in various parts of the House 'that the accepted constitutional principle is that, when a government suffers defeat, either in supply or on any other subject, the proper course for His Majesty's responsible advisers is either to ask His Majesty to relieve them of their office or to ask His Majesty to dissolve parliament.' This view remained current until at least the 1970s. . . . A consequence was cohesion in the division lobbies. Sustenance of the government in office was equated with sustaining the government in every division. The greater the degree of cohesion (or at the least the fewer the defeats), the more this appeared to be borne out in practice. The result was an apparent paradox. On the one hand, the power of the House to ensure effective scrutiny and influence of government, to determine the boundaries in which it could operate, was based upon its power to defeat the government, to deny assent to its measures. On the other hand, given the assumption that a defeat would bring the government down, a majority of the House was not prepared to use it. Hence the ease with which government measures went through and the criticisms levelled at the Commons for failing to fulfil effectively the tasks expected of it. The events of the 1970s served to resolve this paradox.

The belief that a defeat in the division lobbies necessitated the government's resignation or an election was based on no authoritative source nor upon any continuous basis of practice. In that sense, the belief could be described as constituting a constitutional 'myth'. Nevertheless, so long as members continued in this belief, it influenced their behaviour. It took the defeats of the 1970s to make members realise that defeats could be imposed upon the government without there necessarily being any wider constitutional implications. The constitutional reality, as it had been since 1841, was that a government was required by convention to resign (or dissolve) in the event only of losing a vote of confidence; in the event of losing a division on an item central to its policy, it had the discretion as to whether to resign (or request a dissolution) or seek a vote of confidence from the House; in the event of defeat on any other matter, it had to consider only whether to accept the defeat or seek its reversal at a later stage. This distinction was given clear recognition by Stanley Baldwin in the House of Commons in April 1936. The response of the governments of the 1970s to the defeats suffered was in line with precedent. The popular view that there was a deviation from previous practice is incorrect. What changed was not the basis of the government's response but the number of defeats. Whereas previous defeats had been few and far between, and did not impact themselves upon members' consciousness, the defeats of the 1970s were too numerous to be ignored. Members began to realise the implications of their own actions and to realise that they could effect changes in the measures of government without necessarily threatening its life. This was to generate a change in attitude and to resolve the paradox of the House depending upon a power it was not willing to use. Members proved willing to overcome the constraints of party to employ the power that resided with them. Government could no longer rely upon the loyalty of its own backbenchers to see all its measures through in the form desired. (Nor upon the electorate and the electoral system to provide it with an overall majority.) In consequence, members restored to themselves the means by which they could achieve more effectively their function of scrutiny and influence.

Influence and scrutiny – or 'controlling' and 'calling to account' – are functions of Parliament which depend largely on the acceptance by ministers of the Crown of their collective and individual responsibility to Parliament. The responsibility of ministers is the mainspring of the working relationship between Parliament and government.

2 Individual ministerial responsibility

'One of the fundamentals of our system of Government', wrote Lord Morrison (*Government and Parliament*, 3rd edn 1964, p. 332), 'is that some Minister of the Crown is responsible to Parliament, and through Parliament to the public, for every act of the Executive'. According to this convention, every minister is responsible to Parliament for his own official conduct, and a minister who heads a department also has ultimate responsibility for everything done by his department.

A convention in these terms is necessary, first, to enable Parliament to make good the 'explanatory accountability' of government (see p. 345 above): for every branch of the government's business there must be an identifiable minister who has an obligation to answer and explain to Parliament. The performance by Parliament of its functions of controlling the executive and holding it accountable for errors depends on getting from ministers the relevant facts and explanations. A Canadian Royal Commission underlined this in saying:

Full disclosure of all relevant information is an essential requirement for full accountability by government to both Parliament and the people. [*Final Report of the Royal Commission on Financial Management and Accountability*, 1979, p. 29.]

The obligation to answer is not legal but political or conventional and it is by no means complete or unqualified, as we shall see when we come to parliamentary Questions and the role of select committees.

Secondly, the convention of individual ministerial responsibility is traditionally supposed to fix the blame on the minister for every failure of departmental policy or administration, whether it is the minister himself who was at fault, or a civil servant, or if the failure resulted from a defect of departmental organization. The minister must submit to the judgement of Parliament, and if the failure is a serious one, should resign from office without waiting for a vote of censure.

Crichel Down

The traditional view of ministerial responsibility seemed to be vindicated by the resignation in 1954 of the Minister of Agriculture, Sir Thomas Dugdale, following the notorious case of Crichel Down. An account of these events has already been given (pp. 77–8 above). The Minister resigned after widespread criticism, in Parliament and outside, of inefficient and high-handed behaviour by officials of his department. He said in the House (HC Deb. vol. 530, col. 1186, 20 July 1954):

I, as Minister, must accept full responsibility to Parliament for any mistakes and inefficiency of officials in my Department, just as, when my officials bring off any successes on my behalf, I take full credit for them.

But this seemingly unequivocal demonstration of individual ministerial responsibility in its traditional sense was in fact blurred by some of the attendant circumstances. First, civil servants concerned in the case had been named and criticized in a report published shortly before the Minister's resignation (*Report of the Public Inquiry into the Disposal of Land at Crichel Down*,

Cmd 9176/1954): it was not only the Minister who had to take the blame. Secondly, the Minister himself (and two junior Ministers) had taken a personal part in the transactions relating to Crichel Down, and the Minister was to admit to the House that his decisions had been taken with knowledge of the main facts of the case. (See Lord Boyle of Handsworth (1980) 58 *Pub. Adm.* 1 at 10–11.) In the Crichel Down debate on 20 July 1954 the Home Secretary attempted to clarify the convention.

House of Commons, 20 July 1954 (HC Deb. vol. 530, cols. 1285–7)

The Home Secretary (SIR DAVID MAXWELL FYFE): . . . There has been criticism that the principle operates so as to oblige Ministers to extend total protection to their officials and to endorse their acts, and to cause the position that civil servants cannot be called to account and are effectively responsible to no one. That is a position which I believe is quite wrong, and I think it is the cardinal error that has crept into the appreciation of this situation. It is quite untrue that well-justified public criticism of the actions of civil servants cannot be made on a suitable occasion. The position of the civil servant is that he is wholly and directly responsible to his Minister. It is worth stating again that he holds his office 'at pleasure' and can be dismissed at any time by the Minister; and that power is none the less real because it is seldom used. . . .

I would like to put the different categories where different considerations apply. I am in agreement with the right hon. Gentleman who has just spoken, that in the case where there is an explicit order by a Minister, the Minister must protect the civil servant who has carried out his order. Equally, where the civil servant acts properly in accordance with the policy laid down by the Minister, the Minister must protect and defend him.

I come to the third category, which is different. . . . Where an official makes a mistake or causes some delay, but not on an important issue of policy and not where a claim to individual rights is seriously involved, the Minister acknowledges the mistake and he accepts the responsibility, although he is not personally involved. He states that he will take corrective action in the Department. I agree with the right hon. Gentleman that he would not, in those circumstances, expose the official to public criticism. . . .

But when one comes to the fourth category, where action has been taken by a civil servant of which the Minister disapproves and has no prior knowledge, and the conduct of the official is reprehensible, then there is no obligation on the part of the Minister to endorse what he believes to be wrong, or to defend what are clearly shown to be errors of his officers. The Minister is not bound to defend action of which he did not know, or of which he disapproves. But, of course, he remains constitutionally responsible to Parliament for the fact that something has gone wrong, and he alone can tell Parliament what has occurred and render an account of his stewardship.

A convention of resignation?

In Sir David Maxwell Fyfe's statement the traditional view of ministerial responsibility is tempered with realism, and no explicit reference is made to a ministerial obligation to resign in atonement for departmental misconduct. The traditional view was in any event defective in that it did not take account of the great increase in the work of government departments in modern times, which has made it impossible for ministers to control directly or even know about the bulk of departmental business. It has also been shown that the traditional view, with its emphasis on the sanction of ministerial resignation, does not accord with the facts of political life. Professor S. E. Finer looked for ministerial resignations in the period 1855–1955 that had been 'forced by overt criticism from the House of Commons' and so might be attributed to the convention of ministerial responsibility. He found that there had been only twenty such resignations in the century, 'a tiny number', as he wrote, 'compared with the known instances of mismanagement and blunderings' (op. cit. below, p. 386). The following passage gives his conclusions.

S. E. Finer, 'The Individual Responsibility of Ministers' (1956)
34 *Pub. Adm.* 377 at 393–4

The convention implies a form of punishment for a delinquent Minister. That punishment is no longer an act of attainder, or an impeachment, but simply loss of office.

If each, or even very many charges of incompetence were habitually followed by the punishment, the remedy would be a very real one: its deterrent effect would be extremely great. In fact, that sequence is not only exceedingly rare, but arbitrary and unpredictable. Most charges never reach the stage of individualisation at all: they are stifled under the blanket of party solidarity. Only when there is a minority Government, or in the infrequent cases where the Minister seriously alienates his own back benchers, does the issue of the individual culpability of the Minister even arise. Even there it is subject to hazards: the punishment may be avoided if the Prime Minister, whether on his own or on the Minister's initiative, makes a timely re-shuffle. Even when some charges get through the now finely woven net, and are laid at the door of a Minister, much depends on his nicety, and much on the character of the Prime Minister. Brazen tenacity of office can still win a reprieve. And, in the last resort – though this happens infrequently – the resignation of the Minister may be made purely formal by reappointment to another post soon afterwards.

We may put the matter in this way: whether a Minister is forced to resign depends on three factors, on himself, his Prime Minister and his party. On himself – as Austen Chamberlain resigned though possessing the confidence of his Prime Minister and his party, whereas Ayrton remained in office despite having neither. On the Prime Minister – as Salisbury stood between Matthews, his Home Secretary, and the party that clamoured for his dismissal. On the party – as witness the impotence of Palmerston to save Westbury, Balfour to save Wyndham, Asquith to save Birrell. For a resignation to occur all three factors have to be just so: the Minister compliant, the Prime Minister firm, the party clamorous. This conjuncture is rare, and is in fact fortuitous. Above all, it is indiscriminate – which Ministers escape and which do not is decided neither by the circumstances of the offence nor its gravity. A Wyndham and a Chamberlain go for a peccadillo, a Kitchener will remain despite major blunders.

A remedy ought to be certain. A punishment, to be deterrent, ought to be certain. But whether the Minister should resign is simply the (necessarily) haphazard consequence of a fortuitous concomitance of personal, party and political temper.

Is there then a 'convention' of resignation at all?

A convention, in Dicey's sense, is a rule which is not enforced by the Courts. The important word is 'rule'. 'Rule' does not mean merely an observed uniformity in the past; the notion includes the expectation that the uniformity will continue in the future. It is not simply a description; it is a prescription. It has a compulsive force.

Now in its first sense, that the Minister alone *speaks* for his Civil Servants to the House and to his Civil Servants for the House, the convention of ministerial responsibility has both the proleptic and the compulsive features of a 'rule'. But in the sense in which we have been considering it, that the Minister *may be punished, through loss of office* for all the misdeeds and neglects of his Civil Servants which he cannot prove to have been outside all possibility of his cognisance and control, the proposition does not seem to be a rule at all.

What is the compulsive element in such a 'rule'? All it says (on examination) is that if the Minister is yielding, his Prime Minister unbending and his party out for blood – no matter how serious or trivial the reason – the Minister will find himself without Parliamentary support. This is a statement of fact, not a code. What is more, as a statement of fact it comes very close to being a truism: that a Minister entrusted by his Prime Minister with certain duties must needs resign if he loses the support of his majority. The only compulsive element in the proposition is that if and when a Minister loses his majority he ought to get out rather than be kicked out.

Moreover, even as a simple generalisation, an observed uniformity, the 'convention' is, surely, highly misleading? It takes the wrong cases: it generalises from the exceptions and neglects the common run. There are four categories of delinquent Ministers: the fortunate, the less fortunate, the unfortunate, and the plain unlucky. After sinning, the first go to other Ministries; the second to Another Place; the third just go. Of the fourth there are but twenty examples in a century: indeed, if one omits Neville Chamberlain (an anomaly) and the 'personal' cases, viz., Mundella, Thomas and Dalton, there are but sixteen. Not for these sixteen the honourable exchange of offices, or the silent and not dishonourable exit. Their lot is public penance in the white sheet of a resignation speech or letter. (Sir Ben Smith is the only exception: neither shuffle nor white sheet for him, but highly uncommunicative disappearance: Sir Winston put it as *spurlos versunken*, 'sunk without trace'.) It is on some sixteen or at most nineteen penitents and one anomaly that the generalisation has been based.

Between 1955 and 1982 there were only two resignations of senior Ministers (Profumo and Jellicoe) that can be put down to an acknowledgment by the Ministers concerned of their responsibility to Parliament (the resignation of Maudling in 1972 would not seem to fall into this category) and in each case the resignation was connected with the Minister's own conduct, not the actions of his department. In 1982 the unexpected Argentine invasion of the Falkland Islands and public and parliamentary criticism of the role of the Foreign and Commonwealth Office was followed by the resignations of the Foreign Secretary (Lord Carrington), the Lord Privy Seal (Mr Humphrey Atkins), who had been the spokesman for the Foreign Office in the House of Commons, and a Minister of State who had conducted the negotiations with Argentina on the Falkland Islands question. These resignations were an admission of responsibility to Parliament for a failure of policy, afterwards attributed in part to defects in the machinery of government, misjudgments by ministers and officials of Argentine intentions, and faulty decisions by ministers. (See *Falkland Islands Review*, Cmnd 8787/1983).

Letter of Resignation from Lord Carrington, Secretary of State for Foreign and Commonwealth Affairs, to the Prime Minister, Mrs Margaret Thatcher, 5 April 1982

Dear Margaret

The Argentine invasion of the Falkland Islands has led to strong criticism in Parliament and in the press on the Government's policy. In my view, much of the criticism is unfounded. But I have been responsible for the conduct of that policy and I think it right that I should resign. As you know, I have given long and careful thought to this. I warmly appreciate the kindness and support which you showed me when we discussed this matter on Saturday. But the fact remains that the invasion of the Falkland Islands has been a humiliating affront to this country.

We must now, as you said in the House of Commons, do everything we can to uphold the right of the islanders to live in peace, to choose their own way of life and to determine their own allegiance. I am sure that this is the right course, and one which deserves the undivided support of Parliament and of the country. But I have concluded with regret that this support will more easily be maintained if the Foreign Office is entrusted to someone else.

I have been privileged to be a member of this Government and to be associated with its achievements over the past three years. I need hardly say that the Government will continue to have my active support. I am most grateful to you personally for the unfailing confidence you have shown in me.

Yours ever, Peter

(The Minister of State who resigned – Mr Richard Luce – was reappointed to the same office 15 months later.)

The invasion of the Falklands had caused a loss of confidence among parliamentarians and the public in the organization and leadership of the Foreign Office, and for a restoration of that confidence it was believed that ministerial resignations were necessary. But the circumstances were unusual, and most administrative failures are of a more specific kind which do not bring into question the whole departmental organization or the leadership of ministers. It is not likely that a minister's head will be demanded or proffered in such cases. But if the error is serious and has grave consequences, critical attention may be focused on the minister. His response will depend on the factors of personality, party and politics indicated by Professor Finer (above).

The Maze break-out

In September 1983 there was a mass break-out of republican prisoners from the Maze prison in Belfast, an event described in a leading article in *The Times* (8 February 1984) as 'a fearful blow to the authority of the state in Northern

Ireland'. It was serious enough to raise the question of the responsibility of ministers. Those concerned were the Secretary of State in charge of the Northern Ireland Office, Mr James Prior, and the Under Secretary of State responsible for the prison service, Mr Nicholas Scott, who had been in office for only three months at the time of the break-out. His predecessor, Lord Gowrie, had moved to the Privy Council Office as Minister for the Arts.

A report by Sir James Hennessy on security arrangements at the Maze prison (HC 203 of 1983–4) found that there had been deficiencies in the management and physical security of the prison, and that faulty procedures and laxity and negligence of staff had facilitated the escape. For this state of affairs the report held the prison governor to be primarily responsible; there was also some criticism of the prison department of the Northern Ireland Office for its oversight of security at the prison. The Government accepted the report and its recommendations. The prison governor resigned, but no ministers did so. For reasons which may be surmised the Prime Minister was not disposed to press for Mr Prior's resignation; neither did the Labour Opposition wish to see him replaced at the Northern Ireland Office by any other Tory minister.

House of Commons, 9 February 1984 (HC Deb. vol. 53, cols. 1042, 1055–6, 1060–61, 1108)

The Secretary of State for Northern Ireland (MR JAMES PRIOR): . . . There are those who, while they accept this policy [of treating IRA prisoners like all other prisoners] have nevertheless suggested that the circumstances of the escape demand ministerial resignation. I take that view seriously and have given it the most careful consideration. I share hon. Members' concern about the honour of public life and the maintenance of the highest standards. I said at the time of my statement to the House on 24 October, without any pre-knowledge of what Hennessy would find:

'It would be a matter for resignation if the report of the Hennessy inquiry showed that what happened was the result of some act of policy that was my responsibility, or that I failed to implement something that I had been asked to implement, or should have implemented. In that case, I should resign.'

In putting the emphasis that I did on the issue of 'policy', I was not seeking to map out some new doctrine of ministerial responsibility. I was responding to the accusations made at that time that it was policy decisions, reached at the end of the hunger strike, that made the escape possible.

Since the report was published, the nature of the charges levelled at my hon. Friend and myself has changed. It is now argued in some quarters that Ministers are responsible for everything that happens in their Departments and should resign if anything goes wrong . . . I want to make it quite clear that if there were any evidence in the Hennessy report that Ministers were to blame for the escape, I would not hesitate to accept that blame and act accordingly, and so I know, would my hon. Friend [Mr Nicholas Scott]. However, I do not accept – and I do not think it right for the House to accept – that there is any constitutional or other principle that requires ministerial resignations in the face of failure, either by others to carry out orders or procedures or by their supervisors to ensure that staff carried out those orders. Let the House be clear: the Hennessy report finds that the escape would not have succeeded if orders and procedures had been properly carried out that Sunday afternoon.

Of course, I have looked carefully at the precedents. There are those who quote the Crichel Down case. I do not believe that it is a precedent or that it establishes a firm convention. It is the only case of its sort in the past 50 years, and constitutional lawyers have concluded that the resignation was not required by convention and was exceptional.

Whatever some may wish, there is no clear rule and no established convention. Rightly, it is a matter of judgment in the light of individual circumstances. I do not . . . seek to justify my decision on the ground that there are many difficulties in Northern Ireland. There are, but that adds to rather than subtracts from the argument. The question that I have asked myself is whether . . . I was to blame for those prisoners escaping. The Hennessy report is quite explicit in its conclusion that, although there may have been weaknesses in the physical security of the prison and in the Prisons Department, the escape could not have taken place if the procedures laid down for the running of the prison had been followed. . . .

MR PETER ARCHER [Opposition spokesman on Northern Ireland]: . . . The purpose of the debate is not to ask for resignations. . . . We must consider whether Northern Ireland would benefit if a particular Minister resigned. I should not think it right to call for the resignation of the Secretary of State. First, I do not think that he could reasonably have been expected, personally, to have read the minutes [relating to the appointment of dangerous republican prisoners as orderlies]. I believe that he was badly served. Secondly, the right hon. Gentleman may be embarrassed at this; but I cannot envisage him being replaced from among members of the present Administration by anyone more compassionate or more politically sensitive. . . .

The hon. Member for Chelsea [Mr Nicholas Scott] . . . had held responsibility for only three months prior to the breakout. We can see today what a difficult and complicated situation existed . . . I do not seek to convict him. Lord Gowrie is in a different position. In the absence of any explanations today, it is difficult to see how he could justify remaining a member of the Government. . . .

MR J. ENOCH POWELL: The Secretary of State, from the beginning of his speech, recognised the central issue in this debate, that of ministerial responsibility, without which the House scarcely has a real function or any real service that it can perform for the people whom it represents. We are concerned with the nature of the responsibility, the ministerial responsibility, for an event which, even in isolation from its actual context, was a major disaster.

I want to begin by eliminating from this consideration the Under-Secretary of State for Northern Ireland . . . (Mr Scott), because references to him in this context have shown a gross misconception. . . . The fact is that the entire responsibility, whether or not it is delegated to a junior Minister, rests with the Secretary of State. . . .

As the Secretary of State reminded us this afternoon, even before the publication of the report he drew a distinction, which I believe to be invalid, between responsibility for policy and responsibility for administration. I believe that this is a wholly fallacious view of the nature of ministerial responsibility. . . . [E]ven if all considerations of policy could be eliminated, the responsibility for the administration of a Department remains irrevocably with the Minister in charge. It is impossible for him to say to the House or to the country, 'The policy was excellent and that was mine, but the execution was defective or disastrous and that has nothing to do with me.' If that were to be the accepted position, there would be no political source to which the public could complain about administration or from which it could seek redress for failings of administration.

What happened was an immense administrative disaster. It was . . . a disaster that occurred in an area which was quite clearly central to the Department's responsibilities. If the responsibility for administration so central to a Department can be abjured by a Minister, a great deal of our proceedings in the House is a beating of the air because we are talking to people who, in the last resort, disclaim the responsibility for the administration. . . .

The Under-Secretary of State for Northern Ireland (MR NICHOLAS SCOTT): . . . The right hon. Member for Down, South (Mr Powell) . . . outlined a constitutional convention which he might wish existed, which perhaps once did exist, but which, frankly, has not existed in politics in this country for many years. . . .

The Economist (4 February 1984, p. 25) commented on the episode as follows:

According to Mr Prior . . . ministers are answerable for overall policy and for providing resources adequate for its implementation, but cannot be held to blame for the way the rank-and-file carry it out, or even for the failures of senior civil servants who should have supervised them. . . .

So what does ministerial responsibility really mean? In practice, nothing. Ministers cannot get out of answering questions in parliament about their departments – though nowadays this is a largely theatrical accountability. But a minister's only true accountability is to his boss, the prime minister. The reason neither Mr Prior nor Mr Scott resigned over the Maze affair is not Mr Prior's (patently absurd) redraft of the constitution. It is that Mrs Thatcher prefers to have them still in the government. If the public wants to hold anyone responsible, let it vote her out in four years' time.

This is hardly satisfactory. Officials can pass the buck to ministers; ministers feel no obligation to accept it; so there is no penalty for departmental incompetence except the distant ballot box. . . .

Is this scepticism over-stated?

If resignations in deference to ministerial responsibility are rare, the power of the House of Commons to censure and dismiss individual ministers hardly exists except on the plane of theory. Motions of censure can always be defeated by a majority government. They are in any event likely to be treated as putting in issue the House's confidence in the government as a whole, and therefore its survival. (See, e.g., HC Deb. vol. 951, col. 1129, 14 June 1978). A minister threatened with a motion of censure who believed that he had lost the support of party and colleagues would be unlikely to await the formal vote. Nevertheless the power remains in reserve and awareness of it underlies much that is said and done in Parliament; it is one of the conditioning elements in the behaviour of MPs and ministers. This idea was expressed in elevated terms by an MP and former Minister in the course of committee proceedings on a government bill:

House of Commons Standing Committee F (British Nationality
Bill), 12 May 1981, cols. 1916–17

MR J. ENOCH POWELL: Where an Act of Parliament gives discretion to a Minister, it gives him that discretion as a person responsible in all his actions to Parliament. The discretion of a Minister under this Bill or any similar Act is not arbitrary in the sense that it is an irresponsible discretion. He exercises all such discretions in the light of his answerability to Parliament, and any such cases and any such decision can be raised, and theoretically could be made the subject of a vote of censure upon the Minister, in either House of Parliament. . . .

We . . . take it for granted that if in the opinion of Parliament, as the supreme protection of the body of citizens and of every citizen individually, that discretion is exercised unjustly, improperly or unwisely in any way, Parliament is capable of bringing that Minister to account, and willing to do so.

Even if, as in the usual case, the departmental minister is able to disclaim personal responsibility for his department's errors or failures, he is still expected to 'accept responsibility' in the sense that he must give an account to Parliament of the circumstances, take into consideration views expressed in the House, and inform it of disciplinary or remedial action taken. But since the minister is interposed between Parliament and his officials, while his own responsibility for official acts that he did not authorize is diluted, it would seem that there is a constitutional gap. The system does not appear to provide adequately for the accountability of civil servants, who nowadays (as we have seen in chapter 3) themselves formulate policies and take numberless decisions of importance without reference to ministers.

Accountability of civil servants

In constitutional theory the accountability of civil servants is absorbed by the responsibility of ministers to Parliament, with its corollary of the anonymity and exclusively internal (departmental) responsibility of officials. In replying to a report of the Expenditure Committee on the civil service, the Government declared (Cmnd 7117/1978, para. 3)

their belief that the interests of the country will continue to be best served by a non-political, permanent Civil Service working under the close policy supervision of the Government of the day. They distinguish between the responsibility of the Civil Service to the Government and the responsibility of the Government to Parliament. Ministers alone are responsible to Parliament for policy, and any extension of the accountability of civil servants must recognise the overriding responsibility of the Departmental Minister for the work and efficiency of his department. The Government do not therefore favour developments which would detract from the principle that the advice tendered to Ministers by civil servants should be confidential and objective. . . .

Ministerial responsibility can present an effective shield against parliamentary inquiry into decisions taken or advice given by civil servants. In 1979 the Secretary of State for Social Services, purporting to act under statutory powers, directed that the functions of an area health authority, which he considered to be guilty of over-spending, should be taken over by commissioners. The Minister had been advised that he could lawfully take this action, but a court subsequently held (in *Lambeth LBC* v. *Secretary of State for Social Services* (1981) 79 LGR 61) that he had exceeded his legal powers. Afterwards in the House of Commons the Minister was pressed to say what advice he had received from civil servants before taking action, and whether there had been 'repercussions' in his department. (HC Deb. vol. 980, cols. 1640–3, 13 March 1980.) The Minister declined to provide this information, declaring that he accepted full personal responsibility to the House.

The non-accountability of civil servants (outside their departments) is, however, subject to some qualifications.

A direct responsibility of civil servants to Parliament is formally acknowledged in only one instance: the Accounting Officer of a department, who is usually the Permanent Secretary, is responsible for the departmental accounts and answers to the Public Accounts Committee of the House of Commons for the regularity of departmental expenditure and the observance of proper economy.

Senior civil servants are called upon to appear before other parliamentary select committees, in particular the departmental committees set up in 1979, and may be questioned about the work of their departments. But this, again, is constrained by ministerial responsibility and is subject to limits established by the government, as we shall see (p. 385 below).

The actions of civil servants may be the subject of investigation by the Parliamentary Commissioner for Administration. His inquiries into maladministration by government departments may lead to findings that particular civil servants have been at fault, but those concerned are not usually named in his published reports. Soon after the establishment of the office, the Select Committee on the Parliamentary Commissioner took evidence from the Attorney-General on the question whether the identity of a civil servant might be disclosed in its report to Parliament:

> Evidence of the Attorney-General, Sir Elwyn Jones: *Second Report from the Select Committee on the Parliamentary Commissioner for Administration*, HC 350 of 1967–8, Evidence, Q 546

. . . Traditionally, and I submit for very good reason, it is the Minister in charge of the Department who is answerable to Parliament for the workings of the Department. The individual civil servant is, of course, not so responsible. The action of the Department is action for which the Department is collectively responsible and for which the Minister in charge is alone answerable to Parliament. I submit that to attach blame to the individual civil servant, save in certain exceptional cases which might arise where the civil servant had himself affronted a member of the public or something of that kind by his conduct, would run counter to this long established tradition. . . . I submit it is a corollary of the principle that it is the Minister alone who is responsible for the actions of his Department that the individual civil servant who has contributed to the collective decision of the Department should remain anonymous. . . .

A direct accountability of civil servants has from time to time been exacted by committees or tribunals of inquiry which have identified civil servants as being to blame for administrative failures. A notable instance occurred in 1972 when a tribunal of inquiry, established to investigate the collapse of the Vehicle and General Insurance Company, blamed officials in the Department of Trade and Industry by name for failing to exercise adequate supervision over the affairs of the company. The tribunal concluded that the 'ultimate responsibility for the failure of the Department to take action' lay with a named Under-Secretary in the Department. (*Report of the Tribunal of Inquiry on the Vehicle and General Insurance Company*, HC 133 of 1971–2, Summary of Findings, para. (8).) (See also p. 358 above.)

Gavin Drewry, 'Passing the Buck' (1972) 122 *NLJ* 312

Given the ambivalence of the present position of civil servants one can fully understand the resentment at one of their number having to shoulder the blame for the V. & G. debâcle (particularly as it is alleged that he was denied proper opportunity to rebut the charge of 'negligence' made by the Tribunal). As the doctrine of ministerial responsibility becomes increasingly fudged advisers find themselves caught in a cross-fire from 'outsiders' and from Parliament (whose own fire-power has been increased by extensions in the range of investigatory select committees); Ministers can point to vast increases in their burdens of responsibility and shrug blame onto the shoulders of their advisers, while continuing to take credit for successful policy initiatives.

There is an almost schizophrenic attitude to ministerial responsibility. Knowing that Ministers cannot handle all that goes on in their departments we call for both praise and blame to be divided among those who actually perform the tasks of government; yet there is widespread outrage when application of this principle leads (as it logically must) to the public condemnation of a civil servant. Ministerial responsibility lingers on as a mystical incantation emanating from the lips of politicians, half-understood and dangerously uncertain in its application. Perhaps the most important moral to be drawn from the V.& G. case is that we should try belatedly to decide what sort of constitutional relationships we *do* want.

(Consider further the issues raised by the *Sachsenhausen* case, discussed by Marshall, *Constitutional Conventions*, pp. 68–71.)

3 The power of Parliament

We are not now concerned with the 'sovereignty' of Parliament, or that supreme law-making power which belongs not to Parliament alone but to the Queen in Parliament, and which in reality is mainly at the disposal of the government. Our present interest is in the power of Parliament, in particular the House of Commons, to perform its functions of controlling and scrutinizing the executive – these terms being taken in a wide sense: 'controlling' to include influencing or restraining, and 'scrutinizing' (or calling to account) to include extracting information, criticizing, and procuring reparation or redress. (See pp. 345–6 above.) In carrying out these tasks Parliament relies less on its formal powers (e.g. to enforce the production of papers, or punish for contempt) than on the conventional responsibility owed to it by ministers, and the practices and procedures that have crystallized about this convention.

Bernard Crick, *The Reform of Parliament* (rev. 2nd edn 1970), pp. 79–81

Politics, not law, must explain the concept and practice of Parliamentary control of the Executive. In modern conditions any such control can only be something that does not threaten the day-to-day political control of Parliament by the Executive. The hope for any worth-while function of control by Parliament would be grim indeed if it depended on the ultimate deterrent of the vote: the undoubted Constitutional right of Parliament to vote against the Queen's Ministers and the Convention by which they would then resign. But control, on both sides, is indeed political. Governments respond to proceedings in Parliament if the publicity given to them is likely to affect public confidence in the Government, or even if the weakness with which the government puts up its case, even in purely Parliamentary terms, begins to affect the morale of its own supporters (though it takes a very long succession of bleak days for the Government in the House before the country begins to be affected).

The only meanings of Parliamentary control worth considering, and worth the House spending much of its time on, are those which do *not* threaten the Parliamentary defeat of a government, but which help to keep it responsive to the underlying currents and the more important drifts of public opinion. All others are purely antiquarian shufflings. It is wholly legitimate for any modern government to do what it needs to guard against Parliamentary defeat; but it is not legitimate for it to hinder Parliament, particularly the Opposition, from reaching the public ear as effectively as it can. Governments must govern in the expectation that they can serve out their statutory period of office, that they can plan – if they choose – at least that far ahead, but that everything they do may be exposed to the light of day and that everything they say may be challenged in circumstances designed to make criticism as authoritative, informed and as public as possible.

Thus the phrase 'Parliamentary control', and talk about the 'decline of Parliamentary control', should not mislead anyone into asking for a situation in which governments can have their legislation changed or defeated, or their life terminated (except in the most desperate emergency when normal politics will in any case break down, as in Chamberlain's 'defeat' in 1940). Control means *influence*, not direct power; *advice*, not command; *criticism*, not obstruction; *scrutiny*, not initiation; and *publicity*, not secrecy. Here is a very realistic sense of Parliamentary control which *does* affect any government. The Government will make decisions, whether by existing powers or by bringing in new legislation, in the knowledge that these decisions, sooner or later, will find their way to debate on the Floor of one of the Houses of Parliament. The type of scrutiny they will get will obviously affect, in purely political terms, the type of actions undertaken. And the civil service will administer with the knowledge that it too may be called upon to justify perhaps even the most minute actions.

Governments are virile and adult; they are beyond the strict parental control of Parliament. But they are likely to be deeply influenced by well put home truths from the family, if only (or above all) because this may be some sort of clue to their public reputation; and also because, after all, they have to share the same overcrowded house. Defeating the Government or having the whips withdrawn represent, like calling in the police, the breakdown, not the assertion, of normal family control.

Governments deserve praise in so far as they expose themselves, willingly and helpfully, to influence, advice, criticism, scrutiny, and publicity; and they deserve blame in so far as they try to hide from unpleasant discussions and to keep their reasons and actions secret. Parliaments deserve praise or blame as to whether or not they can develop institutions whose control is powerful in terms of general elections and not of governmental instability. This 'praise' and 'blame' is not moralistic: it is prudential. A government subject to such controls is not likely to get too far out of touch with public opinion; it may not, even in Bagehot's sense, attempt to 'teach' public opinion, but it will not destroy it. So Parliamentary control is not the stop switch, it is the tuning, the tone and the amplifier of a system of communication which tells governments what the electorate want (rightly or wrongly) and what they will stand for (rightly or wrongly); and tells the electorate what is possible within the resources available (however much opinions will vary on what is possible) and – on occasion – what is expected of them.

Ours is a system of *party* government in which political parties present themselves and their programmes to the electorate, with the object of winning a parliamentary majority and forming a government committed to the implementation of party policies. In this system it is an essential function of Parliament to sustain the government. Parliament is quite different in this respect from the American Congress which is established, on the principle of the separation of powers, as a separate branch of government with independent powers enabling it to check the executive branch. Ronald Butt has written (*The Times*, 18 May 1978, p. 18):

The essence of effective parliamentary control over government is not simply that the House of Commons should stop a government from doing things. It is that the Commons should positively support and sustain the government of the day – and preferably from the position in which a clear majority of MPs has been elected by the people to do just that.

In practice it is the majority party in the House of Commons which, in speech and vote, performs the function of sustaining the government. This underlines the fact that when we speak of Parliament or the House of Commons doing things, it is often only a part of the House that is meant. Besides being an institution, Parliament is a place in which different political forces, in competition or in combination, pursue a variety of objectives.

So also when we consider Parliament's functions of controlling and scrutinizing the executive, we have to distinguish between the House of Commons as an institution and the forces within it. Generally when the House seems to assert itself as a body against the executive we find only that intra-party disagreement on a specific issue of policy has resulted in temporary defections or an *ad hoc* combination of members. The select committees which seem to speak for Parliament in a dialogue with government are only groups of party members who have temporarily vacated their embattled positions to find common ground in scrutinizing parts of the administration. Parliament, as Ian Gilmour says (*The Body Politic*, 2nd edn 1971, p. 246), is 'rather a place than a body of persons' – a place in which backbenchers and opposition parties (sometimes in strange alliances) can be seen to do the work that, as by a metaphor, is described as the work of Parliament.

This is not to deny Parliament its institutional character, which it possesses in law, as an inheritance of history, and in the convictions of some, at least, of its members who have a sense of being parliamentarians as well as party men or women. It is important to maintain the idea of a shared duty to 'watch and control' the executive, of whatever party.

(a) Opposition

Parliamentary control and scrutiny of the executive is carried out primarily by the opposition parties in the House. In the words of the Houghton Report on Financial Aid to Political Parties (Cmnd 6601/1976, para. 9.1): 'The parties in opposition have the responsibility of scrutinising and checking all the actions of the Executive.'

The legitimacy of opposition parties is confirmed by law, convention and the political culture of the United Kingdom. Opposition is recognized as having rights and is part of the constitutional system – as much part of it as is the government.

Ivor Jennings, *Cabinet Government* (3rd edn 1959), pp. 15–16

Democratic government . . . demands not only a parliamentary majority but also a parliamentary minority. The minority attacks the Government because it denies the principles of its policy. The Opposition will, almost certainly, be defeated in the House of Commons because it is a minority. Its appeals are to the electorate. It will, at the next election, ask the people to condemn the government, and, as a consequence, to give a majority to the Opposition. Because the Government is criticised it has to meet criticism. Because it must in course of time defend itself in the constituencies it must persuade public opinion to move with it. The Opposition is at once the alternative to the Government and a focus for the discontent of the people. Its function is almost as important as that of the Government. If there be no Opposition there is no democracy. 'Her Majesty's Opposition' is no idle phrase. Her Majesty needs an Opposition as well as a Government.

When this passage was written the 'two-party system' – in which a single-party majority government faced an opposition dominated by the other major party – appeared to be firmly established. A system of adversary politics offered the electorate a clear-cut choice between party programmes. Since the 1950s the two major parties have seen a decline in their combined share of the total vote at general elections, although other parties have yet to achieve significant gains of seats in the House of Commons. In 1976–9 the smaller parties were able to bargain for concessions from a minority Labour Government. The new Social Democratic Party has dedicated itself to 'breaking the mould' of adversary politics, and campaigns in alliance with the Liberals for a new political system based on proportional representation. Although majority government has been restored since 1979 the challenge to the two-party system has not faded away, and requires us to contemplate a possible future of multi-party opposition and coalition governments.

Vernon Bogdanor, *Multi-party Politics and the Constitution* (1983),
p. 167

[I]f hung Parliaments were to persist and the strength of minority parties continued to increase, this . . . would undermine the special status of the Opposition and of its Leader. The Opposition would lose the privileges which it enjoyed *vis-à-vis* the minority parties, and the Leader of the Opposition would become merely the leader of one of the Opposition parties. The Commons would cease to be a forum in which the allocation of time was determined bilaterally between government and Opposition; instead the time of the House would come to be allocated on a more proportional basis. Thus not only would a minority government lose its ability to control the Commons timetable, but the opposition would no longer enjoy a near-monopoly of the debating time of the House. Instead, the Commons would be organised by a number of political groups of roughly equal status. It would come to resemble a Continental legislature, since it would comprise a number of mutually competing political groups. Parliamentary politics would be coalitional rather than adversary.

At the present time the constitution accords a special status to the official Opposition and its leader. Since 1937 there has been statutory provision for the payment of a salary to the leader of the Opposition. By the Ministerial and other Salaries Act 1975, s.2(1) and Sched. 2, salaries are now paid – out of the Consolidated Fund, not by annual vote of Parliament – to the leader of the Opposition, the Opposition Chief Whip, and two Assistant Opposition Whips in the Commons, and to the leader of the Opposition and the Opposition Chief Whip in the Lords. The leader of the Opposition is defined by section 2(1) of the Act as follows:

In this Act 'Leader of the Opposition' means, in relation to either House of Parliament, that Member of that House who is for the time being the Leader in that House of the party in opposition to Her Majesty's Government having the greatest numerical strength in the House of Commons . . .

Thus it is by reference to party strengths in the Commons that the leaders of the Opposition in both Houses are designated. Any doubt as to the identity of the leader of the Opposition in either House is settled conclusively by the decision of the Speaker or of the Lord Chancellor respectively (section 2(2), (3)).

The salaries of four members of staff of the Opposition Whips' Office are also paid from public funds.

The status and privileges of the official Opposition and its leader in the House of Commons are supported by rules, conventions and practices of the House. The leader of the Opposition is normally consulted by the prime minister in the event of a national emergency. He and other members of the Opposition front bench are often informed of confidential matters of state. It is customary for Opposition members to chair a number of important select committees, among them the Public Accounts Committee and the Joint Committee on Statutory Instruments.

It was formerly a convention that the Opposition should have at its disposal 29 'Supply days' which were used, not for the government's financial business, but for general debates on subjects chosen by the Opposition. However some of these days were customarily set aside for debates on the armed forces, European Community matters and select committee reports, leaving about 20 at the effective disposal of the Opposition. The formal link with 'supply' was severed in 1982 when House of Commons standing orders were amended so as to allocate 19 'Opposition days' for debates on subjects chosen by opposition parties: the other matters formerly taken on Supply days are now debated in government time. Standing Order 6(2) provides:

Nineteen allotted days in each session shall be at the disposal of the Leader of Her Majesty's Opposition and matters selected on these days shall have precedence over government business. . . .

The official Opposition selects the subjects for debate on most Opposition days, but by convention consults with minor opposition parties and allocates some of the days to them. This prerogative of the leader of the Opposition has not gone unquestioned. In a letter addressed to the Select Committee on Procedure (Supply) in 1981 (*First Report from the Select Committee*, vol. III, HC 118–III of 1980–81, App. 21), the Liberal Chief Whip wrote:

There is . . . no recognised procedure under which we can claim an allocation of Supply [now Opposition] Days. They are effectively in the gift of the Opposition Chief Whip, and can only be secured by agreement with him. Such time is rarely granted until shortly before the Summer Recess. The temptation to make the grant of a Supply Day conditional on, for example, choice of subject, is obvious and I need not dwell on it: suffice it to say that the existing arrangements do not guarantee the freedom of smaller Opposition Parties to challenge the Government when and on whatever matter they choose, within the appropriate allocation of time.

Apart from the formal allocation of Opposition days, the Address in reply to the Queen's speech at the beginning of a session allows for debate on Opposition amendments, and time is always made available for Opposition motions of censure.

Discussions continually take place between government and Opposition 'through the usual channels' – i.e. in communications between the Whips' Offices – on the informal timetabling of bills and debates, the 'pairing' of absent members, and other arrangements for the business of the House.

Donald Wade, *Behind the Speaker's Chair* (1978), p. 24

The expression 'through the usual channels' is used primarily in relation to the arranging of business. It is concerned with the regular management and smooth running of the business of the House with a tacit understanding that, however important the rights of the Opposition may be, the Government must be allowed to govern and to get through its essential legislation. Where some of the fiercest clashes occur is when a Government is alleged by its critics not to represent a majority of the electors and to be introducing legislation, the justification for which the Opposition does not accept. Broadly, however, it still remains true, as stated by Sir Courtenay Ilbert, that 'the existence of every Government, and especially of every constitutional Government, depends on the observance of understandings which proceed on the assumption of a general desire to make the machine work. If these understandings are not observed, the wheels of the machine are stopped and the machinery may be brought to a standstill'. The usual channels work on the general assumption that it is mutually desirable that the machinery should work.

Each week in the House of Commons the Leader of the House, a government minister, announces the business of the House for the forthcoming week in reply to a question from the leader of the Opposition.

House of Commons, 16 December 1982 (HC Deb. vol. 34, cols. 481–2)

MR MICHAEL FOOT (Ebbw Vale): Will the Leader of the House state the business for next week?

The Lord President of the Council and Leader of the House of Commons (MR JOHN BIFFEN): Yes, Sir. The business for next week will be as follows:

MONDAY 20 DECEMBER – Motion on the Christmas Adjournment.

Remaining stages of the Agricultural Marketing Bill.

Motions on the Asian and African Development Banks Orders [and on other Orders and Regulations].

TUESDAY 21 DECEMBER – Debate on the White Paper on 'The Falklands Campaign: The Lessons', Cmnd 8758, which will arise on a motion for the Adjournment of the House.

WEDNESDAY 22 DECEMBER – Debate on the report by Lord Shackleton on the economic potential of the Falkland Islands, Cmnd 8653, on a motion for the Adjournment of the House.

THURSDAY 23 DECEMBER – It will be proposed that the House should meet at 9.30 am, take questions until 10.30 am, and adjourn at 3.30 pm until 17 January 1983.

MR FOOT: First, may I put to the right hon. Gentleman two major matters that have arisen in the past few days? Following yesterday's emergency debate and the Foreign

Secretary's extraordinary statement that he was either unable or unwilling to describe precisely who would have control over the firing of cruise and Pershing missiles if they were ever stationed in this country, we believe that the House should be given an early opportunity to discuss that matter. It is plainly of absolutely supreme importance for the people of this country. Will he assure us that as soon as we return from the recess we shall have in Government time a major debate on disarmament? . . .

Secondly, as a result of the decision that was taken yesterday in the European Assembly about Great Britain's contribution to the budget, all the negotiations on Great Britain's contribution seem to be in jeopardy. It is a matter of prime importance to the House. I presume that an early statement will be made to the House. The best time for that would be on Monday. The Government should make a major statement on how they are to defend British interests in the matter.

There are three other matters that I wish to put to the right hon. Gentleman. When will we have a statement on steel, and will a debate be held? The Leader of the House has so far refused to provide time for a debate on fisheries, but I still ask for a debate on that subject. I hope that the right hon. Gentleman will be able to give me a favourable answer on the question of teacher-training colleges which I raised with him last week.

MR BIFFEN: May I respond in reverse order to the five points that the right hon. Gentleman has made? The issue of colleges of education was raised last week. I understand that preliminary discussions have taken place through the usual channels. Clearly there will be no time for a debate next week. I shall of course bear in mind the possibility of such a debate.

. . . I have said several times that the Government would wish to arrange a debate on the whole fisheries issue. There will be a Council of Ministers meeting early next week. That may well be decisive in resolving the present deadlock between Denmark and other members of the Community. I hope that the debate can take place in the new year.

My right hon. Friend the Prime Minister said a few moments ago that the statement on steel would be made on Monday next week. I cannot offer a debate in the few days remaining before we adjourn for Christmas, but clearly it is a matter that the House will wish to discuss when we return after the recess.

The Economic and Finance Council will consider tomorrow in the light of today's decision the serious position that has arisen in respect of the United Kingdom's contribution to the European Community budget and the refund. I ask the House therefore to wait until the outcome of that meeting is known. That will lead one to decide the appropriate day for a statement. I am sure that we can resolve through the usual channels when that should be. . . .

I note that the right hon. Gentleman would like a further debate on cruise missiles. Doubtless we can consider that through the usual channels.

On the Opposition front bench there is a 'shadow Cabinet' which directs the strategy of the Opposition and organizes its tactical response to forthcoming government business in the House. Members of the shadow Cabinet hold 'portfolios' corresponding to those of ministers of the Crown. A Labour shadow Cabinet is formed by the Parliamentary Committee, consisting of six ex officio members and 15 elected by Labour MPs; a Conservative shadow Cabinet (or Consultative Committee) is appointed by the party leader. The Opposition front bench also includes other MPs who are appointed by the leader of the Opposition as official spokesmen or junior spokesmen on specific areas of policy. The Labour Opposition front bench at the end of 1984 consisted of the Parliamentary Committee or shadow Cabinet of 21 members and 45 other spokesmen.

The front bench team speaks for the official Opposition and its members are expected to observe a convention of collective responsibility and refrain from public dissent from party policies. Compliance with this convention may be enforced by the Leader of the Opposition, as happened when Mr Enoch Powell was dismissed from the Conservative shadow Cabinet in 1968 after a speech on immigration which was considered by Mr Heath to be damaging to the Conservative position on race relations. A more recent instance was the dismissal by the Labour Opposition Leader of three front bench spokesmen for voting contrary to a shadow Cabinet injunction in a debate on the Falklands crisis in 1982. Mr Foot had in the previous year issued a public statement insisting on the convention. This included the following passage (*The Times*, 14 November 1981):

The question of Shadow Cabinet collective responsibility is not one that has suddenly emerged. It is a rule which has been accepted by the Labour Party for generations. . . . A Labour Shadow Cabinet cannot conduct its primary function of directing the fight against our Tory opponents if every decision is subject to debate or different emphasis afterwards by individual spokesmen in the House itself or elsewhere.

The Opposition is under certain disadvantages in delivering its challenge to the government in the House of Commons. The government controls the parliamentary timetable, and possesses weapons for restricting debate such as the closure and the guillotine. The Opposition, however, has its own weapons. A Minister of the Crown once conceded that 'delaying tactics of a strenuous nature' are a legitimate weapon of opposition (Mr Iain Macleod, HC Deb. vol. 655, col. 432, 7 March 1962), and it is one that can be used to considerable effect. If the Opposition considers itself unfairly treated it may withhold cooperation from the government in the conduct of parliamentary business, shutting off 'the usual channels'. It was no idle threat when Mr Jeffrey Rooker, an Opposition spokesman, said in the House on 6 May 1980 (HC Deb. vol. 984, col. 114):

[T]he Opposition will not counsel Labour Members to co-operate in the normal running of business in the House. The Government have a large majority but it will not be possible on many days for them to do what they want when they want to do it. . . .

As a last resort, opposition may be carried to the point of deliberate obstruction: filibustering, contrived points of order, repeated interventions in speeches and other time-wasting devices can be used by an Opposition which considers its rights to have been violated. (See, e.g., HC Deb. vol. 990, cols. 522–50, 6 August 1980). But the confrontation between the parties is not usually taken to these lengths, and in general the government remains in effective control of the proceedings of the House.

The Opposition is unable to match the government in information and resources. An attempt to redress the balance was made on 20 March 1975 when the House of Commons resolved (HC Deb. vol. 888, cols. 1933–4) that provision should be made 'for financial assistance to any Opposition party in this House to assist that party in carrying out its Parliamentary business'. In accordance with a formula then laid down, and revised in subsequent resolutions, opposition parties can claim payments towards expenditure on their parliamentary work, the amounts being related to a party's numerical strength in the House and its electoral support. The money may be used, for example, for the employment of research assistants to frontbenchers and for expenses of the party leader's and Whips' offices. The cost is borne on the House of Commons Vote.

A considerable imbalance of resources remains, and is unavoidable. But opposition needs to be strong and well informed if government is to be accountable, and if the policies of the 'alternative government' are to be realistic. Should the Opposition have its own 'civil service'?

> Douglas Wass, *Government and the Governed: BBC Reith Lectures*
> *1983* (1984), pp. 76–7

I believe there is a good case in principle for improving the efficiency of the Opposition by providing it with the staff to do its job effectively.

The solution canvassed in some quarters is that we should establish a Department of the Opposition, staffed with people who would be rather like civil servants: they would be at the service of the front bench and their salaries would be paid from public funds. The size of such a department might be measured in terms of perhaps a few dozen policy advisers plus ancillary staff and the annual cost [would be] a small sum in relation to the cost of Parliament as a whole. Each shadow minister would have in effect a cabinet of officials. Their business would be to keep a close watch on developments in the area of their chief's portfolio. They would provide advice which enabled him to criticise government policy, and they would put forward constructive alternative proposals. There ought also to be a handful of co-ordinating officials, serving the shadow Cabinet as a whole. . . .

Sir Douglas Wass goes on to outline a number of political and administrative objections to this proposal. A Department of the Opposition would create resentment in a multi-party system and would inhibit the emergence of new parties, so entrenching and solidifying the *status quo*. Some, he adds, would fear that an official staff would 'capture the minds' of the Opposition front bench, so that the political system would 'surrender to the middle ground'. There would be the problem of what should become of the Opposition staff when the Opposition became the government: if they were to move into government as senior officials, and out again with the next change, a political civil service would have been created.

Nevertheless Sir Douglas Wass proposes, as a limited experiment, the secondment of a small official staff to the Opposition, with safeguards to avoid politicization. Might it be better if opposition parties were given more generous assistance from public funds to improve their own supporting services?

The Opposition performs a dual role: it both opposes the government, functioning as 'an orchestration of all discontents' (Bernard Crick, *New Statesman*, 18 June 1960, p. 883), and presents itself to the electorate as an alternative government. It is the latter role which is said to make for 'responsible Opposition', meaning an Opposition which accepts the basic political structure and obeys the rules of the parliamentary game. Acceptance of parliamentary democracy is not, however, incompatible with radical policies for institutional change.

A 'responsible' Opposition, aspiring to power, will criticize the government and expose its weaknesses. It will use whatever strength it has to exact concessions from the government. Continuous scrutiny by opposition parties in a public arena compels governments to defend, to explain and sometimes to moderate their policies.

Ronald Butt, *The Power of Parliament* (2nd edn 1969), pp. 317–18

Just as a Government must anticipate the reactions of its backbenchers and prepare to meet them, so it must do the same in relation to the Opposition. Of course, an Opposition attack is much less menacing than a widespread tide of rebellion within the governing party. Nevertheless, although a Cabinet, to satisfy a particular demand inside its own party, may be prepared to brave the Opposition storm, in many other cases it will modify its policies in the light of what it expects the Opposition case to be. If it suspects that the Opposition will have an attractive case, it will do its best, within broad limits, to make that case less attractive – or to steal and adapt the Opposition's clothes. In this broad sense, therefore, the voice of Opposition contributes to the policy-making of Government in any given Parliament and is not simply a factor in deciding what the composition of the *next* Parliament should be. For example, although Conservative Party opinion prompted the production of the Commonwealth Immigrants Act which became law in 1962, an assessment of Opposition feeling was an important factor in preventing the Government from going further. As it was, the Bill was fought bitterly by the Labour Opposition. This was a generally popular measure but had the Government taken it so far as to have appeared to ordinary people to be unreasonable . . . then many more people might have been swung against it and the Opposition would have been presented with a very much stronger case. To see this point, one has only to try to envisage what shape the measure might have taken had the Labour Opposition not expressed such uncompromising hostility, *in advance*. Indeed, leaving aside the question of the Opposition's part in determining the issues and outcome of any next election, one has only to try to imagine the silence of the Opposition during any Parliament to comprehend what difference it would make to the current conduct of politics.

Apart from the real if indirect effect it has on the evolution of Government policy, the Opposition can also, by a carefully fought and reasoned campaign, get the details of legislation amended. Many, perhaps most, crucial amendments to Bills are in the name of the Minister concerned, yet they may well have arisen from the activity of the

Opposition. Thus the capital gains provisions of the 1964 Labour Government . . . were heavily amended by the Chancellor. Yet the detailed pressure for amendment and the exposure of weak elements in the Government's original proposal came from the Conservative Opposition. The Government's acceptance of some of them cannot be explained in terms of its small majority but rather reflected the Chancellor's understanding that he had to meet a powerful Opposition case.

In British politics, everything depends on the convention that the power of the majority should not be used to steamroller into silence the protests of the minority. If numbers were all that counted, a Government majority could any day silence the minority Opposition, and it is owing less to the formal rules of Parliament than to an acceptance of the spirit of common procedures that it does not do so.

(b) **Backbenchers**

Backbenchers on both sides of the House have a role in the checking of government. Although they generally give their primary loyalty to party they have also other interests and loyalties, and will often speak in the House for their constituencies, or on behalf of outside groups with which they are associated, or to argue the cases of individuals who complain of unfair treatment by government departments. This pleading of special interests, or checking of the detail of administration, is more a function of backbenchers than of organized parties. The procedure and practice of the House provide for it in a number of ways. Besides the daily half-hour adjournment debate and recess adjournment debates, which are used by backbenchers for raising issues of concern to them or their constituents, three full days and one Friday in each session are set aside for debates initiated by backbenchers. In addition, private members' motions and bills have precedence on 20 Fridays and four other half days in each session. Standing Order 9 (emergency debates) provides an opportunity for backbenchers to raise urgent issues on the floor of the House, even though a subsequent debate is only rarely allowed. Backbenchers make frequent use of Question Time in the House (see below) and write to ministers about the grievances of constituents.

Even if much of this backbench activity has no obvious impact on the government, an administration that did not have to submit to it could afford to be less careful and more high-handed.

Important reforms have been brought about by private members' Acts – for example, the liberalization of the law on abortion, homosexual behaviour and divorce, the abolition of capital punishment, and the ending of theatre censorship. Although a private member's bill has no prospect of being enacted in the teeth of government opposition, if the bill has support on both sides of the House the government may stay its hand, help the bill on its way, or promise to introduce a bill of its own. For example, a controversial House Buyers' Bill introduced by an Opposition MP, Mr Austin Mitchell, in 1983, won a second reading with the support of government backbenchers, and was withdrawn only after the Government had given undertakings to review the system of house transfer and the solicitors' conveyancing monopoly, and to introduce legislation.

A government is more concerned to retain the loyalty and support of its own backbenchers than to placate the Opposition. If disaffection should break out among its backbenchers the government's management of the House becomes difficult, the signs of disunity affect its reputation in the country, and it may suffer defeats in the House in circumstances of maximum publicity.

In recent years government backbenchers have shown an increased willingness to use their votes independently – even to inflict defeats on the government, knowing that such defeats do not normally put the government's survival in question. (See p. 350 above.) Between 1970 and 1979 both Conservative and Labour Governments suffered numerous defeats, on the floor of the House and in standing committees, as a result of backbench defection. The Conservative Government that came to power with a large majority in 1979, and substantially increased that majority in 1983, was less vulnerable to defeat, but nevertheless saw its immigration rules voted down by the House on 15 December 1982 (HC Deb. vol. 34, col. 355), has suffered defeats in committee, and has repeatedly had its majority reduced by backbench revolts.

The influence of government backbenchers is not to be measured solely in government defeats. A less obvious but continuous and powerful restraint (or spur) operates on government through the *anticipated reactions* of its backbenchers. Backbench opinion, transmitted through the Whips or expressed in party committees or in private meetings with ministers, indicates to the government the limits of the possible, and may cause it to discard or trim a policy which backbenchers will not support. A famous instance was the Labour Government's abandonment of its proposal to legislate on industrial relations ('In Place of Strife') in 1969 when it became evident that Labour backbenchers would not support the bill. (Opposition in the Cabinet and from the TUC also contributed to this major reversal of policy.) The Thatcher Government has been compelled by backbench opinion to reverse or modify its policies on a number of occasions, on such matters as a register of immigrants (1979), local referendums (1981), green belt policy (1983), provisions in the Rates Bill (1984), and student grants (1984).

Opposition backbenchers, remote from the centres of governmental policy-making, sustain their own front bench as government backbenchers sustain the government. But there are usually groups of Opposition backbenchers who criticize the government from a perspective different from that of the party leaders. When there is consensus between the front benches the independent stance of such groups keeps alive the flame of parliamentary dissent. Opposition to the Falklands campaign in 1982 was principally maintained by dissident Labour backbenchers.

Cross-party combinations of backbenchers can be formidable. It was such a combination (the 'unholy alliance' led by Mr Foot and Mr Powell) that in 1969 defeated a scheme for the reform of the House of Lords which was supported by both Government and official Opposition. At a remove from the battleground of party politics, all-party subject committees of members, often linked with interest groups outside the House, are sometimes able to exercise a significant influence on government policy. (See David Judge, *Backbench Specialisation in the House of Commons*, 1981, pp. 141–4.)

(c) **The House**

There are occasions, not very frequent, when members on both sides of the House of Commons combine to assert the power of the House against what they see as an encroachment by the executive upon its rights or privileges. On these rare but instructive occasions we see the House acting as a body to claim its constitutional authority over the executive. One such instance occurred in 1980.

Following the seizure of American hostages in Iran on 4 November 1979 the United Kingdom Government introduced in the House of Commons on 8 May 1980 the Iran (Temporary Powers) Bill, providing for economic sanctions against Iran. The Minister in charge of the bill assured the House that the bill and orders to be made under it would apply only to future contracts, and would not affect the implementation of those already made by British exporters. The bill was duly passed by both Houses and received the royal assent on 15 May.

On 18 May it was agreed at a meeting of the Foreign Ministers of the member states of the European Community that sanctions should be jointly applied against Iran and should extend to all contracts entered into after 4 November 1979. Since the Iran (Temporary Powers) Act did not apply to contracts already made, the Government proposed to rely upon earlier legislation, the Import, Export and Customs Powers (Defence) Act 1939, under which orders could be made prohibiting the export of goods to Iran under contracts entered into at any time after 4 November 1979. When this decision was announced in the House of Commons by the Lord Privy Seal (speaking for the Foreign Office) he was strongly criticized, from both sides of the House, by members who considered that the House had been misled. After the announcement an Opposition MP sought and obtained leave from the Speaker to move the adjournment of the House under Standing Order 9 'for the purpose of discussing a specific and important matter that should have urgent consideration' and, the required support of not less than 40 members having been given, an emergency debate was set down for the next day. On 20 May the Lord Privy Seal made the following statement to the House (HC Deb. vol. 985, cols. 254–5):

After my statement yesterday about decisions taken on the implementation of sanctions against Iran by Foreign Ministers of the European Community meeting informally in Naples over the weekend, the House made its view very clear that the inclusion of retrospection, however limited, was unacceptable.

The Government have therefore decided that sanctions will not be retrospective. No orders will be laid before the House which ban the supply of goods under arrangements made before the date on which those orders were laid. Last night we informed our European Community partners and the Government of the United States that, in view of the opposition of this House to retrospection, we would no longer be prepared to proceed to apply any element of retrospection among the decisions that we agreed to at the meeting in Naples . . . .

4 Control and scrutiny

(a) Policy and administration

Debates

The main contest between the parties takes place in debates on the floor of the House. Battle is joined on such general issues as unemployment, immigration, or the government's expenditure plans, or debate may focus on specific governmental decisions such as the closure of a dockyard, the deportation of a non-British resident, or the sale of arms to a foreign government.

> R. L. Borthwick, 'The Floor of the House' in S. A. Walkland and
> Michael Ryle (eds.), *The Commons Today* (rev. edn 1981), p. 68

Non-legislative debates are based on three types of motions. Substantive motions are the most concrete. Typically, governments seek approval of their policies in such motions, opposition parties move expressions of regret at omissions or make suggestions for more sensible courses of action. Alternatively, on a Supply Day [now Opposition day] for example, the motion may be critical of the Government who will then propose a more acceptable (from their point of view) set of words as an amendment. Less clear are motions, much favoured by governments, inviting the House to 'take note' of this or that document, though even these may have amendments moved to them. Least precise of all in terms of wording is the debate based on a motion for the adjournment of the House. It may, of course, be an advantage in certain situations not to have a more precise motion before the House. In what is probably the most famous example in this century, the debate of May 1940, the absence of a more precise motion probably helped broaden support against the Government, while in less dramatic circumstances it may be useful to facilitate a very wide-ranging debate (as on devolution early in 1976) or to permit all sides of a divided party to come together, as when the Labour Government was seeking a vote of confidence in March 1976.

Each session begins with a debate on the address in reply to the Queen's speech, continuing over some five or six days, which allows a general discussion of government policy and opposition amendments (one such amendment being at the disposal of minor parties). Debates on policy and administration initiated by the government, opposition parties and back-benchers continue throughout the session, interspersed with debates on legislation and other business of the House. As an exercise in 'control' such debates are most effective when governmental proposals are presented to the House, it may be in a Green Paper, before they have become firm, as a test of parliamentary and public opinion.

Since what is said in a debate rarely affects the result of the vote at its end or induces the government to reverse a decision already taken, it is apparent that debates are not a strong instrument of control. But they are an essential part of the continuous parliamentary scrutiny of government, compelling it to explain and defend its policies and decisions.

Philip Norton, *The Commons in Perspective* (1981), p. 119

[G]eneral debates are . . . not without some uses in helping to ensure a measure of scrutiny and influence, however limited. A debate prevents a Government from remaining mute. Ministers have to explain and justify the Government's position. They may want to reveal as little as possible, but the Government cannot afford to hold back too much for fear of letting the Opposition appear to have the better argument. The involvement of Opposition spokesman and backbenchers ensures that any perceived cracks in the Government's position will be exploited. If it has failed to carry its own side privately, the Government may suffer the embarrassment of the publicly expressed dissent of some of its own supporters, dissent which provides good copy for the press. On some occasions, Ministers may even be influenced by comments made in debate. They will not necessarily approach an issue with closed minds, and will normally not wish to be totally unreceptive to the comments of the Opposition (whose co-operation they need for the efficient despatch of business) or of their own Members (whose support they need in the lobbies, and among whom morale needs to be maintained); a Minister who creates a good impression by listening attentively to views expressed by Members may enhance his own prospects of advancement . . . . A Minister faced by a baying Opposition and silence behind him may be unnerved and realise that he is not carrying Members on either side with him, and in consequence may moderate or even, in extreme cases, reverse his position.

Adjournment debates initiated by backbenchers on local or narrow issues of administration may take place in an almost empty House and attract no publicity, but a minister is obliged to attend and answer what is sometimes a skilfully presented case. If the minister is not often persuaded to change his mind, the debate may serve at least to bring into the open the way in which a decision was reached.

Questions

Any member (other than a minister or, by convention, the leader of the Opposition) may ask Questions of ministers by giving notice to the Table

Office. If an oral answer in the House is required the Question is marked with an asterisk; other Questions are given a written answer. Questions to ministers 'should relate to the public affairs with which they are officially connected, to proceedings pending in Parliament, or to matters of administration for which they are responsible': Erskine May, *Parliamentary Practice* (20th edn 1983), p. 336.

A Question may seek information or request action by the government. The requirement that it must relate to matters for which ministers are responsible to Parliament generally excludes Questions about the activities of local authorities, nationalized industries, other non-departmental public bodies, and the police. A minister can, however, be asked about the exercise of his own powers in relation to these bodies – such as powers of appointment, or to give directions, issue guidance, approve expenditure or call for reports. The Home Secretary is the police authority for the Metropolitan Police and can therefore be questioned about his actions in this capacity, but Questions cannot, in general, be asked about the exercise of police discretion in matters of law enforcement which (by law or convention) are beyond the scope of the Home Secretary's supervisory powers. (Cf. *R.* v. *Metropolitan Police Commissioner, ex p. Blackburn* [1968] 2 QB 118 at 135–6, 138; Geoffrey Marshall, 'Police Accountability Revisited' in David Butler and A. H. Halsey (eds.), *Policy and Politics* (1978), p. 51.)

House of Commons, 13 July 1979. Written answer (HC Deb.
vol. 970, col. *313*w)

Miss Richardson asked the Secretary of State for the Home Department whether it is the practice of the Metropolitan Police to collect, as a matter of routine, details of the organiser, chairman and speakers at political meetings; whether he endorses such a practice . . . if he will indicate the use to which such information is put . . . and who has access to it. . . .

MR WHITELAW: These are operational matters for the Commissioner. I fully support his collecting information necessary for discharging his responsibility for the maintenance of public order.

This restriction upon parliamentary inquiry is subject to the qualification that the Home Secretary, after consulting the Metropolitan Police Commissioner, will report to the House on 'operational matters of major public interest' (HC Deb. vol. 36, col. *312*w, 8 February 1983). Ministers will sometimes respond to Questions about the actions of nationalized industries and other public bodies for which they do not bear responsibility by giving information supplied by the body concerned or requesting it to write to the member.

A minister is not obliged to answer any Question, and there are many matters on which ministers customarily refuse to give answers. Among these are certain broad categories such as confidential exchanges with foreign governments, national security, commercial confidence, information about individual persons and companies, and advice given to ministers by officials. A detailed list of excluded matters was made by the Table Office for a Select Committee in 1972 (see the *Report from the Select Committee on Parliamentary Questions*, HC 393 of 1971–2, Appendix 9). The list consisted of 95 items, among which were: details of arms sales, defence contract prices, forecasts of future levels of unemployment, government borrowing, tax affairs of individuals or companies, forecasts of future overseas aid, telephone tapping, details of air-miss inquiries, Cabinet committees, and 'detailed arrangements for the conduct of Government business'.

Information requested may be refused on the ground that it is not available or could only be obtained at disproportionate cost. Departments apply a general rule that a cost exceeding a certain sum – raised to £200 in November 1982 – justifies refusal.

Since there is no obligation to answer, there is no effective redress for a member who is refused an answer or considers an answer unsatisfactory. The Speaker cannot assist him. The member may raise the matter in an adjournment debate, and is allowed to repeat the Question after an interval of three months. Once in every session ministers may be asked whether they will answer Questions in any previously excluded category. (See HC Deb. vol. 848, cols. 1335–7, 20 December 1972.)

Written answers are given to 'unstarred' Questions and also to Questions put down for oral answer that are not reached in the time allotted on the floor of the House. A considerable amount of information is elicited from the government in written answers. A member can put down any number of unstarred Questions (whereas there are limits on the number of Questions a member may table for oral answer) and can coordinate his Questions to different departments so that a picture is built up of the government's whole operations in the area in question.

Questions for oral answer are taken for about 55 minutes on Mondays, Tuesdays, Wednesdays and Thursdays. Ministers answer in accordance with a rota which is arranged through the usual channels, more time being set aside for the major (or most controversial) departments. (A subject like the Arts may be given only about ten minutes a month.) The prime minister answers for about 15 minutes on Tuesdays and Thursdays.

A member who receives an oral answer can go on to ask a supplementary Question, of which no prior notice need have been given, and other members may put supplementaries if they catch the Speaker's eye.

What are called 'open Questions' are designed not to reveal the subject-matter of the supplementary Question which will follow. This allows the MP to raise a supplementary which is topical on the day when the Question comes up for answer, and also provides an element of surprise. Most open Questions are tabled for answer by the prime minister. Their inscrutable character ensures that they will not be transferred to other, more directly responsible ministers, which might happen if the real purport of the Question were apparent on its face.

House of Commons, 18 January 1983 (HC Deb. vol. 35,
col. 166)

Mr Alton asked the Prime Minister if she will list her official engagements for 18 January.

THE PRIME MINISTER: This morning I had meetings with ministerial colleagues and others. In addition to my duties in the House I shall be having further meetings later today. . . .

MR ALTON: Is the Prime Minister aware that there is evidence that the atomic tests that took place in Maralinga in the south Pacific in the 1950s led to the deaths of some of our service men from cancer? Does she not agree that . . . what is required is a public inquiry and an assurance that compensation will be given to the victims and their relatives?

Twenty-three Questions tabled for 18 January 1983 asked the Prime Minister in identical terms to list her official engagements for the day. Three were reached for oral answer (and supplementaries) and the rest received an identical written answer.

Questions put by backbenchers on the government side may reflect their constituency and other interests or their unease about aspects of government policy, and in this way they play their part in the scrutiny of ministers. Some of their Questions, however, are suggested by ministers themselves, to enable the minister to convey information to the House (often by written answer, entailing no supplementaries). Government backbenchers may also table Questions with the object of balancing hostile Questions asked by opposition members. On one occasion it came to light that civil servants had assisted ministers in the preparation of a 'bank' of favourable Questions to be supplied to sympathetic backbenchers. A select committee which considered this incident advised that

it is not the role of the Government machine to seek to redress the party balance of Questions on the Order Paper, and civil servants should not in future be asked to prepare Questions which have this object. [*Report from the Select Committee on Parliamentary Questions*, HC 393 of 1971–2, para. 36.]

The Government agreed to lay down a new rule in accordance with this recommendation (HC Deb. vol. 847, cols. *462–3*w, 6 December 1972).

Sir Norman Chester, 'Questions in the House' in S. A. Walkland
and Michael Ryle (eds.), *The Commons Today* (rev edn 1981),
pp. 185, 188–9

Question Time . . . comes right at the beginning of the daily business, the Chamber is much fuller than for most of the rest of the day and it is a convenient time for the Press reporters, some answers even being early enough to appear in the evening papers.

There is something for everybody at Question Time – a Minister may shine or be caught out and forty or fifty Members have a chance of getting on their feet and uttering a few words in the Chamber, a rare event for most of them. . . . The fact that most of the information could have been obtained by way of written answer, that few Members are particularly brilliant at asking supplementaries and that few Ministers are caught napping by them still makes it a special occasion. Above all it is not given over to lengthy frontbench speeches, it is largely a backbenchers' affair, and Ministers are there to answer to even the newest and humblest Member of the House . . . .

Thus a large number of [a minister's] own supporters will see how he performs, whether he appears to be on top of his job and gives an air of confidence, and what his attitude is to this or that facet of the work of his department. . . .

It must also be remembered that a Minister personally handles very few of the day-to-day decisions which are taken by his civil servants in his name. These decisions are, of course, made in a way which the official thinks conforms to ministerial policy. A Question about one of these decisions brings the case on to the Minister's desk. The decision may have been taken at quite a low level in the department. It now is looked at by the senior members of the department, even the Permanent Secretary as well as the Minister and one or more Parliamentary Secretaries. The PQ file (each Question is normally given its own file) will normally contain not only a draft answer but also any relevant facts. The Minister has no excuse for not going into the case and satisfying himself that the departmental decision was correct and conformed to his policy. When he examines it he may be surprised, even shocked, and make a different decision or clarify or redefine the policy to be followed in future. This is the internal reality of the public answerability of the Minister.

Private notice Questions, which are not subject to the two days' notice required for ordinary Questions, may be allowed by the Speaker for raising urgent matters of public importance for answer on the same day. The leader of the Opposition normally puts his Questions by private notice.

Select Committees

Besides *ad hoc* committees set up from time to time for particular investigations, the House of Commons has some 25 select committees which are appointed each session in accordance with standing or sessional orders. They include the Committee of Privileges, dating from the seventeenth century, the Committee of Public Accounts, first set up in 1861, and such more recent creations as the Select Committee on the Parliamentary Commissioner and the Select Committee on European Legislation. Not all of these committees are concerned with the control or scrutiny of the executive, but this is the essential function of fourteen select committees established in 1979 'to examine the expenditure, administration and policy' of the principal government departments and the public bodies associated with them.

Governments do not usually regard with enthusiasm the establishment of select committees which can question their policies and investigate the details of administration. The 'departmental' select committees set up in 1979 owe their existence to backbench pressure and the persistence of a reform-minded

Minister and Leader of the House, Mr St John-Stevas, just as an earlier, more limited experiment with specialist committees is associated with Mr Richard Crossman as Leader of the House from 1966 to 1968. The committees established in the 1966–70 Parliament – on Agriculture, Science and Technology, Education and Science, Race Relations and Immigration, Scottish Affairs, and Overseas Aid – did some useful work but were at first regarded with scepticism by many MPs and with suspicion by the Government, which tried to influence the selection of members and the choice of subjects to be investigated. The committee on Agriculture, which showed a particular independence of spirit, was soon wound up. It became evident that too great an assertiveness by the committees would result in counter-measures by the government – a reminder that the traditions of British parliamentary government do not easily accommodate rival institutions which will 'balance' the power of the executive.

Nevertheless it was increasingly realized by backbenchers that in select committees they could take part in a concerted and informed scrutiny of the administration which was more effective than their sporadic efforts on the floor of the House. The system developed in a rather piecemeal way until in 1978 the Select Committee on Procedure recommended a new structure of committees which 'would cover the activities of all departments of the United Kingdom Government, and of all nationalised industries and other quasi-autonomous governmental organisations' (First Report, HC 588–I of 1977–8, para. 5.22). The 14 new departmental committees were established on a firm footing in the standing orders of the House in 1979. The following are the committees, each of which 'shadows' one or more government departments and their associated bodies:

Agriculture
Defence
Education, Science and Arts
Employment
Energy
Environment
Foreign Affairs
Home Affairs
Scottish Affairs
Social Services
Trade and Industry
Transport
Treasury and Civil Service
Welsh Affairs

The Law Officers' Department and the Lord Chancellor's Department are excluded from scrutiny by the committees on the ground that parliamentary inquiry might impinge upon the independence of the judiciary. Committee chairmen have not been convinced that this exclusion is justified, and the Home Affairs Committee has noted that the result is that 'substantial areas of public expenditure such as legal aid and the administration of the courts are not susceptible to scrutiny by any House of Commons Committee' (*First Report from the Liaison Committee*, HC 92 of 1982–3, pp. 12, 85).

If a committee is to keep the work of a department under effective review it may need to conduct simultaneous inquiries through sub-committees, but so far only three of the committees (Foreign Affairs, Home Affairs, and Treasury and Civil Service) have been empowered to set up one sub-committee each.

Each committee now has 11 members (except Scottish Affairs, which has 13) appointed on the nomination of an all-party Committee of Selection which has regard to the balance of parties in the House. It is fortunate that members are not chosen (like those of some other Commons committees) by the Whips and do not hold their places by governmental favour. In a few cases the government has intervened, overtly or behind the scenes, to affect the composition or chairmanship of committees: it is important that such mischief should be resisted. The committees are the preserve of backbenchers: neither Parliamentary Private Secretaries nor frontbench spokesmen are appointed to them, although former ministers may be members. The committees elect their own chairmen, but informal arrangements have ensured that half the chairmanships are held by opposition members. Chairmen serve on a Liaison Committee which coordinates the work of the committees and makes representations on their behalf (on staffing, powers, etc.) to the House.

Each of the departmental committees has power 'to send for persons, papers and records'. This formal power is rarely exercised, the committees preferring to proceed by invitation rather than command, but some initial refusals to appear or provide evidence have led to the service of formal orders by the Serjeant-at-Arms. The committees cannot themselves enforce their orders, but a refusal to comply could be reported to the House which might treat the refusal as a contempt. Ministers, however, can be ordered to attend select committees or produce documents only by the House itself. (See Appendix C to the *First Report form the Select Committee on Procedure*, HC 588-1 of 1977–8, and K. P. Poole (1979) 32 *Parliamentary Affairs* 268.)

The Leader of the House of Commons gave the following assurance on behalf of the Government on 25 June 1979 (HC Deb. vol. 969, col. 45):

> There need be no fear that departmental Ministers will refuse to attend Committees to answer questions about their Departments or that they will not make every effort to ensure that the fullest possible information is made available to them.
>
> I give the House the pledge on the part of the Government that every Minister from the most senior Cabinet Minister to the most junior Under-Secretary will do all in his or her power to co-operate with the new system of Committees and to make it a success.

Both ministers and senior officials appear frequently before the committees, and are questioned at length and in detail. The committees have sometimes had to be content with the appearance of a different minister or official from the one they wished to question, but the Liaison Committee said in 1982 that the undertakings given on 25 June 1979 had been honoured satisfactorily (First Report, HC 92 of 1982–3, para. 48). Nevertheless the committees sometimes have difficulty in getting information and one of them has urged that the government 'should be far more forthcoming with select committees, both about inter-departmental consultations and about their relationships with local government'. (See the *First Report from the Liaison Committee*, above, p. 49.) In 1984 the Government declined to allow the Director of the Government Communications Headquarters and a trade union official employed there to give evidence to the Select Committee on Employment, which was inquiring into a ban on trade union membership at GCHQ. (See *First Report from the Employment Committee*, HC 238 of 1983–4, paras. 6–7).

Governments refuse to disclose certain categories of information to select committees. These were indicated in a Memorandum of Guidance issued to civil servants in 1976 and subsequently revised.

Memorandum of Guidance for Officials Appearing before Select Committees (1980)

9. Officials appearing before Select Committees do so on behalf of their Ministers. It is customary, therefore, for Ministers to decide which officials . . . should appear to give evidence. Select Committees have in the past generally accepted this position. Should a Committee invite a named official to appear, the Minister concerned, if he did not wish that official to represent him, might suggest that another official could more appropriately do so, or that he himself should give evidence to the Committee. If a Committee insisted on a particular official appearing before them they could issue a formal order for his attendance. In such an event the official would have to appear before the Committee. He would remain subject to Ministerial instructions as to how he should answer questions. . . .

15. The general principle to be followed is that it is the duty of officials to be as helpful as possible to Committees, and that any withholding of information should be limited to reservations that are necessary in the interests of good government or to safeguard national security. Departments should, therefore, be as forthcoming as they can (within the limits set out in this note) when requested to provide information. . . . Because officials appear on behalf of their Ministers, Departments might want to clear written evidence and briefing with Ministers. It may only be necessary for Ministers to be consulted should there be any doubt among officials on the policy to be explained to the Committee. However, Ministers are ultimately responsible for deciding what information is to be given and for defending their decisions as necessary, and Ministers' views should always be sought if any question arises of withholding information which Committees are known to be seeking. . . .

23. Committees' requests for information should not be met regardless of cost or of diversion of effort from other important matters. It might prove necessary to decline requests which appeared to involve excessive costs. It may be necessary for a Department to consult their Minister if a particular request seems to involve an

unreasonable amount of extra work. . . .

25. Officials should not give evidence about or discuss the following topics:

i. In order to preserve the collective responsibility of Ministers, the advice given to Ministers by their Departments should not be disclosed, nor should information about interdepartmental exchanges on policy issues, about the level at which decisions were taken or the manner in which a Minister has consulted his colleagues. Information should not be given about Cabinet Committees or their discussions. . . .
ii. Advice given by a Law Officer. . . .
iii. The private affairs of individuals or institutions on which any information . . . has been supplied in confidence. . . .

Officials should also, where possible, avoid giving written evidence about or discussing the following matters. . . .

iv. Questions in the field of political controversy. . . .
v. Sensitive information of a commercial or economic nature, e.g. knowledge which could affect the financial markets, without prior consultation with the Chancellor of the Exchequer; sensitive information relating to the commercial operations of nationalised industries, or to contracts; commercial or economic information which has been given to the Government in confidence, unless the advance consent of the persons concerned has been obtained. . . .
vi. Matters which are, or may become, the subject of sensitive negotiations with governments or other bodies, including the European Community, without prior consultation with . . . the Ministers concerned. . . .
vii. Specific cases where the Minister has or may have a quasi-judicial or appellate function, e.g. in relation to planning applications and appeals, or where the subject-matter is being considered by the Courts, or the Parliamentary Commissioner. . . .

29. Official witnesses . . . should as far as possible confine their evidence to questions of fact relating to existing Government policies and actions. Officials should be ready to explain what the existing policies are and the objectives and justification, as the Government sees them, for those policies, and to explain how administrative factors may have affected both the choice of policy measures and the manner of their implementation. It is open to officials to make comments which are not politically contentious but they should as far as possible avoid being drawn, without prior Ministerial authority, into the discussion of alternative policy. If official witnesses are pressed by the Committee to go beyond these limits, they should suggest that the questioning be addressed, or referred, to Ministers. . . .

(The earlier version of this Memorandum is critically analysed by Peter Kellner and Lord Crowther-Hunt, *The Civil Servants*, 1980, pp. 248–52.)

Lord Crowther-Hunt, in a Memorandum to the former Expenditure Committee (Eleventh Report, HC 535-III of 1976–7, Appendix 48, para. 70), argued for the need to

challenge the convention that the advice civil servants give to Ministers must remain confidential. The Parliamentary Committees . . . must, on most issues, be able to get at that advice and subject it to crucial scrutiny. After all, advice that can stand up to such challenge is likely to be better advice. In any event, the House of Commons can hardly successfully share in the policy making process unless it knows what advice ministers are receiving and what the civil servants believe the options to be.

A former Permanent Secretary, Sir Leo Pliatzky (BBC 'Analysis', quoted by Anne Davies, *Reformed Select Committees: The First Year*, 1981, p. 35), disagrees:

Advice senior civil servants have given should remain confidential because otherwise I think it would be very damaging to giving frank honest advice. I have always claimed and received the privilege of speaking my mind. . . . but it is only possible to do that on the basis that it remains between you and the Minister, and if he rejects it, nobody can say 'Ah but there your Permanent Secretary . . . gave you this very considered advice and you rejected it, why did you do that?' A Minister can't be put in that position.

A committee which is dissatisfied with a department's refusal to disclose information to it may report the matter to the House. The Leader of the House said on 16 January 1981 (HC Deb. vol. 996, col. 1312):

I am entirely prepared to give a formal undertaking that where there is evidence of widespread general concern in the House regarding an alleged ministerial refusal to disclose information to a Select Committee, I shall seek to provide time to enable the House to express its view.

In 1982 the chairman of each departmental committee reviewed the work of his committee in its first three years. (See the *First Report from the Liaison Committee*, HC 92 of 1982–3, Part II.) Their reports showed that each committee had developed its own operating style. The following account draws on the report by the Chairman of the Home Affairs Committee.

The Home Affairs Committee

This Committee has appointed a sub-committee which has so far confined its attention to race relations and immigration, and has been responsible for about half the reports produced by the Committee.

In its first three sessions the Committee issued reports on the following subjects:

1979–80 Proposed New Immigration Rules
Race Relations and the 'Sus' Law
Deaths in Police Custody
The Law Relating to Public Order

1980–81 Home Office Reports
British Overseas Citizens
Vagrancy Laws
The Prison Service
Racial Disadvantage

1981–2 The Commission for Racial Equality
NHS Charges for Overseas Visitors

Police Complaints Procedures
Immigration from the Indian Sub-Continent
Miscarriages of Justice

(The Committee has since published reports on the revised immigration rules, racial attacks, the Representation of the People Acts, British nationality fees, ethnic and racial questions in the census, remands in custody, the Chinese community in Britain, refugees and asylum, and the Special Branch.)

The Committee does not avoid controversial subjects yet has not often divided on party lines. Its report on the much abused 'sus' law, which was unanimous in its recommendation that the offence (of being a suspected person loitering with intent) should be abolished, was debated in the House and helped to bring about the repeal of the law (by the Criminal Attempts Act 1981, s. 8).

The inquiries of the Home Affairs Committee are generally of a non-technical kind and it has made less use than some of the other committees of its power to appoint specialist advisers. For its inquiry into racial disadvantage the sub-committee commissioned research from the Research Unit on Ethnic Relations at the University of Aston. In the course of this inquiry the sub-committee took oral evidence from four other government departments besides the Home Office.

High hopes have been expressed for what the departmental committees might achieve, as when the Leader of the House said that they were intended to 'redress the balance of power' between Parliament and the executive (HC Deb. vol. 969, col. 36, 25 June 1979). But the committees do not make policy or take decisions; they may bear the tokens but do not wield the instruments of power. By no means comparable in strength or influence with congressional committees in the United States, they have been created in the traditional select committee mould as institutions 'which are expected to stay on the sidelines' (Nevil Johnson in Dermot Englefield (ed.), *Commons Select Committees: Catalysts for Progress?* 1984, p. 64).

Nevertheless the committees have an important role in the scrutiny of the executive. Ministers and civil servants are questioned in depth in a way that is impossible on the floor of the House. Departmental activities are investigated, in many hours of questioning, by members who have acquired some proficiency in the subject and can call on the assistance of expert advisers. Inquiries can cross departmental boundaries. Not only the departments themselves but others involved with or affected by their policies – local authorities, political parties, industrialists, trade unions – may be called to give evidence. The committees have prized many facts and explanations from the departments that could not have been extracted in any other way, and their published reports as a whole constitute a considerable body of information about the processes of government. Between the departments and the committees there is a continual dialogue, the departments replying to the committees' reports, and their replies sometimes stimulating further inquiry.

It has been found possible in the committees 'for people of widely disparate views to work together exclusively as parliamentarians' (Mr Edward du Cann, MP, in evidence to the Select Committee on Procedure (Finance), HC 365-vi of 1981–2, Q.459). The committees generally strive for consensus, which adds weight to reports that are often critical of government policy or its administration.

Dilys Hill concludes (*Parliamentary Select Committees in Action*, 1984, p. 29) that the departmental committees

have been a success in altering the perceptions and behaviour of Whitehall. Though they are by no means a fierce threat to Departments . . . the evidence suggests that no big new policy will be made without Ministers and mandarins anticipating very carefully the information that Committees will seek. People are more aware that their decisions may be questioned and while this may not mean that the decision is changed it ensures that the surroundings to that decision are fully explored.

There must also be some effect on the House as a whole. Although few reports are specifically debated in the House, many are relevant to the subject-matter of particular debates. Members of the committees are at least better equipped to play their part on the floor of the House, in the striving for accountability that takes place there.

> *First Report from the Liaison Committee, 'The Select Committee System',*
> HC 92 of 1982–3, para. 12

Not all reports achieve the effects hoped of them. There is little point in suggesting that committees are always right – any more than departments, with their much more extensive support, are always right. But every time a subject is opened up by a committee inquiry, parliamentary interest focuses on a topic not chosen by the Government, the department has to reassess its position and defend it in public, Parliament is shown to be interesting itself in a matter of public concern, Opposition Members get access to Government departments, parties outside the House – and Ministers – are given a parliamentary platform from which they can be heard, the House and country become better informed of the facts, Members of different parties may find common ground for agreement, and a public debate on the matter is stimulated.

Not all parliamentarians have welcomed the development of the system of select committee scrutiny. Some argue that it has a tendency to dilute party politics and to diminish the authority of the House by diverting its efforts into the investigation of administrative minutiae. Remedies of this kind, said a great backbench MP, 'would reduce the party struggle . . . to a technical affair', and would 'plunge us into the kind of coalition methods which would destroy the real clash and battle of democracy in this country' (Michael Foot, MP, in Duncan Crow (ed.), *The State of the Nation*, 1973, p. 193).

What should be the broad objectives of the departmental committees? Can they succeed while party is dominant in the House of Commons? If they succeed, will it be at the expense of a necessary 'clash of parties'?

The Parliamentary Commissioner

The office of Parliamentary Commissioner for Administration (or 'parliamentary Ombudsman') was established by the Parliamentary Commissioner Act 1967 for the investigation of complaints by members of the public of injustice resulting from 'maladministration' by government departments. The model for the new office was the Scandinavian Ombudsman, but unlike the officers of this title in Sweden, Denmark, Norway and Finland the British Parliamentary Commissioner was to be harnessed to the legislature and to function as an extension of parliamentary scrutiny and control. The office was intended, as the Government said in 1965, to provide members of Parliament with 'a better instrument which they can use to protect the citizen' (*The Parliamentary Commissioner for Administration*, Cmnd 2767/1965, para. 4). The Parliamentary Commissioner is an officer of the House of Commons and can undertake an investigation only at the request of an MP, to whom he reports the result. He makes an annual report to Parliament and is supported by a House of Commons Select Committee on the Parliamentary Commissioner, which itself reports to the House on the work of the Commissioner and takes up with the departments any cases in which there has been an inadequate response to the Commissioner's findings.

The linkage with Parliament is a controversial feature of the institution, for the 'MP filter' operates in an arbitrary way – some MPs rarely refer complaints to the Commissioner while others do so frequently – and is a hindrance to the ordinary citizen in need of a clear and simple remedy for grievances against the administration. Direct access to the Ombudsman or equivalent officer by members of the public is allowed in most other countries that have this institution, and there is direct access to the Health Service Commissioners (constituted by the National Health Service Reorganization Act 1973 and the National Health Service (Scotland) Act 1972) and to the Commissioner for Complaints who investigates complaints of maladministration against local authorities and other public bodies in Northern Ireland: see the Commissioner for Complaints Act (Northern Ireland) 1969. Some complainants, unaware of the restriction, apply directly to the Commissioner, who has adopted a practice which mitigates the effect of the present rule. If the complaint seems to be 'clearly investigable', the Commissioner sends it with the complainant's consent to his constituency MP, inviting him to refer it to the Commissioner for investigation.

The Commissioner can investigate the complaint of a member of the public 'who claims to have sustained injustice in consequence of maladministration' (Parliamentary Commissioner Act 1967, s.5(1)), but is not authorized to question the *merits* of a decision taken, without maladministration, in the exercise of discretion (s.12(3)). The Commissioner has stated as follows the four basic requirements a complaint must satisfy if he is to accept it for investigation (*Annual Report for 1983*, HC 322 of 1983–4, para. 17):

(1) the department or authority concerned must be one within my jurisdiction; (2) there must be *some* evidence from which it may reasonably be inferred that there has been *administrative* fault; (3) I have to be satisfied that there is an apparent link between the alleged maladministration and the personal injustice which the aggrieved person claims to have suffered; and (4) I also need to be satisfied that there is some prospect of my intervention, if I find the complaint justified, leading to a worthwhile remedy for the aggrieved person or some benefit to the public at large.

'Maladministration' is not defined in the Act, but its intended scope appears from the 'Crossman catalogue' of procedural improprieties instanced by Mr Richard Crossman in the second reading debate on the Parliamentary Commissioner Bill in the House of Commons: 'bias, neglect, inattention, delay, incompetence, ineptitude, arbitrariness and so on' (HC Deb. vol. 734, col. 51, 18 October 1966). (Cf. *R. v. Local Commissioner for Administration for the North and East Area of England, ex p. Bradford MCC* [1979] QB 287.) The Commissioner cannot investigate if the complaint is simply that a department's decision affecting the complainant was wrong, if there is no suggestion that the complainant's case was mishandled in some way, as by disregarding relevant facts, drawing unjustified conclusions, mislaying information, giving inaccurate or misleading advice – 'and so on'. On the other hand a decision may be so 'thoroughly bad in quality' or 'unreasonable' as to justify an inference of maladministration. (See Frank Stacey, *Ombudsmen Compared*, 1978, pp. 157–8.) A report by JUSTICE has recommended that the Commissioner should be expressly empowered to investigate complaints that the action of a government department was 'unreasonable, unjust or oppressive' (*Our Fettered Ombudsman*, 1977, ch. VII).

The Commissioner has wide powers for carrying out his investigations. He has the same powers as the High Court to compel witnesses to attend for examination and can require any minister or civil servant to provide relevant information or documents. (But material relating to the proceedings of the Cabinet and its committees may be withheld from him.) The courts decline to interfere with the Commissioner's discretion whether to investigate a complaint: *Re Fletcher's Application* [1970] 2 All ER 527.

If the Commissioner finds injustice caused by maladministration he may recommend to the department concerned whatever action he thinks should be taken by way of redress, but he has no power of enforcement. Departments normally act on the Commissioner's recommendations, as by making an *ex gratia* payment to the complainant, or offering an apology, or providing a facility which had been withheld. A department may also revise its procedures or standing instructions for the future. If it appears to the Commissioner that an injustice will not be remedied he may make a special report on the case to Parliament. A demurring department is likely to comply with the Commissioner's recommendation if it is supported by the Select Committee on the Parliamentary Commissioner. (See, e.g., the *Second Report from the Select Committee*, HC 524 of 1976–7, which brought about a departmental volte-face and a remission of tax.)

Case No. C.202/83

This investigation by the Parliamentary Commissioner concerned a complaint by Mr and Mrs A that HM Customs and Excise had given them incorrect advice in connection with a claim for a refund of Value Added Tax paid on builders' materials. They also complained of the length of time taken by the department to correct the error. The investigation established that Mr A had been wrongly advised by an officer of the department that he was eligible for a refund of VAT on building materials that he proposed to purchase. The Commissioner expressed his conclusions on the case as follows (*Sixth Report from the Parliamentary Commissioner for Administration*, HC 388 of 1983–4, pp. 26–7):

Conclusions

When the Chairman [of the Board of Customs and Excise] sent me his comments on this complaint he said that if proper advice had been given to Mr A at an early stage he might well have rearranged his affairs in order, quite legitimately, to avoid the VAT which he had been required to pay. Because of this he offered to make an *ex gratia* payment to Mr and Mrs A representing the amount of VAT that they had paid on the building materials eligible for relief. I conveyed this offer to the Member at the time and I understand that Mr and Mrs A subsequently accepted a payment of £961.67. Although incorrect advice was the root cause of the complaint, the error was compounded by the inexcusable delay in correcting it. Nearly two years passed before Mr A was first told that he was ineligible for a VAT refund even though this had been known some eighteen months earlier. Mr A had planned and incurred expenditure in circumstances where he had had good reason to believe that he would receive a VAT refund on completion of the building. As my investigation has shown, the delay was the result of deliberate inaction by an official who knew that he had made a mistake and yet failed to take steps to rectify it. I was particularly concerned to find that an omission of this sort could have gone unnoticed by senior officials for as long as it did. I was therefore pleased to learn that the [local VAT office] has altered its procedures in order to reduce the possibility of a recurrence. The Chairman has asked me to pass on to Mr and Mrs A his apologies for the exceptionally poor treatment which they received at the hands of his Department – treatment which he said fell well below the standard they hope they normally reach. This I gladly do. And I regard these apologies, the changes introduced at the LVO and the financial remedy already accepted by Mr and Mrs A as a satisfactory outcome of this justified complaint.

The Commissioner receives about 800 complaints a year. In recent years only about 25 per cent have been accepted for investigation, the remainder being excluded by the limiting provisions of the Parliamentary Commissioner Act or as being unsuitable for investigation.

See further Harlow and Rawlings, *Law and Administration*, pp. 199–210, and A. W. Bradley, 'The Role of the Ombudsman in Relation to the Protection of Citizens' Rights' [1980] *CLJ* 304.

(b) Legislation

Legislation as a governmental function has been considered in chapter 6, and an indication was given there of the scope for parliamentary scrutiny.

Primary legislation

The passage of government bills through Parliament is a process in part collaborative and in part adversarial, the mixture depending on the extent to which the bill arouses party controversy. The parliamentary process not only provides the formal legitimation of government legislation but allows for the delivery of an attack on the principle of the bill – mainly at second reading – and for argument on the detail of its provisions – mainly at the committee stage. Ministers are obliged to explain and defend the bill, which is given a public and critical scrutiny. Most government bills presented to Parliament have, however, already been put into firm shape by the responsible department, often in consultation with outside interests (see p. 295 above), and the debates and scrutiny in the House usually have only a modest effect on the outcome of the legislation. Even when the detail of the bill is less firm, the adjustment of its provisions in committee is done chiefly on the government's initiative. Few opposition and backbench amendments are agreed to.

> J. A. G. Griffith, 'Standing Committees in the House of Commons', in S. A. Walkland and Michael Ryle (eds.), *The Commons Today* (rev. edn 1981), pp. 121–2, 130–31

Amendments may have one or more of a great variety of purposes. Whether moved by the Opposition or by a government backbencher, an amendment may be intended to cause political mischief, to embarrass the Government, to discover what are the Government's real intentions and whether (in particular) they include one or more specific possibilities, to placate interests outside Parliament who are angered by the bill, to make positive improvements in the bill the better to effect its purposes, to set out alternative proposals, to initiate a debate on some general principle of great or small importance, to ascertain from the Government the meaning of a clause or sub-section or to obtain assurances on how they will be operated, to correct grammatical errors or to improve the draftsmanship of the bill. If moved by the Government, the purpose of an amendment is most likely to be to correct a drafting error or to make minor consequential changes, to record agreements made with outside bodies which were uncompleted when the bill was introduced, to introduce new matter, or occasionally to meet a criticism made by a Member either during the second reading debate or at an earlier part of the committee stage, or informally.

Not all of these purposes, if fulfilled, are likely to make the bill 'more generally acceptable'. Apart from the trivialities of minor errors, the occasions of an amendment falling within that phrase are when an opposition amendment is accepted by the Government or when a government amendment goes some way to meet an objection. This of course, may, at the same time, make the bill less acceptable to some of the government supporters. This is not to say that committee debates seldom, if ever, result in the improvement of a bill. It is to say, however, that very many amendments are not put forward with that purpose, and of those that are, not all have that effect.

More importantly, much of what takes place during committee on a controversial bill is an extension and an application of the general critical function of the House and there is little or no intention or expectation of changing the bill. The purpose of many Opposition amendments is not to make the bill more generally acceptable but to make the Government less generally acceptable. . . .

If the value of the proceedings in standing committee on government bills is judged by the extent to which Members, other than Ministers, successfully move amendments, then the value is small. It has been as rare for ministerial amendments to be rejected as for other Members' amendments to be successfully moved against government opposition. Party discipline is largely maintained in standing committee. Not surprisingly when the latter rarity occurs it is often on bills concerned with matters of the highest social controversy like race relations or immigration policy. For it is on such matters that the Whip is most likely to be defied.

On the other hand, minor reforms are quite often successfully achieved by persuading the Minister to 'look again' when the matter is before the committee and not infrequently he may propose some compromise on report.

But more important than the making of amendments is the scrutiny to which Ministers and their policies are subjected. Committee rooms are not large and do not have that sense of space and support which can be felt on the floor of the House (though that also can no doubt be at times a very lonely place). For hour after hour and for week after week a Minister may be required to defend his bill against attack from others who may be only slightly less knowledgeable than himself. His departmental brief may be full and his grasp of the subject considerable but even so he needs to be constantly on the alert and any defects he or his policy reveals will be very quickly exploited by his political opponents.

The effectiveness of a standing committee depends largely on the ability of MPs to inform themselves adequately about the background, objectives and machinery of the bill. Outside interests affected by a bill will often supply MPs on the committee with facts and arguments.

It has been questioned whether the adversary proceedings of standing committees are well adapted to the constructive examination and improvement of bills. The Study of Parliament Group said in a Memorandum to the Select Committee on Procedure (First Report, HC 588–III of 1977–8, Appendix 1, Part II, para. 17):

A principal characteristic of Standing Committees is their lack of initiative. They are never able to ask what is the best way of treating a Bill. Whether the Bill has 100 clauses or 2, whether it is likely to be contested on party lines, non-party lines or not at all, whether the Committee has 50 members or 16, it still has to deal with a Bill in a pre-ordained manner. But while many Bills profit from detailed public debate conducted on adversary lines, not all Bills do so. In some cases there may be a very strong case for the public examination of such essential matters as the evidence on which major clauses are based; or the degree, intensity and content of any prior consultation and the relevance of Bills to on-going Departmental policy. For these reasons committees on bills should be given power to send for persons, papers and records and to appoint sub-committees if they so wish and thereby to take evidence.

The Procedure Committee recommended that standing committees should normally be authorized to hold 'a limited number of sittings in select committee form, calling witnesses and receiving written submissions' about the factual and technical background to a bill, before proceeding to the usual examination of clauses and debating of amendments (First Report, above, HC 588–1, para. 2.19). An experiment on these lines was approved by the Commons on the motion of the Leader of the House on 30 October 1980, and a few non-partisan bills – among them the Criminal Attempts Bill and the Matrimonial and Family Proceedings Bill – have been referred to 'special standing committees' which have conducted 'open hearings', examining ministers, civil servants, outside experts and pressure group representatives, before going on to the detailed consideration of clauses. Some important improvements have been made to bills submitted to open hearings, but the experiment has been on a modest scale.

Parliamentary reformers have from time to time urged that Parliament should undertake a 'pre-legislative scrutiny' of government proposals for legislation. The Select Committee on Procedure has suggested (Sixth Report, HC 539 of 1966–7, para. 11) that 'the House should be brought in at an earlier point in the legislative process so as to allow discussion by Parliament of subjects and details of potential legislation before the Government finally prepare a Bill'. Pre-legislation committees of the House of Commons have on rare occasions been set up to consider subjects of possible legislation of a non-party political kind, and the new departmental committees are not prevented from inquiring into legislative proposals. But progress in this direction is likely to meet with resistance from departments, which prefer to prepare legislation within their own walls and in closed consultations with interest groups.

Delegated legislation

Parliamentary control of delegated legislation is severely restricted. Statutory instruments can only be approved or disapproved as a whole, without amendment. In the House of Commons a 'prayer' or motion to annul a negative instrument (p. 314 above) may fail to be debated within the 40-day period fixed by section 5 of the Statutory Instruments Act 1946. Debates on affirmative or negative instruments on the floor of the House take place late at night and are subject to a time-limit of 90 minutes. In practice most instruments are referred, on the government's initiative, to a standing committee where they are debated on a neutral motion which does not allow of any recommendation being made to the House: the committee can only express its disapproval of an instrument by voting that it has not considered it. The effective vote on the instrument is taken subsequently on the floor of the House: indeed once a negative instrument has been debated in the standing committee there is usually no vote on the prayer for annulment. Although the official Opposition can generally secure a debate on an instrument to which it is strongly opposed, the procedures do not provide for an adequate parliamentary consideration of the general run of statutory instruments.

A tehnical examination of all statutory instruments laid before Parliament, and other instruments of a general and not local character, is carried out by the Joint Committee on Statutory Instruments, composed of members of both Houses. (Instruments laid only before the House of Commons are considered by the Commons members of the Committee sitting without the peers.) The Committee determines whether the special attention of each House should be drawn to any instrument on grounds not impinging on its merits or policy – for example, if its drafting appears to be defective, or if it is excluded by the enabling Act from challenge in the courts, or if there is doubt whether it is intra vires, or if it 'appears to make some unusual or unexpected use of the powers conferred by the Statute under which it is made'. (See House of Commons Standing Order No. 104.) Before reporting to the House the Committee must give the department concerned an opportunity to provide an explanation.

Let us look at two examples of the Joint Committee's work.

The Criminal Justice Act 1967, s.60(1), as amended, provides that the Secretary of State may, on the recommendation of the Parole Board, release on licence a person serving a sentence of imprisonment after he has served one-third of his sentence or a 'specified period' of his sentence, whichever expires later. The 'specified period' means (s.60(1)(A)) such period 'as the Secretary of State may by order provide'. Section 60(1)(B) provides that the Secretary of State may, in any such order, 'make such incidental or supplementary provision' as he considers appropriate.

The Home Secretary laid before Parliament a draft Eligibility for Release on Licence Order 1983 which reduced the 'specified' or minimum period of imprisonment that a prisoner must have served to be eligible for release on licence, from the 12 months previously applicable to six months. But the order also provided (Article 1(2)) that the benefit of the reduction in the minimum period should not apply to prisoners already serving sentences when the order came into force.

The Joint Committee on Statutory Instruments drew the special attention of both Houses to the draft order 'on the ground that there appears to be a doubt whether it is *intra vires*' (Eighth Report, HC 41–xii of 1983–4):

... The question is ... whether the power to make 'incidental or supplementary' provision is wide enough to cover what is done in Article 1(2) of this order. The Home Office memorandum argues that it is but admits that the expression 'is not sufficiently precise for there to be no room for doubt as to its scope'. The Committee share the view that there is at least room for doubt. The Home Office memorandum suggests that the words 'incidental or supplementary' are wide enough to cover provisions of a transitional nature such as that in Article 1(2). The Committee accept that they might well be so regarded but consider that the case for relying on these words for transitional purposes is weakened by the fact that it is common practice, in appropriate cases, to use the word 'transitional' as well as the words 'incidental or supplementary' in provisions of this kind. Some significance must therefore be attached to its omission in this case. Furthermore, the relevant powers in this case do not include the power commonly conferred to 'make different provision for different cases' – a power which might also be thought relevant for the purposes of Article 1(2).

In all the circumstances, the Committee feel bound to report that in their view there is some doubt about the *vires* of what is proposed in Article 1(2). Having regard in particular to the considerations mentioned above, it seems to the Committee that the words 'incidental or supplementary provision' cannot be regarded as providing beyond doubt cover for an operation whereby a provision which at present deals even-handedly with all prisoners will in future distinguish between prisoners according to date of sentence. The Committee draw attention to the fact that the distinction thus drawn can produce some capricious-looking results. Thus, under what is proposed in Article 1(2), A and B may both be tried and convicted in December 1983 and both sentenced to 15 months' imprisonment. But if A is sentenced immediately and the sentencing of B is postponed until January 1984, B will be eligible for release on licence after serving six months whereas A will not be eligible until he has served twelve months. . . .

The Home Office, having regard to the Committee's doubt on the question of *vires*, agreed to withdraw the draft order and lay a fresh one before Parliament, omitting Article 1(2).

First Report from the Joint Committee on Statutory Instruments, HC 29–i
of 1982–3

DRAFT MERCHANT SHIPPING (CERTIFICATION AND WATCHKEEPING) REGULATIONS
1982
. . . [T]he Committee draw the special attention of both Houses to the above instrument on the ground that it makes an unexpected use of the powers conferred by the statute under which it is made.

Regulation 9(3) of the draft regulations gives the Secretary of State a widely drawn power not to issue a certificate of service to an applicant who fulfils the necessary conditions. The Secretary of State is not to issue such a certificate unless he is satisfied 'that the applicant is a fit person to be the holder of the certificate and to act competently in the capacity to which it relates'. The Department of Trade, in a memorandum submitted to the Committee, state that before a certificate is refused on this ground 'the Department in practice gives notice to the applicant and gives him an opportunity of making representations on the matter'. The Committee regard it as desirable that such a provision should be explicitly incorporated in the Regulations rather than left to the discretion of the Secretary of State. . . .

In this instance the Department was unyielding.

When a significant technical defect is discovered by the Joint Committee, the department concerned is usually willing to amend the instrument. If it declines to do so, members may use such opportunities as are provided by the affirmative and negative procedures to oppose the instrument in the House. If no parliamentary procedure is prescribed by the enabling Act, other opportunities may be found for raising the question on the floor of the House. But an 'adverse report by the Committee has no effect on the manner in which an instrument is considered, and there is no procedure to prevent a substantive decision [by the House of Commons] before the Committee has completed its consideration' (*First Report from the Select Committee on Procedure*, HC 588–1 of 1977–8, para. 3.8).

(c) Finance

'The real power to have in Parliament is control over money' (Mr Edward du Cann, MP, in Dermot Englefield (ed.), *Commons Select Committees: Catalysts for Progress?*, 1984, p. 38). Parliament exercises a formal financial control over the government in that its authority has to be obtained for taxation and the expenditure of public money. In practice the financial control and account-ability of government depend on a variety of parliamentary procedures of which some have been relatively effective and others decidedly weak. Public finance and expenditure, the process of 'getting and spending', has until recently been neglected by parliamentary reformers. But the raising and expenditure of public money involves choices between different policy goals and can profoundly affect the prosperity of the country and the distribution of wealth in society.

All taxation has to be authorized by Parliament (see p. 62 above). Much of it is provided for in permanent legislation, but income tax is authorized by an annual Finance Act. The House of Commons accordingly has opportunities to debate proposals for taxation when fiscal legislation and Budget resolutions are before it. In the annual Budget, however, Parliament is presented with what is substantially a *fait accompli*: 'Although the tablets of stone on which the Finance Bill is written can in theory be amended during its consideration, in practice the Government's reputation is at stake and so major substantive amendments are rare' (*Sixth Report from the Treasury and Civil Service Committee*, HC 137 of 1981–2, para. 2.1). Parliamentary scrutiny has been modestly strengthened since 1982 by the annual publication, in autumn, of an economic statement or 'green Budget' which includes projections of government revenue for the year ahead and announces some tax changes in advance of the Budget.

The other source of government revenue, borrowing, largely escapes parliamentary scrutiny, although it is of considerable importance in the management of the economy. The Select Committee on Procedure (Finance) has recommended that the House of Commons should be given formal power to approve the government's annual borrowing requirement (First Report, HC 24–1 of 1982–3, para. 44), but the government has not accepted this.

It is a 'principle of the highest constitutional importance', says Erskine May (*Parliamentary Practice*, 20th edn 1983, p. 760), 'that no public charge can be incurred except on the initiative of the Crown'. Money is 'granted' (i.e. expenditure is authorized) by Parliament only on the 'demand' of the Crown. This exclusive financial initiative of the Crown has been an important element in the establishment of the government's ascendancy over Parliament. The rule, as Gordon Reid says (*The Politics of Financial Control*, 1966, p. 44), provides governments with 'a powerful controlling technique', and 'protects parties in government from the political embarrassment of having to vote against a wide range of alternative proposals, initiated in other parts of the House, and designed to appeal to the electorate'. Parliament cannot increase the items of expenditure submitted to it by the government or vote for the expenditure of money on objects of its own choice.

Nevertheless the formal requirement that expenditure must be authorized by Parliament opens up the possibility of an exercise of some control or influence by the House of Commons over the government's spending policies.

The bulk of government expenditure is approved annually by Parliament in voting 'supply' and passing Consolidated Fund Acts and an Appropriation Act. Expenditure that does not require the annual approval of Parliament consists of certain payments charged directly by statute on the Consolidated Fund – for example, judges' salaries and contributions to the European Community – and moneys issued from the National Loans Fund, for example to nationalized industries.

The detailed scrutiny by the House of Commons of the proposed supply expenditure of government departments was abandoned long ago, and the government's Estimates presented to the House came to be passed 'on the nod'. In 1880 the House voted to reduce an estimate by £80, the cost of providing food for the pheasants in Richmond Park (Paul Einzig, *The Control of the Purse*, 1959, p. 271), but a century later a vote of £300 million would be approved without debate. Supply days had come to be used for debating questions of policy or administration chosen by the Opposition rather than for the detailed examination of Estimates. (These are now 'Opposition days', unconnected with the supply procedure: see p. 368 above.)

In recent years efforts have been made to revive the parliamentary scrutiny of expenditure proposals. An annual expenditure White Paper presenting the government's plans for public expenditure for a period of some years ahead is debated in the House. Estimates can now be examined by the departmental select committees (although they are limited in this by other claims upon their time and manpower), and since 1982 three days have been allotted in each session for debates on the Estimates in the House.

For a real improvement in House of Commons scrutiny of the government's expenditure policies and programmes, what is required is nothing less than 'a fundamental restructuring of the whole of the House's financial procedures' (*First Report from the Select Committee on Procedure (Supply)*, HC 118–1 of 1980–81, para. 38). These procedures evolved in past centuries as safeguards against fraud, misappropriation and waste, and are inadequate for an effective parliamentary scrutiny of the government's financial policies in modern conditions.

The Public Accounts Committee

Parliament also needs to check that expenditure by the government has been for the purposes authorized and that value for money has been obtained. Since 1861 this *ex post facto* scrutiny has been carried out on behalf of the House of Commons by its Public Accounts Committee, of which the chairman is always, by convention, a member of the Opposition. After the Comptroller and Auditor General has examined and reported on the accounts of government departments and certain other public bodies, they are considered by the Public Accounts Committee. Senior departmental officials appear before the Committee to be questioned on matters raised by the accounts, in particular those to which the Comptroller and Auditor General has drawn attention. The Committee's reports to Parliament have, over the years, revealed many instances of waste and failure of financial control, and the Committee is said to have 'contributed significantly to the maintenance of high standards in the handling of public money by the Civil Service' (*First Report from the Select Committee on Procedure*, HC 588–1 of 1977–8, para. 8.3).

The importance of the Public Accounts Committee's work appears from its report on the Chevaline project (Ninth Report, HC 269 of 1981–2). The Ministry of Defence embarked on this programme for the improvement of the Polaris missile system in the late 1960s, and the first cost estimate for the project was £175 million. The Secretary of State for Defence informed the House of Commons of the project in January 1980, and announced that the estimated cost had risen to £1,000 million. The Committee decided to investigate Chevaline and in due course reported to Parliament its finding of significant weaknesses in the department's management and control of the project, with serious under-estimates of costs and timescales. The Committee also drew attention to more general grounds for disquiet (para. 15):

In the case of Chevaline a major project costing £1,000 million continued for over ten years without Parliament being in our view properly informed of its existence and escalating costs. Expenditure each year was included in the normal way in the Defence Estimates and Appropriation Accounts; our criticism is that the costs were not disclosed, and that there was no requirement that they should be disclosed. Incidental and oblique references to a Polaris enhancement programme made in Parliament or to Parliamentary committees in our view do not provide sufficient information for Parliament to discharge its responsibility to scrutinise major expenditure proposals and to exercise proper financial control over supply.

The Government in reply agreed to provide the Public Accounts Committee with financial information about major defence projects in future (Treasury

Minute, Cmnd 8759/1982).

It is important that the Comptroller and Auditor General, who audits the accounts of government departments and examines the 'economy, efficiency and effectiveness' with which departments use their resources, should be independent of government. His office was formerly thought to be too closely associated with the Treasury; the Government agreed to a change in the status of the office only under considerable backbench pressure and after a private member's bill to reform the system of state audit had won widespread support from MPs. The National Audit Act 1983 establishes the Comptroller and Auditor General as an officer of the House of Commons who is appointed by the Crown on an address from the House, moved by the prime minister with the agreement of the chairman of the Public Accounts Committee.

(d) **European Community legislation**

With the accession of the United Kingdom to the European Communities in 1972, discussion began of ways in which Parliament might influence the terms of Community legislation which would take effect, or have to be implemented, in this country. The United Kingdom Parliament has, of course, no formal role in the Community's own law-making processes (on which see chapter 5 above) and its influence can only be indirect, through United Kingdom ministers who take part in legislation in the Council of the Communities. There is no scope, therefore, for parliamentary influence on the abundant, but generally less important, legislation of the Commission of the European Communities acting alone. But the Commission's proposals for legislation by the Council of Ministers are published in draft after being submitted to the Council, and are open to parliamentary scrutiny at that stage. There is usually an interval of, at least, several months before Commission proposals are adopted by the Council, although some 'fast-moving' proposals are adopted within a few days.

In 1972 both Houses set up committees to consider how the scrutiny of proposals for Community legislation could best be carried out. The following general observations were made by the Commons Committee.

> *Second Report from the Select Committee on European Community Secondary Legislation* (Foster Committee), HC 463-1 of 1972-3

36. ... [I]t remains central to the United Kingdom concept and structure of Parliamentary Democracy that control of the law making processes lies with Parliament – and ultimately with the elected members of it. It follows therefore that new and special procedures are necessary to make good so far as may be done the inroads made into that concept and structure by these new methods of making law [by the Community].

37. The objective must be to restore to Parliament responsibilities for, and opportunities to exercise its constitutional rights in respect of the making of these

[Community] laws – involving as that must acceptance:–

    (a) by the Government that it necessarily follows that that must be at the expense of some of the freedom of action enjoyed by the Executive since UK entry into the EEC; and

    (b) by Parliament that the scope, means and degree of scrutiny and control must all be attuned to the fact that it is dealing with a new way of making laws which is very different from that to which it is accustomed. . . .

39. Your Committee are aware that there are those who lay great stress on the fact that as the working of the Council is essentially a matter of negotiation it could be a great deal easier for a negotiator to obtain a successful outcome if he is not hedged in by any restrictions and indeed that he may be positively hampered if so restricted; and accept that that will sometimes be so (though not always, for on occasion such limitations must surely strengthen rather than weaken the negotiator's position); but reject entirely any suggestion that the Executive should, for that or any other reason, have an unfettered right to make or alter any part of the law it may choose, subject only to securing the agreement of other Governments to those changes. . . .

44. One of the difficulties which faces Parliament is that the institutions and processes of the Community are so different in their nature and workings from those of the United Kingdom that few of the built-in checks and balances or other constitutional safeguards already at the disposal of Parliament are very readily adaptable, if at all, to its new needs.

45. There is however one notable exception – the doctrine or convention of Ministerial Responsibility.

The part played by the United Kingdom in this new form of law-making is played by Ministers in their capacity as Ministers of the Crown. In that same capacity they are accountable to Parliament for the manner in which they carry out the specific duties with which they are entrusted. This doctrine may therefore be readily adopted and in so far as may be necessary adapted to the purpose in hand. . . .

While not all the specific recommendations of the Foster Committee were accepted, the Government undertook to inform the House promptly of Commission proposals to the Council and to provide explanatory memoranda on their implications for the United Kingdom. In addition the Government would give monthly forecasts of forthcoming business in the Council and ministers would report to the House on Council meetings. Time would be provided for debates and Questions on Community matters.

The Foster Committee recommended that the House should set up a select committee to scrutinize Community legislative proposals and report on them to the House. A similar recommendation was made by the Lords (Maybray-King) Committee. Accordingly both Houses set up scrutiny committees in 1974: the House of Commons Select Committee on European Legislation and the House of Lords Select Committee on the European Communities. The order of reference of the Commons Committee is as follows (Standing Order No. 105):

to consider draft proposals by the Commission of the European Communities for legislation and other documents published for submission to the Council of Ministers or to the European Council whether or not such documents originate from the

Commission, and to report its opinion as to whether such proposals or other documents raise questions of legal or political importance, to give its reasons for its opinion, to report what matters of principle or policy may be affected thereby, and to what extent they may affect the law of the United Kingdom, and to make recommendations for the further consideration of such proposals and other documents by the House.

The Committee does not consider the merits of legislative proposals (or other Community documents submitted to it) but identifies those that raise issues of legal or political importance and recommends some of them for debate in the House.

It is of crucial importance that the House should have an opportunity of debating contentious proposals referred to it by the Committee *before* the British minister has agreed to them in the Council of Ministers. Qualified ministerial undertakings to this effect have been given to the House, and on 30 October 1980 the House itself resolved (HC Deb. vol. 991, cols. 843–4):

> That, in the opinion of this House, no Minister of the Crown should give agreement in the Council of Ministers to any proposal for European legislation which has been recommended by the Select Committee on European Legislation, etc., for consideration by the House before the House has given it that consideration unless –
> (*a*) that Committee has indicated that agreement need not be withheld, or
> (*b*) the Minister concerned decides that for special reasons agreement should not be withheld;
> and in the latter case the Minister should, at the first opportunity thereafter, explain the reasons for his decision to the House.

Qualification (*b*) above has been said by the Leader of the House to be necessary for 'the rare occasion when world and Community events move so fast that there is no time' for a debate (HC Deb. vol. 991, col. 729, 30 October 1980). In the 1979–80 session, for example, there were seven instances of this kind.

Debates on Community legislative proposals are held either on the floor of the House or in standing committee.

The Lords scrutiny Committee has wider terms of reference than the Commons Committee and is able to consider and report on the merits of Community proposals. It has a well-organized structure of specialized sub-committees for dealing with different areas of Community policy, and its Law sub-committee examines the legal implications of Community proposals. The Lords Committee has more time to give to its task, can call upon a wide range of relevant experience, and has developed an effective *modus operandi*.

Parliament has difficulty enough in attempting to keep the government under some measure of control; its efforts to extend its influence to the Council of the Communities encounter even more formidable obstacles. Parliament is not kept fully informed of the course of negotiations between national officials and in the Council of Ministers, and the government insists on retaining its freedom to bargain and make concessions in its dealings with the other member states. 'In the European Communities', says Professor Henry

Schermers, 'international co-operation is so complex and concerns such detailed issues that the national parliaments cannot effectively exert control over it' (in St John Bates *et al.* (eds.), *European Governmental Studies: In Memoriam J. D. B. Mitchell*, 1983, p. 129).

5 The House of Lords

In considering the control and accountability of government we have concentrated on the role of the elected House. We have, however, noticed in passing some of the ways in which the House of Lords takes part in the supervision of the executive – for example, through the work of its Select Committee on the European Communities and its participation in the Joint Committee on Statutory Instruments. The House of Lords has no 'departmental' committees like those of the Commons, but its Select Committee on Science and Technology reviews government policy in this field and it sets up *ad hoc* committees from time to time on subjects like sex discrimination, proposals for a bill of rights, and unemployment.

The Lords have equal powers with the Commons in regard to statutory instruments, other than financial instruments laid before the Commons only, and have therefore a power of veto over most affirmative and negative instruments. This power has hardly ever been used, but in 1968 the Conservative majority in the House of Lords voted to reject an affirmative instrument, the Southern Rhodesia (United Nations Sanctions) Order. The result of this unprecedented vote was that inter-party talks on the reform of the House of Lords were suspended. Having made their protest, the Lords approved a substantially similar Order soon afterwards.

The powers of the House of Lords in relation to primary legislation are substantially restricted by the Parliament Acts 1911 and 1949. A money bill passed by the House of Commons, if sent up to the House of Lords at least one month before the end of the session, may be presented for the royal assent if it has not been passed by the Lords within one month. Any other public bill (except a bill to extend the maximum duration of Parliament beyond five years) may be presented for the royal assent if it has been passed by the Commons in two successive sessions and the Lords have rejected it in each of those sessions, provided that a year has elapsed between the second reading of the bill in the House of Commons in the first session and its third reading in that House in the second session.

Most amendments made in the House of Lords to government bills brought up from the Commons are the government's own amendments, incorporating second thoughts or concessions arising from the proceedings in the lower House or the continuing efforts of pressure groups. Some other amendments are accepted by the government in recognition of their utility or from a willingness to compromise. In these respects the House of Lords performs a useful revising function. Amendments to which the government is opposed are generally defeated when the bill is sent back to the House of Commons, and usually their Lordships, deferring to the democratic character of the elected House, do not insist on amendments with which the Commons disagree. But the House of Lords is capable, as it showed during the 1974–9 Labour Government, of asserting itself to some effect. A Government which lacked a strong base in the House of Commons then had its weakness compounded by a House of Lords which had set aside its customary restraint to impose on the Government's supporters in the Commons a diet of three-line Whips and late nights in the Chamber. The Government was compelled to accede to major Lords' amendments to some of its bills. Even a Conservative Government may find, as the present Government has found, that the House of Lords is not invariably compliant, and that the risk of defeat in votes on government bills may be greater in the House of Lords (when Tory peers rebel or cross-bench peers vote with the Opposition) than in the Commons. A significant defeat was inflicted on the Conservative Government in the House of Lords on 28 June 1984, when an amendment to the Local Government (Interim Provisions) Bill obliged the Government to abandon its scheme to replace elected councillors on the Greater London Council and the metropolitan councils, prior to their abolition, with nominated members.

The House of Lords at present carries out a necessary scrutiny and improvement of bills which have left the Commons after incomplete examination in that House (in particular when a guillotine has been applied there). It may be, however, that the task of revision could be wholly and effectively performed in the House of Commons, if the procedures of that House were radically reformed. As a check and restraint upon the government the House of Lords does not enjoy the legitimacy of a representative chamber, and its permanent Conservative majority (albeit not at present an overall majority, taking cross-bench peers into account) imports an element of imbalance into the constitution.

See generally Hartley and Griffith, *Government and Law*, ch. 11.

8

Parties, groups and the people

The control and accountability of government signified by the expression 'responsible government' are primarily functions of Parliament. The responsibility of government to Parliament is, however, only imperfectly realized in our constitution. In this chapter we shall consider how far the constitution allows for other forms of control and accountability, in which the people as a whole, or representative parties and groups, may take part.

1 The people in the constitution

An ideal conception of a democratic society is that it is one in which the people 'continuously and actively participate' in political affairs (see Graeme Duncan and Steven Lukes, 'The New Democracy' (1963) 11 *Political Studies* 156 at 158). In the real world, societies that fall short of this ideal are nevertheless termed democratic if by their constitutions the people freely elect a government and can at frequent intervals dismiss it and elect another. To this extent, at least, the constitution of the United Kingdom is democratic (see pp. 18–22 above). Periodic elections provide for an accountability of the government to the people – in the sense of the electorate – which therefore has a place in the constitutional system.

According to a modern theory of democracy fathered by Joseph Schumpeter (*Capitalism, Socialism and Democracy*, 5th edn 1976), the intermittent electoral role of the people is as much popular involvement in the practice of government as can take place or is desirable. In this theory the people choose, from competing élites, the government whose business it is to make policies and laws and provide leadership, and do not themselves attempt to decide on issues or influence policy-making. Democracy, says Schumpeter, 'means only that the people have the opportunity of accepting or refusing the men who are to rule them' (op. cit., pp. 284-5). Does this bleak and limited (but its adherents say, realistic) conception of democracy fit the theory and practice of the British constitution? Do elections provide only a retrospective accountability of government, and not the possibility of choosing between or influencing policies? In our representative democracy, what role, and what influence or power, are allowed to the people in the government of the country between elections?

The official or dominant theory of the British constitution has never located a supreme authority in the people and when a concept of sovereignty was invented it was attributed not to the people but to the Crown in Parliament. Since the seventeenth century there have been in England writers, radical politicians and reformers – from the Levellers and Defoe to Thomas Paine and the Chartists – who have claimed sovereignty for the people or have declared the people to be the constituent power of the state, by whose consent political authority was exercised. These ideas, in various forms (and various under-standings of what was meant by 'the people'), flamed by turns bright and dim outside the pale of the pre-democratic constitution. Even the establishment of democracy in the nineteenth and twentieth centuries has not supplanted the official theory with one of popular sovereignty. Yet Dicey was to admit that the electorate had come to possess – or at least to share in – the political as opposed to the legal sovereignty in the state (*Law of the Constitution* pp. 73-6), and to declare, in his arguments for the referendum, that the time had arrived 'for the formal recognition of a principle which in fact, if not in theory, forms part of our constitutional morality' ((1910) 212 *Quarterly Review* 538 at 550). In our own day the idea that the people are sovereign is gaining acceptance, as when Lord Hailsham says that 'the essence of democracy is a statement about sovereignty residing in the electorate' (*The Dilemma of Democracy*, 1978, p. 194). But the traditional view has not been displaced. R. McKenzie and A. Silver wrote in 1968 (*Angels in Marble: Working Class Conservatives in Urban England*) of the 'modest role accorded "the people" in British political culture', and continued (p. 251):

> Though modern constitutions typically locate the source of sovereignty in 'the people', in Britain it is the Crown in Parliament that is sovereign. Nor is this a merely technical point. The political culture of democratic Britain assigns to ordinary people the role, not of citizens, but of subjects.

The unresolved role of the people in the constitution lies at the heart of arguments about the electoral system, referendums, the relation between electors and their representatives in Parliament, and a public 'right to information'. If the people were acknowledged in constitutional theory as the source of political authority, debates on these matters would be conducted in different terms. New ways forward might be opened up, towards greater democracy in the public and semi-public institutions of society.

2 Elections and the mandate

The maximum duration of Parliament is five years (Parliament Act 1911, s.7) and its life can be extended only by an Act to which both Houses have assented. In practice Parliament is normally dissolved, at the request of the prime minister, before it has run its full term, and since the Second World War the average interval between general elections has been approximately three years and five months.

The franchise, which is governed by the Representation of the People Act 1983, is possessed not only by British citizens but by all adult Commonwealth citizens and citizens of the Republic of Ireland who are not disqualified by law (e.g. because serving a sentence of imprisonment) and who are resident in a constituency on the qualifying date. A person may vote only if his name is included in the electoral register for the constituency. (The right to vote is to be extended to British citizens resident abroad, for a period of up to seven years since they were last registered as electors in a constituency in the United Kingdom: see the Representation of the People Bill 1984.) Since 1945 the turnout of voters at general elections has fluctuated between 72 per cent and 84 per cent of the electorate. In the June 1983 election the electorate numbered 42,197,344 and the turnout was 72.7 per cent.

The votes of the electorate in a general election both determine the composition of the House of Commons and – unless the result is a hung Parliament – decide which of the competing parties will form a government. The present system rests on a conviction – now being challenged – of the merits of one-party government based on an absolute majority in the House of Commons. Views about the best system of election will differ according as emphasis is placed on electoral choice of a government, or on the desirability of a truly representative elected House from which a government, reflecting the balance of parties in the House, will emerge.

(a) Review of constituency boundaries

Within the constraints of the existing plurality (or 'first past the post') electoral system it is clearly desirable that votes should be, as nearly as possible, of equal value: a vote in Finchley should be worth as much as a vote in Islwyn. If this is to be substantially achieved, the boundaries of constituencies should be drawn in such a way that their electorates do not differ too greatly in size. Other factors may also have to be taken into account in drawing the boundaries, but it is of the greatest importance that the process should not be influenced by considerations of party advantage.

The House of Commons (Redistribution of Seats) Acts 1949 to 1979 provide for constituencies to be kept under review by four permanent Boundary Commissions, one each for England, Scotland, Wales and Northern Ireland. The Commissions are so constituted as to ensure their freedom from political pressure: the Speaker of the House of Commons is *ex officio* chairman of each Commission and a judge (of the High Court or, in Scotland, the Court of Session) is the deputy chairman. Two other members are appointed by ministers but, following an assurance given to the House of Commons in 1958, these appointments are always made in agreement with other political parties. Expert assistance is given to each Commission by two assessors, the Registrar General for the relevant part of the United Kingdom and the Director General of Ordnance Survey (in Northern Ireland, the Commissioner of Valuation).

Each Commission is required to carry out a general review of constituency boundaries in its part of the United Kingdom at intervals of not less than ten or more than fifteen years, and to report to the Secretary of State the changes it recommends. A Commission may also present a report on a particular area at any time. The Commissions must carry out their reviews in accordance with the rules for redistribution of seats contained in the Second Schedule to the House of Commons (Redistribution of Seats) Act 1949 (as amended). The rules are as follows.

RULES FOR REDISTRIBUTION OF SEATS

1. The number of constituencies in the several parts of the United Kingdom set out in the first column of the following table shall be as stated respectively in the second column of that table –

Part of the United Kingdom	No. of Constituencies
Great Britain	Not substantially greater or less than 613
Scotland	Not less than 71
Wales	Not less than 35
Northern Ireland	Not greater than 18 or less than 16

2. Every constituency shall return a single member.
3. There shall continue to be a constituency which shall include the whole of the City of London and the name of which shall refer to the City of London.
4. (1) So far as is practicable having regard to the foregoing rules–
    (a) in England and Wales,–
        (i) no county or any part thereof shall be included in a constituency which includes the whole or part of any other county or the whole or part of a London Borough;
        (ii) [repealed]
        (iii) no London borough or any part thereof shall be included in a constituency which includes the whole or part of any other London borough;
        (iv) [repealed]
    (b) in Scotland, regard shall be had to the boundaries of local authority areas;
    (c) in Northern Ireland, no ward shall be included partly in one constituency and partly in another.
    (2) In paragraph (1) of this rule the following expressions have the following meanings, that is to say:–
        'area' and 'local authority' have the same meanings as in the Local Government (Scotland) Act 1973; 'county' means an administrative county.

5. The electorate of any constituency shall be as near the electoral quota as is practicable having regard to the foregoing rules; and a Boundary Commission may depart from the strict application of the last foregoing rule if it appears to them that a departure is desirable to avoid an excessive disparity between the electorate of any constituency and the electoral quota, or between the electorate thereof and that of neighbouring constituencies in the part of the United Kingdom with which they are concerned.

6. A Boundary Commission may depart from the strict application of the last two foregoing rules if special geographical considerations, including in particular the size, shape and accessibility of a constituency, appear to them to render a departure desirable.

7. In the application of these rules to each of the several parts of the United Kingdom for which there is a Boundary Commission–

 (a) the expression 'electoral quota' means a number obtained by dividing the electorate for that part of the United Kingdom by the number of constituencies in it existing on the enumeration date;

 (b) the expression 'electorate' means–

   (i) in relation to a constituency, the number of persons whose names appear on the register of parliamentary electors in force on the enumeration date under the Representation of the People Acts for the constituency;

   (ii) in relation to the part of the United Kingdom, the aggregate electorate as hereinbefore defined of all the constituencies therein;

 (c) the expression 'enumeration date' means, in relation to any report of a Boundary Commission under this Act, the date on which the notice with respect to that report is published in accordance with section two of this Act.

Section 2(2) of the House of Commons (Redistribution of Seats) Act 1958 provides:

It shall not be the duty of a Boundary Commission . . . to aim at giving full effect in all circumstances to the rules set out in the Second Schedule to the principal Act, but they shall take account, so far as they reasonably can, of the inconveniences attendant on alterations of constituencies other than alterations made for the purposes of rule 4 of those rules, and of any local ties which would be broken by such alterations. . . .

In 1983 the Boundary Commission for England published the following explanation of its duties and procedure (Third Periodical Report, Cmnd 8797-1, Appendix D).

THE REVIEW OF PARLIAMENTARY CONSTITUENCIES

PART ONE: THE BOUNDARY COMMISSIONS

1. Each of the four Parliamentary Boundary Commissions . . . are required by law to keep under review the parliamentary constituencies in their part of the United Kingdom and, periodically, to conduct a general review.

2. The English Commission's final recommendations must be made in a report submitted to the Home Secretary between 10 and 15 years from the date of the report on their last general review. That was submitted on 21 April 1969, and so the next report must be made between April 1979 and April 1984. The Commission commenced a

general review in 1976 as it had received representations that changes were required to numerous existing constituencies having regard to the new structure of local government, or to provide constituencies which would be of average electorate.

PART TWO: PROCEDURE FOR REVIEW

A. Provisional Recommendations

3. The Commission first formulate a provisional recommendation, usually for a group of constituencies forming a county, a London Borough or metropolitan district.

(*a*) *Advertisement*

4. The law requires the Commission to publish a notice of their provisional recommendations for constituencies in at least one newspaper circulating in each of the constituencies which are affected. The notice has to specify a place in the constituency where details of the recommendations may be inspected. It is the Commission's practice to consult the major local authorities of the area about these arrangements so that notices may be displayed where people are most likely to see them. . . .

(*b*) *Objections and Representations*

5. The notice also states that representations may be made to the Commission within one month of its publication. That is the period prescribed by law, but, wherever possible, the Commission grant a reasonable extension of that period to assist local authorities or others who wish to make representations to do so.

(*c*) *Inquiry*

6. The Commission is bound to hold a local inquiry if representations objecting to the proposed constituency are received from an interested local authority . . . or a body of 100 or more electors.

7. The inquiry is conducted on behalf of the Commission by an Assistant Commissioner who is selected from a panel appointed by the Home Secretary. No statutory procedure is prescribed for the conduct of the local inquiry. The purpose is—

> to ascertain local opinion,
> to hear criticisms of the provisional recommendations,
> to receive counter-proposals, and to enable everyone who wishes to comment on these or on the Commission's proposals to do so.

The Commission are not represented at the inquiry, although a member of the secretariat may be present as an observer. Those who wish to express their views may do so in person, or through a representative, even though they may not have filed written representations.

8. The Assistant Commissioner makes his report direct to the Commission; besides commenting on the various objections received he is fully at liberty to suggest amendments or alterations to the Commission's proposals – or even the substitution of completely different proposals if they appear to him to command wider acceptance than the original proposals.

B. Final Recommendations

9. The Commission then consider the Assistant Commissioner's report and the matters discussed at the inquiry, together with any other relevant information, when formulating their final recommendations. If, in the event the Commission decide to alter the provisional recommendations, the revised proposals are published in the local newspapers and made available for public inspection. If there has been a local inquiry, a copy of the Assistant Commissioner's report is also made available with the documents for public inspection. Representations about these further proposals may

then be made within a one-month period. The Commission are not obliged to hold a further inquiry in respect of a constituency, but they may do so if they consider it necessary to obtain more information or local opinion on certain matters. If the Commission decide to modify their revised recommendations before finally submitting them to the Home Secretary the cycle will be repeated, i.e. the fresh proposals will be published and representations invited again.

C. Order in Council

10. The Home Secretary is under a duty to lay the Commission's report of their general review covering every single constituency in England before Parliament. If the report recommends alterations it must be accompanied by a draft Order in Council giving effect to the proposals. But if the Home Secretary decides to modify the recommendations, he must lay a statement of the reasons for the modifications in the draft Order, for consideration with the report. The Order must be approved by both Houses of Parliament and, if approved, takes effect at the next general election.

PART THREE: RULES FOR REDISTRIBUTION OF SEATS

A. The Rules

11. In formulating recommendations for constituencies, the Commission are required to observe the rules for redistribution of seats. . . . So far as is practicable, a recommended constituency must not fall across the boundary of a county or a London Borough. There is no statutory requirement that constituencies' boundaries must follow the boundaries of metropolitan and non-metropolitan districts. The majority of districts have electorates which are too big, or too small to form constituencies of the right size. Constituencies must be as near the average electorate as is possible, and the Commission allocate the number of constituencies to the counties and London Boroughs accordingly.

B. The Commission's Practice

12. Where possible the Commission propose constituencies which keep within the boundaries of districts with large electorates, so that the constituency lies wholly within one district. Experience has shown that it is often not possible to achieve this result. Conversely, it is often not possible to avoid the division of districts which have too few electors to form a constituency on their own. Such districts have an effect on their neighbours too, for a part of an adjacent district must be added to form a constituency of near-average size. This 'ripple' effect somtimes affects several of the districts in one county as the Commission endeavours to provide equal constituency electorates throughout that area (and throughout England).

13. In general the local political party organisations are based on the district wards; and these wards frequently represent a community with interests in common. It appears, therefore, that any division of district wards between constituencies is likely to break local ties, disrupt political party organisation and be confusing to the electorate, and the Commission have accordingly decided to adhere to the ward basis for forming constituencies in the cases where districts must be divided.

14. The Commission are permitted to depart from the requirements to observe county and London Borough boundaries and to provide equality of electorate if special geographical considerations apply – including in particular the size, shape and accessibility of a constituency. It is generally accepted that this rule applies mainly to Scotland and Wales, and very seldom to England.

15. The Commission are not obliged to give full effect to the rules in all circumstances.

They are directed to take account, so far as they reasonably can, of the inconveniences attendant on alterations of constituencies and of any local ties which would be broken by such alterations. It is sometimes argued that these provisions are intended largely to inhibit change. The Commission are very conscious of the historic and local ties which exist in constituencies, and are not disposed to disturb them merely to achieve some refinement in statistical equality of representation. However, where the electorate of an existing constituency is well above, or below, average, one of the primary objectives of the review is to substitute a constituency with a near-average electorate. Furthermore, where through increase in the electorate, a county has clearly become entitled to an additional constituency, some measure of disturbance in the boundaries of existing constituencies is inevitable. In addition, local government reorganisation has radically changed the boundaries of many English counties, and the duty of the Commission is to reflect those changes when recommending constituencies. . . .

C. Naming and Designation

16. The Commission's recommendations for each constituency must include the name by which it should be known and whether it should be a county constituency or a borough constituency. This decision affects the expenses allowable at elections, which differ according to the classification of a constituency as a borough or county constituency. The Commission consider that where constituencies are composed predominantly of urban areas they will normally be designated as borough constituencies. However, where constituencies contain more than a token rural electorate they will normally be designated as county constituencies.

D. Other Considerations

17. The Commission are sometimes asked to take account of special considerations which affect an area and which, according to those who make the request, justify more favourable representation than that of other parts. The Acts make no provision for special representation on these grounds. Nor do they specify that forecast changes in electorate shall be taken into account. However, the Commission do have regard to perceptible trends in the electorate which would quickly produce constituencies well above or well below the average size electorate for England when deciding between alternative schemes.

PART FOUR: TIMING OF REVIEWS

18. The period required for the English Commission's review is dictated partly by the size of the task and partly by the statutory procedures which are intended to allow full expression of opinions about the proposals at various stages. The constituencies, if approved by both Houses of Parliament, come into operation at the general election which next follows the making of the Order in Council providing the new constituencies. Thus a period of nearly five years could elapse between the Order in Council and the implementation of the new constituencies, which could then last for another 15 years. It follows that any great discrepancy in electorate of a constituency at the time of the initial change could be exaggerated with the passage of time.

PART FIVE: INTERIM REVIEWS

19. The Commissions may also conduct other reviews affecting just two constituencies or a group of constituencies between their general reviews. These interim reviews have in the past reflected changes in local government boundaries, or radical changes in the wards of a district or London Borough, and are intended to produce compatible constituency and local government, or ward, boundaries.

20. The English Commission have followed the established practice of publishing provisional recommendations without prior consultation with local authorities and other local interests. The Commission consider that they should take the initiative in preparing provisional recommendations from all the information available to them. In this way they are not influenced by any particular viewpoint. These provisional proposals are then subjected to full public debate.

21. . . . [T]he Commission are largely dependent in the case of the current review on the progress of the review of district and London Borough electoral arrangements being conducted by the Local Government Boundary Commission for England to provide the wards on which the majority of constituencies are based. . . .

When the Boundary Commission for England began its third general review in 1976 the English electorate had increased by about four million since 1965, the year on which its previous general review had been based. (The qualifying age for the franchise had been reduced from 21 to 18 in 1969). There had been substantial movements of population from inner cities to outlying areas. Great disparities between constituency electorates had resulted.

The Boundary Commission arrived at an average electorate (electoral quota) for England of 65,753 electors by dividing the total electorate for England (in 1976) by the then existing number (516) of English seats. (See rule 7 of the Redistribution Rules, above.) The Commission's application of this electoral quota and the other rules led it to recommend that there should be 523 constituencies in England.

In order to correct the imbalance which had developed between de-populated inner-city constituencies and suburban and shire constituencies where populations had increased, the Commission excised a number of constituencies from inner-city areas. (Eight were extinguished in the area of the Greater London Council.) On the other hand the efforts of the Commission to avoid crossing existing county, London borough or metropolitan district boundaries resulted in many wide divergences from the electoral quota and substantial disparities between constituencies. In London, for instance, the proposed constituency of Hornsey and Wood Green had 84,401 electors (28.36 per cent over the electoral quota) and the neighbouring Hendon South 56,121 electors (14.65 per cent under the quota).

Taken as a whole, the proposed redistribution was unfavourable to the electoral prospects of the Labour Party. When the Boundary Commission for England was about to complete its review and present its report to the Home Secretary, the Leader of the Opposition, Mr Michael Foot, together with the Opposition Chief Whip and the general secretary and national agent of the Labour Party, all of them electors in English constituencies, applied for judicial review, claiming an order of prohibition or injunction restraining the Boundary Commission from submitting its report to the Home Secretary.

It may be noted here that the applicants had acted advisedly in taking proceedings *before* the Boundary Commission had submitted its report. Once the report was in the hands of the Home Secretary he would be under a duty to lay it before Parliament. From that time any legal proceedings might run into difficulties arising from judicial reluctance to interfere with the parliamentary process and also from the restriction upon injunctive relief against a minister of the Crown. (See section 21(2) of the Crown Proceedings Act 1947 and *Harper* v. *Home Secretary* [1955] 1 Ch. 238.) When the Order in Council giving effect to a Boundary Commission's recommendations has been made, after approval in draft by both Houses, it may not be called in question in any legal proceedings: House of Commons (Redistribution of Seats) Act 1949, s. 3(7).

R. v. *Boundary Commission for England, ex p. Foot* [1983] QB 600
(CA)

In their application for judicial review and for an order of prohibition or injunction against the Boundary Commission, the applicants (see above) contended that the Commission had failed to achieve what they argued must be its 'fundamental objective' of creating substantially equal constituencies so that electors should have an equal voice, and more particularly that the Commission was in breach of its duty in failing to exercise its discretion to propose constituencies which crossed county and London borough boundaries.

The Divisional Court (Oliver LJ and Webster J) dismissed the application on the grounds that the applicants had not established that the Boundary Commission had failed in its duty and that, in any event, there had been such unjustifiable delay in bringing the proceedings that it would be inappropriate to grant any relief. Oliver LJ was also of the opinion that the applicants had not shown a sufficient interest in the matter to give them standing to make the application, but Webster J disagreed on this point. The applicants appealed to the Court of Appeal.

SIR JOHN DONALDSON MR (delivering the judgment of the court): . . .
The role of the court
Since a very large number of people are interested in this appeal and since it is most unlikely that our decision, whether for or against the applicants, will meet with universal approval, it is important that it should at least be understood. In particular it is important that everyone should understand what is the function and duty of the courts. Parliament entrusted the duty of recommending changes in English constituency boundaries to the commission. It could, if it had wished, have further provided that anyone who was dissatisfied with those recommendations could appeal to the courts. Had it done so, the duty of the court would, to a considerable extent, have been to repeat the operations of the commission and see whether it arrived at the same answer. If it did, the appeal would have been dismissed. If it did not, it would have substituted its own recommendations. Parliament, for reasons which we can well understand, did no such thing. It made no mention of the courts and gave no right of appeal to the courts.

There are some who will think that in that situation the courts have no part to play, but they would be wrong. There are many Acts of Parliament which give ministers and local authorities extensive powers to take action which affects the citizenry of this country, but give no right of appeal to the courts. In such cases, the courts are not concerned or involved so long as ministers and local authorities do not exceed the powers given to them by Parliament. Those powers may give them a wide range of choice on what action to take or to refrain from taking and so long as they confine themselves to making choices within that range, the courts will have no wish or power to intervene. But if ministers or local authorities exceed their powers – if they choose to do something or to refrain from doing something in circumstances in which this is not one of the options given to them by Parliament – the courts can and will intervene in defence of the ordinary citizen. It is of the essence of parliamentary democracy that those to whom powers are given by Parliament shall be free to exercise those powers, subject to constitutional protest and criticism and parliamentary or other democratic control. But any attempt by ministers or local authorities to usurp powers which they have not got or to exercise their powers in a way which is unauthorised by Parliament is quite a different matter. As Sir Winston Churchill was wont to say, 'that is something up with which we will not put'. If asked to do so, it is then the role of the courts to prevent this happening.

There are undoubtedly distinctions between the position of the commission and that of a minister or local authority taking executive action under statutory powers which affects the individual citizen. The commission have no executive power. Their function and duty is limited to making advisory recommendations. Furthermore the commission's task is ancillary to something which is exclusively the responsibility of Parliament itself, namely, the final decision on parliamentary representation and constituency boundaries. These are distinctions to which we will return when giving further consideration to what action should or should not be taken by the court in the circumstances of this case. At the moment all that need be said is that it is common ground that in some circumstances it would be wholly proper for the courts to consider whether the commission have, no doubt inadvertently, misconstrued the instructions which they have been given by Parliament and, if they have done so, to take such action as may be appropriate in order to ensure that the will of Parliament is done. . . .

Construction of the statutory provisions
(a) *Section 2(1)(a) of the Act of 1949*
Under section 2(1)(a) of the Act of 1949, the commissions are required to submit their reports to the Secretary of State showing the constituencies in which they recommend that their area should be divided 'in order to give effect to the rules set out in Schedule 2 to this Act'. The requirement in this subsection to give effect to the rules is plainly mandatory. We shall however have to consider in a moment the impact upon this requirement of section 2(2) of the Act of 1958.
(b) *The relationship between rule 4 and rule 5*
Turning to the rules themselves, rules 4, 5 and 6 are each concerned with separate matters. Rule 4 is concerned with county and London borough boundaries; rule 5 is concerned with the size of the electorate of each constituency, considered in relation to the electoral quota for that constituency; and rule 6 is concerned with geographical considerations. It is clear, in our judgment, that of these matters, although they may all be properly regarded as interlocking, the requirement in rule 4 that 'so far as is

practicable' constituencies shall not cross county or London borough boundaries must be regarded as taking precedence over the requirement in rule 5 concerning the size of the electorate for each constituency. This appears from the facts that (1) rule 4 is on its face not qualified by reference to rule 5, whereas rule 5 provides that the electorate of any constituency shall be as near the electoral quota as is practicable having regard to the foregoing rules, which of course include rule 4; and (2) the second limb of rule 5 authorises departure from rule 4 only in the circumstances there specified.

This point is not academic in the present case. Mr Williams, for the applicants, asserted in argument that the primary purpose of the rules is to achieve electoral equality between constituencies. On a true construction of the rules, this is not so. The requirement of electoral equality is, subject to the second limb of rule 5, subservient to the requirement that constituencies shall not cross county or London borough boundaries.

(c) *Construction of rules 4, 5, and 6*
The requirements of rule 4 and rule 5 are qualified by the words 'so far as is practicable' or 'as near . . . as is practicable'.

Practicability is not the same as possibility. In part of his argument before us . . . Mr Williams came close to suggesting, particularly in relation to rule 5, that the two were the same. But this is plainly not so. Practicability not merely connotes a degree of flexibility: it contemplates that various matters should be taken into account when considering whether any particular purpose is practicable, i.e. capable in practical terms of achievement. We can see no limit to the matters which may be so taken into account, whether under rule 4 or rule 5, save that they must be relevant to the particular question, having regard to the terms of the relevant statutes and the rules themselves, of which rules 4 and 5 form part. It may be that the test of what is or is not practicable is objective; but in relation to the requirement in rule 5 (with which we are primarily concerned) this is for present purposes theoretical, because the power to depart from the requirement in rule 4 to respect local boundaries only arises if, in the subjective view of the commission, such departure is desirable to avoid any excessive disparity of the kinds specified (see the second limb of rule 5). Exactly the same comment can be made concerning the word 'excessive' itself in this context. It may involve an objective, albeit flexible, standard, but whether it is to be treated as achieved is dependent upon the subjective judgment of the commission. Likewise the question whether there is to be a departure from the strict application of rules 4 or 5 by reason of special geographical considerations is made, by rule 6, dependent upon the subjective view of the commission whether such a departure is thereby rendered desirable. These considerations obviously have an inhibiting effect upon any judicial review of the kind sought by the applicants. We add in parenthesis that, since the Boundary Commissions are not subject to the provisions of the Tribunals and Inquiries Act 1971, they are not required to give reasons for their decision to make any particular recommendation. It follows that it cannot usually be known whether, or if so to what extent, any such decision has been affected by the matters referred to in rule 4; or those in rule 5; or those in rule 6; or, indeed, those referred to in the second limb of section 2(2) of the Act of 1958, to which we will shortly refer. This consideration alone must make it very difficult, indeed usually impossible, to seek judicial review of the kind now sought upon the basis that the commission have failed to construe or apply the rules properly.

(d) *Section 2(2) of the Act of 1958*
Overriding these various points however there is, in our judgment, the impact of

section 2(2) of the Act of 1958. There was considerable argument about the construction of this subsection, both before the Divisional Court and before us. For the applicants, Mr Williams made two submissions, both of which (if accepted) would limit the impact of the subsection. The first (which found favour with the Divisional Court) was that the first limb of the subsection (discharging Boundary Commissions from the duty to aim at giving full effect in all circumstances to the rules) was to be read subject to the second limb of the subsection. On this construction the dispensation in the first limb is effective only to take account of the two matters specified in the second limb, viz. inconveniences attendant on alterations of constituencies, and local ties which would be broken by such alterations. This argument found favour in particular with Oliver LJ in the Divisional Court, because he felt that otherwise no weight would be given to the conjunction 'but' which provides the link between the two limbs of the subsection. We have formed a different view. We consider that the function of the first limb is to do just what it says, viz. to relieve Boundary Commissions from the duty to give effect in all circumstances to the rules, with the result that, although plainly Boundary Commissions must indeed have regard to the rules, they are not strictly bound to give full effect to them in all circumstances. The word 'but' has a role to play because it points the contrast between the dispensation in the first limb of the subsection, and the mandatory requirement in the second limb, that Boundary Commissions shall nevertheless take account of the matters specified in the second limb. So read, we consider that effect is given to all parts of the subsection: whereas on Mr Williams's submission, which we feel unable to accept, no weight is given to the first limb which could, if he is right, for all practical purposes be deleted.

Mr Williams's second submission on the subsection related only to the second limb. It was that Boundary Commissions were required thereby only to take account of the specified inconveniences and local ties when considering *whether* to recommend the alteration of a constituency; but that, once they had decided to recommend an alteration, they were not required to take these matters into account when considering the *nature* of the alteration to be recommended. This submission, which underwent some refinement in the course of argument before us, we are quite unable to accept. We reject it as a matter of construction. Section 2(2) of the Act of 1958 is a statutory provision which modifies the duty placed upon Boundary Commissions under section 2(1) of the Act of 1949. The second limb of section 2(2) of the Act of 1958 requires Boundary Commissions to take account of the specified matters, and this must mean that they are required to take account of them when making the recommendations which are the subject matter of a report to be submitted by them to the Secretary of State. If they are to take account of such matters for that purpose, they must plainly take account of them not only in deciding whether to alter a particular constituency, but for all purposes relative to their recommendations, which must include selection of the particular alteration which they decide to recommend. This view is, in our judgment, reinforced by the fact that we can see no practical sense in imposing any such restrictive meaning as that for which Mr Williams has contended. For these reasons we are unable to accept his argument on this point.

The broad construction of section 2(2) of the Act of 1958 which we prefer places yet another, very substantial, obstacle in the way of judicial review of a decision of a Boundary Commission to make any particular recommendation in a report to the Home Secretary. For the practical effect is that a strict application of the rules ceases to be mandatory so that the rules, while remaining very important indeed, are reduced to the status of guidelines. We also observe in parenthesis that the second limb of section 2(2) of the Act of 1958 underlines (if this is necessary) the importance placed by Parliament on respecting the county and London borough boundaries mentioned in rule 4, which will often also reflect local ties. . . .

The powers of the court to intervene

We have already pointed out that the relevant legislation has provided for no appeal against the commission's recommendations. Furthermore, the discretion in carrying out their functions conferred on the commission by the legislature is a very wide one. However, it is not absolute and unfettered, in view of the existence of the rules.

A long line of cases has established that if public authorities purport to make decisions which are not in accordance with the terms of the powers conferred on them, such decisions can be attacked in the courts by way of an application for judicial review; and furthermore, that even if such decisions on the face of them fall within the letter of their powers they may be successfully attacked if shown to have been 'unreasonable'.

The situation of the commission differs from that of many other public authorities in that, even at the very end of their inquiries and deliberations, they make no final decision; they merely make a recommendation to the Secretary of State who, after making any modifications to their report which he thinks appropriate, has to pass it on to Parliament for final approval or rejection. This distinctive nature of the function of the commission might well make the court in the exercise of its discretion more slow to intervene in regard to their activities than it would be in relation to those of many other public authorities. Nevertheless, it has not been suggested before this court, and in our opinion could not be correctly suggested, that the commission are above the law, in the sense that their activities are never susceptible to review by the courts.

In the present case, it has not been submitted that the commission have exceeded or are about to exceed the letter of their statutory powers. The complaint is more that they have unreasonably exercised or failed to exercise the various discretions conferred on them by statute. This submission necessitates a brief consideration of the meaning of 'reasonableness' in this context.

The Master of the Rolls quoted from Wade, *Administrative Law* (5th edn 1982, p. 362) on the doctrine that powers must be exercised reasonably: within the bounds of legal reasonableness a deciding authority has a genuinely free discretion; a court must not usurp that discretion by drawing the bounds too tightly merely according to its own opinion but must apply an objective standard 'which leaves to the deciding authority the full range of choices which the legislature is presumed to have intended'. His Lordship continued:

What then is this objective standard? The locus classicus on the subject is a passage from the judgment of Lord Greene MR in *Associated Provincial Picture Houses Ltd* v. *Wednesbury Corporation* [1948] 1 KB 223, 230, in which he stated what has become known as 'the *Wednesbury* principle'. Mr Williams expressly accepted that this principle applies so as to govern and limit the powers of the court to intervene in regard to the activities of the commission. We need not cite the passage from Lord Greene's judgment verbatim. For present purposes it will suffice to say that the *Wednesbury* principle would or might in our opinion entitle the court to intervene if it was satisfied that the commission had misdirected themselves in law, or had failed to consider matters which they were bound to consider or had taken into consideration matters which they should not have considered. It would not, however, entitle it to intervene merely because it considered that, left on its own, it might (or indeed would) have made different recommendations on the merits; if the provisional conclusions of the commission are to be attacked on the ground of unreasonableness, they must be shown to be conclusions to which no reasonable commission could have come. The onus falling on any person seeking to attack their recommendations in the courts must thus be a heavy one, which by its very nature may be difficult to discharge.

The issue on this appeal

In relation to the merits, therefore, the issue on this appeal is quite simply whether there is any sufficient evidence that the commission are intent upon making recommendations which go beyond, or differ from, what any reasonable body of men in their position could properly make, exercising the best of their skill and judgment in the light of the instructions given to them by Parliament. If there is such sufficient evidence, it will or may be the duty of this court to intervene in order to ensure either that the commission's breach of duty is made known or, possibly, that it is remedied. If there is not it must be the court's duty to leave the commission to get on with the process entrusted to them, that being their business and not that of the courts.

The case for the applicants

In answering the applicants' case, Mr Simon Brown on behalf of the commission made it plain that, in addition to maintaining the objections to their case on its essential merits, which he and Mr Mummery put forward in the Divisional Court, they would seek to maintain the other submissions relating to locus standi and delay which were advanced in that court. Though strict logic might point to the adoption of another order, we prefer to follow the Divisional Court in considering first the applicants' case on its merits.

The essence of the applicants' case lies in the overriding importance which, as they submit, is to be attached to the first limb of rule 5, which provides that 'The electorate of any constituency shall be as near the electoral quota as is practicable having regard to the foregoing rules. . . .' This, the applicants say, is what the redistribution of seats is all about. This attitude is clearly reflected in their affidavits. . . . That of Mr Foot, for example, refers to disparities in the numbers of the electorates of certain proposed constituencies as offending against what is there described as 'the principle of equal representation for all electors which is required by our modern system of parliamentary representation'. Mr Williams, in opening this appeal, similarly told us that the first main thrust of his argument would be that the commission had paid insufficient regard to the first limb of rule 5. Whilst this provision, which is put forward as the key provision, is expressed to operate subject to rules 1 to 4, it is suggested that of these earlier rules only 4 (which discourages the crossing of boundaries) can pose any real obstacle in the way of achieving something very near to equality with the electoral quota. And even this threat, it is suggested, is much less than it used to be because of the reduced number of boundaries which now have to be taken into account, in the light of recent changes in local authority boundaries and the amendments to rule 4 made by the Act of 1958 and the Local Government Act 1972. Any obstacle to electoral equality produced by rule 4, it is suggested, is then reduced almost to vanishing point by the second limb of rule 5 which permits departure from rule 4 if compliance would produce any excessive disparity between the electorate of any constituency and the electoral quota or between its electorate and that of neighbouring constituencies.

The assertion of this paramount character of the first limb of rule 5 is fundamental to the applicants' case. . . . Mr Williams . . . summed up their complaint by saying that the commission have not achieved what he described as their fundamental purpose of proposing constituencies which are as near as practicable equal. He suggested that the commission have shown a quite excessive reverence for boundaries and districts and have demonstrably failed to pay sufficient regard to the discretion given to them by the second limb of rule 5. Very broadly, these are the grounds on which he submits that their proposals or provisional proposals are open to attack on the *Wednesbury* principle. We now consider how he developed this attack as a matter of fact and law.

First, and we think foremost, he submitted that the draft proposals for a number of constituencies reveal such wide disparities between many of the electorates and the electoral quota that it is obvious *on the face of the proposals* that the commission must have failed to observe the first limb of rule 5, by failing to ensure that such electorates are as near the electoral quota as is practicable having regard to the previous rules. He submitted in effect that the disparities are so great that no Boundary Commission, properly instructed, could reasonably have arrived at the same proposals, if they had had proper regard to this first limb. . . .

We understand that, in the course of argument in the Divisional Court, Mr Williams submitted that, if any given proposal results in an electorate for any constituency which either exceeds or falls short of the electoral quota by more than 10 per cent, this by itself demonstrates that the commission have not complied with rule 5 so far 'as is practicable'. In this court he expressly disclaimed the submission that there is any given percentage of disparity which may never be exceeded. Nevertheless, he submitted that there must come a point at which it is possible to say that in any given instance the disparity between the electorate of a proposed constituency and the electoral quota is, on the very face of it, obviously excessive. For example, by objective standards, in his submission, the disparities of 15·86 per cent and 21·52 per cent in the case of Stoke-on-Trent North and South East Staffordshire respectively are obviously excessive. In the case of these two proposed constituencies, and many other similar proposed constituencies, where substantial disparities of this nature are shown, the court can and must, in his submission, inevitably conclude that the commission have failed to carry out their duties under rule 5. And, in his submission, the court can and should reach this conclusion without reference to any evidence as to the particular circumstances which led them to make the relevant recommendations.

We are prepared to accept the theoretical possibility that in a given instance the disparity between the electorate of a proposed constituency and the electoral quota might be so grotesquely large as to make it obvious on the figures that no reasonable commission which had paid any attention at all to rule 5 could possibly have made such a proposal. We are prepared to accept that in such a hypothetical instance the court might be willing to intervene.

For all this, the submission that the statistics on their face reveal an error on the part of the commission seems to us totally unsustainable on the facts of the present case, for two reasons if no others. First, as we have already pointed out, the guidelines designed to achieve the broad equality of electorates, which are to be found in the opening limb of rule 5, have been deliberately expressed by the legislature in such manner as to render them subordinate to the guidelines given by rule 4, designed to prevent the crossing of boundaries and *not vice versa*. . . . Even if a strict adherence to the principles of rule 4 will produce what is prima facie excessive disparity between the electorate of any constituency and the electoral quota, the wording of the second limb of rule 5 implicitly makes it clear that the commission are to be left with a discretion *not* to depart from the strict application of rule 4, if in all the particular circumstances of the case they consider such departure undesirable. Any doubt about the residual discretion of the commission in this context is removed by the first limb of section 2(2) of the Act of 1958. From a bare reference to the statistics in the present case, we see no reason to assume that the commission did not, consciously and on sufficient grounds, conclude that departure from the strict application of rule 4 was *not* desirable in any of the particular cases where 'excessive disparity' is alleged.

Secondly, and quite apart from this first reason, rule 6 expressly confers on the commission a discretion to depart from the strict application of either rule 4 or rule 5 itself, if special geographical considerations, including in particular the size, shape and accessibility of a constituency appear to them to render a departure desirable. We are wholly unable to say that any of the discrepancies in the cases of Stoke-on-Trent North and South East Staffordshire, already referred to, or of the many other similar discrepancies, are so great that they could not have been justifiable simply by a conscious exercise of the commission's discretion under rule 6 alone. There is no evidence that such discretion was not exercised. . . .

In these circumstances the burden of proof falls fairly and squarely on the applicants to show good grounds on the available evidence for saying that no reasonable commission, if properly instructed as to the relevant facts, could have arrived at the same decisions or proposals.

The Divisional Court apparently understood the submissions made to it on behalf of the applicants as including the submission that the commission erred on the ground that, on the evidence, they *wholly failed* to consider whether they should exercise their discretion under the second limb of rule 5 by proposing constituencies which crossed county or London borough boundaries. We did not understand Mr Williams to put such a far-reaching submission before us, but in any event we think it would be quite unsustainable on the evidence. . . .

Here the Master of the Rolls referred to an affidavit sworn by the deputy chairman of the Commission which declared that the members of the Commission had taken into consideration their power under rule 5 to depart from the strict application of rule 4, if it appeared to them that a departure was desirable to avoid an excessive disparity between a constituency electorate and the electoral quota or between neighbouring constituencies. His Lordship continued:

Before this court, Mr Williams indicated that in this context his submissions had been misunderstood by the Divisional Court and that he did not and does not seek to challenge the truth of these statements made by the deputy chairman, though he would seek to assert that the commission must have misdirected and did misdirect themselves as to the true effect of the rules. . . . If there was ever any doubt about it, this makes it quite clear that the applicants now accept that in every relevant instance the members of the commission have taken into consideration their power under rule 5 to depart from the strict application of rule 4, so that this point does not arise.

The next principal submission made on their behalf by Mr Williams was substantially that the commission had *misdirected* themselves as to the true effect of the rules. The alleged misdirection is that, on the evidence, the commission, contrary to their duty to exercise a full discretion in the matter, had placed a rigid, self-imposed restriction on the exercise of that discretion in regard to constituencies in London and the metropolitan counties by adopting a fixed policy of following and not crossing existing borough or metropolitan district boundaries. The question whether the commission did or did not place a self-imposed restriction on the exercise of their discretion is a pure question of fact to be decided on the available evidence. It seems clear on such evidence that the commission in carrying out their functions have adopted a general policy of trying not to cross London borough or metropolitan district boundaries, so far as they have considered this practicable and consistent with the guidelines given them by the rules. Thus far, however, we can see nothing objectionable about any such general approach, bearing in mind the nature of the primary guidelines under which the commission have to operate. Although metropolitan district boundaries are not mentioned in rule 4, they may well reflect geographical consider-ations (rule 6) and also local ties: section 2(2) of the Act of 1958.

In contrast we readily accept that it would have been objectionable if the commission had adopted a fixed and immutable policy in this context. The two members of the Divisional Court, however, having analysed the relevant evidence with great care and in detail, came to the conclusion in effect that no fixed and immutable policy of this nature had ever been adopted by the commission, but that the commission had done no more than adopt a preliminary and unobjectionable policy, which reflected the provisions of the rules, and from which they consciously reserved liberty to depart in any cases which they regarded as appropriate. Nothing in the argument that has been addressed to us on behalf of the applicants causes us in any way to doubt the correctness of this conclusion of fact. We therefore see no grounds for disturbing this conclusion. . . .

The Master of the Rolls drew attention to various items of evidence which were inconsistent with the applicants' contention that the Commission had adopted an immutable policy of not crossing boundaries, and concluded that the Divisional Court was 'plainly right' in its decision on this point. His Lordship also rejected a submission that the Commission had acted unreasonably in some instances in failing to hold joint local inquiries for neighbouring areas, and continued:

The rest of [Mr Williams's] attack was chiefly directed to particular instances in which he contended that the commission in making their proposals should have crossed district or borough boundaries in order to achieve greater electoral equality. The proposals for the constituencies of Blackburn and Ribble Valley, for example, produce a wide variation between the electoral quota and the electorates of the two proposed constituencies, which could be reduced by transferring two of the Blackburn wards to the Ribble Valley constituency. 'Excessive disparities' in his submission are also to be found among certain constituencies in Avon and Somerset, where the commission should have crossed district borders, with a view to achieving greater electoral equality. Similar submissions were made in relation to Oxford and Wiltshire.

Though the relevant disparities are substantial in some of the instances relied on, they are in no case so large as to point per se to the conclusion that the commission wholly failed to have regard to the provisions of rule 5 relating to electoral equality; and indeed any such conclusion is negatived by the undisputed evidence of the deputy chairman of the commission to which we have referred. Nevertheless, for present purposes we are prepared to assume that in all these instances, as the applicants contend, it would have been 'practicable' for the commission's proposals to achieve greater electoral equality by the crossing of district boundaries. On this basis Mr Williams submits in effect that the relevant proposals cannot possibly be justified by the commission as a proper exercise of their discretions.

The submission is, we think, once again founded on the premise that the overriding objective which must above all others guide the commission in their deliberations is the achieving of electoral equality. In our observations on the construction of the rules we have attempted to make it clear that this premise is in our view an erroneous one. While the achievement of electoral equality is certainly a very important objective, the framework of the rules of 1949 itself makes it plain that as a matter of general policy rule 5 was to be regarded as subordinate to rule 4 and not vice versa. Section 2(2) of the Act of 1958, while explicitly giving the commission a general discretion to depart from the rules in formulating proposals, in effect placed a mandatory obligation on them to take account, so far as they reasonably could, of the inconvenience that would attend alterations of constituencies that might be made for the purpose of achieving electoral equality and of any local ties which would be broken by such alterations.

Though we have before us a number of reports of local inquiries, we do not have before us, and do not know, the totality of the evidence which the commission had before them when they decided not to cross district boundaries in the various specific instances now complained of.

For example, for all we know, they may have considered that there were special geographical considerations, of the nature referred to in rule 6, which compelled or justified a decision not to make proposals which involved the crossing of district boundaries. Alternatively, there may have been other relevant matters, not now in evidence, which led them to exercise the wide general discretion vested in them, as confirmed by the opening words of section 2(2) of the Act of 1958. In the absence of evidence as to all the matters which the commission took into account and of any evidence that they misdirected themselves, we find it impossible to conclude that they have erred in any respect.

It cannot be emphasised too strongly that on this present application the onus does not fall on the commission to justify their proposals, either in general terms or in particular instances, and either by evidence or otherwise. The onus of proof falls fairly and squarely on any person who seeks to challenge their proposals. Furthermore, the onus is a heavy one since the legislature has conferred no express right on any person to challenge the commission's decisions and any attack has to be based on the *Wednesbury* principle.

As in our judgment the applicants have not come near to discharging this onus, it follows that the Divisional Court was right to decide that the application failed on its merits.

In these circumstances we find it unnecessary to express any opinion on the further questions whether the applicants have a sufficient locus standi to present this application and whether delay is by itself a bar to this claim. Indeed, we have not heard full argument on either of these points. Perhaps, however, we should say a very few words in relation to the form of relief claimed. Even though we have not heard full argument on this point too, our clear provisional view is that this would not have been an appropriate case for the court in the exercise of its discretion to grant relief by way of prohibition, even if the applicants had surmounted all other hurdles. The effect of an order for prohibition would have been wholly to preclude Parliament from considering the proposals which the commission, after long and obviously careful consideration, were minded to place before it. Our present view is that in the hypothetical contingency now under discussion, the appropriate course for this court to take, in the exercise of its discretion, would have been simply to express its views as to the legal position in the form of a declaration, which would have been available for consideration, together with the commission's report, both by the Secretary of State and in due course by Parliament.

As things are, however, these further matters do not arise for decision and we express no conclusion on them. . . .

The appeal was accordingly dismissed. The applicants having petitioned for leave to appeal to the House of Lords, an appeal committee of the House, composed of five instead of the usual three Law Lords because of the great public importance of the case, decided unanimously that no arguable ground had been shown on which an appeal to the House could possibly succeed. Leave to appeal was therefore refused. (See Robert J. Waller, 'The 1983 Boundary Commission: Policies and Effects' (1983) 2 *Electoral Studies* 195.)

The rules for redistribution of seats formerly indicated a limit of 25 per cent divergence from the electoral quota, but the present formula ('as near the electoral quota as is practicable') was substituted by the House of Commons (Redistribution of Seats) Act 1947 (repealed and replaced by the Act of 1949). Many people think that a more precise limit upon the Boundary Commissions' discretion should be restored: for example it has been proposed that they should be given 'an overriding instruction that no constituency should have less than half the electorate of any other at the time of redistribution, except for the Scottish Island areas' (*Report of the Hansard Society Commission on Electoral Reform*, 1976, para. 45).

Under the present system the relative value of votes can be much affected by population movements which take place between delimitations. For instance, population changes had produced the result, before the 1983 revision, that the electorate of Buckingham was five times the size of that of Newcastle upon Tyne Central. The most recent review by the English Boundary Commission was based on the 1976 electorate, and its next report could be presented as late as February 1998 (fifteen years after its report of February 1983). The first general election on revised constituencies could be 4–5 years after that. The effects of population movements in the intervals between general reviews have not in practice been much mitigated by the Commissions' power to conduct interim reviews in local areas. (Cf. para. 19 of the English Boundary Commission's explanatory statement, above.)

Our system evidently fails to ensure that votes have equal values. In the United States, on the other hand, the Supreme Court has held that equal representation for equal numbers of people is demanded by the Constitution, and that votes are not to be substantially diluted on the basis of place of residence. 'Legislators', said Chief Justice Warren in *Reynolds* v. *Sims*, 377 US 533, 562 (1964), 'represent people, not trees or acres.' (See also *Wesberry* v. *Sanders*, 376 US 1 (1964).) Some deviation from the equality of votes is, however, permitted if based on legitimate grounds.

The Home Secretary may modify a Commission's recommendations, but in that event must lay before Parliament a statement of his reasons. Parliament cannot amend the draft Order in Council incorporating the proposed boundaries. If either House rejects the draft Order, the Home Secretary may amend it before again laying it before Parliament.

Government modifications were made to a Commission's recommendations in 1948 when the English Boundary Commission had made proposals which gave a preferential weighting to rural constituencies. In 1983 the Home Secretary, Mr Whitelaw, when moving that the English Commission's recommendations should be approved without modifications, said (HC Deb. vol. 38, col. 249, 2 March 1983):

I believe we must retain the public's trust in this vital part of the democratic process. The temptation for Parliament to tinker with a parliamentary Boundary Commission's recommendations will always be there; and sometimes, as in 1948 and 1969, Governments cannot resist it. But every time this happens we damage public confidence in the integrity of our constitutional procedures.

What happened in 1969 was that the Labour Government, instead of following the normal procedure for implementation of Boundary Commission recommendations, introduced a bill which absolved the Home Secretary from his duty and provided for the recommendations to be implemented only in part. The bill was lost as a result of resistance by the House of Lords, whereupon the Home Secretary performed his duty in laying before Parliament the Boundary Commissions' reports together with draft Orders in Council, but asked the Government's supporters in the House of Commons to vote against the Orders, which were duly disapproved. The Government justified its action on the ground that the Boundary Commissions had worked by reference to local government boundaries which were shortly to be extensively revised, following the Redcliffe-Maud Report (p. 208 above). But since the recommended boundary changes were believed to be disadvantageous to the Labour Party's election prospects, the Government was widely criticized for acting from political bias. (Cf. the recent rebuttal by Mr Merlyn Rees, a Home Office junior Minister at the time: HC Deb. vol. 38, col. 266, 2 March 1983.) On a subsequent occasion there were allegations that a Conservative Government was expediting the redistribution process so that the 1983 election might be held on boundaries more favourable to the Conservative Party. (See HC Deb. vol. 995, cols. 279 *et seq.*, 3 December 1980, and correspondence in *The Times* on 10 and 14 December 1981.) Whether or not allegations of these kinds are well founded, it is unfortunate that the process of boundary revision is regularly attended by political controversy. Even though bias is not attributed to the Boundary Commissions themselves, the system is open in various ways to infection by considerations of party advantage. There is a strong case for a fundamental re-examination, perhaps by a select committee of the House of Commons, of the principles and machinery of boundary delimitation.

(b) **Fairness of the contest**

In a general election the electorate chooses, not only members of Parliament, but policies and a government. The free choice of the electorate may be impaired if the competing parties have unequal opportunities of making their policies known to the people, because of differences in financial resources or access to the media of communication. Electoral law and practice should as far as possible ensure that in these respects none of the parties is at an unfair disadvantage in the election campaign. It is also in the public interest that new political groups or independent candidates are not prevented from entering the contest to challenge the policies of established parties.

The election deposit

Every candidate in a parliamentary election is required to deposit a sum of money with the returning officer, and this sum is forfeited if the candidate fails to poll more than a prescribed percentage of the votes cast in his constituency. The amount of the deposit was fixed at £150 in 1918, and the threshold below which the deposit was forfeited was 12.5 per cent of the votes cast. In 1983 the Home Affairs Committee of the House of Commons considered the requirement of the deposit (First Report, HC 32–1 of 1982–3, para. 70):

Though it is sometimes argued that there is no reason why any individual who wishes to stand for Parliament should be prevented from doing so by financial considerations, there are valid reasons for imposing some form of constraint. Candidates in parliamentary and European elections automatically acquire a number of advantages and privileges, such as free postage for their election addresses, free use of publicly maintained buildings for public meetings, the right to veto broadcasts relating to the constituency which they are contesting and, not least, a great deal of publicity. These privileges are capable of being abused, and it is generally accepted that a deposit of £150 would do little to prevent any number of frivolous or deliberately disruptive candidates from participating in election campaigns and distributing propaganda of a racially inflammatory or otherwise anti-social character. . . .

Although the Committee found that there had been little serious abuse of electoral privileges, it was of the opinion that a safeguard was needed (e.g. to discourage candidates who set out to confuse voters by assuming a name similar to that of a well-known candidate) and proposed that the deposit should be increased to £1,000. The Government accepted this recommendation, and also decided that the votes threshold should be reduced to 5 per cent (e.g. 2,500 votes in a poll of 50,000). (The majority of the Home Affairs Committee had proposed 7.5 per cent.) A Representation of the People Bill was introduced at the end of 1984 to give effect to these and other changes in electoral law: in the course of its passage the Government accepted an amendment fixing the deposit at £500.

The requirement of a deposit may discourage some serious independent candidates and creates difficulties for the less affluent political parties, deprived at least for the period of the election campaign of what may add up to a substantial sum. For these reasons it has several times been proposed that the deposit should be abolished and that there should instead be a large increase in the number of supporting signatures required for a nomination – from the present 10 to, say, ·5 per cent of tne electorate (250–400 in most constituencies). The Government has declined to adopt this solution, mainly on the ground that candidates who would poll only a handful of votes might yet have little difficulty in obtaining the additional number of signatures to a nomination ('Representation of the People Acts', Cmnd 9140/1984, para. 5.4). But the exaction of a substantial deposit may shut out fresh ideas and make it difficult for a new political movement or minority group to take the parliamentary way of advancing its cause.

Election expenditure

The power of money could undermine the fairness of the electoral contest if there were no restriction on expenditure in the campaign. This was appreciated as early as 1883, when a Corrupt and Illegal Practices Prevention Act established a ceiling for expenditure by each candidate. The limitation of control to *constituency* expenditure has remained a feature of subsequent legislation.

Election expenses may in general only be *paid* by the candidate's election agent, and no expenses may lawfully be *incurred* 'with a view to promoting or procuring the election of a candidate' in holding public meetings, issuing advertisements or circulars, or otherwise presenting the candidate or his views to the electors, except by the candidate, his election agent, or persons authorized by the agent: see the Representation of the People Act 1983, ss.72–75. (Expenditure directed to *preventing* the election of a particular candidate falls within the prohibition as promoting the election of other candidates: *Director of Public Prosecutions* v. *Luft* [1977] AC 962.) These provisions are the basis for the recording and control of election expenditure. The Act limits the amount of expenditure on the conduct or management of the election in any constituency to £2,700, plus 3·1p for every registered voter in a county constituency or 2·3p for every registered voter in a borough constituency (s.76): these sums may be varied by statutory instrument to take account of inflation.

The legal limits on constituency expenditure appear to be substantially effective, and indeed in recent elections the average expenditure per candidate for all the parties has been well below the permitted maximum. (For the 1983 election see David Butler and Dennis Kavanagh, *The British General Election of 1983*, 1984, p. 266.) But expenditure on the national campaign is not limited by law, even though national leaders and issues have come to dominate election campaigns. In *R. v. Tronoh Mines Ltd* [1952] 1 All ER 697, McNair J decided that the prohibition of unauthorized election expenditure (then contained in the Representation of the People Act 1949) did not extend to general propaganda in support of a political party, even if it incidentally assisted particular candidates of that party. (Cf. *Meek* v. *Lothian Regional Council* 1983 SLT 494.)

The main parties spend substantial (but not vast) sums in the national campaign on such things as public opinion research, poster campaigns, cinema and press advertising, and broadcasting. (Broadcasting time is provided without charge for party political broadcasts, but production can be a costly item.) The Conservative Party has the largest resources and is able to spend more than other parties on nation-wide campaigning. Pressure groups also intervene in election campaigns: the biggest spenders among them are the groups fostering free enterprise which publish advertisements disparaging policies of the Labour Party. This situation, it has been observed,

restores the premium on wealth which it has been the object of legislation over the last ninety years to neutralize, but we need to remember that the sums involved are small when compared with the advertising budget of most major firms, and the cost of election campaigns in many other countries.

(Peter G. J. Pulzer, *Political Representation and Elections in Britain*, 3rd edn 1975, pp. 90–91.) An unofficial commission sponsored by the Hansard Society for Parliamentary Government concluded that this branch of electoral law was seriously out of date.

> *Paying for Politics: the Report of the Commission upon the Financing of Political Parties* (1981), paras. 6.2–6.3

In the 19th century, a general election was seen largely as a contest between individual candidates, and spending by party headquarters was a comparatively negligible factor. The law restricting the expenditure of individual candidates controlled, therefore, virtually all election spending. Today it controls only a relatively small part of such spending. The law ignores two vital features differentiating contemporary election campaigns from campaigns in the 19th century; the nationalisation of politics, and the fact that campaign activity is not restricted to the immediate pre-election period.

The law treats a general election campaign as no more than the sum of a number of simultaneous constituency campaigns, and limits only such expenditure whose purpose is to promote the election of a particular candidate in a particular constituency. Moreover, it assumes that election expenses are incurred only during the immediate pre-election period and not at other times.

We believe the law in this sphere to be seriously out of date and therefore propose a statutory limitation upon election expenditure by the national political parties, to apply to all spending by the parties and not merely to expenditure incurred during the immediate pre-election period.

Two of our members, however ... do not consider the statutory limitation of expenditure by parties to be desirable since its present level is not excessive by international or any other standards. They also consider it impractical as companies, trades unions, organisations and individuals can give significant non-financial help to the parties in countless ways which could not possibly be evaluated in monetary terms.

The media

The fairness of the electoral contest is also put in question by partisanship in the media of communication. Most Fleet Street organs display a political bias, sometimes combined with an attempt at objectivity. In election campaigns the national press consistently gives preponderant support to the Conservative Party. (For the 1979 and 1983 general elections, see David Butler and Dennis Kavanagh, *The British General Election of 1979* (1980), ch.12 and *The British General Election of 1983* (1984), ch.9.) There is uncertainty about the specific effects of newspaper comment and propaganda on voting behaviour, but it has been suggested that although the media 'may not persuade the public directly; nevertheless they affect what people know, and what they think is important' (James Curran and Jean Seaton, *Power without Responsibility*, 1981, p. 273).

The Royal Commission on the Press gave some consideration to the political partisanship of the press in its Final Report in 1977, observing (Cmnd 6810, para. 10.126):

There is no doubt that over most of this century the Labour movement has had less newspaper support than its right wing opponents and that its beliefs and activities have been unfavourably reported by the majority of the press. . . . We do not feel able to pronounce on whether there is political bias at work in drawing up the agenda for discussion and comment. This would require difficult value judgements to be made about politics and society, as well as about the press. Within the terms of the agenda actually drawn up, however, the evidence we have had does not suggest that in either the national or the regional press at present the balance against Labour is a strong one.

But in recent years concern has been increasingly expressed about the tendency of a capitalist press and other media to uphold established viewpoints and propagate a conservative political consensus. The demand is heard for greater independence and diversity of the press. The Royal Commission which reported in 1977 (above) was not in favour of public measures to correct political partisanship in the press, and was concerned about the government involvement which would follow from the establishment of a public launch fund to help new newspapers. It expressed its 'firm belief . . . that the press should be left free to be partisan', restrained only by the law and a strengthened Press Council (Addendum to ch.10, para. 11). On the other hand the authors of the minority report, convinced of a 'manifest political imbalance in Britain's national press', argued for governmental measures which would achieve greater diversity in the press without prejudice to its freedom: *Minority Report* by Mr Basnett and Mr Goodman. (See also James Curran (ed.), *The British Press: A Manifesto*, 1978, ch.4.) A permanent weighting of press comment on one side of the political divide cannot be good for the health of democracy. The Labour movement, convinced that it does not get a fair hearing in the British press, has discussed the establishment of a new national daily newspaper and local newspapers which would express the left-wing viewpoint; but the difficulties are formidable.

Facilities for making election broadcasts on radio and television are offered by the broadcasting authorities (BBC and IBA) and allocated to political parties by the Committee on Party Political Broadcasting, an informally constituted body comprising representatives of the broadcasting authorities and the main parties (including the nationalist parties in Scotland and Wales). Under its rules minor parties qualify for a broadcast if they have 50 or more candidates in the field on nomination day. The Committee deliberates in secret and acts upon precedents established by itself. In 1983 no agreement was reached in the Committee and the broadcasting authorities themselves made the allocation, applying a ratio of 5:5:4 to the main parties, with equality for the Conservatives and Labour and the lesser allocation to the Alliance. The same ratio was applied as a 'working guideline' in current affairs and news programmes. (See David Butler and Dennis Kavanagh, *The British General Election of 1983* (1984), p. 148.)

Extensive radio and television coverage of the election occurs in news programmes, reports from party press conferences, interviews of party leaders, etc. Broadcast programmes relating to the election are exempt from the prohibition of unauthorized expenditure imposed by section 75(1) of the Representation of the People Act 1983 (see above). But section 93(1) provides that a candidate may not take part in a broadcast about his constituency for the purpose of promoting his election unless every other candidate in the constituency consents. This means that a candidate can (in effect) veto any broadcast in which another candidate in his constituency takes part. (Cf. *McAliskey* v. *British Broadcasting Corporation* [1980] NI 44.) Section 93(1) also makes it an offence to broadcast an item about a constituency without the consent of any candidate taking part in the item: see *Marshall* v. *British Broadcasting Corporation* [1979] 1 WLR 1071.

Section 2(2) of the Broadcasting Act 1981 obliges the Independent Broadcasting Authority to ensure that the programmes broadcast by them maintain 'a proper balance' in their subject-matter. In *Wilson* v. *Independent Broadcasting Authority* 1979 SC 351, the Court of Session held that this required the Authority to give balanced treatment to the opposing sides in the referendum campaign on Scottish devolution: 'balance' would not be achieved by allowing one broadcast to each of the three parties campaigning for a 'Yes' vote and one to the only party campaigning for a 'No' vote, as the Authority had proposed. Section 4(1) of the Act further obliges the Authority to satisfy themselves that, so far as possible, due impartiality is preserved in programmes about matters of political controversy or of current public policy. No equivalent duties are imposed by statute on the BBC, but the Board of Governors of the Corporation, in a resolution of 8 January 1981, reaffirmed their recognition of a duty 'to provide a properly balanced service which displays a wide range of subject matter', and their intention 'to treat controversial subjects with due impartiality' both in news services and in programmes dealing with matters of public policy. These assurances are incorporated in an Annex to the Licence and Agreement between the Secretary of State for the Home Department and the British Broadcasting Corporation (Cmnd 8233/1981).

The duties of balance and impartiality are important for it would be rash to deny the possibility of an influence of television, in particular, on political attitudes and the outcome of elections. The findings of a recent report suggest that television may have had a significant influence on the result of the 1983 general election: Gunter, Svennevig and Wober, *Television Coverage of the 1983 General Election* (1984). (See also Appendix E to the *Report of the Committee on the Future of Broadcasting*, Cmnd 6753/1977.) But the formal requirements of balance and impartiality leave a great deal to the judgement of the broadcasting authorities. Ministers take the view that the 'question of equity in broadcasting is a matter for the broadcasting authorities themselves' (Under-Secretary of State, Welsh Office, HC Deb. vol. 953, col. 12, 3 July 1978) and there is no effective accountability to Parliament in this respect. Neither will the courts intervene in a matter of judgement of the broadcasting authorities, unless their decision is so unreasonable as to be perverse (see *Attorney-General, ex rel. McWhirter* v. *Independent Broadcasting Authority* [1973] QB 629), or they have misconstrued their legal obligations (see *Wilson* v. *Independent Broadcasting Authority*, above).

(c) The Electoral System

The electoral system in use affects both the 'value' of a vote in terms of its efficacy to secure the election of a preferred representative to Parliament, and also the likelihood that the government elected into power will reflect the interests or policy preferences of the electorate. The system adopted in the United Kingdom for elections to the House of Commons is that known variously as the plurality, 'first past the post' or relative majority system. Some other Commonwealth countries and the United States also make use of this system, but in most countries, in Europe and elsewhere, different systems are preferred.

In the plurality system, voting takes place in single-member constituencies and the candidate with most votes is elected. It is not the object of this system to produce an elected House which will be a 'mirror of the nation' in the sense that it fairly represents the different parties, interests or viewpoints in society. For many years the system has supported the alternation in government of two main parties, usually assuring to one or other of them an absolute majority in Parliament. The tendency of the plurality system to disfavour small parties (unless their support is regionally concentrated) and to give a disproportionate benefit in seats won to the party with the largest share of the popular vote, has worked in favour of single-party government. Parties have been able to come forward with policies for government, not for bargaining, and general elections have had virtually the character of referendums in which the people have decided which party should form the government. Richard Rose wrote in 1974 (*The Problem of Party Government*, p. 115):

The argument for the existing procedure is simply stated: the British electoral system is intended to manufacture majority government. It does this by giving disproportionately more seats to the most successful party. The element of distortion in the ratio of votes to seats is usually considered a small price to pay for the greater advantage of fixing responsibility for government upon a single party with a majority in the House of Commons. A purely proportional allocation of seats in accordance with votes would result in neither the Conservative nor Labour party gaining a majority in the Commons. The weakest rather than the strongest of the three parties, the Liberals, could decide who governs.

In this century the plurality system has worked reasonably well, at least in the period from 1931 to 1970 when an overwhelming majority of voters gave their support to the two main parties. In the ten general elections held in that period the two major parties together won an average of 90.74 per cent of the vote (their joint share never falling below 85 per cent). In all but one of those elections the party that formed the government – including the National Governments of 1931 and 1935 dominated by the Conservatives – had won more votes than any other party: the exception was the 1951 election, won by the Conservatives although Labour had a ·8 per cent larger share of the total vote. Every government in that period had an absolute majority of seats in the House of Commons. Thus the system was manufacturing majority government, and since the great majority of those voting (the turnout of voters then averaging 76.71 per cent) gave their votes to one or other of the two main parties, it seems a reasonable inference that those parties stood for a range of viewpoints that were widely held in the community.

The plurality system may, then, be credited, no doubt in combination with other factors, with the continuation for much of this century of stable, single-party government enjoying broad popular support. On the other hand critics of the plurality system observed that parties were not fairly represented in Parliament in proportion to votes cast for them, and that the Liberal Party, with substantial but dispersed support among voters, was invariably excluded from a share in government. A party could achieve power having won less than 50 per cent of the total vote, and indeed this had become the normal case.

In recent general elections the distorting effects of the plurality system on parliamentary representation have become more apparent. In each of the two 1974 elections the Liberals, with over 18 per cent of the total vote, won only 2 per cent of the seats, and it was observed that more than ten times as many votes were needed to elect a Liberal MP as to elect a Labour or Conservative MP. Mirroring the 1951 result, the February 1974 election was won by the Labour Party with a smaller share of the total vote than the Conservatives, and Labour took office as the first government since the Second World War not to have an absolute majority in the House of Commons.

The 1979 and 1983 general elections again produced majority government, but the latter election gave a striking demonstration of the disproportionality that may result from the plurality system.

The 1983 General Election

Electorate: 42,197,344
Votes cast: 30,670,905 (72.7% turnout)

Party	Votes	% of total vote	Seats won
Conservative	13,012,602	42.4	397
Labour	8,457,124	27.6	209
Liberal/SDP Alliance	7,780,587	25.4	23
Plaid Cymru	125,309	0.4	2
Scottish National Party	331,975	1.1	2
Others (Northern Ireland)	963,308	3.1	17

The Conservative Government Elected in 1983 with 42.4 per cent of the total vote had an absolute majority of 144 seats in the House: on a principle of strict proportionality the Conservatives would have had not 397 but 276 seats, and would have been unable to form a majority government. The Conservative and Labour Parties together won only 70 per cent of the total vote – their lowest combined share since 1923 – but took 93 per cent of the seats. The Liberal/SDP Alliance was strikingly penalized by the dispersion of its support over the country: its 25.4 per cent of the vote won for it only 23 seats (3.5 per cent); Labour with 27.6 per cent of the vote, concentrated to better advantage, won 209 seats (32 per cent). A strictly proportional representation for the Alliance would have been 165 seats and for Labour 179 seats.

These results showed that the plurality system may discriminate severely against third parties, which naturally regard their under-representation in the House of Commons as unfair. It is also objected against this system that a party can be put in power with much less than a majority of votes and may govern without having to accommodate its policies to the interests of a majority of voters represented by the other parties in Parliament (the argument of 'elective dictatorship'). Other questionable features of the plurality system were emphasized by the 1983 general election. Most MPs elected on that occasion were supported by a minority of the voters in their constituencies: an extreme instance was the election of a Democratic Unionist in Mid Ulster with only 30 per cent of the vote. Like previous general elections that of 1983 distorted the regional representation of parties, yielding a substantial under-representation of Labour voters in southern shires and of Conservative voters in northern industrial cities.

In recent years many have advocated the introduction of proportional representation in place of the plurality system. The case against the present system is summed up in the following passage.

> *The Report of the Hansard Society Commission on Electoral Reform,*
> June 1976, para. 58

The Case Against the Present System
This has been presented to us as follows:
  (a) The stability of government provided by the present system is more apparent than real. In three cases since 1945 new elections were needed within 18 months.
  (b) While 'fairness' of representation is not the only, and perhaps not even the most important criterion of electoral systems, there is a threshold beyond which 'unfair' representation borders on the suppression of sizeable minorities. If and when 25% of the electorate no longer vote for one of the major parties, this threshold has been crossed and change is needed.
  (c) More particularly, and whatever the case for the 'largest organised minority' may be, a democratic electoral system must protect the majority of electors, or at least of voters, from flagrant minority rule. For example if fewer than 40% of voters (29% of electors) can impose their will on the other 60% or more, distortions are no longer a question of 'fairness' but of elementary rights of citizens.
  (d) The present electoral system is obviously in keeping with the tradition of adversary politics, by which the opposition tends to oppose the government on most, if not all, major issues and reverse policy when it comes into power. This tradition has, however, led to considerable instability as well as a tendency for the major parties to give undue weight to their extreme wings. An electoral system which makes possible a parliamentary majority based on less than 40% of the votes possible, has encouraged such developments.
  (e) There is undoubtedly widespread disaffection with the electoral system. The clearest index of this is the fact that one out of every four voters now finds the parties favoured by the system unacceptable. While there are arguments against the findings of opinion research in this matter, the fact is that in a recent (Marplan) survey, almost 60% of those interviewed when told what the result of proportional representation would have been at the last election, said that they would have preferred this result to the one actually attained. . . .

(The Hansard Society presents the case *for* the present system in para. 57 of the *Report.*)
Critics of the plurality system often condemn not only what they see as its

unfairness, but also the 'adversary politics' of alternating single-party governments which it fosters. Professor S. E. Finer, for example, says that proportional representation would have the advantage of inducing 'greater moderation in policy', since the major parties would usually be unable to form governments unless they cooperated with parties 'taking a more central political stance' (S. E. Finer (ed.), *Adversary Politics and Electoral Reform* (1975), pp. 30–31. See also S. E. Finer, 'Adversary Politics and the Eighties' (1982) 1 *Electoral Studies* 221.)

The defects of the plurality system are examined by Vernon Bogdanor, who comes to the following conclusion:

Vernon Bogdanor, *The People and the Party System* (1981), p. 205

The claims made for the plurality system . . . can no longer be sustained. It is now less likely than it ever was to provide for strong majority government, but even if it did, that would not necessarily ensure good government. To defenders of the plurality system a majority government is 'strong' if it has a majority in the House of Commons. But if this does not correspond to broad popular support in the country, it will lack the authority necessary to implement its policies successfully. In theory, the plurality system should encourage the parties to broaden the basis of their support by seeking consensus, but there is no mechanism to prevent parties moving away from the centre, or misrepresenting the opinions of those who vote for them.

Moreover, the system positively incites sectional appeals and highlights areas of conflict rather than reconciliation. In industry and in local government, it makes problems intractable by manufacturing disagreements beyond the real differences of opinion felt by the electorate. Indeed, by putting unrealistic alternatives before the electorate, it paradoxically obscures the very real choices which need to be made in an advanced industrial society. It therefore provides neither stability nor effective choice. And it handicaps two groups – minorities and women – whose growing desire for self-expression is an important feature of life in contemporary Britain.

The plurality system thus frustrates rather than fulfils the aspirations of the British electorate which, although increasingly alienated from the two main political parties, remains thoroughly wedded to moderate constitutional government and is distrustful of doctrinaires. Class and regional divisions in political attitudes are still important, but by no means as important as the electoral system makes them appear. The electoral system makes it difficult for the parties to co-operate, although numerous surveys have shown that the voter is sceptical of party shibboleths and would like politicians to operate on a broader basis of agreement. The voter seeks a consensus which the electoral system prevents him from achieving. That is the nub of the criticism of the plurality system. It is difficult, therefore, not to conclude that the balance of the argument lies conclusively in favour of reform; for, whatever services the plurality system may have performed for the country in the past, today it forms an obstacle to both national unity and social progress.

Proportional representation would be likely to bring about coalition governments and a more consensual style of politics, parties of the left or right having to temper their policies and reach accommodations with parties of the centre. It is said that a new politics of this kind would accord with a broad consensus which exists in society at large and is now artificially polarized by a two-party system. But others believe that to renounce 'adversary politics' is to disregard real divisions of interest in society and to evade a necessary confrontation of ideas in the pursuit of a centralist compromise. Those in particular who wish to see the transformation of society are less disposed to favour 'coalition politics'.

Not everyone agrees that proportional representation would produce governments that were more representative of the views and interests and the electorate.

J. A. Chandler, 'The Plurality Vote: A Reappraisal' (1982) 30
Political Studies 87, 88–91

The relative merits of some form of proportional representation as opposed to the plurality vote must involve the question of whether a coalition of parties, which between them have summed up a majority of votes, is more representative than a single party government based on a minority of votes. A major problem exists here since although it cannot be questioned that at the time of an election a single party will at least represent all those who voted for that party, it is by no means evident that a coalition will fully represent the interests of all those who voted for one of the members of that coalition. . . .

In order to determine whether a coalition will always represent the electorate more faithfully than a single-party government based on a minority of votes it is necessary to note that the answer will depend on the kinds of motive that influence an elector's choice. A voter may favour or oppose a party on the basis of its policies. It must however be recognized [that many] electors cast their ballot according to attitudes of trust, loyalty or expectation which are motives that cannot be analysed in the same manner as policy preferences. The following discussion will therefore firstly consider the problem on the assumption that voters are influenced by party policy, and, secondly, as if they made their choice on the basis of trust or loyalty towards their chosen party.

The problem of whether the policy interests of electors are better represented by a single-party government holding a minority of votes or a majority coalition would clearly be answered in favour of the coalition if all its members agreed to fully accept each other's policies. Although such an amicable agreement between parties is unlikely they will normally be in accord on many fundamental policies and principles. The three largest parties in Britain all firmly support the maintenance of parliamentary democracy and a pro-Western defence policy. An elector will not, however, determine his voting preference with reference to issues on which parties are agreed as these policies will be represented by any government that forms. The extent to which a coalition may be more representative than a single-party government must be evaluated in relation to those policies on which parties differ at the time of an election.

Coalition partners will resolve their policy differences either by agreeing to follow a compromise proposal or, more negatively, by abandoning the policies on which it is impossible to reach an agreement. Ideological hostility and tactical considerations frequently lead coalitions to adopt the more negative alternative. The tendency in states governed by coalitions to forward few legislative initiatives has been a significant and at times problematic characteristic of such regimes. The French Fourth Republic collapsed partly due to the inability of its parties to carry forward much needed legislation. The Italian political system suffers a similar immobility on account of the problems of developing new policies within the framework of coalitions.

A coalition that fails to forward any of the distinctive proposals made by its members may be acceptable to a voter whose sole interest in an election is to prevent a party from carrying out particular policies. There can however be few voters who wish only to retain the status quo at the time of an election and have no thought even of repealing legislation enacted by the previous administration. Electors are more likely to support a party on account of its distinctive policies and will therefore find that their interests are not represented within a coalition that has abandoned the distinctive policies that determined their vote.

Coalitions are rarely wholly negative and will frequently develop policies through a process of negotiations among member parties. It cannot however be assumed that the resultant policies will be more representative of the electorate's interests than those of a single-party minority government. Coalition policies cannot simply take the form of a half-way compromise between contending parties. Many, if not the majority, of disputes over policy are zero-sum conflicts. Proposals to nationalize all major ports, to close direct grant schools or impose fines for unofficial strike action must either be accepted or rejected since half measures make little practical sense. A move to half nationalize the docks or abandon half the direct-grant schools is hardly likely to produce an outcome desired by many electors. Rather than attempt an impossible half-way compromise on many issues, parties in conflict will agree to trade the concession of one policy for another. A frequent agreement will therefore be 'if I let you do X then you must let me do Y'. The governing coalition in Belgium established in June 1978 was for example based on an agreement between the Christian Social Party and the Nationalist parties that the Nationalists would accept a programme of economic austerity in exchange for the Christian Social Party's acquiescence towards proposals for a measure of regional devolution. The pact between the Labour and Liberal parties in Britain in 1977 illustrates both the trading of policies and the negative approach of many coalitions. The agreement effectively rested on the abandonment of distinctive Labour party policies such as further nationalization of industries in exchange for gaining the support of the Liberals without having to accept any of their major distinctive policies such as electoral reform.

Where the trading of policies takes place the results will not produce proposals supported by the majority of the electorate. If party X gains 40 per cent of the vote, then a dispensation from Party Y with 20 per cent of the vote, to allow it to carry out one of its chosen policies in exchange for forwarding one of its own, does not entail that policies of X and Y have now gained the support of 60 per cent of the electorate. All that can be said is that two policies have been enacted and that one of these appears to have been supported by a party that received 20 per cent of the vote whilst the other received 40 per cent. The extent to which such a situation represents the interests of the electorate should be contrasted with a situation in which the party with 40 per cent of the vote is able to govern alone. The party would at least be able to satisfy fully 40 per cent of the electorate in respect to all its policies whilst satisfaction would not be given to policies supported by only 20 per cent of the electorate.

It has so far been suggested that in many cases a single-party government can represent the policy interests of electors more efficiently than a coalition. Calculations as to the extent a coalition represents attitudes of trust and loyalty towards a party are more difficult to formulate and present problems similar to those faced by Utilitarians who set out to establish a felicific calculus. A measure of enlightenment can be given through the following model. Assume in an election that 40 per cent of the voters supported the Conservative party on the grounds that they trusted the organization to govern in their interests whilst for similar reasons 40 per cent voted for the Labour party and 20 per cent for the Liberals. It can be suggested that voters will have a first preference for a government wholly from their own party but would, as a second preference, accept a coalition that contained their party. The election under a pluralist vote of a Labour or Conservative administration would therefore satisfy the first preference of 40 per cent of the electorate and give no satisfaction to 60 per cent of voters. If, under a system of PR, a coalition government was formed between one of the larger parties and the Liberals then 60 per cent of the electorate would be satisifed to the extent that their second preference would be achieved whilst 40 per cent of the electorate would still be unsatisfied. What calculus can determine whether the greatest satisfaction is obtained and therefore better representation of the electorate achieved if only 40 per cent of voters gain their first preference or 60 per cent their second preference? The answer to such a question would depend upon the degree to which each voter's first or subsequent preferences are more desirable than preferences of a lower order. But such differences are unmeasurable and because they are there will always be a fundamental defect in the case for substituting a PR system for the present plurality system.

Proponents of the adoption of a system of PR in Britain rest much of their case on the assumption that a government that is supported by a minority of the electorate lacks a mandate to govern. The idea that an administration can only govern legitimately if it receives the magical qualifying figure of over 50 per cent of the votes cast only makes sense when two choices are to be made. If three travellers bound for a common destination arrive at a cross roads and dispute among themselves as to the way ahead, with one insisting that it is to the right, another that it is to the left whilst the third demands straight on, there is no way that the dispute may be resolved by reference to a majority mandate nor does it make sense to suggest that one may be forged by a compromise requiring the travellers to stand still or to return along the road from whence they came. Where an electorate is asked to make a first preference from three or more alternatives it will frequently be the case that no one choice gains majority support and it is clearly a fallacy to assume that a combination of two or more of the choices will necessarily produce the required majority. It may be argued that the decision must be made by reference to second preferences but without a calculus to determine the extent to which a second preference is more acceptable than a first preference there can be no guarantee that the result would produce the maximum possible satisfaction.

Chandler argues further that the plurality system is more likely than proportional representation to produce governments that are responsive to public opinion throughout their tenure of office (p. 92):

Within a plurality system a relatively small loss of votes will result in a disproportionately large loss of seats for the largest parliamentary parties and will be likely to threaten their ability to form part of a government. Any party operating under such conditions must take great care not to alienate many of their supporters at the time of the last election unless they can be replaced by new converts to their cause. In comparison a party operating under a system of PR could afford to alienate a much larger number of voters before suffering a correspondingly large loss of seats and a threat to its chances of holding or obtaining power.

Some varieties of proportional representation

The single transferable vote (STV) version of proportional representation has much support in the United Kingdom. Although not used on the continent of Europe or in many countries elsewhere, it applies in the Republic of Ireland and for elections to the upper house of the Australian Parliament (the Senate). STV was in use in Northern Ireland from 1920 to 1929 and was re-introduced in 1973 for local government elections in the province and for elections to the Northern Ireland Assembly. It is also used for the election of Northern Ireland's representatives in the European Parliament. Both the Liberal and the Social Democratic parties favour the adoption of STV in Britain.

STV is based on large, multi-member constituencies. If this system were to be introduced in the United Kingdom it is likely that most constituencies would have three, four, five or six members, with the five-member constituency of about 300,000 voters as the norm. The voter indicates an order of preference among the candidates named on the ballot paper. The following is a concise explanation of the method of counting the votes.

Electoral Reform: First Report of the Joint Liberal/SDP Alliance Commission on Constitutional Reform (1982), Annex 2

How Votes are Counted under the Single Transferable Vote
The first thing to be done is to calculate the 'Electoral Quota'. In a constituency which returns one member, this is one vote over 50% of the valid votes – no candidate can be elected unless he has more than half the votes. In a two member constituency, it is one vote over 33.33%, and so on for larger constituencies. For a 5 member constituency it is one vote over 16.66%. What happens next? The *first preference* votes are counted. Any candidate whose first preference votes meet the quota is declared elected. But he may have got *more* first preferences than he needed to get elected. So that the surplus is not wasted, the Returning Officer then counts all the *second preferences* recorded by the voters who give him their first preference, and transfers the appropriate percentage of them to the other candidates who have not yet reached the Quota, in proportion to the preferences given to each of those candidates. (He obviously cannot transfer them at their full value, one for one, because it is only the surplus which can be transferred; they have to be scaled down.) This may bring another candidate above the quota, in which case he is elected, and the process is repeated. Other candidates may then reach the quota (and be elected), but a point may be reached when there are still seats to be filled, but none of the remaining candidates has reached the quota and there are no more surpluses to be distributed. At this point, the Returning Officer starts eliminating candidates from the bottom, i.e. he counts the second preferences for the candidate with the lowest number of votes and transfers them to other remaining

candidates till either someone reaches the quota or no further transfers are possible; if that happens the candidate(s) with the highest number of votes are elected even if they have not reached the quota.

(There are variants of the method explained above for transferring surplus votes in accordance with voters' preferences. For a full account of the system see, e.g., Vernon Bogdanor, *What is Proportional Representation?* (1984), ch.5.)

A feature of STV which may increase the power of the voter is that he can express a preference between candidates who are members of the same party: in this respect a general election also functions as a *primary* election of those who will be a party's representatives in the legislature. The voter can also choose to vote across party lines, giving his preferences to candidates, of whatever party, who support a particular cause that he favours. The adoption of the system could result in the election of more women and members of ethnic minorities to Parliament.

But some of the merits claimed for STV are speculative in a United Kingdom context. The Hansard Society Commission on Electoral Reform in its 1976 Report (above) noted that the system has never been used in a country with a population as large as that of Britain. The Report also said (para. 106) that it was uncertain to what extent voters would be able to discriminate between candidates of the same party by reference to their political standpoints: 'The selection of candidates will still be made by the political parties, and certainly in Ireland there is no conscious attempt to produce a slate of candidates across the political spectrum within a party. . . .' STV could have a 'localizing' effect on politics and the behaviour of MPs, who would be at risk of displacement by candidates of their own parties and liable to be unseated as a result of second preferences recorded by voters of other parties. It can also be objected to STV that second and lower preferences have the same weight as first preferences.

An alternative form of proportional representation, widely used in Western Europe, is the list system, which is designed to achieve a representation of *political parties* in proportion to votes cast rather than – as with STV – a fair representation of the decisions of *voters*, irrespective of their support for parties. There are several kinds of list system. In most varieties, each party presents regional or local lists of its candidates, placed in an order of the party's preference, to electors in multi-member constituencies. Votes are cast for parties, and seats are distributed between the parties in proportion to their shares of the votes, a party's seats being allotted to its candidates in the listed order. The system can be – and usually is – adjusted to allow the voter to express a preference between candidates on the party list, so that the party's order of preference can be varied. There are several different procedures for allocating seats to the parties in proportion to the votes cast for them.

List systems benefit the party machines which draw up the lists. Voters cannot prevent their votes from assisting candidates on the list of whom they disapprove, and cross-party voting is not normally possible. Pure list systems have not been much favoured by supporters of proportional representation in the United Kingdom. (A regional list system was, however, proposed – and rejected – in 1977 for the election of British representatives to the European Parliament: see HC Deb. vol. 941, cols. 298 *et seq.*, 13 December 1977.)

West Germany uses a hybrid system of which a modified form has been proposed by the Hansard Society Commission on Electoral Reform for adoption in the United Kingdom. Under the Hansard Society's 'additional member system', three-quarters of the members of the House of Commons would be elected in single-member constituencies by the present plurality system. An elector's vote would count both for the candidate and for his party, and in the interest of greater proportionality one quarter of the seats in the House would be allocated to the parties, on a regional basis, in proportion to their shares of the vote. The additional seats in each region would be given to candidates who had failed to win seats but had done best (in terms of the percentage of the vote obtained by them in their constituencies) among the defeated candidates of their party in the region. The *First Report of the Joint Liberal/SDP Alliance Commission on Constitutional Reform* (above) draws attention in para. 43 to flaws in the Hansard Society Commission's scheme:

There would as under the West German variant be two classes of members, though under the Hansard Society scheme the additional members instead of being drawn from party lists would be taken from candidates who had been *losers* in constituency elections. The choice would seem to be capricious and unfair both as between candidates and between constituencies. A loser from one party might gain an additional seat though he had fewer votes than a loser from another party. A loser in a three-or-four-cornered fight would have a worse chance of gaining an additional seat than a loser from the same party in a straight fight in another constituency, though he might have come nearer to winning the constituency seat. As between constituencies, some would have two or even more members, while others would have only one. Moreover, the Hansard Society scheme gives no incentive for constituencies to adopt women candidates or candidates from ethnic minority groups.

(See further Vernon Bogdanor, op. cit., pp. 68–73.)

(d) **The mandate**

'For responsible government to exist some control must be exercisable by the electorate over the actions of government' (Jack Lively, *Democracy*, 1975, p. 42). Do elections provide a means of such control? Are governments bound, in accordance with a 'doctrine of the mandate', to carry out policies which have received the endorsement of the electorate?

In a system of representative government the question of the mandate becomes a question of the nature of representation. Our constitution does not embody any one theory of representation, but is generally said to reject the notion that a parliamentary representative is a delegate of the electors and bound to act in accordance with their instructions. The words of Edmund

Burke are often invoked, in his speech to the electors of Bristol in 1774 (*Works*, new edn 1826, vol. III, pp. 19–20):

> But *authoritative* instructions; *mandates* issued, which the member is bound blindly and implicitly to obey, to vote, and to argue for, though contrary to the clearest conviction of his judgment and conscience, – these are things utterly unknown to the laws of this land, and which arise from a fundamental mistake of the whole order and tenour of our constitution.

L. S. Amery expressed a similar idea in a more recent time in saying that our system is one of 'government of the people, for the people, with, but not by, the people' (*Thoughts on the Constitution*, 2nd edn 1964, pp. 20–21), and the Kilbrandon Commission declared that politicians 'are elected to use their own judgement on behalf of the people' (Cmnd 5460, para. 1236). Members of Parliament do not regard themselves as delegates with specific commissions from the voters who elected them or from local party organizations. The Committee of Privileges of the House of Commons has repeatedly affirmed the freedom of speech and action of MPs, and in 1947 the House itself resolved (HC Deb. vol. 440, col. 365, 15 July 1947) that

> it is inconsistent with the dignity of the House, with the duty of a Member to his constituents, and with the maintenance of the privilege of freedom of speech, for any Member of this House to enter into any contractual agreement with an outside body, controlling or limiting the Member's complete independence and freedom of action in Parliament or stipulating that he shall act in any way as the representative of such outside body in regard to any matters to be transacted in Parliament; the duty of a Member being to his constituents and to the country as a whole, rather than to any particular section thereof.

The independence of the member must however be seen in the context of party government. The disciplined party system of our day is based on the loyalty of MPs who have stood before the electors as representatives of parties. (The Representation of the People Act 1969 acknowledged this fact in allowing the party affiliations of candidates to be stated on the ballot paper: see now the Representation of the People Act 1983, Sched. 1, rule 19.) Parties declare their policies to the electorate in manifestos and public statements; electors generally give their votes to parties rather than to candidates distinguished by their personal qualities. David Butler and Donald Stokes observe (*Political Change in Britain*, 2nd edn 1974, p. 28):

> Before party labels were placed on the ballot paper in 1970, virtually every voter was able to make the link between candidate and party, even though many knew nothing else about him: they perceived that to vote for a candidate was to vote for a government of his party, one which he would sustain in power throughout the life of a Parliament.

Unless the 'new democratic theory' is accepted (p. 406 above) which concedes to the people nothing more than the occasional choice of a team of leaders who will apply whatever policies they think best, an election may be regarded as a choice not only between parties and leaders but between alternative pro-grammes or policies. This provides a justification for a 'principle of the mandate' which all political parties recognize in some degree – the principle that a party, if elected, is both authorized and bound to implement specific commitments included in its election manifesto.

The principle of the mandate can be over-stated and there are those who deny its validity. Objections to it are influenced by scepticism about the reality of the supposed approval given by the electorate to the policies of the successful party in a general election. The electoral system does not provide for an expression of views on specific policies but only for a choice between entire party programmes. Policies included in a programme are selected by party organizations and do not necessarily reflect the issues of greatest interest or concern to the public. Moreover there is evidence from empirical research that many voters do not know what are the policies of the different parties, agree with only some of the policies of the party they support, and prefer some policies which are in fact espoused by opposing parties. (See, e.g., Peter G. J. Pulzer, *Political Representation and Elections in Britain* (3rd edn 1975), pp. 122–3.) Manifestos are not widely read and in any case contain many statements of a very general nature, such as promises to 'return more choice to individuals and their families' or 'actively pursue dialogue with the Soviet Union and China'.

But it would be wrong to dismiss the principle of the mandate as unfounded. Party manifestos do also include quite specific undertakings: for example the 1983 Conservative manifesto promised abolition of the GLC and the metropolitan councils, legislation for secret ballots in trade union elections, and the transfer of named state-owned enterprises to private ownership; the Labour manifesto promised withdrawal from the European Community, a Freedom of Information Act, and the repeal of Tory employment legislation. Manifesto commitments are reinforced in public statements and are the stuff of argument in the election campaign. A party's programme and the terms of its appeal to the electorate help to constitute the character or image which it has in the public view, and to generate expectations about its behaviour in office. Opinion surveys of reactions to the 1979 manifestos 'left no doubt of the striking popularity of the Conservatives' proposals and the extent to which they had got across to voters', say David Butler and Dennis Kavanagh (*The British General Election of 1979* (1980), p. 162). On the basis of recent survey evidence, John Clemens (*Polls, Politics and Populism* (1983), p. 9) concludes that 'most electors no longer vote automatically for a party to which they feel a sense of belonging. . . . They now vote on specific issues, and according to how well alternative party policies on these issues seem to match their personal interests.' (See also Bo Sarlvik and Ivor Crewe, *Decade of Dealignment* (1983), pp. 248–9, 263–4, 280 and ch. 14.)

Jack Lively, *Democracy* (1975), pp. 39–40

Does the claim that the primary function of the electorate is to produce a government mean then that the consideration of 'issues' never determines the voters' choice? . . . [T]he claim is implausible. A preference for one party rather than another can hardly be divorced from beliefs about what the party stands for or expectations about how it will act if it forms a government. There may be various grounds for these expectations – promises made by the parties, their past performances in office or their general ideological stances. There may be various motives inspiring voters' preferences – self-interest, prejudice or general ideological commitment. Even if a voter's expectations are quite unreal, even if he is unaware in detail of the policy differences between parties, even if he is dominated in his choice by prejudice or impulse, his vote may still be decided by a preference for one sort of government or set of policies rather than another.

Perhaps it is not unreasonable to interpret the result of an election as a demand addressed by the electorate to the winning party to govern broadly in terms of the party programme, as presented in the manifesto and in public declarations by the party leaders. The parties themselves take pains over the drafting of manifestos and evidently believe that they are presenting the electorate with a choice of policies. The principle of the mandate has had greater potency in the Labour Party than in other parties, and the manifestos of the Conservative Party are generally less specific about policies. But in practice Conservatives do not treat express manifesto commitments as having no special importance. In 1984 Mrs Thatcher defended the Government's policy of abolition of the GLC and metropolitan county councils against Tory rebels by an appeal to the mandate (*The Economist*, 14 April 1984, p. 32). It was a Tory peer (Lord Salisbury) who enunciated the doctrine that the House of Lords should not exercise its powers of delay in respect of legislation which was part of the electoral programme of the government. (See also Lord Carrington, HL Deb. vol. 265, cols. 737–8, 29 April 1965). Graeme Moodie sums up in saying (*The Government of Great Britain* (3rd edn 1971), p. 211):

[I]t is clear that a government's electoral program is and should be neither a straitjacket nor even a complete blueprint, and that the idea of a mandate is vague at best and must be handled with extreme caution. It is nonetheless significant. The doctrine reflects a widespread belief that a party program should be reasonably full and that for the successful party subsequently to depart radically from its spirit and intentions is dishonourable. The mere existence of the doctrine, moreover, suggests that, for much of the time, these expectations are satisfied, and emphasizes that the parties normally possess distinctive general approaches of which the parties' programs and behavior are interconnected manifestations.

(See also Ivor Jennings, *Cabinet Government*, 3rd edn 1959, pp. 503–9.)

We may conclude with C. S. Emden, *The People and the Constitution* (2nd edn 1956), p. 315, that the constitutional system 'includes a principle of mandate of an elastic character'. Manifestos do not cover everything: some issues are left vague or unmentioned, and governments have to deal with problems that were not foreseen. The realism of manifesto commitments is put to the test in government, and adjustments may have to be made. But in general governments take their manifestos seriously. This is confirmed by Dennis Kavanagh in a recent study, 'The Politics of Manifestos' (1981) 34 *Parliamentary Affairs* 7 at 14:

In spite of the charges about broken promises, there is an impressive degree of correspondence between [a] party's election pledges and subsequent performance when in office (in terms of legislation, reviews of policy, committees of inquiry and regulation). In 1964, the Conservatives could boast of having kept 92 of the 93 pledges made in 1959 and by 1974 many of the 1970 manifesto's specific proposals had been acted on. By 1979, in spite of Labour's lack of a clear majority in the Commons for much of the Parliament, more than half of the manifesto pledges had been fulfilled. . . .

The manifesto may be considered an instrument of democractic control, even though of a weak kind (see p. 345 above), and as contributing to the accountability of government in that success or failure in implementing manifesto commitments becomes part of the argument in the following election campaign.

The courts have had occasion to pronounce on the principle of the mandate in the context of local government. In *Bromley London Borough Council* v. *Greater London Council* [1983] 1 AC 768 (p. 234 above) the principle was summarily dismissed by the Court of Appeal, Oliver LJ saying that 'whatever other considerations may be taken into account by a statutory body such as the council in exercising its powers, an advance commitment to or so-called mandate from some section of the electors who may be supposed to have considered the matter is not one of them' (pp. 789–90). In the House of Lords a more measured judgment on the question was given by Lord Diplock in saying (p. 829) that members of a local authority must not

treat themselves as irrevocably bound to carry out pre-announced policies contained in election manifestos even though, by that time, changes of circumstances have occurred that were unforeseen when those policies were announced and would add significantly to the disadvantages that would result from carrying them out.

A different emphasis was given by the House of Lords to a local mandate in *Secretary of State for Education and Science* v. *Tameside Metropolitan Borough Council* [1977] AC 1014 (p. 211 above) in which Lord Wilberforce, referring to the electoral commitment by the Conservative majority on the local council to retain the grammar schools in its area, said (p. 1051) that the council was 'entitled – indeed in a sense bound – to carry out the policy on which it was elected'. (See also Lord Dilhorne at p. 1055 and Lord Salmon at p. 1067 and the comment by McAuslan, 'Administrative Law, Collective Consumption and Judicial Policy' (1983) 46 *MLR* 1 at 14–15, 16–17.)

What would be the role of manifestos in a system of multi-party politics and coalition governments?

3 The people and government

The people elect and dismiss governments, but do they exercise any influence or control over government between general elections? Are governments 'responsive' to the views and demands of the people?

It seems clear enough that governments are not indifferent to public opinion and take account of it in their decision-making. A government is, in a sense, engaged in a continuous election campaign and is influenced, throughout its term of office, by its assessments of electoral consequences. The 'rule of anticipated reactions' (Carl Friedrich, *Constitutional Government and Politics* (1937), pp. 16–18) may lead a government to refrain from actions which it is thought would provoke widespread unpopularity, evasion or non-cooperation among the public. As Jock Bruce-Gardyne and Nigel Lawson say (*The Power Game* (1976), p. 184):

All governments are continuously influenced by *anticipated* public opinion. The act of deference, however, occurs within the secrecy of the Cabinet room, so the people never learn of the triumphs they have won. The people complain that their opinions are ignored, while ministers are frustrated by the constraints of (real or imagined) popular sentiment.

(See also Ivor Jennings, *Cabinet Government*, 3rd edn 1959, pp. 475–80.)

Of course the government may be wrong in its assessment of public opinion. On many specific issues the public will be sharply divided in its opinions, on others it will be generally indifferent, and again a widely held opinion may fail to be publicly expressed, or what is represented as public opinion may be only that of an articulate minority. But this is not to say that public opinion, however crudely expressed or interpreted, has no impact on government.

By-elections may give the government an idea of its standing with the public, and have been known to stimulate policy initiatives or changes of course: the Crowther (afterwards Kilbrandon) Commission on the Constitution was set up at least partly in response to by-election gains by Scottish and Welsh Nationalists in 1966 and 1967 (see chapter 4 above). But by-election (and municipal election) results usually provide at most only a generalized verdict on the government's popularity, not a popular judgement on specific national issues.

Lines of communication lead from the constituencies to the government through the party organization and MPs' post-bags, but a more reliable source of information about public opinion on particular issues is nowadays provided by opinion surveys. Although by no means an exact science, the technique of opinion polling has been greatly refined in recent decades, and political parties frequently commission opinion surveys and make use of polls in planning the tactics of election campaigns. It is not easy to assess the influence of opinion polls on government policy-making, but when they provide evidence of popular support for a policy they may encourage the government to stand firm. (See Frank Teer and James D. Spence, *Political Opinion Polls* (1973), pp. 136–43.) It would in any event not be right for governments to respond in an undiscriminating way to shifts and swings of public opinion recorded by polling organizations: they need at least to satisfy themselves of the strength and stability of popular opinions and demands. The government has moreover a wider responsibility for the public interest and must take account of minority opinions and interests as well as those of the majority.

Referendums

It is rare for a general election to be fought on a single main issue, and the result of an election indicates, at most, an undifferentiated approval of a whole range of policies. Only a referendum makes it possible for the electorate to give a clear judgement on a single issue of immediate relevance.

Our constitution embodies the principle of representative, not direct, democracy, and the referendum is not a normal feature of the system. Various statutes have provided for local referendums on the promotion of private bills, the Sunday opening of cinemas, the establishment of public libraries, and 'local option' for the licensing of public houses. Local polls on Sunday opening of licensed premises are still held at intervals in Wales under the Licensing Act 1964, ss.66, 67.

National referendums have from time to time been proposed for contentious issues such as Irish home rule (Dicey was among those who argued for a referendum on home rule at the turn of the century), and Empire free trade (1930). In 1911 the Conservative Opposition made an unsuccessful attempt to amend the Parliament Bill so as to provide for referendums on bills of constitutional importance (e.g. those affecting the Crown or the franchise or the powers of either House of Parliament). It was not until 1972 that Parliament approved the use of a referendum other than for a local government matter. The Northern Ireland (Border Poll) Act 1972 provided for a referendum in which the electors of Northern Ireland voted on the question whether the province should remain part of the United Kingdom or be joined with the Republic of Ireland. It was then intended that 'border polls' would be held at regular intervals. The Northern Ireland Constitution Act 1973 now provides that Northern Ireland shall not cease to be part of the United Kingdom without the consent of the majority of the people of the province voting in a referendum. (See chapter 4 above.)

Stanley Alderson, *Yea or Nay? Referenda in the United Kingdom*
(1975), pp. 37–8

The British (Conservative) Government's purpose in holding the plebiscite was not to determine whether Northern Ireland should remain in the United Kingdom. At the time that was regarded as a foregone conclusion. It was to take the border out of politics. During the fifty years ofNorthern Ireland's existence, the main issue between the parties had been Partition. . . . The hope was that, being able to vote for or against unification in periodical referenda, Northern Irish electors would vote Left or Right at elections, when the predominant parties would have members and supporters of both religions.

With all these arguments in favour of the Border referenda, the Commons had agreed to them only reluctantly. The most persuasive argument was that, since the Northern Ireland Parliament was suspended at the time proposed for the first one, the electors could not express their opinion without resort to unnatural practice. The precedent set in Northern Ireland prepared the Commons for the EEC referendum.

The United Kingdom joined the European Communities in 1972 without the terms of entry being submitted to the people for approval. In its manifesto for the February 1974 general election the Labour Party undertook that it would renegotiate the terms of membership, and that if the negotiations were successful, 'the people should have the right to decide the issue through a General Election or a Consultative Referendum'. This commitment was reaffirmed in the Labour Party's manifesto of October 1974. After the election the Labour Cabinet decided that the question of membership, which divided both the Government and the party, should be resolved in a referendum rather than in another general election. In March 1975 the renegotiations were concluded and the Government announced that it would recommend the British people to vote in favour of staying in the Community: 'The Government will accept their verdict' (*Report on Renegotiation*, Cmnd 6003, para. 153). A Government White Paper on the Referendum (Cmnd 5925/1975) was debated in the House of Commons on 11 March 1975.

House of Commons, 11 March 1975 (HC Deb. vol. 888, cols. 291–3)

MR EDWARD SHORT (Lord President of the Council and Leader of the House of Commons): Whatever view we may take on Britain's membership of the European Community, I hope that we would all agree that this is much the most important issue that has faced this country for many years. Whether we decide to stay in or to come out, the effects on our economy, on our political and parliamentary systems, on our influence in the world and, indeed, perhaps eventually on our whole way of life will be profound not just for ourselves, but for future generations.

How should a decision of this importance have been taken? The right hon. Member for Sidcup (Mr Heath) had it right when he said that such a decision should be taken only with the full-hearted consent of Parliament and the British people. In our system we accept decisions with which we do not agree, but only if we are satisfied that they have been arrived at fairly and democratically.

MR PATRICK CORMACK (Staffordshire, South-West): In Parliament.

MR SHORT: Unfortunately, the last Government's handling of the European issue did not match their previous promises. They had no mandate to take us in, merely to negotiate – 'nothing more, nothing less'. The result is that the consent of the British people has not, in fact, been secured. The issue continues to divide the country. The decision to go in has not yet been accepted.

That is the essence of the case for having a referendum. Only by means of a referendum can we find out whether the British people do or do not consent to our continued membership. A General Election could not give us this answer, because this is an issue within the parties, not between them. . . .

I understand and respect the view of those devoted to this House and to the sovereignty of Parliament who argue that a referendum is alien to the principles and practices of parliamentary democracy. I respect their view, but I do not agree with it. I will tell the House why.

This referendum is wholly consistent with parliamentary sovereignty. The Government will be bound by its result, but Parliament, of course, cannot be bound by it. Although one would not expect hon. Members to go against the wishes of the people, they will remain free to do so.

One of the characteristics of this Parliament is that it can never divest itself of its sovereignty. The referendum itself cannot be held without parliamentary approval of the necessary legislation. Nor, if the decision is to come out of the Community, could that decision be made effective without further legislation. I do not, therefore, accept that the sovereignty of Parliament is affected in any way by the referendum. Some argue that decisions on national issues should be taken wholly and exclusively by Members of the two Houses of Parliament. In general, we would all agree with that. But Governments are elected on their whole programme and it would be neither appropriate nor practicable to have referenda on individual parts of the package. Moreover, if Parliament's decisions are found to be wrong, a subsequent Parliament can reverse them, as we have been doing since February last year. But that surely does not apply to this matter.

Our membership of the European Community is a unique issue because it profoundly affects our relationships with other countries as well as our whole standing and status in the world. It is unique because in time it could become almost irreversible, not for legal reasons but because, as we are already finding, the longer we stay in the harder it will be to come out, and the harder it will be to find any adequate design for living outside. . . .

Legislation was necessary to provide for the first nation-wide referendum to be held in the United Kingdom. In the referendum held in accordance with the Referendum Act 1975 the electorate voted on 5 June 1975 on the question, 'Do you think that the United Kingdom should stay in the European Community (the Common Market)?' 67.2 per cent of those voting (in a turnout of 65 per cent of the electorate) voted for staying in the Community.

The referendum settled the controversy about membership of the Community for a time, but as it turned out not permanently. The Labour Party's 1983 election manifesto included a commitment to withdraw from the Community, and some Conservative MPs remain opposed to membership.

Arguments for the 1975 referendum had relied on the 'unique significance' of the issue of Community membership. But within a short time the Government was constrained by backbench pressure to provide in the legislation for devolution to Scotland and Wales that referendums should be held in the two countries on the question whether devolution should be implemented. (See pp. 203–4 above.)

J. Barry Jones and R. A. Wilford in David Foulkes, J. Barry
Jones and R. A. Wilford (eds.), *The Welsh Veto: The Wales Act 1978
and the Referendum* (1983), pp. 217–18

[T]he decision to refer the devolution issue to the Welsh and Scottish electorates was
not taken because it was a profound constitutional issue but because it fitted only
imperfectly into the traditional, if simplistic, left-right mould of British party politics.
In this respect it had much in common with the EEC Referendum which was employed
not as a constitutional device but as a political expedient. But the cases are not perfectly
parallel. The EEC Referendum was adopted on the Government's own initiative and
then pushed through a hesitant and dubious House of Commons. By contrast, the
devolution referendums were extracted by backbenchers from a reluctant Government
whose Parliamentary authority was threatened by an unlikely alliance of Conservatives, Liberals, Nationalists and Labour backbenchers largely drawn from North-
East constituencies. Nevertheless, neither experience appears to have fundamentally
undermined the parliamentary system of Government; the artifice of designating
referendums as merely 'advisory' is generally perceived as having safeguarded the
central concept of parliamentary supremacy. Even the massive rejection of the Wales
Act, approved by Parliament and in receipt of the Royal Assent, has conspicuously
failed to precipitate any apprehensions that parliamentary sovereignty had been
violated. Doubtless, the widely shared view that the Government's Welsh devolution
policy had been passed by an 'artificial' majority content to destroy the proposals at the
subsequent referendum has much to do with that complacency. However, the bizarre
precedent of the Commons endorsing legislation of which it fundamentally disapproved was a further indication of the growing compatibility of the referendum with
the parliamentary representative system of government.

Since three referendums have been held on questions of national policy since
1972, and there is existing provision for a referendum in the Northern Ireland
Constitution Act 1973, it can no longer be said that the referendum is
something alien to the British constitution. The view is now commonly
expressed that proposals for major constitutional change should be subject to
'the people's veto' in a referendum. There may, however, be disagreement as
to which issues qualify for submission to the people under this head. As Nevil
Johnson says, 'the major difficulty is defining what counts as a constitutional
matter', and he adds: 'Ultimately, it is impossible to escape from the difficulty
presented by an informal constitution. Nobody knows quite what is in it'
('Types of Referendum' in Austin Ranney (ed.), *The Referendum Device*, 1981,
pp. 25–6).

What other kinds of issue might appropriately be resolved by an appeal to
the people? Is it true to say that 'the arguments against the referendum are also
arguments against democracy'? (Vernon Bogdanor, *The People and the Party
System* (1981), p. 93.)

Before any referendum is held, questions of principle and procedure have to
be settled – for example, whether a majority of votes in favour of a proposal is
to be sufficient, or is to be effective, say, only if it constitutes a specified
percentage of the electorate. (Cf. the 40 per cent rule of the Scottish and Welsh

referendums, p. 204 above.) If referendums are to become a normal part of constitutional practice, should certain ground rules be fixed for them in advance by legislation? It has been suggested that an independent Referendum Commission should be established which would be responsible for drafting the question to be submitted to the people and for supervising the conduct of referendums. (See, e.g., *The Referendum and the Constitution*, Conservative Research Department, 1978, pp. 8–9.)

4 Political parties

The system of parliamentary government in the United Kingdom is one of *party* government. Yet as Jean Blondel remarks (*Voters, Parties and Leaders*, 1963, p. 87), political parties in Britain are 'private associations to which the law does not give more rights and duties than to other private organizations'. The law of the constitution does not regulate political parties and indeed barely acknowledges their existence. But the working of the constitution depends on parties, which are 'the chief motivating force of our main governmental institutions' (Memorandum of Dissent to the Kilbrandon Report, Cmnd 5460–1, para. 311). The authors of the Memorandum considered that any scheme for constitutional reform must concern itself with the political parties.

> *Report of the Committee on Financial Aid to Political Parties*, Cmnd 6601/1976, para. 9.1

Effective political parties are the crux of democratic government. Without them democracy withers and decays. Their role is all pervasive. They provide the men and women, and the policies for all levels of government – from the parish council to the European Parliament. The parties in opposition have the responsibility of scrutinising and checking all the actions of the Executive. Parties are the people's watchdog, the guardian of our liberties. At election times it is they who run the campaigns and whose job it is to give the voters a clear-cut choice between different men and different measures. At all times they are the vital link between the government and the governed. Their function is to maximise the participation of the people in decision-making at all levels of government. In short they are the mainspring of all the processes of democracy. If parties fail, whether from lack of resources or vision, democracy itself will fail.

Parties are important in a study of the constitution because they bring about the election of MPs, provide governments and opposition to governments, and are engines (though not the only ones) for the creation of government policies. Any consideration of the extent to which the constitutional system provides for 'government by the people' must take account of the organization and functioning of political parties.

Selection of candidates

Since independent members are rarely elected to the House of Commons (none was elected in June 1983), the selection of candidates by the political parties is a crucial factor in determining the membership of the House. The parties' rules for the selection of candidates differ, but in each case selection is a function of the constituency party, subject to a degree of control by the national organization. The Labour Party's rules provide for a 'mandatory reselection' procedure between elections, applying to existing MPs as well as other prospective candidates.

In general few local party members take part in the selection process. A short list of prospective candidates is drawn up by a small executive or selection committee and the candidate is chosen by a rather larger executive council (Conservatives) or general management committee (Labour) or by those attending a general meeting of the constituency association (Liberals). In the Social Democratic Party, the final selection is made by a postal ballot of all members of the area party (which covers a number of parliamentary constituencies). Richard Rose observes that in the major parties the candidate is chosen by a group of anything from 20 to 200 persons and that most MPs are 'effectively selected by fewer voters than in the days before the 1832 Reform Act'. (*The Problem of Party Government*, 1974, p. 257.)

The parties exercise an important power in selecting their candidates. Selection in a safe seat is virtually equivalent to election, and many of those selected will serve for long periods in Parliament. Among them will be future holders of ministerial office and prime ministers. The selection procedures used by the parties are therefore a matter affecting the public interest, and it may be argued that candidates should be chosen in a more democratic way by a procedure of primary election in which all local party members could take part. (At present only the Social Democratic Party uses this method: a proposal for reselection by ballot of party members was defeated at the Labour Party Conference in 1984.) The author of the following passage urges the adoption of primary elections as a means of securing 'the fair and open choice of candidates for Parliament'.

Peter Paterson, *The Selectorate* (1967), pp. 170–71

[O]nly the primary seems to me to satisfy all the conditions for an honest and fully democratic system. These conditions are that as many genuine supporters of a party as possible should be given the opportunity to participate in the making of the candidate they are expected to work for and vote for: that the selection system must be fair to the whole range of political tendencies within a party; that hole-in-corner manoeuvring, favouritism, nepotism, and the activities of pressure groups should be discouraged, and an image of honesty and open-dealing presented to the electorate at large, that the legitimate interests of the local activists who maintain the fabric of the party year in and year out, the 'voting supporters' and the national leadership must all be balanced; and that equality of opportunity should be guaranteed to all those who wish to serve in Parliament.

This is a formidable list, but I believe that every point can be satisfied by the primary election. There can be no guarantees on the type of candidate who might be expected to win through a primary election contest because this is impossible to forecast, but nor is there any guarantee under the present arrangements. The necessity for a continuation of the short list should reassure the hard-core political activists that they will not be completely disinherited, and, indeed, their role, together with that of the constituency agent, would still be vital.

In the primary, the parties would have a first-class alternative to the present exclusive selection franchise, a means of bringing about a revival in terms of their mass influence, a possibility of a quickening interest and awareness among voters, and a form of participation – participatory democracy, in fact – that could prove satisfying and rewarding for all who bother to join a political party. Candidates would be able to prove themselves in actual combat without the risk of their unsuitability being discovered only when a Parliamentary election arises, and the scope provided by the present system for skullduggery and foul play would be reduced or even eliminated. Majority party members in that great mass of constituencies known as safe seats, who now have little say in choosing the candidate who inevitably becomes their MP can have restored to them some element of political choice; and the highly dangerous road of 'scientific' selection, using the techniques of personnel psychologists to help choose our legislators, a repugnant idea, would be avoided. Finally, and not least important, the quality of British democracy, which has become extremely *ersatz* over the years, could be vastly improved.

What is proposed by this author is the 'closed' primary, restricted to party members: there would need to be rules to prevent 'raiding' by a party's opponents who joined the party in order to vote in the primary and influence the result. Critics of the primary argue that it would be expensive, would weaken party discipline (since MPs would depend less on the party organization than on the votes of party members), and would make over the choice of candidates to those who had taken no part or interest in the work and policies of the party. (But see further Peter Paterson, op. cit., ch. 11.) It would go against the British tradition for the law to compel political parties to adopt a system of primary elections. However the Blake Report took the view that the interference with freedom of association resulting from legislation on this subject 'would be less damaging than the limitation on freedom of choice which the present situation involves' (*Report of the Hansard Society Commission on Electoral Reform*, 1976, para. 48).

Party policy

Political parties are all engaged to some degree in formulating policies. Parties that aim to take office, whether alone or as part of a coalition, will devise a comprehensive range of policies for government. Some minor parties have more limited objectives which they hope to achieve through pressure and bargaining. The parties have their own procedures and conventions for the making of policy.

In the Labour Party responsibility for the development of policy rests with the National Executive Committee (NEC) which submits proposals to the party conference, a body on which affiliated trade unions, constituency parties, Socialist societies and cooperative and professional organizations are represented. The NEC, which is elected by the party conference, is the chief orginator, interpreter and guardian of party policy but the actual work of policy formation is done by sub-committees and working parties of the NEC. Clause v of the constitution provides:

1. The party conference shall decide from time to time what specific proposals of legislative, financial or administrative reform shall be included in the party programme.

No proposal shall be included in the party programme unless it has been adopted by the party conference by a majority of not less than two-thirds of the votes recorded on a card vote.

2. The National Executive Committee and the Parliamentary Committee of the Parliamentary Labour Party shall decide which items from the party programme shall be included in the manifesto which shall be issued by the National Executive Committee prior to every general election. The joint meeting of the two committees shall also define the attitude of the party to the principal issues raised by the election which are not covered by the manifesto.

The arrangement by which the manifesto is settled jointly by the NEC and the parliamentary leadership – the Cabinet or the shadow Cabinet as the case may be – has sometimes resulted in sharp conflict as to the policies to be included in the manifesto. In recent years attempts have been made to change the constitution of the party so as to vest sole control of the manifesto in the NEC and to bind the Parliamentary Labour Party to implement party policies. In this critical controversy, which has wider constitutional implications, pursuit of the legitimate aim of greater accountability of the party leaders to the membership threatens to result in what a commentator has described as the 'absurdity' of government policy being 'determined by a body that carries no responsibility for putting it into effect' (Barry Hindess, *Parliamentary Democracy and Socialist Politics*, 1983, p. 112.)

The Conservative Party has traditionally placed a higher value upon authority and leadership than upon ideology or programmes, and policy-making is under the firm control of the leader of the party, supported by his or her colleagues in the Cabinet or shadow Cabinet. The annual conference has no responsibility for the formation of policies. An Advisory Committee on Policy is responsible to the party leader, who appoints its chairman. Through it advice is channelled from the many policy groups; further policy advice is provided by the Conservative Research Department. The leader consults the party chairman, ministerial or shadow Cabinet colleagues, the parliamentary party, and other party members and organizations, but takes the final decisions, including those on the content of the election manifesto. A Conservative Party pressure group – the Set the Party Free Charter Movement – campaigns for more democratic party procedures and a more direct involvement of the parliamentary party and national membership in the formation and review of party policy.

The official policy of the Liberal Party is declared in resolutions of the Assembly (or annual conference) of the party, which consists of representatives of constituency associations and recognized bodies, and *ex officio* members including Liberal MPs, peers, candidates and agents. Between meetings of the Assembly declarations on policy may be made by the smaller Council, which includes representatives of the parliamentary party, constituency associations and other sections of the party. The Parliamentary Liberal Party in the House of Commons is an autonomous organ of the party and Liberal MPs are not formally bound by official party policy. The leader of the party (who is elected by the party membership in constituency ballots) is responsible for the election manifesto.

In the Social Democratic Party policy proposals are submitted by a Policy Sub-Committee of the National Committee of the party to the Council for Social Democracy, the party's 'parliament', consisting of elected representatives of area parties and all SDP members of Parliament. The Council is responsible for adopting the policy of the SDP; major issues of policy may be submitted to the whole membership of the party in a consultative ballot. The Policy Sub-Committee draws up election manifestos on the basis of policies adopted by the Council. MPs are required to have regard to official policy and the manifesto, but the party's constitution provides that they 'shall not be mandated nor subject to direction or control by any organ of the SDP'.

Not all party policies find their way into manifestos and not all manifesto commitments are carried out. When a party's leaders take office as the government it usually happens that some party policies are abandoned as unworkable or are modified under the pressure of events. Other influences than party, some of them powerful, are brought to bear on the government, and other agencies – the civil service and pressure groups – generate policies which the government may find itself constrained to adopt. The party leadership acquires an increased autonomy in office, and may not be unwilling to jettison items of party policy that it dislikes. In these circumstances some members of the party may believe that they have been betrayed: this has been the complaint of the Labour left under recent Labour Governments. (See Barry Hindess, op. cit., pp. 107–13.)

Financial resources

Party government needs strong and well-organized political parties, capable of carrying out the study and research necessary for the formulation of realistic policies, and able to present them effectively to the public. These things cannot be done without adequate financial resources. The Houghton Committee recommended in 1976 that a system of state aid for political parties should be introduced.

Report of the Committee on Financial Aid to Political Parties,
Cmnd 6601/1976

9.6 ... [T]he parties must be able to carry out at least a reasonably efficient job of research, policy formulation, publicity and communication to standards which match the expectations and requirements of today's electorate, and which are commensurate with the problems now facing the country. In effect, we are arguing that there is a minimum level of activity and efficiency for political parties, and that it would seriously hamper the working of democracy and the machinery of government if they fell below this level for any length of time.

9.7 What particularly impressed us on our visits to Europe was not so much the details or history of the various schemes for state aid, which are obviously influenced by local circumstances, as the realisation, brought home to us as we visited party offices and talked to party and government officials, of how much could be done to improve the effectiveness of parties in their role of political and national leadership if adequate resources were available.

9.8 By contrast, the evidence we have gathered in this country shows that party organisation is in a number of cases weak at national level, and at local level generally exists on a pitifully inadequate scale of accommodation, equipment, trained staff and resources. Membership fees are low; fund-raising takes up too much time; organisation is frequently inadequate; and the level of political activity is far below what is needed to gain the attention and interest of the general body of the electorate, especially the young. Our considered view is that British political parties frequently operate below the minimum level of efficiency and activity required.

The Committee was of the opinion that it would not be in the public interest for the Conservative and Labour Parties to become increasingly dependent on the support, respectively, of business and the trade unions. The other parties, moreover, were at a disadvantage in having no equivalent institutional support. The Committee concluded that 'a modest injection of state aid is the best, and perhaps the only, way of arresting the run-down of the parties, and of starting the process by which their effectiveness can be raised to an adequate level' (para. 9.17). It recommended that an annual grant should be paid to the central organization of each party, based on the party's electoral support, and that every candidate who polled at least one-eighth of the votes cast should qualify for a limited reimbursement of election expenses. No action was taken to implement the Houghton proposals. A few years later the Hansard Society's Commission upon the Financing of Political Parties proposed a scheme by which the parties should be able to claim state aid related to their popular support, measured by individual contributions of money to the parties (*Paying for Politics* 1981). (See p. 372 above as to financial assistance for opposition parties in their parliamentary work.)

5 **Pressure groups**

'Every modern country', said Duguit in the early part of this century, 'is a mass of groups' (*Law in the Modern State*, tr. F. and H. Laski, 1921, p. 116). Pressure groups are bodies of persons organized to exert influence or pressure upon government without themselves seeking, through the electoral process, to assume governmental responsibility. In general they are clearly distinguishable from political parties, which hope to enter government, or at least to establish for themselves a strong base in Parliament by contesting elections.

Pressure groups have grown in number and following while the membership of political parties has declined. It has been remarked that 'approximately half the electorate belong to one or more organisations which sometimes seek to influence British government'. (Richard Rose, *Studies in British Politics*, 3rd edn 1976, p. 335.) Many find that they can urge their views more effectively by the methods of group pressure than through membership of a political party. R. T. McKenzie (in R. Kimber and J. J. Richardson (eds.), *Pressure Groups in Britain*, 1974, p. 280) was in no doubt

that pressure groups, taken together, are a far more important channel of communication than parties for the transmission of political ideas from the mass of the citizenry to their rulers.

Pressure groups are like political parties in expressing the demands of sections of the public, but unlike most parties they campaign for a specific interest or cause rather than for a wide range of policies. It is usual to distinguish two kinds of pressure groups. 'Interest' or 'sectional' groups represent people with social or economic interests in common, and their main purpose is to protect and further those interests. Among them are producers' groups, such as trade unions, industrial and commercial associations, the National Farmers' Union – and the two 'peak' organizations, the Confederation of British Industry and the Trades Union Congress. Some other organizations in the numerous and varied class of sectional groups are:

> the British Medical Association
> the Building Societies Association
> the Consumers' Association
> the Indian Workers' Association
> the Institute of Directors
> the Law Society
> the Methodist Conference
> the National Tenants' Organization
> the Police Federation
> the Ramblers' Association

The main concern of many sectional organizations is to provide services to their members, and some also control entry to a trade or profession and seek to maintain standards of competence: it may be only occasionally that they resort to lobbying and the tactics of pressure. But some sectional groups are engaged in a continuous dialogue with government, and many try to maintain a constant moderating influence upon the government departments whose policies may affect their interests.

The other kind of pressure group is the 'promotional' group, which is an organization of persons for the promotion of a cause which its members support. These too are of great number and variety. Here are a few examples:

> the Campaign for Nuclear Disarmament
> the Child Poverty Action Group
> the Council for the Protection of Rural England
> Friends of the Earth
> the Howard League for Penal Reform
> the Joint Council for the Welfare of Immigrants
> the National Abortion Campaign
> the National Council for Civil Liberties
> the National Society for the Prevention of Cruelty to Children
> Shelter

Many of the promotional groups put much of their effort into giving assistance to people in need, but all seek by publishing information, mounting public campaigns, or exerting direct pressure on government, to achieve legal reforms or the expenditure of public money or other favourable official response to the cause advocated. Some promotional groups have only a brief life, campaigning on transitory issues like the closure of a hospital or entry into the European Community, but others continue for many years, like the needs or injustices which gave rise to them.

Pressure groups sometimes work through or in alliance with political parties, hoping in this way to influence the policies of an existing or future government. This strategy has been followed by the Campaign for Nuclear Disarmament in relation to the Labour Party. It achieved a notable success in 1980 when a resolution drafted jointly by CND and the Bertrand Russell Peace Foundation, demanding that the next Labour manifesto should include a commitment against a nuclear defence policy and a pledge to close down nuclear bases in Britain, was approved by the Annual Conference of the party. (See Ben Pimlott and Chris Cook (eds.), *Trade Unions in British Politics*, 1982, p. 230.)

The trade unions have had close links with the Labour Party throughout its history. The unions affiliated to the party provide the bulk of its income, have a preponderant vote in the party conference and elect 12 of the 29 members of the party's National Executive Committee. The leader and deputy leader of the Labour Party are chosen by an electoral college in which affiliated trade unions have 40 per cent of the votes (the constituency parties having 30 per cent and the Parliamentary Labour Party (PLP) 30 per cent). In 1972 a Liaison Committee, representing the NEC, the PLP and the Trades Union Congress, was established to bridge the political and industrial sections of the

Labour movement and coordinate views on industrial and economic policy. Ministers serve on this Committee when the Labour Party is in power. Over the years the affiliated unions and the TUC have had a significant influence on the making of Labour Party policies on issues affecting their interests.

Sectional groups do not enjoy a similar organic relationship with the other political parties, but business interest groups, while not affiliated to the Conservative Party, are 'aligned' with it (S. E. Finer, *Anonymous Empire*, 2nd edn 1966, p. 52) and are able to influence party policy in economic and industrial matters.

Apart from groups like ratepayers' and council tenants' associations which are concerned with local government, pressure groups concentrate their efforts on the centres of decision-making in Westminster and Whitehall. Drawn to the substance of power, they cluster most densely about the departments and agencies of central government, where some of them achieve a particular legitimacy and consultative status. As W. J. M. Mackenzie says, every public body 'has its penumbra of organized groups which form its particular public' ((1955) 6 *British Journal of Sociology* 133 at 138). The pressure groups admitted to this favoured role are those able to offer the administration something in return. Many groups have specialized information and expertise which the administration lacks. Some government policies cannot be implemented without the cooperation of representative organizations and their members so that the government, accustomed to rule, is compelled to bargain. (The administration of the National Health Service, for example, needs the cooperation of the medical profession, represented in particular by the British Medical Association.)

Between the 'insider' groups and government there are channels for regular, informal consultation. In addition, client groups are often represented on committees of inquiry or working parties set up by government departments, or on the numerous advisory bodies, many of them created by statute, which give advice on specific areas of policy – on food hygiene, it might be, or building regulations, or waste management, or support for exporters.

Government legislation often bears the stamp of successful pressure by outside interests, and is sometimes virtually the product of negotiation with affected groups. (As to pre-legislative consultation see pp. 295, 312 above.) Some policies are not so much influenced by *pressure* as produced in a joint effort by a government department and one or more groups with which it shares a common interest. (For example, a continuous dialogue takes place between the Ministry of Agriculture and the National Farmers' Union on questions of agricultural policy.) The close relationships between departments and pressure groups has led observers to speak of a 'colonization' of government by groups, or of 'policy communities' composed of government departments and insider groups.

The two peak producers' organizations, the Confederation of British

Industry (CBI) and the Trades Union Congress, have laid claim to, and generally been granted, a privileged association with government involving regular and wide-ranging consultations. The relationship has been institutionalized, notably in the establishment in 1961 of the National Economic Development Council (NEDC), a non-statutory tripartite body which was expected to reach agreement on plans for economic growth. It is composed of ministers, representatives of private industry nominated by the CBI, and members nominated by the TUC.

In the continuous discussion with pressure groups, and more especially in the institutionalized arrangements with organized capital and labour, some have discerned a 'bias towards corporatism', or a 'sharing of the state' between elected governments and the governing institutions of the two sides of industry. This is the thesis of Keith Middlemass, who concludes (*Politics in Industrial Society*, 1979, p. 460) that 'the nineteenth-century concept of the state is wholly outdated':

> The modern state is composed not only of government and the state apparatus but includes the governing institutions; the degree of their inclusion serves as a means of distinguishing them from other institutions and interest groups merely contiguous to the state.

Decision-making in the economic sphere may be effected not only through parliamentary forms but in the processes of discussion between the government and sectional groups: agreements within the 'policy community' provide an alternative legitimation for some government policies. However the tripartism of government, business and labour in economic policy-making has not been a constant feature of British government in recent times, and at present it is quiescent, with a distancing of the relationship between the Government and the Trades Union Congress. The main tripartite organization, the NEDC, appears to have moved away from consideration of the broader (and more contentious) economic issues. But indications of a 'corporatist bias' are still to be seen in British government.

Malcolm Harrison, 'The Coming Welfare Corporatism', *New Society*, 1 March 1984, 321 at 322–3

On the usual definitions, corporatism is a form of political representation and state intervention. Public status is conferred on specific interest groups and other organisations which take part in regular negotiations with state agencies. Outside organisations are charged with carrying out public policy, and they are involved in formulating it. Obviously, in this sense, all modern governments are corporatist to some extent. Corporatist bargaining occurs especially where governments need outside expertise, finance or sources of loyalty. In Britain, corporatist political arrangements exist alongside democratic institutions. But they may displace them from dominance in some areas. This is what is now happening in social policy.

Selected organisations now have *privileged access* to Whitehall. When house builders or building societies become agents for government, they participate in determining planning or housing policy. Housing welfare groups stand largely ignored outside the charmed circle of decision-makers.

Another general characteristic of corporatism is *de-politicisation*. Issues are taken out of the realm of open electoral politics, and moved into the sphere of quiet negotiations behind closed doors, or dealt with by supposedly private markets. Major interests interact with each other and with civil servants, by-passing elected representatives. The importance of local government is reduced as its finances are undercut, and as central government asks for more account to be taken of private economic interests. Local political representation and decisions have become less important in welfare and social planning.

At Westminster, too, there is less chance to oversee what is going on. For example, private financial institutions now play an important role in inner city policy. Yet government gives MPs little information about the outcome. Building societies in the inner cities are a clear example. Parliament is by-passed. Ministers can argue that owner-occupation is a private matter, and that government need not closely monitor the changes. If discreet talks produce a response from the societies to some request by government, this may be seen merely as a public-spirited action by independent bodies. In reality these agencies are now a major vehicle for public policy. The most adventurous of the building societies, the Abbey National, already has its own inner city programme, covering the 'adoption' of over 150 housing action or improvement areas.

At central government level, such bodies are therefore *incorporated* into the very process of governing. They are expected to influence clients or members in the interests of some agreed national policy. Values important for social order are strengthened. Certain notions about entitlements, forms of provision, and property, become firmly established. For example, in housing, welfare is increasingly seen in terms of the right to own or pass on the ownership of a dwelling rather than the right merely to a roof over one's head. . . .

Welfare corporatism creates a useful illusion. Many policies which benefit the privileged do not appear on the agenda of open policies. Despite 'fiscal crisis', indirect state support has continued or increased, at the same time as the less privileged have faced a diminishing of resources. This transformation of welfare has been hidden. The privileged feel their advantages are individual and just. They think they arise from the operations of the market or from private household virtues, rather than from government. By contrast, the poor are stigmatised as recipients of charity given through visible public intervention.

(The ideas in this article are more fully developed in chapters 1 and 2 of M. L. Harrison (ed.), *Corporatism and the Welfare State*, 1984.)

Groups may fail to attain a favoured, consultative relationship with the government because they are not considered sufficiently representative or sufficiently 'responsible'. Again, a group may have objectives which are more congenial to a government of the Left than of the Right, or vice versa. The CBI and the Institute of Directors are able to influence the Thatcher Government on the subject of employment legislation, whereas a Labour government would be more likely in a matter of this kind to reach an accommodation with the TUC.

Pressure groups also look for support in Parliament. Many MPs are sponsored by trade unions; other have links with business organizations or act as parliamentary advisers for outside groups like the Police Federation. A number of pressure groups have succeeded in establishing all-party committees or groups in the House of Commons to look after their interests – among them are the Disablement Group, the Roads Study Group and the Scottish Whisky Industry Group. Opposition frontbenchers, lacking the resources of the civil service, often depend on groups to provide them with the expertise and information needed for the scrutiny of government bills.

Public campaigns and parliamentary pressure organized by groups have induced governments to legislate, and have put on the statute book such measures as the Televison Act 1954 (providing for commercial televison) and the Vaccine Damage Payments Act 1979. Pressure groups have also had an important role in the enactment of private members' legislation, such as the Abortion Act 1967, the Unsolicited Goods and Services Act 1971 and the Protection of Children Act 1978.

Pressure groups are an important part of the machinery by which government is controlled in the modern democratic state. They are a means by which citizens can express their demands upon government between elections and they help to make government responsive to bodies of opinion and interests which it might otherwise disregard. They contribute, therefore, to a more *participatory* democracy and to better-informed government. At the same time it must be remembered that organized groups are of unequal resources and strength, and that some interests in society have no representative organization. 'Functional' representation has to be supplemented, and the wider public interest safeguarded, by party and Parliament. It is important too that the groups admitted to a share in policy-making should be truly representative of their members. If their participation in the processes of government is to be accepted as legitimate there is a need, as Bernard Crick says, 'to ensure that pressure groups themselves are genuinely participative, representative and democratic' (J. A. G. Griffith (ed.), *From Policy to Administration*, 1976, p. 67).

In recent years some pressure groups have adopted a 'test case strategy', assisting individuals to bring cases in courts or tribunals with the object of establishing precedents which will result in changes in administrative practice favourable to the interests of a whole class of persons. The Child Poverty Action Group (CPAG) has pursued this strategy with the objectives and mixed results described by Harlow and Rawlings, *Law and Administration*, p. 604 *et seq.* In an important recent case, *R. v. Secretary of State for Social Services, ex p. Greater London Council, The Times*, 16 August 1984, Woolf J recognized the representative capacity of the CPAG in acknowledging its *locus standi* to bring proceedings on behalf of unidentified claimants of supplementary benefit.

6 Open government

If the principle of responsible government is to be maintained, there must be sufficient public access to information about governmental activities and decisions. Openness in government is necessary if Parliament, groups and the public are to be able to contribute to the making of policy, and if the actions of government are to be properly scrutinized and evaluated, and the decision-makers held accountable.

> Royal Commission on the Constitution, vol. II, Memorandum of
> Dissent by Lord Crowther-Hunt and Professor A. T. Peacock,
> Cmnd 5460-I/1973, para. 136

To command the support of the people it is essential that the processes of government and decision-making should be as open as possible. This is a vital characteristic of any democracy. If people do not know what is going on they are not able to bring their influence to bear before final decisions are taken. The greater the secrecy, the greater the sense of exclusion from the decision-making process and the greater the difficulty of gaining public acceptance for the decisions arrived at – and very probably, too, the worse the decisions. No doubt it will always be necessary to impose some limitations on the principle that in a democracy all decisions should be 'open decisions openly arrived at'; but in a mature democracy those limitations must clearly be kept to an absolute minimum.

British governments have traditionally maintained a high degree of secrecy about their operations. The political culture has not in the past included any idea of 'participatory democracy' which could have supported claims by individuals or groups to be provided with information about government. Governmental secrecy is fortified by a Draconian body of law – the Official Secrets Acts 1911–39 – and this has been only partially mitigated by conventional practices of consultation and disclosure (see, e.g., pp. 149, 312 above). Some of the principal conventions of the constitution – in particular those of collective and individual ministerial responsibility – have contributed to the maintenance of governmental secrecy. The courts admit no right at common law to obtain information about the processes of government, except to the extent that a party to litigation needs such information to prove his case – and then only if the court is not persuaded that the public interest precludes disclosure of the information: see p. 114 above. Indeed some judges take the view that a valid ground of objection to the disclosure of information in legal proceedings is 'to protect from inspection by possible critics the inner working of government while forming important governmental policy'. (Lord Wilberforce in *Burmah Oil Co. Ltd* v. *Bank of England* [1980] AC 1090, 1112. See also Lord Scarman at 1145 but contrast the remarks of Lord Keith at 1134.) The House of Lords has acknowledged that there is a public interest in the free flow of information, but has held that in law it may have to yield to some other interest, such as that of preserving confidentiality: *British Steel Corporation* v.

Granada Television Ltd [1981] AC 1096. Lord Wilberforce said in this case (p. 1168):

As to an alleged 'right to know', it must be clear that except in a totally open society (if any such exists) limitations on this not only exist but are considerable, whether one is concerned with the operations of government, or of business, one's neighbour's affairs or indeed any other activity.

(Compare the dissenting speech of Lord Salmon.)

In most circumstances, therefore, it is entirely in the discretion of the government whether and to what extent official information should be made available to the public or to interested organizations. In recent years concern has been widely expressed that governments are unduly restrictive in withholding information from the public (and from Parliament) and that secrecy is sometimes maintained, not for reasons of the public interest, but to protect the government from criticism or embarrassment.

In 1968 the Fulton Committee on the Civil Service observed that the administrative process was 'surrounded by too much secrecy' and that 'the public interest would be better served if there were a greater amount of openness' (Cmnd 3638, para. 278). The Government in its response drew attention to measures already taken to disclose more information (*Information and the Public Interest*, Cmnd 4089/1969). Among these was the practice, begun in 1967, of issuing 'Green Papers' setting out policy proposals and inviting public comment and discussion before decisions were taken. But even if there had been some improvement in openness, the Government itself acknowledged that more should be done. Unfortunately the Franks Committee appointed in 1971 was restricted by its terms of reference to considering the operation of section 2 of the Official Secrets Act 1911 (penalizing wrongful communication of information) and could not examine wider issues of open government. The Committee did however insist that a democratic government has an obligation to explain its aims to the people, provide the justification for them and give the arguments for and against proposed courses of action:

A government which pursues secret aims, or which operates in greater secrecy than the effective conduct of its proper functions requires, or which turns information services into propaganda agencies, will lose the trust of the people. [Franks Report, Cmnd. 5104/1972, para. 12.]

In 1976 the Prime Minister, Mr Callaghan, announced in Parliament that in future more background information on major policies would be published. This undertaking was followed by the 'Croham Directive', an instruction to heads of departments circulated by Sir Douglas Allen (afterwards Lord Croham), Head of the Home Civil Service.

The Croham Directive, 6 July 1977

During the debate on the address on 24th November last, the Prime Minister announced that it would be the Government's policy in future to publish as much as possible of the factual and analytical material used as the background to major policy studies. . . . I am writing in terms which the Prime Minister has specifically approved to let you know how his statement affects present practice and to ask you to ensure that your Department gives effect to it. . . .

2. The change may seem simply to be one of degree and of timing. But it is intended to mark a real change of policy, even if the initial step is modest. In the past it has normally been assumed that background material relating to policy studies and reports would *not* be published unless the responsible Minister or Ministers decided otherwise. Henceforth the working assumption should be that such material *will* be published unless they decide that it should *not* be. There is of course no intention to publish material which correctly bears a current security classification or privacy marking; at the same time, care should be taken to ensure that the publication of unclassified material is not frustrated by including it in documents that also contain classified material.

3. In effect, what is proposed is an increase in the already considerable amount of material put out by Departments. The additional material will mainly consist of deliberate presentations in the later stages of discussion and development of new policy. Some of these will probably, as now, take the form of Green Papers. . . . While most material will be released on the initiative of the Department, probably through HMSO, some of lesser importance, or of interest to a limited audience, may well be put out through other means such as publication in magazines or in response to specific requests in the same way that a good deal of unpublished material is already made available to bona fide researchers. In some cases it may be preferable simply to publicise the existence of certain material which would be made available to anyone who asked. Consideration should also be given to the issue of bibliographies or digests so that interested parties are advised what material is available.

4. In adopting the working assumption described in paragraph 2 above for policy studies . . . the normal aim will be to publicise as much as possible of the background material subject to Ministerial decision once they have seen the study and reached their conclusions on it. When Ministers decide what announcement they wish to make, therefore, they will also wish to consider whether and in what form the factual and analytical material may be published, since there may, as the Prime Minister made clear in his statement, be circumstances in which Ministers will not wish to disclose such material. . . .

It has been suggested that the Croham Directive was 'expressly designed to head off more radical demands for a public *right* of access'. (Annabelle May and Kathryn Rowan (eds.), *Inside Information: British Government and the Media*, 1982, p. 20.) The Directive does not authorize publication of official advice to ministers, which is protected from disclosure by the convention of ministerial responsibility. While the Directive has increased the flow of information, it has had only a modest effect in opening the processes of government to public scrutiny. A renewed assurance was given to Parliament by a Minister of State in the Civil Service Department on 20 June 1979 that 'it will be the practice of this Government to make as much information as possible available, including background papers and analytical studies, relevant to major policy decisions'

(HC Deb. vol. 968, col. 1316); but a prime ministerial minute on the subject sent to ministers on the same date was withheld from publication.

Experience has taught that in the provision of information, administrative convenience too often prevails over public benefit. Nor can ministers be relied upon to make an objective judgement, unsullied by considerations of party advantage or personal reputation, of what should, in the public interest, be disclosed or withheld. The Australian Senate Standing Committee on Constitutional and Legal Affairs concluded in 1979 (*Freedom of Information*, para. 3.7):

The essence of democratic government lies in the ability of people to make choices: about who shall govern; or about which policies they support or reject. Such choices cannot be properly made unless adequate information is available. It cannot be accepted that it is the government itself which should determine what level of information is to be regarded as adequate.

In 1978 a report by JUSTICE (the British Section of the International Commission of Jurists), in considering the need for access to government information, raised the questions, 'But how much information, how many files are to be opened up and at what cost to the taxpayer?'

Freedom of Information: A report by JUSTICE (1978)

3. These are important questions for which partial solutions have been found in some countries, though in very different contexts from our own. They are difficult questions which give rise to conflicting opinions among those opposed to secrecy. An example will demonstrate the difficulties.

4. In the course of an enquiry as to the medical efficiency of some new drug, the early stages will throw up many adverse opinions and doubts which subsequent and more up-to-date research may show to be unfounded. If the whole of the enquiry were conducted in public the bad news, to which undue importance was attached in the early stages, would be likely to be remembered, while the good news might never receive equal publicity. It can be argued that the public should be told everything and left to reach its own conclusions, but on the other hand there is a strong case for saying that in the pursuit of 'openness' damage will have been done which could have been spared those who were deterred by the bad news and missed the good.

5. We do not think the situation can be met merely by any general declaration in favour of 'openness'. We believe that, however high-sounding, its application is bound to be circumscribed by massive limitations and exceptions and its enunciation by itself would raise expectations that are not likely to be fulfilled under our present arrangements. Our approach to the whole topic has been dominated by practical considerations. At the risk of appearing conventionally pragmatic, we believe that there are no rigid formulae which will provide for the multiplicity of situations where the public ought or ought not to be granted access to official information. The more precise area and ambit of such access will require to be worked out and developed over a period of years. Nor can we disregard the time likely to be consumed in attempting to introduce complex legislation modelled on the lines of the relevant legislation in the United States and Sweden.

6. For these reasons we have reached conclusions which can, we think, be put into effect without legislation. If their implementation proves to be a success, whatever Government is in power will be the more ready to extend the ambit of their operation by detailed legislation, and it is our hope that there will eventually be such legislation. A small but immediate success, however undramatic, in facilitating access to official information, even on a modest scale, is much to be preferred to a prolonged and indefinite controversy over a *statutory right* on a larger scale, a controversy which may produce no practical results. . . .

JUSTICE proposed that a Code of Practice should be introduced which would govern the disclosure of official information, and that the Parliamentary Commissioner for Administration should be given jurisdiction to investigate complaints of non-observance of the code.

Proposed Code of Practice (JUSTICE 1978)

(1)   It is essential to the effective working of a democratic society that the public should be adequately informed about the actions and decisions taken by the Government and other organs of public administration of the United Kingdom. The paramount criterion should be that the public may, by being adequately informed, have the opportunity of understanding and evaluating the nature of, and the reasons and grounds for, such actions and decisions. Accordingly, with certain necessary exceptions, all documents containing information on such matters should, so far as is reasonable and practicable, be disclosed within a reasonable time to any person requesting their disclosure.

(2)   This Code of Practice applies to all government departments and other authorities to which the Parliamentary Commissioner Act 1967 applies.

(3)   Servants of the Crown and other officers and persons responsible for disclosing information in accordance with this Code should disclose sufficient information to satisfy the criterion stated in paragraph (1).

(4)   Documents will not be disclosed if:–
    (a)   the case falls within paragraphs (9), (10) or (11) below; or
    (b)   there are reasonable grounds for believing that the public interest would be adversely affected by disclosure.

With these exceptions, documents should be disclosed where the information they contain relates to decisions on matters of policy or to other acts or decisions (whether of an executive or quasi-judicial character) of any authority to which this Code applies. Information relating to any matter on which a decision has not yet been reached should also be disclosed unless disclosure is likely to prejudice consultation or negotiation with persons or bodies directly affected by the ultimate decision, or to affect the outcome adversely to the public interest: in either of these cases there will be no disclosure until a decision is reached.

(5)   In determining whether or what disclosure should be made it is immaterial that the person requesting disclosure is or is likely to be in dispute with the government department or other authority from which disclosure is sought. On the contrary, all practicable assistance in the form of generous disclosure should be given to any such person since disputes or misunderstandings may well arise from misinformation or inadequate information. So far as is practicable, all information should be disclosed

which might be of advantage to the person requesting disclosure, either with a view to redressing a wrong or which could be helpful in understanding the reasons for a decision.

(6) No regard shall be had to the nature of the applicant's interest in seeking disclosure.

(7) Any complaint of failure to disclose a document or class of documents which ought, in accordance with this Code, to have been disclosed shall be treated as a complaint of maladministration at the instance of the person requesting disclosure and, if he claims to have sustained injustice in consequence thereof, his complaint may be investigated by the Parliamentary Commissioner for Administration in accordance with the provisions of section 5 of the Parliamentary Commissioner Act 1967.

(8) Arrangements shall be made within every government department and other authority to which this code applies for the preparation and publication of a document in ordinary language giving information about the documents or classes of documents which, or copies of which, will be disclosed in accordance with this Code; as to the persons responsible for dealing with applications for disclosure, and as to the charges, if any, which may be made.

(9) Documents containing information relating to matters listed below shall be exempt from disclosure to the extent that they contain such information, so that there shall be disclosure of that part of the document which contains no reference to or indication of matters which may not be disclosed. There will be no disclosure of information:–

(a) relating to defence, foreign relations or internal security;

(b) relating to law enforcement;

(c) which could be privileged against disclosure in litigation;

(d) entrusted in confidence to a government department or other authority to which this Code applies whether or not required by or under any enactment to be disclosed to any such department or authority;

(e) the disclosure of which would infringe the privacy of an individual;

(f) which, if disclosed, could reasonably expose the person disclosing it to a significant risk of proceedings for defamation.

(10) Cabinet and Cabinet committee documents as a class are exempt from disclosure.

(11) There will be no disclosure of any document which comprises advice or comment tendered by any person in the course of his official duties to a Minister or servant of the Crown or other officer of an authority to which this Code applies to the extent that the document contains such advice or comment.

The Labour Government agreed in principle to the adoption of a code of practice, but expressed reservations about authorizing the Parliamentary Commissioner to check its observance (*Open Government*, Cmnd 7520/1979, paras. 65-70). The Government fell soon after, and the present Thatcher administration is opposed to the idea of a code of practice.

Many advocates of open government consider that nothing less than a statutory right of access to official information will be effective. Legislation providing for public access to government documents exists in a number of countries. Sweden has had a statute of this kind since 1766, and there are enactments giving rights of access to official information in the other

Scandinavian countries, France, the Netherlands, the United States, Australia, Canada and New Zealand. In the United Kingdom several private members' bills providing for access to official documents have been introduced in recent years, but all have lapsed. The 1983 election manifestos of the Labour Party and the Liberal/SDP Alliance included commitments to legislate for open government.

The response of British governments to proposals to establish a statutory 'right to know' has been guarded or negative. The growing campaign for freedom of information will not, however, be deflected by such assurances as that '[i]n our system of government the executive is under continuous scrutiny by Parliament, and Members of Parliament have a variety of means and opportunities for seeking information about government policies and actions' (*Reform of section 2 of the Official Secrets Act 1911*, Cmnd 7285/1978, para. 14). Is there more substance in the objection that 'it would be a constitutional novelty for this country if the provision of information in general policy areas, with their largely political content, were made a matter for legal . . . judgement rather than of accountability to parliament' (*Open Government*, Cmnd 7520/ 1979, para. 56)? Doubts about the desirability of a Freedom of Information Act have been expressed on various other grounds. Might such an Act be mainly of benefit to organized interests, furthering the development of pressure group politics, rather than bringing gains to the general public? Would it be compatible with existing conventions of the constitution, in particular those of ministerial responsibility and civil service anonymity and impartiality? Would the administrative and financial costs be prohibitively high? Might the legislation be evaded by recourse to informal discussions and unrecorded decisions? But if these doubts could be resolved and a well-designed Freedom of Information Act were passed, the control and accountability of government might be significantly strengthened.

Index

DATE DUE